DIMENSIONS OF AGING

DIMENSIONS OF AGING:
Readings

Jon Hendricks
C. Davis Hendricks
University of Kentucky

Winthrop Publishers, Inc.
Cambridge, Massachusetts

Library of Congress Cataloging in Publication Data

Main entry under title:

Dimensions of aging.

    Includes index.
      1. Gerontology—Addresses, essays, lectures.
I. Hendricks, Jon   II. Hendricks, C. Davis

4HQ1061.D55   301.43′5   78-23536
ISBN 0-87626-180-2

Cover design by Ann Washer

© 1979 by Winthrop Publishers, Inc.
  17 Dunster Street, Cambridge, Massachusetts 02138

10 9 8 7 6 5 4 3 2

For Alex and Klaus

Contents

Section 6
Aging Tomorrow: Prospects, Policy, Ethics   347

Preface

It is no exaggeration to say the scope of gerontology looms impossibly broad. In the process of researching the existing literature for our *Aging in Mass Society: Myths and Realities,* we came to appreciate the seemingly unending parade of materials confronting new and seasoned readers. While the critical reception granted our earlier work has been encouraging, we realize that even a well-honed text can never do justice to all that gerontologists have to offer. We are also quite aware of the spate of recent anthologies intended to provide an instant overview of the field. Having carefully considered a number of these we experience some trepidation over the prospect of adding still another. Yet the very frustration which arose from our attempt to integrate, to some degree, the diverse perspectives of gerontologists working in a variety of academic disciplines and applied programs serves as justification for the present volume.

This work is designed to be didactic in two senses. On the one hand, readers from traditional academic backgrounds coming to the study of aging and life-span development will find the going less than comfortable unless they have previous exposure to the holistic nature of human existence. Acknowledging that biological scientists have as much to learn from their social science breathren as the latter from the former is fairly easy; implementing the exchange is somewhat more problematic. With so much to learn in one's own area, what hope is there of mastering a truly interdisciplinary perspective? Gerontology is rapidly maturing, we hope, with the attendant cognizance of the myriad factors, and their interplay, which are the aging process. The ground has been broken for interdisciplinary endeavors, now our work must proceed with building an initial and substantial foundation.

In a second sense our efforts and those of our colleagues depend on the titillation, capture and challenge of curious, questing minds. Your comments are not only welcome, but are essential to the dynamics of our future development in gerontology.

Readers will note the interdisciplinary focus, indeed the very organization of this work, parallels our text. We have not altered the view we expressed there for reasons which should be readily apparent. We remain convinced of the utility and the necessity of an interdisciplinary approach. The guiding light of our late night labors has been the creation of a workable combination of biological, psychological and sociological perspectives to be used in addressing the whys and hows of the aging process. Often the information provided by diverse research is not only complex, but appears contradictory. Nonetheless, it is an exciting task to make sense of what is itself a multifaceted, by no means singular, process.

Should *Aging in Mass Society* and this anthology be used together, their complementarity is intentional. This work was designed to offer a number of original readings which inform and shape the text's discussion. Should you explore one before the other, it is our hope that you will seek out the second to fill in the lean spaces of the first. In either case, we feel these selections stand as landmark contributions by their authors.

The more mature one becomes, the more nearly impossible it is to acknowledge all those who have shared in one's development. For their intellectual relentlessness, we owe our colleagues a debt of gratitude which can never be repaid. In particular, Alex Simirenko and Klaus Riegel have directly influenced or served as examples in ways only we four realize. First and foremost, however, has been their willingness to revise their own hard-won views when new, fertile perspectives become available. Isolating potential materials for inclusion is a never ending task, for which Cathy McAllister served as an able assistant. The person on whom we relied for the entirety of their project and to whom we also owe an incalculable debt is Carolyn Anderson. She has exhibited enviable strength and enthusiasm during the periods of intense work and frustration which come with every task. Paul O'Connell and the staff at Winthrop, especially Sharon Bryan, have been helpful, encouraging and reassuringly competent. We are most appreciative to all of you who have contributed to the gerontologists we are becoming.

DIMENSIONS OF AGING

INTRODUCTION

Concerning Old Age: Interdisciplinary Dimensions

Old? What is old? Everything ages; the only alternative to old age is a "premature" death. Everyone reading these words will age in a number of highly predictable ways. From the most minute molecular process to the way we handle information, look at the world, and interact with one another, process and change are part of what it is to be alive. Interpretations of and attitudes toward the changes taking place vary widely. To respond to the question, "What is old?" gerontologists draw on studies and insights from the biological sciences, social sciences, and the humanities. None of these alone is sufficient to describe or understand the process of aging. While human aging has many parallels with the way other biological organisms age, only humans can analyze the process of their own aging. Accordingly, gerontology—the study of the entire aging process—is a multifaceted specialty drawing from traditional bodies of literature while building its own.

While it is usually the case that students of gerontology specialize in one particular area, it is also necessary for them to acquire some rudimentary grasp of the perspectives taken by others who also look at the aging process. The readings selected are intended to provide exactly this kind of overview. They have been included either as the most recent literature available or, in the case of some older articles, because they are seminal contributions to the conceptual development of gerontology. While textbooks can provide a summary view of the study of aging, these primary sources allow the reader to hear directly from those espousing one stance or another, and to participate in drawing whatever conclusions appear warranted.

Another point needs to be made clear at the outset. Oftentimes it is assumed, albeit mistakenly, that gerontology focuses exclusively on the elderly and has little to offer those who consider themselves a long way from old age. Nothing could be further from the truth; most gerontologists agree, not only would they be stinting their responsibility if they took such a position, but they would also be reducing their chances to affect responses to the process of aging. Gerontologists have so far concentrated their attention on the middle and later years but there is no reason they must continue to do so; as our knowledge expands, so will our focus. Among other things it is important to bear in mind that very little in life happens automatically, people do not simply find themselves biologically beyond the peak of their capabilities or socially well adjusted whenever their lives change in one direction or another. The problems encountered are not necessarily unique to the aging process; nevertheless, the possibility for addressing the plight of many offers justification for the investigations that are reported in this text. The opportunity for intervention enhances our appreciation of what it is to become old.

As a topic of interest gerontology is as old as our history; as a systematic inquiry it is considerably younger. In the thirteenth century Roger Bacon initiated the first lines of investigation into the physical components of the aging process but the ground he tilled remained fallow until the seventeenth century, and it was well into the nineteenth century before any appreciable body of information began to accumulate. Only early in the present century did the process of aging become an object of intensive research. Social gerontology, concentrating as it does on societal and cultural components of aging, is a young discipline. The psychologist G. Stanley Hall published his *Senescence, the Last Half of Life,* in 1922, but it was not until the end of World War II that some progress was first made toward an understanding of the social side of the aging process. What was a handful of publications in the 1940s is today a landslide. Journal entries on aging now number well over five thousand annually, with no peak in sight. Of course, not all of this literature furnishes generalizeable leads promoting better understanding, but the field is maturing and becoming more self-critical, paving the way for more insightful studies and research.

STEREOTYPES AND ATTITUDES

Every culture provides a set of prescribed behaviors related to aging. These norms cover not only what rights and responsibilities accrue to people of a given age, but indicate, within certain broad limits, what are considered inappropriate modes of behaving. Throughout the early and middle years of life most people are presented with opportunities to try on various social roles in advance of the time these are fully assumed. The various phases of courtship, for example, from the occasional date to going steady, becoming engaged, to getting married, are a progression which permits the individuals involved to see what each next step means in terms of interpersonal relations. If at any time the relationship begins to feel too confining, it may be terminated before the next step is taken. Old age represents an exception to this model, since little in life is preparatory to being defined as an "older person." Treating old age as a distinct phase of life, set off from all that has gone before, does little to smooth the transition into the later years. Old age is a subject blurred by stereotypes and anxieties perhaps more so than any other stage of life. In this country, for example, it is not at all uncommon to hear the elderly described in largely negative terms. Either they sit and ruminate over a bygone youth receding into the mist, or they are old fogies turned to pasture, no longer making any contribution to society. Bigotry of this type is sadly misinformed, yet it is so pervasive that it has been given a label—ageism—like many other common prejudices (Butler and Lewis, 1977). Assumptions that all old people are destined for an institution, are beset by serious health problems, are "senile," or are necessarily conservative are all examples of ageism. In point of fact, not one of these notions is true. Only about five percent of those over sixty-five years of age are in institutions; chronic health conditions do not limit their activities across the board; there is no such mental illness as senility; the elderly are not necessarily any more conservative than anyone else. According to any number of criteria, the elderly are quite robust, exhibiting positive coping mechanisms that younger people would do well to emulate.

While there is no denying that many people do experience very real problems as they age, far too often the most serious difficulties they have to contend with are the confining and unsympathetic attitudes towards older people. Asking old people what life is like for them and asking younger people what they expect life to be like for an older person is a revealing experience. In a study commissioned by the National Council on the Aging, carried out by the Harris polling organization, younger respondents consistently felt the problems encountered by the old were far worse than did the elderly themselves. Furthermore, for every older person who finds life to be more of a hardship than he or she expected, there are at least three who claim it is not nearly as onerous as they had anticipated (Harris, 1975).

THE OLDER POPULATION

As the ranks of those over sixty-five swell, and as the "graying of America" continues, many of the myths of aging are sure to be dispelled. Today the elderly, defined as those sixty-five and over, account for over 10 percent of the population in this country. In 1900 they made up four percent of the population, and in 1790, when the first census was taken, they accounted for barely two percent of all Americans. With a net increase in their ranks of 1400–1600 every day, by the year 2000 there will be thirty-one million Americans over 65, eight million more than there are today; by the year 2030 there will be more than fifty-two million. Rapid changes, no matter how you count. One reason for the dramatic increase in percentage is the declining birth rate combined with lowered mortality rates for the early years of life. Both of these trends are concomitants of increasing industrialization and the medical advances which go along with modernization. As the age distribution of a country changes, other fundamental realignments are necessary; a country with a very low median age will have needs different from those of a country where the average age is appreciably higher. An example of three countries with differing age distributions is shown in Figure 1. In less industrialized but rapidly developing Mexico, marked by high birth rates but a declining death rate, the bulk of the population is in the lower age categories. The median age there is approximately seventeen years. Prior to its recent economic development Mexico, like all other non-industrialized countries, had a much

Figure 1

Age-sex composition for three types of population structures.

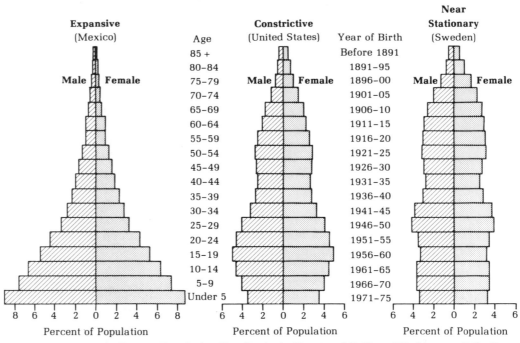

Source: *Population Handbook*, A. Haupt and T. Kane (Washington, D.C.: Population Reference Bureau, Inc. 1978).

higher death rate than it does now. A very small percentage of the population survived into their sixties or beyond, shown by the relatively small size of the top of the population pyramid.

Sweden, also shown in Figure 1, has long been an industrial nation. In the years following its modernization, death rates began to decline, followed shortly thereafter by a falling birth rate, then the population as a whole began to age. The rate of economic growth slowed eventually, while the population structure became relatively stabilized. Today the median age is over thirty-five years, and a sizable contingent of its populace is in the sixth decade or beyond. With zero population growth long a reality, Sweden's population distribution is not likely to exhibit much more aging in the foreseeable future.

The United States, with an age distribution falling between those of the other two countries, has characteristically had a relatively young population. If the patterns established since the turn of the century continue, as most demographers assume they will, the trend will be toward a pyramid looking more or less like Sweden's. The only exception to what otherwise has been a consistent aging of the United States was produced by the post-war baby boom which temporarily shifted the birth rate higher. The median age in 1900 was approximately twenty-four years, with four percent of the people over sixty-five. The current median age is twenty-nine years, and as has already been noted, over one-tenth of all people in the United States are beyond their sixty-fifth birthday. Looking ahead to the next turn of the century, the median age will be between thirty-two and thirty-seven years, with the proportion over sixty-five years at least 11.5, and perhaps as high as 13 percent. In the first three or four decades of the twentieth century these figures are likely to climb even higher. Median age in the year 2030 will be between thirty-one and forty-two years, with the number and percentage of those over age sixty-five at least double what it is now (United States Census, 1977).

Since the Brotman selection in Section 6 explains how various projections are derived, it should be sufficient now to note that the inexactness of the figures cited is due to as yet unknown birth rates. If we merely replace ourselves, the population will become stabilized and our population pyramid will be nearly vertical. If population growth is more than zero, the picture will reflect a concentration in the younger ages, and if fewer births occur the median age will rise.

What is the point in presenting what are admittedly general estimates, figures which cannot be checked for nearly half a century? Why should we even bother with what may be the case fifty years down the road? Phrasing the answer in terms of another question might be the most expedient response. What will be the country's priorities, and how will these be established if as a nation we are significantly older than we are presently? During the 1950s a major investment was made in building public schools and training teachers

Figure 2

Median age of the population 1970–2050.

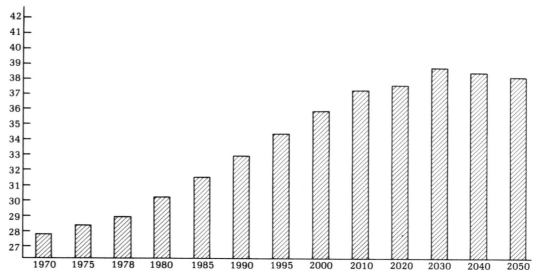

Source: *Current Population Reports,* Bureau of the Census, "Projections of the Population of the United States: 1977–2050" (Washington, D.C.: U.S. Government Printing Office, 1977). (Converted from numerical data, estimates based on zero population growth.)

to staff them. Today schools are being closed nearly as rapidly as they were once built, teachers are looking for new careers, companies which experienced tremendous economic growth catering to the boom babies are searching out new markets, and zero population growth has become a popular credo among young adults. At the same time, the costs of providing for an expanding number of elderly are increasing daily, both for themselves and for workers who contribute to Social Security knowing full well their monies are being redistributed to pay current benefits as quickly as they are withheld from their incomes.

Profiles of the population, such as that presented here, are an essential ingredient of planned social change. In order to insure a maximally satisfying life for young and old, it is necessary to have some historical and analytic grasp of the dynamics of aging. Past, present, and future changes affecting people over the course of their lives are all interconnected, demanding of the gerontologist a kind of wide angle vision which is not easy to develop. The readings selected for inclusion here, and the organization of the material itself, are aimed at providing a holistic perspective on the process, one which cuts across usual academic boundaries. Somewhat greater emphasis is placed on the social and psychological dimensions than on other aspects, but for gerontologists working in these areas, as for the biologist who moves outside the laboratory, there is no excuse for not having at least a rudimentary acquaintance with the overall character of the life process. We cannot afford, nor can we justify, an artificially delimited conceptualization of what it means to age.

REFERENCES

1. HARRIS, L. and ASSOCIATES. *The Myth and Reality of Aging in America.* Washington, D.C.: The National Council on the Aging, Inc., 1975.
2. U.S. CENSUS BUREAU. *Current Population Reports,* Series P-25, No. 704, "Projections of the Population of the United States: 1977–2050." Washington, D.C.: U.S. Government Printing Office, 1977.

SECTION 1

In the Country of the Old: Historical and Cross-Cultural Perspectives

It has become relatively common these days to set the backdrop for a discussion of aging by painting a historical picture of the elderly, whether in one's own society or in those of other times and other places. Although tacit recognition has been given historical analyses of the aged and aging, how important are they, really, to our attempts to understand the processes of growing old? Not surprisingly, we find a range of responses, from an almost complete denial of the relevance of historical examination to those who would advocate the impossibility of understanding today without being thoroughly grounded in knowledge of yesterday.

It is not unusual to look to the past to clarify the present. We need reassurance about the present, we are curious about the uniqueness of our own positions, and we often hope that the past will reveal some information which may help us address immediate problems. One of the most important and interesting goals of the analysis of any aspect of life is the discovery of effective modes of intervention. Because we are so centrally involved in such a search, in this instance an appreciation of the role of aging in our lives, historical analyses can never be totally objective. The investigator is intimately involved not only with the subject matter of the investigation, but also with the methods employed. The way in which we phrase a question necessarily shapes the answers we will obtain. If one is of the mind that the elderly have always fared well until modern times, because they have been supported and well cared for by familial and social structures, there is certainly enough data available to lend support to such a view. On the other hand, as will emerge from the following selections, there are other views which have been taken with respect to the role of aging indicating that many of the choices assumed to exist for old people centuries before were not practically available. The evidence from which historians attempt to generalize is rarely complete, often representing only the views of or information relevant to a particular social class, sex, or age stratum in society (Achenbaum, 1974).

Historical and cross-cultural consideration of the aged and aging does not reveal simply sets of numbers and fragmented observations about the status of old people in society. Somehow such explorations should enable us to gain a feel for what it was like to be old in a different place or at a different time. This, after all, is part and parcel of true understanding (Kastenbaum and Ross, 1975). It is well to remember that human behavior and social structure are inextricably related to individual and social values and beliefs. An examination of one often suggests the shape of another. It is one thing, for example, for the elderly to be treated as worthy and respected members of society when very few survive to be elderly. But if as today, many people survive into old age, the feelings of obligation and responsibility are quite different.

One of the most problematic yet most enticing facets of historical and cross-cultural investigation involves the synchronization of historical circumstances with individual experiences of aging. The selections to follow should be read with this question in mind: how, in fact, did an individual's social experience relate to his or her personal experience of growing, maturing, and aging? An individual's position is related not only to his or her particular social position and history, but is influenced as well by the cumulative experience reflected in the larger social history. A person's life experience cannot be understood by exploring just a single family or community; the investigator must assume a larger world view.

The popularization of historical investigations came about in part because the commonalities, face-to-face interaction, and the integration of human experience all appeared to be on the decline. With industrialization and increasing technological sophistication, specialization and often rather inflexible categorization occurred. What once may have been experienced as a more or less natural process became a stereotyped category. Growing old became something other than the inevitable result of being born; rather, to be old meant to be needy of certain types of security, to be incapable of performing certain occupational, physical, and mental tasks, and to be part of an identifiable group of "others."

Now we come full circle, for now we ask not only what it meant to be old in the past, but what it will mean for us in the future. As we will see, these questions have always been asked; it is the answers which vary according to time and place.

It will also become apparent that attitudes toward aging have always been ambivalent. Nonetheless, general themes emerge which will enable us to evaluate the selections in other sections of this text with a more intelligent, perhaps a more enlightened perspective. The societies described in this section seem to reflect more unified world views than any we are able to identify today.

Just as historical probing and curiosity is generally prompted by practical limitations which are perceived either in an individual's life or in the societal responses to social experiences, several of the selections to follow deal specifically with those factors which were related to changes in the society in question. The reader should not lose sight of the fact that the search for continuity and integration which has always been present is still central to gerontological endeavors. While the many disciplines which constitute gerontology often appear difficult to reconcile, the goal which generally surfaces is the eventual integration of understanding, experience, and active intervention in the way we grow old.

The first selection in this section considers aging in the Orient. Gino Piovesana argues that both China and Japan exhibit several orientations toward the aged which differ from Western perspectives but are similar to one another. Some of the important factors to emerge include the correlation between aging and wisdom, the crucial importance of the elderly in familial roles, the fundamental unity of the family, and the existence of a strong tradition of ancestor worship. Although Japan differs in many respects from China, several cultural themes spring from the same source. The reader is offered a description of the contrasting forms of political power and social organization, which the author feels are associated with differences in the social attitudes and treatments of the elderly in China and Japan. Piovesana discusses the generalizations often made regarding aging and family relations in Oriental societies, attempting to paint a picture which reveals historical perspective and a foreground filled with some modern day observations.

A contrasting perspective of society's attitudes towards the elderly is offered in Andrew Achenbaum's thought-provoking discussion of changes occurring in nineteenth century America. The ideal and the actual conditions were often at odds, because the American elderly, once the focus of a romantic, supportive orientation on the idealistic level were gradually subjected to a more pessimistic and negative evaluation in the years following the Civil War. The last half of the nineteenth century witnessed the rise of bureaucratic and specialist mentalities in the realms of medicine, science, economics, and labor. American medical research, for instance, was directed and nurtured almost exclusively by the work of European physicians. Descriptions became increasingly more precise, and explanations reflected the emerging biological orientation of what was to be known as "germ theory." As a result of a combination of these factors, old age was soon cast as a time of irritability, debility, and childish refusal to conform to cultural conventions—a time best suited for dying, not living. Add to this the increasing growth of bureaucratic organizations apparently composed of anonymous members who saw little value in the ways of the elderly, and both older people and their ways came to be characterized as obsolete. According to Achenbaum, the complex interweaving of technical and scientific innovations, bureaucratic orientation, and rapid social changes in the economic arena insured the elderly's loss of esteem, worth, and self-respect.

The third article, by Peter Stearns, argues that old age rarely enjoyed a prestigious position in pre-industrial societies. Using France for a case study, Stearns develops his premise, painting a rather gloomy picture of old age prior to the twentieth century. Reiterating a theme found in Achenbaum's work, Stearns maintains that few people could actually expect to grow old. Early death was a common and accepted occurrence. Analysis of European and early Greek and Roman writers lends support to the notion that old age was less than venerated, less than pleasurable. After identifying several negative attitudes toward aging, Stearns traces their persistence and pervasiveness into the experience of this century. He does feel confident that a new literature with a fundamentally different orientation toward aging has begun to emerge. While the traditional perspectives will not be radically altered in the course of a generation or two, pessimism may yet give way to a sense of vitality. In large measure, Stearns concludes what occurs in future decades is dependent on our own perspectives and on our attempts to modify the traditional orientations which we have been taught.

The final selection in this section, by Donald Cowgill, formulates a conceptual overview of aging and modernization. He defines modernization as the transformation of a society from a relatively rural orientation toward one which is predominantly urban. This transformation brings with it a modification of the sources of power, the types of technology, institutions, societal perspectives, and role complexes. Numerous factors are presumed to impinge upon and in turn be affected by development or modernization. These include economic changes, health and related technological changes, specialization of work roles, differing generational relations, and a larger number of older people in the society. In addition, the residential concentration of people within the society shifts, so that modernization is generally characterized by an increased pattern of urbanization. Related to urbanization, of course, is geographic mobility. The latter implies a new set of social relations, encompassing both parent-child relationships and the potential separation of work and home life. Cowgill concludes with several possible alternatives to the familiar theme that modernization or progress inevitably implies a deterioration of the status and esteem of older people in society. As he indicates, there are no simple answers to the question of how the elderly will be valued in the future.

REFERENCES

1. ACHENBAUM, W. A. "The Obsolescence of Old Age in America, 1865–1914." *Journal of Social History*, 8, Fall (1974): 48–62.
2. KASTENBAUM, R., and ROSS, B. "Historical Perspectives on Care." In *Modern Perspectives in the Psychiatry of Old Age*, edited by J. G. Howells, pp. 421–49. New York: Brunner/Mazel, 1975.

The Aged in Chinese and Japanese Cultures

Gino K. Piovesana

"The Orient" and "Oriental" are primarily geographical terms, and when speaking of the civilization of the East one has to use the plural form because there is no such thing as Oriental culture. Nakamura Hajime has rightly pointed out the superficiality of generalizations such as the "Oriental mind" or the "mystico-intuitive" Oriental soul. Indians, Chinese, Tibetans, and Japanese reveal very distinct characteristics in their ways of thinking and their attitudes even within some common religious background, which, it may be remarked in passing, appears to be common only because it is not analyzed in detail and depth (Nakamura, 1964, pp. 623–44). This paper comprises a discussion of traditional attitudes toward aging only in China and Japan where the common background, of Confucianism has enhanced the position of the old man in both societies (no attempt has been made to discuss the changes caused by recent developments). It is mostly within the family that old age receives special consideration in China and Japan. Yet because the family structure of both societies far transcends the limits of the family, reverence toward the aged has been a distinct characteristic of China and Japan.

Notwithstanding their differences, both societies possess this feature in common, as we shall see.

AGING IN CONFUCIANISM

Chinese thought and attitudes on aging are expressed in three books of the Chinese classics of Confucianism. In the best known of these, the *Confucian analects*, Confucius characterizes his own progress in sagacity in the following manner, giving at the same time the rationale why aging deserves our unqualified respect:

> At fifteen, I had my mind bent on learning. At thirty, I stood firm. At forty, I had no doubts. At fifty, I knew the decrees of Heaven. At sixty, my ear was an obedient organ for the reception of truth. At seventy, I could follow what my heart desired, without transgressing what was right [*Chinese classics*, I, *Confucian analects*, Bk. II, Ch. 4].

The strict correlation between aging and progress in wisdom could not be better indicated. Age meant accumulation of wisdom, and a man at seventy was considered to have reached almost a blessed state of moral learning and practical conduct. Later commentators of Confucius' sayings had some difficulties with this passage. When Confucius was almost divinized in later centuries, it was said of him that "he was born with knowledge, and did what was right with complete ease." Thus the above quotation was explained as if Confucius were speaking not of himself but of the common man in search of knowledge. Yet Confucius and his early followers who compiled the *Confucian analects* thought differently, and, commentators' casuistry aside, the belief that only age warranted progress in wisdom has been the characteristic of every Chinese sage and writer and the cardinal tenet of Confucian morals.

Although age as such is considered a necessary condition of moral progress, it is in the context of family relationships that it received most detailed explanation, aged parents deserving most consideration. Our quotation from the *Confucian analects* is soon followed by the teaching on filial piety, which does not mean merely supporting one's parents: "Dogs and horses likewise are able to do something in the way of support—without reverence; what is there to distinguish the one support given from the other?" (*Chinese classics* I, *Confucian analects*, Bk. II, Ch. 7). In Confucianism, reverence is a technical term and is akin to a religious feeling combined with awe and respect. Filial piety, however, is dealt with in another well-known Confucian classic which bears the specific title *Classic of filial piety*. There it is stated that "Filial piety is the root of all virtues, and the stem out of which grows all moral teaching" (*Sacred books of the East*, III, *Hsiao Ching* [*Classic of filial piety*], p. 466). This general principle is explained in several short chapters in which filial piety is taught to the Son of Heaven—the emperor—to princes, and to major and minor officials of the empire, down to the common man, for "nothing is greater than filial piety." The ruler and the ruled, the rich and the poor, the literati and the ignorant peasant—all had to profess this virtue. It was not only a private virtue, but a civic norm upon which rested the well-being of the realm. More practical norms to fulfill the obligations of filial piety were prescribed in another classic, *The book of ritual*, which also deals with the care of old people in general (*Sacred books of the*

East, Li Chi [*The book of ritual*], xxvii–xxviii, pp. 464–68; 229–30).

Because of the overwhelming role of Confucianism in shaping Chinese society, Chinese civilization has been characterized as a family culture and a culture of the old man (Lang, 1968, p. 10). China's heroes were neither the knights of medieval Europe nor the samurai of Japan, but literati and officials. Their qualifications increased with age because long years of study and experience were required to master the intricacies of Confucian learning and to acquire expertise in affairs of the empire—all based on preserving ancient traditions and regulated by meticulous procedures. To old age was attached a special sanctity also because only the aged could have the sense of the golden mean, another cornerstone of Confucian wisdom. Realistic and practical as the Chinese have always been, they were obviously aware of senility problems. Therefore, to avoid any excess and to reach a reasonable balance in everything without which no virtue could exist, *The doctrine of the mean* was taught in another sacred book of China (*Chinese classics, Chung Yung* [*The doctrine of the mean*] I, Pt. 2).

ANCESTOR WORSHIP AND AGING

Confucianism is a very broad term which embodies many cultural traits of ancient China. Not all of what commonly passes as Confucianism was initiated by Confucius: ancestor worship antedates Confucius, who, moreover, is known to have lacked interest in discussions concerning the condition of spirits after death. Confucius was concerned with an earthly-bound social ethic and not with transcendental beings and truths. He wanted to bring peace and order to a country divided by fighting lords. Priding himself on being a restorer of old traditions and not an innovator, Confucius retained ancestor worship, which, after all, canonized filial piety. To pay due respect to one's ancestors was considered very beneficial for the living, too, for it fostered the stability and the continuity of the family. For the common man, ancestor worship constituted the main component of Chinese religious life which was always centered in rites and ceremonies for the dead. Ancestor worship was likewise incorporated by Buddhism and Taoism—religious beliefs in China, as well as in Japan—since none of these religions found ancestor worship antagonistic to its religious tenets. Different names are used for the spirits of the dead, called in Japan *hotoke* by Buddhists and *kami* by Shintoists. However, to respect both the *hotokes* and the *kamis* is a basic virtue of every Japanese. In China a very common name for Buddhist monasteries was *Kuan Hsiao Suu* or Monastery for the Glorification of Filial Piety, and filial piety headed the ten Taoist virtues. The incorporation of ancestor worship into other religions was facilitated by the fact that it itself was not an "institutional" religion such as Buddhism, Taoism, and Shintoism, all of which have an independent theology, worship, and priesthood of their own. Ancestor worship is a "diffused" religion which relies upon other social structures to communicate its basic ideas and cult (Yang, 1967, pp. 294ff.). Ancestor worship was naturally centered in the family, and from the family it drew its main vitality, with institutional religions giving it ritualistic support.

Both aspects of ancestor worship, the religious and the earthly, were prominent features of Chinese and Japanese societies. This worship certainly redounded to improving the condition of the family on earth, in some cases keeping the family tradition alive for centuries. Japanese military families have left interesting historical records in the so-called *kakun*, or family instructions (laws), willed by the founder of the family. They were strictly followed by descendants and kept alive by retainers as well. When in the eighteenth century merchant families reached great prosperity and even political power, they were guided by "family instructions" in which the spirit of Japan's incipient

capitalism can easily be read. They were faithfully transmitted to the modern *zaibatsu* or the large-scale family concerns, the backbone of Japanese modernization.

Reports to the ancestors on important decisions the head of the family had to make constituted another side of ancestor worship which served to keep the tradition of the family alive. It is a custom even now in Japan that the emperor and the prime minister report to the ancestors of Japan at the Ise Shrine on important events of the country. The head of even a modest family never fails to obtain the blessing of the departed on occasion of a marriage, a long trip, and the like. In the family *butsudan* ("the altar of the Buddhas") or in the *kamidana* ("the altar of the Shinto gods"), tablets bearing the ancestors' names are preserved. But even in the absence of an altar in the house, family temples keep the tablets, where at least once a year special rites are performed. How much all this is a religious duty is a moot question into which it is not necessary to enter here. What is clear is that by honoring the ancestors a link is kept with the past, and the living too are more respected—the older members of the family being considered on the threshold of ancestor worship.

THE CONFUCIAN TRADITION IN JAPAN

Japan as a cultural entity is, like Korea and Annam, a "cultural variant" of the East Asian tradition mothered by China. Although Japan belongs to the Chinese sphere of cultural influence, she was never wholly captured by the Confucianism imported from the mainland around the fifth century of the Christian era. Japan was politically never conquered by China, and Confucianism was juxtaposed with nativist traits and did not alter the political structure of Japan. The warrior-aristocratic structure of Japanese society was never challenged by Chinese political ideas evolved by Chinese Confucianists. In this sense Japan was less receptive than Korea. In respect for the aged, however, the Japanese were not inferior to the Chinese. Filial piety took, as we shall see, a distinctive Japanese character—an adaptation to Japanese conditions of the original Confucian belief.

The Confucian classics were brought into Japan as early as A.D. 404–405, although it is only with the Taiho code (702) that we are able to assess the impact of Confucianism on Japan.* A Confucian Academy was established, and books like the *Confucian analects* and the *Classic of filial piety* became mandatory texts. The Taiho legislation codified filial piety in more than one article. An official, for example, had to leave office during the period of mourning for parents (three years), and also when the sickness of parents required his presence near them. In the case of an official living far from home, a leave of absence was provided every three years to allow him to perform his duties which included preparing his parents' bed for a restful night and inquiring about their health in the morning. The part of the Code which deals with criminal offenses lists six cases of unfiliality to be met by measured punishment. Offensive words and deeds top the list, followed by failure to support parents and lack of proper behavior during the mourning period, ending with crimes of adultery with concubines of a grandfather or father.

The part of the Code dealing with civil matters is prefaced by an injunction to governors of provinces to make a tour of their districts once a year to acquaint themselves with people who had become distinguished as a dutiful son, an obedient grandson, a righteous husband, or a virtuous wife. The reward for the meritorious was exemption from taxes. Many examples of such virtuous deeds are given in ancient Japanese chronicles. The *Zoku Nihongi, The ancient chronicle of Japan,* for instance, records ten cases of dutiful sons for the years 714–722 (Sakamoto, 1965, pp. 47–49). In March 757, Fuji-

wara no Nakamaro, following the example of the T'ang dynasty Emperor Hsuan-tsung, published an edict whereby all subjects had to provide themselves with a copy of the *Classic of filial piety,* almost a dream then in Japan considering the level of literacy even among aristocrats. Fujiwara no Nakamaro is, however, an interesting case because he deposed Crown Prince Doso who allegedly behaved impolitely during the period of mourning. Filial piety was also the reason why Oi, the new Crown Prince, was chosen, and the same rationale was used by the Empress Koken when in 758 she handed over the throne to Crown Prince Oi. The empress could take her leave to observe the period of mourning only by abdication.

Political expediency aside, it is obvious from the above examples how respect for parents was held in high esteem in ancient Japan. Japanese Buddhism in this did not compare with Confucianism. Shinran (1173–1262), the founder of a popular Buddhist sect, said, for instance, that he had never recited his *Nembutsu* prayer with his parents in mind. Buddhist books used to praise a man who left his elderly mother to become a monk, certainly a mortal sin for any Confucianist and a crime in the eyes of most Japanese. Buddhism, although it gave the Japanese consolation in time of death, never offered a social ethic which was based solely on Confucian norms. Confucianism, moreover, in the course of becoming accepted, was modified to fit the Japanese political structure. Thus, for example, the theory of dynastic changes by revolution when the emperor was no longer fulfilling the Mandate of Heaven was never accepted in Japan. To be sure, military rulers were demoted, but emperors (who had no political power) were left unscathed by warring lords fighting for political supremacy. Filial piety, too, underwent some adaptations in Japan, coming in second best after loyalty to the lord or the ruler of the land.

The China envisioned by Confucius was not a land of warriors. His perfect gentleman was not a samurai, and martial virtues

---

* Before the Taika Reform (645) and the use of the Chinese calendar, Japanese chronology is very approximate.

were not fostered by Confucianism. As the Chinese saying goes: "Good iron is not used for nails; a good man does not become a soldier." Japanese society was different, however, and conflicts between duties toward parents and the lord were bound to arise. To settle the matter as early as 827, the *Keikoshu* (a collection of prose and poetry) stressed (in the twentieth *kan* or "book") the priority of loyalty over filial piety. With the developing of feudalism in medieval Japan and during the Tokugawa period (1600–1867), warrior bravery prevailed over the Confucian civic virtues. Yet, if we exclude cases of obvious conflict, the samurai spirit blended well with Confucianism, and certainly did not lessen respect toward parents and elders in general. As a matter of fact, the warrior spirit and Confucianism formed what is called the modern *kazoku seido* or "the familial structure" of the prewar Japanese state centered in the emperor.

However, before we discuss modern Japan, the best known and most respected Tokugawa Confucianist, Nakae Toju (1608–1648) must be mentioned. Nakae, the "Saint of Omi," as he is often called from the name of the province from which he came, wrote the popular and widely read *Dialogues with an old man* (*Okina mondo*). In this book as well as in more learned works, Nakae extolled the virtue of filial piety and the respect due to parents in particular. The very title of the book clearly indicates the Confucian belief that only men advanced in age could impart wisdom. Naturally, this prestigious source was often used by other Confucianists. Some quotations from Nakae's *Dialogues* have so permeated Japanese society that they cannot be passed over in silence:

> Filial piety is the root of man. When it is lost from one's heart, then one's life becomes like a rootless plant, and if one does expire instantly, it is nothing but sheer luck. . . . Filial piety is what distinguishes men from birds and beasts. When men are not filial, Heaven will visit upon them the six major pun-

ishments. It was said in ancient times that a man without filial piety turned into a man with a dog's head, clearly indicating that he was a beast. . . . Filial piety is the summit of virtue, and the essence of the Way in the three realms of heaven, earth, and man. What brings life to heaven, life to earth, life to man, and life to all things, is filial piety [Tsunoda, 1958, pp. 383–84].

It is clear, especially from the last sentence, that for Nakae filial piety was an eternal and universal principle, the origin of everything, the underlying moral power in the universe. Nakae is usually credited with spreading the notion that the duties of filial piety were but a reciprocal payment for the debt children had toward parents who had brought them into the world and cared for them during their helpless infancy. It was an obligation "higher than the heavens and deeper than the seas," as Nakae himself wrote, which naturally meant that it was limitless and by definition incapable of repayment. Tsuda Sokichi, a great authority on Chinese and Japanese Confucianism, has maintained that to equate filial piety with this basic sense of obligation is more characteristic of Japanese than of Chinese moralists. Be that as it may, it is obvious that Japanese Confucianists cultivated filial piety as much as their colleagues in China. Chinese and Japanese societies were, however, quite different, which explains why filial piety took different forms.

AGING AND FAMILY IN CHINESE AND JAPANESE SOCIETIES

China by 2000 B.C. passed from a tribal organization to feudalism which ended with the Warring States Period (fifth to third century B.C.). By the middle of the third century B.C., the Chinese empire began to take shape, and Confucianism, which had been born during the Warring States Period, was to become the ideological backbone of the empire. It was almost a thousand years later that the neo-Confucianism of Chu Hsi became the official learning of the empire, as a result of the enforcement of the examination system for Chinese officials, with examinations based upon Chu Hsi's new commentaries on the Confucian classics. Yet the basic tenets of the most popular classics such as the *Confucian analects* and the *Classic of filial piety* molded Chinese society well before Confucianism became the official learning.

Much is made of the ideological nature of Confucianism. Imperial China was an agrarian society, which needed a large peasant class and a centralized government with a powerful bureaucracy to solve the problems of land irrigation and flood prevention by means of large-scale public works. Confucianism was, no doubt, a viable ideology to uphold the structure of the empire. "The root of the empire is in the State; the root of the State is in the family; the root of the family is in the individual." This famous saying by Mencius well epitomized the basic political philosophy of Confucianism, which postulated an individual brought up to respect the father, obedient to the authorities outside the family, and, ultimately, to the emperor. In the *Classic of filial piety* it is hinted that "the filial piety with which the superior man serves his parents may be transferred as loyalty to the ruler" (*Sacred books of the East*, III, *Hsiao Ching* [*Classic of filial piety*], p. 483). Yet this point cannot be stressed too much, because in China filial piety was never identified with loyalty as was the case in Japan. In this sense Confucianism was made an ideology much more in Japan than in China, as we shall soon see in more detail.

First, however, some general considerations on aging and family relations in China. As a sociologist says: "Since Chinese society in general has placed strong emphasis on age considerations, as well as those of kinship, it is not odd that age considerations play a considerable part in role differentiation within the family" (Levy, 1949, p. 48). Both "absolute" and "relative" age groupings have been emphasized in China. According to the same expert, "Chinese society's orientation to age is one which invests increasing age with increasingly higher status" (Levy, 1949, p. 48). This is in marked contrast with the industrial West, in particular the United States, which is a youth culture. In the West honor to aged people is a "matter of sentimentality. In China extreme age lends to judgment a weight of validity which is lacking in the West" (Levy, 1949, pp. 63–64). The word *lao* (old) was an honorific term used as a prefix for persons who at times were, absolutely speaking, not aged at all. The prefix "old" gave the honor of age to what followed. Thus the father of a friend was referred to as "old elder brother of my father" although old age and family relationship were both non-existent. In China as well as in Japan there is no single term for brother or sister. The terminology of the family was carried over to denote the relationship between friends (a friend of considerably older age being also called "uncle" or even "father"), while in the West, especially in the United States, close relationship between father and son tends to take over the terminology of friendship and business, as manifested by terms such as "pals" and "partners." In China the reverse process is characteristic, family relationship determining all the others (Levy, 1949, pp. 134ff.).

Experts on Japanese society emphasize even more the use of "displaced" terminology. As one says, "the habit of modelling the structure of social groups outside the family . . . on the pattern of the family, has been developed [in Japan] with a consistency rare in other societies" (Dore, 1958, p. 94). Even today and despite Japan's modernization which demands more impersonal forms of association, the *oyabun-kobun* ("father-part and son-part") system or organization exists in business, trade unions, political parties, academic institutions, athletic teams, and even among criminals. The elder person, accorded the title father, is naturally not related in terms of kinship to his followers, and the *aniki-bun* ("elder-brother-part") is only metaphorically attributed to older members of the group. But what cements these social units is not so much filial duty, or younger-toward older-brother relationship. Loyalty is the real bond, a derivation of the feudal fealty which has been characteristic of much of Japan's history.

The Chinese family was a self-contained unit, but in Japan the family was part of a larger grouping. At the top was the feudal lord, and loyalty toward him came first. A typical anecdote about Confucius tells the story of a feudal lord (still extant at the time of Confucius) who boasted of the loyalty of his subjects, instancing as proof the fact that a son would not fail to report his father if the latter had committed a crime. Confucius replied that in his state citizens were more virtuous because there no son would ever accuse his father. Japan's history is, however, the story of military rulers, of warring barons, and of Tokugawa feudalism which lasted to very recent times. Loyalty to the feudal lord was essential to a society of samurai, who lived by the sword and were in constant danger of death. Japanese Confucianists never had the prestige and the authority which the Chinese literati had. Japanese Confucianists rationalized their warrior society by advocating *chuko ippon*, "unity of loyalty and filial piety."

This unity was not orthodox Confucianism but it certainly helped Japan's modernization. Industrialization directly sapped the solidarity of Chinese society, based exclusively as it was on the family unit. The modernization of Japan instead was fostered by a family structure which extended to the political realm, making the emperor the head of what was called a *kazoku kokka,* or the "family structure of the state."

Feudalism in Japan ended officially in 1868 when the power of the Tokugawa military rulers was restored to the emperor; fiefs were abolished, and local lords renounced their privileges in favor of the new state. The Emperor Meiji and more so his new ministers, the so-called oligarchs, launched Japan into a rapid and superimposed modernization. The Japanese family was not subverted in the process because its cohesion was sublimated into the great family which was the new Japanese nation. Divided feudal loyal-

ties were unified under the aegis of the emperor who became the new symbol of national unity. The family-state system was undoubtedly artificially fostered by the oligarchs for it was a very convenient tool for Japan's rapid development.

Some early-Meiji-period intellectuals tried to reject the traditional family system and Confucian ethic in general. Fukuzawa Yukichi in particular distinguished himself by his attacks on Confucianism and its ideas on the family (Blacker, 1964, pp. 67ff.). Others, however, thought differently, especially those in government service like Motoda Eifu. They succeeded in 1890 in having promulgated the Imperial Rescript on Education which sanctioned the new morals for Japanese youth, a "teaching bequeathed" from ages past, "infallible for all ages and true in all places." The imperial house represented the direct descendants from the divine progenitors of Japan, and since the other families were somewhat related to and dependent upon such lofty ancestors, the whole nation formed a great family.

This ideology took more explicit shape in 1910 when new textbooks on Japanese morals were prepared. Scholars in government service, such as the philosopher Inoue Tetsujiro and the constitutionalist Hozumi Yatsuka, worked out the details of the family-state concept of national polity. Jurists had previously (1890–1898) debated the new Civil Code which was then in preparation. Traditionalists opposed innovators who wanted to change the customary family laws under the impact of French civil codes. Hozumi Yatsuka published in 1891 an article, typical of the conservative viewpoint, bearing the title: "The Emergence of the Civil Code and the Destruction of Loyalty and Filial Piety" (Rabinowitz, 1968, pp. 17–43). The dispute centered mainly on the headship of the family—the head of the family, according to Japanese tradition (which was much stricter than in China), having all parental rights.

Behind the dispute was the thesis that the rights of the head of the family were but representative of the power and authority of the head of the great family which was the nation. To tamper with the former was to impugn the latter. In the 1930s when militarist nationalism took over Japan, the family-state concept reached its climax. In a book published by the Ministry of Education which in a few years sold more than two million copies the following is stated:

> Filial piety directly has for its object one's parents, but in relationship toward the emperor finds a place within loyalty.... Our country is a great family nation, and the Imperial Household is the head family of the subjects and the nucleus of national life.... In China, too, importance is laid on filial duty, and they say that it is the source of a hundred deeds. In India, too, gratitude to parents is taught. But their filial piety is not a kind related to or based on the nation. Filial piety is a characteristic of Oriental morals; and it is in the convergence with loyalty that we find a characteristic of our national morals, and this is a factor without parallel in the world [Tsunoda, 1958, p. 789].

The book in question was the *Kokutai no Hongi* or *The fundamentals of our national polity,* published in 1937. In 1941, the *Shimin no Michi* (*The way of the subject*) reinforced and carried to its ultimate conclusions the loyalty due to the state on the part of Japanese subjects. Until the defeat of Japan in World War II, the family-state concept, referred to as the unique "national polity" (*kokutai*) of Japan, was extolled by politicians and schoolmasters, and in countless publications. After 1945, a natural reaction set in, and progressive intellectuals in particular attacked the family-state ideology as the source of all evils which had brought upon Japan the miseries of war and defeat. Now a much more sober evaluation of the family structure of Japanese society is in the offing—Japan's rapid modernization and even her postwar economic miracle being connected with the family system.

A return to the good points of a family system, which has always linked the present family with past and future generations, seems to be a quest of contemporary China and Japan, notwithstanding their great cultural and social changes. This would appear to be a lesson for the West, where the past or the traditional tends to be disconnected with the present and the future. But a national identity cannot exist without a link with a traditional past.

REFERENCES

BLACKER, C. *The Japanese Enlightenment: a Study of the Writings of Fukuzawa Yukichi.* London: Cambridge University Press, 1964.

Chinese Classics. Translated by J. Legge. London: Oxford University Press, 1893–1895.

DORE, R. P. *City Life in Japan.* Berkeley: University of California Press, 1958.

LANG, O. *Chinese Family and Society.* Handon, Conn.: Archon Books, 1968.

LEVY, M. J., Jr. *The Family Revolution in Modern China.* Cambridge: Harvard University Press, 1949.

NAKAMURA, H. *Ways of Thinking of Eastern Peoples: India–China–Tibet–Japan.* Honolulu: East-West Center, 1964.

RABINOWITZ, R. W. "Law and the social process in Japan." *Transactions of the Asiatic Society of Japan* (3rd series) 10 (1968).

Sacred Books of the East. Translated by J. Legge. London: Oxford University Press, 1879–1885. (Republished, Delhi: Motilal Banarsidas, 1968.)

SAKAMOTO, T. *Nihon ni okeru rinri shiso no tenkan* (*The Development of Ethical Thought in Japan*). Tokyo: Yoshikawa Kobunkan, 1965.

TSUNODA, R. et al., eds. *Sources of Japanese Tradition.* New York: Columbia University Press, 1958.

YANG, C. K. *Religion in Chinese Society: a Study of Contemporary Social Functions of Religion and Some of their Historical Factors.* Berkeley: University of California Press, 1967.

The Obsolescence of Old Age

W. Andrew Achenbaum

During the last third of the nineteenth century, no dramatic event or theory suddenly transformed prevailing perceptions of the elderly's position in society. Many Americans continued to acknowledge the aged's worth and to idealize their usefulness.[1] Some writers, in fact, sought to demonstrate that novel ideas inspired and popularized by Charles Darwin's monumental *Origin of Species* (1859) warranted assigning the aged a favorable place in society. Inferring that Darwinism lent support to the romantic claim that old age represented the culmination of life, Americans sometimes blended a mixture of antebellum notions and current scientific belief about evolution, and argued that the elderly deserved respect because their contributions were unique and their achievements distinctive.[2] Hence, once again we find the resilience of positive opinions about old people's presumed value despite the ceaseless reworking of the normative and intellectual foundations of American culture at large.

Nevertheless, with growing frequency after the Civil War, Americans began to challenge nearly every favorable belief about the usefulness and merits of age that had been set forth by republican and romantic writers and that still appeared in contemporary literature. Instead of depicting the elderly as stately and healthy, more and more observers described them as ugly and disease-ridden. Instead of extolling the aged's moral wisdom

Reprinted by permission from *Old Age in the New Land: The American Experience Since 1790* (Baltimore, Maryland: The Johns Hopkins University Press, 1978). Copyright © 1978 The Johns Hopkins University Press.

and practical sagacity, popular and scientific commentators increasingly concluded that old people were incapable of contributing anything to society. By the outbreak of World War I, if not before, most Americans were affirming the obsolescence of old age.

The period roughly between 1865 and 1914, therefore, constitutes an important transition in the history of ideas about growing old. (More precise dating is impossible because the flowering of predominantly unfavorable perceptions about old people's worth occurred in medical and business circles, among other groups, at different moments and developed at dissimilar rates.) It is not the first time that definitions of the aged's usefulness altered; there had been subtle continuities and changes since at least the 1790s. Nor did scientists or essayists discover any liability or disadvantage associated with old age that earlier observers had not already catalogued. But the era does mark a watershed in which the overall estimation of old people's worth clearly changed.

How, then, do we account for this significant change in perceptions? Why did Americans after the Civil War conceptually strip the aged of roles once described as essential and assign them no new functions to compensate for the loss? It is tempting to say that the answer lies in the shift from romanticism to realism. That is, the evanescence of the romantic sensibility, especially its emphasis on subjective experience, its pious overtones, and its idealistic world view, was eventually displaced by a more objective, secular, and dispassionate perspective.[3] However, this shift taking place in high culture is too diffuse and its timing is too imprecise to explain satisfactorily how and when new ideas arose in the specific sphere of defining older people's roles and places in American life. And while negative opinions about the elderly's worth were consonant with the pessimistic version of Social Darwinism articulated during the latter decades of the nineteenth century, they were neither solely dependent upon or derived from it.

The obsolescence of old age cannot be fully understood by referring to broad cultural tendencies alone. Rather, it is necessary to delineate and explain the interplay of a particular set of attitudes and circumstances, which vitiated the generally complimentary concepts of older people's status and caused new ones to emerge. As I shall show, the unprecedented disesteem for the elderly reflected and resulted from the impact of new scientific, bureaucratic, and popular ideas converging with innovations in medical practice, the economic structure, and American society itself.

One of the reasons why antebellum America had considered elderly men and women useful was because they exemplified the rules of conduct then considered the surest way of enjoying a ripe old age. Although the aged remained living proof that adhering to prescribed modes of behavior enhanced the possibility of a long life, writers after 1865 gradually became less willing to claim that the elderly possessed the most efficacious means of promoting longevity. Specialized scientific knowledge seemed to promise even greater success than enlightened common sense in increasing life expectancy and preventing disease.

Efforts to improve public health and to promote hygiene received tremendous support after the Civil War. States began creating and authorizing boards of health to establish and regulate more sanitary living standards and to investigate the causes and prevent the spread of contagious diseases. The discovery of different bacteria and the reformulation of the germ theory in the latter half of the nineteenth century, moreover, provided a sounder rationale for combating disease than had been available to earlier sanitary reformers. In addition, observers asserted that reductions in infant and child mortality and increases in life expectancy could be attributed to better infant care and improvement in nutrition at early ages as well as to advances in caring for the sick and infirm.[4] Success in applying new ideas and techniques led Americans to believe not only that people were living longer than ever before but also that more gains could be expected in the future. Improved life expectancy, writers increasingly concluded, "depends on no mysterious law of development. . . . It is the necessary result of agencies so obvious and so powerful in our civilization that we need statistics not so much to prove their existence but to measure their results."[5]

Physicians, biologists, and sanitary engineers, therefore, assumed a greater and highly technical role in studying and advancing the principles conducive to increasing longevity and improving hygiene. Americans after the Civil War still acknowledged the importance of moral and sensible deportment, but they steadily preferred to rely on the advice of experts rather than the insights of experience.[6] As more and more Americans deferred to the collective wisdom of professionals, the value of older men and women as promoters of healthful living decreased.

And yet, through the articles and ideas they contributed to magazines like *Harper's* and *Popular Science Monthly* as well as their own professional journals, scientists and doctors did more than displace the elderly from their long-standing societal function as examples of healthful lifestyles. Advances in American medical theory and practice during the last third of the nineteenth century also legitimized the invidious distinction people were making between desiring a long life and wanting to grow old. The practical question was "not whether we can push the natural age of man to ninety or one hundred years, but whether we can keep our bodies so pure and active, and so preserve the integrity of our mental powers, that between fifty and ninety, our place will not be in seclusion, but in some degree, at least, in the full tide of world's activities."[7] In contrast to earlier medical opinions, scientists gradually concluded that the debilities of age were not simply the result of natural decay, but stemmed from more deplorable causes.

It is important to note that the first important changes in medical ideas about old age occurred across the ocean, especially in France and Germany. Many researchers designed their investigations on the principle, circulating in Europe since the second quarter of the nineteenth century, that it was important to correlate localized pathological lesions with symptoms in identifying particular diseases. Such studies received added impetus after 1858, when Rudolph Virchow demonstrated that one could actually observe pathological lesions in cells under a microscope. Virchow not only improved the possibility of refining localized pathology but also endeavored to synthesize the prevailing concept of pathology with an older and more holistic theory of pathology by stressing the need to observe the total bodily reaction to specific, localized diseases.[8]

The most influential work on old age published in Europe during the 1860s and 1870s was Jean-Martin Charcot's *Leçons cliniques sur les maladies des vieillards et les maladies chroniques* (1876), a systematic study of the relationship between old age and disease among inmates at a large public hospital for women in Paris. Charcot's major finding was that there were some diseases that arose from the general physiological modifications of an aging body, a second group of diseases that existed at other periods of life but presented special characteristics and dangers in old age, and a third class of diseases from which old people seemed to be immune.[9] His clinical work indicated that the degeneration and weakening of the cells of specific organs and vessels during the latter stages of life caused specific diseases. Hence, Charcot documented both the importance of identifying localized structural lesions and recognizing that the bodily reactions associated with diseases at other ages did not always manifest themselves in old

age: "In old age, the organs seem, as it were, to become independent of one another; they suffer separately, and the various lesions to which they may become subject are scarcely echoed by the anatomy as a whole."[10]

Charcot's work was not a radical departure from existing ideas about diseases in old age; Charcot acknowledged, for example, that scientists had been studying the pathological manifestations of old age for more than a century. Nor was he the first to gather together in a systematic manner evidence indicating that specific diseases existed in old age.[11] At the time of its publication, however, Charcot's work was considered the most extensively researched exposition based on the belief that one could understand diseases in old age only by clinically investigating localized structural lesions. Charcot's publication was not only accepted as the standard monograph on the subject but also was well circulated; a second edition was published in 1874. It is significant for my purposes that Charcot's study of the diseases of old age was the only European work of its kind to be translated into English.[12] In 1881, William Tuke translated Charcot's lectures for the New Sydenham Society in London, and two New York doctors published an American edition the same year. For the majority of doctors in the United States who were not bilingual, the English translations of Charcot's lectures provided their first full-length contact with current European ideas about the pathological aspects of growing old.

The timing of the translations themselves, moreover, gave Charcot's work an importance as a model for future research in the United States far beyond its actual merits. By 1881, American medical theory and practice had advanced sufficiently to permit doctors to engage in research using the same theoretical framework and clinical techniques on which Charcot had based his inquiry.[13] An increasing number of physicians during the post–Civil War period were familiar with the concepts, methodology, and instruments necessary to study structural pathology. Doctors and scientists interested in doing research received professional encouragement and rewards for their work and could associate with medical faculties and hospitals willing to support pure research. Medical schools at Harvard, Pennsylvania, Columbia, Johns Hopkins, and Michigan and hospitals in metropolitan centers and elsewhere began to receive greater financial support from the private sector to underwrite research. Thus, when the first English editions of Charcot's work appeared, the American medical profession was predisposed to accept and then develop its premises and findings.

This does not mean, of course, that American doctors after the Civil War suddenly embraced all new medical ideas or rushed into laboratories to look at lesions under microscopes. Most doctors, in fact, were more inclined to continue the antebellum practice of recommending ways to postpone the effects of old age than they were to devote years to investigating its causes. Articles on old age in popular and scientific journals as well as in family medical guides typically offered practical advice on personal habits, diet, and exercise.[14] Prescribed medications further demonstrate the persistence of traditional practices: homeopaths and other sectarian physicians still offered recipes for home remedies to cope with minor ailments; some orthodox doctors continued to recommend opium as an analgesic for the elderly.[15]

Nevertheless, new ways of conceptualizing, researching, and treating diseases in old age began to circulate with increasing frequency and significance in the United States during the last decades of the nineteenth century. For example, once American doctors began to accept new European ideas about senile pathology, they needed precise, not general, terms to define its manifestations. "Senility," which was once simply a synonym for "old age" as a stage of life, now referred specifically to the "weakness and decrepitude characteristic of old age." The word gradually gained pathological connotations; it is suggestive that the American biologist Charles Sedgwick Minot noted in his definition of "senility" for the *Reference Handbook of Medical Science* (1885) that he chose to "follow Charcot closely." Doctors

also enlarged their lexicon to describe diseases peculiar to old age.[16] These new definitions underlined the growing interest in defining the pathological aspects of old age as unique and localized entities. In addition, more and more American investigators following in the direction elucidated by Charcot began to research and operate on the ailments and diseases of old age.[17] Case studies of senile gangrene, senile bronchitis, senile pneumonia, and senile chorea among other disorders appeared in medical journals. Refined clinical observations of localized lesions also facilitated surgeons' efforts to relieve the suffering of their aged patients.

Some research proved to be controversial and unsuccessful. For example, Dr. Charles E. Brown-Séquard, a French-American scientist chiefly known for his research on the nervous system and adrenal glands, attributed senility to "diminishing action of the spermatic glands," and reasoned that injecting semen into the blood stream of old men might restore lost vigor. In 1889, at the age of seventy-two, Brown-Séquard injected himself with a mixture of water, semen, and testicular fluids and claimed, "I regained at least all the strength I possessed a good many years ago."[18] The effect lasted four weeks. Brown-Séquard's formula appeared on the market within months as "Pohl's Spermine Preparations." Despite the enthusiasm greeting the initial findings, general interest waned after high expectations were not met. The seminal experiment was not rejuvenating: the drug's effect wore off quickly and did not restore complete physical strength. It also was not totally effective: Dr. Brown-Séquard died five years later even though he injected himself regularly with his mixture. Brown-Séquard had not discovered the elixir of life; by studying an aspect of senile pathology, he only had devised a way to excite the nervous system. But his failure neither deterred other scientists from pursuing new lines of inquiry nor discouraged them from publishing revolutionary ideas about the nature of disease in old age.

Indeed, around the turn of the century, Elie Metchnikoff, a bacteriologist working in Paris, believed that he had discovered the cause of old age: poisonous microbes accumulating in the intestines produced toxic reactions that, he claimed, caused the human organism to degenerate and eventually to die. He recommended as an antidote that people drink sour milk, because the lactic acid in it prevented putrefaction in the intestinal tract. Metchnikoff noted that sour milk was a staple in the diet of Bulgarians, who were thought to be Europe's healthiest and longest-lived people. Popular confidence in this panacea was somewhat shaken by the scientist's death at seventy-one. Subsequent research, moreover, invalidated Metchnikoff's hypothesis that a pathologic phagocytosis caused senescence.[19]

Elie Metchnikoff's significance in the history of medical ideas about old age, however, transcends both his particular theory and his specific therapy for degeneration in old age. Metchnikoff built his theory on Charcot's work, but differed from his predecessor on one essential point: "The senile degeneration of our organism is entirely similar to the lesions induced by certain maladies of a microbiotic origin. Old age, then, is an infectious, chronic disease which is manifested by a degeneration, or an enfeebling of the noble elements, and by the excessive activity of the microphages."[20] Whereas Charcot verified the existence of a senile pathology, Metchnikoff characterized old age as an atrophy *sui generis*.

Metchnikoff's assertion that old age itself was a chronic, infectious disease was well publicized and had a significant, and sometimes paradoxical, impact on medical research and popular thinking at the beginning of the twentieth century. Some researchers, sharing Metchnikoff's opinion that old age was a curable disease, hoped to eradicate toxic disturbances located in various parts of the body. Sir Victor Hursley, for example, concentrated on the degeneration of the thyroid gland; Dr. Arnold Lorand stressed the simultaneous deterioration of several ductless glands.[21] However, many doctors doubted that scientists could ever cure old age precisely because they agreed with Metchnikoff that it *was* a progressive disease. Nihilism flourished among those believing

that "the ravages of years remain as irreparable in the twentieth century as they were in the time of Solomon."[22] The general public, meanwhile, kept informed of debates and developments in the medical sciences by reading articles on old age in encyclopedias and popular journals. Regardless of their optimism or pessimism about the advances made or anticipated in aging research, all these articles confirmed that experts had not yet succeeded in making old age more healthy and attractive, and thus they provided a scientific basis for dreading the coming of age. "If there is any disease in the world it is this. No one looks forward to it with eager anticipation. Nobody welcomes it, nobody enjoys it. . . . It is a disease, that is to say it is essentially a pathological condition. . . . But for it there exists no therapy, no cure."[23] Contrary to previous judgments, attaining old age no longer seemed either a remarkable or a desirable achievement.

By the first decade of the twentieth century, therefore, specialists had not only superseded the elderly as experts in health matters but had also convinced the general public that old people suffered incurable pathological disorders. The ultimate result of living a long life, medical evidence confirmed, was often more deleterious than useful. Consequently, new scientific theories and data forced people to reevaluate their opinions about the elderly's value in other capacities.

"NOT ALL OF THE CENTENARIANS ARE PARAGONS OF ALL THE VIRTUES."

Scientists, almanac compilers, philosophers, and other commentators increasingly challenged the antebellum assumption that surviving to old age proved a person's inherent goodness and sagacity. "Survival was a precondition of progress, but it did not insure progress or define its essence. . . . Survival was a brute fact, not a moral victory."[24] Thus people became less inclined to claim that wisdom necessarily improved with age. In fact, they claimed to have data confirming that old age was a dreadful stage of life ravaged by diseases and debilities that eventually destroyed all cerebral powers.

Research published after the Civil War seemed to demonstrate, contrary to earlier opinions, that people's intellectual faculties declined with age. Sir Francis Galton, an English biologist and statistician, and an American named George M. Beard conducted research in the 1860s and 1870s indicating that people's mental capabilities were greatest between the ages of thirty and forty-five. Significantly, they attributed the decline in intellectual accomplishments after sixty to pathological disorders common to old people.[25] Subsequent studies corroborated their findings. According to W. A. Newman Dorland's The Age of Mental Virility (1908), for example, man's creative power developed steadily to the age of sixty and then fell off. "While in the vast majority of cases [of people over sixty] declining physical and mental ability progressed pari passu to the cessation of life, there loom up, amid the general wreck of bodily and cerebral powers some striking instances of remarkable vitality and virility, standing out, like beacon lights of hope, far beyond the period of normal decay."[26] Writers cited such evidence, which was consistent with current theories about senile pathology, to substantiate the idea that old age corroded the mental capacities of most men and women.

Many observers claimed, moreover, that old people often compounded their difficulties by making themselves inaccessible to new ideas or alternate ways of doing things. In Principles of Psychology (1890), for instance, William James argued that people became more and more enslaved to familiar conceptions and established ways of assimilating ideas as they grew old. "Old-fogyism, in short, is the inevitable terminus to which life sweeps us on."[27] James's reference to "old fogyism" is suggestive. Although the word "fogy" was occasionally used before the Civil War, it did not yet refer exclusively to old people. According to the lexicographers of Webster's dictionary, who cited it for the first time in the 1880 edition, a "fogy" was a "dull old fellow; a person behind the times, over-conservative, or slow:—usually preceded by old."[28] By the latter decades of the nineteenth century there was a special term to describe old people who would not, or could not, keep up with the times.

The very factors that accounted for old people's declining mental capacities and decreasing ability to absorb new information seemed to explain their unpleasant personality traits. As George Beard explained: "The querulousness of age, the irritability, the avarice are the resultants partly of habit and partly of organic and functional changes in the brain."[29] They also provided plausible reasons for questioning an earlier assumption that people invariably gained in moral stature as they aged. "Not all of the centenarians," one commentator pointedly observed, "are paragons of all the virtues."[30]

Old people's unwillingness to conform to cultural conventions, in turn, confirmed the evolving contention that their behavior was not always exemplary. Physicians recommended, for example, that men over fifty and women over forty-five curtail their sex lives. They justified abstention with medical evidence couched in moral tones. Dr. John Harvey Kellogg contended that seminal fluid deteriorated in old age. "Even at its best, its component elements could only represent decrepitude and infirmity, degeneration and senility."[31] The children of old men, he claimed, were feeble and died prematurely. Women, on the other hand, should recognize that menopause signaled the end of sexual activity.[32] Older people who defied the dictates of nature could expect to suffer the consequences. "When the passions have been indulged and their diminishing vigor stimulated, a horrid disease, satyriasis, not infrequently seizes upon the imprudent individual, and drives him to the perpetration of the most loathsome crimes and excesses."[33] Others claimed that emotional numbness, loneliness, physical pain, mental anguish, and economic difficulties often drove the elderly to desperate measures. Dr. Elie Metchnikoff, for example, reported that elderly men committed suicide more frequently than young men and that the aged poor were more likely to take their lives than those who were financially secure.[34]

Contemporary medical research and everyday observations, therefore, persuaded Americans to reject the antebellum notion that being old intrinsically bestowed better judgment or guaranteed moral behavior. "Years do not make sages;" the *New England Almanac for 1872* informed readers, "they make only old men."[35] Reaching this verdict, however, did not automatically lead to the deduction that old people were physically, mentally, or morally incapable of contributing to society. The conviction that old age was a period of economic obsolescence arose primarily in the minds of observers and participants in big business.

"THE SUPERANNUATED MAN"

The rise of large-scale business and organizations is one of the major factors affecting life in late nineteenth-century America. Although the slow transition from an agrarian to an industrial-based economy had already begun, the big business corporation as well as a variety of other economic institutions and government offices did not grow in size and scope until after the Civil War. These new structures had a profound effect. "Corporate structures gradually altered the meaning of property, the circumstances and motivations of economic activity, and the careers and expectations of most citizens."[36] Accompanying the evolution of these organizations was the emerging idea that bureaucratic principles should be employed to ensure that workers performed tasks competently and punctually and to establish channels of authority and responsibility. Efficiency had become the *sine qua non* of any successful enterprise by the turn of the century. Consequently, impersonality symbolized a bureaucratic order in which functions and procedures, not particular men, were indispensable.[37]

Precisely because the rise of large corporate structures and the formulation of bureaucratic principles were incremental processes, Americans did not instantly or completely overturn favorable assessments of the aged's worth in the marketplace. Some writers as late as 1900 still affirmed that old people had vital roles to play. Even if the elderly were not actively directing operations, their experience assured them a place as consultants; at the very least, they could perform ancillary tasks.[38] And yet, observers of the emerging industrial order did become more articulate over time in describing how new conditions and ideas were reducing Americans' dependence on older workers' seasoned experience to ensure economic success.

> In the search for increased efficiency, begotten in modern time by the practically universal worship of the dollar . . . gray hair has come to be recognized as an unforgivable witness of industrial imbecility, and experience the invariable companion of advancing years, instead of being valued as common sense would require it to be, has become a handicap so great as to make the employment of its possessor, in the performance of tasks and duties for which his life work has fitted him, practically impossible.[39]

An unmistakable shift was occurring in perceptions of the elderly's value in the labor force.

A new trend in discharging employees after they had attained a certain age provides one of the clearest indications that ideas about old people's usefulness were changing. The practice had precedents: some states had set retirement ages for judges in the antebellum period. And yet, infirmity, debility, or an employer's displeasure were the only reasons why older workers had normally been forced to quit their jobs; age per se had not been a decisive factor in leaving the labor force before the Civil War. Then, between 1861 and 1915, the federal government and especially private industry began to design and implement policies that discharged workers because they were considered too old to stay on the job.

The first federal retirement measure became law in December 1861, when Congress passed an act requiring any naval officer below the rank of vice admiral who was at least sixty-two to resign his commission; the retirement age for naval officers was raised to sixty-four in 1916.[40] The earliest policy applying to sailors entitled them to retire, because of age or infirmity, on half pay after twenty years of service. There was no fixed age for retirement for sailors until 1899, however, when a minimum age (fifty), not a maximum limit, was imposed.[41] A measure passed in 1869 permitted, but did not require, a federal judge to retire after serving ten years and attaining the age of seventy on a pension equal to his salary at the time of retirement.[42] "An Act to promote the efficiency of the Revenue-Cutter service" (1902) required all incapacitated officers to be dropped from service by the president; all officers were required to retire at sixty-four. Because these were the only retirement policies instituted at the federal level by World War I, it is fair to conclude that the practice of retiring government officials was still in the embryonic stages and affected only a limited number. Nor were there any uniform standards in the measures established: specific acts set different retirement ages for each group; receiving a pension was not always contingent on having served a certain number of years.

Retirement policies in the private sector also were in the formative stages. Transportation companies inaugurated the earliest pension programs. In 1875, the American Express Company permitted workers past sixty to receive some compensation upon retirement. The Baltimore and Ohio Railroad retirement policy (1884), which stipulated minimum age (sixty-five) and service (ten years) requirements, has been called the "pioneer in this country in the movement to pension its employees."[43] There was considerable variation in the pension programs instituted. For example, although most corporations did not require workers to contribute to pension funds, contributory programs did exist. The age of retirement and the number of years of service required for an employee to be eligible for a pension also differed from company to company. Nevertheless, it is apparent that an increasing number of firms appreciated the need to establish some sort of policy to remove older workers from the labor force. Although only eight companies instituted programs between 1874 and 1900, twenty-three others began policies between 1901 and 1905, and twenty-nine more offered employee retirement pensions between 1906 and 1910. Ninety-nine additional corporations initiated policies between 1911 and 1915.[44] The idea of requiring people to retire or offering them the option to do so because they had attained a particular age was gaining acceptance in the private sector.

Disesteem for older employees' worth clearly motivated a company's decision to exact mandatory retirement. As F. Spencer Baldwin, an economics professor at Boston University, explained:

> It is well understood nowadays that the practice of retaining on the pay-roll aged workers who can no longer render a fair equivalent for their wages is wasteful and demoralizing. The loss is twofold. In the first place, payment of full wages to workers who are no longer reasonably efficient, and in the second place, there is the direct loss entailed by the slow pace by the presence of worn-out veterans, and the consequent general demoralization of the service.[45]

From management's viewpoint, retirement systems improved efficiency and morale by removing expendable workers. From a larger perspective, it was claimed that corporations that offered job security, merit promotions, and adequate compensation in old age "inevitably attract the highest grade of men and women, and obtain from them the most efficient work."[46]

The meanings of "retirement" and "superannuation" changed to embrace the policies implemented by large-scale organizations. The primary sense of "retire" in 1828—to withdraw from public notice—had become obsolete according to the lexicographers of the 1880 edition of Webster's *American Dictionary*. Instead, they attributed a new meaning to the verb: "retire" among other things meant "to cause to retire; specifically to designate as no longer qualified for active service; as to *retire* a military or naval officer." An additional definition was added to the verb "superannuate": "To give pension to, on account of old age, or other infirmity."[47] Note the derogatory attitude toward old age displayed in both definitions. Retirement now meant that people reached a stage of their careers at which they were *no longer qualified* for gainful employment because of age. Reaching old age entitled a person to a pension just as other disabilities qualified workers for special considerations.

The unprecedented devaluation of older workers' usefulness was felt even more deeply and pervasively in the marketplace than was signified by new retirement policies and dictionary definitions. Many writers commented on "the tendency—visibly increasing in this country—of relegating the older and middle-aged men to the oblivion of an 'innocuous desuetude.'"[48] Laborers and craftsmen over forty-five who were worn out or displaced by machines found reemployment opportunities limited. Taking an inferior job was not always a satisfactory solution, writers warned, since workers rarely regained steps taken backward.[49] If employment prospects were poor for those in their fifties, they were even worse for people in their sixties. "The things that most promote the welfare of the wage-earning class militate most against old age employment . . . The old man today . . . slow, hesitating, frequently half-blind and deaf, is sadly misplaced amid the death dealing machinery of a modern factory."[50] The evidence reveals similarly negative sentiments about older workers outside the factory gates. Civil Service employees over sixty were said to retain only "partial efficiency" despite years of service; older clergymen, lawyers, or doctors, it was said,

were rarely offered new opportunities for service or advancement.[51] While recognizing that men often ceased working more abruptly than women, commentators noted that society often made both sexes feel superfluous. "We soothe our souls and say to ourselves, 'Grandmother is comfortable and content.' We rarely ask if grandmother is useful and happy."[52] Writers described their contemporaries as treating older women as if they were baubles with only negligible jobs to fulfill.

Thus by the turn of the century, even those who asserted that the elderly *could* contribute something to society admitted that they no longer reflected the opinions of most Americans.[53] Changing circumstances and new priorities seemed to have diminished the aged's worth as veterans of productivity and enhanced the purported value of youth. "Not all the sandwich men in our large cities or the sitters in our public parks are victims of intemperance or shiftlessness; they are, in many cases, the product of an industrial and economic system that thrives only on young blood."[54] This observation was not confined to the economic sphere. Modern conditions, people increasingly believed, required youth, not age, to assume the roles of advancing society and putting life into perspective.

"OLD AGE, LIKE DEATH, IS MERELY INCIDENTAL."

Although Americans after the Civil War generally considered it axiomatic that the human condition improved as society progressed, this did not mean that the human life cycle necessarily followed the same pattern of development. "The dominant aspect of evolution was to be not the genesis of species, but the progress of Civilization."[55] Progress had a dual nature. Blessed with infinite possibilities, civilization was ultimately evolving to its most perfect culmination. Human development, on the other hand, was finite. The retrogression and eventual demise of man was viewed as a necessary and inevitable law of nature that insured the continual unfolding of mankind's destiny.[56]

This concept of evolutionary progress had ominous implications for the aged. New scientific theories and economic realities convinced Americans that individuals declined in old age as human existence marched on. Because they perceived the elderly to be afflicted with pathological disorders and no longer able to keep up with the pace, it is not surprising that writers claimed old people had lost their grasp on the meaning and nature of societal development. Presuming it to be a law of nature that an individual's connection with societal progress relaxed with the coming of age, Americans gradually discounted the value of old people's insights and claimed that young people were in the best position to understand the meaning of life.

> Old men cherish a fond delusion that there is something mystically valuable in the mere quantity of experience. Now the fact is, of course, that it is the young people who have all the really valuable experience. It is they who have constantly to face new aspects of life, who are getting the whole beauty and terror and cruelty of the world in all its fresh and undiluted purity.... Old age lives in the delusion that it has improved and rationalized its youthful ideas by experience and stored-up wisdom, when all it has done is to damage them more or less—usually more.[57]

More and more people came to the conclusion that digesting a lifetime of experience in old age served little purpose. Circumstances seemed to be changing too rapidly to warrant copying the practices of the past; the elderly often imitated or reiterated earlier insights anyway.[58] Youth's enthusiasm, versatility, self-confidence, and pluck, it was said, more than compensated for the lack of seasoned experience. Psychologist G. Stanley Hall captured the heightened sense of importance attached to "youth" as a vital social asset in his monumental work, *Adolescence* (1905). "Despite our lessening fecundity, our over-schooling, 'city-fication,' and spoiling, the affectations we instill and the repressions we practice, [youth] are still the light and hope of the world."[59] Historians point to the economic, educational, and religious changes occurring in the latter quarter of the nineteenth century as factors leading to the tremendous value placed on youth. Because of young people's ambiguous relationship to a society that simultaneously abhorred and participated in the quest for power and order affecting every aspect of existence, radicals and conservatives alike could agree on the appropriateness of that stage of life as a symbol of regenerative power.[60]

Consequently, Americans after the Civil War increasingly challenged the antebellum notion that youth should heed the wisdom of age, and proposed instead that youth was the most exalted stage of life. "As a rule the energy which moves the world in the right direction is that of young men, and correspondingly and naturally the only deference and respect worth having or that can bring satisfaction and happiness to the recipient go to them."[61] This is not the first time in American history, of course, that people celebrated young men and women's zest and potential. Furthermore, pages of advertisements for hair dyes or "physical culture rejuvenation" programs and advice columns recommending that older women wear brighter clothes or stop knitting in the far corner of the parlor represent variations on an age-old phenomenon: many Americans have been trying to look and act younger than their years ever since Ponce de Leon first searched for the fountain of youth.[62] And yet, while it would be incorrect to claim that the cult of youth instigated or even necessitated the depreciation of age, it is clear that the changes in the social as well as economic structure of society, coupled with new ideas about the meaning of progress and experience, forced Americans to reevaluate the relative merits of both age groups and to reach a new verdict. "The whole world is charged with youth," most were concluding by the turn of the century. "Old age, like death, is merely incidental."[63]

The association of death with age as well as the implication that both were incidental to the twentieth-century world of the young is tantalizing. Before we can accept such an observation as representative of the period, far more research must be done on the history of attitudes toward death per se. Nevertheless, primary resources and recent scholarship do suggest that new attitudes toward death may have exaggerated Americans' exultation of youth and denigration of age. Advances in science and technology did not mitigate youth's fear of death, but they apparently lessened the risk of dying young: actuarial statistics computed at the time indicated that the death rate was declining after the Civil War for all age groups under fifty. Improvements in sanitation and public health promised more favorable mortality rates for all but the elderly.[64] Writers reasoned, moreover, that the potential problems of overcrowding and cultural stagnation in a world "overshadowed by too many hoary Methuselahs" made the elderly's demise societally beneficial. In addition, there was an acceptable biological explanation for death among the aged: life was finite because worn-out tissues became increasingly vulnerable to pathological disorders and decay.[65] There was even psychological evidence suggesting that the old, unlike the young, were reconciled to dying. According to a study conducted in 1896 on the relationship between old age and death, a majority of old people thought life was most enjoyable in youth, but would not care to live life over and longed for death.[66]

Hence, theories propounded and evidence presented by biologists, statisticians, public health experts, and psychologists among others confirmed that old people were in the best position to understand the meaning of death. Had the republican and romantic assumptions about the need for all people to come to grips with their own mortality continued to prevail, Americans might still have recognized that old people's perceptions on dying were a valuable asset. But unlike their predecessors, people tended to ignore the potential usefulness of old people's proximity to death. Perhaps they had no other choice, given their belief that youth

had a monopoly on all valuable experiences. As William James noted in *The Varieties of Religious Experience* (1901), the reality of death poignantly reminded people that "old age has the last word: the purely naturalistic look at life, however enthusiastically it may begin, is sure to end in sadness."[67] Because the aged had the last word about the inevitability of death, they were excluded from a world awed by the vitality of youth, a world that increasingly chose to deny the existence of death. "Slowly and with difficulty the septuagenarians climb the steep hill leading to the great temple of youth.... They beat at the doors, and alas! these do not open. They crave only admittance, and a stool in a quiet corner, but the ruthless revellers turn a deaf ear."[68] The young refused the old admission into their world. Youths no longer considered it vital to acknowledge the wisdom and talents of age; they discounted its worth, feared its association with death and excluded it from their midst.

Because of changes after the Civil War in societal patterns and cultural trends, Americans by the outbreak of World War I no longer claimed that the elderly exclusively fulfilled roles that would guarantee them respect. As efforts to increase life expectancy and improve hygiene became more technical and successful, specialists gradually replaced the aged as promoters of healthful longevity. New ideas about pathological disorders weakening the intellectual capacities and moral faculties at advanced stages of life, which the elderly's own seemingly aberrant behavior confirmed, undermined older people's functions as guardians of virtue. Science alone, however, did not condemn the elderly to uselessness. Americans increasingly perceived that the rise of large-scale organizations and the implementation of new bureaucratic principles not only reduced the need to tap the aged' assets but also accentuated their handicaps. In fact, the growing belief that society was changing at a progressively quicker rate further reduced the estimated value of the elderly's cumulative experience; "youth" was thought to be most attuned to modern conditions and most capable of ensuring continued progress. Thus, the stage of life once characterized as the culmination of human existence had become obsolescent.

The unprecedented devaluation of old people's worth is fraught with irony. For it was the lingering romantic notion that every stage of life was unique that encouraged writers, faced with different circumstances and armed with new ideas, to revise the value system implicit in earlier conceptions of the stages of life. Observers between 1865 and 1914 increasingly explained that the heightened worth of youth arose in response to, and as a product of, a new realistic era. Yet writers justified youth's importance by appropriating the assets previously ascribed to the old. Hence, they increasingly contended that the elderly lacked the very experience, wisdom, and power that earlier generations had once claimed made it sensible for youth to honor, or at least heed, age. Perhaps even more ironically, this new, objective, tough, vigorous realism was premised in part on the denial of death. Death had not lost its sting, of course, but new ideas and conditions prevailing in society did enable contemporaries to reach the conclusion that the reduced probability of dying young was a clear indication of the march of progress in the United States. Hence, more and more Americans in the last decades of the nineteenth century overcame death by ignoring it in youth and associating it with age.

NOTES

1. See, for example, Horace Bushnell, "How to Make a Right and Ripe Old Age," *Hours at Home* 4 (December 1866): 106–8; "Ideal of Old Age," *Living Age* 122 (17 March 1874): 704; Henry Wadsworth Longfellow, "Morituri Salutamus," in *Complete Poetic Works of Henry Wadsworth Longfellow*, Cambridge ed. (Boston: Houghton Mifflin Co., 1922), p. 314; "Fruitful Age," *Godey's Lady's Book* 41 (December 1875): 566–67; S. G. Lathrop, ed., *Fifty Years and Beyond; or, Gathered Gems for the Aged* (New York: F. H. Revell, 1881); Margaret E. White, *After Noontide* (1888; reprint ed., Boston: Houghton Mifflin, 1907), p. 33; "Can We Spare the Old Men?," *Independent* 55 (2 July 1903): 1580–82; J. Madison Taylor, "The Conservation of Energy in Those of Advancing Years," *Popular Science Monthly* 64 (February 1904): 349; "Some Grand Old Women," *World Today* 21 (July 1911): 886; and M. M. Pattison Muir, "Some Compensations of Age," *Living Age* 276 (22 March 1913): 740–43.

   It is important to note that favorable estimates of the aged's place in society were not confined to middle-class, white, native-born writers. Religious bodies, such as the various branches of Judaism, and sects, such as the Quakers and Shakers, described the aged's status in positive terms because of their spiritual tenets. Several immigrant groups also maintained respect for the aged in the new land in accordance with cultural assumptions they had adhered to in the old world. See, for instance, Virginia Yans-McLaughlin, *Family and Community* (Ithaca: Cornell University Press, 1977), pp. 256–57.

2. W. H. DePuy, *Three Score Years and Beyond* (New York: Nelson and Phillips, 1873), pp. i–iii, 7; Nathan Allen, "The Law of Longevity," *Medical Record* 9 (1874): 108–11; Edward Henry Sieveking, *The Medical Adviser in Life Assurance* (Hartford: N. P. Fletcher, 1875), p. 97; George Murray Humphry, *Old Age: The Results of Information Received Respecting Nearly Nine Hundred Persons Who Had Attained the Age of Eighty Years, Including Seventy-four Centenarians* (Cambridge: Macmillan and Bowes, 1889), pp. 140–41; and John M. Keating, *How to Examine for Life Insurance* (Philadelphia: W. B. Saunders, 1891), pp. 177–78.

3. For more on this shift, see John Higham et al., *History* (Englewood Cliffs, N.J.: Prentice-Hall, Inc., 1965), pp. 92–95, and Stow Persons, *American Minds* (New York: Holt, Rinehart and Winston, 1958), pp. 201–3, 217–38.

4. Gert Brieger, ed., *Medical America in the Nineteenth Century* (Baltimore: The Johns Hopkins University Press, 1972), pp. 255, 278; Charles E. Rosenberg, *The Cholera Years* (Chicago: The University of Chicago Press, 1962), pp. 5, 228; Barbara G. Rosenkrantz, *Public Health and the State* (Cambridge, Mass.: Harvard University Press, 1972), pp. 5, 72–77, 107.

5. Charlton T. Lewis, "The Influence of Civilization on the Duration of Life," *Sanitarian* 5 (May 1877): 175, 197. See also "Longevity," *Science* 7 (29 January 1886): 109; *"Do We Live Longer?"* *Independent* 53 (28 March 1901): 741; "Longevity," *Johnson's Universal Encyclopedia*, 8 vols. (New York: A. J. Johnson, 1894), 5:348; Langdon Kain, "Man's Span of Life," *North American Review* 166 (April 1898): 493.

6. This argument is consistent, I believe, with the finding that there was an increasing contemporaneous reliance on "professional" judgments pervading American culture itself. For fuller analyses of this point, see Charles E. Rosenberg, *No Other Gods* (Baltimore: The Johns Hopkins University Press, 1976), pp. 2–4; Burton Bledstein, *The Culture of Professionalism* (New York: W. W. Norton, 1976), pp. 80, 90, 99.

7. Nicholas Smith, *Masters of Old Age* (Milwaukee: The Young Churchman, 1905), pp. 1–2. See also "Of Growing Old," *Atlantic Monthly* 71 (March 1893): 305; Robson Roose, "The Art of Prolonging Life," *Popular Science Monthly* 35 (October 1889): 766–73; "When Does a Man Become Old?," *Current Literature* 32 (February 1902): 191; Henry M. Friedman, "Problems of Life," *Medical Record* 86 (7 November 1914): 796.

8. Lester Snow King, *Growth of Medical Thought* (Chicago: University of Chicago Press, 1963), p. 218; Thomas Bonner, *American Doctors and German Universities* (Lincoln, Neb.: University of Nebraska Press, 1963), p. 111. It is worth noting that the concept of disease specificity itself is quite old: it had been expressed in more general terms even before Morgagni of Padua demonstrated in 1761 that disease processes were often localized in organs. See Richard H. Shryock, *Medicine and Society in America, 1660–1860* (New York: New York University Press, 1960), pp. 63–64.

9. Jean-Martin Charcot, *Clinical Lectures on the Diseases of Old Age*, trans. Leigh Hunt (New York: William Wood, 1881), p. 24. For more on Charcot, see Joseph T. Freeman, "Medical Perspectives in Aging," *Gerontologist* 5 (March 1965), pt. 2, pp. 21–22; and M. D. Grmek, *On Ageing and Old Age* (Den Haag: Uitgeverig Dr. W. Junk, 1958), pp. 71–72, 78.

10. Charcot, *Clinical Lectures*, p. 26.

11. For instance, Karl Friedrich Constatt, working in an obscure German village, published *Die Krankheiten des hoheren Alters und ihre Heilung* in 1839. This compendium of diseases of old age rested, however, more on personal speculative philosophy than clinical observations. In addition, Maxime Durand-Fardel published a *Traité clinique des maladies des vieillards* (Paris: Bailliére, 1854), which some medical historians consider to be sounder than Charcot's work even though it did not enjoy the attention Charcot attracted. See Frederic D. Zeman, "Life's Later Years: XI," *Journal of Mt. Sinai Hospital* 13 (1946–47): 246–49 and idem, "Life's Later Years: XII," ibid. 16 (January–February 1950): 308–12.

12. There was at least one work, already published in English, that shared Charcot's assumption that subtle, latent changes in the aged organism modified ordinary diseases and produced peculiar symptoms. See John Gardner, *Longevity: The Means of Prolonging Life after Middle Age* (London: Henry S. King, 1874), pp. iii, 18–19, 28–35, 144, 157–58.

13. The factors summarized here are developed more fully in Richard H. Shryock, *Medicine in America* (Baltimore: The Johns Hopkins University Press, 1966), pp. 22–30, 168–69; Bonner, *American Doctors*, pp. 29–39, 69, 109–11; Joseph F. Kett, *The Formation of the American Medical Profession* (New Haven: Yale University Press, 1968), pp. vii, 180.

14. See, for example, Samuel G. Dorr, "Care and Treatment of Old People," *Buffalo Medical Journal* 35 (1896): 145–48; George W. Post, *Cottage Physician* (Springfield, Mass.: King-Richardson, 1898), p. 585; Joseph G. Richardson, *Modern Family Physician and Home Guide* (Rochester: Rochester Book Company, 1889), pp. 1095–96; D. A. Sargent, "Exercise and Longevity," *North American Review* 164 (May 1897): 556–61; William G. Anderson, "How a Woman Renewed Her Strength," *Ladies Home Journal* 28 (January 1911): 12.

15. On home remedies, Post, *Cottage Physician*, pp. 585–86, is typical. See also J. Y. Dale, "Opium as a Hypnotic in Old Age," *University Medical Magazine* 6 (1894): 322–24.

16. Charles Sedgwick Minot, "Senility," in *Reference Handbook of Medical Science*, ed. Albert H. Buck, 7 vols. (New York: William Wood, 1885), 6: 388. See also Richard Quain, *A Dictionary of Medicine* (New York: D. Appelton & Co., 1883), p. 1416; George M. Gould, *Illustrated Dictionary of Medicine, Biology and Applied Science*, 5th ed. (Philadelphia: P. Blakiston & Co., 1903), p. 1315; Christian A. Herter, *Biological Aspects of Human Problems* (New York: Macmillan Co., 1911), pp. 112–19.

17. Zeman, "Life's Later Years: XII," pp. 65–66.

18. Newell Dunbar, ed., *Dr. Brown-Séquard's Own Account of the "Elixir of Life"* (Boston: J. G. Cupples Co., 1889), pp. 22–28. Brown-Séquard proposed, but never tested, that a mixture of crushed ovaries could be used to restore vitality to women.

19. Elie Metchnikoff, *Prolongation of Life* (New York: G. P. Putnam's Sons, 1908), pp. 36, 72, 161–81.

20. Idem, "Old Age," in *Smithsonian Institution Annual Report, 1903–4* (Washington, D.C.: Government Printing Office, 1905), p. 548. Metchnikoff was not the first scientist ever to classify old age as a disease; variations on this idea had been circulating since at least classical Rome. But the theory as Metchnikoff formulated it seemed particularly credible because it was consistent with other medical principles in vogue in late-nineteenth-century America. In that particular context, Metchnikoff's ideas were more widely discussed and accepted in both medical and nonprofessional circles than they might have been at an earlier point in time.

21. See, for example, Charles G. Stockton, "The Delay of Old Age and the Alleviation of Senility," *Journal of the American Medical Association* 45 (15 July 1905): 169; Arnold Lorand, *Old Age Deferred* (1910; reprint ed., Philadelphia: F. A. Davis, 1912), pp. 51, 90, 114; Marshall Langton Price, "Ancient and Modern Theories of Age," *Maryland Medical Journal* 49 (February 1906): 45–61; Elie Metchnikoff, *The Nature of Man* (New York: G. P. Putnam's, 1905), p. 261.

22. The quotation is from L. Menard, "Remedies for Old Age," *Scientific American Supplement*, no. 1756 (28 August 1909), p. 138.

23. Carl Snyder, "The Quest for Prolonged Youth," *Living Age* 251 (10 November 1906): 323. See also "Growing Old," *Godey's Lady's Book* 86 (February 1873): 147; *Encyclopedia Americana* (1904), s.v. "diseases of old age"; J. G. Bandaline, "The Physiology of Old Age," *Current Literature* 35 (September 1903): 344; Harriet Paine, *Old People* (Boston: Houghton Mifflin Co., 1910), pp. 171–72.

24. For more on this point, see John C. Green, *The Death of Adam* (Ames: Iowa State University Press, 1959), p. 335; David W. Marcell, *Progress and Pragmatism* (Westport: Greenwood Press, 1974), pp. 102, 115–16, 129, 143.

25. Francis Galton, *Hereditary Genius* (London: Henry King, 1869); idem, *Inquiries into the Human Faculty* (London: Macmillan Co., 1883); George M. Beard, *Legal Responsibilities in Old Age* (New York: Russells', 1874); idem, *American Nervousness* (New York: G. P. Putnam's Sons, 1881).

26. W. A. Newman Dorland, *The Age of Mental Virility* (New York: The Century Co., 1908), pp. 31, 70–71. See also B. W. Richardson, "Memory as a Test of Age,"

Scientific American 65 (10 October 1891): 224; Nathaniel Southgate Shaler, *The Individual: A Study of Life and Death* (New York: D. Appelton & Co., 1901), p. 275; Samuel Butler, *Life and Habits* (1877; reprint ed., London: A. C. Fifield, 1911), pp. 170, 295–99.

27. William James, *Principles of Psychology*, 2 vols. (New York: Henry Holt & Co., 1890), 2: 1910. See also "Young World," *Outlook* 105 (4 October 1913): 256.

28. *An American Dictionary of the English Language* (1880), s.v. "fogy."

29. Beard, *American Nervousness*, p. 250. See also J. T. Trowbridge, "Old Man Gram," *Harper's Magazine* 56 (January 1878): 225–28; "Restlessness in Age," *Living Age* 240 (9 January 1904): 124–25; Ada Cambridge, "The Retrospect," *Atlantic* 103 (January 1909): 133.

30. Kain, "Man's Span of Life," p. 472. See also "Age vs. Youth," *Scribner's Magazine* 40 (August 1906): 251. New words were coined to describe the aged's eccentricities. According to Harold Wentworth and Stuart Berg Flexner, *Dictionary of American Slang* (New York: Thomas Y. Crowell, 1967), the earliest use of "geezer" and "fuddy duddy" in America date around 1900.

31. John Harvey Kellogg, *Plain Facts about Sexual Life* (Battle Creek, Mich.: Office of the Health Reformer, 1877), p. 92. This "fact" also appeared in the 1881, 1889, and 1903 editions of this influential and popular guide.

32. Idem, *Plain Facts for Young and Old* (Burlington, Iowa: Segner and Condit, 1881), p. 123. See also Carroll Smith-Rosenberg, "Puberty to Menopause," in *Clio's Consciousness Raised,* ed. Mary Hartman and Lois Banner (New York: Harper Torchbooks, 1974), pp. 23–38.

33. Kellogg first diagnosed satyriasis in 1881. See also Colin A. Scott, "Old Age and Death," *American Journal of Psychology* 8 (October 1896): 120–21.

34. Metchnikoff, *Nature of Man*, p. 131. Interestingly, Metchnikoff does not cite statistics on women committing suicide. It is worth noting that Emile Durkheim's study of suicide (1897) stated that suicide "achieves its culminating point only at the final limits of human existence" (Emile Durkheim, *Suicide*, ed. George Simpson [New York: Free Press, 1968], pp. 101–3).

35. *New England Almanac* (January 1872), p. 22. See also "Old Age," *Living Age* 182 (31 August 1889): 531; "The Intellectual Effect of Old Age," ibid. 184 (25 January 1890): 250–51; "Centenarians," ibid. 221 (20 May 1899): 532.

36. Thomas C. Cochran, *American Business* (New York: Harper and Row, 1968), p. 51; Elisha P. Douglass, *Coming of Age of Business* (Chapel Hill: University of North Carolina Press, 1971), pp. 287–88; Melvyn Dubofsky, *Industrialism and the American Worker* (New York: Thomas Y. Crowell, 1975), pp. 1–29; Louis Galambos, "The Emerging Organizational Synthesis in Modern American History," *Business History Review* 44 (Autumn 1970): 288.

37. Robert Wiebe, *Search for Order* (New York: Hill and Wang, 1968), pp. 145–63; Glenn Porter, *Rise of Big Business* (New York: Thomas Y. Crowell, 1973), p. 21. On the efficiency craze, see Samuel Haber, *Efficiency and Uplift* (Chicago: The University of Chicago Press, 1964), and Daniel Nelson, *Managers and Workers* (Madison: University of Wisconsin Press, 1975), esp. ch. 4.

38. See, for example, Peter Finley Dunne, *Mr. Dooley's Opinions* (New York: R. H. Russell, 1901), p. 183.

39. "Independent Opinions," *Independent* 75 (28 August 1913): 504.

40. U.S., *Revised Statutes*, 2d ed., sec. 1443. U.S., *Statutes at Large*, vol. 39, sec. 579.

41. U.S., *Revised Statutes*, 2d ed., sec. 4756. See amendments in U.S., *Statutes at Large*, vol. 23, sec. 305, and ibid., vol. 30, sec. 997.

42. U.S., *Revised Statutes*, 2d ed., Sect. 714.

43. Lee Welling Squier, *Old Age Dependency in the United States: A Complete Survey of the Pension Method* (New York: Macmillan Co., 1912), pp. 74–82, 110–20; Alden Hatch, *American Express* (Garden City: Doubleday & Co., 1950), p. 89. See also the forthcoming works by William Graeber and Carole Haber.

44. Murray Webb Latimer, *Industrial Union Systems in the United States and Canada*, 2 vols. (New York: Industrial Relations Counselors, 1932), 1: 50.

45. F. Spencer Baldwin, "Retirement Systems for Municipal Employees, *Annals of the American Academy of Political and Social Science* 38 (1911): 6; Alcott W. Stockwell, "Problem of Superannuation in the Civil Service," *Putnam's Magazine* 7 (1909–10): 565–71. See also Gilman M. Ostrander, *American Civilization in the First Machine Age* (New York: Harper Torchbooks, 1972), p. 263.

46. Burton J. Hendrick, "The Superannuated Man," *McClure's Magazine* 32 (December 1908): 117.

47. See Webster, *American Dictionary, s.v.* "retirement," "superannuation"; and *Zell's Popular Encyclopedia* (Philadelphia: T. Ellwood Zell, 1871), p. 954.

48. Dorland, *Mental Virility*, pp. 3–4. See also "The Spectator," *Outlook* 67 (20 April 1901): 899; Emerson G. Taylor, "The Best Years," *Reader Magazine* 9 (December 1906): 67; E. P. Powell, "Passing of Old Age," *Independent* 77 (9 March 1914): 344.

49. See, for instance, Forbes Lindsay, "The Man of Fifty," *Harper's Weekly* 53 (16 October 1909): 15; John A. Fitch, "Old Age at Forty," *American Magazine* 71 (March 1911): 655–56; Edward T. Devine, *Misery and Its Causes* (New York: The Macmillan Co., 1909), pp. 124–25.

50. Hendrick, "Superannuated Man," p. 118. For comparable trends in management, see David Brody, *Steelworkers in America* (Cambridge, Mass.: Harvard University Press, 1960), pp. 25–26.

51. For material on civil service employees, see Franklin MacVeigh, "Civil Service Pensions," *Annals of the American Academy of Political and Social Science* 38 (1911): 4; and U.S., Congress, House, *Report on Retirement of Superannuated Civil Service Employees*, 62d Cong., 2d sess., 1912, H. Doc. 732. On other professionals, see "How to Grow Old," *Nation* 83 (1 November 1906): 365; Marthe Bruère, "Growing Old Together," *Good Housekeeping* 58 (January 1914): 87; "Old Age and War," *Outlook* 108 (11 November 1914): 567.

52. Martha Bruère and Robert Bruère, "The Waste of Old Women," *Harper's Bazaar* 47 (March 1913): 115. See also "The Leisured Class," *Living Age* 250 (14 July 1906): 120; Richard Washburn Child, "What Shall We Do with the Old?," *Everybody's* 21 (September 1909): 356; and Margaret E. Sangster, "Another Talk with Old Ladies," *Ladies Home Journal* 17 (May 1900): 34.

53. N. E. Yorke-Davies, "Why Grow Old?," *Popular Science Monthly* 43 (June 1893): 230–31; An Elderly Woman, "The Land of Old Age," *Harper's Bazaar* 40 (August 1906): 675; "Work and Long Life," *Outlook* 104 (2 August 1913): 737; Amelia E. Barr, *Three Score and Ten* (New York: D. Appelton, 1915), pp. 241–43; Marcus M. Marks, "Retirement from Business," *Review of Reviews* 36 (November 1907): 557–58; John F. Cargill, "The Value of Old Age," *Popular Science Monthly* 67 (August 1905): 313.

54. Hendrick, "The Superannuated Man," p. 120.

55. John Fiske, *Man's Destiny Viewed in Light of His Origin* (London: Macmillan, 1884), pp. 25–30. See also Humphry, *Old Age*, pp. 10–11; Shaler, *Individual*, pp. 62–63; Herter, *Human Problems*, pp. 178–79; Charles Horton Cooley, *Social Process* (1918; reprint ed., Carbondale: Southern Illinois University Press, 1966), p. 56; Brooks Adams, *The Law of Civilization and Decay* (1896; reprint ed., New York: Alfred A. Knopf, 1943), p. 31. For more on the general point, see Frederic Cople Jaher, *Doubters and Dissenters* (New York: The Free Press, 1964), pp. 3–14, 20–27; and Marcell, *Progress and Pragmatism*, pp. 31–36.

56. Cooley, *Social Process*, p. 408. See also T. E. Young, *On Centenarians; and the Duration of the Human Race* (London: Charles and Edwin Layton, 1899), pp. 130–31; M. G. Watkins, "Old Age," *Living Age* 221 (5 October 1901): 59; Herbert Spencer, *The Principles of Biology*, rev. ed., 2 vols. (1899; reprint ed., New York: D. Appelton, 1904), 2: 413; James Mark Baldwin, *Individual and Society* (Boston: The Gorham Press, 1911), p. 156; "The Tragedy of Age," *Harper's*

Bazaar 47 (May 1913): 222; *Independent* 75 (28 August 1913): 503.

57. Randolph S. Bourne, *Youth and Life* (1913; reprint ed., New York: Books for Libraries Press, Inc., 1967), pp. 12–14. Samuel Butler had anticipated Bourne's assertion in *Life and Habits* (London: Trübner & Co., 1877), p. 299. See also "Old Men, by One of Them," *Living Age* 192 (5 March 1892): 630; Washington Gladden, *Ruling Ideas of the Present Age* (Boston: Houghton Mifflin, 1895), pp. 9–10; Shaler, *Individual*, p. 262.

58. Dorland, *Mental Virility*, p. 24; Sangster, "Another Talk with Old Ladies," p. 34; James, *Principles of Psychology*, 2: 401; James Quayle Dealey, *The Family in Its Sociological Aspects* (Boston: Houghton Mifflin, 1912), p. 90.

59. G. Stanley Hall, *Adolescence*, 2 vols. (New York: D. Appleton & Co., 1905), 1: 50 and 2: 60. See also "A Secret of Youth," *Outlook* 86 (6 July 1907): 498; Jane Addams, *The Spirit of Youth and the City Streets* (New York: Macmillan, 1909), pp. 140–42; Edwin L. Sabin, "In Praise of Age," *Lippincott's Magazine* 89 (May 1912): 715.

60. Joseph F. Kett, *Rites of Passage* (New York: Basic Books, 1977), esp. chs. 5 and 8; John Higham, "The Reorientation of American Culture in the 1890s," in *Writing American History* (Bloomington: Indiana University Press, 1970), pp. 79–88; John Demos and Virginia Demos, "Concept of Adolescence in History," *Journal of Marriage and the Family* 31 (November 1969): 632–36.

61. "What Dr. Osler Really Said," *Scientific American* 92 (25 March 1905): 243; Edmund Osgood Brown, *De Senectute* (Chicago: The Lakeside Press, 1914), pp. 35–36; Beard, *Legal Responsibilities*, pp. 19–21; Andrew Lang, "In Love with Youth," *Living Age* 245 (6 May 1905): 381; "On Growing Old," *Living Age* 251 (24 November 1906): 464–65.

62. For hints aimed at women, see Martha Cutler, "How to Remain Young," *Harper's Bazaar* 43 (September 1909): 131; "A Word for the Modern Old Lady," *Atlantic Monthly* 100 (July 1907): 283–84; and "Eternal Youth," *Scribner's Magazine* 43 (March 1908): 378. For hints aimed at men, see Alvin Wood Chase, *Dr. Chase's Recipes* (Ann Arbor: A. W. Chase, 1866); advertisements in the *North American Review Advertiser* 156 (January–June 1893): 43, 52; and Sanford Bennett, *Old Age, Its Cause and Prevention: The Story of an Old Body and Face Made Young*, 2d ed. (New York: The Physical Culture Publishing Co., 1912), pp. 40–42.

63. "Young World," *Outlook* 105 (4 October 1913): 257. See also James Payn, "The Backwater of Life," *Living Age* 205 (1 June 1895): 572; G. S. Street, "The Persistence of Youth," *Living Age* 231 (30 November 1901): 569.

64. "On Death," *Hesperian* 1 (December 1895): 267; Joseph Jacobs, "The Death of Dying," *Fortnightly Review* 72 (August 1899): 264–66; Shaler, *Individual*, pp. 227–28, 239; Joslyn Gray, "Nox Dormienda," *Atlantic Monthly* 91 (January 1903): 103–6. For actuarial evidence presented at the time, see Karl Pearson, *The Chances of Death and Other Studies in Evolution*, 2 vols. (New York: Edward Arnold, 1897), 1: 1–41; John K. Gore, "On the Improvement in Longevity in the United States during the Nineteenth Century," *Proceedings of the Fourth International Congress of Actuaries* 1 (1904): 32–53.

65. See Newman Smyth, *The Place of Death in Evolution* (London: T. Fisher Unwin, 1897), pp. 173–74, on the social need for the elderly to die. On aged death, see Post, *Cottage Physician*, pp. 586–87. Works by August Weismann, collected in *Essays upon Heredity and Kindred Biological Problems* (1891; reprint ed., Oxford: Clarendon Press, 1899), were influential in shaping a new scientific conception of the biological process of death.

66. Scott, "Old Age and Death," pp. 91–92. See also Metchnikoff, *Nature of Man*, p. 131; Cambridge, "The Retrospect," pp. 131–32.

67. Williams James, *The Varieties of Religious Experience* (1901–2; reprint ed., New York: New American Library, 1958), p. 121. See also Shaler, *Individual*, p. 200; Scott, "Old Age and Death," p. 109; William Knight, "De Senectute,"

Living Age 250 (23 December 1905): 750, 753.

68. B. A. Crankenthorpe, "The Plaint of the Old," *Living Age* 200 (10 March 1894): 606. See also Margaret Deland, "The Wickedness of Growing Old," *Harper's Bazaar* 39 (February 1905): 101; and Elderly Woman, "The Land of Old Age," in three parts in *Harper's Bazaar* (August, September, December 1906): 675, 777, 1149–50.

The Evolution of Traditional Culture Toward Aging

Peter N. Stearns

Old age is an age-old problem, and a distinct culture has surrounded it for centuries. Western civilization may have taken an unusually nasty attitude toward the old, but as this is not a cross-cultural comparison we can only suggest this, not elaborate upon it. Simone de Beauvoir's book, in its strongest section, dramatically demonstrates the hostility with which old age was viewed by top intellectuals, Seneca and the like, from ancient times onward. Popular culture reflected similar values: old age was a horror and old people a great nuisance. Far from the traditional veneration for old age which one might expect to find in France—which I had expected to pursue, in fact, in launching this study—one finds almost unmitigated disdain. This disdain persisted well into the contemporary era, among those who dealt with older people, among old people themselves most tragically, and among those who contemplated growing old.

From *Old Age in European Society: The Case of France* (New York: Holmes & Meier Publishers, Inc., 1976). Copyright © 1976 by Peter N. Stearns, by permission of Holmes & Meier Publishers, New York and Croom Helm Ltd. Publishers, London.

This is why we begin with culture—not the great writers, but those who purported to address themselves to old people, who were popularizers and mirrors of widespread societal attitudes. Obviously there is danger in dealing with 'culture' in this sense. The manuals and articles utilized were not widely read; only one, in the nineteenth century, went through more than three editions. But they did proliferate, which suggests some growth in readership and social concern. What is important, however, is not their direct impact so much as their correspondence with more elusive general attitudes. This was a widespread set of values, whatever their precise connections, and the values failed to sustain the old in either pre-modern or modern society.

Two preliminaries, however, to the ultimate connection between published material and popular opinion, which posits that from intellectual to villager, ancient attitudes persisted into recent times. Old people were not new—in other words, traditional wisdom had not been formed in a vacuum or only at the upper-class level. And, obviously, traditional veneration of the elderly (which is predicated in part on their presumed rarity) is largely mythical. Which latter means in turn, to anticipate a bit, that our problems in dealing with old people go far deeper than the evils of capitalism or the hedonism of modern youth; they lie deep in our cultural heritage and it will require heroic efforts, led by the contemporary elderly themselves, to undo the web.

There is a basic demographic confusion which pops up in the most surprising scholarly writing. "At the beginning of the century the expectation of life of women in our countries was about forty-five. At present it is an average seventy-five or more. Thirty years longer to live."[1] We have already seen in the French case that the implication that few people lived to what we would call old age in pre-industrial times is untrue. Life expectancy has increased because, primarily, of the massive decline in infant mortality. If an ordinary person survived age two (before which his or her chances of dying were 50 percent) the prospect of living into the fifties, at least, was pretty good. Yet we have a pervasive impression that the only old people in Western society were the rich and unusual: "The small group of people who lived into old age . . . was generally composed of the aristocracy or the wealthy middle class."[2] Simone de Beauvoir has similarly stated that the old barely existed until the late eighteenth century (which makes her elaborate tracing of a culture of old age a bit futuristic) and that then their gradual appearance was purely an upper-class phenomenon.[3] The fact is, as we have seen, that among adults in a pre-industrial village (where admittedly half the population was by definition normally under two) a good 6 to 8 percent were "elderly," using this term loosely as being over fifty-five. The percentage of elderly actually decreased in the late eighteenth century and into the nineteenth, because of the larger number of surviving children, though longevity seems to have improved a slight bit. But in late eighteenth century France a statistical projection, admittedly tentative, indicated that only 34 percent of the population between twenty and thirty-nine would die before reaching forty, and that on attain-

ing adulthood one had a 36 percent chance of reaching the general area of old age (fifty-five to sixty years of age). The old were definite fixtures in a pre-industrial setting, and often annoying ones.

For these figures are not tossed about simply to confound a demographic confusion, though it would be delightful if otherwise intelligent people would stop using terms like "scarcity value" to distort the situation of the pre-industrial elderly. The point is that the elderly were about, at all levels of society, and in considerable numbers. Attainment of one's sixties, while impressive, was hardly rare enough to call forth outpourings of awe. And all groups in society, not just the upper classes, had to develop attitudes and behavior patterns toward the elderly, which is what this section is all about. Traditionalism was not developed in a vacuum.

This relates to the second preliminary, already mentioned because it is so vital in interpreting the evolution of the elderly. Veneration of the old—esteem for the white-bearded patriarch or the sage grandmother dispensing wisdom from her rocking chair—could not develop from sheer rareness. Yet the social science literature on aging depends heavily on the notion that with modernization the number of old people increases and their worth is diminished among other things because they are so common.[4] Numbers increase, to be sure, but percentages go down in the intermediate period of demographic revolution and rise only in the later nineteenth century after capitalism's callous ways are well established. But the literature goes on with more persuasive arguments, particularly with regard to the twentieth century. Improved health is granted, but this merely allows more people to reach old age and find it disappointing. Material standards have risen, but not so rapidly as those of other groups in the population. Above all, in a culture that measures worth by productivity and does not depend on experience for wisdom, the role the elderly play has shrunk. Family decay leaves them isolated, where once they ruled the clan. Popular assumption echoes this theme of declension; public opinion polls in France as late as the 1940s revealed that a majority believed that longevity itself had declined in modern times.[5] Modernization and deterioration seem inextricably intertwined for the elderly.

This is not a logical connection. We can grant immense problems for the elderly at the present time, but we do not have to assume that their lot has ever been strikingly good in Western society. History is wrapped up in the difficulties of old people, but because of traditional mistreatment more than modern innovations.

Yet the few cultural historians who have touched on the subject of aging have tried to confirm the deterioration motif. A recent article on American culture picks up the point nicely. Middle-class magazines portrayed the elderly with great sympathy and appreciation until the later nineteenth century, when the stress began to switch to the miseries and inutility of old age.[6] The venerable patriarch, still smithying under the spreading tree, became a social drone. There may be some truth in this, but two initial caveats: first, it does not explain the outburst of American "it's fun to be old" literature which appeared in the 1920s, of which more later. And second, it does not compare neatly with a more traditional society such as France, where one might expect veneration of old age to continue for a longer period. Simone de Beauvoir's work presents a slight variant on the same theme. She also notes deterioration in the view of the elderly by the end of the nineteenth century, but believes that briefly, in French culture, there was a pride in age, when authors like Victor Hugo (if only for self-justification, as they lived in health into their eighties) gloried the old and found virtue in age. This outlook was to end with the youth-oriented twentieth century, so that whatever twists are taken with pre- and early-nineteenth-century material, we return inexorably to the theme of deterioration.

This approach is basically incorrect, for the old have consistently been treated unkindly in Western culture with exceptions, which can include Hugo, Longfellow, but also Cicero, to be found proving the rule.

And here, before launching on nineteenth century attitudes more precisely, which largely mirrored traditional themes for the simple reason that these were not rethought, let us dip into probable pre-modern attitudes, which is why we venture an initial cultural chapter in a social history of the elderly in the first place.

Picture the aging villager. We know he/she was not rare. Extraordinary individuals may have maintained great power, if they preserved their health and/or could claim access to unusual wisdom, not excluding magical powers or more prosaic talents such as midwifery (which in countries like England and France involved however only appointment by the local pastor and the fact of having had children oneself).[7] The old might preserve a place. But the more typical situation involved such mundane matters as the probable loss of teeth by age forty-five. This meant that someone, typically the youngest daughter who would not marry among other things because of a decade or more of care of an aging parent, had to chop up food and spoon it down the elderly gullet. False teeth became a common purchase among the lower classes only after 1850. The old might cling to property ownership, long after they were judged incapable of making sensible decisions about its use or actually working the fields. We can jump to the end of the nineteenth century when a French peasant expressed a typical attitude. Writing of his father's demise he remarked only: "When in 1891 after the death of my father, I became free to act as I wanted..."[8] So many peasants did retire, but in so doing they commonly had to protect themselves carefully against the ambitions of their children; this was a major area of peasant law, for the aging parent who did not bind his property to support him as he grew too weak to till the land often found himself near starvation. Hence the careful legal provisions turning over cottages and produce to the elderly as they bequeathed the main property to the more capable successor generation.[9] The old were a nuisance. The commonplaces that prevailed about aging were largely pessimistic. Older widows, as we will see, were an object of special suspicions, not only in bouts of witchcraft mania but in normal times; an attempt at remarriage was regarded as inappropriate, often attended by rowdy charivari, while at the same time the widow, having fulfilled her function of bearing children and yet incapable of caring for property, was regarded as a village misfit. This is why a traditional society such as France long maintained a legacy of suspicion about aging which has yielded only in the past half century, and then slowly and incompletely, to new attitudes. It was in fact newer, more youth-oriented cultures such as that of the United States (and perhaps transformed cultures as in the Soviet Union) that proved more flexible in their thinking about what old age is or might be.

Yet one other point about pre-industrial culture in France and elsewhere. If the old were not statistically rare, few people could sensibly contemplate growing old. Death was omnipresent in the village. Infants died at rates of 50 percent or more; summer, the worst period in terms of infection and malnutrition (note the contrast with the modern cycle, when old people are most likely to die in winter) was a time of death. A mid-nineteenth-century Sicilian peasant saw eight of his playmates die when he was six, and only about half of the infants born at his age had even survived to six. Childhood was a time of fear, and few people could think of longevity. In a large Italian village a funeral occurred every three days, and more often during the summer. Death had to be accepted as normal, but it was mourned and remembered—and fought, with peasant remedies. For the young adult, the expectation that half one's children would die simply enhanced the disinterest, the disbelief, in aging.[10]

Peasant culture thus provided a durable basis for concentration on the now. Being elderly meant being an economic drain and was unrealistically unexpected, because of the pervasiveness of death at other age levels. This is the final element of the pre-industrial outlook that would at once coincide with more formal culture and persist, as in the new urban working class, literally to the present day.

We turn now to the written word, with a pledge to return to evidence of correspondence between the published word and popular attitudes. The written image was, as already noted, not new; it corresponded to popular attitudes but also to most classical dictums about old age. What was new, in nineteenth century France, was the number of pamphlets and articles on the subject, part of the general expansion of publishing more than of any recognition that old age posed novel problems or that the old were increasing in numbers. Census takers noted the increased proportion of older people in the later nineteenth century, but who reads censuses? And they misconstrued the cause to boot, claiming better health rather than the simple effect of declining birth rates. The first public discussion of the social problems of aging came only after World War Two, when France was feeling low; here it was recognized that a sluggish birth rate and, now, rising longevity would produce a less vibrant population, which combined correct demographic facts with the traditional view of the old as useless which really must serve as our main theme.[11]

The increased writing on aging in the nineteenth century had two specific sources. First, the rise of science and medicine, which will be detailed more fully in the next chapter. Buffon and others gave new scientific cachet to the investigation of centenarians,[12] with the basic theme that most people do not manage to live out their normal lifespan.[13] More specific of course was the concern of doctors. Discussions of menopause, for example, began in the eighteenth century and increased steadily, and continue to the present. Doctors accounted for many of the pamphlets and books designed to tell people how to live a long life and what, if anything, to do with it. Some of their works won modest popularity, for the second source of the new materials on aging was the fact of a growing number of articulate older people, particularly in the middle classes, who wanted advice about this phenomenon, from presumed experts, just as they sought advice on child rearing and marriage. At an admittedly lower level, then, we have the characteristic groping for guidance, produced by a larger group of people who were aware that they would become old or were indeed old, and wanted some control over their lot: a middle-class characteristic above all. Hence a book like Noirot's *L'Art de Vivre Longtemps*, published in 1868, went through eight editions. *La Verte Vieillesse*, written by a Lyons doctor in 1920, was widely read. In combination, the popularized works on aging by doctors, self-appointed experts, plus a few more conventional productions by old men themselves, eager to tell the whole world how they'd done it,[14] account for a substantial body of modern literature. All of this made the culture of aging more accessible than ever before.

And, in terms of the permeation of culture, the literature can be tested by its currency in general periodicals and, by the twentieth century, through direct statements by old people and their organizations. It had currency, even when its products were not directly read. There are traces of rebellion against it, but these have been arduous and remain incomplete partly because the culture is so persuasive, and by no means entirely incorrect in its description of old age. But it represents a self-fulfilling picture, which is why we must begin with it and ultimately deplore it.

Despite a new audience and more scientific authors, the outlook toward old age changed little from the eighteenth century to the interwar period. Gloom prevailed even as Victor Hugo hailed his undeniably persistent virility. Balzac portrayed the miseries of retirement; Lamennais, Péguy, and many others talked of age as a foul infirmity. One cannot look to literature for a pervasive new current of optimism. The classics were endlessly repeated, admittedly with some internal contradiction as old age had not been a subject of antique unanimity. One could be mildly optimistic with Cicero, deeply aggrieved with Juvenel or Seneca. This classical framework was not altered because old age, while commanding some new attention, was not held to be important enough to merit serious new thought. The one partial exception to this statement, clinical pathology, ironically confirmed the classical pessimism. The ongoing culture of aging left the increasing numbers of people who were old bereft of much constructive advice about what they could do with the remainder of their lives.

The repetition of past wisdom was endless. Cicero and Seneca are perhaps less surprising than half-baked medical references to the cures and definitions of Hippocrates and Galen. Lacassagne, the Lyons doctor who made a good thing out of this 1920 manual, invoked not only these classics but also Montaigne (who had aged loudly but gracelessly) and Pascal. And one manual fed on another; Reveillé-Parise, who produced an uncomfortable amalgam of medical and conventional wisdom at mid-century, was constantly cited.[15]

From the classics one learned that old age began at fifty-five to sixty (forty-five to fifty for women). This conventional wisdom, derived from the age ladder of Hippocrates, was endlessly repeated. According to Hippocrates, a springtime of old age might be defined up to seventy; a green old age from seventy to seventy-five; "real" old age, seventy-five to eighty; ultimate, eighty to ninety; and caducity, ninety onward—by which time death was both certain and welcome.[16] Reveillé-Parise, in a slightly clinical variant in which he had to stress physical decay, put the green period from fifty-five to sixty-five, admitting only that it might extend longer in individual cases; in this period, physical decline might be compensated by intellectual faculties that could be at their height even though, the clinician returning, the brain had become smaller and was receiving less blood.[17] The figures themselves may seem unsurprising, since they correspond roughly with our own notions of the onset of old age, save in the special case of women. What must be stressed however, is that once old age occurred, whatever the labels attached to its various stages, it was not seriously distinguished from senility. As Reveillé-Parise's modifications of the classical scale suggest, if a fertile period of old age was identified it involved pushing back the beginning of aging itself into what we would call later middle age.

This had a more dramatic and more obviously inaccurate corollary. Since old age could be defined so neatly, its arrival was believed to be quite sudden. Reveillé-Parise paints a picture of mature, robust health and appearance all at once giving way to the symptoms of age; hair grayed and fell out (sometimes a simultaneity was suggested that could best be explained by a change in color as the hair left the head and drifted to the floor); teeth fell out; organs deteriorated; wrinkles came, and so on. The pathologists correctly noted that the actual deterioration of organs was gradual, but they did not dispel the idea of a sudden change—most severe, of course, for women with the onset of menopause. The view survives, in the French term "coup de vieux," "the blow of age." Cosmeticians advise on how to conquer the coup, and even some doctors continue to stress that few people avoid it (though downplaying its brutality, in comparison with their nineteenth century counterparts).[18] The "coup de vieux" concept makes a stark contrast between normal adulthood and age, to the inevitable disadvantage of the latter. It emphasizes, again repeating classical wisdom, the irrevocability of a feeble old age.

To be sure, one could prepare for the last stage of life, and somewhat contradictorily, given the desire to define specific stages of aging, the classical legacy was more benign when it came to the question of how to reach old age in the first place. Cicero's wisdom was endlessly repeated, for again there was little new thinking, but with specified exceptions discussed below it was normally sound enough. Moderation was the key. The manuals argued about how much heredity played a role. It was generally agreed that short people, and thin people, had the best chance. Obesity was bad. Thick feet promised an early old age, as did a slow pulse. Noirot, the most popular of the manualists, argued against too much brain work; others

were less sure. "The immoderate exercise of the intellectual facilities can only tire the brain and exhaust that organ; intellectual work pushes back the limits of life."[19] Most were convinced however that precocity was doomed to early demise. Athletes, also, were given low marks, because they spent themselves too early. But these factors of heredity or identifiability largely revolved around the moderation theme. Prepare for old age early, certainly by thirty-five or so. "The wisdom of young men is the wealth or well-being of mature men, and health itself for old men." Limit the passions, including sexual appetites. Exercise regularly but moderately— hard breathing should be avoided as "the first sign of fatigue of the heart."[20] Keep the eating down, particularly of meats, and obviously be moderate with wine. Get good air, and breath deeply (though presumably not too hard).[21] Maintain active interests but get lots of sleep; artists died young because of their irregular nocturnal habits. This same current of advice, though sensible enough in itself, produced a constant temptation to regard old age as a sickness, which could be prepared for only by the greatest prudence. Most medical manuals explicitly discounted the old-age-sickness equation and then proceeded to argue on its base.[22] Hence travel, for example, was bad. Reveillé-Parise noted: "Old people are like old furniture; they last only so long as they stay put." But there were warnings against vegetating, and the manuals uniformly opposed the idea of complete retirement.[23] The old had to feel useful and maintained "an absolute need for an occupation, a task."[24] Prudence could even conquer unfavorable heredity, so long as one did not wait until the onset of old age itself. Sobriety, nothing in excess—these were the keys to the kingdom.[25]

Recommendations changed almost not at all well into the twentieth century. Lacassagne, in 1920, added the desirability of regular medical visits to the list of virtues and an interest in "scientific advances" to the contemplations available to the old, but little else had been altered. Thus the image of old age itself changed not at all; it might be slightly delayed by moderation, but this idea itself was not new. The preservation of the classical canons, even if sound, raised important problems for actual behavior in an urbanizing society, both for the old and for those contemplating the prospect of aging. Modernization brought rising material expectations that could easily conflict with the counsels of moderation. Manuals noted, for example, the contradiction between growing meat consumption and the proper preparation for old age. There resulted an interesting debate over the relationship between aging and modern times, which is significant particularly in its implicit contradiction with what modern people, prior to old age at least, were interested in doing with their rising wealth and their hedonism.

Beginning in the nineteenth century, there were many who began to believe that with modern ways longevity had deteriorated. As early as 1842 it was claimed that the modern lifestyle was "richer in worries and frustrations than in happiness," which was why man "as now constituted" could not live to the Biblical term of 200 years.[26] Elie Metchnikoff, arguing for greater medical efforts to achieve man's natural life span, accepted Biblical claims as late as 1903; hence modern man did not live as long as his progenitors. The standard geriatric treatise published a few years later accepted the same opinion, noting that modern people hastened their own demise.[27] An advocate of "hippocratic" medicine repeated this in 1940, for the traditional, almost mercantilistic belief that the body had a set amount of energy readily lent itself to the idea of increased modern depredations due to the new pace of life.[28] A more generalized variant on this argument was that average lifespan had improved, thanks to medical advance, but the number of people surviving to advanced age had declined. More popular opinion certainly accepted the idea. The *Gazette de Médecine* in 1861 listed the departments having the largest number of centenarians, noting with approval that most were rural but adding, with genuine astonishment: "One is

amazed to see the Seine included." A woman's magazine admitted that many people used to look old at thirty but added, with the facile lack of consistency so common in discussing aging, that the modern generation had forgotten how to age properly.[29]

At the same time, however, modern medicine had to be given its due for measurable improvements. Hence Reveillé-Parise disputed the idea that the traditional countryside was healthier than the newer city, pointing out that peasants neglected proper hygiene and were poor and overworked. He and Noirot both rejected the Biblical claims, contending that each Biblical year was a mere three months in modern terminology. Average lifespan was in fact slightly higher than in the past, despite the popular tendency to exaggerate the vitality of earlier ages. But having said this both manuals went on to undermine their own hypothesis. Noirot blasted modern education as detrimental to long life: "A precocious education kills in their buds the highest aptitudes of life and exhausts the sacred source." He added that farmers, with their access to good air, lived longer than city workers. Noirot did admit that poverty was more detrimental to survival than wealth, but he repeated classical advice in noting that excessive wealth was itself a killer, not only through its support for overeating but also because of the monotony it caused. For Reveillé-Parise Paris was a jail, while the nineteenth century was turning everything to "haste, hurry, torment," all hostile to long life. Certainly the old should seek the peace of the countryside. A few students of the centenarians contended that intellectuals lived longer than any other category,[30] but most saw the poor peasant as the likeliest to survive.[31] Few observers, then, even when they declared an official optimism, really set the basis for compatibility between longevity and the modern lifestyle. Many went on to add that the modern world worsened the position of those who did reach old age. Chateaubriand was one of many who, quite early in the nineteenth century, pointed to those gloriously undefined "old days" as a period in which the elderly had been part of a community in contrast to their modern isolation.[32]

One thus emerges with a very callous image of old age. Assuming one survived by rigid self-discipline, there was scant reward. The conventional wisdom produced no reason to want to survive. The physical picture was bleakest. At most it could be noted that some individuals experienced a partial rebirth in their eighties, "like those rare trees that flower again in autumn, for the second time."[33] Hence some attention was paid to unusual phenomena such as a return of hair, menstruation and other more or less desirable characteristics of younger adulthood. This aside, the theme of decay, and attendant ugliness, was universal and, in most accounts, given considerable detail.[34] For Reveillé-Parise, the centenarian was a "ruin of himself," a mere vegetable. Old age was a total transformation of the organism. Even the most optimistic could only note that a few organs might be spared from loss of recuperative ability. Old age, was "the retrograde period of human life, the age of decline or of involution," a state "midway between disease and health," "the last, sad revolution which leaves only ruins behind."[35] The theme is a constant, from the late eighteenth century onward. The old could only be pitied for their infirmities but even this was qualified by revulsion at the ugliness of a wrinkled, toothless creature.

But what of the mental state and special virtues of the elderly? Here lay Cicero's consolation and Buffon's pleasure in age, and the advantages were not ignored in the new literature of the nineteenth century.[36] The *Gazette de Médecine*, strongly disapproving an essay on the evils of old age, claimed that while the body aged the spirit never did.[37] References to creative older people were common: Michelangelo, Voltaire (who would have lived still longer if vanity had not tempted him to take his final trip to Paris), and later Hugo. "The old man, whose intelligence continues to glow like a torch, the old man who still has productive energies,

can guide men and create and manipulate ideas, preserves his value."[38] But here was already the opening wedge of dispute, for the old genius was by definition atypical. For the common run of humanity, a special kind of mental activity had to be claimed. Noirot, granting bleakly that the old had nothing more to hope for on earth, characteristically stressed the power of memory, which could continue to entertain.

Experience was hailed as well.[39] The old might be less quick, less open to innovation, but, as Reveillé-Parise put it, "One cannot deny that the essential mode of intelligence and of its infinite applications belongs to mature age."[40] Most important the aged were not distracted by passions, since their very survival depended on serenity and their physical decay left them no energy anyway. "The moral side is the beautiful side of old age. We cannot age without our physique losing, but also without our morality gaining; it is a noble compensation."[41] Hence the old were counted upon for benevolence, patience, acts of charity, as well as a self knowledge impossible to youth. Calm, then, replaced passions which might be held of little value anyway. Hopefully the old man could serve a vital role also in guiding a respectful family.

This preservation of classical and religious wisdom must not be belittled. But without meaning to simplify or unify the modern experience unduly, it is obvious that the calm, resigned life of the mind being urged was not calculated to make old age attractive to more modern urban kinds of expectations, and it had never been accessible to most older people anyway. The manuals that advised an interest in science or history were simply not talking to the interests of the bulk of the older population, a problem that still pervades contemporary guidance literature. Ciceronian advice on contemplation perhaps might benefit a retired postal employee but there is little evidence that it usually does—which may reflect as much on Cicero as on the postal service. Important also was the fact that few manuals even specified what one's intelligence was to be exercised upon. By the turn of the century some were picking up the theme that a happy old age depended on a young, innovative spirit, open to new ideas and interested in what was going on around, but this was not yet the common approach. As late as 1924 the old were urged to be resigned, neither optimistic nor pessimistic; they should accept the inevitable and learn to die well.[42] And this from an observer who urged the morality and intelligence of old age. The lack of focus in the praise of the mentality of old people remained a serious handicap.

Furthermore, intellectual capacities were also subject to the image of doom. Few guides could avoid dwelling on the mental drawbacks of the elderly and some stressed them exclusively. The theme of mental decay gained increasing precision as medical knowledge increased. Old age was not benevolent in any form, physical or moral. The old were selfish, wrapped up in their own concerns. They lost their memories as well as their creativity. They were avaricious; this vice was given extraordinary attention.[43] Here is a clear connection between the manuals and popular culture—and, admittedly, the behavior of some old people as well. In a property conscious society, where inheritance was all, avarice was an easy sin to identify; it meant among other things that the old clung to property for support in a hostile world, possibly for self-identification. The only remedy, as we have suggested earlier from the pen of a peasant, was more timely death. The elderly were believed to have lost all their good sense, which is why no one would listen to them anyway. If they acted old, it was noted in the 1860s, everyone shunned them, and if they acted young everyone laughed at them.

There was no escaping the dilemma. The main thrust of the old age culture was that the aged were distinctively senile whether constructive or not. Michel Lévy, like most manual writers, while admitting that a few old people stayed alert, was forced to conclude that most saw their minds decay gradually, leading them to a vegetal existence cut off from the world. Reveillé-Parise was less aware of the dilemma of the old, although he too dealt with individual variation. He wanted to be on the side of Cicero and the angels. The old should be esteemed, their intelligence was of the kind appropriate for leadership roles, they should enjoy peace and honor in their age. But, inexorably, their brains did decay—"The faculties of intelligence share equally in this universal deterioration"—and they were commonly victim of all the vices attributed to them.

One final attribute, on which there was universal agreement, no sex; after a life of moderation, abstinence. This was not a new admonition. Like most of the sexual advice for which the Victorians have been blamed, it had ancient lineage and simply achieved wider currency given the new interest in, but failure to rethink, the phenomenon of aging. It was admitted that some men could maintain sexual activity, and cases of an octogenarian siring a child by a young woman were noted with a certain Gallic pride. But the eroticism of the old was much more commonly condemned as both disgusting and unhealthy. This applied also to those menopausal women who experienced erotic dreams and appetites. Genital decay was an essential attribute of old age, though this seemed clearest for women. "Old age begins with the cessation of the genital function."[44] Even where capacity remained, the mind should rule the passions—here was one action for which the elderly were certainly responsible. There might be beauty in the result; with age, "love takes on an entirely moral character, liberated from the servitudes of animality."[45] More commonly, however, danger was emphasized, once "the hour of genital repose has sounded."[46] From 1807: "Abuses of the hymen harm even the most robust people,"[47] and the author went on to excoriate the stereotypic dirty old man. From 1873: "Like our hair, our desires should wither."[48] From 1911: "Each sacrifice to Venus is, for the old man, a spadeful of earth on his head."[49] From 1931: No more sex after sixty or sixty-five; "the genital secretions should remain to the profit of the organism that produces them." [50] And here of course was the basis of the admonitions, a combination of the conventional stigma placed upon lust on the part of older people and a belief that genital fluids were part of the vital essence, perhaps the vital essence itself. Folklore, as evidenced by hostility to remarriage, particularly of widows, and medical traditions easily combined here. Noirot, urging continence early, on behalf of "the vital fund," [51] went on to illustrate how much longer monks and neuters lived than the generality of mankind. His recommendations at least had an air of practicality. Men could keep active, as with hunting; it was no accident that Diana was goddess both of chastity and the chase. Women could knit. And for both sexes (one assumes, in default of the monastery or castration; here too, logic was not the strong point of manual writers who poured out their scattered tidbits of conventional wisdom) there was marriage. It was long noted that married people lived longer than single. Noirot had isolated the cause: "By excluding the attraction of novelty, marriage shelters man from artificial overexcitement." [52] Only a few guides, by the twentieth century, either extended the period before which sexual activity should stop or recognized that occasional intercourse, so long as spurred solely by natural desire, might be all right. [53]

It is not anachronistic to poke a bit of fun at the manuals' approach to sex, for again it countered interests that steadily increased with modernization. But the recommendations on sex are just an extreme example of the general approach: no rethinking of the canons of behavior for older people and therefore a growing gap between what was desirable, indeed what was probably practiced by some, and what was advised. The gap had potentially tragic consequences, for clearly many old people acted upon the advice. The conventional wisdom created few reasons for wanting to live to old age and thus enhanced the difficulty of adjustment

for those who, usually to their surprise, reached that state.

And if little was offered to the elderly in general, absolutely nothing was held out for the stronger sex. A few functions might be found for old men, but none for women. There was, of course, the problem of explaining the well-known fact that women lived longer than men, though all the manuals proudly noted that the very old, the centenarians, and the really creative among the elderly at any age were all male. Women engaged in less physical labor, competition, and war; for some writers this explained their edge. Or maybe it was because they talked more, which preserved their interest in the little things of life. Or because they were more sedentary—which allowed them to use less oxygen—more sober and less ambitious, with no passions other than love. Whatever the reason it was almost universally agreed that female longevity was a disaster. A few commentators reverted to the plea for morality. The obvious physical losses entailed in menopause might be compensated by ethical gains; friendships might be more easily formed when sexual rivalry was absent. But this was a slender reed, for morality while desirable for men was essential for women and few seemed sure they could bear the burden. Hence Dr. Pinel, early in the nineteenth century, noted menopause as "most sad and melancholy . . . if an elevated character does not replace, by pure enjoyments, the reign of frivolous pleasures and the attractions of a dissipated life." [54] Menopause was certainly the key to the dilemma: "nature refuses her one part of the attributes of her sex." "An old woman is for nature only a degraded being, because she is useless to it." [55] The obvious basis of this view was the association of life forces with sexual functions; women began to age sooner, more definitely than men did. Relatedly aging early marked the appearance of women. The theme of ugliness was extremely pervasive, for the menopausal woman was held likely to be obese, wrinkled, with deteriorated skin and hair. Reveillé-Parise, whose professional work was mainly among old women, found their appearance "disgraceful," though he admitted that a few looked good with white hair.[56] Furthermore, it was assumed that bad appearance bothered women more than men, because of their earlier commitment to successful flirtation. "In general one can divide the life of women into three periods: in the first, they dream of love; in the second, they make it; in the third, they regret its passing."[57] Of course, it was possible to point out the functions the grandmother could perform in the family, with maternal affection replacing youthful ardor; and religion was widely urged. But few would have disagreed with Reveillé-Parise that, for women, "old age is a terrible period."[58] It began early for women, whom nature then cruelly allowed to outlive men.

The special judgments on women confirm the general inappropriateness of the guidance given to older people well into the twentieth century. That portion of the population most likely to survive was left virtually functionless, indeed derided. Here too, the conventional wisdom, if unusually harsh in France, remained virtually unchanged. Manuals in 1920 would differ little from those of 1820, which is why some can range freely over a century or more in citing examples of common views. It was in fact in 1920 that Lacassagne's pamphlet stated starkly that most people who lived to seventy were physical and mental wrecks and wished they were dead.

It is clear, then, that France, far from being a source of admiration for patriarchs, or even tolerant of matriarchs, maintained an official culture that held old age in pity perhaps, but in scant respect. As already suggested, countries with a less traditional culture, even a culture that can with some qualifications be termed youth-oriented, might produce a more varied, if not completely contrasting, approach. It was in the 1920s that a spate of optimistic, if perhaps unrealistic, pamphlets began to appear in the United States urging the infinite number of activities open to old people. But what of the relation between the culture expressed in old age manuals, often backed by the authority of "science," and actual outlook? If the preservation of classical admonitions was increasingly irrelevant to the urban, modernizing experience, they had continuing impact nevertheless, for middle-class readers of manuals often believed what they read; they could easily think, for example, that urban life would poison their old age even if they could not afford to escape it. And we have suggested a parallel popular culture, which was not caused by reading but which stemmed from many shared assumptions.

Signs of persistence of the popular culture abound, even when we stress the most advantaged social groups, even as we move to the present day. The culture had ample resonance in more general literature aimed at the middle classes. The *Gazette des Femmes*, in 1841, faithfully reproduced the notion that aging had deteriorated compared to the past, in part because of the modern woman's disgusting rage for cosmetics. Grandmothers were used as figures of sage advice, to be sure, but even in this literary ploy, grandma (by her sixty-sixth year) carefully refused to disclose her age, lest she shock her younger advisees.[59] The religious motif, more common in the magazines than in old age manuals, might lead to a greater stress on the ageless soul,[60] but otherwise there was little difference in the culture; in fact it could lead to attacks on any effort to prolong life. Even an article specifically on cosmetics noted that once one was fifty, there was no hope, "no way to repair the irreparable outrage of the years."[61] Truly, as another article noted, while praising the grandmotherly role, "The people dethrone kings and time dethrones women."[62] There is no reason, judging by widely read magazines, to disagree with Reveillé-Parise, who noted that the general opinion associated age only with illness and imminent death, expecting no enjoyment in it; even many older people, in his view, held this outlook.[63] As an article in the *Revue des deux mondes* put it a half-century later, "One cannot hope to become old. It should be easier to die with some hope left."

But for our purposes the more significant point is the persistence of these attitudes well into the twentieth century. They were to be seriously qualified after World War Two, but even now they reappear. A doctor in 1950, although noting some medical advance, including hormonal treatments that might, just might, allow women to enjoy sex after menopause, concluded that the old are cautious and selfish as their brain atrophies faster and faster after the onset of age. Pension groups, particularly between the wars, repeated the same laments, undoubtedly with an eye toward public sympathy but with an undercurrent of self-conviction as well; hence one magazine stated that even before sixty many people had lost their strength, and this in a magazine that was actually offering its readers gardens for sale, vacation plans, and the like.[64] Somewhat more optimistically, La Vieillesse heureuse returned to Cicero, in 1956; admittedly the elderly had no strength save their morality, but this should give them wisdom and authority which in turn merited the regaining of traditional respect. Certainly the medical view was widely accepted: "Old age is a mosaic of deterioration." Troisième Age, now the largest periodical aimed at older people, began in its first year, 1959, with the plea for automatic retirement at age sixty, which would allow France to have a young labor force and recognize the fact that the old are incapable of heavy responsibilities and fatigues.

This view was to change, but it was amplified in this first statement: aging begins at forty-eight, the critical period; stabilizes a bit in the decade after fifty-five, then becomes full of anxiety and deteriorating health; only at seventy-two comes serene incapacity, which leads calmly to death. With the same kind of contradiction that was now developing in public self-perception, the journal in the same year stressed that the "life of old people is worth living" but that the industrial revolution had destroyed the affectionate family which had placed the elderly at the center of its love. General MacArthur was also cited, to compound the complete lack of consistency, on the possibility of an active,

productive life into one's seventies and eighties. But MacArthur had yet to conquer France and he had never promised to return there; more pervasive, in the magazines produced to an extent for the elderly, was the traditional pessimism, at least until the 1960s, as in the case of a journal that pleaded for sympathy for those over sixty, "at the age when one can no longer do anything." "Old age is the sad age when everyone, recalling what he was and thinking of what he's become, measures his deterioration and suffers."[65]

The opinions of organs of retirees form a probable framework for the outlook of the old themselves. In 1927, retired teachers in the Creuse established an amicale, which put out a tiny periodical bulletin noting how little participation they were able to solicit. (Again, the contrast with the United States, where retirees' groups became active before 1900, is marked; a cultural difference is inescapable.) The old in France simply did not view themselves capable of active association, and some were even fearful of any deviation from the daily routine. Many healthy retirees stayed away from the annual banquet, claiming that the food and excitement (shades of Galen) would hurt their health. The organization's leader urged against this, noting that all diets were provided for and a calm atmosphere was maintained to aid digestion. But even his own pitch suggests the deep roots of the traditional outlook toward age. What did one do at the banquets? See old friends of course, but mainly recall one's youth, "which gives the illusion of reliving a bit the bygone days" and lets one forget for just a moment the routine of suffering and mourning. There were even some jokes, though of course no one laughed uproariously, just mildly; the charm of the occasion was a bit "melancholy." But next year—for things were changing—there was going to be singing, and maybe someday the group would dance as they used to when they were young.[66]

Here, admittedly in a single example, we catch the poignancy of the situation of the elderly, even teachers, some of whom might retire at fifty-five. The culture had penetrated deeply, and even those who began, toward the teens of this century, to propose the first organizations of retirees, shared much of the outlook of debility. Even more of their colleagues failed to join at all, which produced local groupings, even in the 1960s, claiming no more than 110 members (under 1 percent of the retirees in the region) less than half of whom ever showed up for any activity.[67] Hence the accurate claim: if the old unite, "by their number they can defend their rights"; but the sad admission that most remained isolated, believing that they were impotent to defend themselves.[68] The interwar period did spur associations of retirees, because the pressures of inflation and then depression created obvious and horrendous problems for people on fixed pensions. But almost none was formed among any group save state functionaries, despite the existence of a host of private plans. And even the functionaries were often led by men still on the job, whose motives, as we shall see were mixed.[69] When we look at retiree efforts per se, the more common picture is that of the Fédération générale des retraités, section de l'Ain. Begun in 1935 with thirty members, it had constant problems finding leadership and had grown to but two hundred members even by 1957. Nancy claimed greater power, arguing in 1934 that it had eight hundred members; but it could muster only two hundred people for a demonstration for a pension increase.[70] Thus promptings to join, even in a period of great crisis, vastly exceeded actual growth of organizations. The fact that organizations did spring up and find some support should not be minimized; for individuals this could signal a real change in one's sense of the possibility of an active role in modern society. But far more, the history of organizations agitating specifically even for the middle-class elderly reflect, again, the common outlook which the old apply to themselves, resulting here, to paraphrase a well-known title, in a culture of political despair. As one retired engineer said four years ago: "At my age, what should I do with my little voice?"[71]

And there is little doubt that this sense of impotence was and is greater in France than in countries like the United States, which operated from a more open, or at least more ambiguous, set of attitudes toward the elderly. The French lagged even in the formation of groups for art work, sewing and the like, designed for the elderly. The first significant citations of such groups (obviously not precluding quite informal ones, among friends, far earlier) come in the 1950s,[72] and the common formation of "Third age clubs" is literally but a few years old.[73] A 1965 survey of retired functionaries found 80 percent spending most of their time at home, though half claimed to want (but lacked) an active club where they could meet people.[74]

A sad picture, and one which suggests, accurately I think, that vital aspects of behavior, particularly until very recently, reflect the fact that the elderly held much the same view of themselves that the pervasive culture advised them to. They were ugly, selfish, impotent, and had best stay out of sight; their health was extremely fragile even if there were no overt symptoms of specific disease; so for a host of reasons organizational activity would be a danger and a waste.

This, then, is theme one suggested by the traditional culture. Widely shared attitudes persist and cause behavior; insofar as they are promulgated by popular and/or authoritative publications, they find reinforcement, but the roots go deep into fear of aging and hostility to the old. They long dominated the outlook of those who dealt with the elderly; this we will shortly see in discussing groups as diverse as medical researchers and radical labor leaders. They continue to overwhelm the old themselves in many social groups, particularly the lower classes; this also we will return to shortly.

But there is an irony in the culture toward aging, as expressed in manuals and general magazine articles. After World War Two it did a somersault. The basic message now is that age can be conquered. Old people are urged to avoid the behavior of the traditional elderly: "It's time to change this record. Act young and you will be young." Travel is recommended and in general the old are prompted to be open to change: "To depart from routine at our age is a very good way . . . of remaining young."[75] Sex, once disdained with horror, is now strongly encouraged as normal and healthy. In retirement an old person can make a new life, develop new interests. Or if a person chooses to continue to work his capacities will remain considerable. The very definition of age has changed; in a typical reshuffling one manual views the years forty-eight to sixty as a time of transition, sixty to seventy-eight or eighty as one of calm, eighty to ninety-two as active old age, with senility coming only after this.[76]

There are a number of reasons for this change in outlook. The American example is one. Much of the new literature is copied from the United States, since the outpouring of happiness material has continued since the 1920s. Beauticians urge their female charges to copy the exercising, face lifting, and cosmetic practices of American women. While one proudly proclaims that France alone shares with the United States the honor of having a "third woman," between old and young—a woman who by all appearances might be thirty just as easily as fifty-five— she also bemoans the three centimeter edge in hip slimness that the average American woman preserves over her French counterpart.[77] The general openness of older Americans to sports, travel, and retirement groups is often commended.[78] Also praised is the presumed American practice of regular medical checkups, which as we will see began to be urged in France only recently. Greater American readiness to find interests even in their advanced years is perceived, however inaccurately, by the general public. One poll indicated considerable enthusiasm among French retirees to go to the United States to "recycle," though there is little evidence of practical follow-up to this interest.

Changes in French society bolster the new image. Medicine, though partly itself derivative, is one to which we turn shortly. The old are in fact more active, less ugly. The declining significance of property ownership as the basis of status and power is another factor of vital importance. An adjective that is never, now, applied to the old is miserly, despite its canonization from classical times onward. The young no longer have to wait for inheritance to begin their own adulthood. Generational tension remains but this fundamental feature of agricultural and traditional bourgeois society is gone. It is easier to feel responsible for one's parents, even reluctantly, than to hope for their death. Not coincidentally, whereas in the mid-nineteenth century on a *per capita* basis a person over fifty was four times as likely as a member of any other age group to be murdered (forming, despite their small size in the total population, the largest group of murderees), old people now comprise the smallest group of murder victims.[79] Straws in the wind, perhaps, but indications of a real correspondence between the change in the tone of the literature devoted to old age and actual social behavior, even in its less extreme manifestations.

Yet the basis for the new literature lies primarily in new behavior developed by old people themselves, particularly among the elements of the middle class. The existence of the new literature guides us to a more fundamental evolution in the outlook held by many older people and, to some extent, by those who deal with them. We must of course be attentive to the persistence of traditional motifs, for such a deep-rooted culture cannot die within a single generation. And it is premature to say that the evolution of the elderly in modern society, after over a century of gloom, has had a happy ending. The relationship between the new literature, easy to trace in its joyous acceptance of old age, and the actual outlook of older people, must preoccupy us as we assay an account of how the elderly have actually evolved in subsequent sections. Neither traditional pessimism nor recent optimism exactly hits the mark. There is movement, however, there is transition, won against the painful odds posed by customary assumptions, and this shows in most though not all of the social facets of aging. Even partial breakthroughs, against undiluted pessimism, can only be welcome.

NOTES

1. Evelyne Sullerot, "Woman's Role in Modern Society from the Sociological and Economic Point of View," in Regional Trade Union Seminar, *Employment of Women* (Paris, 1968), p. 91.
2. Evelyne Sullerot, *Women, Society and Change* (New York, 1974), p. 46.
3. Fernand Boverat, *Le vieillêssement de la Population* (Paris, 1946).
4. P. Flourens, *De la longévité Humaine* (Paris, 1854), p. 39.
5. See also de Parcieux, *Essai sur les probabilités de la durée de la vie humaine* (Paris, 1746).
6. A. Lacassagne, *La verte vieillesse* (Lyons, 1920).
7. H. Guéniot, *Pour vivre cent ans* (Paris, 1931), pp. 26ff.
8. J. H. Reveillé-Parise, *Traité de la vieillesse Hygiénique, Médical et Philosophique* (Paris, 1853), pp. 77–78.
9. Charles Vidal, *Le vieillard* (Paris, 1924), pp. 11ff.
10. I am grateful to Rudolph Bell in his paper "The Persistence of Fatalism and its Demographic Base in Modern Rural Italy," and other works in progress, for these insights.
11. Reveillé-Parise, *Traité*, p. 383.
12. P. L. Jacob, "Conseils aux femmes sur la conservation de leur beauté," *Journal des femmes* (1843), pp. 167, 461; see also Janine Alaux, *101 Trucs pour Vaincre le Coup de Vieux* (Paris, 1973).
13. L. Noirot, *L'art de vivre longtemps* (Paris, 1868), p. 272.
14. Vidal, *Vieillard*, p. 82.
15. Lacassagne, *Vieillesse*, p. 322.
16. André Léri, *Le cerveau sénile* (Lille, 1906), pp. 3–4 and *passim*.
17. Reveillé-Parise, *Traité*, pp. 270ff.; see also Lacassagne, *Vieillesse*, ix.
18. Dr. Scheffler, *Comment on défend sa jeunesse* (Paris, n.d.), p. 35.
19. G. Rauzier, *Traité des maladies des Vieillards* (Paris, 1909), pp. 14ff.
20. Elie Metchnikoff, *Etudes sur la nature humaine* (Paris, 1903), p. 339.
21. Rauzier, *Traité, passim*.
22. Charles Legoncourt, *Galérie des centenaires anciens et modernes* (Paris, 1842), p. 114.
23. Paul Carton, *Le guide de la Vieillesse* (Paris, 1951), pp. 30ff.
24. *Gazette de Médecine* (1861), p. 74.
25. Noirot, *Art*, p. 64.
26. Ibid., p. 290.
27. Rauzier, *Traité*, p. 324.
28. Carton, *Guide, passim*.
29. For more fundamental optimism see Jean Finot, *La philosophie de la longévité* (Paris, 1900), p. 42; A. Lorand, *La vieillesse, moyens de la prévenir et de la combattre* (Paris, 1914). This last work, translated from the German, was notably more advanced than French medical treatises in its openness to possibilities of cure, its recommendations for regular sexual activity and so on; but it maintained the greater health of rural over urban people. Doubtless the fact that doctors rarely saw rural patients aided this impression, as did the widely current cultural prejudices against the city.
30. M. Philibert, *L'echelle des ages* (Paris, 1968), p. 199.
31. Alfred Sauvy, *Les limites de la vie humaine* (Paris, 1961), p. 12.
32. Reveillé-Parise, *Traité*, p. 69.
33. E. Monin, *Hygiène, et médecine journalière* (Paris, 1823), p. 363.
34. Michel Lévy, *Traité d'hygiène publique et privée* (Paris, 1844), I: 114.
35. M. A. Legrand, *La longévité à travers les ages* (Paris, 1911), p. 194.
36. Noirot, *Art*, p. 256.
37. "Les Peines de la Vieillesse," *Gazette de médecine* (1863), p. 219.
38. Reveillé-Parise, *Traité*, p. 92; see also Emile Demange, *Etude clinique et anatomie pathologique sur la vieillesse* (Paris, 1886).
39. Flourens, *Longévité*, p. 54.
40. Reveillé-Parise, *Traité*, p. 16.

41. Lacassagne, *Vieillesse*, pp. 282–83.
42. Vidal, *Vieillard*, p. 103.
43. J. A. Millot, *La Gérocomie* (Paris, 1807), p. 98.
44. August Lumière, *Sénilité et rajeunissement* (Paris, 1932), p. 139.
45. Guéniot, *Pour vivre*, p. 71.
46. Noirot, *Art*, pp. 227–28.
47. Millot, *Gérocomie*, p. 98.
48. Noirot, *Art*, p. 243.
49. Legrand, *Longévité*, p. 147.
50. Guénoit, *Pour vivre*, p. 71.
51. Noirot, *Art*, pp. 143ff.
52. Ibid., p. 243.
53. Charles Vidal, *Etude médical, physiologique et philosophique de la femme* (Paris, 1912), p. 143.
54. Ph. Pinel, *La médecine clinique* (Paris, 1802), *passim*; Millot, *Gérocomie*, p. 360.
55. *Gazette de santé* (An 13), p. 123; for an early expression of the standard view, C. A. Goubelly, *Connaissances nécessaires sur la grossesse, sur les maladies laiteuses, et sur la cessation des règles* (Paris, 1785), II, pp. 362ff.
56. Reveillé-Parise, *Traité*, p. 59.
57. Ibid., p. 63.
58. Ibid., p. 137.
59. *Gazette des femmes*, June 12, 1841.
60. *Revue de la famille*, April 15, 1875.
61. Jacob, "Conseils", pp. 164ff.
62. Anais Ségalas, "La vieille femme," *Journal des femmes* (1847), p. 554.
63. Reveillé-Parise, *Traité*, pp. 108, 137.
64. *Cri du retraité*, 1930 and 1934.
65. *Echo de la vieillesse*, 1958.
66. *Bulletin trimestriel de l'Amicale des retraités de l'enseignement public du Creuse*, 1933.
67. *Annuaire des retraités des organismes sociaux de la région Montpellier-Languedoc-Roussillon*, 1960.
68. *Bulletin du département de Seine-et-Oise*, 1933; *Tribune des fontionnaires*, 1926ff.
69. *Cri du retraité, passim.*
70. *Bulletin trimestriel du groupement des retraités civils de l'Est*, 1934.
71. Anne Lauran, *L'Age scandaleux* (Paris, 1971), p. 49.
72. *Echo de la vieillesse*, 1958.
73. *Troisième age*, 1972.
74. "Les cadres retraités vus par euxmêmes," *Revue française du travail* (1968). In terms of membership in formal associations of the elderly only 38 percent of French males and 18 percent of females could be listed in 1972, and these often inactive. Groups involving upper- and middle-class elements here, not surprisingly, as in other areas of activity could claim a distinct lead, but even here only a minority was involved.
75. Léon Binet, *Gérontologie et gériatrie* (Paris, 1961); Jean Daruc, *Vieillessement de la population et prolongation de la vie active* (Paris, 1958); René Berthier, *Nouvel age de vie* (Paris, 1973); M. Shrem, *Des anneés, oui; vieillir, non!* (Neuchatel, 1965).
76. P. Baumgartner, *Les consultations journalières en gérontologie* (Paris, 1968), pp. 79 and *passim*.
77. Alaux, *101 Trucs, passim.*
78. *Troisième age, passim.*
79. For congenital pessimists it can be noted that, perhaps replacing murder, old people, particularly males and mainly in the sixty to sixty-nine age group, are vastly disproportionate victims of automobile attacks upon pedestrians. (After seventy apparently there is greater acceptance of immobility, perhaps greater recognition of elderliness by drivers, and much more caution when the forces of stop and go encounter each other; *per capita* death rates by vehicular death go down dramatically), *Statistique de la France, mouvement de la population*, 1952ff. For percentage murder figures, same source, 1856 to the present.

Aging and Modernization: A Revision of the Theory

Donald O. Cowgill

The book *Aging and Modernization* (Cowgill and Holmes, 1972), developed a theory of aging in cross-societal perspective. The theory emerged from a comparison of the role and status of older people in fifteen different societies which differed widely among themselves in degree of modernization and modernization was utilized as the chief independent variable. Thus the theory as it emerged was essentially a descriptive statement of the changes in role and status of older people with increasing modernization.

However, it was expressed in twenty-two discrete propositions each of which enunciated a correlation between a pair of variables. In thirteen of those propositions modernization was explicitly used as one of the paired variables and it was assumed to be the independent variable. Thus modernization was declared to be associated with later onset of old age, increased use of chronological criteria, increased longevity, aging populations, increased proportions of females and widows in the population, increased proportions of grandparents, lower status of the aged, decline in leadership roles of the aged, decline in power and influence of the aged, increased ambiguity of the role of widows and an increase in the extent of disengagement of older people from community life. In eight further propositions,

From Jaber F. Gubrium, ed., *Late Life: Communities and Environmental Policy* (Springfield, Illinois: Charles C. Thomas, Publisher, 1974). Reprinted by permission of the publisher.

modernization was not explicitly made one of the paired variables, but the independent variables were assumed to be closely related to modernization if not integral aspects of it. Thus rapid social change, mobility, urbanization, literacy, decline of ancestor worship, break up of the extended family, loss of useful roles for the aged and increased proportions of aged in the population were declared to be associated with lower status of the aged. Reexamination indicates that only one of the propositions utilized an independent variable which could not be subsumed under the general rubric, modernization. An individualistic value system appears to be at least partly independent of the forces of modernization.

This article is an attempt to refine that theoretical statement in several ways: (1) a more precise explication of concepts, (2) differentiation between major or primary variables and intervening variables, (3) more explicit attention to functional relationship among the variables, and, most importantly, (4) an effort to develop the interrelation among all of the variables within a single integrated system. Such a revised statement should provide a more meaningful and significant theoretical formulation.

THE CONCEPT OF MODERNIZATION

Stated in its most general form, utilizing the most general independent and dependent variables, the theory holds that with increasing modernization the status of older people declines. However, such a proposition cries out for explicit definition of the term "modernization."

However, one will search the literature in vain for a single, concise, generally accepted definition of this much used term. One gains the impression that the meaning is so broad and all-encompassing that most authors avoid an explicit definition and merely give illustrative facets of what must be viewed as a more general process. I plead guilty to this approach in our book where the nearest we come to a definition is to state that it encompasses level of technology, degree of urbanization, rate of social change, and degree of westernization (Cowgill and Holmes, 1972:2). Such a statement is useful in that it points to significant aspects of the process, but it is not a definition.

Some, in valiant attempts to define the term get caught up in what appear to be tautological statements. For example, Dore (1969) defines modernization as "... the transformation of one's own society or segments of it in imitation of models drawn from another country or society." Bendix (1968) is only a little more explicit in indicating what kind of countries are the models when he says that it is a process whereby "backward" countries imitate "advanced" countries. Nettl (1968:56–57) is not much more helpful: "Modernization is the process whereby national elites seek successfully to reduce their *atimic* status and move towards equivalence with other 'well-placed' nations." Such statements are little better than the assertion that modernization is the process of becoming modernized.

Others who have sought to give more meaningful referents in their delineations have usually been trapped by their limited disciplinary perspectives. Perhaps the most common perspective is an economic one which holds that modernization is primarily a matter of technology, a succinct illustration of which is the following: "A society will be considered more or less modernized to the extent that its members use inanimate sources of power and/or use tools to multiply the effects of their efforts" (Levy, 1966:11).

Those who have this perspective tend to equate modernization with economic development or at least that stage of development which is characterized by "self-sustaining growth" (Rostow, 1963). This tends in turn to lead to the employment of a vast array of economic indicators to measure it. These include not only the usual GNP per capita and kilowatts of electricity per capita but indicators of production of steel or cement, use of tractors, telephones, radios, television, consumption of paper, protein, sugar, or cereals (Janossy, 1963; Ehrlich, 1971). Others following a political scientist's perspective see modernization chiefly in terms of the development of political institutions concentrating on such things as the disappearance of tribalism, the concentration of political power, the emergence of nationalism, the development of an articulate public opinion and even citizen participation (Cf. Eisenstadt, 1966a; Lerner, 1958). If the latter two qualities seem to have a western flavor, such appears to be the reality; as pointed out by Nettl (1968:45–50), much writing on the subject does implicitly follow the assumption that modernization is the imitation of western democratic nations. A common sociological perspective gives emphasis to institutional differentiation calling attention not only to the increasing separation of the major social institutions from each other—familial, economic, political, and religious—but also elaboration, specialization, and differentiation within each institutional area as well (Cf. Etzioni, 1964; Coughenour, 1969). Others see modernization as mainly a change in attitudes and values (Waisanen, 1968) and this leads to attitude surveys and psychological tests as measures of it (Inkeles and Smith, 1970; Barndt, 1969; Armer and Schnaiberg, 1972; Stephenson, 1968).

Perhaps the most eclectic treatment of the concept is that of Eisenstadt (1966a). While he stresses institutional differentiation, he is careful to incorporate all institutional areas including such peculiarly modern ones as education, science, and leisure. He also encompasses the psychological and cultural aspects of the process including changes of values. The work is quite eclectic and comprehensive, but one will search in vain for a concise, usable definition.

A somewhat less detailed and more meaningfully focused treatment of the subject is that of Lerner. In his discussion in the *International Encyclopedia of the Social Sciences* (1968), he falls into the tautological trap: "Modernization is the current term for an old process—the process of social change whereby less developed societies acquire characteristics common to more developed societies," but elsewhere he calls it "... the infusion of 'a rationalist and positivist spirit'" (1958:45). However, his main thesis has stressed the four interrelated processes: urbanization, literacy, mass media, and political participation. Urbanization comes first and gives rise to literacy which in turn leads to the demand for and the use of mass media; rising levels of education elicit informed opinions on public affairs and the demand for participation.

Weiner (1966), like Eisenstadt, catalogs an extensive range of aspects of modernization without giving a definition.

Having failed in the attempt to find a ready-made definition and in the search having gained a fuller appreciation of the vast all-encompassing nature of the process which has led many to avoid the attempt and others to fall short, I am probably foolhardy to assay the task myself. However, I want to be as explicit as possible in what follows and that requires definition of terms.

Modernization is the transformation of a total society from a relatively rural way of life based on animate power, limited technology, relatively undifferentiated institutions, parochial and traditional outlook and values, toward a predominantly urban way of life based on inanimate sources of power, highly developed scientific technology, highly differentiated institutions matched by segmented individual roles, and a cosmopolitan outlook which emphasizes efficiency and progress. There are two fundamental aspects to this definition: (1) It is the transformation of a *total* society; no part of the society is left untouched. (2) The change is *unidirectional*; it always moves away from the rural

traditional form in the direction of the urban, highly differentiated form. This is not to assert that the process is uniform; on the contrary, as Nettl (1968:42–57) has pointed out, just as each society is unique in specific content at the start of the process, so it will be uniquely selective as the process goes on and certainly none should expect a uniform, standard outcome.

For Parsons (1964) the unidimensional nature of this change takes on the quality of a functional imperative when he calls it an "evolutionary universal." And the same idea is contained in Levy's (1966:744) characterization of modernization as a universal social "solvent." He asserts that whenever there are contacts between the members of a traditional society and those of a modern society, the structures of the traditional society begin to dissolve and to change in the direction of the modern society. Eisenstadt (1966a:1) appears to have the same quality of compulsive inevitability in mind in the opening sentences of his book:

> Modernization and aspirations to modernity are probably the most overwhelming and the most permeating features of the contemporary scene. Most nations are nowadays caught in its web. . . .

This statement also calls attention to another quality of the process, namely, that it is international in scope. Indeed, Eisenstadt (1966a:15–19) goes on to note that while in any given society one aspect of modernization is the eclipse of tribalism and the emergence of "mass-consensual orientation" in the form of nation-states, it is not confined within any set of political boundaries, its thrust and impact are truly international.

One point on which there appears to be consensus is that while modernization began in a limited number of western countries who are still leaders in the process and within these societies it was a self-generating autochthonous process, for the late-comers in the rest of the world it has now become largely a matter of imitation (Cf. Eisenstadt,

1966a:67; Nettl, 1968:42–57; Levy, 1966:744; Coughenour, 1969; Dore, 1969; Bendix, 1968).

The acknowledgement that modernization is the transformation of a total society carries with it some problems of utility. How can one discuss the relationship of modernization to some particular phenomenon without treating the total society, an enterprise which becomes prohibitive in terms of time and space? Obviously there is need for selectivity and abstraction in any such undertaking. In the current case we shall need to abstract from the total range of societal changes those which are salient to the subject of aging. We shall also attempt to differentiate among societal changes which are major and minor, on the one hand, and those which are relatively independent and relatively dependent, on the other.

At the outset we shall affirm that the major independent, and most salient societal changes which are subsidiary aspects of modernization—salient to the conditions of older people are: (1) scientific technology as applied in economic production and distribution, (2) urbanization, (3) literacy and mass education, and (4) health technology (the application of scientific technology in the range of environmental control, nutrition, and curative medicine). In many respects it is difficult to differentiate between the effects of scientific technology as applied in economic production and distribution, on the one hand, and its effects in the areas of public health and medicine, but we believe that with respect to aging, this is an important distinction.

MODERNIZATION AND AGING

The general thesis of the book was that modernization results in, *inter alia*, a relatively lower status of older people in society. Each of the major salient aspects of modernization appears to conduce to this effect and the following discussion seeks to analyze the causal sequences.

It is ironical that one of the most salient aspects of modernization with reference to aging is the development of health technology. Within this area we include all public health technology arising in consequence of the germ theory of disease, all aspects of modern knowledge of nutrition, and all aspects of curative and surgical medicine. The ironical aspect of this is that in none of the treatises on modernization is this aspect given more than passing notice. Yet, certainly in all contemporary development plans, health technology is given high prominence, backed up by significant budgetary allocations, and health programs are among the earliest and most liberally supported programs of assistance offered by the most modernized to so-called developing nations.

The most immediate, and sometimes dramatic, effect of such programs is the prolongation of life in these societies. In the initial instance the saving of life is most effective in infancy and childhood, consequently the most immediate impact when these measures are applied rapidly, as they have been in developing countries since World War II, has been not only a population explosion but also a "younging" of the population, i.e., a rapid increase of the child population. Theoretically this could have major significance for intergenerational relations but, so far as I know, this phenomenon has not been subjected to empirical study.

However, in the long run the application of modern health technology results in an aging of population, since it not only results in a prolongation of life of the young, but also (and perhaps this is an integral aspect of modernization) eventually a reduction of the birth rate which in turn reduces the ratio of children in the population. The combination of increased longevity followed by decreased fertility eventually results in the aging of the population (i.e., the increase in the proportion of the population in the upper age brackets).

Just how and when and to what degree this results in an increase in intergenerational competition for jobs (roles) is certainly unclear from present research, but that such competition eventually develops does seem clear and it is also clear that out of such conflict of interest, within the setting of an impersonal, highly-differentiated society with the emphasis on youth and new occupations, older people are eventually pushed out of the labor market. In the modern world this has led to the phenomenon which we know as retirement.

In a society which values the work role above all others and metes out its rewards on the basis of this role, retirement from it is likely to be prejudicial to the perpetuation of those rewards both material and non-material. Thus monetary income is drastically reduced (Riley and Foner, 1968) and whatever prestige and honor (psychic income) was ascribed to the position fades. The loss of income is probably a fairly accurate index of the decline of status, but in a society which tends to use consumption patterns as status symbols, the loss of income itself contributes to the decrement in status.

Therefore it appears that the introduction and application of modern health technology tends ultimately to contribute to the undermining of the status of older people in society. Figure 1 shows the analytical sequence in simplified form. However, the reader should note that the Work Ethic appears as an extraneous variable, important for the result, but not an intrinsic part of the sequence.

There will be further discussion of this exogeneous variable later.

A second salient aspect of modernization is economic modernization, more commonly called "development." This includes a broad range of economic changes which can be dissociated from other aspects only by intellectual abstraction. These are so profound that some see modernization as consisting entirely of them, while others, adopting a Marxian view, see them as the precipitating causes of modernization.

I can only illustrate the elements included in this aspect of modernization. It would certainly include: the increasing application of inanimate sources of power, the extensive application of new inventions in agricultural production, industrial production, transportation, communication, and distribution. These obviously led to and were intertwined with profound changes in the work world including factory organization and the separation of work from the home; they included the creation of new occupations and increasing specialization and professionalization; they included the increasing scale of operations in all spheres and consequent bureaucratization of organization, the proliferation of special interest associations, the impersonalization of relationships, including employer-employee relationships, and increasing interdependence withal (Cf. Eisenstadt, 1966a; Levy, 1966).

Out of this melange of developments, one which appears highly salient in its ultimate consequences for older people is the emergence of many new specialized occupations. It is highly significant that most of these new occupations emerge in cities and remain fundamentally urban in context. One of the most firmly established principles of demography is that the most mobile members of a society are its youth. It is they who are attracted by new frontiers including the job

Figure 1

Simplified analytical sequence.

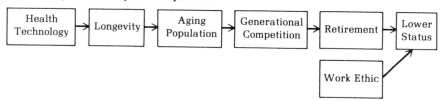

frontiers of the city. It is they who take the new jobs and acquire the training to fill them, leaving their parents behind both geographically and socially. Generally speaking the new occupations carry greater rewards in both money and status. Consequently there is an inversion of status, with children achieving higher status than their parents instead of merely moving up to the status of their parents as in most pre-modern societies. This not only leaves the parents in older, less prestigious, perhaps static and sometimes obsolete positions, it also deprives them of one of the most traditional roles for older people—that of providing vocational guidance and instruction to their children.

Some of the pressure toward early retirement occurs because of shifting patterns of vocational application resulting in static conditions or even declines in the demand for some types of workers. Usually these are the very lines of work in which older workers are concentrated. And again, retirement within this social and cultural setting is fraught with insecurity, is usually accompanied by loss of income and its attendant lower status. And again, the Work Ethic is a persistently conditioning, perhaps extraneous, factor.

Furthermore, the work role is only one of the roles which is lost in modernizing societies; other familial and community roles also tend to be eroded and with the decline of useful, prestigious roles the status of older people declines (Rosow, 1967; Cowgill and Holmes, 1972:11).

A greatly oversimplified sequence of influences flowing from changes in technology is shown in Figure 2.

The third major aspect of modernization with respect to aging is urbanization. Although this clearly is a process which is closely interrelated with economic development, it is at least partially independent and has significance for aging which extends to facets which were not discussed in connection with economic development.

We did call attention to the separation of work from home and to the geographical separation of youthful urban migrants from their parental homes. This puts a heavy strain upon bonds of the extended family which has been so prevalent in so many traditional societies. I am not contending that the extended family completely disappears in modern societies nor that relations with kin are unimportant; I am asserting that urbanization does tend to break up the extended family as a household unit, to increase the spatial separation between generations and to establish neolocal marriage and the nuclear family as the norm. Recent findings of moderately frequent contacts between adult children and aged parents do not warrant the conclusion that nothing has changed. Weekly visits across town are profoundly different from constant association within the same household. The current mode of calling the occa-

Figure 2

Simplified sequence of influences.

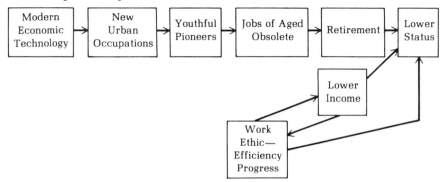

sional contacts between selected remnants of kin networks the "modified extended family" (Litwak, 1959–64; Sussman, 1965; Shanas, *et al.* 1968) must not blind us to the profound impact of urbanization upon the family.

It does produce residential segregation of the generations and, while this is certainly not synonymous with isolation, it most assuredly reduces the frequency and intimacy of contact; it militates against immediate availability of help in time of crisis; it decreases not only the extent of interaction but also the amount of interdependence in daily activities. This makes aged parents peripheral to the nuclear families of their adult children (Williams, 1970), it fosters independence of the generations from each other and this ecological reality is moved to a moral obligation when, as in Western society, it is undergirded by the Protestant Ethic which makes individual independence and self-reliance a moral virtue. The prevalence of such an ethic is attested by much research in Western industrialized societies (Cf. Streib and Thompson, 1960; Shanas et al. 1968).

Urbanization not only induces geographic mobility, it also accelerates social mobility (Smelser and Lipset, 1966). One aspect of this is the emergence of new social classes and a restructuring of the status system (Cf. Coleman, 1968) tending toward a much more fluid situation and a blurring of class lines. Another aspect which is more relevant to the present discussion is the intergenerational mobility whereby children move up through the system (upward mobil-

ity is much more frequent than its opposite in a modernizing society) with the inevitable consequence that they ultimately achieve a status which is superior to the maximal achievement of their parents. To the extent that they internalize the values of the society, and the more successful ones are very likely to espouse those values, the children consciously or unconsciously feel superior to their parents.

The inversion of status is accentuated by geographic separation as the youths move to the cities and the old folks stay behind because, at least in the early stages of modernization, urban comes to mean "modern" and rural means "traditional" or "backward" (de Briey, 1966).

When to this inversion of status based on active work roles is added the humiliation of retirement, the contrast and debasement of the older generation is exaggerated. If to this combination of factors is added the further insult of enforced dependency, severe mental conflicts tend to occur (Clark, 1967).

Recapitulating the chain of forces stemming from urbanization bearing on the status of the aged, we have Figure 3.

A fourth salient aspect of modernization with respect to aging is education (Cf. Smelser and Lipset, 1966:29–42). In premodern societies most of the population is illiterate and thus their knowledge of the world is severely limited. Their knowledge of the past beyond their own personal experience was confined to verbal recitations of other living persons whose experience tran-

Figure 3

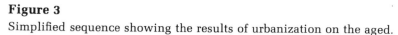

Simplified sequence showing the results of urbanization on the aged.

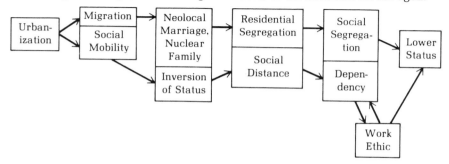

scended their own or who were repositories of oral tradition. This tended to provide an important role for older people and to reinforce their status in that type of society.

Early in the process of modernization one always finds measures being undertaken to promote literacy and to advance education. In fact, Lerner (1958:60–65) suggests that after the initial impact of urbanization, the second significant aspect of modernization is the spread of literacy and, as a matter of fact, literacy is sometimes used as an index of modernization especially during its early stages (Cowgill and Holmes, 1972:306). Closely interrelated with efforts to promote literacy are programs to extend the educational level of the populace, sooner or later taking the form of public mass education of the child population to a prescribed minimal level. Paralleling these developments are training programs conducted either by employers or by technical schools designed to develop skills in particular jobs.

The main targets of such programs are always the young; in the case of mass public education, children; in the case of technical education, teenagers or young adults. The major consequence of this is that once a society is launched into the process of modernization, no matter what its stage of development, adult children are always more highly educated than their parents. In the early stages this may manifest itself in a situation in which most of the younger generation are able to read while their parents are not and the parents have to rely on the expertise of their children to keep them informed about current events as well as communicating with their own kin who have moved away to the city. At another stage we may find that most of the children have had an elementary school education while their parents are barely literate. At a still later stage we may find that most of the children have completed secondary school while their parents only completed primary school. In the United States of America, probably in an advanced stage of modernization today, it is fairly accurate to say that the average older person (sixty-five and over) has about an elementary

school education (the last illiterate generation has already passed from the scene); their children, currently in middle age, are on the average high school graduates; their grandchildren, just now completing their formal education, will have the advantage of several years college.

The continuation of a condition in which the children always have greater skill than their parents and know more than their parents, including more about their own past history, cannot avoid fostering a different relationship between generations and different roles in the society as compared with a traditional society in which the situation is reversed. The obvious tendency will be for the child generation to be in a superior status vis-a-vis their parents, and for the child generation to occupy positions according them higher status in the community than had been achieved by their parents.

Furthermore it appears that once launched into the process of modernization, the rate of social change continually accelerates. This implies that the generation gap continually becomes wider and places the older generation at a greater and greater disadvantage tending further to depress its relative status in society (Moore, 1966; Cowgill and Holmes, 1972:9).

When, as in the most highly modernized societies, we approach a stage of development in which not only are past forms of education and socialization inappropriate but the young must be socialized for a future which is unknown (Cogswell, 1970) it is evident that the older generation is deprived of much of its earlier socializing role and is incapable of sharing the experiences and problems of the younger generation. The generation gap becomes a nearly unbridgeable chasm.

This generalization speaks to the situation while both generations are still active participants. When we add to this discrepant status some actual deterioration of the status of the older generation with retirement and/or dependency the generation gap may become rather wide indeed. Certainly under these circumstances there can be no mystique

Figure 4

Simplified sequence showing the results of the generation gap on the aged.

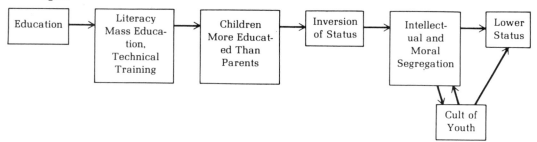

of old age. There can be no reverence deriving from superior knowledge and no awe based on recognition of superior power.

This generation gap produces a real intellectual and moral segregation of the aged in modern societies. The sequence in simplified form is shown in Figure 4.

In this instance the extraneous factor is labeled "Cult of Youth" but it is a companion of and partially derivative from the Work Ethic with its emphasis on efficiency and progress. But it extends beyond the usual dimensions of that concept to include not only an emphasis on vigor and athletic prowess but a dominating value on youth itself. Youth becomes the symbol of and means to progress. When choices between generations are forced, youth is given priority. We have already seen this in two contexts: in applying modern medical technology the early thrust is toward the reduction of infant and child mortality, and in the application of modern education the main targets are children and youth. We could add that in the spending of local community resources through such devices as community chests and united funds there is further conclusive evidence of the prevalence of this value system. And, be it noted, this is not something created by the pressures of youth; these are values which are prevalent throughout modern societies, concurred in by all generations and implemented by the power structures of the societies. This is what is called here the Cult of Youth. It is a conditioning factor which operates interactively within the total system to

accentuate the decline of the status of the aged (Havighurst and Albrecht, 1953).

However, there is a related but quite different phenomenon which is often called Youth Culture. This is an indigenous intra-generational development in which a particular youthful generation creates to a recognizable degree its own culture—its own idiom, its own standards of dress and behavior, and its own organizations. Some of this is in rebellion against what is perceived as the archaic standards and values of old fashioned and "ignorant" parents. It occurs within the context of a mass urbanized society where the generation gap has become very wide, where tradition has been debunked, and where each generation to a considerable extent evolves its own culture and is guided by the standards of its peers (Riesman, 1950). Smelser and Lipset (1966:42) see a functional relationship between their "other-directedness" and economic development. The term "youth culture" is probably a misnomer because it connotes that the current generation of youth are behaving as they do because they are young and that there is likely to be some continuity to these patterns, that oncoming contingents will adopt the culture and behave the same way because they have now become a part of youth society. This is a static and dated view of what is really a very dynamic, ever-changing condition. Since the term "youth culture" first came into vogue its content has made several drastic shifts; we have already had several generations of different youth cultures. It is temporally myopic to see the culture of any particular generation as "youth culture"; to the extent that there is any permanence to it, it will be carried forward by that generation into adulthood, becoming in succeeding years the young adult culture, then the culture of middle age, then of later middle age and finally of old age. A more realistic appraisal of this stage of modernizing society indicates a succession of increasingly segregated generations (segregated from each other physically, socially, psychologically, intellectually, and morally) each in turn inventing and evolving to a significant degree its own culture. Given the pressures toward segregation of the generations surely such an eventuality is predictable.

Those who are speculating about the incipient emergence of a "subculture of aging" (Cf. Rose, 1965) are subject to the same myopia while looking in the opposite direction. The cultural characteristics of the current generation of older people are attributes of a generation; they are not attributes of old people. Those who have hopefully or fearfully looked for emerging self consciousness and mutual peer loyalty among the aged have so far had little evidence on which to base their hopes or fears. As a matter of fact, there is much evidence that many people born before the turn of the century still refuse to classify themselves as old or aged. However, I doubt whether many of these would reject being classified with their generation.

It may be that future older generations will develop more self consciousness of generational identity and perhaps more loyalty to their peers. Such a development would appear not unlikely in the context of increasing numbers and proportions of older people and increasing segregation.

Throughout the previous discussion the Work Ethic has been treated as an extraneous variable, perhaps not inherent in or essential to the process of modernization. This is of course a moot point. Weber (1958) gave a different interpretation many years ago. According to that view Western capitalism arose on the foundation provided by the prior emergence of Protestantism whose leaders espoused and promulgated an ethic of individual salvation demonstrated by hard work, frugality and self-reliance. One does not have much difficulty in defending the proposition that the rise of Western capitalism signaled the beginning of modernization. One can also agree with Weber, as Eisenstadt (1966b, 1968) does, that in the particular historical setting in European society where both developments were initiated Protestantism did play a significant role. But these two propositions do not force us to the conclusion that either Protestantism or capitalism are essential to the continuing process of modernization. It would be tenuous indeed to argue that the modernization of Japan should be attributed to Protestantism and by the same token the extensive modernization of Russia can scarcely be identified with capitalism. Indeed these and other illustrations of modernization appear to demonstrate that neither Protestantism nor capitalism is an essential ingredient in the process. However, it does appear that all societies which have advanced very far in the process have by diffusion or independent invention acquired a value system which incorporates the motivating forces analogous with those provided by Protestantism in Europe. Parsons (1960:162) asserts that one of the most crucial non-economic factors underlying the industrial type of economy is "drive" and Bendix (1966) finds the analogue in Japan in the reactions of samurai after the Meiji restoration. Certainly industriousness, frugality, accumulation of savings (capital), rational organization of work, efficiency, time-consciousness, a secular outlook, orientation toward this world and hope of individual achievement in it, rising expectations and standards of living are a part of the value system associated with economic development and modernization.

I have sought to capture the most salient aspects of this "new cultural outlook" (Eisenstadt, 1966a:5) in the term "Work Ethic." The concept is obviously derived from the Protestant Ethic but these values can no longer be attributed to any single religious orientation or event.

This still does not resolve the issue of its role in the process—whether as a major, primary variable or as a facilitator and conditioning agent. Myrdal (1968) assumes a Weberian stance when he holds that South Asia will not succeed in its economic development without a fundamental change of values. Weiner (1966:5–12) acknowledges the Weberian view but points out that the opposite view, supported by considerable research on cognitive dissonance, is that attitudes change when they get out of consonance with behavior, i.e., they tend to follow rather than lead.

The present treatment is a compromise between these views. It holds that while the Work Ethic is a significant factor in the process and while it does have an important role in motivation, it is not the primary nor even one of the major salient aspects of modernization. Nevertheless it is a very important conditioning factor and because of its pervasive cultural nature it has impact and modifying effect upon the operation of each of the major salient aspects of modernization as they affect the status of older people.

In summary, the thesis is that modernization does tend to diminish the relative status of older people in their society and that this relationship is not a mere statistical correlation, it is a functional relationship which can be analyzed. Selecting the four most salient aspects of modernization, we have sought to delineate the causal chain linking each with the ultimate outcome—diminished status for the aged. Figure 5 integrates the four chains into a single system. This shows parallel influences through and between the

Figure 5

Aging and modernization.

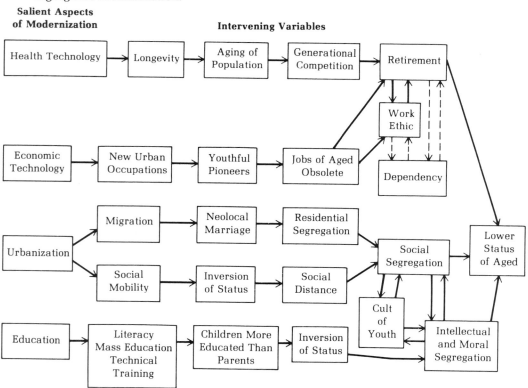

four chains converging in a single direction and tendency. Thus the introduction of modern health technology, modern economic technology, urbanization, and rising levels of education, all operating within a climate which incorporates the Work Ethic and a Cult of Youth, tend to have a depressing effect on the status of the aged in society.

THE FUTURE TREND

Until very recently the evidence for the general proposition that modernization tends to diminish the status of the aged was largely anecdotal and impressionistic. Palmore and Whittington (1971) recently found for the United States that not only was the status of the aged lower than the younger population in terms of several socioeconomic indicators but it had also declined significantly between 1940 and 1969. The theorem is still more convincingly demonstrated by Palmore and Manton (1973) in a study just completed which correlates indicators of modernization with indicators of status in thirty-one countries. As indicators of modernization they used gross national product per capita, percent of the labor force in agriculture, change in the percent of the labor force in agriculture, percent illiterate, percent of youths in school, and percent of population in higher education. It may be noted that these indicators include measures of three of the four salient aspects of modernization treated above—economic technology, urbanization, and education; again health technology was slighted. The relative status of the aged was measured by indexes which measured the difference in employment, occupation and education of the older population (sixty-five and over) as compared with the general adult population (twenty-five to sixty-four). The correlations gave rather decisive indication that the relative status of older people was lower in the more modernized countries.

However, Palmore and Manton found on more intensive analysis that for two of the indicators of status—occupation and education—the relationship was curvilinear. The

relative status of the aged declined through most of the range of modernization represented by the thirty-one countries, but at the most advanced stages the relationship turned positive. This suggests that while modernization is detrimental to the status and interests of the aged in its early stages this trend may "bottom out" in later stages of modernization and from then on there is some comparative improvement in the status and condition of older people.

These are encouraging symptoms fostering some hope that modernization does not inevitably and unendingly sacrifice the interests of the aged on the altar of progress. Perhaps there comes a time when they begin to share in the fruits of that progress.

In the light of the theory presented in this paper it is interesting to speculate about the possible bases for this reversal of the trend and to search for further symptoms of it. One possibility for which there is some impressionistic support is that there is a softening of the Work Ethic; that work is no longer such a high virtue and that not working does not connote such disgrace. With declining work hours and increasing leisure, even during the prime working years, it is reasonable to believe that increased leisure in old age in the form of retirement would be less destructive to one's status. A second possibility is that only after a society reaches a certain stage of affluence is it able or willing to provide adequate incomes to non-productive members such as the aged retired and this occurs long after the extended family has lost its capability for adequately fulfilling this function. Another possibility is that illiteracy may be the most serious handicap of an aged generation vis-a-vis younger literate generations and when illiteracy disappears even among the aged the degree of their handicap is decreased. A similar possibility which pertains also to the education variable is that societies in advanced stages of modernization may approach a point of diminishing returns in terms of further increases in the amount of education to be provided to the oncoming generations. Beyond this point the differential in the levels of education of the generations begins to decline. This is strongly indicated in the data of Palmore and Manton (1973). A final possibility which will be mentioned here, though this certainly does not exhaust the possibilities, is that with increased numbers and proportions of the aged and with increased segregation there may be an increasing self-awareness in the older generation and increasing group pressure on behalf of their interests. Cutler (1973) finds that increased awareness of status decline is associated with increased demands for governmental assistance and increased support for organized political activity. These various possibilities are obviously not mutually exclusive and certainly most if not all of them could occur concurrently.

SUMMARY

This chapter has sought to extend and develop a theory of aging which was stated elsewhere in elemental form (Cowgill and Holmes, 1972). It has sought to abstract the most salient aspects of the general process of modernization and analyze the ways in which these aspects taken severally and in concert contribute to the general tendency for the relative status of the aged to decline with modernization. The salient aspects which were examined were the introduction of modern health technology, the introduction of modern economic technology, the increase of education, and urbanization. Each of these prime factors was found to initiate a chain reaction which tended to diminish the status of the aged. The effects were amplified by the presence of the Work Ethic and the Cult of Youth. However, new evidence indicates that this trend may "bottom out" in advanced stages of modernization and from that point on the relative status of the aged may begin to improve. The evidence suggests that this may be happening in the most modernized nations today.

REFERENCES

ARMER, MICHAEL, and SCHNAIBERG, ALLAN. "Measuring Individual Modernity: A Mere Myth." *American Sociological Review* 37 (1972): 301–16.

BARNDT, DEBORAH. "Changing Time Conceptions." *Summation* 1 (1969): 17–28.

BENDIX, REINHARD. "A Case Study in Cultural and Educational Mobility: Japan and the Protestant Ethic." In *Social Structure and Mobility in Economic Development*, edited by Neil J. Smelser and Seymour Martin Lipset. Chicago: Aldine Publishing Company, 1966.

BENDIX, REINHARD. "Proba Definicji Modernizacji" [Towards a Definition of Modernization]. *Studia Socjolgiszno Polityczne* 25 (1968): 31–43.

CLARK, MARGARET, and ANDERSON, BARBARA GALLATIN. *Culture and Aging.* Springfield, Ill.: Charles C. Thomas, 1967.

COGSWELL, BETTY E. "Socialization and Modernization." Paper presented at International Congress of Sociology, September 14–19, 1970, at Varna, Bulgaria.

COLEMAN, JAMES S. "Modernization: Political Aspects. In *International Encyclopedia of the Social Sciences*, edited by David L. Sills, vol. 10. The MacMillan Company and The Free Press, 1968.

COUGHENOUR, C. M. "Modernization, Modern Man and Social Change." Paper presented at Rural Sociological Society, 1969.

COWGILL, DONALD O., and HOLMES, LOWELL D., eds. *Aging and Modernization.* New York: Appleton-Century-Crofts, 1972.

CUTLER, STEPHEN J. "Perceived Prestige Loss and Political Attitudes Among the Aged." *The Gerontologist* 13 (1973): 69–75.

DE BRIEY, PIERRE. "Les agglomerations urbaines et la modernisation des etats du tiers monde." *Civilisations* 15 (1966): 454–70.

DORE, R. P. "The Modernizer as a Special Case: Japanese Factory Legislation, 1882–1911." *Comparative Studies in Society and History* 11 (1969): 433–50.

EHRLICH, E. "Comparisons internationales de developpement economique." *Analyse et Prevision* 11 (1971): 81–107.

EISENSTADT, S. N. *Modernization: Protest and Change.* Englewood Cliffs, N.J.: Prentice-Hall, 1966.

EISENSTADT, S. N. "Problems in the Comparative Analysis of Total Societies." In *Transactions of the Sixth World Congress of Sociology* 1:187–202. Published by International Sociological Association. Louvain, Belgium: Impriemerie Nauwelaerts, 1966.

EISENSTADT, S. N. *The Protestant Ethic and Modernization.* New York: Basic Books, 1968.

ETZIONI, AMITAI, and ETZIONI, EVA, eds. *Social Change.* New York:Basic Books, 1964.

HAVIGHURST, ROBERT J., and ALBRECHT, RUTH. *Older People.* New York: Longmans, Green, 1953.

INKELES, ALEX, and SMITH, DAVID H. "The Fate of Personal Adjustment in the Process of Modernization. *International Journal of Comparative Sociology* 11 (1970): 81–114.

JANOSSY, F. The problem of measuring the level of economic development: a new method of estimation, Budapest, 1963.

LERNER, DANIEL. *The Passing of Traditional Society: Modernizing the Middle East.* New York: The Free Press, 1958.

LERNER, DANIEL. "Modernization: Social Aspects." In *International Encyclopedia of the Social Sciences,* edited by David L. Sills, vol. 10. The MacMillan Company and The Free Press, 1968.

LEVY, MARION J. *Modernization and the Structure of Societies.* Princeton, N.J.: Princeton University Press, 1966.

LITWAK, EUGENE. "The Use of Extended Family Groups in the Achievement of Social Goals." *Social Problems* 7 (1959–60): 177–87.

MOORE, WILBERT E. "Aging and the Social System." In *Aging and Social Policy,* edited by John C. McKinney and Frank T. de Vyver. New York: Appleton-Century-Crofts, 1966.

MYRDAL, GUNNAR. *Asian Drama.* New York: Pantheon, 1968.

NETTL, J. P. *International Systems and the Modernization of Societies.* New York: Basic Books, 1968.

NETTL, J. P., and ROBERTSON, R. *International Systems and the Formation of National Goals and Attitudes.* New York: Basic Books, 1968.

PALMORE, ERDMAN, and WHITTINGTON, F. "Trends in the Relative Status of the Aged." *Social Forces* 50 (1971): 84–91.

PALMORE, ERDMAN, and MANTON, KENNETH. "Modernization and Status of the Aged: International Correlations. *Journal of Gerontology,* 29 (1974): 205–210.

PARSONS, TALCOTT. *Structure and Process in Modern Societies.* Glencoe, The Free Press, 1960.

PARSONS, TALCOTT. "Evolutionary Universals in Society." *American Sociological Review* 29 (1964): 339–57.

RIESMAN, DAVID. *The Lonely Crowd.* New Haven: Yale University Press, 1950.

RILEY, MATILDA W., and FONER, ANNE. *Aging and Society: An Inventory of Research Findings.* New York: Russell Sage Foundation, 1968.

ROSE, ARNOLD M. "The Subculture of the Aging: a Framework for Research in Social Gerontology." In *Older People and Their Social World,* edited by Arnold M. Rose and Warren A. Peterson. Philadelphia: F. A. Davis Company, 1965.

ROSOW, IRVING. "And Then We Were Old." *Transaction* 2 (1965): 20–26.

ROSTOW, WALT W. *The Economics of Take-off into Sustained Growth.* New York: St. Martin's Press, 1963.

SHANAS, ETHEL; TOWNSEND, PETER; WEDDERBURN, DOROTHY; FRIIS, HENNING; MILHØJ, POUL; and JAN STEHOUWER. *Old People in Three Industrial Societies.* New York: Atherton Press, 1968.

SMELSER, NEIL J., and LIPSET, SEYMOUR MARTIN. *Social Structure and Mobility in Economic Development.* Chicago: Aldine Publishing Company, 1966.

STEPHENSON, JOHN B. "Is Everyone Going Modern? A Critique and a Suggestion for Measuring Modernism." *American Journal of Sociology* 74 (1968): 265–75.

STREIB, GORDON F., and THOMPSON, WAYNE E. "The Older Person in a Family Context." In *Handbook of Social Gerontology,* edited by Clark Tibbits. Chicago: The University of Chicago Press, 1960.

Sussman, Marvin B. "Relationship of Adult Children with Their Parents in the United States." In *Social Structure and the Family: Generational Relations,* edited by Ethel Shanas and Gordon F. Streib. Englewood Cliffs, N.J.: Prentice-Hall, 1965.

Waisanen, Frederick B. "Actors, Social Systems, and the Modernization Process." Paper presented at Carnegie Seminar, April, 1968, at Indiana University.

Weber, Max. *The Protestant Ethic and the Spirit of Capitalism.* New York: Charles Scribner's Sons, 1958.

Weiner, Myron, ed. *Modernization: The Dynamics of Growth.* New York: Basic Books, 1966.

Williams, Robin M., Jr. *American Society.* New York: Alfred A. Knopf, 1970.

SECTION 2

From the Inside Out: Physiological and Health- Related Events

Underlying all other aspects of the process of aging is the inescapable fact that as biological organisms we begin to age as soon as we begin to live. Why this should be cannot yet be answered definitively. Nonetheless, we become increasingly vulnerable to offsetting stimuli of all types as we pass through life. In their search for an explanation, biological researchers have unravelled many of the mysteries about how our bodies operate; much of the information obtained has already been useful in ameliorating the physical infirmities responsible for early mortality in less medically advanced times and places.

Despite the efforts of investigators around the world, little is yet known which might ultimately bring about the longed for retardation of the processes of senescence. Biologically, we are complex systems, carrying with us not only the accumulated results of our genetic heritage but the consequences of a lifetime of stress, trauma, and chronic diseases. Each of these plays an independent as well as an interactive role in determining the parameters of the aging process as we see it in ourselves and those around us. As members of a species, the genetic package of our heredity contributes to the lifespan or maximum period we may expect any one of us to live; it is doubtful whether much can be done to increase this beyond the 120 or so years most biologists now agree upon. The secondary factors arising from the actual experience of living directly affect our life expectancy or the number of years people in particular circumstances may reasonably anticipate (Busse, 1977).

As complicated as the biological side of aging is, it is by no means entirely a downhill trip. It is true however, that after age thirty—the benchmark used by biologists and physiologists to measure subsequent changes—many of our body's functions do begin a gradual, decremental decline, which eventually appears as an increased incidence of physical complaints and chronic health conditions. For example, despite their most vigorous efforts, individuals of fifty simply cannot tone their bodies to the same level as is possible for a thirty-five-year-old. A person of eighty or so has the approximate muscle strength of a twelve-year-old adolescent (Birren, 1959). Fortunately, we do not have to live by muscle strength alone, and the losses incurred need not be incapacitating. Exertion itself is unavoidable; since it requires not merely strength but a coordination of respiratory functions, circulatory capacity, and the nervous system, it becomes more of an effort as the various systems and the ability to integrate them undergo degenerative changes. The mechanisms by which molecular and cellular alterations are translated into declining physiological functioning are not clearly understood, but most experts agree that the link is there. Their attention has been directed to discovering the causes of aging at the cellular level first, before proceeding to systemic level explorations. Despite repeated attempts to isolate a magic drug, elixir, or hormone which might delay the onset of old age, no successful treatment has as yet been found (Shock, 1974).

In his award-winning discussion of biological aging, Daniel J. Wallace begins by examining the history of research efforts intended to solve the mysteries of the aging organism. From the time of the ancient Egyptians, to the Greeks and Romans, on through to eighteenth and nineteenth century scientists, most researchers invested their time and effort in what was essentially a Hippocratic concept, a disease-model explanation of aging—a point of view which has not yet passed entirely out of vogue. As eminent a personage as King George III (1738–1820), the man so disliked by the American Revolutionaries, was diagnosed as suffering "the Climacteric Disease," or more simply, aging, when he was ravaged by an incapacitating emotional illness (Livesley, 1977). Many of the unfavorable attitudes held by professionals and nonprofessionals alike stem from just this confusion of the normal process of aging with its pathological concomitants. As Wallace notes, aging was not often a primary interest among physicians or physiologists until after World War II, even though the term *geriatrics* was coined in 1914 to describe such a focus. Attention was directed to the process, of course, but seldom was it considered a scientifically respectable enterprise (Birren and Clayton, 1975). A remarkable growth in the range and sophistication of the explanatory frameworks took place in the period following the war. Wallace is critical of the lack of productivity these have had so far in highlighting the etiology of aging. Selecting four of what he considers the more viable possibilities, he suggests what effect these could conceivably have on life expectancy. Whether or not these gains would prove beneficial to humanity is a question left to the readers.

The issue of extensions in life expectancy is also taken up by Strehler. Amplifying the thrust of Wallace's remarks, Strehler sets forth a four-fold division of what he labels *gerontogeny*, or the means of enhancing longevity. The physical health domains are basic, but advances in mental health, social effects, and economics are also essential. The author suggests that a major rethinking of priorities in each of these areas is required before anything resembling a golden era can be achieved. As will be seen in Section 6, many of the questions raised by Strehler also trouble those who are more broadly concerned with social policy and ethics.

Questions of health and its relationship with life satisfaction prove to be more intransigent than might at first be assumed. In what may be one of the most extensive studies of the concerns of older people, the Harris polling organization found health to be far and away the most threatening problem identified (1975). Even so, roughly half of those over sixty-five do not feel impeded in their daily lives by any chronic limitations. The remainder, however, may be not only inconvenienced but suffer from protracted and painful disabilities; the number experiencing significant disabilities increases dramatically as individuals move into the later years of adulthood. Not surprisingly, the economically disadvantaged—white and nonwhite—and women experience the most serious problems. As Estes vividly points out, circulatory problems, especially heart disease, hypertension, cerebral hemorrhages, cancers of various types, and crippling arthritis are real specters in the health picture for older people. Not only must the elderly contend with these conditions themselves, but they are forced to negotiate with a medical bureaucracy characterized by a shortage of professional help. Medicare has not turned out to be the panacea many of its advocates had hoped and, as will be seen in the last section on social policy, a major revision is overdue.

Physicians have long recognized that distressing events tend to compromise a person's ability to ward off or recover from illness. A considerable volume of literature evaluating the role played by stress, both physical and social-psychological, has accumulated in recent years. In the past few years a new dimension, that of apparently ordinary life-change events, has been added (Gunderson and Rahe, 1974). While studies of young and middle-aged people have become plentiful, gerontologists have felt that insufficient attention has been focused on the relationship between health status and those events common to the second half of life (Busse and Pfeiffer, 1977). In an attempt to remedy that situation, Garrity and Marx provide a thoroughgoing review of the effects of life-change on the health experienced and manifested by the elderly. As they so cogently suggest, there is a vast array of displacing stimuli likely to result in a breakdown of physiological functioning, though these are not necessarily the ones usually assumed to be the most serious. Retirement is one such event. The notion that it has a negative impact on health is widely held, yet Garrity and Marx uncover little which would serve to substantiate this. While neither the authors nor the works they surveyed detail the exact physiological mechanism by which stress is transcribed into a physical response, they suggest possible linkages with the body's hormonal and neuroendocrine systems.

The final selection in our overview of physiological and health-related events offers an examination of nutrition and lifestyle as they interact in the lives of older people. Food intake and eating patterns are essential in maintaining well-being. This is true because they furnish an avenue for social integration as well as good nutrition. In 1972 the federal government, responding to pressures to improve the dietary status of older people, initiated legislation which would provide nutritionally balanced meals to all needy individuals over age sixty. Insuring the availability of adequate intake is one thing; remolding the habits of a lifetime is quite another. Meals usually satisfy more needs than those of hunger alone. Reporting the results of his investigation of nutrition and lifestyle, Todhunter identifies a number of social factors which must be considered if the goals of the federal program are to be realized. While this study was carried out in a particular locale, the implications and conclusions are applicable in widely differing contexts.

As biological organisms we will all experience certain events in common. To date however, the intricacies of the issues involved have precluded very much in the way of conclusive data or pragmatic application. Whether scientists will break the code which determines the parameters of normal aging is still an open question. New avenues must be explored before our chances of significantly extending life expectancy will be increased. Since our bodies do not age in a vacuum, insulated from environmental and social inputs, the complexities of any solutions are multiplied beyond what might be possible for controlled populations in laboratory settings. One theme which emerges from these and similar reports is that even so basic a biological fact of life as age is interwoven with social and psychological variables. It is unrealistic to expect any gerontologist or even any one research team to be able to tie together all the factors influencing the process of aging. Many years of interdisciplinary research will be required before the potential for intervention can be achieved. Nonetheless, intervention must remain our goal if the scientific community is to justify the tremendous expenditures already incurred. Far more important than the mere financial outlays are the human costs, a factor which will continue to escalate as the number of people living into their sixth, seventh, and decades beyond continues to increase.

REFERENCES

1. BIRREN, J. "Principles of Research on Aging." In *Handbook of Aging and the Individual,* edited by James Birren. Chicago: University of Chicago Press, 1959, pp. 3–42.

2. BIRREN, J. and CLAYTON, V. "History of Gerontology." In *Aging: Scientific Perspectives and Social Issues,* edited by D. S. Woodruff and J. Birren. New York: D. Van Nostrand Company, 1975, pp. 15–27.

3. BUSSE, E. W. "Theories of Aging," In *Behavior and Adaptation in Late Life,* edited by E. W. Busse and E. Pfeiffer. Boston: Little, Brown and Company, 1977, pp. 8–30.

4. BUSSE, E. W. and PFEIFFER, E. "Psychiatric Disorders." In *Behavior and Adaptation in Late Life.*

5. GUNDERSON, E. and RAHE, R. H. *Life Stress and Illness.* Springfield, Ill.: Charles C. Thomas, 1974.

6. LIVESLEY, B. "The Climacteric Disease," *Journal of the American Geriatrics Society* XXV, 4 (1977): 162–166.

7. SHOCK, N. "Physiology of Aging." In *Aging: The Challenge to the Individual and to Society,* edited by W. C. Bier. New York: Fordham University Press, 1974, 47–60.

The Biology of Aging

Daniel J. Wallace

The first objective in this overview is to discuss the biology of aging from the historical aspect and to trace the reasons for the lack of productivity of this approach up to the present. Next to be considered are the reasons for undertaking research on aging, the levels of this research, the models, the theories for the etiology of aging, and the possible factors which may affect the lifespan. Finally, we discuss some of the philosophic arguments and implications of research on aging.

YESTERDAY'S RESEARCH ON AGING

The ancient Egyptians approached the problem of aging with attempts to find a rejuvenating elixir. In pre-Biblical times, the Chinese considered aging to be a function of how proper a life one had lived (cf. the Taoist *yin* and *yang*). The Hindus believed in continuous reincarnation which eventually led to a state of Nirvana for a fortunate minority. In the Bible, the ninetieth Psalm states that man's natural lifespan is three-score and ten years—a figure that has hardly changed to this date! The twelfth chapter of Ecclesiastes also includes a philosophic discussion of the aging process.

The Greeks were the first to postulate a cause of aging. Hippocrates (460–377 B.C.) called aging an irreversible and natural event

From *Journal of the American Geriatrics Society* 25, 3 (1977), pp. 104–111. Copyright © 1977 by the American Geriatrics Society. Reprinted by permission.

that was caused by a decrease in body "heat." He was also the first to write about diseases found in the elderly. Galen (A.D. 130–201) further elaborated on this theory and stated that aging was primarily caused by a change in the body's humors which produced increased dryness and coldness. His most significant contribution was his belief that aging goes on throughout one's lifespan and does not appear only toward its end.

The ideas of the Greeks and the Romans greatly influenced world thought for fifteen hundred years. These teachings could not be challenged. The Catholic Church discouraged research or discussion on the subject of the etiology of aging, and the universal belief in the hereafter took away much of the willpower to talk about aging. Nevertheless, the Jewish philosopher Maimonides (1135–1204) stated that life was predetermined and unalterable but that our lifespan could be prolonged by taking suitable precautions. Roger Bacon (1210–1292) was the first European after Galen to write anything of substance about aging, and he spent much of his life in prison on account of these concepts as well as his other efforts. His monograph, "Cure of Old Age and Preservation of Youth," viewed aging as a pathologic process that could be halted by good hygiene. He adhered to the Greek model of decreased innate "heat" causing increased dryness and producing aging. But he also theorized that aging was the result of the wear and tear of living and believed that the Catholic Church ultimately determined one's natural lifespan.

The first renaissance in research on aging occurred when investigation superseded empiricism. Leonardo da Vinci (1452–1519) performed autopsies on old men and young children, described the anatomic findings, and attempted to explain some of the pathologic findings. Francis Bacon and others endorsed the ancient theories, but added to the myths by postulating that aging was caused by the presence of a "vital spirit"—an hypothesis that was copied by others. Santorio in the 1620s utilized most of the foregoing theories in his works but observed that aging manifested itself through the hardening of fibers and the progressive consolidation of earthy material within one's body.

The advent of microscopy and investigational inquiry had little impact on the aging discipline. Alchemists and mystics continued to try to discover the "fountain of youth," a concept of Hindu origin. In the eighteenth and nineteenth centuries scientists first began seriously to elucidate the physiologic and anatomic processes of aging, even though mystics and eccentrics still dominated the field. Erasmus Darwin (1731–1762) believed aging to be due to failure of the body to respond to nervous and muscular stimuli following a loss in irritability of these tissues. Xavier Bichat (1771–1802) conceptualized disease in all tissues as being a representation of the same process, regardless of which organ was involved. Aldred Warthin (1866–1932) felt that, with time, man lost intrinsic energy which was part of an involutional process. Hufeland (1762–1836) spoke of a vital force which activated and deactivated all body processes. Elie Metchnikoff (1845–1916) believed that "autointoxication," and hence aging, could be successfully dealt with by preventing intestinal putrefaction. Charles Brown-Séquard (1817–1894) injected animal testicular extracts into his own body when he was seventy-two years old; the results were disappointing.

Some physiologists were performing serious work. In 1854, Durand and Fardel described the anatomic and physiologic changes in man relative to time by systematically covering each organ system. In the 1860s Charcot (1825–1893) initiated more sophisticated studies. His central belief ("Life

is a vital force of limited duration") and his works mark the point of turning away from philosophy toward physiology. Canstatt then showed that with time, cells die which are not replaced. At the turn of the century, C. S. Minot studied mortality rates with the use of statistical analysis. Seventy-five years earlier a mathematician named Gompertz (1779–1865) deduced several equations that were applicable to the study of mortality.

For years after 1900 very few people studied aging as a primary interest. There was no geriatric medical journal until 1945, and no international gerontologic conference until 1950. Geriatrics, a word coined by Nascher in 1914, is a recognized subspecialty only in Great Britain. Nascher proposed ten possible etiologies of aging, and Warthin mentioned 11. So little investigation was done of these theories that as late as 1963 a gerontologist philosopher wrote: "Our age is no closer to accounting for the ultimate cause of aging than was any past age. It may be that empiric science is not the appropriate medium for its discussion."[1]

Increasing interest in research on aging over the last ten years, along with the involvement of well trained and respected immunologists and cell biologists in gerontologic research, led to the formation of the National Institute on Aging within the National Institutes of Health in October 1974, with a fifteen million dollar budget. This allotment averages out to four cents per American as compared with five dollars per American spent on cancer and cardiovascular research.

WHY UNDERTAKE RESEARCH ON AGING?

In 1963, Kohn summarized actuarial data to show that, if cancer were cured, the human lifespan would be extended by as much as three years.[2] If cancer, cardiovascular disorders and all other disease could be cured, the lifespan would be extended by ten to fifteen years to a maximum average of ninety years. Hence the intrinsic process of aging is responsible for one's demise or provides the

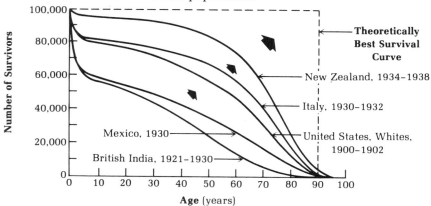

Figure 1

Survival curves for various populations.

Source: "Ageing: The Biology of Senescence," by Alex Comfort. Copyright ©
1956, 1964 by Alex Comfort. Adapted by permission of Holt, Rinehart and
Winston.

diathesis for the terminal event. In 1956,
Comfort showed through population studies
(Fig. 1) that the medical improvements made
in this century only allow more people to
live through their early and middle years; the
same percentage live to be ninety in the
Third World as in Western countries.[3] Theoretically, if all disease could be cured, the
best we could hope for would be a "squaring
of the box" shown in Figure 1; everybody
would drop dead at midnight of their ninetieth birthday. It is noteworthy that if this
were accomplished, the world's population
would increase by only 15 percent, implicat-
ing birth rates as the controlling factor. Acceptance of the finiteness of the human lifespan has only recently occurred in academia.
The previous noncompliance was largely due
to widespread acceptance of the early work
of Alexis Carrel (1873–1944) which demonstrated that chick embryo cell explants could
be kept alive indefinitely. Revelations that
the findings of the Nobel prize-winning
"father of tissue culture" were invalid because critical information was kept from him,
were released simultaneously with the papers of Leonard Hayflick showing that human diploid embryo fibroblasts had a finite
lifespan in tissue culture of 50 ± 10 pas-

sages.[4,5,6] Subsequent studies showed that
animal cells had tissue-culture lifespans that
were almost proportional to their in vitro
lifespans—chicks twenty-eight passages,
mice eighteen passages, Galapagos turtles
100 passages—and that cells from human
adult skin fibroblasts lived less than fifty passages in proportion to their age.[7]

In 1973 Cristafalo devised the "Cristafalo Index" which enables one to predict how
many more passages an early or middle passage cell will live.[8] The implications are both
exciting and frightening. Current studies are
aimed at determining whether the rate-limiting factor is metabolic time, passages, or
divisions.

In summary, man has a finite lifespan
and research on aging is performed to elucidate why and how this happens and what
interventions are possible.

LEVELS AND PARAMETERS OF AGING

Aging can be defined as a change in living
systems due to the passage of time. In order
to categorize better some of the parameters of
aging, we must consider the process as oc-

TABLE 1

Aging—some current theories and a list of parameters.

THEORIES OF AGING

(None of these concepts is mutually exclusive of the others, and many additional theories are possible.)

1. Genetic theory. A failure in DNA replication, transcription or translation may be responsible for aging, as may a malfunction in RNA or related enzymes. This could be pre-programmed or random.
2. The autoimmunity theory. Forbidden clones or a similar mechanism are capable of a minor attack on a variety of tissues, and this arises with greater frequency with aging.
3. Free radical theory. An increase in unstable free radicals produces deleterious changes in biologic systems, such as chromosome changes, accumulations of pigments, and alterations in macromolecules such as collagen.
4. A vertically transmitted ubiquitous tumor virus, slow virus, or ordinary virus may play a role in the aging process.

PARAMETERS

(These theories must fulfill certain criteria in order to be valid. A given theory must explain how changes in the following parameters occur.)

a. Anatomic criteria (e.g., shrinking nucleus, big nucleolus, fragmented Golgi bodies, vacuole accumulation).
b. Biochemical criteria (e.g., increased histone, lactate and lipofuscin; less ATP; de-repression of certain enzymes).
c. Physiologic criteria (e.g., loss of hair, hardening of blood vessels, more collagen cross-linking, loss of blood-making bone marrow).
d. Behavioral criteria (e.g., senility changes in sensory-motor capacities, mental function, drives and personality).

curring on several levels. Vertically, it can be viewed on a molecular level, then a cellular level, and finally on a tissue level; or horizontally, on an anatomic, biochemical, physiologic, and behavioral level (Table 1). For research purposes, the horizontal level is much more practical.

Anatomically, in the aging cell the nucleus shrinks, the Golgi bodies become fragmented, the nucleolus is large, and there is an accumulation of vacuoles. With each tissue type there are slight modifications. Let us take connective tissue as an example. With aging, collagen shows increased rigidity from cross-linking (which impedes metabolite transit); it becomes less soluble and shows increased thermocontractility. Elastin demonstrates increased degradation and accumulation of pigments with time. Mucopolysaccharides are predominantly hyaluronic acid in the fetus, but chondroitin sulfate in the adult.

Biochemically, with the passage of time, the cell shows increased lactate, histone and lipofuscin, decreased adenosine triphosphate and variations in certain enzyme systems. Cristafalo and others have worked out what happens to many of the metabolic pathways with time (Table 2).[9]

Physiologically, there is loss of hair, hardening of blood vessels, increased collagen cross-linking and less blood-making marrow with age. This can manifest itself clinically with graying of the hair, wrinkling of the skin, increased skin pigmentation and decreased muscle mass. Some organs increase in size with age (prostate), some decrease (brain). There is wide variance in the decrements detected by tests of function with time. Between the ages of thirty and ninety

TABLE 2

Examples of variation with cell age of a diploid cell's metabolic properties.

INCREASES WITH AGE	NO CHANGE	DECREASE WITH AGE
Glycogen content	Glycolysis	Pentose phosphate shunt
Lipid synthesis	Glutamic dehydrogenase	Glycolytic enzymes
Acid phosphatase band 3	Nucleohistone content	Nucleic acid synthesis
RNA turnover	Respiratory enzymes	Ribosomal RNA content
Membrane-associated ATPase activity	Permeability to glucose	Rate of histone acetylation

Adapted from Cristafalo

in a healthy male, nerve conduction velocity decreases by 10 percent, cardiac index by 30 percent, and maximal breathing capacity by 50 percent. Thus, it is difficult to assess one physiologic parameter and try to apply it to the whole body.

Behaviorally, there are changes in sensory motor capacities, in mental function and capacity, and in drives, personality and social roles.

There is a reduction in functioning of the sensory processes (decrease in vision, hearing of high-pitched sounds, balance, taste, smell) and in psychomotor performance (reaction time, speed and accuracy, complex performance). Sensory impairment of vision or hearing in old people may well lead to secondary desocialization. Thus, the old person may become paranoid merely because he has a defect in hearing, and a memory defect may lead to social rejection.

Also seen are decreases in intelligence, learning, memory, thinking, problem-solving and creativity. There is an increased tendency to dwell in the past, with diminished capacity for new and imaginative lines of thought, a lowering of the general interest level, loss of adaptability, and increasingly rigid adherence to routine. Emotional responses are cooled, e.g., the death of near relatives and loved ones is taken with much less show of feeling. There is increased possessiveness and preoccupation with money, and an increased interest in creature comforts such as food and warmth. Egocentricity is common. The self-concept tends to remain stable in later life. This is due to inward orientation of the personality, and the fact that former roles can still be used as part of the self-concept. Self-esteem is more volatile among older people; nevertheless, it is more stable than might be expected.

Mental capacity is based both upon ability to perceive new relationships (impaired in old age) and upon continued habits in a particular field, no longer requiring insight or perception for successful operation (not impaired in old age). There is a wide range of variation: some people are old in middle age, others young in old age.

New neurotic behavior is rare; it is almost always a sign of organic cerebral disease. In old age there is usually an exaggeration of previous personality traits.

Hunger can withstand increased deprivation; sex drives take the form of sexual fantasies or auto-erotic activities as a compensatory mechanism for decreasing function; and activity in general decreases. Attitudes become slightly more pessimistic as age increases and attitudes toward death become slightly more favorable. With advancing age there is an increasing continuity, consistency, and simplicity of the personality. Statements of poor health are often rationalizations of other issues.

Ten percent of our population is over age sixty-five, compared with 4 percent in 1900. The most important factor in maintaining mental skills into old age seems to be an environment which allows the mental faculties to be consistently exercised. It would seem that although older people undergo certain significant physical and psychologic changes with age, these changes usually are more of an inconvenience than a true handicap.

MODELS OF HUMAN AGING

If one states that "hypothesis X" is the cause of all aging, it must be shown that it etiologically accounts for all the aforementioned anatomic, biochemical, physiologic, and behavioral factors. Since in vitro models are not entirely satisfactory, we must search for practical human in vivo models. Because a longitudinal study of a population group from birth to death would outlive any investigator, other approaches must be viewed. (The NIH Gerontology Research Center in Baltimore is making longitudinal studies; results of their work so far are quite revealing.)[10]

In addition to tissue culturing, five in vivo models are being used to study aging. Progeria (Hutchinson-Gilford disease) is a rare and tragic disorder that turns infants into miniature ancients with gray hair, balding scalps, wrinkled skin, fragile bones and atherosclerosis. Most of the fifty patients described in this century died in their teens. When cells from a progeria patient are grown in tissue culture, they seldom live for longer than a few passages. For some reasons, these patients seem to lack an HL-A system.[11] Werner's syndrome is another rare disease in which there is accelerated aging characterized by autosomal recessive inheritance, short stature, hair loss, early graying, cataracts, diabetes, metastatic calcifications, osteoporosis, and atherosclerosis. Involvement is usually apparent during the teenage years, and death usually occurs around age forty. Juvenile-onset diabetes might also be considered a disease of accelerated end-organ aging. The cells of these patients live for shorter periods in tissue culture than those of controls[12] and very few patients with juvenile diabetes live to be older than fifty. The placenta is the most short-lived human organ, and the study of post-dated and even a full-term placenta reveals evidence of cellular aging with atherosclerosis, numerous thromboses, and histologic senescence. This is especially true in preeclampsia and eclampsia. (Parenthetically, because their work was performed on mice and not humans, Daniel et al. were able to transplant cells to different hosts and study their in vivo cellular lifespan.)[13]

The fifth model of aging involves the study of longevity in certain long-lived population groups. I prefer to call this a "pseudomodel" because population groups whose average lifespan exceeds ninety years do not exist. A group of Ecuadorian Indians living in the Andes simply have not been properly studied. The Hunza living in the Kashmir have no birth records or written language and so their claims cannot be documented. Most of the claims of extraordinary longevity have been pressed by the Soviets concerning the Abkhazians in the Caucasus mountains of Georgia. In 1974, Zhores Medvedev, a noted Soviet gerontologist now based in London, exposed the fallacy of most of their arguments.[14] He showed that the number of centenarians in Russia decreased from 29,000 in the 1926 census to 19,000 in the 1970 census despite a population increase of seventy million (and a decrease from nine thousand centenarians in Georgia to five thousand). In Christian areas of Russia, birth records were recorded in church registers, but 90 percent of the churches in Georgia were destroyed during the revolution. In Moslem areas, there was a tendency to use a ten-month year. Furthermore, passports were not issued with birth dates shown until 1932, and many persons had lied about their age to avoid the draft in World War I and during the revolution. It was socially more respectable to say that one was older than one actually was. Stalin was a Georgian, and Georgian longevity was good state propaganda. Indeed the Abkhazians do live in an environment where a greater proportion of the group live to be 90, but claims of extraordinary longevity cannot be substantiated.

THEORIES OF AGING

The four most viable theories for the etiology of aging are listed in the upper portion of Table 1. Theory I proposes that aging is genetically induced. It could be pre-programmed or could occur randomly. If pre-programmed, some force in the universe has determined exactly how long each organism is going to live and, through a redundancy of message repetitions in the cistrons, operons or genes, one's fate is played out.[15] This is in contrast to the "random" genetic theory, which has different levels of application. Orgel's error hypothesis implies a breakdown of the genome with age, which causes the production of error-containing proteins.[16] These proteins can: (a) be inert and deprive the cell of a necessary function; (b) be lethal and kill the cell; or (c) become antigenic. Random gene mutations can also produce errors.[17] Strehler et al. trace the key to an increased deficiency of a transfer RNA enzyme with age.[18] Hayflick's laboratory is now engaged in putting old cytoplasm into young nuclei and vice versa; results to date show that the nucleus has control over cellular aging.[19]

The autoimmune theory is unique in its insistence that reactions between cells rather than within cells cause aging. The body may "reject" itself through several mechanisms. New antigens may be stimulated by the production of defective proteins, or with age there may be a loss of immune tolerance, thus producing an increased response to antigens with age. Soon after birth, cells undergo immune diversification and shortly thereafter the thymus atrophies. A milieu of prolonged histo-incompatibility reactions may produce aging. Progeria can be explained as a runt disease in which maternal lymphoid cells cross the placenta, and juvenile diabetes as a disorder in which the islets of Langerhans bind insulin with an antihuman globulin, thus producing an altered insulin. Several objections have been raised to the autoimmune theory. First, most plants and invertebrates have either a primitive immune system or none at all, and yet they undergo senescence. Furthermore, most but not all humans acquire more autoantibodies with age, and in vitro work has not necessarily supported the autoimmune theory. Kay has modified the theory to state that the immune system is a rate-limiting but not controlling factor in aging.[20] She has postulated that an age-related decrease in T-cell (thymus-controlled) but not B-cell (bursal) immune surveillance allows the ingress of viruses whose enzymes modify host glycoproteins, rendering them immunogenic and permitting the replication of viruses incorporated into the genome of cells during infections early in life.

Harman is the chief proponent of the free radical theory.[21] He believes that free radicals, which are substances released by polyunsaturated fats, act with cell membranes and certain enzymes to produce oxidative reactions which disrupt the cell membranes, damage mitochondria and lysosomes, produce chromosome changes, cause accumulation of pigments, and alter collagen. Therefore, antioxidants such as vitamin E and the food additive butylated hydroxytoluene (BHT, found in most potato chips, among other foods) could theoretically slow the aging process.

The most recent theory emphasizes the role of the remarkable RNA tumor virus, which has a helical formation with a nucleocapsid and shell that is unique in its ability to be transmitted horizontally (person to person) and vertically (genetically from mother to progeny). It has been identified in at least twelve species ranging from snakes to mice, and probably in man. The viral genome may exist in every cell of every organism. It is capable of making fifty proteins, only fifteen of which have been described. Included among these are two group-specific antigens made in the nucleus. They form C-particles when they bud off, and also reverse transcriptase (the revolutionary enzyme which can cause RNA to make DNA). The proteins are expressed in the fetus and repressed at birth. Environmental stress, certain hormones, lymphocytic choriomeningitis virus and polyoma virus can de-repress the genome and cause the cell to make an oncogene-transforming protein (hence, cancer), or perhaps an aging-inducing protein. In my work with the Special Virus Cancer Research Group at the University of Southern California, some of these interactions were studied (Fig. 2).[22,23] When a C particle buds off the

Figure 2

The oncogene and "aging" gene hypothesis: a suggested mechanism for the RNA-tumor-virus-hypothesis.

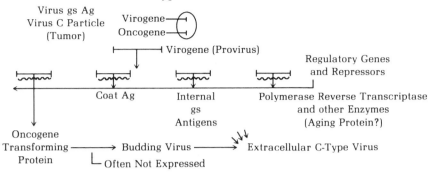

cell membrane, it could impart antigenic properties to other cells or alter the cell membranes. RNA tumor viruses have been implicated causally in oncogenesis, autoimmune disease such as systemic lupus, and slow virus disease such as amyotrophic lateral sclerosis.[24,25,26,27]

The relationship between cancer and aging should be mentioned. It is incorrectly but widely believed that there is a direct relationship between them as regards incidence. Certain tumors are found only in children and rarely in adults, and the incidence of cancer decreases yearly from ages five to fifteen. Although the incidence of cancer deaths rises proportionately from ages fifteen to eighty-five, after age eighty-five the percentage decreases in comparison with deaths due to other diseases.

Of the foregoing theories, all, none, or a combination of them may prove to be correct.

LIFESPAN-ALTERING FACTORS

A disproportionate amount of funding for research on aging seems to be directed toward determining how much the lifespan can be extended if certain altering factors are relied upon, as opposed to conducting basic research into the theories of aging. These altering factors include: 1) radiation, which can decrease the lifespan; 2) temperature,

e.g., in poikilotherms, cold can increase the lifespan, though homeothermic Eskimos show accelerated aging in some organ systems; 3) antioxidants such as vitamin E and BHT, which can help clean up free radicals; 4) the intervention of drugs, e.g., hydrocortisone can extend the life of human cells in tissue culture by several passages, and it is claimed (though not proved) that a Roumanian procaine preparation called Gerovital H3 can retard senility and aging; 5) a reduction of caloric intake in rats may increase their lifespan, but the specifics of the effect of dietary manipulation on longevity in humans remain to be determined; 6) hormones may influence longevity (e.g., eunuchs in China were believed to age more rapidly than uncastrated males) and various hormonal interventions are being studied; 7) exercise in moderation is helpful in prolonging the lifespan; 8) too much stress is harmful; 9) a germ-free environment, if feasible, is salutary; and 10) manipulation of the calcium factor may prolong the lifespan, if it is confirmed that alterations in calcium metabolism give rise to such disorders as osteoporosis, cataracts, and skin wrinkling.

PHILOSOPHIC FACTORS

Gerontologists must be introspective about their work and able to answer some basic questions about why they carry on research in aging. The German embryologist Weismann stated in 1891 that men and women are purposeless after their reproductive periods have passed and that death is simply an acquired secondary adaptation to this process. Both Comfort and Strehler challenge this concept because they believe that there is no inherent property of cells which precludes perpetual self-replenishing and function.[28] If we increase the world's population 15 percent by "squaring the box" shown in Figure 1, and thus enable everybody to live to age ninety, would we be adding thirty years of senility to the lifespan? Would we prevent this by concentrating on the development of a "soma" as described in Huxley's *Brave New World*? As cures for cancer and other diseases are discovered, increasing emphasis will be placed upon understanding the intrinsic aging process. If the cause of aging and its cure are ultimately elucidated, should anything be done about it? It seems evident that, with appropriate guidelines, research on aging can be conducted with maximal benefits for humanity.

NOTES

1. R. L. Grant, "Concepts in Aging: an Historical Review," *Perspectives on Biological Medicine* 6 (1963): 430.

2. R. R. Kohn, "Human Disease and Aging," *Journal of Chronic Diseases* 16 (1963): 5.

3. A. Comfort, *The Biology of Senescence* (New York: Holt, Rinehart and Winston, 1956).

4. L. Hayflick and P. S. Moorehead, "The Serial Cultivation of Human Diploid Cell Strains," *Experimental Cell Research* 25 (1961): 585.

5. L. Hayflick, "Limited in vitro Lifetime of Human Diploid Cell Strains," *Experimental Cell Research* 37 (1965): 614.

6. L. Hayflick, "Aging Under Glass," *Experimental Gerontology* 5 (1971): 291.

7. L. Hayflick. "The Longevity of Cultured Human Cells," *Journal of the American Geriatrics Society* 22 (1974): 1.

8. B. B. Sharf and V. J. Cristafalo, "Cellular Senescence and DNA Synthesis," *Experimental Cell Research* 76 (1973): 419.

9. V. J. Cristafalo, "Animal Cell Culture as a Model System for the Study of Aging," in *Advances in Gerontological Research*, edited by B. L. Strehler (New York: Academic Press, 1972), vol. 4, pp. 45–79.

10. A. H. Norris, R. Andres, and N. W. Shock, "Comparison of Longitudinal and Cross Sectional Estimates of Changes in Physiological Function," *Proceedings of the Eighth International Congress on Gerontology*, (Bethesda, Md.: Federation of American Societies for Experimental Biology, 1969), vol. 2, p. 18.

11. D. P. Singal and S. Goldstein, "Absence of Detectable HL-A Antigen in Cultured Fibroblasts in Progeria," *Journal of Clinical Investigations* 52 (1973): 2259.

12. S. Goldstein, J. W. Littlefield, and J. S. Soeldner, "Diabetes Mellitus and Aging: Diminished Plating Efficiency of Cultured Human Fibroblasts," *Proceedings of the National Academy of Sciences* 64 (1969): 155.

13. C. W. Daniel et al., "The in vivo Lifespan of Normal and Preneoplastic Mouse Mammary Glands: a Serial Transplantation Study," *Proceedings of the National Academy of Sciences* 61 (1968): 53.

14. Z. Medvedev, "Caucasus and Altay Longevity: a Biological or Social Problem?" *Gerontologist* 14 (1974): 381.

15. R. Holliday, "Growth and Death of Diploid and Transformed Human Fibroblasts," *Federation Proceedings* 34 (1975): 51.

16. L. E. Orgel, "The Maintenance of Accuracy of Protein Synthesis and its Relevance to Aging," *Proceedings of the National Academy of Sciences* 67 (1970): 1476.

17. Z. Medvedev, "Repetition of Molecular-Genetic Information as a Possible Factor in Evolutionary Changes of the Lifespan," *Experimental Gerontology* 7 (1972): 227.

18. B. L. Strehler and M. D. Bick, "Leucyl Transfer RNA Synthetase Changes During Soybean Cotyledon Senescence," *Proceedings of the National Academy of Sciences* 64 (1971): 224.

19. W. E. Wright and L. Hayflick, "Nuclear Control of Cellular Aging Demonstrated by Hybridization of Anucleate and Whole Cultured Normal Human Fibroblasts," *Experimental Cell Research* 96 (1975): 113.

20. M. M. B. Kay, "Autoimmune Disease: the Consequence of Deficient T-cell Function?" *Journal of the American Geriatrics Society* 24 (1976): 253.

21. D. Harman, "Prolongation of Life: Role of Free Radical Reactions in Aging," *Journal of the American Geriatrics Society* 17 (1969): 721.

22. D. J. Wallace, "Aging and RNA Tumor Viruses," *Clinical Research* 22 (1974): 198A.

23. D. J. Wallace, "Aging Yesterday and Today," *Gerontologist* 14 (1974): 110.

24. G. J. Todaro and R. J. Huebner, "The Viral Oncogene Hypothesis," *Proceedings of the National Academy of Sciences* 69 (1972): 1009.

25. H. J. Temin, "The RNA Tumor Viruses," *Proceedings of the National Academy of Sciences* 69 (1972): 1016.

26. P. E. Phillips, "The Virus Hypothesis in Systemic Lupus Erythematosis," *Annals of Internal Medicine* 83 (1975): 709.

27. M. B. Gardner et al., "A Spontaneous Lower Motor Neuron Disease Apparently Caused by Indigenous Type C RNA Virus in Wild Mice," *Journal of the National Cancer Institute* 51 (1973): 1223.

28. B. L. Strehler, *Time, Cells, and Aging* (New York: Academic Press, 1962), pp. 219–21.

REFERENCES

ANDREW, W. *The Anatomy of Aging in Man and Animals.* New York: Grune and Stratton, 1971.

ATCHLEY, R. C. *The Social Forces in Later Life.* Belmont, Calif.: Wadsworth, 1972.

BROCKLEHURST, J. C. *Textbook of Geriatric Medicine and Gerontology.* London: Churchill-Livingstone, 1973.

GOLDSTEIN, S. "The Biology of Aging." *New England Journal of Medicine* 285 (1971): 1120.

MEDVEDEV, Z. "Aging and Longevity." *Gerontologist* 15 (1975): 196.

TIMIRAS, P. S. *Developmental Physiology and Aging.* New York: Macmillan Company, 1972.

WALFORD, R. L. *The Immunological Theory of Aging.* Baltimore: Williams and Wilkins, 1969.

Implications of Aging Research for Society

Bernard L. Strehler

The success, until now, of the human species in controlling the resources of this planet for its own benefit is based on two features unique to man. The first of these is a brain capable of assimilating experience in memory, organizing such experience into abstract categories, making predictions based on regularities in nature, inventing structures (machines and societies) that have modified nature in man's interest, and finally the communication of subjective experience between members of the species symbolically through written and spoken languages. The second uniquely human feature is a sufficiently long lifespan to make the above-mentioned qualities of the human brain useful. We are the longest lived of the highly evolved animals.

These two evolved properties go hand in hand, for there would be little evolutionary value to a brain capable of storing decades of experience and manipulating this data logically if there were insufficient longevity to use this mental ability; conversely, a relatively puny body unprotected by the brain's predictive and inventive powers would not survive even to reproductive maturity. Long-lived tortoises can hide within their armor; longevous birds (usually predators) can fly above their natural enemies, and ancient bristlecone pines tower over competing species for nourishment, resist insects

with toxic oils, and outlive fires with thick, slow-burning bark. But man dominates through wit and inventiveness.

Not the least of man's inventions is the system of arriving at understanding of general rules of nature, science, whose application has made possible industrial societies and tentative probings of outer space and the inner mind. In view of the revolutionary events of the first three quarters of this century, it would not be surprising to witness, during the last quarter, the conquest of the two most perplexing puzzles: 1) the nature of the neural processes that give rise to the sense of self; and 2) the molecular-cellular bases of the slow decline that returns dust to dust. Unless the aging process differs in some mysterious and totally unforeseen way from other puzzles man has solved in the past, it is essentially inevitable that he will, before long, understand aging's sources, and with that understanding will come a considerable measure of control. The effects on the individual and society of that control will be even more pervasive than the revolutions that followed the invention of modern democracy, the steam and internal combustion engines, means to generate and distribute electricity, the transistor, nuclear reactors, digital computers, and the understanding of DNA—most of which were fathered in our country.

From *Federation Proceedings* 34 (1975) pp. 5–8. Reprinted by permission.

EFFECT DOMAINS OF GERONTOGENY

Societies are often not ready for scientific windfalls. What predictions, possibilities, and problems will societies encounter when the age-old puzzle yields? Some are easily foreseen; others can only be fantasized.

Gerontogeny is defined here as the development of means to achieve an enhanced healthy longevity. Its effects in various domains of life will depend on the degree of such life extension, which cannot be predicted on a sound basis until more is understood of the basic process itself.

The duration of life depends on the interaction of two variables; the effects of environment, and the intrinsic changes that occur during aging within a living system. Essentially all of the increase in life duration that has occurred during the twentieth century is due to an improved environment, particularly in the public health and pharmaceutical domains. Figure 1 shows the general trend in survivorship curves that has occurred in the last one hundred years. It can generally be described as an asymptotic approach to the so-called "rectangular" survival curve. Assuming uniform genetic qualities a species will approach a rectangular survivorship curve as its environment improves. In the extreme case, for a genetically homogeneous population living in a homogeneous environment, all individuals would die at precisely the same maximum age, like a myriad of "wonderful one-horse shays."

In heterogeneous populations, such as the human species, different maximum longevities are to be expected even in ideal environments, because different genetic en-

Figure 1

Human survivorship trends from ancient times to the present. These idealized curves illustrate the rapid approach to the limiting rectangular curve that has occurred during the last 150 years. The inset on the upper right lists major factors responsible for these transitions. Note that life expectancy for males has not changed since 1950 in the 50+ age group but that female survivorship has improved during this period, partially, at least, because of better treatment of reproductive system malignancies.

Transition	Major Factors in Transition
A → B	Improved Housing, Sanitation, Antiseptics
B → C	Public Health, Hygiene, Immunization
C → D	Antibiotics, Improved Medical Practice, Nutrition, Health Education
D → E	Recent Biomedical
D → F	Breakthroughs

A–D Male or Female Survivorship
E Male Survivorship
F Female Survivorship

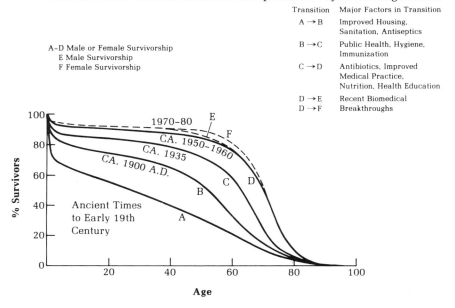

Figure 2

Composite origins of present rectangular survivorship curve in the United States. Genetic predispositions to specific causes of death express themselves during different epochs of the total lifespan; the expression of these qualities appears to derive in considerable part from a general deterioration in a variety of structures and functions that has as its common denominator poorly understood "basic" aging processes. Among these the most important is a general decline in the rate at which reparative-homeostatic processes can proceed maximally. One common denominator may be the gradual loss of DNA recently reported by Johnson et al. in post-mitotic cells.

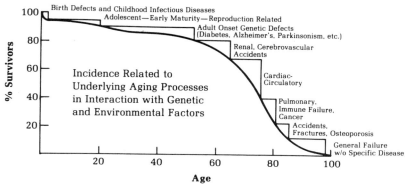

dowments will lead to death from different inherent defects at different times. Figure 2 shows the compound rectangular survivorship that presently exists. The light lines represent different genetically limited rectangular curves, the heavy line the average curve produced by such heterogeneity. Figure 3 depicts the shape of survivorship curves if genetic defects could be compensated for through "heroic" measures such as the hoped for conquest of cardiovascular disease, cancer, and the like. It also shows what would occur if the intrinsic rate of aging were retarded to 90 percent, 75 percent, and 50 percent of its present rate, the first two probably within reach in our lifetimes. In the remainder of this presentation the middle figure, a 25 percent reduction in the rate of aging, will be used as a basis for the anticipation of effects of aging research on society within the lifetimes of those now approaching adulthood.

Domain 1: Physical Health

There is no way to increase longevity in an hospitable environment except by improving the health state at all post-mature ages. Increased longevity, due to a retardation of the aging processes, will thus inevitably improve the health status of all age groups after age twenty-one. (In the absence of aging the longevity of newly mature twenty-one-year-olds would exceed 2,000 years.)

Professional pessimists can take little comfort from their predictions of a society populated by ancient, wrinkled, toothless, decrepit, incontinent, mindless, Dorian Gray-like bodies, for such will not exist. It will take about as long to go through a terminal illness at age one hundred fifty as it does at sixty-five today. The real effect will be to increase the total number of years an individual spends in a healthful, and hopefully productive, state.

Figure 3

Past, present, and potential human survivorship curves. (*A*) Ancient times to early 19th century. (*B*) Present survivorship curve. (*C*) Range of curves to be expected if the "major killers" were conquered (circulatory and neoplastic diseases). The basic reason that such conquest, the major direction of present biomedical research investment, would produce such a relatively minor change in survivorship derives from the fact that deaths due to "accidents," a measure of general homeostatic capacity, cause the same rate of death at about age 84 as do *all causes of death*, including the major killers, at age 68–72. Thus, a 15-year increment in longevity is the maximum to be expected from such research unless a retardation of aging is included in the therapeutic measures developed. (*D*) Survivorship that would derive from an 8–12 percent decrement in rate of aging, possibly derivable from pharmaceutical, dietary, and immunological manipulations. (*E*) Hypothetical survivorship produced by a 20–30 percent decrease in rate of aging, potentially attainable through a 2–4 C decrease in body temperature. (*F*) Longer range hypothetical survivorship potentially derivable from a combination of factors in curves *D* and *E* plus means for reinstituting repressed gene functions and/or reinsertion of deleted portions of the genome. The basic conclusion to be derived from this graph is that an adequate investment in basic studies of the aging processes' origins, coupled with appropriate therapeutic measures should produce benefits in terms of added healthful and productive years far in excess of those to be expected from the major lines of biomedical research investment that exist today.

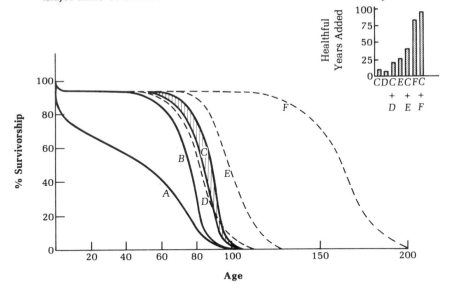

Domain 2: Mental Health

Because we are the species most blessed (or cursed?) with the ability to predict the future, we are incapable of ignoring, in our innermost selves, the fact of our own impermanence. As a rule this awareness is suppressed or consciously ignored, like most unpleasant realities. But the ultimate reality is no less real than the April 15th income tax form. Although no one seems to have made a study of the effect of the individual's impermanence on this earth as a contributing factor to mental anguish and disease, one suspects that it is at least as important as many childhood hurts, insufficient self-esteem, marital incompatibility, impotence, frustrations in career fulfillments, and so on, as a lingering source of mental disquietude and illness. It is accordingly more than likely that the postponement of aging's infirmities will decrease the incidence of mental disease and postpone the occurrence of age-related mental illness, e.g., depression.

Domain 3: Social Effects

Biologists are not professionally schooled in such nebulous subjects as the intricacies of social forces. At best we are speculative spectators who are as confused by the premises, methods, and predictions of social scientists as they themselves sometimes seem to be. Nevertheless, there are some rather obvious societal consequences of greatly increased lifespans. These range from poly-generational families to a decrease in intergenerational conflicts. It can be argued that much of the social upheaval of the last decade in the United States resulted from a disproportionate number of persons in the young adult category. Even today there is evidence of a changing emphasis as the post-war baby boom dies away. Enrollments in primary schools are decreasing; there is a surplus of teachers; in the next decade the population implosion will reach academia, with uncertain results. The extension of the average lifespan to one hundred or one hundred twenty-five will make five-generation families a commonplace. Moreover, these concurrent generations will have much more in common than do the three-generation families that now exist. The average chronological age will be about sixty, though the average physical state will be about thirty-five to forty.

The greatest benefit of such a social restructuring will be a greater sense of coherence and continuity in society, for the great preponderance of individuals will be in the productive, post-mature years, and the understandable conflicts that arise between the providers and the receivers in society should fade materially into the background. A potential danger that cannot be ignored is that the innovativeness of youth will be smothered by more established age groupings. It would be more than unfortunate if the blessing of increased healthful longevity were to be mixed with social inflexibility. On the other side of the ledger is the fact that a longer exposure to life permits a broader perspective among the more experienced—usually referred to as the "wisdom" that accompanies age.

Related to the above is the problem of tenure in positions of power. It would be disastrous to vest power to fashion social practice and policy in the limited hands and minds of those who acquired it at chronological age forty-five—a fact all too well understood by younger faculty and reaching the proportions of ironic comedy if a Stalin, a Mao, or even some domestic statesmen were to hold political power for ten decades!!!

Domain 4: Economic Effects and Poly-Careers

The most extreme changes in society that will result from substantial life extension are in the economic area. The existing patterns and trends toward early retirement versus productive employment will doubtless require rethinking. In today's industrial-technological societies, an individual contributes about half of his lifetime to the production of goods and services. For professionals about twenty-five years of dependence (childhood, education, and so on) are spent before the "loan" begins to be repaid to the community. Assuming retirement at sixty to sixty-five and ten years of life beyond that, just about thirty-five years are spent in "production." It is improbable that retirement at sixty-five followed by forty to one hundred forty years of retirement-community living will be tolerated either by the "work force" or those who have retired with the energy implicit in a mind and body equivalent to today's thirty-five- to forty-year-old. This means, in effect, that retirement will be postponed until well after eighty to one hundred years of age, a grim prospect for those whose joys and creativity are at the level of the Archie Bunker prototype.

An obvious solution, which may well ensue, is the expansion of leisure time at all ages, accompanied by multiple and successive careers. Today's biological limitations make it difficult for all except the gifted, daring, or foolish to give up the security of an established career to develop a new career interest. But if one had four successive twenty-five-year periods in which to develop different skills and expertise, no such limitation would need to exist. Compulsory retirement might well be from one career to another.

Certain professions, particularly medicine, would benefit from extended periods of practices beyond what is now possible. For an excellent physician, extended experience is almost as important as excellent training, for one has to see many different kinds of illness in order to recognize subtle symptoms, and this kind of expertise can only be acquired over an appreciable period of time. In no professional area does an extended lifespan offer such a beneficial side effect as in medicine. The wisdom that accompanies age would, in this case at least, be highly useful to us all. Another benefit would derive from the actual costs per year of life of medical care. If, as described earlier, the effect of extending lifespan is to add to the "healthy middle years," and terminal illnesses cost about what they do now, the average expenditure per person/year of life will be correspondingly less than it presently is—a positive economic fallout.

The greatest problem posed by an extended lifespan is how to supply the economic needs of persons, assuming retirement at some age. If one, as a rule of thumb, accepts 70 percent of the income level in the pre-retirement years as adequate for the post-retirement years (fewer expenses), it is clear that an individual must accumulate a retirement investment from which he could derive the above at the then existent interest rates, after inflation. Thus, a retirement income of $20,000 per annum would require an investment of about $400,000 at a return of 5 percent, over and above inflationary erosion, and this assumes also that there would be no use of the accumulated capital during the retirement years. This would require about $5,000 per annum to be accumulated (investment plus interest) over an average forty-year working lifetime or alternatively, with interest, about $1,500 per annum for a seventy-year working lifespan.

Obviously, the more one accumulates per year, the earlier one can retire at the above-mentioned $20,000. Or, alternatively, if one chooses to work for a more extended period the decrement in usable resources during the working period would be correspondingly less. At any rate, while the above calculations are based on today's rate of return from investment and ignore the justifiable subsidies from the public treasury that social security benefit increases represent, as well as their magnitude in the future, it is more than obvious that both the business (particularly insurance) sector and the public bodies that are parts of the equation should begin now, if not yesterday, to make projections for the future. To base investment, governmental or private, on today's lifespan is to ignore rather clear handwriting on the palace wall, and the dislocations of a retirement income crisis could make the 1974 energy crisis look like an afternoon tea.

One of the factors that should reduce the economic load implicit in the above is the fact that most persons thrive on some kind of creative activity, whether it is called "work" or not. This is why new avenues to successive careers should be prepared for by individuals and society. In the absence of ready means to develop new outlets and interests, the result will be ennui for all except the very few. Who would want to be chairman of a study section, the department, the board or even the Supreme Soviet for one hundred years?

While undoubtedly the preceding discussion can at best be only an improbable approximation to what life will be like thirty-five to one hundred years from now, the greatest enemy in this writer's opinion will not be insecurity, poor mental or physical health, or even anonymity. It will be ennui, boredom, and the destructiveness that follow in their wake.

TO REACH THE GOLDEN ERA

Why are all these biological and human possibilities not being pursued with the vigor and inventiveness their potential promises? The answer is perhaps a kind of societal senescence. Could those who control policy and funding for the necessary fundamental research needed to bring the reality within reach of those of us now alive themselves be ensnared in time's net? Is the parochial promotion of professional status and career the moon behind which a sun of understanding lies? Are the available funds so necessary for the pursuit of today's ephemeral problems that we stand blindfolded before a lovely unfolding landscape?

As my late friend, Leo Szilard, who was as captured by this possibility as he previously was by the potential for nuclear fission, observed: "There are times when I would like to shout 'Help!' but all that comes out is 'Ha'!" Hungarians are like that!

REFERENCES

Because so little substantive work has gone into the anticipation of this problem, the relevant bibliography is minimal. It includes:

COMFORT, A. *The Biology of Senescence.* Boston, Mass: Routledge & Kegan Paul, 1964.

PALMORE, E., ed. *Prediction of Life Span.* Lexington, Mass: Heath, Lexington, 1971.

ROSENFELD, A. *The Second Genesis.* Englewood Cliffs, N.J.: Prentice-Hall, 1969.

STREHLER, B. *Time, Cells, and Aging.* New York: Academic Press, 1962.

STREHLER, B. "Myth and Fact." *Center Magazine* III (1970): 4.

WHEELER, H. "The Rise of the Elders." *Saturday Review.* Dec. 5, 1970.

Health Experience in the Elderly

E. Harvey Estes, Jr.

When is a person healthy? When is he ill? These questions are difficult ones at all ages, but for the older person the answers are especially obscure. Many an older person has low back pain, stiff joints, or diminished hearing yet considers himself in the best of health. Experience has taught him that these

From E. Busse and E. Pfeiffer, eds., Behavior and Adaptation in Later Life (Boston: Little, Brown and Company). Reprinted by permission.

are common symptoms, that there is little to be done for them in a curative sense, and that life can be pleasant in spite of them, once the anxiety about their potential significance has been put aside.

No attempt will be made here to cover all the illnesses of the elderly. But certain broad areas important to the health care of the elderly, as well as some of the diseases that have an increased incidence in this age group, are discussed.

ILLNESS PATTERNS IN THE ELDERLY

Acute Illnesses

One characteristic of older persons is that they are apparently less often affected by acute illness than are younger people (Table 1). When such illness occurs, however, it usually leads to more days of restricted activity than does illness in younger persons (Table 2). Older women spend about five more days per year in restricted activity due to acute illness than do their male counterparts (thirteen and eight days respectively, at age sixty-five and older). The data in Tables 1 and 2 were obtained by household interviews conducted by the National Center for Health Statistics on a probability sample of the civilian population of the United States. *Restricted activity* was defined in this study as a substantial reduction in activity normal for that day and covered restrictions up to and including complete inactivity.

Why there should be a decreased incidence of acute illness in the elderly is not clear. A greater degree of immunity to common respiratory pathogens, a diminished level of awareness of symptoms, and a diminished concern, leading to less acknowledgment of illness are all possibilities.

As in all other age groups, the group of illnesses consisting of upper respiratory infections, influenza, and other respiratory ailments accounts for the majority of the episodes of acute illness and for most of the days of disability in the elderly. Injuries are the second most common cause of illness and days of disability. Contusions are the most frequent type of injury, followed by fractures, sprains, and dislocations. Digestive disorders are the third most frequent type of acute illness in the elderly. These three categories alone account for four-fifths of the acute illness problems of the elderly (fifty-eight, fourteen, and seven percent respectively).[1]

Thus the majority of the acute illnesses seen in the elderly are relatively simple in terms of the techniques and professional skills required for diagnosis and treatment. They do not differ substantially from acute illness in other age groups in this respect. However, the superimposition of these illnesses on patients with underlying senility and chronic disease leads to greater disability as measured by days of restricted activity.

Chronic Illnesses

The exact incidence of chronic disease in the elderly is not known due to the inadequacy of methods of obtaining information. The two general types of survey techniques used are (1) a clinical examination of a sample population and (2) a questionnaire given to a sample population. Diseases requiring medical tests or observations (such as hypertension and diabetes mellitus) appear more

TABLE 1

Number of acute illnesses per 100 persons per year, by age.

AGE	NUMBER OF ILLNESSES
Under 5	372
5–14	290
15–24	239
25–44	204
45–64	144
65+	109

Source: *Acute Conditions: Incidence and Associated Disability, United States, July 1971–June 1972.* National Center for Health Statistics, Series 10, No. 88, January 1974. Table 11, p. 22.

TABLE 2

Days of restricted activity associated with acute illnesses per 100 persons per year, by age.

AGE	DAYS OF RESTRICTED ACTIVITY
Under 5	1,151
5–14	896
15–24	833
25–44	883
45–64	928
65+	1,092

Source: *Acute Conditions: Incidence and Associated Disability, United States, July 1971–June 1972.* National Center for Health Statistics, Series 10, No. 88, January 1974. Table 12, p. 23.

frequent when a clinical examination is used, whereas those diseases that are largely self-diagnosed (such as chronic sinusitis) appear more frequent when a questionnaire technique is used.[2]

On the basis of data from an examination-type survey, the chronic illness seen most frequently in the elderly is heart disease.[3] Over half of persons over age sixty-five (575 per 1,000) suffer from this disorder, with hypertensive heart disease and coronary artery disease leading the list of specific types. Arthritis is seen only slightly less often, and again over half the persons examined were affected (515 per 1,000). Osteoarthritis was the specific type seen in over ninety percent of these cases. The incidence of other frequently diagnosed chronic disorders per 1,000 is as follows: obesity, 380; abdominal cavity hernias, 212; cataracts, 148; varicose veins, 148; hemorrhoids, 142; hypertension without heart disease, 142; and prostate disease, 135 per 1,000 males.

The incidence of all chronic disease, including relatively mild and non-disabling diseases, rises steadily with advancing years. Under age fifteen there are four hundred chronic diseases per one thousand population, and at age sixty-five there are four thousand per one thousand population, a tenfold rise in incidence.[4] Thus there are multiple chronic illnesses in many older members of the population.

With respect to the disability caused by these chronic diseases, this is, as expected, more severe in the elderly. In the survey being discussed, about thirty percent of those over age sixty-five considered themselves to be limited in one or more daily activities (moving about, feeding themselves, climbing stairs) as a result of chronic disease.[5] The limitation was usually at the level of inconvenience or discomfort, with a much smaller number requiring assistance from others. Less than one percent of persons surveyed were limited in their ability to feed, dress, and bathe themselves or perform toilet functions, but when limitation was present, help was usually required. Locomotion could usually be carried out with help, though with difficulty. Two-thirds of those reporting lim-

itation of ability to move about were still able to function without aid. Three-fifths of those reporting limitation of ability to climb stairs were able to function alone. Of particular importance is the fact that travel on public conveyances was an exception to this trend. Three-fourths of those who reported limitations in this function required help to travel or were unable to travel at all. This fact has obvious implications in planning for delivery of proper medical care to an elderly population.

MORTALITY AND ITS CAUSES IN THE ELDERLY

The average length of life in the United States in 1969 was seventy years, a figure that has remained essentially the same for fifteen years.[6] On the average, the female outlives the male by seven years (seventy-four versus sixty-seven years). This average expectation of life at birth is strongly influenced by infant and childhood mortality and therefore gives little information about the expectation of life at a given age.

At age sixty, the average remaining years of life are 18.1; at age sixty-five, 14.8 years; and at age seventy, 11.8 years. The same trends exist as in the preceding paragraph. For example, at age sixty the average remaining lifetime for white males is 16.0 years, for white females 20.5 years, for non-white males 14.9 years, and for nonwhite females 18.5 years.

The twenty most important causes of death in the elderly are listed in Table 3. Arteriosclerotic heart disease is the most important cause of death in all age ranges, with cerebral and subarachnoid hemorrhage as the second in rank order. Hypertensive heart disease is the third most common cause of death from sixty-five to eighty-four, and though it remains an important cause of death beyond eighty-five years, it is outranked by generalized arteriosclerosis and cerebral thrombosis and embolism.

While most of the twenty listed causes of death show an increasing death rate with progressively older age ranges, neoplasm of

TABLE 3

Age-specific death rates per 100,000 population per year, by cause, 1959–1961.

CAUSE	ALL AGES	65–74	75–84	85+
Neoplasm, stomach	12	67	123	156
Neoplasm, colon	16	87	167	220
Neoplasm, lung	22	123	105	74
Neoplasm, breast[a]	14	55	82	135
Neoplasm, prostate[a]	7	45	116	171
Diabetes mellitus	16	96	167	174
Subarachnoid and cerebral hemorrhage	60	261	749	1,686
Cerebral embolism and thrombosis	32	152	517	1,341
Other CNS vascular diseases	8	34	137	449
Arteriosclerotic heart disease	278	1,433	1,306	6,878
Endocarditis and myocardial degeneration	29	118	438	1,465
Other heart disease	11	47	116	277
Hypertensive heart disease	35	179	446	933
Other hypertensive diseases	7	26	81	221
General arteriosclerosis	18	56	300	1,394
Chronic and unspecific nephritis	6	21	45	101
Influenza and pneumonia	32	102	316	999
Emphysema	5	33	43	46
Senility, ill defined	7	22	49	183
Accidents, falls	11	33	137	513

[a] Incidence per 100,000 males and females. Incidence per 100,000 of the particular sex at risk would be approximately double the reported rate.

Source: Modified from E. A. Duffy, and R. E. Carroll. *United States Metropolitan Mortality 1959–1961.* P.H.S. Publication No. 999-AP-39. Cincinnati: National Center for Air Pollution Control, 1967.

the lung is a notable exception. The death rate from this cause declines with older age ranges. The death rate from emphysema is also noteworthy in that it is relatively constant with progressively older age ranges.

SOME DISEASES AFFECTING THE ELDERLY

Arteriosclerotic Heart Disease

There is some evidence that mortality from arteriosclerotic heart disease increased for several decades, reached a peak in the 1960s, and has begun to decline. This raises many questions regarding the influence of external factors on both the incidence of, and

the response to, coronary atherosclerosis. There is also a notable variation in mortality in various areas of the United States. The states in the northeast have one and one-half times the incidence seen in the central plains states. These facts serve only to remind us that this disease, though a well-defined entity, still has many unknown facets.

The underlying pathological lesion is coronary artery obstruction, which begins as an intimal lipid deposition early in life and is progressive in nature. The process is spotty in location and affects certain areas preferentially (first portion of the anterior descending branch of the left coronary artery; first part of the right coronary artery; the right coronary artery as it bends at the acute margin). Superimposed on this chronic, progressive process are other related processes that may cause a sudden increase in the degree of obstruction. Subintimal hemorrhage into the hypervascular base of a lipid deposit may cause a thrombosis within the narrowed lumen. Thrombosis may also occur without subintimal hemorrhage.

Potential collateral channels exist at all ages, but channels interconnecting coronary arteries become more frequent and of larger size with advancing years. The interplay between advancing obstructive disease, increasing collateral channels, and the anatomical location of the obstructive disease is an important determinant of acute myocardial infarction. About one-third of cases of acute infarction terminate fatally before medical attention is obtained; in another 20 to 30 percent of cases the patient dies within the period of acute hospitalization, the highest risk being within the first twenty-four hours. These deaths are of several types. Most are due to acute arrhythmia, and the rest are due to congestive failure or cardiogenic shock. The advent of coronary care areas within community hospitals is a significant development, since continuous monitoring of cardiac rhythm and a staff especially trained for emergency treatment of arrhythmic events have produced a significant reduction in the mortality from arrhythmia. However, the mortality from cardiogenic shock and congestive failure remains essentially unchanged.

Presbycardia. The existence of a specific disease of the heart related to aging and involutional changes in the heart muscle and independent of the presence of coronary artery disease has been proposed by William Dock.[7] This high incidence of coronary artery lesions in the elderly makes it difficult to judge the independent effect of involutional changes in heart muscle, but rare cases are seen in which no other apparent cause of congestive heart failure can be found.

Complete Heart Block. At one time, the occurrence of complete heart block, particularly in an older person, was considered an-

other manifestation of coronary artery disease. More recent observations have shown that the appearance of stable atrioventricular block in older patients is usually a result of an idiopathic fibrotic change in the upper interventricular septum, extending downward and interrupting the common bundle. Heart block due to coronary artery disease is seen but is usually accompanied by a clear clinical event, such as a myocardial infarction. Thus stable atrioventricular block may represent a form of heart disease related to aging, in that it is caused by an extension of a fibrotic process that is normally present in the upper septum but slowly increases with time, occasionally extending into the conduction system.

Cerebral Thrombosis and Hemorrhage

Table 3 shows the rising incidence of both cerebral thrombosis and hemorrhage with increases in age. Ischemic infarction of the brain and intracerebral hemorrhage are listed as separate entities, in spite of the frequent difficulty in antemortem clinical differentiation between the two. It is also noteworthy that both entities are strongly related to the presence of arterial hypertension.

Ischemic infarction is usually ascribed to progressive vascular narrowing, leading to slowed vascular flow and thrombosis. Intracerebral hemorrhage is a result of arterial rupture, but the events leading to the rupture remain obscure. R. W. R. Russell has suggested that hemorrhage may be caused by a rupture of small microaneurysms that he has found to be present in certain sites in the brain in close correlation with advancing age and arterial hypertension.[8] Such lesions are seen in greatest numbers in older patients with hypertension, and the sites of occurrence are similar to the sites of cerebral hemorrhage. Russell suggests that such lesions are a direct result of damage associated with age and hypertension.

Thrombosis is often seen in the sac of such aneurysms. Hoobler has suggested that the evolution of these aneurysms could produce small nonhemorrhagic strokes related to thrombosis.[9] He thus explains the reduced incidence of both ischemic infarction and intracerebral hemorrhage seen with antihypertensive therapy.

Osteoporosis

Osteoporosis, characterized by a thinning of the cortex of long bones and thinning of the vertebral bodies due to decreased formation of bone matrix, is not usually listed among the most common ailments of the elderly in response to trauma. It has many causes, including immobilization, decrease in estrogen production (postmenopausal osteoporosis), and steroid administration. A specific form related to senility is recognized. Its etiology remains obscure, but diminished androgen production probably plays an important role.

Except for back pain, the condition is usually asymptomatic and is usually an incidental finding or is discovered as a result of a fracture. It is more severe in the spine and pelvis than elsewhere and may lead to vertebral collapse. Normal levels of serum calcium, phosphorus, and alkaline phosphatase usually distinguish it from other bone disorders. However, differentiation from multiple myeloma presents special problems, since alkaline phosphatase levels may not be elevated in multiple myeloma, and the radiological picture may be indistinguishable. For this reason, bone marrow aspiration should be performed in cases of unusual osteoporosis, especially when accompanied by anemia or proteinurea.

CONSTRAINTS TO PROPER HEALTH CARE IN THE ELDERLY

As discussed in previous sections of this chapter, the elderly patient suffers from relatively few illnesses that are unique to his age group. The special problem of the elderly is that a given illness is usually superimposed on an assortment of pre-existing chronic illnesses and on organ systems that have lost their wide margin of reserve capacity. The elderly patient thus represents a delicately balanced mechanism in which even a "minor" illness can lead to major consequences.

This fragile state of affairs poses problems for both elderly patients and their physicians. The patient has multiple problems, and treatment for one may produce adverse effects on the other. Aspirin prescribed for arthritic pains may cause a flare of a peptic ulcer, or a diuretic prescribed for mild congestive failure may cause a painful exacerbation of gout. "Usual" doses of medications may also cause unusual effects. A sedative dose of a barbiturate may cause mental confusion, for example. The physician (and his patient) may be unprepared to accept the chronic nature of the medical problems, resulting in discouragement, frustration, and even anger.

In treating elderly patients, many physicians wisely follow a general policy of extreme caution in prescribing drugs, changing activity routines, or removing the patient from familiar surroundings. Patience and understanding on the part of physician, family, and patient is highly rewarding.

Manpower and Facilities

The elderly patient faces many problems in seeking assistance for health and illness problems. First, a physician may not be available. Second, the patient usually has several medical problems (e.g., hypertension, prostatic hypertrophy, and glaucoma), and each of these problems may require the services of a different specialist. Third, he has difficulty in obtaining guidance in matters of general hygiene and the application of techniques to prevent illness (e.g., dietary measures, exercise), as well as in obtaining advice for minor day-to-day illnesses, due to the lack of primary care physicians, or the crowding of the physician's schedule, or both.

Many recent publications have noted a growing shortage of physicians.[10,11] In addition, most (approximately two-thirds) of today's physicians are specialists, and they are therefore less available to the patient as a personal physician than the generalists whom they have replaced.

Maldistribution of physician manpower is also a growing problem and is particularly likely to affect the elderly. The younger physician usually settles in a practice location that is most likely to provide good hospitals, capable colleagues, and good living conditions for his family. These conditions are most often found in areas of economic growth and higher per capita income.[12] The older, declining areas of large cities and the smaller towns and rural areas are the areas that have failed to attract new physicians. These are the same areas in which older persons are found in greater proportion.

Such areas are often dependent on elderly physicians. For example, in North Carolina's rural counties, 40 percent of the physicians are over age sixty, and 20 percent are over age seventy.[13] It should be recognized that an ill-defined but very important service of a personal physician is that of providing an interface with, and an input pathway into, the increasingly complex system of medical care. Even though an elderly physician may be unable to provide the special skills required for certain illnesses, he can nevertheless provide the access to these skills. The loss of a physician of many years because of illness, retirement, or death often forces the older patient to seek entry into the health care system with no guidance, and he often has to consult a new, much younger physician who may not transmit the same sense of security as the older man.

Medical facilities are also becoming more complex as they are arranged and equipped to deliver more complex medical treatment. While this is a laudable development, it also creates problems. The physician is much more dependent on the services of these facilities—in clinics, hospitals, and the like—than in the past and has largely abandoned the practice of seeing the patient in the home. The advantage of the available laboratory and radiographic facilities in hospitals and clinics for proper diagnosis and treatment is obvious. However, as noted earlier, the older patient is often limited in his ability to drive and to utilize public transportation, and a high percentage of the elderly require assistance to travel. Even when transportation is arranged, the complexity of the hospital or clinic may deter the older patient from utilizing its services unless compelled to do so.

Another major problem is the lack of a specific cadre of physicians who understand and are able to deal with the health and medical problems of the elderly as a specialty. There are very few training programs in geriatrics and few role models among existing physicians. These physicians are badly needed as medical directors of nursing homes and other facilities responsible for the care of those who are no longer capable of independent living.

Economic Factors

Most older persons face the unknowns of the future (an unknown span of life, an unknown degree of economic inflation, unknown expenses) with a fixed amount of savings or income. Medical care is costly and is becoming more so month by month. It is therefore not difficult to understand why many older persons, with a fixed reserve to cover an unknown period of years, delay or avoid altogether seeking medical care for economic reasons. Medicare has provided a partial answer to the problem, but by uncovering personnel shortages and inadequate facilities, it has undoubtedly forced all medical care costs even higher.

A wider scattering of family members in modern society has heightened the economic threat of illness. Family members who were once available to care for an ill mother or father may now live in distant cities. For many, hospitalization or professional nursing care is now the only alternative—and that one requires considerable financial outlay.

Attitudinal Factors

Most older persons today, perhaps to a greater extent than later generations, have grown up with a conception of themselves as strong, productive, and independent, relying on no one. Hard work and "something for a rainy day" are important components of their value system. Many wish to retain enough of their material goods to pass along an inheritance to their heirs. The acceptance of illness, with its dependency on others, is extremely difficult, and denial of illness is common, particularly in men.

Fear of discovery of a fatal or progressive illness is another common factor leading to delay or avoidance of medical care. A questionable symptom or sign is ignored until pain or other symptoms force a medical consultation, or until concern by other family members leads to the same result. While the consequences of such denial are difficult to quantitate in terms of greater mortality, greater disability, and greater overall cost, these are presumed to result.

SUMMARY

The acute illnesses of the elderly are not unique in type but result in more prolonged disability and probably constitute an increased threat to life because of restricted organ system reserve. Chronic disease is relatively common but usually results in mild limitation in function. Some few illnesses seem directly attributable to aging and its effects. The problems that have led to poor delivery of health care to the population at large have a more profound effect on the elderly.

NOTES

1. U.S. Bureau of the Census, *Statistical Abstract of the United States, 1967.* 88th edition (Washington, D.C.: U.S. Government Printing Office, 1967) Table III, p. 84.

2. B. S. Sanders, "Have Morbidity Surveys Been Oversold?" in *Chronic Disease and Public Health,* edited by A. M. Lilienfeld and A. J. Gifford (Baltimore: Johns Hopkins University Press, 1966).

3. Commission on Chronic Illness, *Chronic Illness in a Large City,* vol. IV (Cambridge, Mass.: Harvard University Press), p. 539.

4. *Chronic Illness in a Large City,* p. 51.

5. *Chronic Illness in a Large City,* p. 64.

6. U.S. Department of Health, Education, and Welfare, *Vital Statistics of the United States, 1969,* vol. II, sec. 5. National Center for Health Services. (Washington, D.C.: U.S. Government Printing Office, 1974).

7. W. Dock, "Presbycardia or Aging of the Myocardium," *New York State Journal of Medicine* 45 (1945): 983.

8. R. W. R. Russell, "Pathogenesis of Primary Intracerebral Hemorrhage," in *Cerebral Vascular Diseases, Sixth Conference,* edited by J. F. Toole (New York: Grune & Stratton, 1968).

9. S. W. Hoobler, "Cooperative Study on Stroke and Hypertension," in Toole, *Cerebral Vascular Diseases.*

10. R. Fein, *The Doctor Shortage: an Economic Diagnosis* (Washington, D.C.: Brookings Institute, 1967).

11. J. V. Warren, "The Problem of Providing Health Services," *Annals of Internal Medicine* 69 (1968): 951.

12. E. H. Estes, Jr., "The Critical Shortage—Physicians and Supporting Personnel," *Annals of Internal Medicine* 69 (1968): 957.

13. Research and Evaluation Division, *General Information for Regional Study Committees* (North Carolina Medical Program, 1968).

The Relationship of Recent Life Events to Health in the Elderly

Thomas F. Garrity
Martin B. Marx

INTRODUCTION

From time to time one hears or reads of deaths which occur in people who have recently experienced some traumatic life event. George Engel collected the accounts of 170 such deaths.[1] They tell of people who died soon after the deaths of loved ones as, for example, the sixty-one-year-old woman who collapsed immediately upon receiving news of her sister's sudden death and died shortly thereafter of cardiac arrest. There was the eighty-eight-year-old man without known heart disease who, upon learning of the sudden death of his daughter, developed acute pulmonary congestion and died as his physician reached his house. About 50 percent of the deaths reported by Engel followed the death of an important friend or relative, or the threatened loss of such a person. One account tells of a forty-year-old father who "slumped dead as he cushioned the head of his son lying injured in the street beside his motorcycle," and another of the sixty-seven-year-old woman who died "while waiting to hear news of friends in a disastrous nursing home fire." Most of the accounts related by Engel involved deaths preceded by important life events, such as the loss of a good reputation, a job, or an expected benefit. Several accounts also described deaths following positive life events, such as the sixty-year-old prisoner who "collapsed and died when

he returned home to his family after serving a fifteen-year sentence," and the fifty-five-year-old man and his eighty-eight-year-old father who both died upon meeting after a twenty-year separation.

These are dramatic illustrations of the possible links between human cognition and apparent physiological response. They serve to illustrate a particular theory which is to be examined in this chapter and ultimately applied to the situation of the aged. The theory, simply stated, holds that life events which require some degree of adaptation, some departure from the stability of everyday life, tend to bring about negative changes in health.

THE LIFE CHANGE-HEALTH CHANGE PARADIGM

The life change-health change hypothesis has roots in the biological works of Walter B. Cannon in the 1920s[2] and those of Hans Selye in the 1930s.[3] Both of these scientists developed perspectives that became useful in explaining the apparent links between man's cognitions, especially those relating to threatening stimuli, and physiological responses. Cannon's "fight-flight" concept described man's innate capacity to mobilize stored physical energy very quickly in the presence of some external threat.[4,5] For example, when confronted suddenly by an attacking angry dog, one experiences instantaneous increases of heart rate and blood

Original paper prepared by the authors for this volume.

98   From the Inside Out: Physiological and Health Related Events pressure along with myriad other metabolic changes which support increased energy expenditures capable of facilitating counterattack (fight) or escape (flight) from the animal. In this case man's cognitive faculty in the brain is capable of surveying and appraising the environment for its threat potential and communicating appropriate neural and hormonal signals to the various bodily organs which support needed physical responses.

Hans Selye described the processes mobilized by the body to deal with a broad spectrum of physical and symbolic challenges to the organism. He described a "general adaptation syndrome" of physical responses identifiable in man and lower animals which come into play when physical insults to the organism occur. These include secretion of hormones from the adrenal cortex, some of which promote and some of which retard inflammatory processes useful in limiting damage resultant from the insult. This adrenal response has organism-wide impact and is ordinarily beneficial in helping the organism cope with and adjust to external stressors. The general adaptation response is also evoked by symbolic stressors such as threat of injury or loss of one's good reputation; in such instances adrenal cortical activity is also activated. Unfortunately, such normal, healthy adaptive responses can themselves cause illness when activation is prolonged, intensified or otherwise deranged.

While Cannon and Selye suggested the interplay between mind and body in stressful situations, others worked hard to specify more exactly the nature of this relationship. Franz Alexander, a psychoanalyst and researcher, was one of these early contributors. He hypothesized that specific personality profiles and pyschic conflict situations brought on specific illnesses. For example, Alexander proposed that the personality predisposed to development of peptic ulcer was one with strong dependency needs rooted in early life experience, but which was involved in a life style very demanding of self-assertion, independence, and initiative-taking.[6] In Alexander's model, the conflict led to chronic emotional distress and hypersecretion of hydrochloric acid in the stomach.

The early tendency in psychosomatic medicine to attempt to link emotions and personality configurations with specific illnesses[7] has given way to the belief that psychophysiological disturbance results from an almost limitless variety of stressful stimuli which can cause a large array of illness outcomes.[8] Psychophysiological arousal is thought to increase the susceptibility of the organism to illness and injury from infectious, chronic, degenerative, and emotional diseases. Hence, stress is thought to be capable of lowering resistance to disease producing microorganisms, of setting into motion physical processes capable in the long run of damaging structure and function of bodily organs and of causing failures in coping with life challenges.

It was out of this perspective of psychosomatic medicine that the life change-health change theory grew. In 1949, Thomas H. Holmes and his associates began to develop a method for measuring the amount and strength of recent life change experienced in individuals and for studying the effect of such change on health.[9] It is Holmes' conviction that life changes, both desirable and undesirable, cause a break in the stability and equilibrium of life.[10] Thus, the adaptation process may place the individual under a psychophysiological strain which, in turn, is thought to increase the likelihood of a negative change in health.

The diagram in Figure 1 presents a simple schematic of the model being discussed. The relationship between recent life events and negative health changes is mediated by psychophysiological strain. Simply stated, life changes stress the person, causing the organism to struggle emotionally and physically to cope with the change; this struggle results in health breakdown. The diagram suggests two other elements for consideration in this model. It is not unusual for some people with many recent life changes to remain healthy. At least part of the explanation

Figure 1

Schematic representation of the life change–health change paradigm.

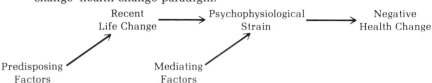

Recent Life Change → Psychophysiological Strain → Negative Health Change

Predisposing Factors

Mediating Factors

for this resistance may be found in personal and environmental factors which increase the individual's coping resources. For example, a person with strong bonds of love and respect with one or a few friends may use them as a source of emotional and informational support for dealing with challenging life disruptions. Such resources, if effectively used, might prevent the person from experiencing psychophysiological strain and, consequently, onset of illness. In a similar way, certain personality strengths could act to lessen the strain resultant from life change. Hence, a complete representation of the life events-health change model must include mediating factors capable of reducing the impact of events on health. Conversely, certain environmental and personal factors may potentiate the life change-health change relationship.

Figure 1 also suggests the existence of factors which influence the occurrence of life change events themselves. Clearly, some of the changes which life brings are largely out of man's control—a home destroyed in an earthquake or flood, the death of a friend, the closing of a place of employment, for example. Nonetheless, many life changes are controllable, such as the taking of a new job, marrying, and moving to a new residence. It is possible that certain personal and environmental factors promote "change-seeking" behavior. Casual observation of friends and associates reveals that some seem most content in relatively quiet and unchanging lifestyles while others seek excitement, change, and a frenetic pace of life. Hence, no complete picture of the life events-health change model can exclude mention of factors that predispose to life change experience.

State of the Art

By 1967, Thomas H. Holmes and his colleague, Richard H. Rahe, had developed an instrument useful in measuring recent life change experience.[11] Their Social Readjustment Rating Scale (Table 1) included forty-three commonly reported life change events. Using a large panel of judges, the authors were able to determine and assign values or weights to each item in proportion to the "relative degree of necessary readjustment" required by each event. The ratings by judges ranged from one hundred for the readjustment required after the death of spouse to eleven for minor violations of the law. This approach to the measurement of life change has been criticized for not covering a sufficient range and variety of life change events, for assigning readjustment weights which only weakly approximate. the individual responses of most research subjects, for including desirable as well as undesirable life changes, and for other reasons.[12] Nevertheless, several studies of the rating scale have demonstrated that in various cultures around the world and with people of differing social and personal characteristics, the rankings of various life changes were quite consistent.[13,14,15] Furthermore, the Social Readjustment Rating Scale has proven a reliable predictor of illness outcomes.

An extensive program of studies undertaken by Rahe and his colleagues has shown that the extent of life events experienced by young naval personnel in the six months prior to a six-month cruise is predictive of their illness rate during sea duty.[16] These findings inspire some confidence because of the use of a rigorous prospective

TABLE 1

The Social Readjustment Rating Scale of Holmes and Rahe.*

RANK	LIFE EVENT	MEAN VALUE
1	Death of spouse	100
2	Divorce	73
3	Marital separation	65
4	Jail term	63
5	Death of close family member	63
6	Personal injury or illness	53
7	Marriage	50
8	Fired at work	47
9	Marital reconciliation	45
10	Retirement	45
11	Change in health of family member	44
12	Pregnancy	40
13	Sex difficulties	39
14	Gain of new family member	39
15	Business readjustment	39
16	Change in financial state	38
17	Death of close friend	37
18	Change to different line of work	36
19	Change in number of arguments with spouse	35
20	Mortgage over $10,000	31
21	Foreclosure of mortgage or loan	30
22	Change in responsibilities at work	29
23	Son or daughter leaving home	29
24	Trouble with in-laws	29
25	Outstanding personal achievement	28
26	Wife begin or stop work	26
27	Begin or end school	26
28	Change in living conditions	25
29	Revision of personal habits	24
30	Trouble with boss	23
31	Change in work hours or conditions	20
32	Change in residence	20
33	Change in schools	20
34	Change in recreation	19
35	Change in church activities	19
36	Change in social activities	18
37	Mortgage or loan less than $10,000	17
38	Change in sleeping habits	16
39	Change in number of family get-togethers	15
40	Change in eating habits	15
41	Vacation	13
42	Christmas	12
43	Minor violations of the law	11

* Table 3, p. 216 in T. H. Holmes, and R. H. Rahe, "The Social Readjustment Rating Scale." *Journal of Psychosomatic Research* 11 (1967). Reprinted by permission.

study design which eliminates biases possible in the less demanding retrospective design used in most earlier studies. Also, the use of a captive and confined shipboard population minimizes the effects of externally introduced sources of illness. Furthermore, the findings of Rahe in this American sample have been largely replicated in studies of Norwegian sailors.[17]

The relationship between recent life events and illness has been documented in a range of study populations and for a range of illness outcomes. In relatively young populations, illness outcomes have generally included minor illness, such as, upper respiratory infections and accidental injuries.[18,19] However, the review of Rabkin and Streuning summarizes that "modest but statistically significant relationships have been found between mounting life change and the occurrence or onset of sudden cardiac death, myocardial infarctions, accidents, athletic injuries, tuberculosis, and the entire gamut of minor medical complaints."[20] They also point out that psychiatric symptoms and disorders have been significantly predicted by life change scores.

While it is not the purpose of this presentation to comprehensively review the findings or the criticisms of this theoretical model, it should be understood that the theory is not without its critics. In addition to the criticisms of the Social Readjustment Rating Scale mentioned already, some have argued that the "statistically significant" correlations found in most of this research are clinically trivial. Some have wondered if even these associations are misleading and explainable without reference to the life events-health change theory. For example, it seems possible that the relationship could be due to the tendency of some individuals to report many problems, be they of health or life in general. Such a propensity would build in a significant life change-health change correlation, but would not support the psychosomatic links between the two.[21] It is also possible that the life change-health change relationship results from a correlation between the high life events score and the high utilization of health service regardless of actual health status. In this case, the apparent life change-health change relationship would really be indicative of a relationship between life change and care seeking behavior rather than actual illness. In spite of this sort of conjecture, the weight of evidence continues to suggest a real link between life change and health. But further research on a number of aspects of the model is needed.

Most of the research to date has used relatively young adult and middle-aged study groups to demonstrate the relationship between life events and illness outcomes. Studies of children, adolescents, and the aged have been rare. Do the correlations found in young adult groups between life events and illness persist for these different age groups? Likewise, few of the studies of this theoretical framework have examined the role of predisposing and mediating factors in the model pictured in Figure 1. We also still need to learn if there are more productive approaches to measuring recent life events than the Social Readjustment Rating Scale. For example, would it be better to permit each research subject to supply his own life change weights to each item of change he has experienced than to impose the weights derived from the 1967 anonymous judgments of the Holmes and Rahe subjects? Are there some dimensions of life change which are more pathogenic than others? For example, are uncontrollable life changes more damaging than controllable ones? Finally, with rare exception,[22] there is almost no research yet on possible interventions for reducing illness likelihood after life change has occurred.

RECENT LIFE EXPERIENCES AND THE ELDERLY

Given the large amount of research already done on the life change-health change model, it is interesting that application of this paradigm to the elderly is so rare. Published studies of the model have focused primarily on young populations such as college students[23] and naval shipboard subjects. In these young study groups, the negative health outcomes have generally included rather minor, non-life-threatening kinds of illness. Such studies have raised questions about the generalizability of these results to older populations and people experiencing more serious illness.[24] Several studies of hospitalized patients have begun to answer this objection, at least in middle aged subjects.[25,26] These studies include a greater age mixture of subjects with the average age in the forties and fifties instead of the twenties as was the case in the college student and naval studies. The results indicate that in these middle-aged subjects with illness sufficiently serious to warrant hospitalization, life changes mounted in the year prior to hospitalization. These studies and others have included subjects over sixty years of age in proportion to their presence in the populations being studied and the results have generally supported the life change-health change hypothesis.[27,28] (The recent prospective study of Goldberg and Comstock fails to find the expected relationship between life change and illness in the samples representative of two communities.)[29]

In the remainder of this chapter, we review a number of studies which suggest the validity of the life change-health change hypothesis in the elderly and the desirability of applying this model to research with the elderly. One of the only direct applications of the Holmes and Rahe method of summated recent life change to the elderly was reported in 1974 by Wilson and Maddox using data from the Duke longitudinal study of aging.[30] With 180 white, middle-class men and women, ranging upon entry into this prospective study from forty-five to seventy-one years of age, it was found that recent life events predicted psychological symptoms tapping disturbed mood and life dissatisfaction. The life events measure, however, failed to predict psychophysiological disturbance such as bodily symptoms usually associated with psychological distress. The failure of this study to replicate the findings of other investigators[31,32] of links between life change and psychophysiological symptoms may indicate the non-applicability of the model to the elderly or, as the authors suggest, the results may be an artifact of the concentration in this study of higher social class subjects who are less likely to express distress through somatic complaints. On balance, this study offers modest evidence that, in the elderly, recent life change leads to certain types of psychological disturbance.

While the Wilson and Maddox study is the only application known to us of the Holmes and Rahe method in an elderly population, there are a number of studies of single traumatic life changes and their health impact on the aged. The health impact of retirement, of change of residence, and of death of a close relative (usually spouse) are the three categories of life change we shall discuss. Studies in these three areas are reviewed with the hope of better understanding their implications for the life change-health change hypothesis.

Retirement As Life Change

Retirement, in the popular conception, has widely been viewed as a negative life change which often heralds the end of the worker's "productive" life and the beginning of a period of enforced idleness. Stories of retirees who are unhappy with this life change, who have "time on their hands," and who make life miserable for those around them are often heard. Furthermore, it has been conjectured that such a state of maladaptation may somehow be an instrumental antecedent of illness and premature death.

One methodological barrier to the empirical study of the retirement-health (and mortality) issue is the fact that retirment itself may frequently be precipitated by failing health. Hence, if the data showed that the early post-retirement period has a greater than expected incidence of illness and death, at least two explanations could be postulated: first, the life change caused psychophysiological distress which leads to negative changes in health, or second, there are more sick people within the pool of recent retirees because the retirement was brought about by

an illness and, therefore, one would expect higher rates of disease and death among recently retired persons as compared to persons of similar age who continue to work. Adequate studies would need to take into account a number of possible alternative explanations.

Although retirement is only a single change item on the Holmes and Rahe list of forty-three life events, it implies other changes also on the list. Retirement, for example, implies "change in financial state," "change in living conditions," "revision of personal habits," "change in work hours and conditions," "change in recreation," "change in social activities," and "change in sleeping habits." Other changes mentioned on the Holmes and Rahe list might also occur as a result of the retirement, including "change in the number of arguments with spouse," if for no other reason than the increased hours of mutual exposure every day. Also, some "change in residence" often occurs shortly after retirement. The literature on the health effects of retirement, therefore, is a logical place to search for evidence bearing on the life change-health change hypothesis in populations of the elderly.

A 1969 study of retirement and health by Ryser and Sheldon dealt with five hundred retirees of both sexes, ranging from sixty to seventy years of age and generally representative of the population of retirees in Massachusetts.[33] The authors studied such objective health measures as hospital admissions, visits to physicians and presence of common psychophysiological symptoms. Subjective health measures included perceptions of, and satisfaction with, present health status and perception of physical limitations and changes. Over all, the authors found no evidence of mounting or increased health problems since retirement. In fact, a substantial number of respondents subjectively perceived their health as improved since retirement. Eighty percent reported that the amount of contact with physicians had remained essentially the same since retirement as compared to the pre-retirement period. Only 10 percent were seeing the doctor more often. Also confirmed was the well documented relationship between health and socioeconomic status, namely, the well educated, upper income subjects were most likely to experience better health.

There is impressive support for the findings of the above study elsewhere in the literature. Ryser and Sheldon pointed to several studies which support the contention that health does not fail markedly after retirement, and in a substantial proportion of retirees actually improves.[34] They noted that Heyman and Jeffers in a study of 180 aging respondents found far more subjects reporting improved health after retirement than declining health.[35]

Palmore's 1971 review statement agrees with the results described above.[36] He pointed to the work of Myers, who found that the elevated mortality rates of recently retired workers was accounted for by the voluntary retirement of those who were ill.[37] Myers also found that the mortality rise did not occur among those forced to retire at a given age. Tyhurst similarly found no rise in mortality following retirement from a Canadian communications company.[38] Palmore cited several research projects which indicate that general health status is largely unaffected (possibly even benefited) by retirement.[39,40]

In summary, Atchely states of the stereotype that retirement leads to sickness and death in older people that, "This is definitely untrue. There is absolutely no evidence that retirement has *any* deleterious effects on health. If anything, people show a tendency toward *improved* health upon retirement."[41]

Hence, the research literature on the health effects of retirement gives us no support for the life change-health change hypothesis. To say that retirement may often represent a "desirable" life change to the individual in no way explains away these non-supportive findings since the paradigm specifically includes positive life events. Indeed, such negative results may be one of the reasons that social gerontologists have not adopted the life change-health change paradigm in their research.

Residential Relocation As Life Change

Change of residence is a second major area of life change frequently experienced which suggests itself as a source of evidence bearing on the life change-health change model. As with young and middle-aged adults, older adults move for many reasons. However, while the young make residential moves to accommodate changing jobs, increasing family size or living space needs, for investment purposes and to reflect improving socioeconomic status, the elderly move because of lessened need for space or the lessened physical and financial ability to manage large quarters. While the young may define residential change as symbolic of improved status, the meaning of moves for the elderly are often decidedly negative. For the elderly, a move may signify loss of independence and ability to control one's own affairs as when the move is into an institution of some sort or even into the home of a relative. The move may be the result of deteriorating financial or physical status or the decline of once comfortable housing to slum conditions. Even when residential relocation is to objectively better environmental conditions, the break in continuity may cause it to be defined as something negative.

In a series of studies begun in 1961, Lieberman has identified a phenomenon which appears to have bearing on the life change-health change paradigm.[42] In this early study, the records of 860 applicants to the Orthodox Jewish Home for the Aged of Chicago were examined. The death rate of those on the waiting list before actual admission was 10.4 percent, or less than half the mortality rate of people during the first year after admission which was 24.7 percent. Lieberman's analysis excluded age and initial health status differences between those on the waiting list and those admitted as the cause of the difference. While it is possible that the staff of the Home made subtle distinctions to admit sicker people sooner than the robust, this explanation has no documentation in Lieberman's data. The author suggests that the rigors of early adjustment in the Home may be the explanation for these interesting findings. Certainly the latter interpretation coincides with the life change-health change hypothesis.

In a study of one hundred mentally and physically well elderly awaiting admission or newly admitted to one of three sectarian homes for the aged and a comparable control group of elderly not anticipating entrance into a home for the aged, Tobin and Lieberman again found physical (including mortality) and behavioral effects among those experiencing new institutionalization.[43] Of the eighty-five people who finally entered a home, forty-one (48 percent) showed a marked physical or behavioral decline, including thirteen deaths. The control group, on the other hand, experienced marked deterioration in but six of the thirty-five controls, or 18 percent of its members (number of deaths not given). The authors learned that the first two months in the new setting were, for almost all subjects, the most difficult ones, fraught with feelings of vulnerability, decreased hope, increased preoccupation with the body, increased helplessness, and more involvement in hostile interactions with others. They also found that the elderly who took active coping stances in these trials of adaptation were least likely to decline; the passive did poorly by comparison.

A discussion of three other studies of Lieberman and his colleagues pointed to similar declines in physical and behavioral well-being in the early adjustment of relocated elderly individuals.[44] In these studies, between 48 and 56 percent of the aged subjects experienced marked decline. In the first of these studies, forty-five physically and psychologically well elderly were forced to relocate from a small hotel-like institution to a larger "quasi-military" institution for the aged. Twenty-three of these individuals experienced marked decline, including four deaths. The second relocation study examined a group of patients from a geriatric mental hospital who were moved into a variety of community based institutional and semi-institutional settings. Of the eighty-two aged transferees, forty showed marked decline, including two deaths. Finally, in a study of the mass transfer of elderly mental hospital patients to a variety of other institutions, 237 of the 427 patients suffered marked decline, including seventy-eight deaths. While Tobin and Lieberman explicitly noted the probability that such decline and mortality rates were due to the trauma caused by the discontinuity in individuals' lives, they suggested that other explanations may also be operative, such as the damaging nature of certain aspects of institutional life.[45] They also proposed three strategies which might be useful in preventing or lessening the deleterious impact of relocation: careful selection of candidates for relocation based on knowledge of the characteristics of those who do not tend to thrive after relocations of different sorts; preparation programs designed to ease the transition by helping transferees establish expectations and coping behaviors; and environmental construction which minimizes the need for radical and rapid adjustments by newcomers.[46]

Stimulated in part by the findings of Lieberman, Aldrich and Mendkoff examined the mortality experience of 180 patients transferred because of the closing of the Chicago Home for Incurables.[47] All subjects had been in residence for at least one year before transfer. The majority of transfers were to nursing homes, though a few moved into hospitals, homes of relatives and independent living situations. The new situations were of either "substantially the same or better quality" care and accommodation as compared to the Home. The actual one year post-transfer mortality experience was 32 percent. The anticipated mortality rate, based on the experience of comparable patients in the Home during the previous ten years, was only 19 percent, a statistically significant difference. Further analysis revealed that the major difference in mortality rates occurred in the first three months after the transfer during which time the post-transfer mortality rate "was more than three times as high as the expected death rate." During the last nine months of the first post-transfer year, the observed and expected mortality rates were about equal. These data agree with Tobin and Lieberman's observation that adjustment distress is greatest after early relocation.

Blenkner and co-workers randomly assigned 164 non-institutionalized older persons who were "likely to come to the attention of welfare and health agencies" to a study group which received intensive social work attention and a comparison group which continued with no special social work attention beyond what would have ordinarily existed.[48] Among other findings, it was noted that those receiving the intensive care of social workers were more frequently institutionalized during the study period than the comparison group, despite the increased availability of supportive "outpatient" services for the study group members. It was also learned that the mortality rate of the study group (25 percent) was somewhat higher than that of the comparison group (18 percent). About half of the deaths in the study group occurred within the first three months of the acceptance for service.[49] The researchers speculate that even the imposition of needed and helpful services causes significant changes in life patterns which may be lethal.

Lieberman's reviews cited additional studies supportive of the hypothesis that relocation of the elderly raises risk of mortality,[50,51] but he also draws attention to several studies which show declines in physical and emotional health status without any increase in death rate. Lawton and Yaffe, for example, found greater decline in physical health in a relocated group than in a comparison group,[52] while Miller and Lieberman found physical problems (hospitalization, restricted activity) and psychological disturbance (confusion, memory defects) in a large proportion of the recently relocated.[53]

Lieberman[54] identified several studies which did not find the major rises in mortality rate or declines in physical and psychological status associated with relocation.[55,56]

He feels that this pattern of positive and negative findings may indicate the need for a clearer understanding of the factors which mediate the health effects of relocation. Certain characteristics of the individual such as personality traits,[57,58] coping style,[59] cognitive function,[60,61] socioeconomic status, age, sex, health, and the like may modify vulnerability to negative outcomes. Likewise, certain conditions, such as the degree of preparation for the change[62,63,64] or voluntary versus involuntary relocation may affect the likelihood of negative health outcomes.[65] Lieberman's thinking here is similar to the line of thought expressed earlier in relation to the complete life change-health change model, namely, we need to learn more about intervening factors which heighten or reduce the influence of life change on health.

In summary, residential change for elderly people, especially when it entails movement into some sort of care-taking institution or from one institution to another, appears to involve some increased risk of premature death or non-fatal decline in physical health and psychological well-being. The data are not unanimous in support of this proposition, but they are sufficiently numerous and powerful to warrant at least tentative support for such a theory.

Death of a Loved One As Life Change

Of all individual life change experiences, the one most likely to cause negative health outcomes is death of a loved relative or friend. The ability of this event to distort health and the heavy demand it places on people of all ages to adjust is reflected in the wealth of literature, especially psychiatric and medical, describing the effects of bereavement.

There is evidence that the struggle to readjust after the death of a loved one entails an increased mortality risk. The study of Rees and Lutkins provides one example of "the mortality of bereavement."[66] The town of Llanidloes and its vicinity in Wales is served by a single group practice comprised of 5184 patients. During the period of study, about 370 people died whose close relatives were available for study. A study group of bereaved close relatives was established along with a control group of comparable people who had not recently experienced a death in the family. The bereaved group experienced a mortality rate of 4.76 percent during the first year after the death, while the control group experienced a rate of only 0.68 percent, a seven-fold difference. In the following year the difference narrowed greatly, the bereaved group having a 1.99 percent mortality and the control group having a 1.25 percent mortality experience. Incidentally, male survivors fared worse than female survivors, with rates of 6.4 percent and 3.5 percent respectively. The mortality impact appeared greatest on widowed persons in the bereaved group; they had a 12.2 percent death rate.

Hinton supports the notion of increased risk of death during bereavement.[67] He argues that in addition to the deleterious physical effects of emotional strain, self-neglect and suicide contribute to "the mortality of bereavement." He cites several studies which demonstrate elevated mortality rates among the bereaved. Young and his co-workers in England found that elderly (above 55 years of age) widowers ran a 40 percent higher risk of dying in the first six months after the death of the spouse than married men of similar ages.[68] While the elevated death rate may be due to several factors, including self-neglect, common infection contracted with the deceased, or common lifestyle with the deceased, the authors favor the view that emotional distress causes organic damage or physiological dysfunction leading to death. Cox and Ford, stimulated by these results, used British actuarial data to examine the mortality experience of widows (of all ages below seventy), and found an unexpected rise in mortality in the second and third years after the death of the spouse.[69] The authors caution that this apparent discrepancy in lag time between death of spouse and death of survivor in the two studies may

be accounted for by the way the actuarial data of the second study were gathered and compiled. Kraus and Lilienfeld, in a study based on mortality data for married, single, divorced and widowed men and women of ages twenty through seventy-four garnered from the National Office of Vital Statistics in 1956, found a striking elevation in mortality in young (under thirty-five) widowed men and women in comparison to their married counterparts.[70] This heightened risk diminishes with age in all demographic categories according to the data. Such studies using census information and actuarial data are useful but not nearly as sensitive to important variations such as length of time since death as the Wales study of Rees and Lutkins.

What is being suggested here is that the adaptation struggle after such a traumatic life change as death of a loved one may exact a heavy toll—quite possibly, death. While death is the most dramatic physical outcome of this life event, it is not the only one. Other minor and serious physical problems have long been recognized as aspects of the grief process. Lindemann early described a variety of physical symptoms of grief, including tightness in the throat, shortness of breath, loss of appetite, and muscular weakness.[71] He described these sensations as occurring in waves of increasing and waning intensity. He also observed that in morbid or distorted grief reactions, serious diseases may develop, such as ulcerative colitis or rheumatoid arthritis.[72] Asthma attacks have also been mentioned as a possible result of grief.[73] Hinton lists several physical symptoms of bereavement as probable correlates of depression: fatigue, insomnia, loss of appetite, loss of weight, muscular pains, indigestion, constipation, dizziness, and headache. The commonness with which such physical symptoms occur following death of a loved one helps to explain the three-fold increase in visits to the physician for psychiatric symptoms during bereavement, the seven-fold increase in use of sedation, and the 50 percent increase in physician visits for non-psychiatric symptoms such as arthritis reported by Parkes.[74]

Decrements in mental health and well-being after the loss of a loved one are well recognized. Lindemann, in his seminal work, identified several common manifestations of emotional disturbances in bereavement.[75] Preoccupation with the image of the deceased, including dreams, guilt about real and imagined failings in relation to the deceased, hostile reactions and irritation toward others, restlessness, and ineffectiveness of actions are all normal, common responses of the survivor. Somewhat less common reactions include acquisition of symptoms and mannerisms of the deceased, radical alteration of social relationships such as withdrawal, and other self-damaging behavior. Kübler-Ross described five phases commonly experienced by survivors and those anticipating the loss of their own life.[76] Initially, shock and denial act to protect the person from the sudden impact of the revelation of loss or impending loss. Subsequently, anger toward God, others and the injustice of fate is often seen. Bargaining with God, care-givers and others expresses the need to gain control of a situation which is largely uncontrollable. Bargaining may also be an expression of guilt over past failings which are thought to be partially responsible for the present or impending loss. Depression follows when finally the inevitability of the loss is acknowledged and mourning over the loss begins. Finally, after mourning the loss, the depression lessens and life once again seems worthwhile; the loss is incorporated as an important but not disabling part of one's life. While Lindemann believed that the most severe symptoms of acute grief last four to six weeks,[77] others, such as Hinton, say it is not uncommon to find survivors still seriously depressed beyond a year after the death of the loved one.[78] The psychological symptoms of bereavement are generally self-limited and normally resolved without psychiatric intervention. Support of friends and family and occasionally general attention from one's family physician are usually sufficient to bring the bereaved through the crisis. Prolonged reactions and those which are extreme in either their expression or repression of grief may require professional psychological assistance.

In summary, there can be little doubt that death of a loved friend or relative is a life event which commonly precipitates both physical and psychological dysfunction in people of all ages. There is also some evidence that mortality rates are stimulated by the strain incurred during bereavement especially among older people.

Physical Mechanisms

We know very little about the physiological links between exposure to multiple recent life events and negative physical outcomes. As suggested in our discussion of psychosomatic theories, there seems to be a broad consensus that when one assesses some stimulus as immediately or potentially threatening, emotional and physical response processes aimed at adapting to or coping with the stimulus are set into motion. We can observe anxiety, fear, anger, and hypervigilance, while changes in cardiovascular function, energy mobilization, hormone secretion, and activity of the central nervous system are identified.

A study of a small number of middle-aged and older patients hospitalized for heart attack helps to illustrate several points made above, and also typifies the response of people experiencing relocation strain. Klein and his co-workers had come to expect an increase in patient medical and emotional problems around the time of patient transfer from the intensive coronary care unit to the general medical wards for further recuperation.[79] Transfer occurred because the intensive care given in the cardiac unit was no longer needed as cardiac function stabilized during the first several days after the attack. However, patients often became anxious about the transfer, feeling that the move might place them in danger if further heart trouble were experienced. It was found that catecholamine levels in blood and urine increased as patients became more upset over the transfer. These hormones (adrenalin and noradrenalin) are produced in greater quantity whenever an individual experiences increased strain. It was also found that a variety of physical disturbances tended to occur in conjunction with these emotional and hormonal responses. In a series of seven transferred patients studied intensively, five experienced a rise in catecholamine excretion and each of these patients also experienced some cardiac dysfunction ranging from minor rhythm disturbance to recurrent heart attack and death. Subsequently, a program was implemented to prepare patients for transfer and provide emotional support before, during and after the move. In a series of seven prepared patients, only two developed increased catecholamine levels and none experienced cardiac complications. We present this example to provide an illustration of the links between emotions, physiological function, and illness outcome. Such linkages help explain the increased illness and death reported as people struggle to adjust to relocation, loss of a loved one, and other significant life changes.

The neuroendocrine mechanisms just alluded to have been studied primarily in animals and young and middle-aged humans. It seems reasonable to withhold judgment about their operation in elderly people until definitive work has been completed. However, Stenback summarizes our present state of knowledge.[80] Work has been done which indicates decreased neural sensitivity and excitability of the cerebral cortex, the hypothalamus and the reticular formation in the aged.[81] Also chemical substances used in neural transmission are synthesized at a lower rate in the elderly. Such changes in the elderly induce an increased sluggishness in the influence of higher brain regions over lower ones and over peripheral organs. However, these decrements are compensated for by the slower inactivation of noradrenalin at neural receptors, thus causing prolonged recovery time following stress.[82] Stenback also notes that the function of the hormonal system (except gonads) is not radically diminished by aging.[83] At the peripheral organs, furthermore, reduced neural sensitivity is compensated for by increased sensitivity to

hormones.[84] These data, preliminary and sparse as they are, give no reason to doubt the applicability of the neuroendocrine mechanism to older people. On the contrary, Engel points to the heightened effects of psychosomatic mechanism on physical systems which are increasingly fragile because of advancing age. The coronary vessels, for example, are likely to exhibit advanced atherosclerosis in the aged. Intense psychophysiological arousal is far more likely, it would seem, to cause heart damage under this circumstance than in the younger, less compromised coronary system.

SUMMARY

This chapter introduced the proposition that the experience of many and significant life changes is frequently followed by breakdowns in physical and emotional health. The origins of this model were traced to the 1920s and 1930s in the work of Walter Cannon and Hans Selye, early researchers in the area of psychosomatic medicine. By the 1950s, Thomas Holmes had developed the life change-health change paradigm into a distinct area of research and theory within the psychosomatic field. In the past thirty years the validity of the model has found support in its application to subjects of several nationalities experiencing a variety of physical and emotional health problems, both minor and severe. The quality of research has also been improving with a shift from the weaker retrospective study designs to stronger prospective ones. Although numerous problems remain, as critics of the area attest, guarded optimism persists that the paradigm will be borne out and strengthened with further research. Major efforts are still needed in gaining an understanding of the factors which promote and inhibit the translation of life change experience into illness.

In the second part of this chapter, the possible usefulness of the life change-health change model in studies of the elderly was examined. In view of the dearth of research applications of this model in populations of the aged, analogs of the model were sought in studies of the health effects of three important life events heavily studied in literatures of gerontology and behavioral medicine, namely, retirement, residential relocation, and death of a loved relative or friend. Little support was discovered in the literature for the popular notion that retirement leads to health breakdown and premature death. On the contrary, there was some evidence that health actually improves after retirement. The literature on relocation and death of loved ones, on the other hand, offered considerable evidence for a life change-health change linkage. The physiological mechanisms suspected of translating life change experience to physical illness were reviewed and it was concluded that such mechanisms could be operative in the aged. In some regards, the physical situation of the elderly might make them even more vulnerable to the deleterious impact of these psychosomatic mechanisms.

NOTES

1. G. Engel, "Sudden and Rapid Death During Psychological Stress." *Annals of Internal Medicine*, 74 (1971): 771–782.

2. W. Cannon, *Bodily Changes in Pain, Hunger, Fear and Rage.* (New York: Appleton, 1929).

3. H. Selye, *The Stress of Life.* (New York: McGraw-Hill, 1965).

4. Cannon, *Bodily Changes in Pain, Hunger, Fear and Rage.*

5. W. Cannon, *The Wisdom of the Body.* (New York: Norton, 1939).

6. F. Alexander, *Psychosomatic Medicine: Its Principles and Applications.* (New York: Norton, 1950).

7. H. G. Wolff, "Protective Reaction Patterns and Disease." *Annals of Internal Medicine* 27 (1947): 944–969.

8. G. Moss, *Illness, Immunity and Social Interaction.* (New York: Wiley, 1973).

9. T. H. Holmes, H. Goodell, S. Wolf, and H. G. Wolff. *The Nose. An Experimental Study of Reactions Within the Nose in Human Subjects During Varying Life Experiences.* (Springfield, Illinois: Charles C Thomas, 1950).

10. T. H. Holmes, and M. Masuda. "Life Change and Illness Susceptibility." In *Stressful Life Events,* edited by B. S. Dohrenwend, and B. P. Dohrenwend. (New York: Wiley, 1974), 45–72.

11. T. H. Holmes, and R. Rahe. "The Social Readjustment Rating Scale." *Journal of Psychosomatic Research* 11 (1967): 213–218.

12. J. Rabkin, and E. Streuning. "Life Events, Stress, and Illness." *Science* 194 (1974): 1013–1020.

13. M. Masuda, and T. H. Holmes. "The Social Readjustment Rating Scale: A Cross-Cultural Study of Japanese and Americans." *Journal of Psychosomatic Research* 11 (1967): 227–237.

14. D. Harmon, M. Masuda, and T. H. Holmes. "The Social Readjustment Rating Scale: A Cross-Cultural Study of Western Europeans and Americans." *Journal of Psychosomatic Research* 14 (1970): 391–400.

15. T. Woon, M. Masuda, N. Wagner, and T. H. Holmes. "The Social Readjustment Rating Scale: A Cross-Cultural Study of Malaysians and Americans." *Journal of Cross-Cultural Psychology* 2 (1971): 373–386.

16. R. Rahe, "The Pathway Between Subjects' Recent Life Changes and Their Near-Future Illness Reports: Representative Results and Methodological Issues." In *Stressful Life Events,* 73–86.

17. R. Rahe, I. Floistad, T. Bergan, R. Ringdahl, R. Gerhardt, E. Gunderson, and R. Arthur. "Subjects' Life Changes, Symptom Recognition and Illness Reports in the Norwegian Navy." Unit Report, U.S. Navy Medical Neuro-psychiatric Research Unit, San Diego, (1973).

18. R. Rahe. "Life Change Measurement as a Predictor of Illness." *Proceedings of the Royal Society of Medicine* 61 (1968): 1124–1126.

19. S. Bramwell. "Personality and Psychosocial Variables in College Athletics." Medical Thesis, University of Washington (1971).

20. Rabkin and Streuning, "Life Events, Stress, and Illness."

21. T. Garrity, G. Somes, and M. Marx. "The Relationship of Personality, Life Change, Psychophysiological Strain and Health Status in a College Population." *Social Science and Medicine* 11 (1977): 257–263.

22. J. McNeil, and B. Pesznecker. "Altering your Response to Stress." *Washington State Journal of Nursing* 49 (1975): 9–12.

23. M. Marx, T. Garrity, and F. Bowers. "The Influence of Recent Life Experience on the Health of College Freshmen." *Journal of Psychosomatic Research* 19 (1975): 87–98.

24. Rabkin and Streuning, "Life Events, Stress, and Illness."

25. R. Rahe, L. Bennett, M. Romo, P. Siltanen, and R. Arthur. "Subjects' Recent Life Changes and Coronary Heart Disease in Finland." *American Journal of Psychiatry* 130 (1973): 1222–1226.

26. A. Wyler, M. Masuda, and T. H. Holmes. "Magnitude of Life Events and Seriousness of Illness." *Psychosomatic Medicine* 33 (1971): 115–122.

27. R. Payne. "Recent Life Changes and the Reporting of Psychological States." *Journal of Psychosomatic Research* 19 (1975): 99–103.

28. T. Theorell, "Selected Illnesses and Somatic Factors in Relation to Two Psychosocial Stress Indices—A Prospective Study on Middle-Aged Construction Building Workers." *Journal of Psychosomatic Research* 20 (1976): 7–20.

29. E. Goldberg, and G. Comstock. "Life Events and Subsequent Illness." *American Journal of Epidemiology* 104 (1976): 146–158.

30. R. Wilson, and G. Maddox, "Relating Life Change to Psychological Distress: Further Research." Paper read at meetings of the Southern Sociological Society, Atlanta (1974).

31. B. P. Dohrenwend, and B. S. Dohrenwend. *Social Status and Psychological Disorder: A Causal Inquiry.* (New York: Wiley, 1969).

32. J. Myers, J. Lindenthal, and M. Pepper. "Social Class, Life Events and Psychiatric Symptoms: A Longitudinal Study." In *Stressful Life Events,* 191–205.

33. C. Ryser, and A. Sheldon. "Retirement and Health." *Journal of the American Geriatrics Society* 17 (1969): 180–190.

34. Ibid.

35. D. Heyman, and F. Jeffers. "Effect of Time Lapse on Consistency of Self-Health and Medical Evaluations of Elderly Persons." *Journal of Gerontology* 18 (1963): 160–164.

36. E. Palmore. "The Promise and Problems of Longevity Studies." In *Prediction of Life Span,* edited by E. Palmore, and F. Jeffers. (Lexington, Mass: Heath, 1971), 3–11.

37. R. Myers. "Factors in Interpreting Mortality After Retirement." *Journal of the American Statistical Association* 49 (1954): 499–509.

38. J. Tyhurst, L. Salk, and M. Kennedy. "Mortality, Morbidity and Retirement." *American Journal of Public Health* 47 (1957): 1434–1444.

39. W. Thompson, and G. Streib. "Situational Determinant: Health and Economic Deprivation in Retirement." *Journal of Social Issues* 14 (1958): 18–34.

40. C. Schneider. "Adjustment of Employed Women to Retirement." Doctoral dissertation, Cornell University (1964).

41. R. Atchley. *The Social Forces in Later Life.* (Belmont, Calif.: Wadsworth, 1972).

42. M. Lieberman. "Relationship of Mortality Rates to Entrance to a Home of the Aged." *Geriatrics* 16 (1961): 515–519.

43. S. Tobin, and M. Lieberman. *Last Home for the Aged.* (San Francisco: Jossey-Bass, 1976).

44. M. Lieberman. "Relocation Research and Social Policy." *The Gerontologist* 14 (1974): 494–501.

45. Tobin and Lieberman, *Last Home for the Aged.*

46. Leiberman, "Relocation Research and Social Policy."

47. C. Aldrich, and E. Mendkoff. "Relocation of the Aged and Disabled: A Mortality Study." *Journal of the American Geriatrics Society* 11 (1963): 185–194.

48. M. Blenkner, M. Bloom, and M. Neilsen. "A Research and Demonstration Project." *Social Casework* 52 (1971): 483–499.

49. M. Blenkner. "Environmental Change and the Aging Individual." *The Gerontologist* 7 (1967): 101–105.

50. A. Goldfarb, S. Shahinian, and H. Turner. "Death Rates in Relocated Aged Residents of Nursing Homes." Paper read at meetings of Gerontological Society, New York, 1966.

51. D. Kay, V. Norris, and F. Post. "Prognosis in Psychiatric Disorders of the Elderly." *Journal of Mental Science* 102 (1956): 129–140.

52. M. Lawton, and S. Yaffe. "Mortality, Morbidity and Voluntary Change in Residence." Paper read at meetings of American Psychological Association, Washington, D.C. (1967).

53. D. Miller, and M. Lieberman, "The Relationship of Affect State and Adaptive Capacity to Reactions to Stress." *Journal of Gerontology* 20 (1965): 492–497.

54. M. Lieberman. "Institutionalization of the Aged: Effects of Behavior." *Journal of Gerontology* 24 (1969): 330–340.

55. F. Carp. "The Impact of Environment on Old People." *The Gerontologist* 7 (1967): 105–108.

56. B. Stotsky. "A Controlled Study of Factors in a Successful Adjustment of Mental Patients to a Nursing Home." *American Journal of Psychiatry* 123 (1967): 1243–1251.

57. Aldrich and Mendkoff. "Relocation of the Aged and Disabled . . ."

58. Miller and Lieberman. "The Relationship of Affect State and Adaptive Capacity Reactions to Stress."

59. Tobin and Lieberman. *Last Home for the Aged.*

60. Goldfarb, Shahinian, and Turner. "Death Rates in Relocated Aged Residents of Nursing Homes."

61. A. Goldfarb. "Predictors of Mortality in the Institutionalized Aged." In *Prediction of Life Span,* 79–93.

62. J. Zweig, and J. Csank. "Effects of Relocation on Chronically Ill Geriatric Patients of a Medical Unit: Mortality Rates." *Journal of the American Geriatrics Society* 23 (1975): 132–136.

63. D. Aleksandrowics, "Fire and its Aftermath on a Geriatrics Ward." *Bulletin of the Meninger Clinic* 25 (1961): 23–32.

64. L. Novick. "Easing the Stress of Moving Day." *Hospitals* 41 (1967): 64–74.

65. Lawton and Yaffe, "Mortality, Morbidity and Voluntary Change in Residence."

66. W. Rees, and S. Lutkins. "Mortality of Bereavement." *British Medical Journal* 4 (1967): 13–16.

67. J. Hinton. *Dying.* (Baltimore: Penguin, 1967).

68. M. Young, B. Benjamin, and C. Wallis. "The Mortality of Widowers." *Lancet* 2 (1963): 454–456.

69. P. Cox, and J. Ford. "The Mortality of Widows Shortly After Widowhood." *Lancet* 1 (1964): 163–164.

70. A. Kraus, and A. Lilienfeld. "Some Epidemiological Aspects of the High Mortality Rate in the Young Widowed Group." *Journal of Chronic Diseases* 10 (1959): 207–217.

71. E. Lindemann. "Symptomatology and Management of Acute Grief." *American Journal of Psychiatry* 101 (1944): 141–148.

72. E. Lindemann. "Modifications in the Course of Ulcerative Colitis in Relationship to Changes in Life Situations and Reaction Patterns." *Proceedings of the Association for Research in Nervous and Mental Disease* 29 (1950): 706–729.

73. N. McDermott, and S. Cobb. "Psychogenic Factors in Asthma." *Psychosomatic Medicine* 1 (1939): 203–244.

74. C. M. Parkes. "Effects of Bereavement on Physical and Mental Health—A Study of the Medical Records of Widows." *British Medical Journal* 2 (1964): 274–279.

75. Lindemann. "Symptomatology and Management of Acute Grief."

76. E. Kübler-Ross. *On Death and Dying.* (New York: Macmillan, 1969).

77. Lindemann. "Symptomatology and Management of Acute Grief."

78. Hinton. *Dying.*

79. R. Klein, V. Kliner, D. Zipes, W. Troyer, and A. Wallace. "Transfer from a Coronary Care Unit." *Archives of Internal Medicine* 122 (1968): 104–108.

80. A. Stenback. "Psychosomatic States." In *Modern Perspectives in the Psychiatry of Old Age*, edited by J. Howells. (New York: Brunner-Mazel, 1975).

81. V. Frolkis. "Regulation and Adaptation Processes in Aging." In *The Main Problems of Soviet Gerontology*, edited by D. Chebotarev. (Kiev: USSR Academy of Medical Science, 1972).

82. N. Verkhratsky. "Characteristics of Catecholamine Metabolism During Aging." In *Ninth International Congress of Gerontology in Kiev—Reports and Introductory Lectures*, Vol. 1 (1972).

83. D. Gusseck. "Endocrine Mechanisms and Aging." In *Advances in Gerontological Research*, Vol. 4. Edited by B. Strehler. (New York: Academic Press, 1972).

84. Stenback. "Psychosomatic States."

Life Style and Nutrient Intake in the Elderly

E. Neige Todhunter

A major factor in enabling the elderly to continue independent living is their ability to obtain or prepare meals adequate to maintain their nutritional health. Comparatively few studies have been made to determine the adequacy of the diets of older age groups. There have been some at the local and others at the national levels (USDA Household Consumption Survey, 1965; Ten State Survey; and "HANES"). Still fewer investigations have attempted to determine the factors that contribute to dietary inadequacy by looking more closely at the life styles.

The investigation partially reported here* was undertaken to identify factors that influence the food practices, acceptance, and attitudes of elderly persons, and to determine the extent to which group feeding programs are needed, and should be modified, according to region, socioeconomic status, ethnicity, sex, and other possible factors.

This investigation was made during February to December, 1973. These dates are important because of the marked increase in food prices since that time, and some findings reported here might be different if the same study were repeated today.

THE SAMPLE AND METHODS USED

The sample of individuals sixty years and over of non-institutionalized persons in middle Tennessee included both males and females, and blacks and whites, with different educational levels, socioeconomic backgrounds, and living conditions, from both rural and urban areas, who were willing and

From M. Winick, ed., *Nutrition and Aging.* Copyright © 1976, John Wiley & Sons, Inc. Reprinted by permission of John Wiley & Sons, Inc.

* "Food Acceptance and Food Attitudes of the Elderly as a Basis for Planning Nutrition Programs," E. Neige Todhunter, Faye House, and Roger Vander Zwaag (Vanderbilt University). Tennessee Commission on Aging (Nashville, Tenn.: June, 1974), p. 178.

competent to be interviewed. The total group of 529 persons interviewed had a mean age of 73.6 years, median 72.3 years, mode 75 years, and a range of 60 to 102 years (Table 1).

All data were obtained by personal interview and all interviews were by the same qualified dietitian, familiar with regional terminology and food practices, skilled in establishing rapport, and experienced in working with the elderly. The interview was limited to questions that could be answered in about sixty minutes, and thus could be completed without tiring the respondent. A twenty-four hour food recall was obtained and intake of seven nutrients was calculated.

DATA TREATMENT

For a few questions where the replies varied with the individuals a hand count was made. All other data were keypunched on cards and computer analyses were made. All data are presented as percentages of the total group or of subgroups (race and sex). Averages have not been used because we believe this tends to obscure major differences within the groups or between groups.

DESCRIPTION OF THE SAMPLE

Living Conditions

More than half the total group (54 percent) lived alone, either because they were single (11 percent) or because they were wid-

TABLE 1

Characteristics of the sample.

CHARACTERISTIC	TOTAL NUMBER	MALE	FEMALE	BLACK	WHITE	RURAL	URBAN
Age[a]							
60–64	65	27	38	14	51	20	45
65–69	105	34	71	30	75	26	79
70–74	121	39	82	52	69	17	104
75–79	117	42	75	36	81	18	99
80–84	71	20	51	22	49	13	58
over 85	49	23	26	19	30	·6	43
Education							
none	10	9	1	7	3	2	8
grades	279	106	173	135	144	51	228
high school	145	44	101	18	127	29	116
college	73	16	57	10	63	14	59
degree received	22	10	12	3	19	5	17
Marital status							
single	56	11	45	11	45	9	47
married	169	112	57	47	122	59	110
widowed[b]	304	62	242	115	189	33	271
Living							
alone	287	58	229	111	176	20	267
with spouse	167	109	55	47	117	57	107
with relatives	67	15	52	13	54	20	47
with friend	11	3	8	2	9	4	7

[a] One urban white female age not given.
[b] Includes also divorced or separated.

owed, divorced, or separated. The highest percentage of single individuals was among white women.

Two-thirds of the group were renters, and 44% lived in apartments. All participants had food preparation and food storage facilities; electricity was used by 95%. Approximately three-fourths of each subgroup made food purchases at supermarkets and the remainder mainly at neighborhood stores. About 40% shopped once a week and 36% from two to four times per week. Black women shopped least frequently, probably because of transportation problems and distance from food markets (three miles for half of this subgroup). The majority of each subgroup were within one-half mile of markets and public transportation systems.

Financial Status

No direct question regarding amount of income was asked but from information available about sources of income and rent, it was possible to make a reliable estimate of income. Twenty-nine percent of the total group had an individual income below $1800, 20 percent between $1800 and $2400, 28 percent between $2400 and $5000, and 22 percent over $5000. More blacks were in the lowest income group.

Money spent on food was $5.00 or less per week by 9 percent (mainly blacks) and between $5.00 and $10.00 by 48 percent, and 24 percent spent $10 to $15 per week.

Aloneness

Aloneness was considered because of the possible effect on food practices. To live alone does not necessarily mean loneliness, which is largely dependent on the interests and inner resources of the individual. A high proportion lived alone, but only 7 percent of the total group never had any visits with relatives (and this was about the same by race and sex). Daily visits with relatives were the normal occurrence for 44 percent of the total group, with males having the highest percentage and black women the lowest (25 percent). Religious affiliation was high for both

sexes and races and there was church attendance by 69 percent of the total group, with the highest percentage being the black female group (76 percent).

About 13 percent of the total group did not participate in recreational activities of any kind, and 22 percent of the black women had no recreation. The highest percentage of each subgroup engaged in recreation that did not involve others (such as walking, gardening, sewing, fishing, reading, and music listening).

Volunteer services in the community were participated in by 13 percent, more often by females than males. About 12 percent had some employment, either at regular hours or irregularly.

Loneliness did not seem to be a major problem for this group; however, no information was obtained on their inner feelings.

Those who lived alone and those who lived with others (spouse, relatives, or friends) when compared as subgroups did *not* differ in dietary adequacy.

Health Status

The health of individuals may influence their current food practices. Health of participants in this study was evaluated from their responses to the interviewer regarding how they felt physically, what they thought their ailments were, what their physician had told them, their dental condition, their use of prescribed medication and vitamin or mineral supplements, and their mobility and physical ability to prepare food.

More than 50 percent of males, both black and white, claimed to feel healthy, but only 30 percent of the black and the white females answered affirmatively. Incidence of arthritis was higher among women (30 percent) than men (13 percent). None of the black men expressed a desire to lose weight; 10 percent of the black women considered themselves overweight. Eighty-four percent of all participants said they had normal mobility.

Based on reports by participants of their physicians' diagnoses, a higher percentage of black women reported diabetes, heart disease, hypertension, and arthritis than any other subgroup. More black men and women reported hypertension than the white group. Sixty percent of the total group said they "feel good"; fewer white women gave this response than any other subgroup. More white women than any other subgroup took medication, and also used vitamin and mineral supplements (22 percent).

Ten percent of the total group were edentulous, and 16 percent of the group said they had chewing problems.

These health factors might be expected to affect the food practices, but this was not apparent in the dietary ratings of the groups.

FOOD PRACTICES AND BELIEFS

The Recommended Dietary Allowances (RDA), 1974, of the National Research Council are not requirements; they are allowances intended for use in planning group meals. They cannot be used for judging dietary adequacy for individuals. They were used in this study as a basis of comparison of individuals when grouped by race, sex, age, income, education, and health factors. The percentage in each group whose individual calculated nutrient intakes were 66 percent or more of the RDA have been classified as "satisfactory."

Nutrient Intakes

Intakes for seven essential nutrients are shown in Table 2.

Protein. More than 80 percent of males, both black and white, and white females, had "satisfactory" ratings, but only 70 percent of the black females achieved this rating. One-half of the total group met or exceeded the RDA, but only one-third of the black females met the RDA for protein.

Calcium. Two-thirds of the total group had "satisfactory" ratings; fewer black females had this rating.

Iron. There was a marked difference between the numbers of men and women in iron intakes; 78 percent of males (black and white) but only 48 percent of white females and 37 percent of black females met the "satisfactory" level.

Vitamin A. More than half the total group had less than "satisfactory" intakes, but over 40 percent of blacks (both male and female) met the RDA.

Thiamin. More than half the total groups were below "satisfactory" rating, and blacks (male and female) had the least number with this rating.

Riboflavin. Riboflavin was the nutrient of lowest intake by the total group, with little difference between races or sexes.

Vitamin C. Intakes of vitamin C were "satisfactory" for two-thirds of the total group, with black females having the largest number with the "satisfactory" rating (72 percent).

Comparison of dietary ratings by age groups, between those with and without problems in chewing food, between those who did and did not "feel poorly," and between those living alone or with others showed no appreciable differences.

Dietary ratings were influenced by level of formal education and by income (Table 2), which is in agreement with findings in national and other surveys. The number of satisfactory ratings for all nutrients improved up through the group having some high school education. As income increased, more participants met the adequacy standard for all nutrients.

The above dietary data have been presented from the point of view of the percentage of each subgroup who had ratings of satisfactory or better. The problem of adequate nutrient intake is further emphasized if one studies how many individuals had diets providing less than one-third the RDA for various nutrients. In this classification it was found that one-fifth the total group had less than one-third the RDA for vitamin C, one-

TABLE 2

Percent by sex, race, age, education, and income with dietary rating of satisfactory or better for seven nutrients.

SAMPLE DESCRIPTOR	PROTEIN %	CAL-CIUM %	IRON %	VITAMIN A %	THI-AMIN %	RIBO-FLAVIN %	VITAMIN C %
Race and sex							
Total group	84.6	66.7	54.9	44.1	43.0	37.0	67.1
Males, black	88.7	64.5	67.7	46.7	32.5	37.1	56.5
Males, white	91.0	69.7	77.9	45.9	59.0	37.7	65.6
Total males	90.2	67.8	74.4	46.1	51.1	37.4	62.5
Females, black	70.4	57.5	37.1	46.3	23.1	27.8	72.2
Females, white	86.7	70.1	47.9	41.5	45.7	41.1	68.4
Total females	81.5	65.9	44.3	42.8	38.5	36.8	69.5
Age Groups							
60–70 years	88.1	63.0	57.3	41.6	49.5	37.0	67.7
71–80 years	80.4	66.4	54.5	46.8	37.8	36.2	66.8
over 80 years	87.7	67.5	51.0	41.8	41.8	38.8	64.4
Education, formal							
None	70.0	50.0	30.0	20.0	10.0	20.0	50.0
Grade School	80.5	63.7	50.7	40.6	38.0	36.6	58.3
High School	88.3	66.2	60.0	48.3	46.2	32.4	75.2
College	94.6	75.3	58.9	49.3	54.7	43.8	79.8
Degree received	86.3	86.4	72.7	54.5	59.1	59.1	90.9
Income							
Low	78.8	65.4	42.3	27.9	30.8	36.5	58.7
Middle	82.8	62.4	50.7	46.6	38.9	34.4	62.9
High	89.6	72.1	66.2	49.8	53.7	40.3	76.1

third the RDA for riboflavin, and one-fourth the RDA for vitamin A.

These data indicate that there are differences in the diets consumed by males and females and also differences between those of blacks and whites. More diets of blacks were satisfactory in vitamin A, and low in thiamin than for whites. More black women had diets of lower rating in protein, calcium, and iron but higher in vitamin C than any other subgroups.

Study of actual foods consumed indicated that size of servings rather than choice of foods was a major factor influencing the nutrient intake.

Beliefs about Food and Health

In response to a question about what foods are "good for health" approximately 14 percent of black males and females and white males said all foods were good; only 5 percent of white females gave this response. Vegetables were named more often than any other food by both races and sexes, and this belief was consistent with their actual practice. Foods usually considered "health foods" were not mentioned.

Pork was most frequently mentioned as "bad for health." Foods high in fat or fried foods were named by more than 10 percent of each subgroup and most frequently by black males (20 percent). Sweets (desserts and candy) also were considered in this category by about 10 percent of the participants.

Approximately 90 percent of each subgroup believed their own diet was good and that the food they ate affected the way they felt; 84 percent of each subgroup said they had a good appetite for meals.

The use of vitamin or mineral supplements was comparatively low. It occurred in about 15 percent of the white males and females and was almost negligible among blacks.

Willingness to try new foods was expressed by 60 percent of each subgroup. More than 50 percent of white males and females and 75 percent of black males and females, believed food had "less taste" than it used to have. Approximately 70 percent of each subgroup had made some changes in food habits, mostly in recent years, for reasons of health, aloneness, beliefs, and a few for financial reasons.

Companionship was considered the most important factor at mealtime by 41 percent of white females, 34 percent of white males, 27 percent of black males and 25 percent of black females. "Food you like" and the way it is cooked were rated important by 30 percent of white females and 36 percent of black females.

More than 50 percent of the total group had a favorable attitude to the need for food and did not economize by reducing food expenditures. More blacks than whites did economize on food. Meat was the food first to be economized on.

Breakfast was eaten regularly by over 90 percent of the group, was eaten at home, and was the favorite meal for more than one-third of each subgroup.

Comparatively few meals were eaten away from home and least often by black women.

Interviewees were asked to name their favorite foods and most disliked foods (no check list was given; these were spontaneous answers). Meat of some kind was mentioned most frequently (beef by 37 percent, chicken by 24 percent, and pork by 10 percent); next in frequency was green beans (32 percent), greens (25 percent), and potatoes (16 percent). Fifteen percent said they had no dis-

liked foods. Many different foods were listed as disliked, but cottage cheese was most frequently mentioned (by 13 percent). Few could give any reasons for disliking a food; taste was most frequently mentioned, but dislike of some vegetables was because of their texture or because "they disagree with me."

Fresh produce was preferred by all subgroups, but canned foods were used by 85 percent and frozen foods less frequently by blacks.

Between meal eating, or snacks, was the regular practice of only 37 percent of the total group. The kind of snack foods used were predominantly protein-rich foods or dairy products; beverages were infrequent snack choices.

SUMMARY

The life styles of the elderly population under study indicate that they had positive attitudes toward health in general and toward food and eating. Their food habits and beliefs were free from faddism, they were willing to try new foods and to change at least some of their food habits, and they had a good appetite for meals. Meal patterns and choice of foods, snacks, and food likes were toward foods of high nutritive value. They had comparatively few food dislikes, and the majority ate three meals a day.

Many of the participants in this study had nutrient intakes of less than two-thirds the 1974 RDAs. Food choices, meal patterns, and beliefs about food suggest that economic factors strongly influenced dietary adequacy and limited the food choices and size of servings. Black females appear to be the most disadvantaged group.

All of these findings are a strong indicator of the need for group feeding programs for the elderly. Such meal programs should provide at least one-third of the daily nutrient needs, and should be pleasurable experiences using foods appropriate to the food habits and beliefs of the specific groups, their locale, and their cultural-economic backgrounds. These programs should also be accompanied by realistic nutrition education programs designed to provide guidance in buying and using foods of highest nutritive value within their resources. The need for such programs becomes increasingly urgent because of today's rapidly increasing food prices.

SECTION 3

Psychological Dialectics: Development and Encounters Along the Way

INTRODUCTION

The range of topics and issues which can conceivably be included in a psychological orientation toward aging is exceedingly diverse. Similarly, the theoretical frameworks representatives of the discipline might bring with them are also widely varied. For example, a psychologist who focuses on aging might draw from any of the specialties listed in Table 1. Clearly each of these possible orientations is deserving of extended discussion in its own right; however, we shall confine our attention here to a brief look at a developmental approach and some of the social dimensions related to it.

Adjusting to the myriad and unending challenges confronting us in the course of life is no small task. It requires a flexibility not easily achieved without conscious effort being made time and time again as the years pass by. Psychologists have formulated many developmental models, each of which attempts to lend some order and predictability to the transient stages of an individual's life course. Most of the models rely on one of two metaphors, either an *organistic* or a *mechanistic* conception of human behavior. The former treats a person's actions as a negotiated compromise, with changing events given meaning by those attending to them. The second perspective assumes that people

TABLE 1

Varieties of psychological orientations to aging.

TRADITIONAL TAXONOMY	BEHAVIORAL PROCESSES	CONTEMPORARY ORIENTATION
Associationalism	Sensation	Physiological
Structuralism	Perception	Learning
Functionalism	Attention	Cognitive
Behavioralism	Memory	Bio-Behavioral
Gestalt	Information Processing	Ecological-Field
Trait	Cognition	Role-Personality
Psychoanalysis	Personality	Developmental
	Social	

Adapted from *Handbook of the Psychology of Aging*, J. E. Birren and K. W. Schaie, eds. © 1977 by Litton Educational Publishing, Inc. Reprinted by permission of Van Nostrand Reinhold Company.

are primarily reactive agents, responding to external stimuli, the absence of which implies relative stability in life. Change is thought to be quantitative, rather than qualitative, as in the organismic paradigm. New information can be unlearned in much the same fashion as it was learned in the first place. Lest the reader assume these two views are the guiding force behind all psychological research on the aging process, it should be emphasized that there is a great deal of conceptual transition currently afoot in the field. What appears to be emerging is a dialectical orientation which seeks to overcome the separation inherent in the organismic and mechanistic approaches. It is likely that the next few years will see an extension of the dialectical synthesis of the constructive unfolding of successive stages or phases of human life. Such a view will undoubtedly include attention to intrinsic psychological and biological factors as well as to cultural and social aspects of behavior (Riegel, 1977).

Perhaps the best known of the sequential perspectives presently enjoying some currency in the psychological community is that of Eric Erikson (1950). Basing his eight-stage model on his Freudian training coupled with the early work of Charlotte Buehler, who herself proposed a five-level trajectory, Erikson suggests there are distinctive life tasks to be faced in each successive phase of development as personalities evolve throughout life. Each phase has its own unique crises and is organically related to the preceding phases. Successful adjustment depends on what kinds of resolutions are made, then carried on to the next developmental plateau. Subsequent attempts to validate Erikson's paradigm have resulted in several refinements and reformulations (see for example, Peck, 1968; Gould, 1975; Levinson et al., 1978), but for the most part the notion that life is a progressive unfolding has survived intact. Although the timing of the transitions has been of concern, the more important questions are of sex-linked differences between women and men. Women do not yet appear to suffer the same occupational or health-related stresses as men; instead they must cope with expressive and familial crises. Interestingly, there is some disagreement as to who encounters the most threatening hurdles and who is most likely to devise a new coping strategy (Lowenthal, 1975; Neugarten, 1968). Obviously, how one meets the world at any period of life cannot be anticipated without attention to the social and cultural trappings defining appropriate alternatives. Socialization, or adaptation to developmental stages, is a lifelong and culturally molded process. As the trend toward human equality continues, there is every reason to assume that the women and men of the future will experience themselves and life in a manner which need not necessarily replicate what has historically been the case.

The goal characteristic of each life stage is the integration of personal skills and needs with socially prescribed roles and expectations. In their summary of the developmental tasks, crises, and research themes identified by the psychological literature dealing with later life, Newman and Newman provide a workable framework for a discussion of cognitive abilities, social relationships, and psychopathology of older people. As they point out, an absence of precise passage times and the tendency to lump together the last several decades of life are not conducive to an advantageous perception or restructuring of the lifeworld for the elderly. Despite the vagueness of their coverage of the later years, most developmental models agree that change is intrinsic to the lifecourse. They also emphasize that aging is in no way a predominantly negative journey. With the formulation of appropriate coping styles, many psychological functions reveal marked stability and, in some cases, improvement during a period the uninformed often describe as bleak. In their landmark research, Schaie and his associates (Baltes and Schaie, 1974; Schaie, 1975) have demonstrated that what were previously thought to be decrements in mental performances are instead artifacts of testing situations and situational constraints imposed on older individuals. In short, the presence of a built-in age bias in both traditional testing instruments and setting plays a major role in causing the elderly to look deficient. Pulling together much of the existing research, Newman and Newman dispel many of the myths enshrouding cognitive and emotional adaptation. In addition, they offer a glimpse at one example of a responsive environment designed to accommodate older people in a way which will enhance their abilities to achieve and preserve satisfactory adjustment.

Charting the course of successful aging is synonymous with maintaining a balance between personal and social resources on one hand and perceived demands and obligations on the other. In referring to the possibility of an incongruity or instability between individual and societal timetables, gerontologists often use the phrase *age-status asynchronization*. It is thought the risk of maladjustment is exacerbated without a feeling of permanence or consistency. In speaking to the particular developmental patterns of women, Jan Dynda Sinnott discusses the complex of roles available to them and the function they serve in promoting feminine resilience in old age. While she concentrates on socially defined roles, the link between Sinnott's thesis and the necessity of providing supportive symbolic cues in each sequential life cycle stage should be apparent. There is a pervasive propensity to assume that roles appropriate to a woman's developmental needs are found largely within the context of her familial participation. Sinnott notes, however, that from girlhood to grave impermanence is the name of the game for a woman, with instability a constant component of her adaptive strategy. If it is true that men are more seriously challenged as they approach old age, perhaps there is a lesson to be learned from the kind of fluid adjustment pattern Sinnott identifies as characteristic of a woman's experience (see also Kline, 1975).

The mid-life confrontation between idealized expectations and the reality of what is experienced or in store for tomorrow is apparently more of a problem for men than for women. David Gutman's assertion that cultural factors are the mediators of adjustment indicates a means for ameliorating the negative consequences of developmental imperatives. Despite a number of masculine traits which appear to be impervious to cultural disparities, sex-role prescriptions do vary. In societies where power and dominance are pre-eminent, middle-aged and older men will continue to struggle against the passivity and receptivity which life's unfolding currents hold for them. As a consequence, psychosomatic illness, alcoholism, and other symptoms of emotional strife are likely to remain familiar companions of male passage through the lifecourse. As both Sinnott and Gutman imply, a breakdown of traditional sex roles may well enrich the lives of the elderly of both sexes.

The accumulation of developmental stresses and maladaptive responses makes the later years a period of high risk. Regardless of whatever personal strengths an individual may possess, old age is a time when many of the support systems previously available are no longer; consequently, the potential for emotional distress is increased. Furthermore, physiological impairments of the brain or other parts of the body leave persons susceptible to organic disorders which interfere with normal psychological functioning. The interaction of these two distinct types of disorder poses serious diagnostic problems; there is little agreement among specialists whether the symptoms presented by older patients parallel those expected of their younger counterparts suffering the same condition. Because classification of mental and psychological conditions is a complex and speculative business, the descriptions furnished by Jack Weinberg in his condensation of the principal clinical states is necessarily topical. It would require several volumes to give each one the attention it deserves. Readers interested in additional information should turn to any of the worthwhile sources available in the gerontological literature (for a summary see Pfeiffer,

1977.) As Weinberg argues, no easy assessment of the relative importance of internal factors versus social or cultural values is possible.
Depriving older people of a sense of mastery, of control over their own
life situations, cannot but help increase the strain the elderly experience. The variety of ways in which a person deals with stressful
dimensions of his or her life range from what surely appears to be the
most desirable and normal pattern of social adjustment to the most
bizarre, seemingly abnormal modes of behavior. However, Weinberg
does well to remind us that any such behavioral accommodation serves
a purpose. Even the most unorthodox of behaviors function to maintain
or protect individuals from challenges beyond their capacity. How to
assist people who are experiencing some disability poses a never ending riddle; optimally, of course, therapy ought to be directed toward
a return to personally satisfying lifestyles.

Pharmacological approaches to dealing with the older patient are
a commonplace form of therapy. Drugs are big business among the
elderly and there is no denying that medication often provides a viable
means of dealing with long-term problems. Unfortunately, drugs are
also frequently misused, either deliberately, by those administering or
taking the medication, or inadvertently, through the development of
psychological or physiological dependencies. In commenting on the
flow of drugs through the country's more than 23,000 nursing homes,
former Senator Frank Moss, author of much of the legislation to insure
accountability in the nursing home industry, notes that there is virtually no monitoring of how medication is handled. Moss asserts that
tranquilizers alone are the basis of a $100 million enterprise, consti-
tuting nearly 20 percent of all drugs administered in nursing home
facilities. All too often these tranquilizers are utilized more for the
staff's benefit, to control demanding patients, than for the patients
themselves. None of this is to say that all medication procedures are
necessarily insidious or that they do not provide a valuable avenue for
treatment. There are innumerable occasions when the use of psychotropic agents, stimulants, vasodilators, anticoagulators, hormones, and
so on, represents the primary hope of many elderly. As diagnostic
protocols become even more refined, problems with inappropriate prescriptions will surely diminish. It would be a mistake, however, to
assume that pharmacological advances alone are sufficient to remedy
functional or organic psychological disorders.

There is an emerging concern with the drug taking behavior of
community-based old people. There is relatively little information regarding the pervasiveness of drug use in general or the extent of
misuse; on the whole, we know the elderly fall into what epidemiol-
ogists refer to as a high risk category (Garta and Gaetano, 1977). David
Guttmann and his colleagues, responding to a 1975 drug conference
call for detailed information, have conducted a pilot investigation in
the Washington, D.C., area of drug taking behavior among old people.

In the study reported here, Guttmann looks at the dimensions of both alcohol problems and of legally available medications. Not too surprisingly, demographic, socioeconomic, and personal image factors differentiate the users and non-users once the crucial variables of health and physical disabilities are taken into account. Knowledge of alternatives apparently makes scant difference, even though intelligence *per se* is a significant factor in predicting who takes drugs and who does not. As Guttmann reminds us, there are many "myths" pertaining to the use of drugs by the elderly, but little information is available to bolster them. Part of the reason for the mystification, according to Guttmann, lies in the spiraling tendency toward the "medicalization" of many aspects of the human condition.

REFERENCES

1. BALTES, P., and SCHAIE, K. W. "The Myth of the Twilight Years." *Psychology Today* X, 7 (1974): 35–40.
2. BALTES, P., and WILLIS, S. "Psychological Theories of Aging and Development." In *Handbook of the Psychology of Aging*, edited by J. Birren and K. W. Schaie, pp. 128–54. New York: Van Nostrand Reinhold Company, 1977.
3. GARTA, G., and GAETANO, R. J. The Elderly: Their Health and the Drugs in Their Lives. Dubuque: Kendall/Hunt, 1977.
4. GOULD, R. "Adult Life Stages: Growth Toward Self-Tolerance." *Psychology Today* 8, 9 (1975): 74–78.
5. KLINE, C. "The Socialization Process of Women: Implications for a Theory of Successful Aging." *The Gerontologist* 15, 6 (1975): 486–92.
6. LEVINSON, D. J., et al. The Seasons of a Man's Life. New York: Alfred Knopf, 1978.
7. LOWENTHAL, M. F. "Psychosocial Variations Across the Adult Life Course: Frontiers for Research and Policy." *The Gerontologist* XV, 1 (1975): 6–12.
8. NEUGARTEN, B. "The Awareness of Middle Age." In *Middle Age and Aging*, Chicago: University of Chicago Press, 1968, pp. 93–98.
9. PECK, R. C. "Psychological Developments in the Second Half of Life." In *Middle Age and Aging*, pp. 88–92.
10. PFEIFFER, E. "Psychopathology and Social Pathology." In *Handbook of the Psychology of Aging*, pp. 650–71.
11. REIGEL, K. F. "History of Psychological Gerontology." In *Handbook of the Psychology of Aging*, pp. 76–102.
12. SCHAIE, K. W. "Age Changes in Adult Intelligence." In *Aging: Scientific Perspectives and Social Issues*, edited by D. Woodruff and J. Birren, pp. 111–24. New York: Van Nostrand Company, 1975.

Later Adulthood

A Developmental Stage

B. M. Newman
P. R. Newman

Pablo Picasso lived to be ninety-one years old. When he was seventy-nine he married his second wife, Jacqueline Roque, with whom he enjoyed twelve years of married life. During the last twenty years of his life he remained productive and energetic, persistently experimenting with new art forms.

As the expected lifespan continues to expand, the period of later adulthood will become increasingly long and will afford opportunities for experiencing new relationships, developing skills, and discovering personal potential. We see the years from fifty until death as a period of continued psychological growth during which the person must adapt to new roles and discover creative outlets for his leisure time, as well as prepare himself for the end of life. The primary integrating theme of this life stage, no matter how long it lasts, is a search for personal meaning. The adult begins to assert the competence and creativity attained during middle adulthood as he enters this stage. As life progresses, the motivations for achievement and power give way to a motive for understanding, reminiscent of the toddler's needs to know "why" and the later adolescent's need to challenge and experiment with life

From B. M. Newman and P. R. Newman, eds., *Development Through Life* (Homewood, Illinois: The Dorsey Press, 1975). Copyright © 1975 The Dorsey Press. Reprinted by permission.

roles. The individual is still confronted with these essential problems of definition and explanation during later adulthood. At this stage, the adult may begin to apply the wealth of his experience with growth, his perspective on time, and his adaptation to life crises to a personality satisfying conceptualization of the question of life's meaning.

For some, the period of later adulthood ends in a state of physical or mental deterioration or both, which impedes further psychological growth. The onset of senescence may result in a dramatic loss of memory, reasoning capacities, and problem-solving abilities, as well as an increase in fantasy activity, physical deterioration, and helplessness. These chronic problems of aging cast a shadow of depression and hopelessness on the years of later adulthood, particularly as they are viewed by younger people. They may cause serious psychological and financial problems for children as they observe their parents' progressive decline. The older person begins to feel alienated from his environment and uncomfortable about his severe loss of capacities. Psychological growth, as we have been describing it, comes to a close at this point. While the events of senility may have a powerful impact on others, they mark the end of significant development for the adult. It should be stressed that most adults continue to function at a high level, remaining intellectually competent and socially involved throughout later adulthood.

THE DEVELOPMENTAL TASKS

Redirection of Energy to New Roles and Activities

The end of parenthood is an event which demands a redirection of energy. Within the cycle of family development, the role of grandparent may also require a renewal of skills which have been stored in the attic, along with the bottle sterilizer and the potty chair. Grandparents begin to renew their acquaintance with the delights of childhood—including diapering the baby, telling fairy tales, taking trips to the zoo, and having the pleasure of helping hands with the baking, the gardening, or the carpentry. The utilization of grandparents' skills, their patience, and their knowledge may be as much in demand or even more in demand in the grandparent role than they were in the parent role.

In the occupational sphere, the adult may find himself in an administrative or mentor role. He may be in charge of organizational or community efforts to improve the lot of others. He may be required to teach his skills to novices or to design training experiences for groups of subordinates. On the job, he will be one of the senior workers who, perhaps, informally, must socialize or teach younger workers about such job-related issues as pacing, the authority hierarchy, the permanence or transience of the job itself, and the existence of potential occupational hazards.

The new roles described above occur before the cessation of one's career. At the time of retirement, there is a demand on the individual to fill his time. Many possibilities for redirection are open at that point. Some people have anticipated this and have activities in mind that they look forward to engaging in as the demands from the work setting decrease. For others, the event of retirement comes without preparation or anticipation. These adults may experience some anxiety or depression at the end of their work. For these individuals, redirection of energy to new roles is a much more complex process of adaptation which involves personal introspection about their areas of skill, their outlook toward the future, and their assessment of existing social relationships. In order to identify activities and interests that will be personally satisfying, they must stop to assess their life goals and select new directions that will bring them into greater harmony with their personal philosophies.

Let us just note here that, as in the case of Picasso, some people never retire and therefore never face this particular aspect of development. Individuals who are self-employed or who are in some creative profession where age is not a relevant variable may continue at the same work until death. They may discover new skills, they may redefine their work goals, they may reconceptualize their standards of success, but they do not ever abandon their occupational role.

At the point of retirement, many individuals elect to adopt a variety of leisure activities to fill their time. Some people decide that tennis, golf, fishing, cards, boating, or administrative work related to these leisure activities will occupy the remainder of their lives. Such an investment in leisure activities may not be considered a new role; the retired businessman does not think of himself as a golfer. However, the investment in the pursuit of these sports can be quite intense. Adults may select a location for retirement that fosters their particular leisure interest. They may plan vacations that allow new experiences related to their favorite sport. In sum, the involvement with a leisure-time activity can actually become a full-time preoccupation.

One new role that has begun to emerge for the person who has terminated his primary life work activity is that of retiree. Current publications such as *Modern Maturity* define an older age group with common interests as an age role, in much the same ways as *Seventeen* defines early adolescence as an age role. There are groups of people in the life stage of later adulthood who have formed active voting blocks and maintain lobbies which attempt to promote the passage of legislation which is in the interest of older people. Within many companies there are similar groups of retirees who, as former employees of that company, attempt to administer pension plans and to influence company policy. The presence of these groups is evidence of the continued vigor of older adults and of their ability to identify and promote issues related to their own welfare.

National policy, in fact, attempts to promote the ability of older people to direct their energies to an unlimited variety of new roles. The national Social Security Act was designed to provide a minimum income to people of age sixty-five or beyond. Benefits now may be obtained by women and by some men at their own request prior to the age of sixty-five, and social security benefits may be received continuously until death. While to some the benefits of social security seem to be inadequate, for others they represent an important source of income in the absence of a salary. Because of the certainty of this minimum income, older adults have the freedom to invest their energy in any way they see fit. They may wish to stop work, continue some form of part-time work, accentuate the role of grandparent, or begin some new roles. They do not need to work steadily in order to survive.

The most difficult adaptation to a new role occurs when an adult loses a spouse. For many older people, this loss causes severe disruption, as well as grief and depression. While some adults remarry, many others remain unmarried and identify themselves as widows or widowers. They must learn to function socially as well as in their own household without the presence of a marriage partner. Adaptation to this role requires resilience, creative problem-solving, and a strong commitment to a belief in one's personal worth.

We have indicated a number of new roles that require adaptation during later adulthood. The circumstances of life, such as grandparenthood, an administrative promotion, retirement, or illness, force most older adults to redirect their energy. For a few, the decision may be more internally motivated, as with the woman who seeks employment when her children return to school or the grocer who goes to night school to work on a college degree. The dominant theme is the vision of oneself as participating in a continued state of growth rather than decline.

Acceptance of One's Life

During middle adulthood, people begin to be aware that they have lived more years than they expect to live in the future (Neugarten, 1968). This realization stimulates a process of self-assessment through which the goals and ideals of childhood, adolescence, and adulthood are reviewed and progress toward those goals is evaluated. Due to the process of goal setting, in which aspirations exceed accomplishments, most people find that they have set some goals which they have failed to attain. While they may have had considerable achievements in some areas, they may still fall short of their level of aspiration in other directions.

By later adulthood, evidence about one's successes and failures in the major tasks of middle adulthood—marriage, child rearing, and work—has begun to accumulate. There is an abundance of real data upon which an individual can determine his own adequacy with respect to these roles. As the child-rearing role ends, adults have an opportunity to determine the degree of harmony in their own marriage relationships. They can assess whether or not they have successfully responded to the changes in their relationships or whether the marriage itself has deteriorated with the departure of the children from the home. In viewing their own children as mature adults, parents are able to determine whether they have helped their children to be able to meet the challenges of intimacy, work, and child rearing with creativity and morality. In the work role, older adults can begin to estimate the degree to which their productivity has matched their abilities and the extent to which they have kept up with their private goals for occupational accomplishment.

During later adulthood, the individual is inevitably vulnerable to some degree of discouragement about the limitations of his accomplishments. He must be able to accept the realities that present themselves and to realize that there is a necessary discrepancy between his accomplishments and his goals. The process of accepting one's past life as it has been can be a difficult personal challenge. One must be able to incorporate certain areas of failure, crisis, or disappointment into one's self-image without being overburdened by a sense of inadequacy. One must be able to take pride in areas of achievement, even when those accomplishments fall short of expectation.

There appear to be a number of responses to the challenge posed by this life task. Some adults become extremely depressed in thinking about their past and resign themselves to a future of unhappiness. The illnesses, deaths, and personal crises of their past become dominant preoccupations. No current experiences can quite compensate for a general feeling of discouragement.

Other older adults respond by becoming rigidly self-confident. They see their own life as an example for younger people and are unable to tolerate any implication of failure. Often, in encountering these adults, it may be felt that they have achieved a sense of self-righteousness at the expense of compassion. In order to protect their self-image, they reject all doubts and present an impression of total confidence.

Both of these strategies make it impossible for the older person to change during later adulthood. An alternate type of response would be for the older adult to accept the areas of disappointment or crisis but put them in perspective with his personal achievements. For most adults, this approach would probably result in an overall balance tending toward self-pride but not self-aggrandizement. A more flexible attitude toward one's life history allows one to conceive of new directions for growth and to feel optimistic about the possibility for success in these areas.

In the preceding chapter we discussed the concept of a philosophy of life which emerges as the adult engages the developmental tasks of middle adulthood. It is this unifying philosophy which aids the older adult in coming to terms with his own life accomplishments. Whether it be a religious or personal philosophy, some systematic network of beliefs and values will help the adult to understand the meaning in his own existence, regardless of the nature of his personal achievements. In the realm of accomplishments, few people actually are able to contribute to a significant improvement in the quality of life. Nonetheless, people find value in their own existence by seeing their life as part of some larger, more abstract, and infinite order.

Developing a Point of View about Death

It is inevitable at this stage of life that serious, frightening, and unhappy questions about death will fill the individual's thoughts. For most people, their own stage of middle adulthood is the period when their parents die. During later adulthood, their peers die. These events are sources of psychological stress which involve the adult in the emotional process of grief and mourning, as well as the cognitive strain of trying to accept or understand these deaths.

It would appear that the evolution of a point of view about death requires some capacity to absorb the loss of one's close relatives and friends, as well as the capacity to accept one's own death. We suggest that the former task may be even more difficult than the latter, in that the death of peers begins to destroy the social group of which the adult is a member. Losing one's friends and relatives means a loss of daily companionship, a shared world of memories and plans, and a source of support about values and social norms. The circumstances surrounding the death of others may also prove to be very frightening. One sees people suffer through long illnesses, die abruptly in the midst of a thriving and vigorous life, or die in an absurd, meaningless accident. In each instance, the adult who survives must ask himself about the value of each of these lives and subsequently about the value of his own life. He is also left with a growing set of possibilities about the circumstances of his own death.

Several contemporary works, such as *The American Way of Death,* have pointed out the degree of anxiety and fear that most adults associate with death. The elaborate arrangements for a burial service; a viewing of the body; selection of a coffin or urn, gravestone, or a cemetery site; and provision for care of the grave allow adults to work through the reality of their own death by focusing on aspects of it over which they can have some control. The details of the funeral and the burial may not bring the adult closer to an emotional acceptance of death, but they do give him some feeling of certainty about the events immediately following his death. In fact, some people think of their funeral as a last social statement. All plans surrounding the death are designed to heighten the perception of the individual's social status and moral virtue. The event of death is a direct contradiction to the cultural values of activity, productivity, and individuality. In order to disguise the feeling of death as a final failure, the individual may attempt to maintain an illusion of competence by planning out the circumstances of his funeral.

The development of a perspective about death is a continuous process which begins in childhood and is not fully resolved until later adulthood. The earliest concern with death, during the early-school-age period, reflects an inability to conceive of an irreversible state of lifelessness. By middle-school-age, the child has a rather realistic concept of death but is unlikely to relate that concept to himself or to others close to him (Anthony, 1972).

A person's thoughts about his own death do not become very realistic or focused until sometime during later adolescence. Before that time, the individual has not yet established an integrated identity. Thus, he is unlikely to project himself into the distant future or to conceive of his own mortality. In the process of forming a personal identity, the individual asks questions about mortality, the meaning of life, and the possibility of life after death. During this stage, a point of view about death begins to form. Because the older adolescent is deeply preoccupied with his own uniqueness, he may tend to have a heightened sense of his own importance. He also sees himself at the very beginning of his adult life. At this stage, death may therefore be anticipated with great fear. Some adults never overcome this fear of death, which is associated with a deep narcissism and sense of self-importance.

During early adulthood, intimate personal bonds are formed which are expected to endure. The individuals' concerns about death at this stage include some anxiety about the possible death of the other person and emerging feelings of responsibility for the other person. One's own death has greater consequences once an individual has linked his personal fate with that of another. Thus, a point of view about death must involve some sense of being able to provide for one's partner or to feel confident that they can survive in one's absence. One's view about death broadens from a preoccupation with one's own mortality to an appreciation of one's relationships and interdependencies with other people.

During middle adulthood, people not only recognize that about half of their life has already been lived, but the issue of death becomes increasingly concrete as their parents and older relatives die. At the same time, adults begin to have a larger impact on their families and communities during this stage. Changes in the point of view about death may include a sense of effectiveness and vitality which lessens the threat of death as a blow to narcissism, as well as some discouragement about how little time is allotted for the accomplishment of personal goals. The degree to which an individual gains satisfaction from his own contributions to future generations will determine the extent of his anxiety about death during this stage. Achievement of a sense of generativity should allow him to feel that his impact will continue to be felt even after death.

Ideally, during later adulthood, the presence of ego concerns with respect to death should become minimal. The individual comes to accept his own life as it has been lived and begins to see death as a natural part of the life cycle. Death no longer poses a threat to his value as a person, to his potential for accomplishment, or to his desire to influence the lives of others. As a result of having accepted one's life, one can accept its end without fear or discouragement. This does not imply a willingness to die, but a resignation to the fact of death. The older adult can appreciate that the usefulness of his contributions does not necessarily depend on his physical presence.

Concern about death is a persistent theme throughout the adult years. To some extent, the success with which the individual resolves each psychosocial conflict will determine his resultant point of view about death. One who resolves the crisis of early adulthood in the direction of isolation, for example, would never be able to conceive of the significant impact his own death might have on others. With the successful resolution of the final stage of adult life, the individual becomes more invested in the preservation of a quality of life and less invested in the perpetuation of his own life.

Summary

The three developmental tasks of later adulthood suggest a need for a realistic balance between active engagement and contemplation. Some energy is directed toward experimentation with new roles or elaboration of roles which have had lower priority during the middle adulthood years. The tasks of life acceptance and development of a point of view about death, which stimulate the processes of evaluation and recollection, also require concerted energy. These tasks move the person toward a broader conceptualization of the meaning of life which can accommodate both personal failures and personal successes. Successful accomplishment of the tasks of later adulthood depends on the resilience, openness, and intellectual complexity of the adult.

THE PSYCHOSOCIAL CRISIS

Integrity versus Despair

The end of this final stage of life comes at a different time for each person. It is difficult, therefore, to continue the assumption that the psychosocial crisis is resolved at the end of the stage. Nonetheless, it appears that the attainment of integrity can only come after some considerable thought about one's life meaning. Integrity, as it is used in Erikson's theory, refers to an ability to accept the facts of one's life and to face death without great fear. The older person who has achieved a sense of integrity views his past in an existential light. He appreciates that his life and his individuality are due to an accumulation of personal satisfactions and crises. He can accept this record of events totally, without trying to deny some facts or overemphasize others. Integrity is not so much a quality of honesty and trustworthiness, as we might use the terms in daily speech, but an ability to integrate one's sense of past history with one's present circumstances and to feel content with the outcome.

The opposite pole of this crisis is despair. It is much more likely that adults will resolve the crisis of integrity versus despair in the negative direction than that infants will resolve the crisis of trust versus mistrust in the negative direction. For the infant to experience trust, he must depend on the benevolence of a responsible care-giver who will meet his essential needs. In most cases this care-giver is present, and the infant learns to rely on him or her. The older adult, in order to experience integrity, must incorporate a lifelong sequence of conflicts, failures, and disappointments into his self-image. This in itself is a comparatively difficult process. In addition, the older adult must face some degree of devaluation and even hostility from his social community. The negative attitudes expressed by family members, by colleagues, and by younger people about the incompetence, dependence, or old-fashioned ways of older people may lead many of them to feel quite discouraged about their self-worth. The gradual deterioration of certain physical capacities, particularly the loss of hearing, impaired vision, and limited motor agility, feeds into the older person's sense of frustration and discouragement.

All these factors are likely to create a feeling of regret about one's past and a continuous, nagging desire to be able to do things differently. The individual who resolves the crisis of later adulthood in the direction of despair cannot resist speculating about how things might have been or what he might have done if only conditions were different. Thus, despair makes an attitude of calm resignation about death impossible. Either the individual seeks death as a way of ending a miserable existence, or he desperately fears death because it makes any hope of compensating for past failures impossible.

The Central Process: Introspection

In order to achieve a sense of integrity, the individual must engage in a great deal of deliberate self-evaluation and private thought. The final achievement of a sense of integrity results from an ability to introspect about the gradual evolution of life events and to appreciate the significance of each event in the formation of the adult personality. This state can only be reached through individual effort. One may even have to isolate oneself temporarily, shutting out the influences of potentially competitive or resentful associates.

Of course, the process of introspection will be affected by selectivity of memory, the dominant value orientation, and the general quality of supportiveness or destructiveness in the social milieu. Given these contaminants to a purely objective self-assessment, the individual must engage in repeated soul-searching efforts to sort out his life and to come to terms with some of the discordant events which will inevitably be a part of his history. He must determine whether the essential nature of his personal identity has survived through time. He must evaluate the quality of his close relationships and determine the degree to which he was able to meet the needs of others. He must identify those

contributions that represented a serious effort to improve the quality of life for others. Finally, he must determine the extent to which his philosophy of life has been accurately translated into a pattern of significant actions.

Ultimately, the attainment of integrity is a result of thought. The adult's thoughts about his life will generate a predominant stance toward his feelings of personal contentment and worth. The final outcome of this process of introspection is not a direct translation of the number of positive or negative events in one's life or the number of successes and failures in one's efforts to achieve. There are some adults who have experienced grave lifelong trauma or are seriously physically handicapped and can still maintain an attitude of contentment with their lot in life. On the other hand, there are adults whose life has been comparatively conflict-free who still view their past with great dissatisfaction and resentment. Resolving the conflict of integrity versus despair is a process of achieving an attitude of self-acceptance through private introspection.

Examples

Retirement. Retirement serves to stimulate the adult's introspective capacities. Once the day-to-day preoccupations of the work role are removed, the individual is freer to let his thoughts wander and to begin to focus on personal interests that may not be highly work related. Retirement may spark a number of thoughts about one's work role, job satisfaction, early training, and eventual occupational contributions. In seeking solutions to the problem of how to redirect one's energy after retirement, introspection will focus on one's personal interests and skills, and some evaluation of the available resources for pursuing new directions. Retirement usually means an increase in time that is unscheduled. Much of that time, at least at first, is filled with the private activity of introspection.

For some, the time released by retirement is an unwelcome burden. These adults may not be ready to retire, or they may feel discouraged by the sudden uselessness that accompanies a lack of work. Under these conditions, introspection might be more likely to dwell on the injustice of the retirement regulations, anxiety about how to maintain a certain financial level, and regrets about the lack of personal control one is able to exert in such an essential matter. Most men feel glad to be relieved of the expectation for daily work. Those who do not feel content about this new phase of the life cycle are unlikely to find sources of compensation in their own introspection. Retirement may, in fact, facilitate the development of a sense of despair.

The Role of Grandparent. Most older adults take great satisfaction and pride in their grandchildren. Grandchildren symbolize an extension of personal influence which will most assuredly persist well beyond one's own death. To this extent, grandchildren help older adults to feel more comfortable about their own death. They have concrete evidence that some thread of their life will persist into the future.

Grandchildren also stimulate older adults' thoughts about time, the changing of cultural norms across generations, and the patterning of history. In relating to grandchildren as they grow up, they discover elements of the culture that remain stable. Certain stories and songs retain their appeal from generation to generation. Certain toys, games, and preoccupations of children of the current generation are remembered by grandparents from their own childhoods. On the other hand, grandparents become aware of changes in the culture which are reflected in new child-rearing practices; new equipment, toys, and games designed for children; and new expectations for children's behavior at each life stage. The communication adults maintain with their grandchildren allows them to keep abreast of the continuities and changes in their culture as they are reflected in the experiences of childhood. Through their grandchildren, adults can avoid a sense of alienation from the contemporary world.

Some adults interpret the role of grandparent as that of one who passes on the wisdom and cultural heritage of their ancestry to the children. In the process of fulfilling this role, the older adult must attempt to find meaning in his experiences and to communicate this meaning to children in ways that they can understand. There are many avenues grandparents select in order to educate their grandchildren. Story telling, special trips, long walks, attending religious services, or working on special projects are all activities that allow grandparents some moments of intimacy with their grandchildren. During these times, grandparents can influence the thoughts and fantasies of their grandchildren. The process of educating one's grandchildren involves a deep sense of investment in those experiences and ideals that are believed to be central to a fruitful life.

The many ways in which grandchildren can contribute to a feeling of integrity suggest that the absence of grandchildren, or the failure to establish a relationship with grandchildren, may easily serve as a source of despair for some adults. Many older people who do not have children of their own find surrogate children in whom they can invest their energy. Those who are unable to establish an intimate relationship with any young children may find themselves growing out of touch with the content of contemporary culture and discouraged by the finality of their death.

Reminiscence. As people advance in age, they tend to reminisce about their pasts. This process of nostalgic remembering allows the adult to recapture some of the memorable events in his life history. Reminiscence may serve to increase the adult's feelings of youth, competence, attractiveness, and closeness to others. On the other hand, some adults tend to dwell on sad events and allow earlier disappointments to preoccupy their current thoughts.

The process of reminiscence appears to lend continuity to the older adult's self-concept. He can trace the path of his own development through time and identify moments which are of central importance to the crystallization of his personal philosophy. We see reminiscence as an integrating process which has positive value for an eventual attainment of integrity. In excess, however, reminiscence can dominate reality. In that case, the adult's past life takes precedence over current circumstances. No new events can compete with past memories in engaging the adult's attention and energy. Under these conditions, a realistic acceptance of one's total life history is not possible.

Summary

Retirement and grandparenthood are examples of events in later adulthood which bring about a redirection of energy to new roles. They also can stimulate the adult's thoughts about the meaning of his past life and thereby facilitate work on the achievement of a sense of integrity. Integrity comes about only after extensive introspection and self-evaluation. It includes a cognitive sense of certainty as well as an emotional state of calm acceptance. Despair, on the other hand, is a sense of regret about one's personal history. Given the cultural resistance against aging, it is not difficult to understand why older adults might resolve this final crisis in a negative direction.

INTEGRATION OF RESEARCH FINDINGS

Changes in Cognitive Functions with Aging

Introspection has been identified as the central process in the resolution of the final life crisis, integrity versus despair. In order to appreciate the adult's capacity for introspection, it is necessary to be aware of the characteristics of intellectual functioning that are observed during later adulthood. The adult's memory, his reasoning, his information, his problem-solving abilities, and his mental rigidity or fluidity all influence his capacity to introspect and to assess his past history.

For a long time, psychologists have painted a picture of declining intellectual ability that begins in early adulthood and continues until the end of life (Birren, 1964). This approach is based on an analysis of intelligence test scores which show a pattern of decline from age thirty on. But as Birren himself points out, the definition of intelligence that is used in the design and application of these intelligence tests refers to capacities that are predictive of school-related success. The criteria for assessing adult intelligence are necessarily more heterogeneous than the ability to succeed in the school curriculum.

In attempting to define intelligence in a slightly different way, several researchers have looked at the pattern of productivity in the work setting (Dennis, 1968; Lehman, 1953). Lehman, in examining high-quality production, reported that the decade of the thirties is the peak for productivity of a very high quality. Work which is rated as "worthy" was observed to peak somewhat later and decline gradually. Dennis, in considering total work productivity, identified the decade of the forties as the most productive period. He differentiates patterns of productivity among a variety of professions. Among those he studied, productivity of scholars in the humanities continued at a high level until the seventies, while for those in the creative arts, the decline after forty was comparatively rapid. These data may reflect a pattern of expectations about productivity as well as an indication of intellectual capacity. Those adults who anticipate retirement at age sixty-five would not be likely to invest a great amount of energy in their work as they approach that age.

Kimmel (1974), in his assessment of the fate of intellectual capacities, has identified a number of areas in which decline has been recorded with age. He suggests that older subjects are likely to perform more slowly as a result of slowed reaction time. Referring to Reed and Reitan's (1963) distinction between information and problem-solving ability, he suggests that problem solving declines but information does not. With regard to memory, Botwinick (1967) has described a gradual increase in the number of people whose

TABLE 1

Example of a set of samples permitting all comparisons deducible from the general developmental model.

		TIME OF TESTING 1955	1960	1965
Time of Birth	1910	Sample 3 Age 45	Sample 5 Age 50	Sample 6 Age 55
(Cohort)	1905	Sample 2 Age 50	Sample 4 Age 55	
	1900	Sample 1 Age 55		

Source: K. W. Schaie, "Age Changes and Age Differences," in Bernice Neugarten (ed.), *Middle Age and Aging*, pp. 558–562 (Chicago: University of Chicago Press, 1968).

memories decline at each age level. Botwinick (1970) also suggests that short-term memory is more seriously affected by aging than long-term memory is. Thus, an older person may find it more difficult to store newly acquired information and then retrieve it than younger subjects would. Kimmel identifies a gradual deterioration of the central nervous system at about age sixty or sixty-five which would account for declining intellectual capacity.

A new trend in the research on cognitive capacities during aging has begun to cast doubt on the view that capacities decline with age. Riegel and Riegel (1972) have presented the notion that the older adult group really consists of two distinct subgroups, those who are healthy and will survive and those who are sick and will soon die. Their data indicate that there is rather rapid intellectual decline among people who are nearing death. This decline enables them to predict who, in their sample, is likely to die before the next testing point. The data also suggest that a cross-sectional study of intellectual capacity is contaminated by the inclusion in a single group of those who will soon die and those who will survive. Intellectual functioning appears to remain at a constant level until shortly before the person is going to die, at which point there is a rapid deterioration.

Another approach to the question of intellectual functioning in the aging process

has been taken by Schaie (1965, 1970, 1972, 1973; Schaie and Labouvie-Vief, 1974). In his work, he has tried to take into account the discrepant results of longitudinal and cross-sectional studies of cognitive functioning in the developmental process. Longitudinal studies have generally reported IQ maintenance and, in many cases, IQ gains throughout the life cycle (Bayley, 1968; Bayley and Oden, 1955; Nesselroade, Schaie, and Baltes, 1972; Schaie and Labouvie-Vief, 1974). In contrast, cross-sectional studies have reported patterns of IQ decline (Botwinick, 1967; Horn, 1970; Jones, 1959). Schaie's strategy has been to combine these methods by selecting cohorts of Ss who are compared across age groups at a single point in time and within age groups at two points in time. The research design for this sequential pattern is pictured in Table 1.

The advantage of this method is that it permits taking into account age differences in cognitive functioning that might be due to cultural changes in education, sources of stimulation, or emphases in child rearing rather than to developmental maturation. Kuhlen (1963) has identified a variety of sources of cultural influence which might make comparisons between cross-sectional groups inappropriate. The Schaie model allows for some control on those sources of error in making inferences about the developmental process. This paradigm also permits short-term longitudinal studies of age change with several populations. A comparison of the changes in performance among samples 3, 5, and 6 is a traditional ten-year longitudinal study, while a comparison of changes in performance among samples 1, 2, and 3 is a traditional cross-sectional design. A comparison of samples 1, 4, and 6 allows for generational control, as does a comparison of samples 2 and 5.

In Schaie's most recent research report (Schaie and Labouvie-Vief, 1974), using this combined longitudinal and cross-sectional design, he found patterns which clearly contradict the assumptions about age-related decrement but which add a new dimension of complexity to attempts to summarize the fate of cognitive capacities with age. On some cognitive dimensions, there were stable, developmental increases in performance. On other dimensions, there were clear cohort differences. Ss of the same chronological age performed quite differently, depending on the time of the measurement and the presence of environmental influences which might differentially reinforce or devalue that dimension.

We are left with the conclusion that the pattern of cognitive development is not unidimensional and stable but is subject to the preponderance of environmental influences which might differentially affect adults of different generations. In fact, we may eventually conclude that the generational changes in child rearing, education, nutrition, and occupational training will be most significant determinants of adult intelligence. Attempts to attain a normative pattern of intellectual development during adulthood may result in an awareness of constant cohort differences (Baltes and Labouvie, 1973).

The research in this area has been conducted with the use of traditional intelligence tests which have focused on the assessment of mental abilities. There are other cognitive functions which have been given minimal attention in the study of the aging process. For example, we have identified introspection as a critical intellectual skill which is of heightened importance during later adulthood. At one time, this capacity

represented the primary tool of psychologists for the study of psychic life (James, 1890). The growing interest in cognition has stimulated a new series of efforts to describe the process of introspection and the manner in which introspective knowledge is acquired. (Natsoulas, 1970; Radford, 1974). One aspect of introspective activity has been described by Butler (1968) as the life review. The process Butler discusses involves reminiscence about one's past life. He supports our earlier contention that this review process is a positive and potentially growth-producing activity which helps the older adult to integrate and resolve unresolved conflicts.

Another area of cognitive functioning to which we referred in the chapter on middle adulthood is the capacity for creativity. The necessity for a redirection of energy in later adulthood requires creative problem-solving, particularly with respect to the creation of a facilitative social environment and the structuring of leisure time. Dellas and Gaier (1970), in their review of the literature which attempts to identify creative individuals found no evidence to associate age and creativity. Creative people appear to be differentiated by their style of life rather than by their intellectual abilities. We would expect, then, that an investigation of the development of creative processes in later adulthood would demonstrate the active use of creative thinking in response to the particular tasks which confront the older adult. The use of creativity would most likely be stimulated by the need to redirect energy, the challenge of developing a point of view about death, and the search for personal meaning.

Self-Attitudes of the Aging Adult

Throughout this book we have looked, in detail, at the individual's attitudes toward himself. We have discussed self-esteem, the self-concept, self-evaluation, and self-acceptance. These self-related concepts are central to the gradual evolution of the individual's personality because they capture the ways in which he differentiates himself from others and the degree of satisfaction or tension he experiences with regard to his own personal characteristics. It is crucial, therefore, in trying to appreciate the point of view of the older adult as he faces the challenges of later adulthood, to identify the dominant attitudes he holds which might influence his self-esteem and his self-concept. This final review of research will cover two topics: (1) the patterns of changes in self-esteem that have been observed among older adults, and (2) the sources of self-esteem that are most relevant to the aged.

Changes in Self-Esteem. The research we reported in the previous chapter suggested that older adults tend to feel more satisfied with their marriage and parenting roles, their work accomplishments, and their overall life style than younger adults do (Gurin, Veroff, and Feld, 1960). In a comparison of attitudes of older and younger people toward older people, Streib (1968) has reviewed the results of a number of studies. Several studies examined attitudes toward the older person as a worker. In each of these polls, older people were seen as competent by younger Ss, supervisors, and themselves. Four surveys of adults sixty years of age or over found that the majority of older adults perceive themselves not as "elderly" but as "middle-aged." Streib concludes that neither younger people nor older people have a generally negative attitude toward older adults.

We suggest that the resistance to seeing oneself as elderly implies that respondents are making some distinction between being an older adult who is still active, healthy, and involved (the "middle-aged" older adult) and being one who is irritable, ill, and passive (the "elderly" older adult). Two studies (Jyrkila, 1960, and Busse, 1961) have found that older adults who perceived themselves as "old" were more maladjusted than those who saw themselves as young or middle-aged. In fact, both young and old subjects have negative views about old age (Bennett and Eckman, 1973). Older adults appear to defend against these negative attitudes by identifying themselves as younger. In general, older adults do not identify themselves as members of some devalued minority group. In contrast, Streib's evidence suggests that they may, in fact, be somewhat over-represented in the elite, decision-making groups of their communities.

We would expect, then, that the self-esteem of older adults, particularly those who had resolved the crisis of integrity versus despair, would be high. Two studies of the relationship between self-attitudes and age have bearing here. Mason (1954) compared self-judgments of people over sixty who were institutionalized with those of older people who were living independently. The environmental circumstances were more highly related to feelings of self-worth than was chronological age, *per se.* Mason did find a general expression of negative self-worth, however.

Bloom (1961) asked adult males to respond to an adjective checklist. Self-acceptance was defined by the number of positive adjectives checked, and self-rejection was defined by the number of negative adjectives checked. Bloom reported a curvilinear relationship between self-acceptance and age which indicates that self-acceptance rises between ages twenty and fifty, peaks at fifty, and begins to decline at sixty. According to these studies of self-esteem, the morale of the older adult appears to be rather low. But if this is the case for the fifty and sixty-year-olds, what of those who live to seventy or beyond? Does the sense of discouragement persist throughout the last life stage? Coles (1971), in a review of *American Centenarians,* discusses the basic themes which emerged in interviews with men and women who had reached their 100th birthdays during 1969. These older people demonstrated a calm resignation to the variability and the patterning of life events. Cole describes them as "shrewd and humble." They were not disoriented, dogmatic, or self-righteous. Rather, they appeared to be content with their lot and pleased to have lived so long.

There is the problem here of collecting data from respondents who are at different points in a psychosocial stage and trying to make generalizations about the entire group of subjects at that stage. Two contradictory lines of research must be integrated—one in which older adults express feelings of competence and satisfaction, and another in which adults report feelings of low self-esteem and lack of worth. Those in the age group fifty-five to sixty-five are likely to be experiencing the greatest stress as they cope with physical ailments, retirement, and the newness of feelings of growing old. These subjects are also representative of two groups, the survivors and the nonsurvivors (Riegel and Riegel, 1972), which are likely to differ greatly in self-attitudes. If Bloom's study had included several older age groups, a new positive direction in self-esteem might have been observed. Similarly, if Schaie's model of research on intellectual functioning were applied to personality research, such a design might demonstrate longitudinal increases in self-esteem after sixty-five but cross-sectional decreases due to generational factors. Self-esteem during later adulthood appears to be directly influenced by environmental conditions, particularly health, housing, and companionship, which would have to be controlled in any cross-sectional study.

Fluctuations in self-esteem reflect the individual's conscious awareness of new life tasks which pose serious challenges to his skills. In later adulthood, the individual's capacity to regain a positive feeling of worth depends on the existence of a supportive social environment and the ability to integrate past life events successfully.

Sources of Self-esteem. What are the conditions that support a feeling of life satisfaction in later adulthood? A serious debate has arisen around this question. We will present both perspectives and then offer a synthesis of the problem.

In 1961, Cumming and Henry introduced a theory of adaptation to aging which they called the disengagement process. They argued that as death is an inevitable end, it is to the benefit of both the individual and the society to gradually disengage from social roles and withdraw from social interaction in order to accept this eventuality more easily. Disengagement theory argues that older people who are less invested in their social community, their social relationships, and their social responsibilities will experience higher morale than those who continue to remain involved with their social milieu. Several factors contribute to the gradual diminution of the life space, including retirement, widowhood, the departure of children from the home, and the death of peers. These events stimulate a perception of a limited social context which is responded to by a gradual loss of involvement in these and other relationships. Cumming and Henry describe the aging process as one of increased egocentrism, including a dominance of personal motives, increased expressivity, and declining concern with reality.

A number of social scientists have proposed evidence and theory in opposition to the concept of disengagement. Rose (1968) has suggested three central criticisms of the disengagement theory. First, there is evidence that disengagement represents not a new adaptation during later life but a continuation of a lifestyle. Maddox (1968), in a discussion of activity level and life satisfaction among the elderly, has suggested that individuals who are high or low in activity generally maintain that ranking through repeated observations. Subjects who displayed the disengagement pattern, that is high satisfaction and low activity, were the very oldest ones. Maddox points out that they may have arrived at this pattern through several paths, not just as a new adaptation to old age.

Rose's second criticism of the theory is that adults who are engaged in their social environment experience greater satisfaction than those who are not engaged. Havighurst, Neugarten, and Tobin (1968) have reported an analysis of the Cumming and Henry sample after seven years. This sample consisted of one cohort between the ages of fifty and seventy in 1956, when the first interviews were conducted, and another cohort between the ages of seventy and ninety in 1958, when they joined the study. Havighurst et al. attempted to differentiate between social engagement and psychological engagement. The former refers to activity in daily interactions and in life roles, and the latter to a personal investment in these relationships and a readiness to engage the complexities of social reality. Both of these dimensions were found to decrease with age. This supports the disengagement process. On the other hand, measures of life satisfaction and emotional attitude toward social activity showed that those who are most active are most satisfied, and those who are least active are least satisfied with life. There is no decrease in life satisfaction with age, but a strong expression of regret in the loss of role activity. Thus, older subjects appear to be able to accept their current loss of activity, albeit with some dissatisfaction, and still maintain their overall sense of self-esteem. These data point out the strong value that is placed upon social interaction and role activity among older adults. The fact that they can adapt to a decrease in activity does not support the notion that they wish it, but rather indicates that they can be resigned to it.

The final source of criticism of the disengagement theory Rose proposed is that disengagement may reflect a current condition rather than a psychological necessity. This is the argument to which Rose devotes most of his attention. Many of the cultural conditions which may now serve to force elderly people into a more restricted social environment are likely to change. As the lifespan increases and retirement comes earlier, people in good health will be unwilling to limit their activities severely. Increases in economic security through Social Security legislation will provide the financial resources for continuing participation in social events. New forms of engagement, particularly the political identity of the older adult and interest in cultural, scientific, and artistic hobbies, will serve to replace work as an involving role. All these potential opportunities for the elderly will encourage adults to redirect rather than to disengage their energy.

We see the pattern of life involvement which is observed during later adulthood as the result of personality characteristics, physical limitations accompanying aging, and environmental resources or supports for a particular lifestyle. While the pattern may appear to demonstrate a reduction in social involvement, as in the Cumming and Henry study, this may reflect the particular generational conditions of the elderly subjects in that study which predisposed them to low involvement, as well as the cultural environment which encouraged their withdrawal from social activity.

Another source of self-esteem that has been documented in the literature is the ability to maintain an intimate relationship with another person. In a study of 280 adults aged sixty and older, Lowenthal and Haven (1968) have reported that the ability among the aged to have and maintain a close relationship with a peer is significantly related to the maintenance of high morale, positive psychiatric status, and an absence of depression. Part of the satisfaction of such an intimate relationship most likely derives from the values, experiences, and knowledge shared between the two intimates. Another component of the intimate relationship may well be the sexual intimacy that is experienced. Masters and Johnson (1968) have provided a convincing argument that satisfying, erotic experiences are still possible for seventy- and eighty-year-old adults. The most significant factor for the continuation of sexual satisfaction is the opportunity to maintain sexual activity. Thus, the continuity of an intimate relationship, particularly a heterosexual relationship, can be seen to play a central role in the maintenance of a positive self-attitude.

As Freud once explained in response to a facetious question about the definition of healthy personality, love and work are the two essential components of positive mental health. The aging adult seeks to maintain a personal sense of value through a continuation of intimate bonds with significant others and a redirection of energy to new roles.

Summary

The research on intellectual development and self-attitudes during later adulthood represents a real change in our understanding of the aging process. First, there is strong evidence of intellectual stability rather than decline during later adulthood. Second, adults prefer to remain active in later adulthood, and they value their involvement in the social community. Third, although negative attitudes toward aging persist, older adults resist the implications of those attitudes by denying that they are old.

The research also has significant implications for the models of research on developmental change. The concept of the generational cohort suggests an interaction between developmental age and environmental circumstances which will affect adaptation at each stage. Particularly when biological regularities are less obvious, development proceeds as a response to social expectations, personal proclivities, and situational characteristics.

NEW ROLES FOR OLDER PEOPLE: A MODEL FOR A MULTI-AGE DAY CARE PROGRAM

One of the problems we have identified as a task for older adults is to discover new activities and roles which will substitute for the loss of roles that dominated the middle adult years. The need to retain a sense of effectiveness, status, and usefulness in the community is often frustrated by an inability to identify groups or settings that desire the involvement of the elderly.

A design for a day care center intended to meet the predominant needs of the child during the period of toddlerhood could easily be expanded in order to serve a wider group. School-age children whose parents are at work could go to such a center after school and find comfort, companionship, recreation, and intellectual stimulation. Young adolescents could participate in this kind of center as part of their school curriculum. By accepting responsibility for the continuous care of younger children, they would gain valuable experience in preparation for the adult parenting role, as well as providing a significant service to the community. Older adults also could be encouraged to participate in the day care program

in a variety of capacities. They might be asked to read, play, or talk to a small group of younger children. They might be able to give instruction to older children in skills they had acquired: needlepoint, electronics, horticulture, cooking, and auto mechanics all could be presented to small groups of school-age children through the expertise of the elderly. Older adults might be able to take children for medical appointments away from the center or on short walks, bus rides, and other field trips. If the director of such a center were sensitive to the resources that the older citizens in the community could provide, the center could become a new forum for informal education. Children would have an opportunity to learn from the older, more skilled members of the society some of the time-honored talents and arts of the culture.

There are also many ways in which an intergenerational day care center could meet the needs of adults. They would be able to find peer companionship through their participation in this setting. They would be included in the meals and activities of the center. There might be a center bus that could provide transportation for older participants, as well as for the younger ones. The opportunity to give affection and knowledge to children would most certainly be reciprocated by expressions of warmth and love.

Such a day care program would be a real asset to the psychosocial development of the entire community. Age groups would not be alienated from one another. Children whose parents could not care for them would be given love, care, and perhaps a great deal more stimulation than could be provided at home. Adolescents would learn to anticipate their own future development through interactions with younger children and with older adults. They would be less likely to develop negative stereotypes of the elderly if they observed older adults functioning in competent roles. Finally, older adults would find new ways to contribute to the positive growth of their community through the nurturance and education of young children.

There are some difficulties that would be encountered in involving older adults in such a day care program. First, adults may be reluctant to engage in an activity with younger children, fearing that it would tax their energy, patience, or strength. However, the foster grandparent program and the tutoring of elementary school children seem to have engaged older adults quite successfully. The critical issue would be to allow the adults to set their own limits with regard to the amount of time and the kind of interaction they would be able to engage in. Once the limits are established they should be articulated, so the older person knows when he is expected and the day care staff and the children know when to expect volunteers and how long they will be there.

Second, older adults, particularly men, might find the prospect of participating in a day care program demeaning. They might resist an image of themselves as "babysitters." Community leaders, the center director, and the parents of children who attend it would all have to help affirm the significance of the project and its dependence on the participation of the adult community.

An often unanticipated problem in efforts to involve the elderly is the availability of transportation from home to center. A separate budget item might have to be included for this particular need.

Conflicts in value orientation, intergenerational communication, and authority relations are bound to emerge in such a pro-gram. The director of the center would have to anticipate the presence of conflict and design training sessions with volunteer workers as well as with staff workers. The training sessions would serve two purposes: (1) to provide information about techniques of working with children and ideas for activities, and (2) to allow for the expression of frustration and conflict, if they exist, in order to develop techniques for turning the energy of the conflicts toward constructive rather than destructive goals.

CHAPTER SUMMARY

We hope to have conveyed a sense of the continued potential for growth during this final stage of development. Variability in the patterns of adjustment during later adulthood results from the persistence of personality characteristics and the range of circumstances which can befall an older person. Certain regularities can be anticipated in the termination of old roles and the establishment of new ones. Consolidation of attitudes toward one's own life and toward the reality of one's own death can bring about a new perspective about life and may lead to a more universalistic moral orientation.

The negative circumstances which confront many older adults and the devaluation of the aged in our culture make the

TABLE 2

Summary of chapter.

Developmental Tasks	1. Redirection of energy to new roles and activities
	2. Acceptance of one's life
	3. Developing a point of view about death
Psychosocial Crisis	Integrity v. Despair
Central Process	Introspection
Examples	a. Retirement
	b. The role of grandparent
	c. Reminiscence
Integration of Research Findings	1. Changes in cognitive functions with aging
	2. Self-attitudes of the aging adult
Applied Topic	New roles for old people:
	A model for a multi-age day care program

positive resolution of the psychosocial crisis of this stage quite difficult. Despair may arise from experiences of alienation, illness, helplessness, or poverty, all of which trouble the aging adult. On the other hand, research suggests that most adults maintain their intellectual capacities and their social involvements. Adults are oriented toward personally satisfying strategies to avoid despair and to strengthen their feelings of adequacy. These strategies may include reminiscence, involvement with grandchildren, participation in leisure-time activities, or the creation of new social, political, and professional roles. The experience of growing old will continue to change as the physical, emotional, and educational characteristics of each aged generation changes.

REFERENCES

ANTHONY, S. The Discovery of Death in Childhood and After. New York: Basic Books, 1972.

BALTES, P. B., and LABOUVIE, G. V. "Adult Development of Intellectual Performance: Description, Explanation and Modification." In The Psychology of Adult Development and Aging, edited by C. Eisdorfer and M. P. Lawton, pp. 157–219. Washington, D.C.: American Psychological Association, 1973.

BAYLEY, N. "Cognition and aging." In Current Topics in the Psychology of Aging: Perception, Learning, Cognition and personality, edited by K. W. Schaie, pp. 97–119. Morgantown: West Virginia University Library, 1968.

BAYLEY, N., and ODEN, M. "The Maintenance of Intellectual Ability in Gifted Adults." Journal of Gerontology 10 (1955): 91–107.

BENNETT, R., and ECKMAN, J. "Attitudes Toward Aging: a Critical Examination of Recent Literature and Implications for Future Research." In The Psychology of Adult Development and Aging, edited by C. Eisdorfer and M. P. Lawton, pp. 575–97. Washington, D.C.: American Psychological Association, 1973.

BIRREN, J. E. The Psychology of Aging. Englewood Cliffs, N.J.: Prentice-Hall, 1964.

BLOOM, K. L. "Age and the Self-Concept." American Journal of Psychiatry 118 (1961): 534–38.

BOTWINICK, J. Cognitive Processes in Maturity and Old Age. New York: Springer, 1967.

BOTWINICK, J. "Geropsychology." Annual Review of Psychology 20 (1970): 239–272.

BUSSE, E. W. "Psychoneurotic Reactions and Defense Mechanisms in the Aged." In Psychopathology of Aging, edited by Paul H. Hoch and J. Zubin. New York: Grune & Stratton, 1961.

BUTLER, R. N. "The Life Review: an Interpretation of Reminiscence in the Aged." In Middle Age and Aging, edited by B. L. Neugarten. Chicago: University of Chicago Press, 1968.

COLES, R. "Some Very Old People." Integrated Education: a Report on Race and Schools, September–October, 1971.

CUMMING, E., and HENRY, W. E. Growing Old: the Process of Disengagement. New York: Basic Books, 1961.

DELLAS, M., and GAIER, E. L. "Identification of Creativity: the Individual." Psychological Bulletin 73 (1) (1970): 55–73.

DENNIS, W. "Creative Productivity Between the Ages of Twenty and Eighty Years." In Middle Age and Aging, edited by B. Neugarten. Chicago: University of Chicago Press, 1968.

GURIN, G., VEROFF, J., and FELD, S. Americans View Their Mental Health. New York: Basic Books, 1960.

HAVIGHURST, R. J., NEUGARTEN, B., and TOBIN, S. S. "Disengagement and Patterns of Aging." In Middle Age and Aging, edited by B. Neugarten. Chicago: University of Chicago Press, 1968.

HORN, J. L. "Organization of Data on Life-Span Development of Human Abilities." In Life-Span Developmental Psychology: Research and Theory, edited by L. R. Goulet and P. B. Baltes. New York: Academic Press, 1970.

JAMES, W. The Principles of Psychology. New York: Holt, 1890.

JONES, H. E. "Intelligence and Problem Solving." In *Handbook of Aging and the Individual*, edited by J. E. Birren. Chicago: University of Chicago Press, 1959.

JYRKILA, F. "Society and Adjustment to Old Age." In *Transactions of the Westmarck Society*, vol. 5. Turku: Munksgaard, 1960.

KIMMEL, D. C. *Adulthood and Aging*. New York: Wiley, 1974.

KUHLEN, R. G. "Age and Intelligence: the Significance of Cultural Change in Longitudinal vs. Cross-Sectional Findings." *Vita Humana* 6 (1963): 113–124.

LEHMAN, H. C. *Age and Achievement*. Princeton, N.J.: Princeton University Press, 1953.

LOWENTHAL, M. F., and HAVEN, C. "Interaction and Adaptation: Intimacy as a Ritual Variable." *American Sociological Review* 33 (1) (1968): 20–30.

MADDOX, G. L. "Persistence of Life Among the Elderly: a Longitudinal Study of Patterns of Social Activity in Relation to Life Satisfaction." In *Middle Age and Aging*, edited by B. Neugarten. Chicago: University of Chicago Press, 1968.

MASON, E. P. "Some Correlates of Self-Judgments of the Aged." *Journal of Gerontology* 9 (1954): 324–37.

MASTERS, W. H., and JOHNSON, V. E. "Human Sexual Response: the Aging Male and the Aging Female." In *Middle Age and Aging*, edited by B. Neugarten. Chicago: University of Chicago Press, 1968.

NATSOULAS, T. "Concerning Introspective Knowledge." *Psychological Bulletin* 73 (2) (1970): 89–111.

NESSELROADE, J. R., SCHAIE, K. W., and BALTES, P. B. "Ontogenetic and Generational Components of Structural and Quantitative Change in Adult Cognitive Behavior." *Journal of Gerontology* 27 (1972): 222–28.

NEUGARTEN, B. "The Awareness of Middle Age." In *Middle Age and Aging*, edited by B. Neugarten. Chicago: University of Chicago Press, 1968.

RADFORD, J. "Reflections on Introspection." *American Psychologist* 29 (4) (1974): 245–50.

REED, H., and REITAN, R. "Changes in Psychological Test Performance Associated with the Normal Aging Process." *Journal of Gerontology* 18 (1963): 271–74.

RIEGEL, K. F., and RIEGEL, R. M. "Development, Drop, and Death." *Developmental Psychology* 6 (1972): 306–19.

ROSE, A. M. "A Current Theoretical Issue in Social Gerontology." In *Middle Age and Aging*, edited by B. Neugarten. Chicago: University of Chicago Press, 1968.

SCHAIE, K. W. "A General Model for the Study of Developmental Problems." *Psychological Bulletin* 64 (1965): 92–107.

SCHAIE, K. W. "Age Changes and Age Differences." In *Middle Age and Aging*, edited by B. Neugarten, pp. 558–62. Chicago: University of Chicago Press, 1968.

SCHAIE, K. W. "A Reinterpretation of Age-Related Changes in Cognitive Structure and Functioning." In *Life-Span Developmental Psychology: Research and Theory*, edited by L. R. Goulet, and P. B. Baltes. New York: Academic Press, 1970.

SCHAIE, K. W. "Can the Longitudinal Method be Applied to Psychosocial Studies of Human Development?" In *Determinants of Behavioral Development*, edited by F. J. Monks, W. W. Hartup, and J. de Wit. New York: Academic Press, 1972.

SCHAIE, K. W. "Methodological Problems in Descriptive Developmental Research on Adulthood and Aging." In *Life-Span Developmental Psychology: Methodological Issues*, edited by J. R. Nesselroade and H. W. Reese. New York: Academic Press, 1973.

SCHAIE, K. W., and LABOUVIE-VIEF, G. "Generational versus Ontogenetic Components of Change in Adult Cognitive Behavior: a Fourteen-Year Cross-Sectional Study." *Developmental Psychology* 10 (4) (1974): 305–20.

STREIB, G. "Are the Aged a Minority Group?" In *Middle Age and Aging*, edited by B. Neugarten. Chicago: University of Chicago Press, 1968.

Sex-Role Inconstancy, Biology, and Successful Aging

A Dialectical Model

Jan Dynda Sinnott

Crysee Kline, writing in *The Gerontologist* (1975), made several well-documented points about the existence of role inconstancy during the lifespan of women. She hypothesized that it may be this very inconstancy of roles, rather than constancy of roles, which accounts for women's relative resilience during the role changes of old age. I would like to offer a reply to her article, not to challenge it, but to extend her hypothesis. Kline suggested that women are subjected to repeated role discontinuities and learn to adjust to them, thereby learning to adjust to the discontinuities of aging, too. I would like to suggest, based on a review of the data of others, that a person's ability to show *lifespan variations in sex roles* is an indication of a general flexibility which is associated in some way with more successful aging and a longer lifespan.

There appear to be three possible explanations for this association. First, general survival of the fittest may be the operant dynamic, and the flexible person may also be one of the "fittest." Second, it may be that the generally creative and adaptive person survives, and that sex-role flexibility is but one form of that creativity. Finally, it is possible that the biological, psychological, and cultural tasks and expectations conflict for the older adult; therefore, the older adult who

From *The Gerontologist* 17, 5 (1977), pp. 459–463. Reprinted by permission.

is able to make a behavioral *synthesis*, compromising among these factors, is more likely to survive. I expect that the third explanation will prove to be the most useful and that a thesis-antithesis-synthesis model (Riegel, 1976) holds for the relationship between sex-role flexibility and successful aging. I also believe, with Bem (1975), that the ability to synthesize disparate roles, when the need arises, is an indicator of a general flexibility, adaptivity, or intelligent behavior, which, in turn, is related to successful aging.

BIOLOGICAL, CULTURAL, AND PSYCHOLOGICAL TASKS OF OLDER ADULTS

Today we are willing to ask a complex question: what is the function of sex-role behaviors in the adaption of the species, as well as in the psychological functioning of the individual (Block, 1973; Emmerich, 1973)? From observation, experience, introspection, interviews, and social indicators, it appears that the chief *biological* and *psychological* tasks in old age are: to maintain health; to continue to grow; and to achieve integrity (Erikson, 1968). From a *cultural* point of view, the old individual has a function larger than that of continuing and enhancing his or her own life, and that is to carry on the culture of the group (de Beauvoir, 1973).

This last task was a particularly important function when customs were transmitted orally, and social change was slow. When the older adult's wisdom was coupled with the power of seniority, it saved the individual from a loss of status with the decline of his/her physical abilities. It reduced the conflict between biological and social status. The role or tradition maintained might have little to do with the actual biological or psychological need of the old individual involved. It represented a past value investment, resulting from youthful choices which were once meaningful, *and* from a reduction of the conflict engendered when a physically less productive group member remains alive.

Sex roles seem to be a category of traditions maintained by the old individual in spite of their general lack of relevance. The elder might counsel young males to be aggressive and young females to be submissive because such counsel is consonant with the elder's previous behavior, or because such advice appears useful to the culture. All the while, *that* older adult might be violating the stereotype for very (personally) functional reasons. Meanwhile, that older adult, no longer reproducing or contributing through physical work, is still working toward the good of the group by promoting group values and attitudes.

An additional complication occurs in a fast-changing technological society where custom is less valuable. The most *adaptive* strategy, in this case, would be to achieve a behavioral synthesis in which sex roles change or converge.

DATA RELATING SUCCESSFUL AGING AND SEX-ROLE FLEXIBILITY

We have examined studies dealing with the topics of suicide in middle age, aging and mental health, social expectations, personality and aging, sexuality, and social change. The intriguing trend is that, whatever its genesis, successful aging and an androgynous personality seem to go together in our culture.

One piece of evidence is the analysis of Rorschach responses in old age (Ames, Learned, Metraux, and Walker, 1954). The "normal" subjects' Rorschach profiles were highly individualized and did not manifest sex-role-stereotyped responses to any great degree. But the "pre-seniles," and to a great extent the "seniles," responded in a sex-stereotyped way. Longitudinal follow-ups demonstrated that as normals became seniles, their responses fell into the sex stereotyped pattern.

A second piece of evidence is found in the Reichard, Livson, and Peterson (1962) study of aging and personality. In this study eighty-seven men between the ages of fifty-five and eighty-four were interviewed. Subjects were healthy, middle-class urbanites. After extensive testing, five patterns of adjustment were noted, ranging from *mature* to *self-hating*. The men who were best adjusted manifested both activity and passivity, with neither trait dominating. They reported genuine satisfaction from their work and wanted to maintain independence. They also accepted passivity and had an awareness of their feelings and drives. A nurturing role was acceptable, as was that of nurtured one. Reichard concludes that growing old may make it possible for a man to integrate formerly unacceptable feminine drives into his personality due to changing social expectations. Whatever the dynamic, lessening sex-role differentiation was related to more successful aging.

Another study of personality and aging reported by Williams and Wirth (1965) focused on major life styles of the successfully aging. The characteristics deemed most important to successful aging in *either* women or men were autonomy and persistence (*vs.* precariousness or instability), in both work and family relations. Both sexes were represented by individuals who were successful in old age and who demonstrated active, independent orientations while not neglecting nurturant activities.

In testing middle-aged and old men and women with the TAT, Neugarten and Gutmann (1968) analyzed the perceptions each age and sex group held of traits shown by old men or old women in general. This study and others (Neugarten, 1968) pointed out that older men are expected to be more receptive to affiliative and nurturant impulses as they age, while older women are expected to be more accepting of egocentric and aggressive impulses as they age. To some degree, we see an androgynous sex-role *ideal* which is accepted by many age groups.

When Neugarten, Crotty, and Tobin (1964) classified old men and women into personality types and then related types to life satisfaction, *integrated* men and women were the most satisfied. Integrated men and women combined aggressive and passive-dependent drives, had insight into themselves and their feelings and impulses, and accepted both family and work roles.

Other studies, for example, Britton and Britton (1972) and Jacobson (1974), have obtained similar indications of lessening sex-role differentiation in old age. Finally, Jewett's study (1973) should be mentioned. He investigated the personality traits of especially long-lived individuals. Their longevity was related to the ability to combine independence, interest in work, activity, and strength with adaptability, nurturance, family concerns, and acceptance of emotions.

INTERPRETATION OF THE STUDIES

In spite of some flaws, the studies cited above have been generally accepted as valid by students of aging. The question of cause and effect in studies of personality and longevity is a difficult one. The only statement that can logically be made is that survival and satisfaction in old age are often *concomitant* with adoption of sex roles which combine traits culturally defined as masculine and traits culturally defined as feminine. Perhaps long-lived individuals and those satisfied in old age have always been nonconformist in this respect. Perhaps their sex roles have been modified due to recently changed situational demands, such as children leaving home, retirement, or age status expectations. Mallea-

bility in such basic roles argues that sex roles are, for the most part, learned, and perhaps less central to identity than was expected by earlier theory.

Which of the possible explanations for the association between sex-role flexibility and successful aging received the most support?

The first general approach, i.e., that the "fittest" survive and role flexibility equals fitness, seems to be supported. "Survival" can be conceptualized either as longer life or as a better quality of life. There is evidence in all the studies cited to support the position that sex-role-flexible persons live longer and age more successfully. However, the first approach does little to elucidate the dynamic behind the association.

The second general approach was that the creative, flexible person survives, and that sex-role flexibility is but one form of creativity. There is evidence in the Jewett study that creative older adults also demonstrate sex-role flexibility. The profiles of integrated, peak-living, self-actualizing individuals described by Maslow (1964) include a generalized creativity. However, aging, longevity, and sex-role flexibility were not examined *specifically* in these studies. Barron's (1968) and Arieti's (1976) studies of the creative personality also point to a generalized flexibility and heterogeneity of interests and behaviors in this group. Again, sex-role flexibility is not specifically mentioned and investigated by Barron or Arieti, or by the authors they cite. In the area of cognition and behavioral flexibility, Butler (1973) notes that general flexibility correlates with lack of impairment in old age. It can be hypothesized that the survival value of sex-role flexibility is somehow tied to general creativity and flexibility, a step further toward an understanding of the association between sex-role flexibility and successful old age.

The third possible explanation for the relationship was a more detailed derivation of the second and the first. Biological, psychological, and cultural tasks *conflict* for most older adults; this conflict is apparent in the area of sex roles; the older adult who can arrive at a better synthesis of the conflicting roles and behaviors is creative and flexible and is rewarded by a more successful old age and a longer lifespan. Evidence for the multi-domain conflict surrounding sex-role behaviors and for the co-variance of sex-role flexibility and successful aging was described in the studies cited above. This potential explanation goes furthest in detailing a dynamic underlying this and other adaptive behaviors, and is easiest to operationalize and test.

Riegel (1976) has described the thesis-antithesis-synthesis model which underlies this third explanation. He has also (1975) shown how the dissonance between the biological, psychological, cultural, and environmental demands on a person can lead to adult conflict, and possibly to growth. Other existing theories of lifespan personality development (Looft, 1973) have been unable to incorporate so many varied aspects of adult life in this coherent way. In terms of this model, the older person's biological needs would most likely be congruent with *equivalent* male/female roles, and psychological needs with *disparate* male/female roles. Cultural needs would be congruent with *disparate* male/female roles (in a slowly changing traditional culture) or with *equivalent* roles (in a culture moving toward androgeny as an ideal). To reach a complex role which synthesizes these needs and responses and situational expectations can be a difficult growth experience, associated (direction of causality unknown) with successful aging and longevity when it does lead to growth.

Many views of development in older adults implicitly use this model. When Erikson (1968) speaks of crisis resolution leading to development, he appears to be describing a similar model. Clayton (1975) goes on to interpret Erikson's "crisis" as compromise, precisely what is involved in obtaining one type of *synthesis*. The older individual must successfully *combine* the activities and demands of a lifetime into a congruent whole.

In the area of lifespan sex-role development, Hefner, Rebecca, and Oleshansky (1975) speak of three stages which appear to utilize this model of thesis-antithesis-synthesis: global roles; polarized roles; and tran-scendent roles. These authors, however, do not look at sex-role development from all three *functional* points of view (biological, psychological, cultural) as we have done. Even less dialectical is Bem's (1974) model of androgynous behavior.

It may prove worthwhile to examine Riegel's (1975) model for its utility in examing adult growth *and* adult sex-role development. Successful achievement of synthesis in either or in both may predict successful aging and longevity.

The relationship between androgyny and successful aging appears to be part of a larger pattern of increasing and decreasing sex-role differentiation at points in the lifespan. At birth, the individual behaves androgynously. Sex roles diverge in middle childhood, converge again in the working period of the early twenties, and diverge again during the childraising period. When children have grown, roles again *converge*. This changing lifetime pattern suggests that sex roles are not central to identity and that the adaptive individual usually functions with the ability to modify sex roles and other roles when needed. Block (1973) notes that the most complex stages of Kohlberg's model of moral reasoning, and of Loevinger's model of ego development, among others, delineate behavior that can be characterized as androgynous. She suggests that the individual's integration of sex-role behaviors represents a more advanced level of development. Older adults' behavior helps confirm her point of view.

Why might behavior demonstrating sex-role flexibility *lead* to a more successful long lifespan? Probably, it meets the biological needs of the individual, provides for psychological continuity, and does not antagonize the dominant culture. The normal, healthy (adaptive) old person, manifesting a combined male/female role, is most likely an individual who has incorporated *all* the major values of his or her culture. On the other hand, the pre-senile or nonadaptive old person, manifesting stereotyped masculinity/femininity like that of early childhood, appears to be less flexible, more rigid, and focused on atypical values and behaviors in the culture.

NEED FOR DIRECTED STUDIES

Although we do not know the genesis of the apparent merging of sex roles with age, we have seen some evidence that it does occur and that it does relate to successful aging. The need to study masculinity and femininity, lifespan identity, and the dialectical processes is clear.

Examination of the behaviors of *unsuccessful* aging in the studies cited above tends to confirm that divergent sex roles in old age relate to less successful aging. Many questions arise. To what extent do counselors, clinicians, social workers, and others consider nonstereotyped sex-role behavior deviant in older adults? What effect does this role convergence have on the generally accepted definitions of masculinity and femininity? How integral are sex roles to life-span identity? Is there a developing androgyny for all aging cohorts? Further directed research will answer these questions.

NEED FOR PROGRAM CHANGES

Program changes would concern being aware of role flexibility, or promoting it.

Multidimensional counseling can be made the rule. Biological needs, psychological needs, and cultural forces can be explicitly taken into account in resolving conflicts and in teaching conflict synthesis. Counselors can be made wary of traditional masculinity/femininity scales in tests they might use for assessment, bearing in mind that the scales were developed and scored for younger persons of a given cohort.

Recreation programs offered for older adults can be made much more heterogeneous with respect to sex roles implicit in them. Activities suggested to women and men should be representative of a wide nonstereotyped range of interests. Those working

with the older person could be encouraged to respect the integrity of the person who goes outside the bounds of behaviors stereotypically appropriate for his/her sex and to avoid suggesting that such behavior is abnormal. Some training of the media would be necessary here.

Finally, younger adults might be taught while still in school to think in terms of the roles they will play in later life. It can be pointed out to them that their identity need not rest on certain roles and invariant behavior, but can successfully incorporate many changes in those roles and behaviors.

CONCLUSION: SUPPORT FOR AN EXTENSION OF KLINE'S HYPOTHESIS

The blurring of distinctions between "male" and "female" roles in old age appears to be related to successful aging. Kline argued that practice in role inconstancy was related to successful aging. Anticipating longitudinal and cross-sequential data, I suggest that role flexibility is a sign of a generalized trait, such as adaptivity or intelligence in a broad sense, which, in turn, is related to successful aging and adult development. This trait is an indication that the adaptive older adult can create a meaningful, functional synthesis from conflicting biological/psychological/cultural demands and behaviors. Those who work with older adults can be made aware of the utility of this role flexibility.

REFERENCES

AMES, L. B., LEARNED, J., METRAUX, R., and WALKER, R. *Rorschach Responses in Old Age.* New York: Hoeber, 1954.

ARIETI, S. *Creativity, the Magic Synthesis.* New York: Basic Books, 1976.

BARRON, F. *Creativity and Personal Freedom.* Princeton: Van Nostrand, 1968.

BEM, S. "Measurement of Psychological Androgyny." *Journal of Clinical and Consulting Psychology,* 42 (1974): 155–162.

BEM, S. "Sex Role Adaptability: One Consequence of Psychological Androgyny." *Journal of Personality and Social Psychology*, 31 (1975): 634–643.

BLOCK, J. "Conceptions of Sex Role: Some Cross-Cultural and Longitudinal Perspectives." *American Psychologist*, 28 (1973): 512–526.

BRITTON, J., and BRITTON, J. *Personality Changes in Aging*. New York: Springer, 1972.

BUTLER, R., and LEWIS, M. *Aging and Mental Health*. St. Louis: Mosby, 1973.

CLAYTON, V. "Erikson's Theory of Human Development as It Applies to the Aged: Wisdom as Contradictive Cognition." *Human Development, 18 (1975): 119–128.*

DE BEAUVOIR, S. *The Coming of Age.* New York: Warner Paperback Library, 1973.

EMMERICH, W. "Socialization and Sex Role Development." In *Lifespan Developmental Psychology: Personality and Socialization,* edited by P. Baltes and K. Schaie. New York: Academic Press, 1973.

ERIKSON, E. *Identity, Youth and Crisis.* New York: Norton, 1968.

HEFNER, R., REBECCA, M., and OLESHANSKY, B. "Development of Sex-Role Transcendence." *Human Development* (1975): 143–158.

JACOBSON, O. "The Effects of Selected Personal-Social Factors on Cognitive Functioning in the Aging." Doctoral dissertation, Catholic Univ. America, microfilm No. 74-19, 292, from University Microfilms, Ann Arbor, 1974.

JEWETT, S. "Longevity and the Longevity Syndrome." *Gerontologist*, 13 (1973): 91–99.

KLINE, C. "The Socialization Process of Women." *Gerontologist*, 15 (1975): 486–492.

LOOFT, C. "Socialization and Personality Throughout the Life-Span: An Examination of Contemporary Psychological Approaches." In *Lifespan Developmental Psychology: Personality and Socialization,* edited by P. Baltes and K. Schaie. New York: Academic Press, 1973.

MASLOW, A. *Religions, Values, and Peak Experiences.* Columbus: Ohio State University Press, 1964.

NEUGARTEN, B. (ed.) *Middle Age and Aging.* Chicago: University of Chicago Press. 1968.

NEUGARTEN, B., CROTTY, G., and TOBIN, S. "Personality Types in an Aging Population." In *Personality in Middle and Late Life,* edited by B. Neugarten, Englewood Cliffs, New Jersey: Prentice-Hall, 1964.

NEUGARTEN, B., and GUTMANN, D. "Age-Sex Roles and Personality in Middle Age: A Thematic Apperception Study." In *Middle Age and Aging,* edited by B. Neugarten. Chicago: University of Chicago Press, 1968.

REICHARD, S., LIVSON, F., and PETERSON, P. *Aging and Personality.* New York: Wiley, 1962.

RIEGEL, K. F. "Adult Life Crises: A Dialectical Interpretation of Development." In *Life-Span Developmental Psychology: Normative Life Crises,* edited by N. Datan and L. Ginsberg. New York: Academic Press, 1975.

RIEGEL, K. F. "The Dialectics of Human Development." *American Psychologist*, 31 (1976): 679–700.

SHIELDS, S. "Functionalism, Darwinism, and the Psychology of Women: A Study in Social Myth." *American Psychologist*, 30 (1975): 739–754.

WILLIAMS, R., and WIRTH, C. *Lives Through the Years.* New York: Atherton Press, 1965.

Individual Adaptation in the Middle Years

Developmental Issues in the Masculine Mid-Life Crisis

David Gutmann

CRISIS AND GROWTH

Used together, the two words "male" and "mid-life" have come to imply a third term, "crisis." A crisis of some proportion—at times verging on the lethal—is presumably the mid-life norm for American men. This crisis is generally conceived in depletion terms: physically, as loss of health and vitality; socially, as loss of career opportunities; existentially, as confrontation with death, with finitude, with the sense that final choices have been made and that these are irreversible. For example, in his summary of mid-life crisis theories, Brim (1974) cites this poignant statement: "the hormone production levels are dropping, the head is balding, the sexual vigor is diminishing, the stress is unending, the children are leaving, the parents are dying, the job horizons are narrowing, the friends are having their first heart attacks; the past floats by in a fog of hopes not realized, opportunities not grasped, women not bedded, potentials not fulfilled, and the future is a confrontation with one's own mortality."

Along the same lines, sociologist Michael Farrell and his colleagues (1975) blame the middle-age crisis, particularly among blue collar men, to failures in their work life: there is a loss of job satisfaction and reduced opportunity to find better employment.

From *Journal of Geriatric Psychiatry* 9, 1 (1976), pp. 41–59. Reprinted by permission.

"They find their jobs unsatisfying," Farrell explains, "and they have nowhere to go with their problems. They have less information about the options open to them than middle- and upper-class men do, and even if they had this knowledge, they wouldn't have the financial or educational resources to make sure of such opportunities." Subjects in the age range thirty-eight to forty-eight are beset by other depletions as well: "By this time a man's kids may have started to leave him, causing him to question his reasons for sticking to his marriage or job. His career has usually reached a point where reality spoils his earlier dreams of glory. His parents may die, or require care, raising thoughts of his own advancing age and mortality" (Farrell et al., 1975).

These work related, somatic, and existential depletions can have unconscious as well as conscious reverberations, and revive early fears. Blacker (1974) cites the psychoanalytic literature on this life period: "The usual psychological explanation given for the middle-aged man's distress is related to his concern about decreasing physical powers and sexual potency due to aging. This decrease is said to rekindle fear of castration, and to assuage this fear the male reasserts his masculinity through sexual conquest."

There is much truth in all of this, but the *exclusive* emphasis on deprivation and depletion may be inaccurate, and needlessly depressing. After all, although middle-age, like other major life periods, may imply phase-specific problems and losses, a crisis is not necessarily a disaster, or even a prelude to disaster. In medical practice, "crisis" implies that period during which the issue is in doubt: the patient may get better or he may die; and there are as yet no clear indications toward either outcome. In the more general sense, a crisis period defines the time frame within which familiar opportunities are indeed receding, but also one in which new alternatives—in the world, in the self, or in both—are emerging. That which is novel is always dubious; the sense of crisis may reflect fear of that which is strange, as well as grief over the familiar securities that are being lost. New thoughts, new desires, even new capacities threaten the existing self-establishment; and these may initially be regarded as a threat even though they may actually portend, in their developed form, an expansion of self. A true crisis resolution is achieved when new possibilities, recognized as such, become part of the framework of the self and/or its psycho-ecology.

It is in this more developmental sense that I will discuss the masculine mid-life crisis, viewing it as a time of both inner and outer change, during which energies tied to pre-existing structures are released, with constructive or destructive consequences, depending on the individual's personal and cultural circumstances.

PSYCHOLOGICAL DEVELOPMENT IN LATER LIFE

The developmental dynamisms of middle life can only be identified through comparative, cross-cultural work. Studying these in one society, we cannot disentangle nature from nurture, developmental imperatives from the social circumstances in which they are enacted. Observed in one culture, developmental *causes* can be misread as *consequences* of social pressures. Developmental imperatives can only be highlighted when

we look across societies, varying culture while holding age constant. Those regularities in individual lives that continue to emerge despite the widest possible variation in social circumstances can then logically be referred to as developmental influences.

These intrinsic, nonsituational dimensions of middle and later life have been brought into focus by my cross-cultural studies among various preliterate and agrarian groups: the traditional Navajo of Arizona, the Lowland and Highland Maya of Mexico, and the Druze of the Middle East. I have used open-ended interviews and projective techniques among the middle-aged and older men of these groups, with the aim of establishing some basis for a comparative psychology of aging. In this paper some central findings will be illustrated with TAT data. In addition, the phenotypic outcomes of interaction between developmental processes and particular cultural circumstances will be discussed. Hopefully, this brief review will justify some reasonable optimism concerning the potential benefits for men who successfully transit the mid-life period.

The data pertaining to psychological changes in middle and later life for both men and women have been reported in greater depth elsewhere (Gutmann, 1964, 1969, 1974). To repeat, these changes appear to be developmental in nature in that they occur in predictable sequence across disparate cultures. We find that, by contrast with younger men, older men are more interested in love than in conquest or power, more interested in community than in agency. The younger men see energy *within* themselves as a potential threat that has to be contained and deployed to productive purposes. But the older men see energy as *outside* of themselves, lodged in capricious secular or supernatural authorities. For older men, then, power must be manipulated and controlled in its external form through prayer and other forms of supplication and accommodation. In sum, younger men are businesslike; they do not go out of their way to seek pleasure, nor do they avoid necessary discomfort. They seek pleasure mainly in sex, after working hours, and even their sexual pleasures may have a productive goal: in scarcity societies they ultimately serve procreation, the production of sons who will aid the father in his work and will be his social security in old age.

Older men, by contrast, are more diffusely sensual, more sensitive to the incidental pleasures and pains of the world. Unlike the "phallic" young men, the older men seek pleasure in the pregenital direction; they become particularly interested in food, pleasant sights, sounds, and human associations. Where younger men look at the world instrumentally, older men take some incidental bonus of aesthetic pleasure from their daily routines.

We also find, across a wide range of cultures, that women age psychologically in the reverse direction. Even in normally patriarchal societies, women become more aggressive in later life, less sentimental, and more managerial—they become *less* interested in communion and *more* turned toward agency. Thus, over time and across sex lines a massive transcultural involution takes place: during the post-parental years the husband comes to be more dependent on the wife; he tends to defer to her wishes and requirements, acting toward her as he does toward other sources of security in his life. The older wife becomes something of an authority to the husband; and through these various sex-role changes the normal androgyny of later life is ushered in.

These interage and intersexual developments are best illustrated through reviewing some revealing responses to the "heterosexual" card of the standard TAT, a stimulus used in its original form at all sites. This card, which shows a young man half turned away from a young woman who reaches towards him in a restraining or pleading manner, provides further evidence of the shift from exuberant and outward directed male aggression toward more security seeking, receptive stances.

As Table 1 indicates, younger men— urban American, Mayan, Navajo, or Druze— propose that the young man brushes aside a beseeching or timorous woman and forges out into a dangerous but exciting world of combat, carousing, and mistresses. For younger respondents, the sexes are sharply distinguished: the young man pushes toward some extradomestic periphery without much regard for consequences; inhibition and timidity are mainly located in the woman. But to the *same stimulus* older men propose more anergic, constricted or "pre-genital" themes. In their version, the young woman tends to domineer, or the male protagonist retreats back to her consolation and away from a world in which he has known danger and defeat. In either case, initiative and strength have migrated away from the young man toward the young woman. Finally, for many older men, the male protagonist does not reject the nurturance offered by the young woman but instead dwells with her in a happy, seamless harmony. Potential trouble comes from outside, not within, the dyad and menaces the young man and woman equally.

These age shifts appear to be developmental rather than secular in nature and thus appear with some predictability across a panel of disparate cultures where the drift of generational, cultural change has been different in each case. Within cultures, these changes in sex-role perceptions show up in longitudinal as well as cross-sectional data. When the same "heterosexual" card is shown after a five-year interval to the Navajo and Druze respondents who first reacted to it at time 1, the results are as shown in Table 2: though some "passive" interpretations of the "heterosexual" card have dropped out by time 2 in favor of more active images of the younger man figure, a far greater number of passive images and themes have appeared *for the first time*, replacing more active imagery, by time 2. Clearly, then, the original age X theme distributions of responses to this card reflect psychological changes *within* individuals, and not intercohort differences having to do with generational contrasts in the various cultures. Thus, as they age, men are increasingly prone to assign dominance to the female figure, and to see the younger man as

TABLE 1

The "Heterosexual-Conflict" card: Distribution of stories by age, culture, and theme.

		35–49	50–59	60+
1. Male initiative and dominance: Young man's intrinsic sexual, aggressive, and autonomy needs constitute a problem for a gentle, nurturant young woman and potential danger for himself.	Kansas City	21	12	10
	Navajo	9	7	9
	Lowland Maya	4	1	2
	Highland Maya	2	—	—
	Druze	20	13	7
		56	33	28
2. Domestic problems: Conflict centered around young man's aggression, but direction, scope, cause, or outcome of this aggression is unclear.	Kansas City	1	3	—
	Navajo	4	4	4
	Lowland Maya	7	5	7
	Highland Maya	—	2	1
	Druze	8	8	8
		20	22	20
3. Female initiative and dominance: Young man's anger is reactive to young woman's rejection of him or dominance over him.	Kansas City	6	5	6
	Navajo	—	3	9
	Lowland Maya	7	5	7
	Highland Maya	—	2	1
	Druze	5	4	8
		18	19	31
4. Rationalized male succorance: Menaced by external forces or defeated in his outerworld achievement strivings, the young man looks for or accepts female nurturance and control.	Kansas City	—	1	4
	Navajo	—	1	12
	Lowland Maya	—	1	2
	Highland Maya	1	—	2
	Druze	18	5	22
		19	8	42
5. Untroubled affiliation (or syntonic dependency): Mild, untroubled affiliation between relatively undifferentiated young man and woman.	Kansas City	—	—	—
	Navajo	1	6	6
	Lowland Maya	3	7	12
	Highland Maya	8	3	3
	Druze	11	9	32
		23	25	53

Kansas City	N = 69	N +	136	107	174
Navajo	N = 75				
Lowland Maya	N = 70	+ Chi square (of cell totals) = 42.165,			
Highland Maya	N = 25	df = 8, p < .001			
Druze[a]	N = 178				
Total	N = 417				

[a] Druze group includes Golan (Syrian), Galilean, and Carmel (Israeli) Druze.

her satellite; this intrapsychic change proceeds independently of culture.

The same sex-role turnover is dramatically captured by another card, used among the Druze, which for most subjects elicits concerns around intergenerational and intermale relations and lines of authority. The stimulus depicts what appears to be an older man, arm outstretched, approaching a group of two smaller individuals, usually perceived

TABLE 2

Longitudinal changes in TAT imagery of Navajo and Druze subjects elicited by "Hetero-sexual-Conflict" card.

	NUMBER OF PASSIVE IMAGES DISCARDED IN FAVOR OF MORE ACTIVE IMAGERY AFTER TIME 1[a]			NUMBER OF PASSIVE IMAGES APPEARING ONLY AT TIME 2		
	NAVAJO	DRUZE	TOTAL	NAVAJO	DRUZE	TOTAL
Male aggression in reaction to female dominance	3	1	4	8	3	11
Man is inactive; woman is active and/or dominant	2	2	4	4	7	11
Man and woman react similarly to troubling or pleasant scene	3	2	5	5	7	12
Man is sick; woman is his nurse, or is concerned about him	1	3	4	6	4	10
Man is tired or old (woman may be his daughter)	1	2	3	2	5	7
Man and woman like or love each other. No conflict or role distinctions	1	9[b]	10	8	4	12
	Total number of passive images discarded by Time 2 30			Total number of new passive images by Time 2 . . . . .63[c]		

[a] Time 1 to Time 2 interval is four years in the Navajo case and five years in the Druze case. The Galilean and Carmel Druze, but not the Golan Druze, were reinterviewed for the Time 2 study.
[b] Two thirds of the Druze reversals in this category toward more "active" imagery occur among men younger than age sixty-five; three-fourths of the new perceptions of an affiliative and undifferentiated couple occur in men aged sixty-five and over.
[c] These are not independent entries. A single story may be entered under more than one heading.

as young males. Almost invariably, Druze men below age sixty see the card as depicting boys or younger men. However, a number of men over sixty see the older man as a beggar, asking for food or money from a *woman*, who may or may not indulge him. Again, the tendency to turn a compliant young man into a dominant woman and to turn an authoritative old man into a beggar is not a cohort phenomenon, limited to a particular generation of Druze men; longitudinal studies with this card reveal that nine Druze, all but one over sixty, who saw the older man as an authority at time 1 see him as a beggar at time 2. This intra-individual shift is all the more striking in that Druze values favor fierce self-reliance, and Druze mores do not permit begging for *any* age group, particularly not for the elderly guardians of the society's religion and traditions.

These findings in regard to age shifts in fantasy are in general confirmed by those anthropologists who study more overt and public behavior. In fact, Gold (1960) asked some twenty-six anthropologists, varied in their theoretical interests, to report on *any* age-related changes in sex role in the very different groups with which they had worked. Fourteen out of twenty-six reported a shift, in most cases unofficial (not registered in the formal rules of the society), toward greater female dominance in later life. The remainder reported no change; but in *no* case did the balance swing toward greater male authority over the wife with advanced age. The transcultural consensus is dramatically summed up by a Moroccan parable, which holds that each man is born surrounded by 100 devils, and each woman by 100 angels. However, with each passing year, a devil is exchanged for an angel, so that when he reaches 100 years of age, the man is entirely surrounded by angels, and the woman by devils.

Apparently, then, there is a comprehensive developmental event of middle and later life, involving strongly-bonded mates, that acts to reverse or at least equalize the domestic status of the partners, and tends to redistribute the so-called "masculine" and "feminine" traits among them. This sex-role involution proceeds simultaneously within two individuals who comprise a unified field in regard to this comprehensive developmental sequence. We are not speaking of related but separate developmental events in men and women; in this case, each partner appears to be the context for a symmetrical, developmental change within the other.

Any developmental pattern, such as the sex-role involution of later life, is an *evolved* outcome; as such, it is an adaptation toward species survival. A species persists through *parenting*, through the procreation of viable children, who will in their turn grow to be the parents of viable children. Human parenthood and adulthood are roughly coterminous; by considering the requirements of human parenthood, and the division of labor set by those requirements, we may understand the dynamisms that bring about the sharp sex distinctions of young adulthood, as well as the reversals toward androgyny in later adulthood and old age.

SEX ROLES AND THE PARENTAL EMERGENCY

I have recently proposed (Gutmann, 1975) that the onset of parenthood constitutes a normative crisis for men and women, a period of chronic emergency based on children's vital needs for emotional as well as physical security. Under the average expectable species condition of scarcity and hardship, the forms of sustenance required by children are mutually exclusive; they cannot be adequately provided by the same parent. Sex roles thus reflect a basic division of responsibilities, centered not around some male need to dominate, or around female masochism, but around the survival needs of offspring, of the sort recognized by most subsistence-level groups.

Murdock's (1935) survey of 224 preliterate, agrarian societies indicates that any activities requiring a protracted absence from the home—hunting, trapping, herding, and deep-sea fishing—are almost exclusively performed by males. It is not the capacity for hard labor that discriminates the sexes, but the *site* at which the work is performed. Women can work, often harder than men, at domestic labor, but the military activities that secure the domestic area, as well as extra-domestic forays, are universally the province of men. Young fathers provide physical security to their dependents by leaving home. These sex-linked potentials toward male boldness and female domesticity have to be structuralized long before the onset of parenthood by socialization practices that begin in early childhood.

Barry, Bacon and Child (1957) present data from 110 subsistence societies confirming that self-reliance is routinely fostered in young boys, while nurturance and even dependency are fostered in young girls. These complementary but distinct potentials are mobilized by the onset of parenthood, and in response to this formidable stimulus, the standard reaction for each sex is to surrender to the other the qualities that would interfere with the provision of their special mode of security. Male providers of security give up the dependency needs that would interfere with their courage and endurance in the campaign, hunt, or voyage. Instead they live these out vicariously, through identification with the spouse and children who are the recipients of their nurturance. The wife and children become external representations of the "passive" yearnings that the father must give up in order to provide physical security to others. By the same token, the wife concedes to her husband, and sends out of the house with him, the aggression that could alienate her male provider or that could emotionally damage her vulnerable and needful child. In effect, each sex lives out, through the other, those closeted aspects of their nature that could interfere with adequate performance in their version of the parental role, and that could be lethal to their children.

However, as children take over the responsibility for their own security (and even for the security of their younger siblings), the chronic sense of parental emergency phases out, and the psychological structures established by men and women in response to, and validated by, this crisis are in effect dismantled; then the sex-role reversals that shape our transcultural data occur. Both sexes can then afford the luxury of living out the potentials and pleasures that they had to relinquish earlier in the service of their particular parental assignment. Consequently, as we have seen, there is a mid-life turn toward androgyny, wherein men begin to live out directly and to own as part of themselves those "feminine" qualities—passivity, sensuality, tenderness—previously repressed in the name of exploitation and production. And we find the opposite effect in women: they generally become managerial, achievement oriented, and relatively tough minded, taking over the "masculine" qualities that men surrender. In effect, "masculine" and "feminine" qualities are disturbed not only by sex but by life periods. Men are not forever "masculine"; rather, they can be defined as the sex that shows "masculine" traits before the so-called "feminine" pattern emerges. The reverse is true for women.

In sum, the particular constellations we associate with maleness and femaleness may not pertain to biological sex as much as to parenthood. They lose their distinctness and gender specificity as the psychic structures predicated on and sustained by parenthood are phased out, with varying consequences for men and women.

CULTURE AND DEVELOPMENT IN LATER LIFE

Cultural factors play an important role in mediating between developmental genotypes and phenotypic outcomes of these transformations. Thus, in various traditionalist societies older men gain prestige precisely *because* of the so-called passive tendencies released by their withdrawal from production and parental tasks. Though religious doctrines vary across cultures, the vast majority of folk societies institutionalize the belief that life-sustaining or life-destroying powers originate not in the mundane community, but in the various domains of supernatural power surrounding the community. The power brokers who man the sacred perimeter of the community must, in their own persons, be metaphors of the "good" power that they bring into the pragmatic community so as to sustain their people and ecosystem. Róheim (1930) cites much data from preliterate societies confirming that the power broker typically exhibits abasive and even masochistic behavior before the gods. The gods are arrogant; therefore, the man who would receive their power must approach them as a supplicant rather than as a Promethean rival. Accordingly, in the traditional and religious communities it is the older men, cleansed of sex and aggression, humble in bearing, who intercede for the good influences of the gods, without offending the divinity. The folk culture transforms the older man's passivity and "femininity" into the very pivot of his renewed identity and social power.

In these folk-traditional settings, the psychic contents released by the developmental process of later life are socially *sponsored*, transformed from ego potentials into ego executive capacities. The human ego and the forms of the small, face-to-face society are the products of a conjoint evolution; predictably then, the social age-grading of the life cycle in these societies is isomorphic with the sequential patterning of human potentials from birth to death. In these societies, as Erikson (1959) has shown us, the human ego and its psychosocial ecology are metaphors and extensions of each other.

However, the umbilical connection between the structures of the ego and the institutions of society breaks down in impersonal, urbanized, and technocratic cultures. These societies generate their own power; they require no aging heroes to neutralize and transform the awful powers of the supernatural. In the folk society the old man who is too weak to work can still be a link to the awesome *mana* of the gods, but in the secular society the unproductive older man is in danger of losing his *raison d'être*. Lacking the traditional armature, the sense of vital connection to a transhuman order, our achievement centered society cannot recognize, use, or validate the more sentient contents of the male psyche as they move towards more overt expression in middle and later life. Older women often discover new bursts of vitality, ratified by social opportunity—the "second life" of which Benedek (1952) has written. But for males the new and potentially refreshing contents of the psyche are more apt to become the pivot of crisis and of pathology.

PATHOLOGY: THE FUNCTIONAL EQUIVALENT OF CULTURE

The crisis of the middle-aged urbanized man is exacerbated by corresponding changes in the aging wife. In his earlier years, the husband can externalize and live out the discrepant, "feminine" side of his own nature through indulging and sponsoring his wife's femininity. But as women become more assertive, and eschew the more submissive role toward men, the aging husband loses this "projective ecology." He begins to sense—usually with some discomfort—that so-called feminine traits are a feature of his own internal landscape, and not exclusive to his wife.

The older traditionalist who faces a newly "liberated" wife can find other, circumscribed religious arenas in which to live out his growing passive-dependent tendencies. His dealings with God are usually private, and in any case God's omnipotence justifies quite completely the abasement of a mere human. The aging traditionalist can thus indulge the bisexuality of later life without shame, and he need not make some final choice between the active and passive, the "masculine" and "feminine" sides of his nature.

In contrast, the middle-aged and middle-class American male, whose wife is no longer willing to provide a "projective ecology" for his own feminine potentials, cannot easily find some conventional substitute. He either comes to terms with his own bisexuality—a resolution that is at best difficult in a culture that puts a high premium on "masculine" virtues—or he resorts to pathologic solutions. The older traditionalist can manage his "femininity" through externalization, by assigning responsibility for his dependent feelings to God. But the middle-aged American, who lacks the conventional institutions to sponsor, justify, and use his passivity, must often re-externalize such tendencies via symptomatic routes. He therefore often expresses the sexual bimodality of his nature through idiosyncratic, symptomatic forms that serve to gratify, externalize, and at the same time deny the closeted yearnings unacceptable to a proper man.

Alcoholism, which has been identified as one of the chief syndromes of middle life, serves these multiple functions very well. On the one hand, as McClelland and his associates (1972) have shown us, strong drink is instant *machismo*, concretized (or liquefied) male power. Liquor releases inhibitions on aggression and is accordingly confounded—as "fire water"—with the energy it sponsors. On the other hand, drinking is an oral activity, a recapitulation of infantile modes (the drinkers sucks in male strength), and in sufficient quantities, alcohol reduces the drinker to a state of physical helplessness and dependence. Finally, alcohol allows the drinker to externalize—under the cover story, "It's the liquor talking"—responsibility for *any* actions, whether passive *or* aggressive, that he indulges in in his drunkenness. Clearly then, as a symptom, alcoholism provides for the simultaneous expression, denial, and externalization of the drinker's emergent passivity.

Psychosomatic symptoms, up to and including the heart attacks that proliferate in middle life, can play an equivalent function: in effect, the patient brings his denied passivity to the one major institution in our society that recognizes and even insists on a dependent stance—the hospital. By becoming a patient, the middle-aged man says, "It is not *I* but my diseased organs that ask for help. My spirit is still willing; I cannot help it if my flesh is weak." Again, with this move, the patient dichotomizes his emergent bisexuality, externalizing the needful, damaged, and "feminine" aspects of himself into his weakened body, asking that *it* and not *him* be succored.

Other, perhaps more strongly defended, men may emphasize the denial rather than the covert expression of their emerging proclivities. Though more research is required, these may be the "type A" men (described by Friedman and his associates, 1969) who, out of a desperate need to refute the changes in their psyche and their bodies, drive themselves through overwork to a premature heart attack.*

Other men of this persuasion may escalate their *machismo*, heap chips on their shoulders, and hunt for antagonists, particularly oppressive authorities. Again, they deny certain passive wishes and simultaneously project the responsibility for these onto the objects of such wishes: they accuse their boss of requiring from them the submission they themselves secretly desire.

The increasingly frequent middle-aged divorce, where an older man leaves his wife of twenty years and marries a young wife, is relevant here. The usual interpretation is that the aging divorced male seeks to renew vi-

rility via a new sexual partner. However, I contend that in many such cases the aim is not primarily to enhance potency, but to re-externalize passive features of the personality. The middle-aged wife has come of age: she now refuses to live in her husband's shadow and to be the outward metaphor of his own "softer" nature. Just as some men seek to externalize their unfolding passivity via alcoholism or psychosomatic illness, others try to recreate a lost *status quo ante* and to relocate their "feminine" side in a new external vessel by discarding this now autonomous wife—a wife who further brings out the husband's frightening succorant needs—in favor of a still dependent, still adoring younger woman. Through her, these older men hope to both live out and cordon off the discrepant, questionable aspect of their own nature.

Yet again, crisis and extreme crisis solutions need not be compulsory. Men who resort to the extreme defenses I have described are coerced by the unconscious conviction—one that makes sense, if at all, only during the emergency period of young parenthood—that emotionality, dependency, and aestheticism are utterly incompatible with true manhood. Accordingly, they respond to a potential addition to the self as though it were a profound decrement, a veritable castration. However, seen from a less culture bound and less emergency centered perspective, middle-aged men are not losing a penis, but are regaining lost and hitherto undeveloped capacities for relating, enjoying, and knowing. This country does not need a "greening" of youth; but the counterculture, which has promoted a greater acceptance of sensuality, affiliation, and aesthetic appreciation in the culture as a whole, may bring about a much needed "greening" of the middle-aged American man.

Nevertheless, until cultural change makes the so-called passive and receptive quotient of their nature respectable for senior men, various forms of psychotherapy will have to fill in the gap. To conclude, the developmental perspective on aging, although it grows out of research with nonclinical and

---

* Significantly, the type A characteristics no longer predict coronary disease after age 50. The correlations between character and coronaries weaken at about the point when these driven, masculine-protesting men begin to accept the duality of their own nature.

non-American populations, suggests new directions for psychotherapists treating men in mid-life crisis. The therapeutic task is not to "adjust" the patient to inevitable loss and depletion, but to work with the developmental currents that can, if they are properly sponsored and understood, lead to a more enriched, more multifaceted self.

REFERENCES

BARRY, H.; BACON, M. and CHILD, I. "A Cross-Cultural Survey of Some Sex Differences in Socialization." *Journal of Sociology and Abnormal Psychology,* 55 (1957): 372–432.

BENEDEK, T. *Psychosexual Functions in Women.* New York: Ronald Press, 1952.

BLACKER, K. H. "Frightened Men: A Crisis of Middle Age." Unpublished paper. Department of Psychiatry, Davis School of Medicine, University of California, 1974.

BRIM, O. "Selected Theories of the Male Mid-Life Crisis: A Comparative Analysis." Presented to Division 20, American Psychological Association, New Orleans, 1974 (unpublished).

ERIKSON, E. H. "Identity and the Life Cycle: Selected Papers." *Psychological Issues,* Monograph No. 1. New York: International Universities Press, 1959.

FARRELL, M. et al. Unpublished paper, Department of Sociology, SUNY at Buffalo, 1975.

FRIEDMAN, M. et al. *Pathogenesis of Coronary Artery Disease.* New York: McGraw-Hill, 1969.

GOLD, S. "Cross-Cultural Comparisons of Role Change with Aging." *Student Journal of Human Development* (Committee on Human Development, University of Chicago), 1 (1960): 11–15.

GUTMANN, D. "An Exploration of Ego Configurations in Middle and Later Life." In *Personality in Middle and Late Life: Empirical Studies,* edited by B. Neugarten et al., pp. 114–148. New York: Atherton Press, 1964.

GUTMANN, D. "The Country of Old Men: Cross-Cultural Studies in the Psychology of Later Life." *Occasional Papers in Gerontology,* 5 (1969): 1–37. Institute of Gerontology, University of Michigan, Wayne State University.

GUTMANN, D. "Alternatives to Disengagement: The Old Men of the Highland Druze." In *Culture and Personality: Contemporary Readings,* edited by R. A. LeVine, pp. 232–235. Chicago: Aldine, 1974.

GUTMANN, D. "Parenthood: A Key to the Comparative Psychology of the Life Cycle." In *Life-Span Developmental Psychology,* edited by N. Datan and L. Ginsberg, pp. 167–184. New York: Academic Press, 1975.

McCLELLAND, D. C. et al. *The Drinking Man.* New York: Free Press, 1972.

MURDOCK, G. P. "Comparative Data on the Division of Labor by Sex." *Social Forces,* 15 (1935): 551–553.

ROHEIM, G. *Animism, Magic, and the Divine King.* New York: Knopf, 1930.

Psychopathology

Jack Weinberg

INTRODUCTION

There are realities that transcend the truth. Paradoxical though this may seem it is not so to anyone who has heard the words of the emotionally ill ... the poetry of the anguished mentality which becomes its credo, its reality. The eighty-one-year-old confused and incontinent woman, whose delusion is that she is pregnant, clings to what is to her a reality despite all objectively true findings to the contrary. For truth is objective, while reality is subjective, varying with the individual and becoming clear to anyone willing and able to interpret its meaning. What the old woman was saying was that she harbored her own regressed self within herself and was about to deliver it. If senility is the "second childhood," then she was pregnant with it and at the point of delivery. Viewed from this perspective, her delusion makes sense— her method of expressing it, poetry.

To understand the uniqueness of each person's reality, the young and the old, is the very essence of psychological skill which must deal not only with the individual variance, but also with the shifting and altering quality of this subjective state as the human being grows, develops, and ages. Each period in the lifespan of man forces on him a different reality, based on the altered physiology and the extent of the richness of the human

From J. G. Howells, ed., *Modern Perspectives in the Psychiatry of Old Age* (Larchmont, New York: Brunner/Mazel, Publishers, 1975). Reprinted by permission.

experience. Old age can become an expression of the summation of the human experience, and therein "lies the rub." It can be rich, varied, colorful and, in turn, enriching; conversely, it may be impoverished or empty and serve only to emphasize the futility of life and its meaning to many of the old. However, no matter what one's experiences may be, there is a need for an elaboration upon one's experiences which tend to distort the objective truth, but which add to the uniqueness of the reality which the individual wishes to convey. It is by far more real, for it delineates more clearly to the observer the actual personality of the observed. It is a more "real" reflection of the personality structure of the communicating person than the actual facts warrant or state. What emerges is a romanticized version of events, a dramatization of the facts; the good becomes magnificent, the sad—tragic. It is a poetic interpretation of one's experiences which, in turn, need interpretation by the listener.

Furthermore, we who are engaged in the field of mental illness and health are quite aware of the permutations of time. We work with emotions that have their origins in the person's dim forgotten or repressed past, but which make themselves ferociously felt in the present. No sooner does the patient express an emotion, a feeling, than it is related to his past. His dreams know of no time dimension—they permeate all three and operate as if the individual organism has no cognizance of that which we know as temporal. What is needed most, therefore, in working with the emotionally ill elderly is an understanding of their manifest behavior in the light of their lifelong experiences and affected as it may be by accrued deficits—both extrinsic and intrinsic.

Much too much has already been written on the subject, yet much too much has either been ignored or simply misunderstood. My effort is to make the covert overt, the seemingly bizarre understandable, to point out the order inherent in chaos, and thus make life bearable for the observer and help the observed.

Behavior is the aggregate of observable responses of the organism in its interrelationships. In its predictable form, it is the usual modality by which an individual handles life situations that may arise. It is usually automatic and more often than not defines the character of the person. It is what one expects of one's contacts with another and upon which one projects a continuum of transactions. While minor deviations from the established patterns are allowed for under certain circumstances, the usual set of expectations is that of stability, if not rigidity. Unfortunately, the predictability of behavior presumes a static quality to the source, the human being, who, of course, is in a constant state of change, development and, hopefully, growth. Added to this dilemma is the subtlety of an ever-increasing spectrum of that which is called normal due both to the greater tolerance by society of more and more deviant behavior and the greater understanding that the helping professions bring to the study and alleviation of the human condition.

In view of the above, I have chosen to address myself to the psychodynamics of what I like to call agedness rather than aging. Aging is an ongoing process, therefore difficult of assessment. Agedness, however, is an assumed stance on the part of the organism that may or may not be due to organ dysfunction, but may be behaviorally character-istic of a unified complex of roles, assigned, ascribed and much too often acquired. It may be both character and pathology. It may be independent of any overt manifestations of organic disease and thus present itself as a mode of coping or adaptive behavior most economical to the character structure of the individual. Behavioristically speaking, one may manifest agedness quite early in one's life, though usually it is characteristic of the later periods of the life cycle. Thus it is the manifest behavior of an individual that should interest us and the latent meaning of its content that should intrigue us. For again it is the understanding of behavior, and not only its origin, that can produce the proper responses in dealing with it and with the problems that may ensue.

PSYCHODYNAMICS IN THE AGED

Many clinicians tend to reify the names of abnormal psychological conditions and thus assume their reality as entities. A more consistent clinical view would, to my mind, regard diagnoses as names given to sets of extreme variation of different kinds of behavior. The behavioral modalities subsumed under a diagnostic category are not describable as unitary. It is not the diagnoses that have a reality reference, but rather the behavioral variations the diagnoses describe. In any type of class of behavior one will see extremes, and the laws that govern and describe those extremes also govern and describe the non-pathological functioning. Thus, the idea of continuity between normal and abnormal can be established and have meaning.

We can further assume that no one behavior is unique to a diagnostic category; therefore, individual symptoms are not reliable indices of a psychopathological grouping. When precise and definite etiological factors are isolated and the pathogenesis is well understood, the disease entity itself may certainly be used to define a target population. However, most studies on the psychopathological conditions of aging do not define etiological or pathogenic factors solely, and lacking such forces, lead some of us to what may be described as empirical conclusions on behavioral patterns.

Perception-psychopathology relationships in old age are a case in point. While some regard perception as an independent variable and direct our attention to the effect of disordered perception on personality development and consequent behavior, others view psychopathological conditions as independent variables and regard the perceptual behavior as outcomes or effects. I, for one, an adherent to the latter notion, have long since postulated the *exclusion of stimuli* in later life as an outcome or effect of a psychopathological, if not psychodynamic, condition.

Perception, of course, refers to a perceptual act that transforms a physical stimulus into psychological information. Complex processes are involved in this transformation: reception of the stimulus, registration, the processing of the registered information, and the checking of the information against continued input. Eventually, the human organismal organization is meant to interpret all of the above in the light of its life experiences and affect action. Thus, sensory, cognitive, conceptual, affective, and motor processes are all linked with each other in any given perceptual act. Most of us have long since recognized the crucial significance of perception, its central role in the development of those modulatory and controlling structures designated as the ego or, as I like to call it, the problem-solving self. For the perceptual act reflects the psychological point of contact between a person and his internal and external milieu. Its principal function is to convey information from his environment for integration with other psychological functioning such as memory, judgment, and anticipation. Obviously, too, it also receives and carries information about the nature and consequences of the perceiver's actions. Perception is, thus, a central ingredient in effective adaptation, in the fitting-in process between the individual and his environment.

As the individual develops and moves towards active mastery, he can no longer depend on the instrumentality of others as in infancy, childhood, and adolescence, but must amplify and coordinate the executive potential of his own body parts, which cease to be independent information and pleasure receptors, and take up their collaborative, productive functions. In later life, due to intrinsic and extrinsic vectors, recapitulation of early developmental sequences may take place, moving the individual from productivity to receptivity and, in effect, to dependence on the mastery or the instrumentality of others, an adaptive approach which, in the belief of some, is characterized by gross coercive dependence and/or by the disruption of proper ego functioning.

The threat of organic deficits or destruction within, plus the welling-up of heretofore unacceptable but controlled impulses and the all too frequent deterioration of the individual's socioeconomic status, tax the adaptive capacities of the ego to the utmost. To master the threat of dissolution of its boundaries and to ward off any break with reality, the aging organism, having at its disposal a lowered psychic energy supply and being unable to deal with all stimuli, begins to exclude them from awareness. While, of course, the nature of the receiving organ obviously influences reception, we have seen that perception is not a passive process. The physical stimulus is organized and transformed at the point of reception, and I like to believe that it never goes beyond the point of the sensory receptor.

The infant, too, is faced by the problem of too many stimuli and little ego development to help him cope with them. The very young, however, can and do take refuge in sleep or withdrawal to allow a gradual exposure to the clamor and the slow, measured, developmental integration of stimuli and the evolvement of acceptable responses to them. Then, too, the very young are helped by supportive figures who are ever ready to supply ego judgment and strength to the struggling new organism. Neither of these elements is available to the aging individual nor are they acceptable—hence, the exclusion.

Though it may be argued by some that the mechanism of exclusion of stimuli is identical to the familiar mechanism of denial, it is my belief that this defense is rather different. Denial, in my view, implies that a stimulus has been received, cathected and invested in, and then cathexis is withdrawn. Not so with the exclusion of stimuli. A stimulus may be blocked at the point of entry by a threshold lowered only for those stimuli relevant to one's narcissism, by which, at this point, I mean survival value. The problem is how to assess the rate and extent of the exclusion experimentally so as to utilize this mechanism as a pyschobiological measure of aging.

Based on the above assumptions and on the assumption that our society is neglectful, if not hostile, to the needs of the aged, I have allowed myself psychodynamic formulations on some aspects of their behavior.

The sensory organs envelop each individual with personal spatial boundaries within which messages may be perceived, and which may differ in dimensions and scope for each organ. Tactile language would therefore be the closest and, unless invited or eagerly yearned for, the most encroaching and threatening of all stimuli received. Thermal, olfactory, aural, and visual stimuli, in that order, provide ever-increasing spatial territoriality for meaningful messages of increasing complexity to reach the human being, for him to decode and to give the proper response. Each of these personal spaces may have a "Do Not Trespass" sign, not discernible to others but well delineated for the comfort of each organism.

When cultural determinants are added to these biologically determined boundaries, the problem becomes even more complex. Unless invited, encroachment on one's personal space becomes an invasion of one's privacy. Cultural values, biases, and practices tend to decrease the allowable areas of intrusion, inhibit the sending out and receiving of messages, and thus further thwart the language of communication. The transactional reciprocity between the human organism and its circumambience is a thing of beauty to behold. For, ironically enough, as visual and auditory acuity diminish and the environmental language becomes less discernible, the aged themselves join the vast throngs of the invisible and untouchable in our society.

It is not that I am unaware of the effects of organic deficits. My emphasis is on the effects on sensory organ functioning of one's inner perception of the self and one's ambience. While all may agree with what is here stated, the tendency is to arrive at quick closure on the effects of organic deficits, sacrificing a more comprehensive therapeutic effort on the altar of organicity. Thus, in a recent paper concerning the needs of the elderly for tactile relationships, of the need for intimacy and touch, I wrote, "The sensory organ of the aged person's skin often becomes dull, as if in response to an anticipated deprivation. There is no need to feel, if feelings are to be denied." And again: "Visually the older person is more concerned with messages in his environment dealing with movement. Available data suggest that he relies more heavily on visual information channeled through the periphery of the eye, which magnifies movement, than on information received by means of detailed and clear vision. Psychologically it is as if the older person anticipates some external threat to his being and is alert to ward off an offending object, or in search of a supportive figure" (Weinberg, 1970).

Complicating matters even more is the fact that the behavioral patterns as manifested by the aged are bound to inner secret legends each person has about himself. As psychiatrists, we are engaged in a type of life review of each one of our patients. The life review allows us to perceive the lifestyle, or more often the life-theme, as Binswanger calls it, of the individual. The life-theme of a person, as an example, may be of emptiness and a constant search for the filling of the self, as one may encounter in a depressed individual. What is not so apparent, even to an astute observer, is the personal legend, as I like to call it, that pervades our being and motivates our behavior. I use the term legend, for in all of us the concept of the self as a dynamic force, interacting with the environment, is more often than not tinged with wish rather than reality, and is thus distorted and obscured. When the legend of the self is not in concert with the facts as they are, discomfort and disease make their appearance. The legend leads to a romanticizing of the self and a poetic interpretation of reality, which arouse skepticism and even hostility toward the holder of the dream. There are personal realities, therefore, that transcend the obvious truth.

To move on to another dimension, man recognizes that the existing harmony and interrelationships in the world about him bespeak an interdependence between them. The loss of any of the components or systems calls for a new adaptation and adjustment to the whole. The observation of these phenomena, added to man's own life experience from infancy to maturation in a complex society, makes it quite apparent to him that he cannot exist isolated from other interacting individuals. He can manage to do so for a given period of time, particularly when there is hope that the isolation will eventually end. He cannot manage, though, if the isolation is not self-imposed or if there is no hope of its amelioration. This, however, is precisely the situation faced in later life within our culture. The gradual isolation of the aging organism into a state of aloneness is the great tragedy of aging.

I use the term aloneness because it is descriptive of the intensely experienced inner affect related to the gradual isolation that takes place, and is a physical or geographic state. Aloneness, of course, is a result of a number of factors. A very real one is the dispersal and death of friends and members of the family. Each loss necessitates a rearrangement of the equilibrum that had been set up for comfortable functioning. Each loss, too, releases energy previously invested, but which now needs a new object. The aging person searches for a substitute, but there are no candidates. There is no replacement of family and there are no bidders for his friendship. When the aging individual attempts to reestablish equilibrium by attempting to reinvest the freed libido in new objects in the environment, he meets a wall of resistance. Having no place to go, this freed-up energy is turned inward and is either reinvested in organs or organ systems and appears in the guise of somatic complaints, or is experienced as pain and ruminatory recapitulation of a past life experience. The aged then appear to be egocentric, selfish, and preoccupied with inner rumblings of the self.

Within the final span of years, the aged must also face the twin spectrum of physiological losses and eventual death, of which the above are but a part. Losses may be handled by denial, overcompensatory mechanisms, or projection. Grief may be a constant companion which takes on the appearance of depression. Equally common, and most troublesome to respond to, is one method of dealing with losses—projection. It is most often expressed by complaints of the aged that someone is cheating or lying to them, stealing, or taking things away from them. It is a rebuke and an expression of anger at the fact that internal biological losses are being sustained, that mastery over hitherto controlled functions and impulses is threatened, and influence over one's family and environments is waning. The "thiefs, robbers, and cheaters" are usually members of the family, friends, relatives, and caretakers who can least comprehend the accusations made against them, and who in turn respond in anger, resulting in mutual frustration, distrust, and alienation.

Psychodynamically, the above is quite clear. By taking over functions for the aged, we do rob them of mastery and control. While this may be necessary as a protective device to save the aged from their own judgmental deficits, it does not deny the fact that control of their independent actions is being usurped. The response on the part of the aged is either by rage or accusation, hanging on to any vestige of control, or by denial that may be either vigorous or pitiful, depending on the circumstances. Frequently, the aged will begin to cling to many seemingly meaningless objects. Hoarding is not uncommon, whether it be of food, priceless objects, or trifles. This, too, needs to be understood in the light of ever-increasing losses. The more often the aged person loses close friends—others with whom he has shared life experiences—the greater is his need to hold on to inanimate objects with which he has shared common experiences. These objects replace and are substitutes for cherished reunions and memories when very few, if any, friends are left to meet with and reminisce. Chaotic disorder to the observer may represent organizing strength to the observed old person, so that forebearance should be the guiding rule.

Cultural patterns, too, play a great role in determining variables in human behavior. These include not only moral standards and mores but also more subtle patterns of motivation and interpersonal relationships. Variations in judgment and systems of belief, like religion and philosophies, have been integrated with the other cultural patterns, like child-rearing practices, by the cultural anthropologists. As a result of this synthesis, there is now clearer understanding of the effects of one or the other on the individual and on the cultural patterns he has developed. The values the child accepts, introjects, and incorporates into himself have much to do with defining his attitude toward aging people and later toward himself as an aging person. If in our society the aged are perceived as unattractive, unproductive, old-fashioned, useless, querulous, etcetera, then we in our youth absorb these concepts, make them part of ourselves, and apply them to ourselves in later life. Clearly a built-in system of self-depreciation or denial and dynamic processes determine behavior.

We need, therefore, to examine some specifics of our culture and its value system, along with their continued effects on behavior long after their usefulness to the organism has become anachronistic. No easy assessment of what is defined as culture is available, but this could best be understood by Kluckhohn's approach to the problem (Kluckhohn, 1963). According to her, there are five questions that man, regardless of the level of sophistication of his culture, asks himself, whether he is aware of it or not. These questions can be answered within a given spectrum and while each society may relate to the entire spectrum, it is the inordinate emphasis that is placed on one of these answers that determines the society's value system, its child-rearing practices, its behavior, and its treatment of the aged. A brief examination of one or two of these questions may illustrate my point.

What is man's relationship to time? Which of the three time orientations, past, present, or future, does he value most? There is, of course, no question that we as Americans, or those who attempt to emulate our culture, value the future. Our future-mindedness makes planners of us all. Nothing is left to chance, not even a spontaneous good time. We are so busy planning for the future that, when the future catches up with us and becomes the present, we cannot enjoy it because we are again busy planning for the future. As a result, we cannot have a good time and enjoy the present. We seldom sit anywhere without feeling that we should be somewhere else. How does this affect older persons? Not only are they people without a future and hence not ones to invest in, but having incorporated the valued time orientation, they, the only group in our society meant to do so, are incapable of enjoying the present, while the hope for a better future is a mirage in the twilight of life.

Another question: *What type of personality is valued most?* The "being"—the individual who is mainly concerned with feelings, impulses, and desires of the moment; the "being in becoming"—most interested in inner development and the fullest realization of aspects of personality; or the "doing"—the one principally concerned with action, achievement, and getting things done? It is not too difficult to recognize ourselves in this configuration. We are the doers. While the Mexican mother, valuing the "being" orientation, may happily enjoy her child from day to day, the "doing" mother is too often concerned with his progress. His achievements are a measure of her competence as a mother, an efficient manager, and a force in the community. Doing, too, must have a by-product discernible to one of our senses. We unconsciously depreciate the contemplative aspects of life. One does nothing when one reads or thinks.

Here, again, we can readily recognize the impact of such an orientation on the aging organism. The old have stopped doing, are alien in our eyes and depreciated in their own. Nor have they prepared their lives for a contemplative existence. The effects are often quite devastating, resulting frequently in restlessness and purposeless agitation.

CLINICAL STATES

The specific mental disturbances seen in the older years may be divided into two major categories: (1) organic, in which there is some demonstrable pathology in the brain, and (2) functional personality disorders, in which there seems to be nothing wrong from an organic viewpoint. Under organic disturbances are to be classed the many cases of cerebral arteriosclerosis. The physical symptoms are dizziness, tremors, unsteady gait, tingling sensations, and so forth. Emotionally there appear apprehension, panic, restlessness, sleeplessness, disturbance in consciousness and thinking, memory defects, delusions of threats of bodily harm, nightmares, and depression. There may occur actual violence against people, even against those closest to the individual. All of these symptoms reflect the reaction of the personality to the inwardly perceived threat to its integrity, and the extreme fight that it puts up to master it.

Presenile Syndromes

Alzheimer's disease and Pick's disease, which occur in middle age, are known as presenile psychoses. The onset is in the forties or fifties and is characterized organically by marked diffuse changes in the brain. Psychologically they present symptoms of marked failure of memory, rapidly developing confusion and disorientation, speech difficulties, and complete dementia. Even in these undeniably organic diseases, the individual in the early phases manifests emotional responses and reactions indicative of his struggle against the threat of overwhelming destruction. The individual often overcompensates by euphoric overactivity, grandiose business plans, sexual deviations, and general uninhibited behavior.

The Senile Psychosis

This has been called the "final caricature of old age." It is insidious in onset and may therefore be neglected until it is too late. It begins with a gradual decline in initiative, loss of interest in things which normally are of importance, reversal of the sleep rhythm, failure of memory, concentration and comprehension, and general deterioration with final confusion and formation of delusions. This constitutes a gradual breakdown of the personality into what may be called a second childhood, but minus the charms and easy acceptability of the first.

Infectious disease, acute or chronic, and vitamin deficiencies may bring with them disturbances in the mental functioning of the aging person. There may be delirious types of reaction which in the aged are more sustained than is the case in younger years.

Among the gross functional disturbances seen in the later years are the following.

Involutional Melancholia

This most common disorder of middle life was formerly thought of as a direct reult of the female menopause, or "change of life." In reality, it tends to appear in both women and men as a first attack of mental illness, in women between the ages of forty and fifty-five and in men between the ages of fifty and sixty. In the female the symptoms that present themselves are: nervousness, menstrual disturbances, flushes and chills, excitability, fatigability, weeping and depression, irritability, sleeplessness, memory defects, inability to concentrate, headaches and other vague and indefinite pains. Men show the following: hot flashes, emotional instability with sudden uncontrollable shifts in mood, tendency to break into tears, periods of irritability and sudden anger, physical and mental fatigability, difficulty in concentration, hypochondriacal complaints, and impatience. As the illness progresses, both sexes show marked anxiety, an agitated type of depression, delusions of guilt, and attempts at self-destruction.

Simple Depression

This is another common disorder of the later years. It is characterized by general feelings of desolation and isolation which, in a measure, reflect the reality of the life situation. Feelings of unworthiness, of guilt, and self-punishing attitudes are the rule and psychologically constitute a reaction to the resentment and hostility which these patients feel toward their environment and fellow human beings, but which, for many reasons, they cannot express. Because of this inability, they turn their resentment and hostility inward and tend to be self-deprecatory and self-destructive.

Paranoid States

Paranoid states are characterized by feelings of persecution and apprehension. It is easy for the older person to develop ideas that people and the world are hostile to him and wish to destroy him.

Primarily, however, paranoid states are the result of the resurgence in an individual of primitive hostile impulses toward the world and the people in it, both of which are beginning to fail him. To the average person such hostility is unacceptable and the only defense against it is to project it outward. The individual's hostile ideas thus become delusions of persecution. It is simpler to say that one is hated and not wanted because one

is old, than to admit to oneself and others that one is incapable of coping with overwhelming odds.

The Neuroses

The neuroses occupy a conspicious place in the disorders of later life. The incidence of the neuroses is by far greater than is that of the psychoses, yet little attention is being paid to them because in the neuroses there is no total break with reality. Much too often neuroses have been thought of as precursors to a general physical decline. Nothing could be further from the truth. A neuroses may occur at any period in life and is indicative of a failure in adaptation. Among the common neuroses in later life, the following are the most conspicuous.

Hypochondriasis

Hypochondriasis is the inordinate preoccupation with one's bodily functions and is an especially common disorder seen in the aged of present-day culture. The symptoms are directed mostly to the organs of ingestion, digestion, and evacuation, that is, to the gastrointestinal tract, and also to the heart and circulatory system. This does not mean, however, that the reproductive system or the muscles, bones, and joints are excluded from attention. Hypochondriacal over-concern is often mitigated by the re-education in the range of activities permitted by one's own physical limitations, and by conventions in certain socioeconomic groups which accept an excessive concern with bodily functions as normal behavior. However, with fewer worthwhile things to hold the attention and to divert one from self-concern, it becomes easier to notice and to talk about minor ailments and accidents. In general, the older a person grows, the more experience he has had with illness, operations and accidents, whether his own or those of other people, and the easier it is for him to feel himself to be ill or in danger. Then, too, bodily concern helps to save face when one is beset by failures. "I am ill and therefore I cannot . . ." is a rationalization that is more universally acceptable than the truthful but prestige-shattering "I cannot."

Despite the fact that heart conditions are more numerous and more often fatal than gastrointestinal disease, the elderly person is usually much more concerned with the latter. Psychologically it is believed that this is tied in with an unconscious expression of the person's dependency needs. It is an expression of a desire to be taken care of, just as one had been taken care of when one was young and when a great deal of attention centered about the feeding, digestive, and evacuation processes of the infant. The responsiveness of the gastrointestinal tract at all ages to emotional disturbances, to anxiety, to conflict, to apprehension, to frustration, and to unhappiness is by now well recognized. By his unconscious utilization of the resulting physical symptoms, the older person often attempts to regain attention, affection, and domination.

Anxiety States

Anxiety states are not entirely new experiences for older people. In all probability they have experienced similar reactions, perhaps rather frequently, whenever their security had been threatened or whenever they faced emotional deprivation. Since insecurity and realistic anxiety producing situations are more common in later life, anxiety states can easily arise. An anxiety neurosis is characterized by increased muscular tension with difficulty in relaxation and sleeping, disturbances in the regular rhythm of the heart, gastrointestinal tract and urinary system disturbances, tremors, headaches, excessive perspiration, increased irritability, and a vague sense of impending doom. At times acute anxiety may arise because of guilt feelings resulting from hostility toward one's family when it fails to understand and meet the needs of the older person.

In any event, anxiety is not without its compensating elements. It has long been recognized as a danger signal for something more serious that may supervene. It has a dynamic quality that bespeaks treatability. It is by far better than the seemingly less dis-

tressing attempts at withdrawal from any experiencing of feelings, with its attendant fantasy formation and possible total divorce from reality.

Chronic Fatigue States

These states are at times difficult to diagnose in the aging individual because it is normal for elderly people to tire more quickly and easily and to recover more slowly and incompletely than younger ones. Also, as a rule, sleep in older people is shorter and less sound, and they awaken feeling less refreshed and at times irritable. Fatigue can, however, be a result of emotional frustration. Whenever the prospect of gratification is small, a person is apt to tire quickly and to remain so until something interesting turns up. Since prospects for gratifying experience wane with the years, easy fatigability is therefore common in this age group.

It is a mistake to meet these fatigue states in older people with advice for rest cures or prolonged vacations. Very often it is these very prolonged vacations or rests that produce lethargy and fatigue. A balanced diet of rest, recreation, and occupation gives a starting point for a successful therapeutic effort. One cannot overstress the need for some occupation and satisfying accomplishment geared to the physical limitations of the person involved as a definite therapeutic aid for fatigue based on emotional factors.

Compulsive Disorders

Compulsive disorders and patterns in later life are similar to those occurring in earlier life. The compulsive individual can be recognized by his over-conscientiousness, perfectionism, orderliness, over-attention to details, and doubts about himself and his adequacy. While some of these character traits may be considered as quite praiseworthy, they can readily become troublesome symptoms that undermine the person's efficiency and immobilize him. Such symptoms may take the form of excessive cleanliness and orderliness, and endless and inflexible rituals to guard against mistakes, danger, or evil thoughts. There may be endless counting, the compulsion to do certain things over and over again, checking and re-checking of gas jets, locks, faucets, rituals in food, dress, excretion, and evacuation, excessive washing of hands, etcetera. Compulsions, like anxieties, have some protective aspects to them. Repeated acts of a penitential or conciliatory character may appear in elderly people as a result of or as a protection against erratic, hostile, or vindictive fantasies which arouse guilt in them.

Any attempt to stop these compulsive acts may arouse acute and intolerable anxiety. It must be recognized that these symptoms constitute a last-ditch effort on the part of the individual to ward off complete disintegration. The attack, therefore, should be directed at the environment and not at the symptoms themselves. The treatment of symptoms should be attempted only by a skilled therapist who is thoroughly familiar with psychodynamics and aware of the possible dangers involved in treatment.

Hysterical Neuroses

Such neuroses are not too common in the later years. The classical hysterical picture of the giving-up of function of a part of the body, such as in hysterical paralysis, blindness or deafness, so that the rest of the organism can continue to function unimpaired is relatively rare in the elderly. What one does see is a form of exaggeration of minor physical symptoms which may be present.

Sexual Behavior

Studies uniformly agree that proper health and proper environment (i.e., availability of partners, and, thus, sanction by society) are the most important factors for continued activity of sexual intercourse. This, of course, means that an essential or fundamental fit between behavior and environment exists. When such a fit does not exist, it is brought about by changing behavior to fit the environment or by changing the environment to fit the habitual or accustomed mode of behavior.

Whether environment or behavior will be changed to attain this fit depends upon the kind of organism, its developmental level, and other circumstances. As a general principle, it may be said that the organism will modify its immediately given environment to suit itself to the extent it is capable of doing so. Thus, there is a relationship between the state of the organism and its "docility in the face of environmental restrictions," as phrased by Lawton (1968).

The more competent the individual is, in terms of health, intelligence, ego strength, and social role performance, the less will be the proportion of behavior variance attributed to objects or conditions around him. With a high degree of competence, he will rise above or bend the environment to suit his needs. However, reduction in competence or deprivation of status heightens his behavioral dependence on external conditions and social organization.

In old age a person's competence—physical, mental, social—is reduced, and he becomes more dependent on the environment. To attain the fit with his environment, he engages in a continuous process of behavior change. This does not mean that he never tries to alter the circumstances about him or never succeeds in doing so. It simply means that environmental change takes place infrequently and to a lesser degree than the frequency and degree that behavior is changed to suit the environment.

No one seems to want to touch the older person. Very few seek physical contact with them. Yet there seem to be instinctual and acquired needs for contactual relationships which are sought by all living organisms. We are all too ready to touch and even caress and pat the young, the cat or the dog, but not the aged. Our physical encounters with them are perfunctory, with no warmth or conviction behind them.

Theirs is a psychological hunger that usually remains ungratified. If sensory organs of the skin of the old become dull, as they so often do, it is as if this were in response to an anticipated deprivation. There is no need to feel, if feelings are to be denied. It is an unspoken grievance that needs to be redressed.

In the absence of opportunity for direct sexual gratification, the need for sexual expression may indeed take on many forms. Without thinking of regressive maneuvers related to dynamic formulations of oral, anal, and phallic preoccupation, we should take into consideration the sublimated and socially acceptable expressions such as touch, or tactile contact, which in the younger adult may be acceptable and natural but in the older person is looked upon with curiosity, and often with suspicion and disapproval. The sick old man who reaches out a feeble hand to touch the young female nurse is an "old fool making a pass." The sick younger man with the same gesture may also be making a pass, but he, of course is no "fool." The aged man who reaches out to touch and pat the smooth, inviting skin of a youngster becomes the prototype of the dangerous molester despite the fact that statistically he ranks low on the scale. Nevertheless, it is quite true that the courts may be more lenient with the aged and ascribe their behavior to confusion. (The number of aged molesters is quite negligible when compared to the number of young adult molesters.)

The sexual expressions of the elderly are numerous and diverse. Chronological age is no barrier to the continued sexual life of the old when opportunity and sanction are present. Difficulties arise when, in the absence of the above, sublimated activities are also denied them. Much too often their feeble efforts to establish contactual relationships are misinterpreted and rejected, forcing the old to regressed behavior. Not only must this be understood and placed in proper perspective, but the overt sexual acting out on the part of the elderly must also be understood. In the wake of biological deficits and in the waning moments of one's influence over one's environment, re-establishment of mastery may take on the form of overt sexual acts and aggression.

MANAGEMENT

Remedial measures for all of these difficulties can be gratifying. One must make due allowances for the reduced vigor, agility, and learning capacity of the individual. Beyond that, therapy can be conducted along the lines of therapy at any age level. The skilled therapist who knows the dynamics involved has to be more active and more direct than with other age groups, for the exigencies of time demand shorter methods. This holds as true for therapy directed at the level of personal conflict of insecurity and of rebellion as it does for therapy directed at attitudes, at manipulation of the environment, at social rehabilitation, and so on.

In dealing with the rehabilitation of the mentally ill among the aged, it must be borne in mind that all human beings are to be treated as individuals. While there are character traits and human experiences common to most men and women, the most invariable feature of human beings is their variability. There are no two persons with precisely the same fingerprints, much less any two with exactly the same mind. It is the variance in life experience and in personality, the differences in nuance, which dictate an individual approach to each person. This truth compounds, of course, the difficulties encountered in the treatment of the mentally ill. At the same time, however, it multiplies the challenge and interest of those engaged in rehabilitation.

The question as to what type of therapy is to be employed in treating the older patient is dependent on a number of factors. First of all, one should assess the physical state of the patient, in order to determine how much the aging organism will be able to take. Secondly, one must evaluate the suitability of the individual for therapy from the viewpoint of his earlier adaptation and maladjustments, his capacity for establishing a workable relationship with the therapist, and the degree to which these characteristics are modifiable. Lastly, it is important to determine whether the presenting symptomatology is something new in the life of the individual or whether it is a continuation of a long existing neurotic personality structure. Obviously, all of these determinations require the services of a trained individual. It is the psychiatrist's responsibility to decide as to the type of treatment to be instituted and who is to do the therapy. When therapy is not directly conducted or supervised by a trained psychiatrist, the following techniques should be of help as general guidelines.

Allow the patient to express himself, to talk about himself and his difficulties. Impatience will be interpreted by the patient as a rejection which cannot be tolerated. The attitude should be one of respectful attention and thoughtful consideration despite the fact that the same problem may arise and be discussed over and over again. Empathy—the ability to place oneself in the patient's place without ever identifying with him, not sympathy, is of the essence. The older person does not wish the other person to sympathize with and pity him. He craves respect which will help him to bolster his self-esteem. An insincere approach will be easily discerned by the patient and is apt to lead to insurmountable barriers.

Allay the anxiety and insecurity of the aging patient insofar as this is possible. This requires of the helping person a genuine fondness for the elderly and a willingness to help them. One must, however, be tactful, for the elderly are proud and do not wish to betray their weakness. Therefore, they should be allowed to gratify their dependency needs in a manner that will not make them feel that they are leaning on another person. A condescending, patronizing attitude on the part of the supporting figure will only accentuate feelings of inadequacy and insecurity.

Patients should be helped into activities which will tend to enhance their attractiveness—physical and mental. When an individual is young, he may be physically attractive. When that fails him, achievement in some field of endeavor or continued productivity on a job can enhance the person's attractiveness. For to be wanted increases one's self-esteem and, as a by-product, one's value to others. At the same time, the elderly must be helped in accepting gracefully a curtailment of activities, when necessary, into something meaningful and gratifying rather than merely out of a job and thus out of life. Plan their daily activity with them, and not for them, when life would otherwise become empty. In addition to knowing the patient's own personal and family situation, one should become thoroughly acquainted with the facilities that the community, the church, and social agencies have established for the elderly population. At times the older person needs literally to be led by the hand to participate. The mere pointing out of the presence of such facilities may not be enough.

Finally, one must bring an optimistic attitude to the psychiatric techniques used in working with older people. One must not get too easily discouraged. One should leave the patient at the end of any interview with the feeling that the contact was a gratifying experience and that something had been accomplished during that hour. Only an understanding of and due consideration for the validity of the feelings of the older person can and will accomplish the desired results.

REFERENCES

1. KLUCKHOHN, F. "Dominant and Variant Values Orientation." In *Personality in Nature, Society and Culture,* edited by C. Kluckhohn and H. A. Murray. New York: Alfred A. Knopf, 1963.

2. LAWTON, P. "The Ecology of Social Relationships in Housing for the Elderly." *Gerontologist* 8 (1968): 108–15.

3. WEINBERG, J. "Environment, its Language and the Aging." *Journal of American Geriatric Society* 18, No. 9 (1970); 681–86.

A Study of Legal Drug Use By Older Americans

David Guttman

INTRODUCTION

This study was conducted to explore the patterns of behavior and the problems associated with the medical and nonmedical use of drugs by older Americans. The investigation focused on the assumed differences between elderly users and elderly nonusers of legal drugs, including ethical drugs, (i.e., drugs that can be legally obtained by prescription only), over the counter drugs, and alcohol. Information was also sought on the extent of side effects resulting from the use of various drugs in combination, on whether subjects sought treatment voluntarily in such events, on whether they were able to obtain the drugs they thought they needed, and on whether subjects exhibit any degree of dependence on their legal drugs for the performance of the regular activities of their daily living.

Background

In his Pulitzer Prize winning book, *Why Survive? Being Old in America*, R. N. Butler (1975) states:

> Ultimately, interest must focus on clarifying the complex, interwoven elements necessary to produce and support physical and mental health up to the very end of life rather than our present preoccupation with "curing ills" after they develop. . . .

As the largest consumer of legal drugs in America, the elderly are at risk to dependency problems from a wide variety of ethical and over the counter substances (*The Drug Users* 1968). Although aging is not synonymous with illness, 80–86 percent of the elderly reportedly suffer from at least one chronic disease or condition, compared to only 40 percent of the population under age 65. Many of these conditions can be relieved or controlled with the proper use of prescription or over the counter drugs.

Legal drugs with properties that lead to their self-administration under a wide variety of conditions have the highest potential for misuse or abuse (Schuster and Thompson, 1969). But problems related to the misuse and abuse of prescription drugs by the elderly are not generally recognized, unless or until they reach emergency proportions. Pascarelli and Fischer (1974) report that alcohol in combination with other drugs and nonnarcotic analgesics account for a large number of abuse episodes in the over-fifty age group. Chambers and Griffey (1975) report that older persons are more likely to use sedatives and tranquilizers than younger persons, but less likely to use stimulants.

National Institute on Drug Abuse. *A Study of Legal Drug Use by Older Americans* by David Guttman. A NIDA Services Research Report. DHEW Pub. No. (ADM) 78–495. Washington, D.C: Superintendent of Documents, U.S. Government Printing Office, 1978.

Drug interaction is an important factor in prescription drug misuse. Since some 86 percent of persons over 65 have at least one chronic condition (Lenhart 1976), treatment of these patients is apt to involve a variety of drugs that may produce complex and little understood antagonistic interactions (Wynne 1973). Sedatives, tranquilizers, and antidepressants—classed together as psychotropic drugs—are frequently used in combination, and each of these ethical drug types can inhibit the metabolism of the others (Learoyd 1972; as noted immediately above, sedatives and tranquilizers are more likely to be used by older persons). Furthermore, there may be harmful interactive effects between some commonly prescribed medications and an individual's diet (Wynne 1973).

Socioeconomic factors also play an important role in drug taking behaviors among the elderly. Since most live on fixed incomes, they will frequently turn to over the counter (OTC) preparations and home remedies to avoid the double expense of a doctor's bill and a prescription. Fear, ignorance, and lack of transportation are considered factors contributing to drug misuse or overuse by the elderly.

METHODOLOGY

This paper is drawn from a survey conducted in the Standard Metropolitan Statistical Area (SMSA) of Washingtpn, D.C. in 1976. Using a social area analysis approach, 23 census tracts were selected from the 627 census tracts that make up the entire SMSA, to represent the range of socioeconomic variation within geographic sectors as related to the proportion of the population who are elderly. Using goodness of fit statistics, the 23 census tracts selected were found to be highly representative of the general SMSA population in terms of age, sex, marital status, income, and race.

The universe thus constructed included approximately 5,600 senior citizens aged 60 years or older. Subjects were chosen for the study sample to represent the relative proportions of the elderly within each census tract for each of the five variables mentioned above. Only ambulatory, noninstitutionalized, elderly residents of the community were included in the study sample. The principal types of living arrangements of the subjects were also investigated, to ascertain their possible affects on drug use.

Instruments and Data Collection

Data were collected on an interview schedule consisting of measures of socioeconomic background and decision-making patterns related to the use of drugs. This 28-item schedule was developed specifically for this investigation and was reviewed for substance and relevance by a panel of four authorities in the field of drug abuse research. Furthermore, questions included in the final instrument were pretested on a number of elderly persons from similar census tracts in the Washington, D.C. SMSA as a means of assessing the reliability of the questions.

Participation in the study was voluntary. An initial sample of 1,200 elderly people was identified in the 23 selected census tracts. These 1,200 potential respondents were sent letters explaining the purpose of the study, advising them that they would be contacted to arrange for the interview, and assuring them of confidentiality and anonymity. Of the 959 persons subsequently contacted, 512 or 53 percent declined to take part in the survey. Of these refusals, 72 or 14 percent gave illness as a reason and 363 or 71 percent offered no reason. A telephone survey of a sample of 10 percent of the refusers indicated similar age and sex characteristics as the population of study respondents.

Interviewing took place between February and June 1976 and, despite the rather high rate of refusal, a total of 447 interviews were obtained. Each respondent was contacted by telephone to arrange a time for a home visit and each interview lasted approximately 45 minutes. The interviews were conducted by a team of 11 professionals and doctoral students; all had been trained in the proper use of the instrument prior to the data collection effort.

Statistical Analyses

A correlation design was used as the basic approach to analysis of the data. It was assumed that several of the variables were interrelated and would have a combined impact on decisions made on whether to use or not to use drugs.

The actual analysis consisted of basic descriptive statistics such as frequencies, means, and standard deviations. These were followed by the correlation analysis.

Analysis of patterns of drug use and nonuse yielded eight groups of subjects; for these purposes, drug use was distinguished in three categories—prescription drugs, over the counter drugs, and alcohol—and the eight groups of subjects ranged from persons who reported using all three substance categories to persons who reported using none of the three. Differences in the mean scores of users and nonusers of particular categories of drugs were subjected to one-way analysis of variance (ANOVA); usage patterns were analyzed by cross-tabulations of ANOVAs.

In addition, multiple regression analysis was performed to predict the most significant variables related to drug use.

RESULTS

The sample comprised 40.4 percent male respondents and 59.6 percent female respondents. The average age of respondents was 71.87 years. The average number of years of education was 11.9; this relatively high level of educational attainment was the only major difference between the study sample and the total population of the elderly in the United States (*The Drug Users* 1968). Income levels ranged from less than $200 per month (11.4 percent of the sample) to over $1,000 per month (33.7 percent of the sample), with an average monthly income of about $600; nearly three-fourths of the sample (73.9 per-

cent) felt that their income was adequate to their needs.

Fifty-eight percent of the respondents were married and living with their spouses. Single persons living alone—including those never married, widowed, separated, or divorced—made up the rest of the sample.

Personal health was assessed as good by 54.2 percent of the respondents, average by 29.5 percent, and poor by 16.3 percent. When asked to compare their own health with the health of other people their age, 56.5 percent of the respondents reported they felt themselves in better health than others, 31 percent reported they felt their own health was about the same as others, and 9.8 percent considered their health to be poorer than that of other persons their age.

Patterns of Prescription Drug Use

Nearly two-thirds of the respondents (62 percent) reported that they used ethical drugs—that is, drugs legally available through medical prescription, only. The three most frequently reported types of ethical drugs were cardiovascular (39.3 percent), sedatives and tranquilizers (13.6 percent), and antiarthritic drugs (9.4 percent). These three types of ethical drugs accounted for well over half of all the prescription drugs reported taken by respondents in the 24 hours prior to interview. Another 1.1 percent of respondents reported using antidepressants, which—like sedatives and tranquilizers—are classed as psychotropic drugs. Amount and frequency data on prescription drug use are contained in Table 1.

More than one-third of the respondents reported using between two and four prescription drugs; 5 percent reported using between five and nine prescription drugs. These drugs were obtained legally, i.e., with a physician's script, in nearly all cases (97.4 percent of responses). Only 3 percent reported using prescription drugs more often than their physicians had recommended.

The leading reason given for the use of prescription drugs was poor health during

TABLE 1

Use of prescription drugs by major type of drug.

TYPE OF DRUG	AMOUNT/FREQUENCY	NO. OF PERSONS
Sedative/Tranquilizer	Daily Use	28
	1 or more times weekly	16
	As Necessary	30
Antidepressant	Daily Use	6
	As Necessary	1
Antibacterial	Daily Use	5
	As Necessary	6
Nervous System	Daily Use	10
	As Necessary	2
Cardiovascular	Daily Use	218
	1 or more times weekly	31
	As Necessary	25
Gastrointestinal	Daily Use	37
	1 or more times weekly	1
	As Necessary	13
Masorespiratory	Daily Use	18
	As Necessary	15
Diabetic	Daily Use	16
	1 or more times weekly	1
Genitourinary Tract	Daily Use	7
	1 or more times weekly	1
	As Necessary	2
Topical	Daily Use	13
	As Necessary	7
Analgesic	Daily Use	18
	1 or more times weekly	1
	As Necessary	16
Antiarthritic	Daily Use	44
	1 or more times weekly	2
	As Necessary	8
Hormonal	Daily Use	27
	As Necessary	4
Other Drugs	Daily Use	29
	1 or more times weekly	9
	As Necessary	9

the preceding year (21.2 percent of respondents). This corresponds to the fact that over one-fourth of the respondents (26.6 percent) reported they could not perform their daily activities without their prescription drugs. If those who reported sometimes being unable to perform their daily activities without their prescription drugs (12.7 percent of respondents) are added, then more than one-third of the sampled population of elderly persons (39.3 percent) may be characterized as being to some degree dependent on prescription drugs for the performance of their daily activities.

In the light of these findings, it is interesting that only 12 percent of the respondents admitted having experienced overdose and/or side effects related to their prescription drug use. Those reporting such experiences indicated they had consulted a professional, usually a physician, on how to remedy the situation.

Use of prescription drugs was positively related to both age and knowledge of resources. Those who used more prescription drugs tended to be less satisfied with their lives, tended to use more over the counter drugs as well, and tended to have a lower perception of themselves in terms of intelligence and capability.

Health was the preeminent predictor of prescription drug use. Knowledge of resources, perceived capabilities of other elderly persons, and physical disability were also variables significantly related to prescription drug use.

Use of Over the Counter (OTC) Drugs

Over two-thirds of the respondents (69 percent) reported using over the counter drugs; this is a slightly greater percentage than reported using prescription drugs. Over half (55.4 percent) of all the OTC drugs reportedly used were identified as internal analgesics. Small percentages of respondents reported using other types of OTC drugs and most OTC drugs were reported obtained from a drugstore. Table 2 displays the reported use of over the counter drugs by drug type.

Dependence on OTC drugs for the performance of daily activities was small, compared to dependence on prescription drugs. Only 8 percent of the respondents reported requiring their OTC drugs to perform daily activities.

The great majority (85 percent) of those who reported using OTC drugs also reported that the amount and frequency of use had not changed appreciably in the preceding year

and that they had experienced no medical problems related to their OTC drug use. Only one-sixth of the respondents consulted a physician about the use of OTC drugs, while two-thirds relied on their own judgments and a small percentage sought the advice of spouses, friends, or other professionals. As with prescription drugs, well over two-thirds of the respondents thought they knew what the OTC drugs they used were supposed to do.

Small but statistically significant correlations were found between OTC drug use and respondents' perceptions of their own and others' capabilities. However, significant negative correlations between OTC drug use and health, age, life satisfaction, and the use of prescription drugs tended to reinforce the trend noted earlier: that is, users of both ethical drugs and over the counter drugs tended to be older, less healthy, and less satisfied with life than those who reported no drug use.

Patterns of Alcohol Use

Responses relating to alcohol use were categorized into three groups: 1) the frequent users, i.e., those who reported using alcohol daily; 2) the infrequent or moderate users, i.e., those who reported using alcohol a few times a week to a few times a month; and 3) the nonusers or abstainers, i.e., those who reported using alcohol a few times a year or never. The majority of the respondents (56.2 percent) reported little or no alcohol use. Infrequent or moderate users comprised nearly one-fourth (24.6 percent) of the respondents, while less than one-fifth (18.6 percent) of the respondents reported frequent use.

Twenty percent of the sample reported using all three types of alcoholic beverage, i.e., beer, wine, and liquor. Beer and liquor were reported used by 11.6 percent, while 10.7 percent reported using wine, only. A small percentage of the sample (3.3 percent) reported using hard liquor, only.

Among those who reported alcohol use, about 80 percent gave social or psycho-

TABLE 2

Use of over the counter (OTC) drugs by major type of drug.

TYPE OF DRUG	AMOUNT/FREQUENCY	NO. OF PERSONS
Internal Analgesic	Daily Use	58
	1 or more times weekly	18
	As Necessary	155
Antihistamine	Daily Use	2
	As Necessary	28
Liquid Decongestant	Daily Use	1
	1 or more times weekly	1
	As Necessary	7
Nasal Decongestant (drop/spray)	Daily Use	7
	As Necessary	6
Sleeping Aid	1 or more times weekly	2
	As Necessary	2
Other Preparations:		
Vitamins	Daily Use	30
	As Necessary	6
Laxatives	Daily Use	10
	1 or more times weekly	5
	As Necessary	20
Other Digestive System	1 or more times weekly	3
	As Necessary	11
Other Drugs	Daily Use	13
	1 or more times weekly	2
	As Necessary	12

logical reasons for using alcohol: 27 percent reported using alcohol "to have fun"; 22 percent, "to be accepted by friends"; and 29.9 percent, "to forget about some personal problem." Only 1.8 percent reported alcohol use was a habit. Two percent reported using alcohol to sleep better and 5.1 percent reported using alcohol in sociocultural and religious events, such as the celebration of a holiday.

Only 1.1 percent of the respondents reported having experienced problems related to their use of alcohol, such as blackout, arrest, accident, absence from work, or marital difficulties. All who reported such experiences had sought treatment.

An analysis of simple predictor variables of alcohol use revealed that only one, in-

come, was a significant indicator (.34). Therefore, multiple regression analysis was employed to determine whether several variables together might prove useful in predicting alcohol use.

Three variables were found to have an effect on increasing the correlation coefficient, R^2. These were income, knowledge of resources, and life satisfaction. Income accounted for 10.9 percent of the variance (Multiple $R = 0.33$, $p = 0.05$); that is, the higher the income, the more frequently the respondent tended to use alcohol. The next two most significant factors—knowledge of resources and life satisfaction—together added only 1.5 percentage points to the total amount of variance, 12.05 percent; life satisfaction did not make a significant contribution to the percentage of variance.

Positive relationships also occurred between health and alcohol use, and between family relationships and alcohol use. However, these did not achieve statistical significance.

Combined Use of Legal Drugs and Alcohol

Of the eight respondent groups distinguished by categories of substances used, those who reported using both prescription drugs and over the counter drugs but abstaining from alcohol made up the largest group, 25.3 percent of the sample. Those who reported using prescription drugs, over the counter drugs, and alcohol comprised 17.4 percent of the sample. Five percent of the respondents reported using alcohol, only, and no drugs; 4.8 percent of the respondents—the smallest group—said they abstained from both prescription drugs and OTC drugs, and alcohol.

Mean scores differed significantly among the eight groups of respondents on the variables of health, physical disability, income, and perceived capability.

Health provided the most significant correlation with patterns of legal drug and alcohol use ($F = 10.9$, $p = 0.001$). Those who reported using prescription and OTC drugs and no alcohol recorded the lowest health status; alcohol users tended to consider themselves as having better health than those who used prescription and/or OTC drugs.

Physical disability—defined for this study as being prevented from performing daily activities due to illness—also provided statistically significant variance among the eight groups ($F = 5.518$, $df = 7.428$, $p = 0.001$). Those who reported using alcohol and/or OTC drugs but no prescription drugs recorded the least disability, while those who reported using only prescription drugs or prescription and

OTC drugs but no alcohol were most likely to record the greatest disability.

Income related strongly to legal drug use patterns, as well ($F = 9.4$, $df = 7.418$, $p = 0.000$). All groups reporting alcohol use, either alone or with other drug use, recorded higher incomes; those groups reporting prescription and/or OTC drug use but no alcohol use recorded lower incomes.

Similar trends were also recorded in the relationship of *perceived capability* to drug use patterns. The group of respondents who reported using neither legal drugs nor alcohol and the group who reported using only alcohol recorded the higher perceptions of personal capabilities, while the group that reported prescription drug use only recorded the lowest perception of personal capability. Intellectual capabilities did not appear to be reflected in drug use patterns.

Cross-tabulations of the data revealed several social and demographic variables—including marital status, living arrangements, and sex—were significantly related to legal drug use patterns among the elderly. For example, females in the study sample reported using drugs 2.65 times more often than males (72.2 percent for female respondents, compared to 27.2 percent for male respondents).

Characteristics of the Psychotropic Drug Use Among the Elderly

Since elderly users of psychotropic, or mood altering, drugs (i.e., sedatives, tranquilizers, and antidepressants) are becoming more visible in our society—not only in nursing homes, but in the community as well (Butler 1975)—the data were examined to determine if social and psychological characteristics of this population could be delineated. Data from respondents reporting use of psychotropic drugs were segregated from data from respondents reporting use of all other ethical (prescription) drugs and the two groups thus derived were compared.

Persons who perceived their family relationships as satisfactory reported using psychotropic drugs less frequently and/or in smaller amounts, while those who described their family relationships as unsatisfactory reported using psychotropic drugs in larger dosages and/or more frequently than chance would have predicted. Frequency of reports for psychotropic drug use by perceived quality of family relationships is displayed in Table 3.

Other major findings about use of psychotropic drugs by elderly Americans include:

Almost all those who reported using psychotropic drugs (98.7 percent) indicated that they obtained their ethical drugs through physicians' prescriptions. It will be recalled that 97.4 percent of all those reporting ethical drug use indicated they obtained their drug(s) legally, i.e., with a physician's script.

More of those reporting psychotropic drug use (50.7 percent) than those reporting use of other prescription drugs (39.0 percent) indicated that they could not perform their daily activities without their ethical drugs (i.e., dependency).

Slightly fewer of those reporting psychotropic drug use (28.6 percent) than those reporting use of other prescription drugs (33.7 percent) indicated

TABLE 3

Psychotropic drug use by quality of family relationships.

QUALITY OF FAMILY RELATIONSHIPS	NO. OF USERS	NO. OF NONUSERS	TOTAL
Satisfactory	48	208	256
Unsatisfactory	11	17	28
Total	59	225	284

health as the major reason for their drug use.

The same percentage (12 percent) of those reporting psychotropic drug use and those reporting use of other prescription drugs indicated having experienced medical problems and/or side effects related to their use of ethical drugs.

About the same percentage (90.6 percent) of those reporting psychotropic drug use and those reporting use of other prescription drugs indicated they had no difficulty in obtaining their ethical drugs.

Those reporting psychotropic drug use uniformly indicated that they knew what these drugs were intended to do, while only 78.7 percent of those reporting use of other prescription drugs indicated they knew what their ethical drugs were supposed to do.

A considerably higher percentage of those reporting psychotropic drug use (38.67 percent) than those reporting use of other prescription drugs (26.4 percent) indicated they took several kinds of drugs—both ethical and OTC drugs—in combination. This finding recalls the issue of drug interaction discussed in the *Background* section of this paper.

Those reporting use of psychotropic drugs in combination with other drugs indicated that they consulted a physician prior to combining such drugs more frequently (75.8 percent) than those reporting use of other prescription drugs in combination.

Slightly fewer of those reporting psychotropic drug use (35.1 percent) than those reporting use of other prescription drugs (40.5 percent) indicated that they used alcohol in moderate amounts, i.e., a few times each week to a few times each month. More of those reporting psychotropic drug use (64.9 percent) than those reporting use of other prescription drugs (56.2 percent) indicated they did not use alcohol.

Those who reported using psychotropic drugs also reported using significantly more prescription drugs overall, a possible confounding factor. Yet, interestingly, those who reported psychotropic drug use also indicated they perceived their personal capabilities to be better than those who did not use psychotropic drugs.

Cross-tabulations revealed significant differences on measures of health and physical disability between those who reported psychotropic drug use and those who recorded no such use. According to the data, those who reported using psychotropic drugs also indicated poorer health and more physical disability than those who reported no use of psychotropic drugs. No significant differences were found between those reporting psychotropic drug use and those reporting nonuse in their decision-making processes, i.e., weighing alternatives, seeking information, considering risks, making decisions, and expressing satisfaction (or dissatisfaction) with decisions made. Those who reported use of psychotropic drugs also indicated greater reliance on themselves and less reliance on family members in making decisions. Despite those indications, those reporting psychotropic drug use scored significantly lower on life satisfaction than those reporting no use of psychotropic drugs, and looked upon the present as the worst time in their lives.

Statistically significant differences were also revealed for age and place of birth. Those who reported using psychotropic drugs tended to be younger and native born, while those who reported no use of psychotropic drugs tended to be older and foreign born.

More women than men reported using psychotropic drugs. This finding corresponds to the one reported earlier, that women in the sample reported using legal drugs—both ethical drugs and over the counter drugs—2.65 times more often than men in the sample (72.2 percent for female respondents, compared to 27.2 percent for male respondents). Since women in the sample tended more frequently to be living alone and to be unmarried, the relationship between psychotropic drug use and sex for several of the other psychosocial variables was confounded.

No significant differences were found between those reporting psychotropic drug use and those reporting no such use on measures of employment and volunteer work. This may be due to the fact that less than one-fourth of the sample population recorded either employment (full time or part time) or involvement in volunteer work.

Those who reported using psychotropic drugs also indicated a need for social services, such as counseling, homemaking, legal aid, etc. Their expressed needs included three major concerns: help with housecleaning chores; help with legal matters; and help in establishing and maintaining contacts with other human beings, "to make sure I'm all right."

IMPLICATIONS

The data presented in this report points to beginning identification and differentiation of legal drug use among elderly persons in our society. Characteristics of psychotropic drug use among the elderly have also been drawn from this research. The data gathered on prescription drug use by noninstitutionalized elderly in this study resembles rather closely the findings reported by Lenhart (1976) and by the Task Force on Prescription Drugs (*The Drug Users* 1968).

One of the major implications of this study is that there are specific demographic and psychosocial variables associated with older Americans who use or refrain from using ethical and over the counter drugs. Patterns of legal drug use vary according to marital status, sex, age, living arrangements, and self-perception. This exploratory research indicates that ethical drugs are used heavily by

independent households than move in with their adult children. The ease with which we accept the myth that our aged parents would love to live with us, if only we would let them, is somewhat surprising in view of the preferences articulated by the same parents.

A generally overlooked variable is that of privacy, something we too often assume an older person no longer needs. The absurdity and demeaning nature of this assumption cannot be overemphasized. Further, the question of why society finds it reasonable to deny the continuation of sexual interest and behavior in older adults is beyond the scope of this section. The fact remains that such a perspective is not only dehumanizing but invalid. We are—and, provided opportunities are available, will continue to be—sexual beings, with the attendant need to express our sexuality in both private and public arenas.

A person's physical living arrangements have considerable impact on his or her life. Family support systems are related to the type of housing an elderly person is able to maintain. Satisfaction with housing arrangements is also associated with a number of variables, no one of which as yet has emerged as the best predictor of a sense of well-being. The interaction among feelings of security, belonging, privacy, independence, and a recognized life space is a complex process. At any given time at least one of every twenty elderly lives in an institution of some sort; many more find themselves institutionalized during their later years, even if it is limited to the period immediately prior to death. Considerable attention has been focused on the inadequacies and often inhumane aspects of custodial, profit-seeking institutions, some of which could be more accurately characterized as warehouses for the rejected. The implications of these types of institutions for our collective responsibility can no longer be denied. An increasing sense of social responsibility has prompted more realistic appraisals of the situation.

Despite its inevitability, death remains a mysterious factor. As advances in health care and medical intervention have occurred during this century, most of our experience with death is now associated with elderly relatives or acquaintances. Part of the social stigma encountered by the elderly may derive from the threat this close relation between death and old age poses to other societal members. Similar themes may be found in the early articulation of disengagement theory in gerontology. Cumming and Henry (1961) postulated a mutual withdrawal of the aged and society. They argued that individuals retreated as they perceived the nearness of death and a decline in their coping strategies. The existence, inevitability, and the extent of this phenomenon have been called into question by later theorists.

The very centrality of death implies that many issues confront individuals as they maneuver their life courses, some in clear and forthright fashion, others in a more oblique or peripheral manner. Each person must come to grips with the meaning of death in his or her own life, and with grief triggered by the death of others. Individuals must develop their own styles of dying. Related questions include the meaning of death for a society, the functions of socially acceptable grief work versus grieving that violates social norms, the timeliness of one's death, and the industry that has developed presumably to speak to the needs of those who die and those who continue to live (Kastenbaum, 1977). As the selections here will reveal, these questions are asked and answered differently depending upon one's location in society: ethnic background, family, and socioeconomic status.

Part and parcel of the aging experience is how significant people feel their actions are or will be. Societal recognition, acceptance, even advocacy, of minority group rights are influenced by a host of factors less than clearly defined. Researchers and planners have been frustrated by the lack of reliable data concerning the aged of minority groups. Until this decade, studies of the aging process among minority Americans were few and far between. What little was known was gleaned from ethnographic accounts or generalizations made from research based almost exclusively on the white population. Fortunately, this situation has vastly improved; attention is now being focused on minority groups in their own right. Current criticism, however, derives from the lack of a historical perspective on each subgroup, the tendency to generalize after using only a cross-sectional research design, and the failure to consider the differential opportunity structure for minority group members in American society. The extent to which racial and ethnic characteristics influence aging has not yet been determined; indeed, the problems in doing so are as challenging and pervasive as they ever were.

The social life course of an individual presents numerous relevant opportunities for investigation and intervention. Without the benefit of some theoretical underpinnings, the problems confronting the aging, the availability of varied coping styles, and the impact of social change cannot help but appear fragmented. Gerontology combines a diverse group of disciplines, addressing interrelated phenomena which for the sake of study often must be abstracted from one's unitary experience, thus contributing to a sense of compartmentalization. The first selection, in an attempt to circumvent this tendency, offers a summary of the principal theories of social gerontology.

The initial theoretical efforts by Cumming and Henry in articulating disengagement theory have since been expanded and restated. As is evident in this reading, the trend in theoretical approaches has been toward more processual, developmental models of aging. Activity and subcultural perspectives on aging complement the emergent theories involving labeling, socioenvironmental interaction and age-stratification. All of the theoretical approaches described have been formulated with the goals of understanding and explanation on the one hand and possible intervention on the other. The value of varied theoretical orientations lies in the manner in which we address the world and thus test our premises about social factors in aging.

As was mentioned earlier, the family life of the elderly is of primary influence in determining how they manage to cope with aging. Treas' and VanHilst's article on marriage rates indicates that the propensity of older people to marry has not changed since the early 1960s, although the absolute number of late life marriages has increased. Despite the fact older people who are married are a lower risk population than those who are not, marital prospects continue to decline with every passing year. The authors find that cultural sanctions favoring remarriage are not as salient for the elderly. In keeping with the age-stratification model described in the first selection, socialization to marital and familial roles among the elderly apparently remains unchanged, while allocation to familial roles would indicate late life marriages are potentially more numerous. Possibilities aside, the reality seems to be that the low rate of remarriage among the elderly will remain just that.

If it can be said that older people may be hesitant to become involved in new family situations late in life, the reluctance with which they are willing to discuss sexual needs and desires is even greater. Research indicates that sexual activity is not only possible among the aged, but that sexual interest is often expressed and frequently sexual contact declines only slightly, especially for those who were sexually interested and active at earlier stages of the life cycle. One should not forget that sexuality is but one form of human expressiveness, one which is often linked to the need to express love, affection and security. Sexual activity is rarely simply physical activity. The meaning of sex and touch throughout an individual's life obviously influences the needs that person seeks to fulfill later in life.

Similarly, sexuality manifests itself in different ways depending upon the social context. The equation of sexual capacity with power is not new, although Safilios-Rothschild ably points to an inherent dilemma in American society: on one side, women find that society is technologically able to keep them fit and attractive; on the other, the possibilities for human sexual equality have yet to be realized in either the norms or the prevalent attitudes and interpersonal reinforcements in today's society.

Life choices, personal adjustment, and satisfaction are also reflected in the physical living environment in which one finds oneself. The article by Lawton, Nahemow, and Teaff explores the association among four environmental variables and six indices of well-being. Data were gathered from 2457 tenants residing in different federally funded housing projects throughout the country. The housing variables examined were community size, height of the residence building, whether the housing was public or nonprofit, and the number of units designated for the elderly. Results of the study indicate that factors other than building size and height have impact on tenant well-being, as measured by the indices in this analysis. We must take care in studying satisfaction with specific housing types to consider where the project, home, or institution is located within the community as well as the physical and psychological access of the aged in the facility to the outside world.

A significant concern for anyone, be they parent, child, or forward-looking adult, is the task of assessing the need for institutionalization of a family member or of oneself. A major component of such a decision is the type and quality of care available in particular nursing homes or extended care facilities. Kart and Manard speak to just this crucial issue in their article. According to the literature relevant to this topic, the variables which comprise the concept of quality of care differ from one investigator to the next. Surveys by the federal government usually define quality in terms of factors contributing to safety and health care. Too often, aesthetic, recreational, educational, and personal opinions are completely ignored. The authors examined five characteristics related to quality of care which emerge from the literature. The type of ownership—nonprofit or proprietary—the size of the facility, as well as the socioeconomic status of the facility's staff and residents, coupled with the resources of the institution and the price of health care influence the delivery of services and the determination of the quality of care provided. In addition, the professionalism of the facility's staff, its management and procedures, and the degree to which new social interaction and relationships are fostered are aspects which affect quality of care. As Kart and Manard point out, we may be able to recognize a good facility when we see it, but it is more difficult to say what factors go into making that decision.

Death is a topic of daily concern for many elderly. Victor Marshall provides a survey of the advantages and disadvantages of congregate living arrangements with respect both to interaction and coping styles. Discussion, determination, and acceptance of the appropriateness of one's own death, including the ramifications of it for one's family may be enhanced in such communities. Popular opinion aside, the aged who have and take the opportunity to explore their impending deaths seem willing and able to balance their natural fears with a sense of equanimity. This possibility certainly needs to be examined to further understanding and intervention in our own lives and in the lives of those facing a move to an institutional facility.

While death will always be a unique and personal experience, attitudes toward death are conditioned to some extent by the social context in which people find themselves. Using the concepts and general theoretical perspective of age-stratification theory, Bengtson, Cuellar, and Ragan explore the relationship between orientation toward death and an individual's location in the social structure. Their sample includes members of two ethnic groups plus a number of white elderly. As Marshall's work suggested, despite many preconceptions to the contrary, increasing age appears to be associated with a decreasing fear of death. Survey research techniques coupled with ethnographic data provide a richly detailed portrait of contemporary attitudes toward death among the elderly.

The cultural heterogeneity described in the previous selection is reinforced in the next two articles. Herbert Golden briefly reviews the demographic profile of black elderly in America. He maintains that racism has adversely affected the life chances of blacks to such an extent that those who are among today's aged have a lower life expectancy, lower income, and are twice as likely to be illiterate as their white counterparts. He cautions researchers and observers alike that ethnicity is as important as age, sex, or socioeconomic status in predicting status and family relationships. The admonition that we cannot assume members of a minority group exhibit any more homogeneity within the group than what exists between different groups is becoming more prevalent. This theme is also articulated in the article by Kalish and Moriwaki on elderly Asian Americans.

Asian Americans have long been a neglected minority. They were not included in the orignal plans for the 1971 White House Conference on Aging until just one month before the scheduled meetings. The stereotypic notion that Asian Americans take care of their own and so are rarely in need of outside aid has been pervasive enough to ensure a paucity of data concerning this American minority. Examining historical evidence as well as ethnographic data enables the authors to challenge the myth that elderly Asian Americans are well cared for in ongoing family relationships. The peculiar history of those minority members currently aged is such that many have not lived with their families since arriving in this country. Kalish and Moriwaki conclude with a description of needed social services and the type of agency staffing most likely to succeed in the delivery of these essential services.

The final selection explores the demographic aspects of minority aging in the urban environment of Manhattan. The barriers mentioned in the previous article are examined in greater detail by Marjorie Cantor. She also explores potential avenues for intervention, and for successful delivery of social services. The evidence suggests that such services, even when available, are unlikely to be utilized to their full extent by minority elderly.

REFERENCES

1. CUMMING, E., and HENRY, W. E. *Growing Old: the Process of Disengagement.* New York: Basic Books, 1961.

2. KASTENBAUM, R. J., *Death, Society, and Human Experience.* St. Louis: C. V. Mosby Company, 1977.

3. SUSSMAN, M. B., "The Family Life of Old People." In *Handbook of Aging and the Social Sciences,* edited by R. H. Binstock and E. Shanas, pp. 218–43. New York: Van Nostrand Reinhold Company, 1976.

4. TROLL, LILLIAN. "The Family of Later Life: a Decade Review." *Journal of Marriage and the Family,* 33 (1971): 263–90.

5. U.S. Department of Congress, Bureau of the Census. *Current Population Reports,* Series P-20, No. 287. Washington, D.C.: Government Printing Office (1975).

6. WERSHOW, H. J. "The Four Percent Fallacy: Some Further Evidence and Policy Implications." *The Gerontologist 16* (1, Pt. 1) (1976): 52–55.

Theories of Social Gerontology

Jon Hendricks
C. Davis Hendricks

As should already be evident, understanding the process of aging is impossible without consideration of the connections between aging on the physiological level and the social or cultural setting. For many years social gerontologists have worked alongside their biologically oriented colleagues to unravel the intricacies of becoming old, but only in the past two decades have they attempted to formulate integrative conceptual frameworks of their own to lend some order to the vast collection of empirical findings. Initially, gerontologists interested in either physiological or social aspects of the aging question proceeded piecemeal, focusing attention on problems the larger society defined as relevant, without any overriding concern for theoretical explanation. As the field has matured as a scientific endeavor, the separate branches developed at different rates by adopting the theoretical and methodological tools of earlier kindred disciplines. In the present discussion our concern will be with theories of social gerontology that have gained adherents since the first of them was formulated in 1960.

From J. Hendricks and C. D. Hendricks, *Aging in Mass Society: Myths and Realities* (Cambridge, Massachusetts: Winthrop Publishers, Inc., 1977), pp. 102–128. Reprinted by permission.

THE PURPOSE OF THEORY

Theoretical Frameworks

The description of physiological theories in the previous chapter probably served to reinforce the preconception most people have of theoretical explanation as being the domain either of natural scientists surrounded by their specimens and a vast library or of life scientists in white lab coats carefully scrutinizing a computer printout of performance measures. Regardless of whether theory is defined by attempts at complete explanation and predictive accuracy or simply as a descriptive account of a particular event, theorizing is by no means limited to scientists. In point of fact, the theoretical process is considerably more widespread, constantly taking place in everyday life, from the time language is acquired to the development of a philosophy of life which gives it meaning. The process of naming, the most fundamental theoretical organization, is manifested by us all when as children we learn to identify objects by readily observable characteristics that help us discriminate one from another. Although general conceptual categories already exist in the structure of the language into which we are born, we each discover by experience increasingly diverse events that can be brought together under a general classification. Since others also learn to view the world in roughly the same terms, they, too, develop the same generalizations about it and are able to communicate what they see or feel. The structure of our language itself, therefore, serves as an implicit theoretical framework that not only circumscribes experience but acts as a filter through which individual encounters are perceived, modified, and categorized as examples of more general phenomena.

In a number of important respects, the theories formulated by social gerontologists can be viewed as extensions of the unreflective theorizing carried out in ordinary life. For one thing, gerontologists bring with them to the study of aging a certain taken-for-granted view of life based on their personal experience and the values of their culture. Furthermore, the "objects" upon which social gerontologists fix their attention are not at all like those of the natural scientists, who are free to impose a purely arbitrary order on their observations so long as it is logical and agreeable to fellow scientists. By contrast, the social scientist is faced with a pre-established system of meanings known to and utilized by the very people who are the focus of scientific investigation. It is important to bear in mind in examining the theories promoted by social gerontologists in their efforts to explain and understand the process of aging that the crucial dimensions of their conceptual frameworks are but reflections from the larger social matrix. At the same time, however, gerontologists strive to reach beyond the world of common sense to discover consistent patterns of aging in the social world.

Needless to say, the analysis of human behavior is infinitely complex and requires its own particular approach. Over and above any disciplinary orientation or field of investigation, all theoretical explanations share a common objective of making explicit the order behind what often appears as chaotic or individualistic events. By developing a system of interrelated propositions in a logical and verifiable manner, gerontologists subscribe to a similar goal with the intention of producing an integrative framework capable of providing a coherent explanation ·of why people age the way they do. In his introductory remarks to the first detailed explication of age stratification theory, Brim (1972) fur-

nishes a concise statement of the need for conceptual integration that is equally applicable to other theories of aging. To begin with, an awareness of the *normative* character of aging in a social-cultural context brings about a broad appreciation of individual situations and the patterning fixed upon them by the institutional order in a given society. Once we have an impression of the relative nature of age-related norms, cognizance of their malleability should follow. The realization that aging does not necessarily have to be the way it is offers a justification for interceding in what is often taken to be a predetermined natural process. As Brim points out, the possibility for changing the manner in which we age has the potential of enhancing not only our personal lives but the general welfare of society as well.

Adjusting to Age

Prior to discussing the theories themselves, it is desirable to linger for a moment in order to touch on some of the difficulties involved in accounting for social patterns of aging. Not the least of these has to do with the wisdom behind or the need for a theory applicable to only the later years. There is less than complete agreement among gerontologists themselves that the social nature of aging requires its own explanation. Granted, theories do have a significant heuristic value, aiding as they do in the collection of data and the organization of existing information, plus giving direction for the implementation of policy changes. Still, the question remains as to *why* old age should demand its own, perhaps singular, interpretation. By the time people reach their later years, have they not already weathered innumerable personal changes and life course crises, which ought to leave them well prepared to face whatever ambiguities or anxieties they might encounter in their post-retirement years? In one way, no, since for nearly every other age-related transformation in life, most people undergo what social psychologists call *anticipatory socialization*, the learning of a new role preparatory to actually assuming it. In addition, while it is true that adapting to change is a lifelong process, the adjustments made after one turns sixty or sixty-five are carried out against a backdrop of involutional changes in the physical and social realms. Whether or not it is essential or even possible to devise theoretical explanations is an issue that cannot be resolved here. Let us merely caution that some social scientists have noted the fallacy of inferring each new social problem demands a novel description. With regard to aging, some have suggested a perspective focusing on the nature of the transitional episodes throughout life may be sufficient to account for whatever change takes place during old age. In all fairness, it must be made clear the theories themselves do not seek to explain the totality of social aging; they generally limit themselves to expositions of how people adjust to advancing age. The means by which people reach a satisfactory structuring of their lives after the age of sixty-five are part and parcel of one of the more important unanswered questions about the life cycle. As older people become ever more visible on the national scene, it is predicted that even greater emphasis will be placed on providing an accurate prediction of what awaits us all in our later years (Havighurst, 1968; Maddox, 1970).

In constructing their explanations, social scientists are forced to treat all members of a category as though they are nearly identical. It is the only way by which any useful generalizations can be made, though in the case of human beings, they recognize the risks involved in making such an assumption. The aged do not, however, constitute a homogeneous aggregate; the same factors that are known to differentiate people at the earlier stages of life continue to operate unabated through the later phases. To adequately discuss the social and social-psychological processes integral to the way older people adjust to their situations, it is necessary to distinguish the consequences of aging *per se* from those more appropriately attributed to discontinuities in personal lifestyle or to situational constraints and generational effects. While there is no denying the importance of the latter, they do not actually reflect maturational age changes as much as they do differences between cohorts or individuals (Maddox, 1965; Schaie, 1967). To date, gerontological theory occupies an underdeveloped area within the field, but the last decade has been marked by a rapid growth and sophistication in the depiction of the social variables involved in human aging. The major theories all speak to essentially the same problem and, in a way, complement one another in many important respects.

PRINCIPAL THEORIES IN SOCIAL GERONTOLOGY

The propagation of explicit explanatory models in social gerontology can be dated from the first tentative statement of disengagement theory published in 1960, and particularly from the appearance the next year of Cumming and Henry's *Growing Old* (Cumming et al., 1960; Cumming and Henry, 1961). In the following years, scores of criticisms and reformulations appeared, including separate revisions by the original authors, before the controversy over the applicability of the theory finally began to subside. Although the disengagement model has now been largely discredited, it remains an important milestone in the theoretical literature because of the attention it generated and its role in bringing forth competing perspectives (Hochschild, 1975). An implicit emphasis on active involvement on the part of the elderly as a means of sustaining high morale had been an undercurrent in gerontological discussions for years, but did not receive deliberate explication until after the disengagement notion had sensitized researchers to the value of presenting detailed paradigms. It was inevitable, of course, that variations of these two approaches would prompt still further revisions. Perhaps the best known among these is the conception of an aged subculture formulated by Rose (1965) to account for the type of interaction commonly engaged in by older people. In the following sections each of these will be treated before turning to a brief discussion of a personality continuity theory, an ecological resource model and the recent age stratification perspective increasingly utilized by researchers to explain variations in life satisfaction and aging.

Disengagement Theory

The proposition of mutual disengagement represents the first major theoretical system attempted by social gerontologists. It was originally based on a cross-sectional survey analysis of 275 people ranging in age from fifty to ninety, all of whom resided in Kansas City and were physically and financially self-sufficient. Reflecting the common sense observation that older people are more subject to ill health and to the probability of death than their younger counterparts, Cumming and Henry (1961) assert that a process of mutual withdrawal normally occurs in order to insure both an optimum level of personal gratification as well as an uninterrupted continuation of the social system. Since disengagement is thought to be a normatively governed phenomenon woven into the social fabric of mass society, they conceive of it as quite beyond individual whim or fancy, excepting some limited input into its timing. In setting forth the basic tenets of their theory, the authors refer to the aging process as:

> . . . an inevitable mutual withdrawal or disengagement, resulting in decreased interaction between the aging person and others in the social system he belongs to. The process may be initiated by the individual or by others in the situation. The aging person may withdraw more markedly from some classes of people while remaining relatively close to others. His withdrawal may be accompanied from the outset by a preoccupation with himself; certain institutions in society may make this withdrawal easy for him. When the aging process is complete, the equilibrium which existed in middle life between the individual and his society has given way to a new equilibrium

characterized by a greater distance and an altered type of relationship (1961).

In spelling out the details of disengagement, Cumming and Henry clearly enunciate what is to be regarded as the inevitability and universality of the process. Society retracts because of the need to fit younger people into the slots once occupied by older people, no longer as useful or dependable as they were, and in order to maintain the equilibrium of the system. Individuals, on the other hand, choose to retreat because of an awareness of their diminishing capacities and the short time left to them before death. Although individual or cultural factors may alter the configuration of withdrawal, it is thought that older people everywhere will ultimately experience a severing of their social ties. As the number, nature, and diversity of the older person's contacts with the rest of the world contract, he or she will in effect become the sole judge of what is appropriate, freed as it were from normative control over commonplace behavior. Consequently, with the narrowing of the social life space, disengagement becomes a circular or self-perpetuating process in which there is a continuing shrinkage of interactional opportunities. Men, because of the instrumental nature of the roles with which they have primarily identified, will experience a drastic early constriction and identity crisis following retirement. In comparison, women, who have traditionally had ready access to socioemotional roles not as immediately subject to age-grading and organizational imperatives, encounter relatively fewer stresses. For a combination of experiential and developmental reasons, older people in general are likely to find themselves less motivated to preserve their social positions, while at the same time society will attempt to place younger people whose skills are not yet obsolete in positions held by those nearing retirement. A disjuncture may occur when either the individual or society is not yet ready to begin disengagement, although in most cases societal needs will take priority in initiating the process. When older people suffer severe adjustment problems, it usually implies a lack of synchronization between individual readiness and societal demands. However, as a corollary to the postulate of mutuality, Cumming and Henry did concede the possibility of re-engagement should the individual choose to cultivate a new set of valued skills. Morale will obviously suffer as the disengagement process gains momentum due to the gaps between opportunities and orientation to previous roles, but once the elderly person is able to carve out new concerns and rearrange his or her priorities to fit the new station in life, high morale can conceivably be reestablished (Cumming and Henry, 1961).

Almost from the instant it appeared, disengagement theory engendered a running controversy among social gerontologists. For the most part, criticisms tended to converge around the presumed inevitability and inherent nature of the process. Questions were also posed about the functionality of withdrawal from either the individual or societal standpoint, plus the apparent lack of attention to personality factors and their effect on the whole process (Maddox, 1964; Atchley, 1971). Even Cumming and Henry have expressed misgivings in separate revisions of their original formulation. In her further thoughts on the theory of disengagement, Cumming (1963) backed away from an emphasis on the societal equilibrium and prescribed behavior to concentrate instead on the role of innate biological and personality differences as distinct from externally imposed withdrawal. She no longer viewed societal pressures as sufficient to account for disengagement, though she did reiterate her contention that men and women would undergo sex-linked stylized adjustment. Responding to the theory's critics, Cumming adds a caveat regarding what she terms the *appearance*, contrasted to the *experience*, of engagement. To those who would look simply at activity levels, Cumming suggests it is possible for disengaged people to appear involved, when in fact they are merely going through the motions of interaction, remaining oblivious to or simply shrugging off so-cial sanctions on their behavior. The psychologically engaged, on the other hand, engrossed as they are in social intercourse, would still be responsive to feedback from others. At the same time, Cumming indicates a nascent attitudinal detachment, akin to a desocialization, may begin in middle age, far in advance of actual withdrawal and in the midst of what may for all intents and purposes look like the height of engagement.

Cumming also makes an important distinction between "*impingers*," those who take an assertive stance in their interaction, and "*selectors*," who are more passive, waiting for others to confirm pre-existing assumptions about themselves, while recognizing only those cues that reinforce their views. In later years, impingers are thought to be more anxious about the prospect of disengagement, while the selectors have a capacity to use alternative mechanisms to insulate and maintain their personal orientations. Furthermore, Cumming repeatedly distinguishes men and women along a social dimension, not necessarily related to personality attributes as much as socialization, with men being the more ill-prepared to accommodate themselves to compensating forms of sociability in their later years. In either case, the remaining socioemotional roles assume added importance in maintaining self-conceptions or stimulation, helping both men and women resist shrinkage throughout much of the rest of life. Subsequent research has affirmed Cumming's emphasis on differential disengagement as an avenue for maximizing adjustment in various relationships (Williams and Wirths, 1965; Strieb and Schneider, 1971; Cumming, 1975). As far as the earlier definition of mutuality is important, Cumming (1975) redefines it as ". . . another way of saying the process is normatively governed and in a sense agreed upon by all concerned." She does repeat, nonetheless, her original contention of the interest mass society has in controlling its own vital affairs by removing crucial functions from the role repertoires of older people, though she does not explicitly address the part played by structural conditions.

Henry (1965) also amended his initial view of the disengagement model to lay greater stress on psychological dynamics. Like Cumming, he agreed that they had not satisfactorily resolved all the questions of the process, but rather than focusing on innate temperamental variables, he chose instead to adopt a developmental approach. In essence, Henry's later statement is practically synonymous with the position propounded by Havighurst, Neugarten, and Tobin (1968), who also worked with the Kansas City data, but who arrived at a somewhat different conclusion from that originally implied by Cumming and Henry. Since a general overview of the developmental perspective is offered below, it should suffice at this point to say developmentalists conceive of personality as continually evolving, with adjustments at each successive stage reflecting earlier coping strategies as well as the matrix of environmental factors active at the moment. Most developmental psychologists also see a gradual turning toward greater *interiority* over the course of life; consequently, it is quite natural to expect older people to be less attentive to external events and more attuned to their own inner states. In Henry's restatement, the character of personality coping mechanisms and the focus on interiority are derived from previous experiences that determine the level of engagement or disengagement during subsequent stages of the life cycle. Those people who customarily have dealt with stress by turning inward and insulating themselves from the world will probably continue to manifest a pattern of withdrawal. At the same time, those who remain engaged are likely to have been similarly predisposed over the course of their lives. For this latter group, the nature of activities may change, but generally they will rely on their interaction to resist the centripetal movement inherent in the disengagement model. For all practical and theoretical purposes, Henry's revision of the kernel of disengagement theory can be read as an abandonment in favor of a more developmental approach.

The Activity Perspective

In the course of maturing, children gain a sense of themselves through their socializing experiences and via responses of significant others to various identities tried on in much the way adults try on clothing. By assuming various roles, children are able to participate in the larger world, thereby gradually carving out their own social identities. As adults, people continue to refine and refurbish their self-concepts in their performance of socially valued, or at least legitimated, actions, seeking out what is sometimes referred to as *consensual validation*: the affirmation of their personal sense of worth and integrity. Upon reaching that socially prescribed stage of life wherein they are commonly divested of many of the roles that have been so central to their lives for years, older people experience a narrowing of their social radius, a reduction of their activity levels and, consequently, a loss of or confusion in their sense of who they are. To offset these losses, preserve morale and sustain self-concepts, the activity theory of aging presumes, almost the converse of disengagement, that restitution, in the form of compensatory activities, must take place. By keeping active, it is presumed people will remain socially and psychologically fit. In the words of one researcher, the central thesis of activity theory can be summarized as: ". . . the greater the number of optional role resources with which the individual enters old age, the better he or she will withstand the demoralizing effects of exit from the obligatory roles ordinarily given priority in adulthood" (Blau, 1973).

The proponents of the activity orientation assert that disengagement theory may be applicable to a small minority of the elderly, usually the very old; but for the vast bulk of older people, the continuance of a moderately active lifestyle will have a marked preservative effect on their sense of well-being (Havighurst and Albrecht, 1953; Maddox, 1970). Despite recognition of the fact that not all activities provide sustenance for the self-concept, little attention has as yet been directed to the differences between types of activities or an individual's ability to exert any significant control over either the roles themselves or the performance of those roles. As a result, the theory has received only limited empirical support and has been criticized as an oversimplification of the questions involved. It may hardly be appropriate merely to substitute pastimes, geared to what is thought to be older people's interests and abilities, for those roles they surrendered as they moved beyond middle age. Busying one's self with enterprises meaningless in terms of dominant cultural values, presumably still subscribed to by older people, may not in itself contribute to adjustment (Phillips, 1957; Gubrium, 1973). On the other hand, both longitudinal and cross-cultural investigations of old age have repeatedly found a positive, but by no means incontrovertible, association between morale, personal adjustment, and activity levels (Havighurst et al., 1969; Palmore, 1970).

The first full-bodied, systematic statement of activity theory did not appear until over a decade after the disengagement theory caused such a furor in gerontological circles, and even then its validation proved to be somewhat problematic. Following an explicit definition of the concepts implied, four postulates central to activity theory have been stipulated. First, the greater the role loss, the less the participation in activity. Second, as activity levels remain high, the greater the availability of role support for role identities claimed by the older person. Third, the stability of role supports insures a stable self-concept. Finally, the more positive one's self-concept, the greater the degree of life satisfaction. From these four propositions, six theorems were deduced that specify in detail the relationships implied by the theory. With such an auspicious statement of a theory never more than implied in the twenty years since it was initially suggested, it is indeed unfortunate that the data available to the investigators were insufficient to provide definitive support for the propositions basic to activity theory (Lemon, Bengtson, and Peterson, 1972).

The Aged as a Subculture

Broadly speaking, both the activity and subcultural perspectives on the adjustment problems of the elderly share an underlying interactionist orientation that posits a close relationship among roles, social identities, and the maintenance of self-concepts. However, while the activity approach assumes people continue to adhere to middle-aged standards and expectations as they move into their later years, the latter asserts the development of a distinctive aged subculture. Unfortunately, neither is able to explain the discontinuities assumed to exist between middle and old age. To help clarify the social relations between older people and the rest of society, some social gerontologists have offered the concept of an aged subculture similar in nature to other age status groupings. As conceived by Rose (1965), the initial advocate of this perspective, whenever members of one category interact more among themselves than with people from other categories, a subculture will be generated. In addition, he suggested there are a variety of demographic and social trends contributing to the genesis of an identifiable aged subculture that effectively cuts across all previous statuses to impart to the elderly a sense of group identity over and above earlier memberships. Among the specific factors mentioned by Rose are the sheer numbers of persons beyond the age of sixty-five who are still healthy and mobile enough to interact. With the growth of what some have termed aged ghettos, either retirement communities, inner city neighborhoods or residual rural congregations created when younger people migrate to urban areas, older people live in close proximity to one another. Legally established retirement policies now common in most industrialized societies have blocked major avenues for many older people to retain their integration with the larger society, thereby promoting a greater identification with an aged peer group. Social services designed to assist older people also tend to prompt recognition of their common situation at a time when many have an opportunity to engage in wide-ranging, non-work-related activities for the first time. Rose goes on to note that many attributes of an aged subculture may stem from biological changes, normative expectations and perceptions of older people held by the general population, or from generational differences in socialization, each making its own contribution to an age-graded segregation.

As Rose outlines it, individual involvement in an aged subculture depends on the solidarity of the age group itself, plus the nature and extent of contacts retained with the total society through families, the media, employment or the older person's own resistance to aging. In many instances, the statuses previously so important are not nearly as meaningful in the world of the older person, who is isolated from the spheres of life that imparted status originally. Good health and physical mobility serve to confer status within the aged subculture, while occupational, educational or economic prestige tend to be redefined as less influential than they were during earlier years. Commenting on the development of an aging self-concept, Rose avers that societal institutions, formalized retirement being foremost among them, have imposed an artificial boundary on what is socially recognized as old age. Concomitantly, an aging group consciousness has arisen, fostering an awareness of belonging to a particular group and not simply a chronological category. Participation in voluntary associations has also been a primary mechanism in the development of group self-consciousness, as has the greater puublicity given to the elderly's common predicament or occasional victories. Although there are many who disagree with the idea of an aged subculture, claiming for instance that the elderly do not fit traditional definitions of minority groups, there is an accumulating body of evidence to indicate many of the elements in Rose's framework are indeed extremely powerful factors in delineating associational patterns sponsoring a communal consciousness (Streib, 1965; Rosow, 1967, 1974; Hochschild, 1973).

Whether the social stigma attached to being old or the elderly's own affinity for people their age provides sufficient grounds for a subculture to evolve to the point where older people become a voting bloc as Rose envisions is a question which presently cannot be answered, despite the admitted increase in militancy among older people. It is agreed, however, that there is certainly a strong relationship between peer group participation rates and the adjustment process of the elderly. From the standpoint of activity theory, the occasional person who expresses high morale but low activity levels is a deviant, while from a subcultural perspective he or she may simply be listening to an older drummer. If by engaging in activities governed by performance standards not suitable to their capabilities older people perceive the possibility of failure, they will in all likelihood readjust their interests to reflect their current status, joining with their age peers (Miller, 1965). Neither the disengagement model, the activity theory, nor the idea of an aged subculture has so far proven to be as useful a predictive tool as social gerontologists are searching for, though their underlying utility as heuristic aids remains unquestioned.

Personality and Patterns of Aging

There is a sizeable contingent of social gerontologists who are of the opinion that no monolithic theoretical framework can explain successful aging patterns. To understand why some people have difficulties while others have none is thought to require an appreciation of the interplay between biological, social, and personal changes as they come to expression in an individual's own coping style. To meet the tasks of living, people develop distinctive behavioral and psychological responses which those with whom they interact come to identify as their personality. Over time, characteristic patterns are built up on which people rely in the process of adapting themselves to the new situations and problems they encounter. In a sense, these patterns are stable features of one's self; yet they are dynamic, perpetually evolving, but always rooted in the past (Birren, 1964; Havighurst, 1968). As far as the adaptability of older people to the situations confronted in later life is concerned, those who focus on the persistence of personality traits assert:

> There is considerable evidence that, in normal men and women, there is no sharp discontinuity of personality with age, but instead an increasing consistency. Those characteristics that have been central to the personality seem to become even more clearly delineated, and those values the individual has been cherishing become even more salient. In the personality that remains integrated—and in the environment that permits—patterns of overt behavior are likely to become increasingly consonant with the individual's underlying personality needs and his desires (Neugarten, Havighurst and Tobin, 1968).

Interestingly enough, even though personal adjustment is by definition a highly individualized process, gerontologists have been able to isolate a limited number of *personality types*. In an analysis of adaptive patterns observed among a panel of 87 older men—ranging in age from fifty-five to eighty-four—Reichard, Livson and Peterson (1962) delineated five main types of character structure that describe the majority of men they studied. In each case, all the evidence available to the research team suggested the personalities of the panel members, though distinguished by age-specific criteria, had not changed appreciably throughout most of adulthood. Healthy adjusted men could be classified as members of either the mature, rocking chair, or armored categories, while the less successful agers were more often characterized as either angry or self-haters. *Mature men* are those well-balanced types

who maintain close personal relationships. Being realistic, they accept both the strengths and the weaknesses of their age, finding little to regret about retirement and approaching most problems in a relaxed or convivial manner without having to continually assess blame. *Rocking chair* personalities are passive-dependent agers who are content to lean on others for support, disengage and let most of life's activities pass by their doors. They fret neither about work nor about retirement, though generally they look upon work as pure drudgery, to be escaped if at all practical. Usually they possess some insight into their own feelings, acknowledging their admiration for women, whom they see as experiencing a different sort of life. *Armored men* are those with well-integrated defense mechanisms, which serve as adequate protection. Rigid and stable, they present a strong silent front and often rely on activity as an expression of their continuing independence. Insight is not one of the armored type's stronger qualities, nor are they able to tolerate people who are markedly different from themselves. Still, they represent an adjusted group within the confines of their own personality system. On the other hand, *angry men* are bitter about life, themselves and other people. Aggressiveness is a common response, as is suspicion of others, especially minorities or women. With little tolerance for ambiguity or frustration, they have always shown some instability in work and their personal lives, and now feel extremely threatened by age. Finally, the *self-haters* are similar to angry men except most of their animosity is turned inward upon themselves. Seeing themselves as dismal failures, being old only depresses them all the more.

Ironically, another typology very similar to this one was developed by a group of social psychologists working with the same Kansas City data utilized by Cumming and Henry. Viewing personality systems as a crucial dimension of life satisfaction, Neugarten and her associates utilized sophisticated statistical procedures in order to avoid the methodological criticism that was leveled at Reichard's findings. In a preliminary typology published about the time Cumming and Henry began to express doubts about their own theory, Neugarten, together with various colleagues, outlined four major personality types, each with its own subdivisions (Neugarten et al., 1964, 1968; Neugarten, 1972). In the original version separate patterns were developed for men and women, although subsequently these were combined into one typology resembling that developed by Reichard and her associates. Neugarten's types are labeled *integrated, armored-defended, passive-dependent* and *unintegrated*. In most respects her descriptions parallel Reichard's, with one important modification. Neugarten asked her respondents to evaluate themselves both in terms of their own earlier expectations and in comparison with age peers. Judging from their case histories, it does indeed appear likely, according to Neugarten's position, that aged personalities are most often merely the extensions of middle-age coping styles into later years.

EMERGENT THEORIES IN SOCIAL GERONTOLOGY

Social Environment and Aging

As the quest for a serviceable conceptual framework has expanded, still another contingent of the gerontological community has called for a closer look at the reciprocal relationship between aging and social environments. Generally speaking, the various approaches, though still in the formulative stages, assert contextual analyses that have not received the attention they deserve in studies of the aging process (Bennett, 1970). In essence, their view contends that the values and beliefs endemic to given situations exert an undeniable degree of suzerainty over individuals insofar as they constitute the cultural backdrop against which the elderly test their adaptability to change. Advocating the development of an ecological perspective that stresses the interaction between role alternatives and individual adjustment within social systems, Bruhn (1971) claims it ought to be possible to avoid the negative connotations often associated with chronological age. Whether or not a person does adapt to the inevitable changes of life depends on the nature of alternative exchange mechanisms available within the social environment. Without some idea of their range, it is impossible to evaluate adjustment. Although Bruhn's ecological posture stands out because of its anticipation of age-stratification theory and because of its attention to aging as a dynamic process occurring in a system of structural and processural components, he is not alone in setting forth what will be called here a social environmental model. As conceived by another researcher, three elements are crucial to such a model; an emphasis on normative expectations derived from particular contexts, attention to individual capacities for interaction and a focus on the subjectively evaluated correspondence between ability and what is expected in a particular situation. If all three components are reasonably consonant, older people are much more likely to feel a sense of well-being. Yet since each is constantly changing at its own unique rate, adjustment is always contingent on maintaining supportive environments and individual resources for manipulating unfavorable situations (Gubrium, 1973, 1974).

A useful framework for analyzing the role of personal resources in promoting successful aging is provided by those who conceive of aging as involving a rebalancing of exchange relationships. The thrust of the exchange model is relatively simple: interaction is predicated on all parties maximizing the rewards to be had from their association while minimizing the costs. In other words, people continue to trade in the realm of personal exchange only so long as the benefits of their interaction outweigh the costs. Should the rewards, whether material or nonmaterial, be devalued relative to what must be undergone or foregone in order to achieve them, social contact will subsequently cease. Naturally, an assessment of the costs entailed depends on an appraisal of alternatives for reaching the same goal or a viable substitute (Emerson, 1972). In terms of the interaction of older people, exchange theory explains their shrinking social networks as a realignment of their personal relationships brought about by a debasing of the influence that they are able to exercise over their environments. Without valued skills and finding themselves more often the recipient than the initiator of personal bonds, the only commodity older people have to bargain with in the social marketplace to win acceptance and support from others is compliance. Hence, for example, they may cultivate the appearance of "mellowness" in order to avoid alienating the affections of those upon whom they are dependent for their interpersonal ties (Blau, 1973). The link between the ability to control one's environment and a whole gamut of physiological and social factors needs to be specified in far greater detail; however, the exchange paradigm does at least permit a consideration of these in the adjustment process of the elderly (Dowd, 1975).

What has been labeled the social breakdown theory provides what may be the most systematic statement of the interdependence between older people and their social world. As initially drafted, the social breakdown syndrome referred to the negative feedback generated by a person already susceptible to psychological problems. Once the cycle is initiated, it serves to reinforce everyone's conception of incompetence, thereby insuring even further difficulties (Zusman, 1966). A parallel is assumed by some gerontologists to exist among older people who encounter societal prejudices about aging. As is the case with anyone else surrounded by unfamiliar circumstances, role loss, or drastic change without adequate preparation, older people reach out for some hard and fast cues to advise them as to how they should react. The very fact that they must reach out is then taken by all parties as an indication of failing capacity, a cause for concern. In order to

elicit further interaction, older persons gradually, almost inadvertently, adopt some of the negative characteristics ascribed to them, thus slipping deeper into a dependent status as the cycle is repeated (Figure 1). In adapting the social breakdown model to explain aging in modern societies, Kuypers and Bengtson (1973) assert the continuing adherence to the middle-age values of visible productivity, so prevalent in American society, practically assures an invitation to involvement in the breakdown syndrome.

There are, however, alternatives available that might lessen the probability of social breakdown. Intervention in the cycle through provision of opportunities for older people to enhance their sense of competence in appropriately structured environments, free from the dominance of general societal values, engenders the possibility of breaking the spiral, or of replacing it with what Kuypers and Bengtson term a reconstruction syndrome. By improving environmental supports while facilitating an expression of personal strengths, if in no other way than recognizing the tendency toward inferiority or allowing older people to make independent decisions, the forces leading to breakdown could be ameliorated within a positive interactive environment. Shifting the focus from general theoretical explanations or the narrow emphasis on continuity of personality traits to one that attempts to align personal factors, including self-labeling, with a fluid responsive world will, according to those espousing a social-environmental model, allow for effective participation by older people. In the view of Kuypers and Bengtson, the place to begin is with a model having practical applicability at the individual level, since it is unlikely the larger society will furnish alternative environments when dominant values are what brought about the situation in the first place. Restructuring of the environment will be by no means simple, as all sponsors of an environmental approach realize, but even small gains will improve our chances for insuring a satisfying life among the elderly, paving

Figure 1

The social breakdown cycle in old age.

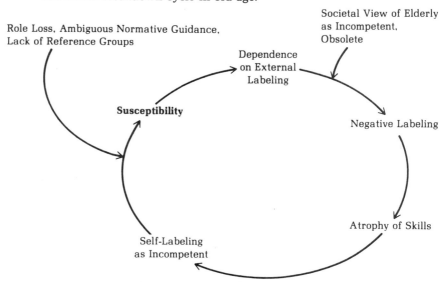

Source: J. A. Kuypers and V. L. Bengtson, "Social Breakdown and Competence: A Model of Normal Aging," *Human Development*, 16, 3 (1973): 190.

the way for the eventual acknowledgement of the potential inhumanity of unresponsive societal institutions.

Sociology of Age Stratification

Age stratification theory adopts a somewhat broader stance than any of the foregoing explanations in an effort to illuminate the myriad linkages among age, personality, and the social systems to which people belong. To speak meaningfully about the status of old age, or for that matter any age, the proponents of an age-stratification model focus on the need to view age not merely as an individual characteristic, but as a dynamic component of every aspect of modern societies (Riley, 1971; Foner, 1975). It takes as its point of departure the seemingly straightforward observation that societies typically arrange themselves into a hierarchy of age strata complete with obligations and prerogatives assigned to members as they move

from one stratum to the next. The particular configuration of one's social roles is dependent on individual attributes, yet at the same time, it reflects certain parameters imposed by structural factors and by the composition of successive biological cohorts. Since each age stratum develops its own characteristic subculture as it moves through time, and because history itself presents subsequent cohorts with their own unique conditions, sequential generations manifest distinctive patterns of aging (Riley, Johnson and Foner, 1972).

The notion of *age grading* discussed earlier, long a familiar concept in the anthropological literature but infrequently applied to modern mass societies, forms the underpinning for the age stratification model. As shown in Figure 2, the age structure of a society is constructed from four primary elements. The first requirement is a population of disparate individuals who can be grouped together on the basis of chronological age or other developmental criteria into a series of age *strata*. As these cohorts move through life, innumerable forces impinge on them to alter the overall size and composition of each stratum and, indirectly, the population as a whole. Second, each stratum, because of actual physical, social or psychological factors, differs from the others in terms of the contributions it makes to ongoing societal needs. *Age-related capacities* of successive strata might vary as a result of the impact of cultural values on the definition of childhood and old age, technological change, or the influence of health factors on physical performance throughout life. Consequently, aging can be viewed either as a movement from one stratum to the next or as an indicator of physical abilities or motivations in other areas of life.

The third ingredient of the model is the patterning and distribution of *social roles*. Age may be a direct linkage—as when biological constraints limit when women may be pregnant, or when age criteria are legally established for voting, holding certain public offices, retirement and so on—or it may operate indirectly—as when there are socially prescribed parameters for given roles. Examples of the latter might include the sanctions regarding the appropriate age for high school students or for those desiring to enter medical school, or the appropriate age for a junior executive. Most often, age-graded roles appear as sets or constellations of roles simultaneously accessible to people within a certain flexible time frame; for instance, parents of pre-school children are not usually found among the retired or those ensconced in the upper echelons of their occupations. In a general but very real sense, the criteria employed in establishing the distribution of age-related roles provide a reliable guide to societal priorities and values. Finally, there is an element of *age-related expectations* intrinsic to the ways in which people react in the roles they perform. Even when a role may not be closed to a person on the basis of age, age nevertheless influences the perceptions of competence and the finer shadings of performance. What is considered suitable behavior ranges along a sliding scale within the larger definition of the role, thereby allowing people to continue in roles for some time without experiencing serious disjunctures or incongruities.

As originally formulated, the age stratification model also posits a series of interrelated processes affecting the degree of articulation between the structural elements

Figure 2

Elements and processes in age stratification theory.

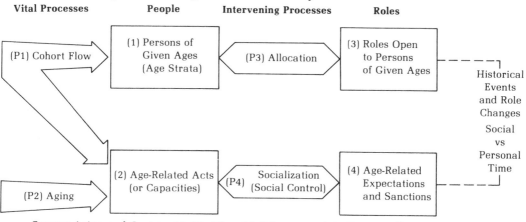

Source: *Aging and Society,* M. W. Riley, M. Johnson, and A. Foner. Vol. 3, *A Sociology of Age Stratification* (New York: Russell Sage Foundation, 1972), p. 9.

and the rhythm or patterning of individual lives. The two most basic and vital processes are said to be cohort flow and what is termed aging. *Cohort flow* refers to all those factors that contribute to the shaping of the age strata; foremost would of course be fertility, mortality, and migration. Perhaps the best way to illustrate the process of cohort flow is the metaphor used by the authors themselves of people stepping on an escalator at birth. How many and what types of people get on at any two points are never identical, although in every instance those arriving at the bottom at the same time move up in a collective fashion. However, they do not remain a completely stable group as they move along; some get off by leaving the area; others, particularly men, by dying; hence, proportionately more women continue the ascent after early adulthood. As they move along, some acquire social attributes that come to distinguish them from others, either enhancing or impeding their likelihood of staying on the escalator for the full ride. Eventually, fewer and fewer people are left on the moving stairs, until all of those who began together are dead. As successive cohorts pass by, they alter conditions to such a degree that later groups never encounter the world in exactly the same way.

Interrelating the ideas of age strata and cohort flow provides a means of conceptualizing the dynamic nature of age in determining social location, but it does not explicitly account for individual exceptions or for how mobility from one stratum to the next occurs. For this purpose the age-stratification model incorporates the concept of *aging* as an endemic process taking place on two levels. Physiological aging, although fundamental, does not occur in a vacuum; rather, it is influenced by innumerable exogenous factors. Some of these are already apparent, and more will be discussed later. It should be sufficient at this point to note that physical aging is by no means an isolated experience. At the same time, aging can be seen as a maturational phenomenon, a measure of acquired experience or knowledge, reflecting the extent of whatever personal resources are available to bolster and guide a person. According to age stratification theory, the nature of aging is inextricably bound up

> . . . by the individual's characteristics and dispositions, by the modifications of these characteristics through socialization, by the particular role sequences in which he participates, and by the particular social situations and environmental events he encounters. Hence, it follows that patterns of aging can differ, not only from one society to another and from one country to another, but also among successive cohorts in a single society (Riley, Johnson, and Foner, 1972).

It is by no means possible to explain the multifarious differences between strata by reference to age alone; therefore, the age stratification model proposes the intervening processes of allocation and socialization to account for the disparities that arise. *Allocation* refers to the process of assigning and reassigning people of various ages to suitable roles. Even though the size and compositions of successive cohorts may change, the functional needs of society persist, necessitating occasional redefinitions of age-appropriate or essential positions in order to redistribute people in the system's role structure. As people age, they also adopt and abandon a sequence of roles. The process of deciding which people will fill what roles is not, however, always conscious, deliberate or immutable. Among the examples of allocative processes we could mention are the number of students admitted to college as determined by age, sex, income levels, race, and so on, or the size of the faculty responsible for their instruction. Similarly, age is an important consideration in apportioning the role of parent for those who wish to adopt a child, in filling an executive position or even for securing certain kinds of fairly menial positions such as stock clerk in a grocery store. In the case of adoption, the age criterion for allocation is often abandoned when the number of children grows too large; or, in the case of new industries, executives may be appreciably younger than in more established spheres. In an overall sense, the criteria used for allocation of particular roles or role complexes reflect both social values and the vital processes inherent in aging.

Socialization, the other intervening process included in the theory, is a means of insuring a smooth transition of individuals from one age status to the next. Sociologists previously discussed socialization almost exclusively within the context of childhood, though it has been widely accepted for a number of years that it is a never-ending process, operative throughout life for every role assumed. The age-stratification model views individuals as well as entire cohorts as molded by socializing agencies independently and together. Some researchers have suggested that in complex industrial societies, the criteria for role assignments have become increasingly ambiguous, and socialization processes weakened to the point of being inoperative. As a consequence, there is an undercurrent of asynchronization, sometimes called role strain or simply personal stress, built into the movement between age strata that requires special attention (Cain, 1964). An example which comes readily to mind is the need for pre-retirement counseling to facilitate the adjustment of older workers to their future and to the new roles which present themselves. Pre-retirement programs are reciprocal in nature, not only helping a person socialize out of the work role, in anticipation of future roles, but at the same time, having a latent socializing influence on company policies regarding older workers.

Finally, age-stratification theory includes, but does not deal extensively with, a set of exogenous processes not directly linked to age structures, but which nonetheless influence the role available. Some role changes may reflect historical events, as in the relatively few blacksmith positions currently found for people regardless of age. Similarly, differences in timing between the lifespan of a social order and the timetables of individuals are thought to add to the strains experienced as part of aging. Although these external factors impinge on the

way people age, they are not explicitly considered by the model. They do, however, serve to remind us that the age-specific elements in society never constitute a complete system, nor can any aspect of aging be adequately understood without reference to the complicated interplay among the factors involved. In spite of the numerous aspects of aging left untouched, the age stratification model offers the most comprehensive theoretical perspective yet developed. Perhaps one of the more significant omissions is any serious discussion of an actor's intentional participation in a process that cannot be mandated entirely by societal constraints. Further, while the authors assert that generations are not limited to mere chronological age groups—that they can be defined by attitudinal variation or perceptual factors—little is made of this important distinction. These unresolved questions do not negate the importance of the age stratification model for greatly expanding the scope of theories and their practical applications in social gerontology.

SUMMARY

Social gerontology has not escaped the common plight confronting most disciplines that attempt to integrate the theoretical with the applied. Solutions nearly always appear couched in the language used to formulate the problems. To date, the theoretical frameworks are neither all that they should be nor what they could be, but the growth of explanatory models witnessed in the last decade or so definitely has laid the groundwork for significant advances in the near future. Our review of the theories promulgated by social gerontologists should provide ample evidence of the continuing search. The insufficiency of unitary models of adjustment to explain the multiple dimensions of aging that must be taken into consideration should also have become apparent (Maddox, 1970). Still, no theory can ever be completely rejected, only disregarded in favor of those that offer a greater utility in the real world of the elderly. As the conditions affecting older people change, gerontologists must construct new models or renovate older ones if their explanations are to be of any scientific or social consequence. Limited as some may be as explanatory devices, each new effort serves to sharpen the issues involved, so that one day deliberate intervention will become a viable means of making life more satisfying for older people.

As one of the original theoretical attempts, disengagement theory, with its assertion that aging is a process of quietly receding from view or at least of withdrawing from active participation, quickly met with criticism from all sides. Especially vocal were those activity theorists who contended older people do not change their minds about the importance of being involved even when they can no longer keep pace with the world around them. In an effort to account for differential adjustment among those who withdraw as well as those who remain active, Rose (1965) suggested the possibility of an aging subculture, very much the counterpart of the widely recognized youth movement associated with the late 1960s. By becoming their own reference group, by recognizing their common predicament, Rose claims older people will develop a new basis for adaptation, even to the point of evolving into a social movement with a political voice. Not content with any of these descriptions of why older people experience and react with the feelings they do, social-psychologically oriented gerontologists expressed reservations, asserting instead that it all depends on a person's psychological makeup and habitual methods of coping. It is true, they noted, that roles themselves may be discontinuous, but people are not; the repertoire of responses developed throughout a lifetime is not suddenly abandoned on the threshold of old age.

Filling the gap between theories that stress social factors and those emphasizing personal ones, the social environmentalists posit a reciprocal process wherein any acknowledgement of personal stress prompts the social environment to label an older person as incompetent, a label frequently inter-nalized by the person. Which people end up their years overcome by despair depends on what kinds of environmental supports are available to them. Finally, the age-stratification theory is an attempt to formulate a whole life conception of aging. A complicated model to say the least, age-stratification views old age as a process of becoming socialized to new or revised role definitions, reflecting a fluid relationship between people, their social contexts and their opportunities. How much change must be accommodated by individual actors is difficult to predict; it is dependent upon an intertwined series of feedback loops revolving around the size of the aging population, the roles available, and differences in the timing of individual and social needs. Before any of the theories reviewed or one yet to emerge adds measurably to our understanding of aging in the modern world, they must each be subjected to thoughtful testing in a variety of cultural contexts.

REFERENCES

ATCHLEY, R. C. "Disengagement Among Professors." *Journal of Gerontology* 26 (4) (1971): 476–80.

BENNETT, R. "Social Context—a Neglected Variable in Research on Aging." *Aging and Human Development* I, (2) (1970): 97–116.

BIRREN, J. E. *The Psychology of Aging.* Englewood Cliffs, N.J.: Prentice-Hall, 1964.

BLAU, Z. S. *Old Age in a Changing Society.* New York: New Viewpoints, a division of Franklin Watts, Inc., 1973.

BRIM, O. G., Jr. "Foreword." In *Aging and Society, Vol. 3: a Sociology of Age Stratification,* by M. W. Riley, M. Johnson and A. Foner, pp. ix–xii. New York: Russell Sage Foundation, 1972.

BRUHN, J. G. "An Ecological Perspective of Aging." *The Gerontologist* 11 (4, pt. 1) (1971): 318–21.

CAIN, L. D., Jr. "Life Course and Social Structure." In *Handbook of Modern Sociology,* edited by R. E. L. Faris, pp. 272–309. Chicago: Rand McNally, 1964.

CUMMING, E. "Further Thoughts on the Theory of Disengagement." *International Social Science Journal* 15 (3) (1963): 377–93.

———. "Engagement With an Old Theory." *Aging and Human Development* 6 (3) (1975): 187–91.

CUMMING, E., DEAN, L. R., NEWELL, D. S., and McCAFFREY, I. "Disengagement— a Tentative Theory of Aging." *Sociometry* 23 (1) (1960): 23.

CUMMING, E., and HENRY, W. E. *Growing Old: the Process of Disengagement.* New York: Basic Books, 1961.

DOWD, J. J. "Aging as Exchange: a Preface to Theory." *Journal of Gerontology* 30 (5) (1975) 584–94.

EMERSON, R. M. "Exchange Theory, Parts I & II." In *Sociological Theories in Progress,* vol. II, edited by J. Berger, M. Zelditch, and B. Anderson, pp. 38–87. Boston: Houghton Mifflin, 1972.

FONER, A. "Age in Society: Structure and Change." *American Behavioral Scientist* 19 (2) (1975): 144–65.

GUBRIUM. J. F. *The Myth of the Golden Years: a Socio-Environmental Theory of Aging.* Springfield, Ill.: Charles C Thomas, 1973.

———. "Toward a Socio-Environmental Theory of Aging." *The Gerontologist* 12 (3, pt. 1) (1947): 281–84.

HAVIGHURST, R. J. "A Social-Psychological Perspective on Aging." *The Gerontologist* 8 (2) (1968): 67–71.

HAVIGHURST, R. J., and ALBRECHT, R. *Older People.* New York: Longmans, Green, 1953.

HAVIGHURST, R. J., MUNNICHS, J. M. A., NEUGARTEN, B., and THOMAE, H. *Adjustment to Retirement.* Assen, The Netherlands: Van Gorcum & Comp. N.V., 1969.

HAVIGHURST, R. J., NEUGARTEN, B., and TOBIN, S. S. "Disengagement and Patterns of Aging." In *Middle Age and Aging.* edited by B. L. Neugarten, pp. 161–72. Chicago: University of Chicago Press, 1968.

HENRY, W. E. "Engagement and Disengagement: Toward a Theory of Adult Development." In *Contributions to the Psychobiology of Aging,* edited by R. Kastenbaum, pp. 19–35. New York: Springer Publishing Company, 1965.

HOCHSCHILD, A. R. *The Unexpected Community.* Englewood Cliffs, N.J.: Prentice-Hall, 1973.

———. "Disengagement Theory: a Critique and Proposal." *American Sociological Review* 40 (5) (1975): 553–69.

KUYPERS, J. A., and BENGTSON, V. L. "Social Breakdown and Competence: a Model of Normal Aging." *Human Development* 16 (3) (1973): 181–201.

LEMON, B. W., BENGTSON, V. L., and PETERSEN, J. A. "An Exploration of the Activity Theory of Aging: Activity Types and Life Expectation among Inmovers to a Retirement Community." *Journal of Gerontology* 27 (4) (1972): 511–23.

MADDOX, G. L. "Disengagement Theory: a Critical Evaluation." *The Gerontologist* 4 (2) (1964): 80–82.

———. "Face and Artifact: Evidence Bearing on Disengagement Theory from the Duke Geriatrics Project." *Human Development* 8 (1) (1965): 117–30.

———. "Themes and Issues in Sociological Theories of Human Aging." *Human Development* 13 (1) (1970): 17–27.

MILLER, S. J. "The Social Dilemma of the Aging Leisure Participant." In *Older People and Their Social World,* edited by A. M. Rose and W. A. Peterson, pp. 77–92. Philadelphia: F. A. Davis Company, 1965.

NEUGARTEN, B. L. "Personality and the Aging Process." *The Gerontologist* 12 (1, pt. 1) (1972): 9–15.

NEUGARTEN, B. L., CROTTY, W. J., and TOBIN, S. S. "Personality Types in an Aged Population." In *Personality in Middle and Late Life,* edited by B. L. Neugarten et al., pp. 158–87. New York: Atherton Press, 1964.

NEUGARTEN, B. L., HAVIGHURST, R. J., and TOBIN, S. S. "Personality and Patterns of Aging." In *Middle Age and Aging,* edited by B. L. Neugarten, pp. 173–77. Chicago: University of Chicago Press, 1968.

PALMORE, E., ed. *Normal Aging.* Durham, N.C.: Duke University Press, 1970.

PHILLIPS, B. S. "A Role Theory Approach to Adjustment in Old Age." *American Sociological Review* 22 (2) (1957): 212–27.

REICHARD, S., LIVSON, F., and PETERSON, P. G. *Aging and Personality.* New York: John Wiley & Sons, 1962.

RILEY, M. W. "Social Gerontology and the Age Stratification of Society." *The Gerontologist 12* (1, pt. 1) (1971): 79–87.

RILEY, M. W., JOHNSON, M. and FONER, A. *Aging and Society, Vol 3: a Sociology of Age Stratification.* New York: Russell Sage Foundation, 1972.

ROSE, A. M. "The Subculture of the Aging: a Framework in Social Gerontology." In *Older People and Their Social World,* edited by A. M. Rose and W. A. Peterson, pp. 3–16. Philadelphia: F. A. Davis Company, 1965.

ROSOW, I. *Social Integration of the Aged.* New York: The Free Press, 1967.

———. *Socialization to Old Age.* Berkeley: University of California Press, 1974.

SCHAIE, K. W. "Age Changes and Age Differences." *The Gerontologist 7* (2, pt. 1) (1967): 128–32.

STREIB, G. F. "Are the Aged a Minority Group?" In *Applied Sociology,* edited by A. W. Gouldner and S. M. Miller. New York: The Free Press, 1965. Reprinted in *Middle Age and Aging,* edited by B: L. Neugarten, 35–46.

STREIB, G. F., and SCHNEIDER, C. J. *Retirement in American Society.* Ithaca, N.Y.: Cornell University Press, 1971.

WILLIAMS, R. H., and WIRTHS, C. G. *Lives Through the Years.* New York: Atherton Press, 1965.

ZUSMAN, J. "Some Explanations of the Changing Appearance of Psychotic Patients: Antecedents of the Social Breakdown Syndrome Concept." *The Millbank Memorial Fund Quarterly 54* (1) (1966).

Marriage and Remarriage Rates Among Older Americans

Judith Treas
Anke VanHilst

Recent years have witnessed a growing popular awareness of late-life romance. Anecdotes of gerontic courtships thwarted by social security restrictions and nursing home rules have become commonplace. A national retirement magazine now features articles like "Retirement Home Marriage" (Woodfin, 1975), while a planned community of senior citizens boasts in a full-page newspaper ad of having had "15 weddings and 65 golden anniversaries" last year (Rossmoor Leisure World, 1975). Masters and Johnson (1966) offer scientific validation of the lasting sexual capacities of older men and women. Despite current interest, no study to date has grounded speculation on autumn love with demographic statistics on marriages contracted by older Americans. By drawing upon U. S. Vital Statistics data for 1970, the most recent year for which detailed marriage registration figures are available, we here assess the frequency of new marriages in old age, document trends, identify those older people

From *The Gerontologist* 16, 2 (1976), pp. 132–135. Reprinted by permission.

most likely to wed, and infer something of the feelings and customs involved in these unions.

DESCRIPTION OF THE DATA

This analysis is based on published data from marriage certificates sampled for forty-seven states and the District of Columbia in 1970. Arizona, New Mexico, and Oklahoma were excluded from the sample, because they do not maintain central marriage files. Published estimates are available for most of the United States on the age, sex, race, previous marital status, and state of residence of bride and groom as well as on the month, state, and type (religious or civil) of wedding ceremony. Since data are aggregated for those sixty-five and older, our subsequent discussion refers to this age group.

Although marriage registration data are considered to be of reasonably high quality, they are not without error. Some error arises from reporting and processing of data. To take an extreme example, 36 percent of marriage records failed to state the race of bride and groom; the item was simply not included on 31 percent of forms, and on another 5 percent respondents failed to give codable information (NCHS, 1974).

Another source of error arises from sampling variation. State totals and distributions are estimated on the basis of sampling procedures yielding at least 2500 records for each state. It is likely that the estimates deviate from actual counts due to random sampling error. In 1970, the difference between the complete count and the sample estimate of marriages was less than 2 percent for all but three states. However, the potential for error is greater for small categories (e.g., the divorced aged). Checks on the data are facilitated by comparisons with other years (and hence other samples), and standard errors for characteristics may be calculated using information supplied by the National Center for Health Statistics (1974).

PROSPECTS FOR LATE-LIFE MARRIAGE AND REMARRIAGE

About 60,000 senior citizens married in 1970. Although the absolute numbers are impressive, these marriages touched relatively few in the population sixty-five and older. It is estimated that there were fewer than three brides out of 1000 older single women; the marriage rate for males, while higher, was estimated to be only seventeen grooms per 1000 older single men (NCHS, 1974). That older persons constituted just 1 percent of all brides and 2 percent of all grooms clearly suggests marriage to be a prerogative of the young (NCHS, 1974). Although some people marry or remarry late in life, they are atypical.

Is this pattern changing? Has a rise in gerontic nuptiality paralleled the increasing popular interest in late-life unions? Marriage estimates for the decade of the 1960s reveal no rising wave of weddings among the aged. More older people are marrying today because there are greater numbers of older people in the population. However, the *propensity* of older people to marry, as indexed by marriage rates, has evidenced no change over time (NCHS, 1974).

The rarity of new marriages for older people may be lamentable since wedlock would seem to have much to recommend it to a high-risk population like the aged. Previous research has shown the married to have an advantage over the unmarried in terms of happiness (Gurin, Veroff, and Feld, 1960), longevity (Gove, 1973), and financial resources (Sherman, 1973). In fact, McKain (1972) has found marriages contracted in advancing years to enjoy considerable success when bolstered by motives of affection, by financial security, and by children's approval. If marriage and remarriage is potentially beneficial for older people, we want to know which older people are most likely to wed. Age, sex, previous marital status, and region are pertinent to late-life marital chances.

Marital prospects of both men and women decline after the mid-twenties and continue to drop off in old age. Although detailed age data on the older population are not available for the nation, crude marriage rates calculated for California in 1971 verify that marriage chances plummet for every five-year interval beyond age sixty-five (Treas and VanHilst, 1975). These rough estimates suggest, for example, that a woman sixty-five to sixty-nine is twice as likely to wed as one seventy to seventy-four. Similar declines, if somewhat less precipitous, are found for men. Such age differences in gerontic marriage rates doubtless reflect the fact that the "young-old" are advantaged in terms of health, vigor, mobility, physical charm, income, and other qualities which facilitate courtship activities and attract mates.

Older men have a substantial edge over women in the marriage market. They are over six times more likely to wed than are their female counterparts. Perhaps men are more motivated to marry. We know that husbands tend to report greater satisfaction with marriage than do wives and that men are more bereft at the loss of a spouse than are women (see Treas, 1975). It is clear that older men have an easier time attracting marital partners than do older women. Women, of course, confront a "double standard of aging" whereby they are defined as sexually unattractive at an earlier age than are men (Sontag, 1972). They also face an increasingly inauspicious sex-ratio. Given sex differences in mortality and widowhood, there are three single women for each unmarried man in the population over sixty-five (U. S. Bureau of the Census, 1972). Furthermore, social norms ordain that men wed brides younger than themselves—a custom which expands the number of potential partners for older men while effectively restricting marital choice for older women. Although one in five grooms sixty-five and older marry women under fifty-five, less than 3 percent of older brides attract such young spouses (NCHS, 1974).

Marital forecasts also differ for those with different marital histories. The divorced are more likely to marry than are the widowed while the never-married aged are least apt to wed. For men sixty-five and older, marriage rates per thousand are estimated to be 3.4 for bachelors, 19.4 for widowers, and 23.6 for the divorced. Comparable rates for their female counterparts are 1.1, 2.3, and 6.1, respectively (NCHS, 1974).

First marriages constitute only six percent of all marriages for older brides and grooms (NCHS, 1974). The rarity of late-life marriage for bachelors and spinsters no doubt indicates the continuation into old age of marital prospects and proclivities which ruled out marriage in younger years. The never-wed category is composed largely of two groups: 1) those who have been unable to attract spouses due to physical, mental, or social handicaps; and 2) those with little interest in or need of marriage. There is hardly reason to expect such life-long inclinations or handicaps to vanish in later years.

More surprising may be the greater likelihood of marriage for the divorced than for the widowed. However, several reasons may be advanced for this. First, divorced persons tend to be younger than widowed ones because of life-cycle differences in the timing of divorce and widowhood and because of the greater vulnerability of recent cohorts to divorce. In the population sixty-five and older, only 23 percent of widows and 19 percent of widowers were under seventy years of age in 1970. Comparable figures for the divorced were forty-three and forty-two percent (U.S. Bureau of the Census, 1972). Second, the divorced may have some life circumstance predisposing them to remarry, since divorced persons are more likely to wed than are widowed ones at every age (NCHS, 1974). Perhaps past conjugal misfortunes do not discourage new nuptials for the divorced. At least, they are not obliged (as are the widowed) to defer remarriage out of respect for the memory of a former spouse. Being less likely to have offspring with whom they must maintain cordial relations or share housing (U. S. Bureau of the Census, 1973), divorced persons may also be relatively unconcerned with preserving an estate for heirs or with winning children's approval of marriage plans. Finally, the divorced category is probably selective of those who are less bound by normative constraints regarding marriage. Perhaps they hold more liberal views on the propriety of new unions for older people. For some, plans to remarry may even have precipitated divorce.

One final indicator of marital propensity in old age is geographic. In the south and west, older men and women are about two times more likely to marry than in the northeast and north central states (NCHS, 1974). Perhaps the mild climate of the south and west facilitates courting, attracts honeymooners, or spawns retirement communities drawing residents who have the vigor and financial means to marry and remarry. However, since regional differences in marriage rates are paralleled for every age group above thirty, it is possible that there are regional subcultures which encourage or discourage (to a greater or lesser extent) late marriage. Such subcultural variations might relate to the preponderance of ethnic Catholics in the northeast and midwest. Lopata (1973), for example, has recounted the negative attiudes of Polish-American widows to remarriage. At the very least, the concentration of celibate Catholic religious workers among the older population of the northeast would act to depress marriage rates.

MATES AND MEANINGS FOR OLDER BRIDES AND GROOMS

Although we have drawn a demographic profile of the senior citizen most likely to marry (presumably a sixty-five-year-old divorced man residing in the southern or western United States), we have yet to tap the rich social meanings and psychological motives which surround late-life weddings. Admittedly, the limited data from marriage registration records are ill-suited to questions of this type. Nonetheless, information on the marital choices of older people and on the wedding ceremony itself do permit some valuable insights on the personal sentiments and social customs which color these unions.

Since the widowed numerically dominate the aged single population, widows and widowers are the most usual marital choices of older people, regardless of their own previous marital status (Treas and VanHilst, 1975). Fully 78 percent of older brides and grooms marry widows. Despite the preponderance of widowed mates (a practical reconciliation to their greater availability), a preference for spouses with like marital histories may be detected. This is most evident for those with the best bargaining position and hence the most options in the marriage market—older men. Bachelors and divorced men are about as likely to wed brides of like status as they are to wed widows. Furthermore, the divorced and never-married women who wed older grooms are younger than are the widows. Marriages between older grooms and never-married women constitute a disproportionate number of those rare May-December unions (NCHS, 1974). Although one in five older grooms chooses a bride under fifty-five years of age, among those wedding never-married women, 36 percent of the widowers, 51 percent of the bachelors, and 65 percent of the divorced grooms choose a bride under fifty-five (NCHS, 1974). In short, older people seem to prefer marital partners with marital backgrounds like their own. Since the pool of older divorced and never-married people is relatively small, most older brides and grooms marry older widows and widowers. Older men are more likely to wed divorced and never-married spouses than are older women, because they either prefer or are in a position to attract younger mates.

Available datta on the marriage ceremony itself indicate that older people attach the same symbolic import to their nuptials as do younger brides and grooms, for their weddings reflect the romantic customs associated with new unions. For example, older brides and grooms favor June weddings over any other month (NCHS, 1974). They are as inclined to honeymoon as are other newlyweds. At least they are as likely to be married in a state where neither partner is a resident (NCHS, 1974). Las Vegas weddings are especially popular, for transient grooms elevate the Nevada marriage rate for sixty-five and over men from a national average of 17 to 402 per thousand (NCHS, 1974). Older people prefer to solemnize their vows with a religious ceremony. Three-quarters of older brides are married by clergy. Only the very young are more likely to choose a church wedding for a first marriage, and no age group exceeds the proportion of older people opting for a religious remarriage (NCHS, 1974). Since fewer older people are divorced, fewer are bound by the standards of propriety demanding a discreet civil ceremony for a second marriage.

DISCUSSION

Although the public and practitioners are becoming increasingly aware of the potentials of new marriages for older people, Vital Statistics data indicate late-life nuptials to be rare and to show no upsurge in popularity. While such events are romantic and some older people have better marital prospects than do others, the infrequency of these unions suggests the barriers to marriage and remarriage in advancing years.

As we have mentioned, old age poses objective limitations to marriage. The scarcity of older single men means many older women who might wish to marry will be unable to find new partners. Furthermore, successful courtship may depend on health, mobility, and adequate income—resources which decline with advancing age.

In addition, our culture offers little impetus to marry in later years. Many of the factors promoting marriage among the young are not pertinent to older singles: premarital pregnancy or the desire for children, escape from parental domination, social validation of adult heterosexuality, and pressure for conformity in the timing of life-cycle events. Instead, there are distinct social pressures against marriage and remarriage in old age. For example, older people are encouraged to protect their estate for offspring—a norm which grants children a potential veto on a

parent's plans for remarriage. One pre-retirement magazine counsels prenuptial agreements since "your heirs will be concerned as to how your marriage will affect their inheritance" (Dynamic Maturity, 1974). Given this cultural climate, it is not surprising that a third of those over sixty in a rural sample frowned on remarriage for their peers (Britton and Britton, 1967). That 81 percent of Lopata's (1973) widows expressed no wish to remarry is testimony both to cultural prohibitions and to their poor marital prospects.

The dearth of late-life unions may also reflect the subjective processes of aging itself. Life-cycle theorists have long emphasized that the last stage of the developmental cycle is marked not by new ventures but by an assessment of past accomplishments in response to a shortened future time perspective (see Buhler, 1968; Erikson, 1968). Given an uncertain future and a cultural silence on the unique virtues and rewards of new marriages in old age, older people may be justifiably reluctant to make the personal investments and accommodations, to assume the grave responsibilities, which new marriages demand. Thus, while marriage may be deemed desirable for older people on a number of counts, there is little reason to expect late-life unions to rise above their presently low levels in the near future.

REFERENCES

BRITTON, J. H., and BRITTON, J. O. "The Middle Aged and Older Rural Person and His Family." In Older Rural Americans, edited by E. G. Youmans. Lexington: University of Kentucky Press, 1967.

BUHLER, C. "The Developmental Structure of Goal Setting in Group and Individual Studies." In The Course of Human Life, edited by C. Buhler and R. Massarik. New York: Springer, 1968.

Dynamic Maturity. AIM's legal guide. 1974, 9, (5), 26.

ERIKSON, E. H. Identity: Youth and Crisis. New York: W. W. Norton, 1968.

GOVE, W. R. "Sex, Marital Status, and Mortality." *American Journal of Sociology*, 79 (1973): 45–67.

GURIN, G., VEROFF, J., and FELD, S. *Americans View Their Mental Health*. New York: Basic Books, 1960.

LOPATA, H. Z. *Widowhood in an American City*. Cambridge, Mass.: Schenkman, 1973.

MASTERS, W. H., and JOHNSON, V. E. *Human Sexual Response*. Boston: Little, Brown, 1966.

MCKAIN, W. C. "A New Look at Old Marriages." *Family Coordinator*, 21, (1972): 61–69.

National Center for Health Statistics. *Vital Statistics of the U. S.: 1970. Vol. III, Marriage and Divorce*. Washington: USGPO, 1974.

"Rossmoor Leisure World." *Los Angeles Times*, 4 April 1975, Part I, 25.

SHERMAN, S. "Assets on the Threshold of Retirement." *Social Security Bulletin*, 36, (1973): 3–17

SONTAG, S. "The Double Standard of Aging." *Saturday Review*, 23 Sept. 1972, 29–38.

TREAS, J. "Aging and the Family." In *Aging: Scientific Perspectives and Social Issues*, edited by D. S. Woodruff and J. E. Birren. New York: Van Nostrand, 1975.

TREAS, J., and VANHILST, A. "Marriage and Remarriage Among the Older Population." Paper presented at the 28th Annual Meeting of Gerontological Society, Louisville, 1975.

U. S. Bureau of the Census. Census of Population: 1970. Subject reports. Final report PC2-4C. Marital Status. Washington: USGPO, 1972.

U. S. Bureau of the Census. Census of Population: 1970. Subject reports. Final report PC92-4B. Persons by Family Characteristics. Washington: USGPO, 1973.

WOODFIN, M. "Retirement Home Marriage." *Modern Maturity*, 18 (June-July 1975): 68.

Sexuality, Power, and Freedom Among "Older" Women

Constantina Safilios-Rothschild

There is no news in the statement that women have been more restricted than men. This has been true in many societies, today and in the past. This is because men have needed to control women's sexuality—and I am referring to more than reproductive consequences. It seems to me that wherever men

From L. Troll, J. Israel, and R. Israel, eds., *Looking Ahead: A Woman's Guide to the Problems and Joys of Growing Older*, © 1977, pp. 162–166. Reprinted by permission of Prentice-Hall, Inc., Englewood Cliffs, New Jersey.

view women primarily as potential sex partners, they are bound to face uncomfortable tensions whenever they interact with them—tensions that can be released only through sexual activity. And since such interminable preoccupation with sexual activity can interfere with the ordinary affairs of life, women judged to be sexually attractive would better be kept in control so that social order can be maintained and social structures can continue to function (Mernissi, 1975; Safilios-Rothschild, 1977.)

Furthermore, it seems to me that men have long realized that women's physical capacity for sexuality does not decrease with age the way men's does, and that this knowledge is threatening. To remove this threat, then, men have had to extend their power in all domains and subjugate women. They could find it easier to handle their desire for and their dependence on women's sexuality, as well as their inferior sexual capacities later in life, when women were clearly subordinate, economically, socially, and politically. They could then set the rules in the sexual domain in such a way as to feel comfortably in control there too (Nissen, 1971).

In "traditional" (non-Western) societies the prevailing low life expectancy—lower particularly for women—resulted in few women ever reaching or surviving menopause. "Old" women were rare. Yet those postmenopausal women who survived were frequently defined as "asexual." Men compensated for this ascription of an asexual status to physiologically sexual women by granting them extra power in the family as well as some of the freedom of movement and behavior usually reserved for men. Because they were seen as asexual and could no longer qualify as potential sex partners, they no longer represented a sexual threat (Bart, 1969). It was probably easy for men to desexualize older women because "sexual objects," like many other possessions, tend to decrease in value with use, exposure to debilitating conditions, and age.

In some countries around the world in which younger women may not leave their home unescorted, older women are free to walk alone at any time of the day or night, to go to bars, to swear, and to interact freely with men. In the Arab world, Sicily, the traditional segments of Greece, Japan, and many traditional societies in Southeastern Asia and Central America, even today, older women enjoy considerable power over all younger women in the family—also over younger men. They often run the entire extended family, especially when they have survived the old men. In other such cultures, older women

who have abdicated their sexuality are finally allowed to earn money by gathering shrimps, or trading fish, or engaging in some other kind of business that requires freedom of movement and interactions with men not allowed to younger women. With sexuality out of the way, men can interact with them almost as they do with other men. Under these conditions, it is not surprising that young women, oppressed by men of all ages and also by older women, usually look forward to middle and old age. Besides, since their sexual experiences are often unsatisfactory and frustrating, partly because their husband rarely considers the woman's pleasure, they are glad when sex is no longer required of them as part of their wifely role (Mernissi, 1975; Bart, 1969; Safilios-Rothschild, 1977).

At another extreme, the older women in Western societies like ours are evolving a very different pattern. Because of increased life expectancy and a host of technological discoveries, many can expect to live long after menopause and, what is more, to experience fewer clear-cut psychological and social changes. "Anti-old age" technology helps women stay slim, maintain a fresh and unwrinkled face, control cellulitis, and, in general, look and stay young and attractive for many years. Hormonal treatments help them escape physiologically determined discomforts as well. Recent investigations report that women's sexual desires, urges, and potential reach a peak between 30 and 35 years of age and remain stable from that time on. As these findings become public knowledge, menopausal and postmenopausal women will no longer be automatically redefined as asexual. I may also add that this new type of older woman is more characteristic of middle- and upper-class women than of working-class women, though time and technology are spreading its effects to wider segments of our society. The hidden part of this reversal, though, may be that the asexual label will no longer guarantee special privileges.

It is still possible and socially acceptable for a woman to refuse to use the technological means that would allow her to stay young and "sexy" looking and to claim the asexual label, although the ensuing advantages are not always clear. It may be that in some situations this choice may make her more acceptable to men in occupational power positions. Ugly women or masculine women in business are viewed as "one of the boys" and don't have as difficult a time balancing their being "female" with competitive assertiveness (Safilios-Rothschild, 1977).

In general, then, while technology allows older women to continue to look young and attractive, especially if they have the time and financial resources to afford it, their overall subordinate status, the existing discrimination against them, and their internalized "feminine" stereotypes prevent them from cashing in on their attractive appearance for sexual fulfillment. They are allowed and even encouraged to continue to look trim and attractive, but most are not allowed sexual expression. They are still effectually a-sexual. If nothing else, they lack the necessary self-confidence to enter and enjoy sexual and love relationships. Furthermore, until very recently, the many unwarranted hysterectomies performed on menopausal American women underlines a view of their sexual obsolescence (Rodgers, 1975).

Look at American women! In their 50s, they are more often divorced and remarried or widowed than still married to their first husbands. With advancing age, widowhood becomes the prevalent state. Until very recently, postmenopausal women who were still attractive did not have the option of marrying a younger man. Since the number of surviving same-age or older men shrinks with age, such women often have to stay single. The number of women who have started feeling more self-confident as a result of their increasing economic status and accomplishments and are able to attract and marry younger men is increasing but still very small. Most older women are sexually frustrated.

If postmenopausal American women without husbands have trouble expressing their sexuality, those who have stayed married to the same husband for over twenty-five years could have even greater difficulty. As Pineo (1961), Feldman (1964), and I have found, few marriages stay vital and alive beyond fifteen years. It is true that there are couples who manage to keep the excitement, the flavor, the tenderness, and the affection throughout life, who continuously discover and rediscover each other's sexual potential. But these couples are few and usually have worked hard to improve and extend their relationship. Most other middle-aged couples do not feel like making love and when they do, it is usually a mechanical, "soulless" activity. Trying to feel earlier satisfaction and excitements does not help. Bored husbands can find the stereotypes about waning female desires a good excuse for sexual withdrawal. They can hide sexual indifference under the cloak of decency and respect for their wife. The same can hold true for wives. If they are no longer excited or even satisfied by their husband's timeworn style of lovemaking, they can cloak their lack of enthusiasm under their "old age." Some of these middle-aged couples find that divorce and remarriage produces psychological and sexual revitalization. Recently, others are following a path to marriage and sex counselors to try to "put new wine into old bottles."

Since we presume that if society permits it, women will want to express and enjoy their sexuality as long as possible, we need to know how older women can reach the point where they will feel comfortable admitting—both to themselves and to others—the existence of these sexual needs and finding ways of fulfilling them.

This point of sexual liberation will not happen until men and women can look at each other as human beings instead of as "sex objects." As long as women's sexual attractiveness is based on perishable flesh, only the exceptional older woman will manage to attract the exceptional "liberated" younger man. Only when being an interesting person becomes an asset—as it is now for men—will older women have a chance. Today's increasing possibilities for women to develop their intelligence and their talents gives us hope that this will lead to their emergence as fascinating people, and that this may, in turn, allow them to enjoy being sexual. And to defy time and age.

REFERENCES

BART, P. B. "Why Women's Status Changes in Middle Age: the Turns of the Social Ferris Wheel." *Sociological Symposium* 3 (1969): 1–18.

FELDMAN, H. *Development of the Husband-Wife Relationship: a Research Report.* New York: Cornell University Press, 1964.

MERNISSI, F. *Beyond the Veil. Male-Female Dynamics in a Modern Muslim Society.* Cambridge, Mass.: Schenkman Publishing Co., 1975.

NISSEN, L. "The Role of the Sexual Constellation." *Acta Sociologica* 14 (Nos. 1, 2) (1971): 52–58.

PINEO, P. C. "Disenchantment in the Later Years of Marriage." *Marriage and Family Living* 13 (January, 1964): 7–13.

RODGERS, J. "Rush to Surgery." *The New York Times Magazine*, September 21, 1975.

SAFILIOS-ROTHSCHILD, C. *Love, Sex, and Sex Roles.* Englewood Cliffs, N.J.: Prentice-Hall, 1977.

Housing Characteristics and the Well-Being of Elderly Tenants in Federally Assisted Housing

M. Powell Lawton
Lucille Nahemow
Joseph Teaff

This research was designed to investigate the relationship between selected physical characteristics of planned housing environments and their neighborhoods (sponsorship, community size, building size, and building height) on the one hand, and tenant well-being, on the other.

A national probability sample of housing for the elderly was studied in order to overcome two major problems which typically limit the generalizability of man-envi-

ronment research: studying a sample of environments large enough to allow adequate variability in environmental characteristics and assembling a large enough group of individual subjects in each environment to allow an effective test of the interaction between environmental characteristics and individual outcome. Two alternative methods of study which are frequently used are not entirely satisfactory: a) contrasting a pair of environments known to differ in one important characteristic in terms of the presumed effect of this environmental difference on the individual—differences in other char-

From *Journal of Gerontology* 30, 5 (1975), pp. 601–607. Reprinted by permission.

acteristics of the environments are difficult to control, however, and they may exert a spurious influence on the outcome criterion; b) using archival data such as census or directory information to characterize a large number of environments—such archives frequently do not contain the information most relevant to the problem; further, it is sometimes extremely difficult to relate these archival data to other information on the individual subject.

Impact of size. In a study of member activity among League of Women Voters chapters, Likert (1961) found that the amount of participation by leaders increased as chapter size increased but that average participation by non-central members decreased with size. Forehand and Gilmer (1964) reviewed several studies suggesting that member satisfaction decreases as size of group increases.

Studies of mental hospitals have found large size to be associated with less patient movement (Cohen and Struening, 1965; Gurel, 1964), shorter post-discharge community tenure (Gurel, 1964), and more "institutional" staff attitudes (Lawton and Cohen, 1975; Moos, 1972).

On the other hand, an equivocal or no relationship between size and quality indicators of nursing home was found by Anderson, Holmberg, Schneider, and Stone (1969), Gottesman (1972) and Levey, Ruchlin, Stotsky, Kinloch, and Oppenheim (1973). Beattie and Bullock (1963) and Kosberg (1973) found large size to be associated with highly judged quality. Curry and Ratliff (1973) found residents of small homes to be less socially isolated but no different in life satisfaction from those in larger homes. On the other hand, Linn (1974) found small size to be associated with highly judged quality in her sample of institutions.

The only study of housing that examined size dealt with family public housing (Newman, 1972). While one might wish for a larger sample of sites, he found some tendency for large project size and for high-rise building type to be associated with a higher project crime rate.

Barker's Undermanning Concept. A special characteristic of size is the concept of "undermanning," developed by Barker (1968), who found that a relatively small pool of available participants necessitates both active recruitment and the use of marginally capable participants. Such an undermanned situation recruits a greater proportion of all eligibles than does a situation where there is a surplus of eligibles, which allows the choice of only the most capable. In a study of schools of different sizes (Barker and Gump, 1964), the concept of undermanning was used to account for the greater proportional involvement of studies in the activities of the smaller schools. Support for the undermanning hypothesis was obtained in research on church-member activity (Wicker, 1969). On the level of community size, Wright (1969, presented in Bechtel, 1974) found a number of associations between size and indicators of involvement.

Many of the above studies have dealt with size in univariate fashion, taking no account of factors such as size of community, characteristics of organization members, or of other organizational characteristics. Not only have these studies dealt with different kinds of members, settings, and locales, but they have also relied upon a variety of criteria of well-being. Thus, it is difficult to compare studies and impossible to generalize from them.

The present study examined four environmental variables—sponsorship, community size, and height of building in relation to measures of the well-being of older tenants. It also tested the undermanning hypothesis as it applies to participation in the organized activities of housing for the elderly.

METHOD

A national probability sample of 3,654 tenants was obtained. These tenants resided in housing projects sponsored under the HUD low rent public housing program and the 202 program. All the public housing projects contained some units specially designed for the elderly (EDUs) and limited to occupancy by the elderly or young handicapped people. The 202 program was for lower-middle income elderly; these projects housed only the elderly and handicapped and were sponsored by private nonprofit organizations such as churches or unions. The projects were all at least three years old as of 1971. These sites were drawn simultaneously from a probability sample of 154 projects located in twelve large geographic areas of the country. The geographic areas themselves represented a probability sample of all geographic areas in proportion to the distribution of tenants in the United States.

Environmental data gathered from all 154 sites included census information on each community, neighborhood characteristics, proximity to resources, site and building characteristics, organizational characteristics of the housing, on-site services offered, administrator attitudes and preferences, and aggregate social characteristics of all tenants living in each site. Individual tenant data were gathered through interviews with approximately twenty tenants from each site. These were conducted in tenants' apartments by trained interviewers in the summer of 1971. The interviewer spent about a week in each site gathering the environmental and tenant data. Every site that was solicited cooperated, and the tenant interview completion rate was 89 percent. Data for this report were those from the 2457 subjects who gave complete responses to all questions.

Measuring tenant well-being. Measures of tenant well-being were tabulated from short interviewer administered questionnaires developed from previous research in fourteen housing sites. The items selected were self-reported items which loaded highest on factors described in Lawton and Cohen (1974). Six indices of well-being were selected for study. Table 1 shows the items used in each index. In an ideal situation one would wish for indices with more items and therefore higher reliability. The items' previously tested reliability, together with the large subject *N*, argue for their usefulness. Another

TABLE 1

Items comprising indices of well-being.

---

1. Friendship in housing (2 items)
   How many people at this housing do you consider very good friends? In the past week how many friends (not relatives) did you visit in their apartment or visited you in yours?
2. Housing satisfaction (3 items)
   How much do you like living in this neighborhood? If you could live anywhere you wanted, where would you like to live? How much do you like living here?
3. Morale (2 items)
   Do you have a lot to be sad about? Do things keep getting worse as you get older?
4. Motility (2 items)
   How often do you go out of this building in warm weather? About how often do you leave the neighborhood?
5. Family contact (1 item)
   How often do you see (the relative that you see most frequently)?
6. Activity participation
   The number of on-site activities named by the subject as engaged in during the past year.

Each index was maintained as a separate criterion in the analysis.

limitation is their dependence on tenants' reports and recall. In a smaller-scale study it would have been possible to utilize ratings done by staff, direct observation, or possibly archival records in the case of activity participation. The survey approach and limitations on the amount of assistance that could be requested from the housing staff simply precluded such possibilities. These data must thus be interpreted in light of the limitations inherent in all self-reported survey data.

The intercorrelations among indices of well-being (Table 2) were all positive but generally low, indicating that different facets of well-being were being measured, as well as reflecting their restricted range of possible scores. Self-reported health, while utilized as an independent variable, is shown in Table 2 as it related to the other indices.

TABLE 2

Correlations among indices of well-being.[a]

	ACTIVITY PARTICI-PATION	FRIEND-SHIP	HOUSING SATIS-FACTION	MORALE	MOTILITY	FAMILY CONTACT
Friendship in housing	.23					
Housing satisfaction	.06	.19				
General morale	.16	.12	.17			
Motility	.18	.08	.04	.22		
Family contact	−.02	−.05	−.08	.00	.06	
Subjective health	.16	.08	.03	.26	.42	.03

[a] Cases for whom all indices were not available were deleted. $N = 2,457$.

Data Analysis

A series of regression analyses was performed in order to ascertain the impact of housing characteristics upon individual satisfaction and well-being. The following factors were considered: 1) whether it was public housing or Section 202 nonprofit housing; 2) the population size of the area (a rural–urban continuum); 3) the size of the project as measured by the number of elderly-designated units (EDU) contained; 4) the number of floors in the residence building.

Since the environmental characteristics of the site and the neighborhood were expected to relate to personal characteristics of the tenants, i.e., more black people may live in cities, it was not advisable to examine the buildings without considering the demographic characteristics of the residents. Regression analysis was performed and in every case key personal variables were entered into the regression equation first so that it would be possible to examine the residual effect of the environmental factors.

The study was cross-sectional and therefore limited in the extent to which causal inferences may be derived. Correlational methods were employed through the hypothesis testing hierarchical multiple regression method described by Cohen (1968). Within this framework, hypotheses were made about the causal order in which independent variables may affect the dependent variables, and multiple regression analyses were performed so that the independent variables enter in the order prescribed by the hypothesis. The critical independent variable becomes the last one to enter the equation, so that its relationship to the dependent variable is independent of all prior-entering independent variables.

In order to ascertain the amount of *unique* variance contributed by the environmental factors, the following personal variables were entered into the multiple regression equation first: age, sex, race, marital status, length of residence in the building, whether or not the person was receiving welfare benefits, and self-reported health. Following the personal variables, the environmental variables were entered into the equation: a) public housing versus 202; b) size of community; c) building size; and d) building height.

RESULTS

Table 3 shows for each index of well-being the percentages of unique variance accounted for by the personal control variables, each of the four environmental variables separately (in the order in which they entered the equation), the set of four environmental variables, and the set of all personal and environmental variables. Relatively small increments in variance may be statistically significant with such a large N. Therefore, only

TABLE 3

Percentages of variance in well-being accounted for by personal and environmental variables entered in hierarchical order.

| | PERSONAL VARIABLES | SPONSOR | ENVIRONMENTAL VARIABLES | | | ALL ENVIRONMENTAL VARIABLES | TOTAL VARIANCE |
			COMMUNITY SIZE	BUILDING SIZE	BUILDING SIZE		
Friendship	3.2*	0.7*	3.4*	0.1	0.1	4.3*	7.5*
Housing satisfaction	2.0*	0.5	2.7*	0.1	1.2*	4.4*	6.4*
Morale	7.6*	0.2	0.0	0.0	0.0	0.2	7.8*
Motility	22.2*	0.0	0.0	0.2	0.7*	1.0*	23.2*
Family contact	3.0*	0.0	0.0	0.1	0.1	0.3	3.3*
Activity participation	10.3*	2.2*	0.6*	0.0	0.4	4.3*	14.6*
df[a]	7,2449	1,2448	1,2447	1,2446	1,2445	4,2445	11,2445

* $p < .01$ and variance increment > 0.5%.

[a] error df for Activity participation is one less than indicated for other indices.

those increments with associated F values that are both significant at the .01 level and that contribute more than 0.5% of unique variance are asterisked. For simplicity of presentation, beta weights and partial correlations are omitted; the directionality of the associations will be identified as each item is presented.

Personal background characteristics accounted for substantial proportions of variance in each index of well-being. This proportion was greater than for environmental variables except for *friendship and activity participation*. With these personal variables controlled, *friendship* scores were higher in 202 projects and in smaller communities; building size and height showed no independent relationship to friendship. *Housing satisfaction* was greater in small communities and in lower buildings. No environmental characteristic was related either to *morale* or to amount of *family contact*. *Motility* was greater in lower buildings. In order to examine *activity participation*, an additional control variable was added, the number of scheduled activities at the site, as reported by the administrator from a list of fourteen activities. Utilizing this control variable in effect measures activity participation in proportion to the number of activities actually offered. With size as the critical (final) independent variable, this was the major test of the undermanning hypothesis. While proportionate participation was higher in 202 projects and smaller communities, no independent effect on participation was found for building size or building height.

To summarize the results in a different way:

202 sponsorship was associated with higher friendship scores and with greater activity participation, with personal variables controlled.

Small community size was associated with higher friendship score, greater housing satisfaction, and greater activity participation, with personal variables, and sponsorship controlled.

Building size was associated with no index of well-being, with personal variables, sponsorship, and community size controlled.

Greater building height was associated with lower housing satisfaction and lower motility, with personal characteristics, sponsorship, community size, and building size controlled.

In the above analyses, building size was measured as the number of EDUs, on the assumption that number of age-peers defined the functional size of the project for the subject. However, about half of the public housing sites contained various types of age mixes. In all of these, the total number of units was considerably greater than the number of EDUs. All of the regressions presented in Table 3 were therefore run, using the total number of units regardless of age as the measure of building size. With one exception, the results shown for EDUs were replicated. *Housing satisfaction*, however, was inversely related to total number of units [r_p = $-$.08, variance % 0.7, F = 15.02 p < .01].

Since age integration occurred in these public housing projects, one may ask whether this social environmental variable might have affected the findings reported above. Another report from this study (Teaff, Lawton, and Carlson, 1973) did, in fact, show that age integration was associated with lower well-being by most of the criteria. However, again, another set of regressions, utilizing a measure of age integration as a control variable, did not change the findings noted above.

Finally, as an alternative to the undermanning hypothesis, one might hypothesize a curvilinear relationship between building size and activity participation. That is, proportionately reduced individual participation might occur in both the largest (overmanned) and the smallest projects (critical mass to support viable activities not reached), with maximum participation in moderate-sized projects. The variance associated with the quadratic component (Cohen, 1968) was not significant for either EDUs or total project size.

DISCUSSION

It must be emphasized that when the amount of variance accounted for by height and size of building is discussed, reference is being made to the *unique* variance after all other factors including the public–private dichotomy and size of community are forced into the regression analysis first. This means that much shared variance which is legitimately associated with these factors is arbitrarily assigned to the control variables. In addition, all relationships are underestimated by the correlational measures, because of the restriction in range of the dependent variables. Therefore, the tests made were conservative on both counts.

The impact of size was smaller than had been anticipated. Studies of the other types of organizations reviewed earlier in this report showed small size to be associated with a variety of positive outcome criteria. Where such a relationship has been found, explanations of the processes that mediate the relationship have been largely speculative; usually it is suggested that large size produces disproportionate increases in organizational maintenance operations such as vertical and horizontal communication among worker levels, personnel problems, or small-group rivalries. Thus, the time available to maintain output-related behavior becomes disproportionately required for maintenance operations.

The undermanning hypothesis is a suggested mechanism which describes the differential effect of size. In the case of housing for the elderly, there is no reason why the same rationale could not be applied. Yet, the relationship did not occur in the present study. Since the total size of projects ranged from ten to well over six hundred dwelling units, one cannot suggest that size was restricted in range. It is worth noting, however, that even though the mean number of activities reported by the manager was 8.3 per site, the mean number in which each tenant participated was 1.3; 45 percent engaged in no activities. The differential between 202 housing (72 percent of tenants participated in at least one activity) and public housing (46 percent) was substantial, accounted for partly by tenant background characteristics and partly by differences in the sites' activity programming. Notably lacking is any measure of managerial quality, which will be examined in later reports. One can only hazard the guess that some of these uncontrolled factors are so much more important determinants of activity that any possible effect of size was too small to be of consequence.

In relation to the test of the undermanning hypothesis, we must acknowledge that Barker (1968) framed this hypothesis to apply to a behavior setting (a "standing pattern" of behavior in a particular physical location or class of locations) rather than to a total organization such as a housing environment. However, Bechtel (1974) reviewed several studies using gross size variables, rather than behavior settings, whose results were consistent with the undermanning hypothesis. A promising direction for future research might include a full behavior setting survey of housing environments in the classical Barker style, which would include formal settings such as specific scheduled activities. Participation in a weekly senior citizens club, for example, rather than participation in overall activities, might give a more precise test of the hypothesis. In such a study one would also be able to examine hypothesized consequences of undermanning other than mere attendance, including degree of penetration, sense of personal gratification, behavior setting entry requirements, and so on.

This study does appear to support undermanning with reference to community size. However, the housing environments' activity programs are usually totally self-contained; to associate activity participation rate with the different numbers of potential participants in the wider community seems tenuous at best. It may be the anonymity and social overload effects of large-community life (Milgram, 1970) that are responsible for the lower participation in cities. This interpretation is consistent with the finding in this present report that the friendship criterion is also higher in smaller communities.

The size and height question.—This study gives little reason to conclude that project or building size bears any essential relationship to tenant well-being. Planning decisions as to the size of a project may thus tentatively be presumed possible on the basis of factors other than impact on tenant well-being.

Even after the variance shared with community size and public–private ownership was partialled out, a statistically significant amount of unique variance due to building height alone remained in two of the six indices of well-being, *housing satisfaction* and *motility*.

Evidently elderly persons are slightly more satisfied in lower buildings, and residing in a high-rise does seem to be associated with reduced motility. The mechanisms behind lesser housing satisfaction and motility in the high-rise building are not clear. Evidence from other work (Nahemow, 1972) suggests that older people's direct preferences are slightly greater for low-rise housing. Familiarity and lifelong experience are undoubtedly factors in such preference. In the case of motility, many of the obvious factors that might possibly cause a spurious relationship between high-rise living and motility were controlled. For example, high-rises are more often built in urban areas, where motility is greater (Langford, 1962); size of community was therefore controlled. One thus may search for noncontrolled mediators, such as the possibility that high-rises may be placed selectively in high crime areas, thus reducing mobility. Another possibility is that the vertical distance from an upper floor to off-site areas may constitute a greater psychological barrier to motility than the horizontal distances occasioned by low-rise sprawl.

It does not appear from these results that concentrated high-rise housing need be disastrous to the well-being of elderly tenants. In fact, it appears to be factors that often co-vary with building height, such as their frequent location in high crime areas, which produce the major effects that have been previously found. High-rise buildings should continue to be built when the circumstances warrant it, but administrators should be alerted to their potential problems. For example, the manager of a high-rise might have to make a special effort to determine which tenants need encouragement to go into the community, or which ones might feel better about their housing situation if they had the opportunity to discuss possible anxieties about high-rise living. Such feelings may change with times as people become adapted to unaccustomed elevators and vistas. In any case, the effect of building height is small enough to enable one to conclude that a satisfying life-style is possible in any building type, given the other positive features of housing for the elderly.

SUMMARY

This research studied four characteristics of housing environments for older people about which there is much debate among planners and designers—the type of sponsorship, the size of community in which the housing is located, the number of people housed in a single project, and the height of the building. The design of the study and the large sample of both tenants and environments enabled an unusual degree of control to be exercised over the many aspects of the settings that might affect the well-being of the tenant. Associations were found between both small community size and nonprofit sponsorship and some indices of well-being. An independent relationship between size and well-being was found only in the case of housing satisfaction, when total project size was considered. On the other hand, tenants in low buildings were more satisfied with their housing and more motile in their environment than tenants in high-rise buildings, with many personal and some other environmental factors controlled. The high-rise is less familiar to this generation's elderly and may constitute a psychological barrier to the enjoyment of their housing and neighborhood milieux. However, the relationships were small enough to enable one to conclude

that the necessity for high-rise construction should not veto the choice of a particular building site. Rather, recognition of the possible problem by management should lead to counteractive administrative efforts to reduce the possible negative effects of high-rise on some tenants.

REFERENCES

ANDERSON, N. N., HOLMBERG, R. H., SCHNEIDER, R. E., and STONE, L. B. *Policy Issues Regarding Nursing Homes.* Minneapolis: American Rehabilitation Foundation, 1969.

BARKER, R. G. *Ecological Psychology.* Stanford, Calif.: Stanford University Press, 1968.

BARKER, R. G., and GUMP, P. V. *Big School, Small School.* Stanford, Calif.: Stanford University Press, 1964.

BEATTIE, W. M., and BULLOCK, J. *Preface to a Counseling Service.* St. Louis: Health & Welfare Council of Metropolitan St. Louis, 1963.

BECHTEL, R. B. "The Undermanned Environment: A Universal Theory?" In *Man-Environment Interactions.* Vol. 8. Edited by D. H. Carson. Milwaukee: Environmental Design Research Assn., 1974.

COHEN, J. "Multiple Regression as a General Data-Analytic System." *Psychological Bulletin,* 70 (1968): 426–443.

COHEN, J., and STRUENING, E. L. "Simple-Minded Questions and Twirling Stools." Journal of Consulting Psychology, 29 (1965): 278-280.

CURRY, T. J., and RATLIFF, B. W. "The Effects of Nursing Home Size on Resident Isolation." *Gerontologist,* 13 (1973): 295–298.

FOREHAND, G. A., and GILMER, G. "Environmental Variation in Studies of Organizational Behavior." *Psychological Bulletin,* 62 (1964): 361–382.

GOTTESMAN, L. *Nursing Home Performance as Related to Resident Traits, Ownership, Size, and Source of Payment.* Philadelphia: Philadelphia Geriatric Center, 1972.

GUREL, L. "Correlates of Psychiatric Hospital Effectiveness." VA Hospital, Washington: Intramural Report 64-5, Psychiatric Evaluation Project, 1964.

KOSBERG, J. I. "Differences in Proprietary Institutions Caring for Affluent and Non-affluent Elderly." Gerontologist, 13 (1973): 299–304.

LANGROD, M. Community aspects of housing for the aged. Ithaca, New York: Cornell University Center for Housing & Environmental Studies, 1962.

LAWTON, M. P., and COHEN, J. "The Generality of Housing Impact on the Well-Being of Older People." Journal of Gerontology, 29 (1974): 194–204.

LAWTON, M. P., and COHEN, J. "Organizational Studies of Mental Hospitals." In Handbook of Evaluation Research, edited by E. L. Struening and M. Guttentag. Los Angeles: Sage, 1975.

LEVEY, S., RUCHLIN, H. S., STOTSKY, B. A., KINLOCH, D. R., and OPPENHEIM, W. "An Appraisal of Nursing Home Care." Journal of Gerontology, 28 (1973): 222–228.

LIKERT, R. W. New Patterns of Management. New York: McGraw-Hill, 1961.

LINN, M. W. "Predicting Quality of Patient Care in Nursing Homes." Gerontologist 14 (1974): 225–227.

MILGRAM, S. "The Experience of Living in Cities." Science, 167 (1970): 1461–1468.

MOOS, R. "Size, Staffing, and the Psychiatric Ward Treatment Environment." Archives of General Psychiatry, 26 (1972): 414–418.

NAHEMOW, L. "National Survey of Housing for the Elderly, 3rd Report." Philadelphia: Philadelphia Geriatric Center, 1972.

NEWMAN, O. Defensible Space. New York: Macmillan, 1972.

TEAFF, J. D., LAWTON, M. P., and CARLSON, D. "Impact of Age Integration of Public Housing Projects upon Elderly Tenant Well-Being." Gerontologist, 13 (1973): 77.

WICKER, A. W. "Size of Church Membership and Members' Support of Church Behavior Settings." Journal of Personality and Social Psychology, 13 (1969): 278–288.

WRIGHT, H. "Children's Behavior in Communities Differing in Size." University of Kansas, Dept. of Psychology, Lawrence, 1969.

Quality of Care in Old Age Institutions

Cary S. Kart
Barbara B. Manard

In a recent study, Gottesman and Bourestom (1974) sought to determine "why nursing homes do what they do." The sampling frame for the study included 169 of Detroit's licensed nursing homes which were not operated by a hospital and not exclusively homes for the aged, rehabilitation hospitals, mental hospitals, or Tuberculosis Sanataria. Forty facilities were selected to represent the total group, and 1144 residents from these facilities constituted the sample population. An observation procedure, used for recording behavior, was employed. Two trained assist-

From The Gerontologist 16, 3 (1976), pp. 250–256. Reprinted by permission.

ants observed residents during twenty-four one-hour segments between 6:30 a.m. and 7:30 p.m. on two days. In each hour the resident was observed for one full minute in a predetermined sequence. Each time a record was made of services given or patient activity, including location, position, and involvement with other people. The results reported from this study show that more than half of the residents' time was spent doing nothing with most of the remaining time spent in personal care or socializing. To the surprise of the authors, only 2 percent of their observations recorded residents receiving a nursing service from a professional or nonprofessional staff member. In fact, over the course of more than 27,000 observations, fewer than one in four (23 percent) sample residents were observed receiving any nursing contacts at all. Residents in this sample who did receive care could be distinguished from others by race, economic status, and some organizational characteristics of the Old Age Institutions (OAIs) in which they resided.

The real issue emanating from Gottesman and Bourestom's research seems not to be "why nursing homes do what they do" but rather, "why don't they do what they are supposed to?" The "supposed to" in this question refers to a characteristic of institutions, variously measured, which is perhaps the most elusive for researchers and practitioners concerned with OAIs: quality of care. Clearly a dirty, crowded, understaffed nursing home in which old people live unhappily and die rapidly is a bad institution. But what is a good one? Should quality be measured in terms of resident satisfaction or professional nursing care? Given limited resources, is it more important to spend money on gardners, interior design, janitorial services, and food quality, or on an abundance of aides, orderlies, and health professionals?

Obviously, no one type of facility will be best for all types of people. However, it is important to recognize the complexity of quality and to deal with its many aspects. Looking at federal and state regulations, we see that the emphasis has been almost exclusively on promoting higher standards of safety and health care. This same regulatory power, and particularly the "certificate of need" program, could be used to influence aesthetic features of facility design, the incorporation of educational and recreational activities into facility programs, and other features related to "quality of life." Thoughtful persons in a position to influence the regulation and development of OAIs will be frustrated by the current state of research into quality.

Researchers have generally taken one of two approaches to the investigation of quality. One method is to devise a list of "probable indicators" of quality and to study what types of facilities rate high. For example, Anderson, Holmberg, Schneider, and Stone (1969) thought that the following would be important characteristics in the quality of nursing homes: the number of patients per room and bathroom; whether or not the facility had been originally designed as a nursing home; the number of staff hours per patient; patient participation in various activities; and the therapeutic orientation of the administration. They found higher quality in facilities with fewer welfare patients, higher costs, rural location, larger size; in those attached to hospitals, those with fewer ambulatory patients, and in accredited facilities. One problem with this approach to the measurement of quality is that we often do not really know what difference it makes to the patient, for example, to have more nurses available. As Gottesman and Bourestom's (1974) study of Detroit area nursing homes showed, only a few patients had any nursing contacts at all, though, based on direct testing, one-half of the sample was either moderately or very confused and 40 percent were reported to need some assistance in activities of daily living.

A second approach has been to study a probable indicator such as crowding or staffing patterns in relation to various outcome measures—resident satisfaction, social participation, staff performance, and the like (Dick & Friedsam, 1964; Lawton, 1974; Schooler, 1969). The problem with this type of investigation is that, as Alexander Pope put it, "we murder to dissect." In other words, if we know that residents are happiest in small homes, new homes, homes with many nurses, and homes in rural areas, we still do not know much about small, new homes, with many nurses, in rural areas.

A third approach, rarely used, is that employed by Taietz (1953) in his admirable study of three homes for the aged, completed some 20 years ago. Taietz selected homes of high, medium, and low quality as determined by professionals working in the area. He found that resident happiness was indeed highest in the home judged to be of the best quality by outside observers; however, he also found that the characteristics that made this home the best in professional eyes were not in many cases what made it the happiest environment for the residents.

We look now at a few of the general characteristics which have interested investigators concerned with quality.

SOME INSTITUTIONAL CHARACTERISTICS RELATED TO QUALITY

Ownership

Several studies have investigated the relationship between quality of care (variously measured) and facility ownership. Anderson et al. (1969) found that more physician hours per patient were provided in the nonprofit than in the proprietary facilities they surveyed. Beattie and Bullock (1964) rated the social milieu, staff attitudes, and other features of eighty facilities in St. Louis which differed by level of care offered. They reported that nonprofit homes rated higher than the others.

Townsend (1962) devised a multiple item index of quality of care and surveyed 173 British institutions for the aged. He reported that voluntary nonprofit homes were best, proprietary homes occupied a middle position, and public homes were the worst.

Levey, Ruchlin, Stotsky, Kinloch, and Oppenheim (1973), in a study of 129 Mas-

sachusetts nursing homes in 1965 and 1969, looked at the relationship between quality of care, ownership, and cost. Three types of facility (noncorporate proprietary, corporate proprietary, and corporate charitable) were rated on a nine component aggregate quality-of-care scale. They found no significant relationship between quality of care and facility ownership. In both 1965 and 1969, the highest per capita per diem costs were reported by corporate charitable homes, and the lowest by noncorporate proprietary homes. When the authors employed a multiple regression technique to explain variation in their 1969 quality-of-care rating, no significant relationship appeared between the dependent variable and ownership. Thus, while cost was found to relate to quality of care and ownership, ownership was not related to quality. Disaggregating the quality-of-care scale into its nine major components and analyzing each score by type of ownership also showed no significant differences among the ownership types. The individual dimensions of quality included measures relating to the personal care of patients, the maintenance of patient records, patient activities, equipment and resources available, nursing personnel and services, and the physical plant.

Other important distinctions among facilities by type of ownership have been reported. Holmberg and Anderson (1968) observed that residents of the nonprofit homes they studied were slightly older and less impaired mentally than those in proprietary homes. The National Health Survey's studies of OAI report that residents in proprietary facilities are in the poorest health and have the shortest mean length of stay compared to residents in facilities under government or nonprofit management (USDHEW, 1968; 1972; 1973).

Size

System size has received much attention as a sociological variable. It is widely believed that size has a pervasive influence on the internal order of an organization (Kasarda, 1974). In OAIs, increasing size may necessitate an increasing commitment of resources to clerical, administrative, and other impersonal activities. This may adversely affect the satisfaction of institutionalized residents. Greenwald and Linn (1971) have suggested that as OAIs get larger, activity and communication decline. Curry and Ratliff (1973) argue that a person's life satisfaction is likely to be influenced by certain aspects of his current environment. They contend that since smaller facilities generally have a more homelike atmosphere than larger facilities, smaller homes create fewer disruptions in accustomed living arrangements. They suggested that this ought to favor resident satisfaction.

Studying a sample of Ohio proprietary nursing homes, Curry and Ratliff (1973) found that the residents of the smaller facilities had more friends within the home, more monthly contacts with these friends, and more total monthly contacts, despite the fact that residents of the larger homes had more living relatives and more contacts with these relatives. This may suggest that increased sociability developed within the smaller homes as a result of the greater proximity of residents.

Socioeconomic Status

The socioeconomic status of an OAI has several components, including the socioeconomic status of the residents and staff, the resources of the facility, and possibly the price of care in the facility. Surprisingly little work has been done relating the socioeconomic status of OAIs to quality of care. The gerontological truism seems to be that upperclass identification implies greater resources, which in turn implies a higher quality of care. Empirical studies partially support this easy assumption.

In a survey conducted in 1969 of 126 Minnesota nursing homes, Anderson and her colleagues (Anderson et al., 1969) found that quality of care was inversely related to the percentage of welfare patients in a facility, and positively correlated with daily per capita facility expenditures. Levey et al. (1973), in a study of Massachusetts facilities, report

that quality of care was higher in facilities that spent more money.

Kosberg (1971, 1973) studied the relationship between organizational characteristics and treatment resources (e.g., professional personnel, equipment) in 214 Chicago area nursing homes. He found only a modest relationship between level of care offered and available resources. However, availability of resources in the facilities was highly correlated with the characteristics of resident populations.

Kosberg assigned a Resource Score to each facility. These scores were correlated with (among other things) the percentage of black residents, the percentage referred to the facility by a public agency, and the percentage supported by public-aid payments. The respective zero-order correlations were −.27, −.48, and −.57. It would seem that the non-affluent and minority elderly are often institutionalized in OAIs lacking in treatment resources. Kosberg also reported that the elderly poor are further inconvenienced by being placed in facilities located further from their families and previous homes than are the affluent elderly.

Social Integration

Very little is known about the attempts of OAIs to promote the development of new social relationships to take the place of other social relationships that have been abandoned in the process of aging.

Jacobs (1969) has reported on the adjustment of a group of forty-six women occupying one-half of a floor in a Jewish home for the aged. Using a conflict model, she views inter- and intra-group conflict as measures of integration and adjustment, respectively. In the institution she observed, conflict promoted interaction, which in turn led to a group cohesiveness and solidarity among the women. Suppression of conflict was seen as a barrier to adjustment for these women.

Lipman (1968), using what he calls a socio-architectural approach, observed the relationship between seating patterns and social interaction in three homes for the aged in England. He found that while sustained verbal interaction was a factor in establishing friendships, the residents' practice of regularly occupying particular chairs and the fixed furniture arrangements seemed to limit the scope and range of possible friendships in the homes. He proposed, from a disengagement perspective, that regular occupation of chairs in fixed arrangements may be preferred manner of coming to terms with enforced proximity to others in institutions.

Bennett (1963) has argued that as institutions for the elderly become more "total," increased regimentation occurs. Administrators may foster a feeling of dependence and inactivity in residents by discouraging close relationships among residents and between them and staff. The end result may be increased feelings of isolation and powerlessness on the part of residents.

Another aspect of social integration involves the relationship between an OAI and its residents and the greater community. Several researchers have dealt with this.

Gelfand (1968) tested the general hypothesis that social adjustment among institutionalized aged is related to the totality of the institution and the more specific hypothesis that adjustment is related to the degree to which residents have access to the outside community. A sample of thirty-two women and men residing in a St. Louis OAI was used. All members of the group were both ambulatory and in good mental health. Rank-order correlations (Kendall's Tau) of .45, .48, and .28 (all $p < .01$) were reported for the relationships between outside visiting and adjustment, sociability and adjustment, and sociability and outside visiting, respectively. The author's explanation of these findings reflected a fourth relationship, that between outside visiting and identification with the home (.21, $p < .05$). He argued that the ability of residents to visit outside the institution increases acceptance of the home and its goals and thus promotes greater social adjustment.

Grant (1970) discussed the relationship between age segregated housing and the satisfaction of the elderly. From his review of the gerontological literature, it appears that age homogeneous housing contributes to high morale and life satisfaction for the aged. However, we cannot generalize from this conclusion to the organization of OAI. Kahana and Kahana (1967), studying a psychiatric facility, found that placing newly admitted patients in an age integrated rather than age segregated ward had a stimulating effect on social interaction.

Professionalism

OAIs vary in the degree of sophistication with which they are managed, the proportion of highly trained professionals on the staff, and the manner in which formally prescribed procedures are carried out. These elements, among others, contribute to what might be called a professionalism factor. We know of no studies dealing specifically with this composite characteristic. However, the results of some related studies suggest that professionalism and some aspects of quality of patient care may be inversely related.

One study of Massachusetts nursing facilities reported a great increase between 1965 and 1969 in the proportion of facilities in compliance with regulatory standards for eight of nine quality-of-care measures (Levey et al., 1973). However, a measure on which compliance declined from 1965 to 1969 related to personal care of the patients. In 1965, 90 percent of all facilities were in compliance on patient personal care (e.g., patient is clean; has clean clothes; is well groomed); by 1969 this had fallen to 78 percent. Similarly, for care of the bedside unit, the percentage in compliance decreased from 60 percent to 55 percent. On facility oriented items (e.g., personnel records, diet orders, and medical records) compliance had improved dramatically.

We have elsewhere emphasized the problems associated with sorting OAIs according to state licensure categories (Manard, Kart, and van Gils, 1975). However, generally speaking, lower level facilities are less professional than higher level ones. Beattie and Bullock (1964) reported that St. Louis facilities licensed as homes for the aged received more favorable observer ratings of administrator's attitudes and of the social milieu than facilities licensed for nursing care, practical nursing care, or domiciliary care. In addition, the personnel of homes for the aged were reported to have more positive attitudes toward the residents than the personnel of other facility types.

CONCLUSIONS

Someone looking for suggestions on how to choose a quality nursing facility for an aged friend or relative might, on the basis of a reading of the above literature review, select an institution that is nonproprietary, relatively small in size, wealthy in resources, sociable, and with a staff that has positive attitudes toward the residents. Unfortunately, such institutions are rare. But, if one could be found, another question would be in order: does the facility provide the appropriate *level of care* for the individual involved? This question points up a fundamental problem with much of the research into quality and which has contributed to the difficulty in generating concensus on quality-of-care components. The problem we refer to is the failure of many concerned with the issue of quality to distinguish between different types of facilities offering different levels of care. One of the major reasons for the failure to arrive at agreement on quality-of-care components which are universally acceptable is the insistence we seem to pursue in lumping all facilities together and all types of patients together.

The serious reader of the quality-of-care literature is already aware that *nursing home* and *rest home* are terms practitioners, the general public, and some investigators commonly apply to a great variety of institutions which we have called collectively, OAIs. In general, distinctions are made between nursing home and rest home on the basis of supposed differences in services offered, and each elicits a different set of images: the nursing home suggests hospital beds and uniformed staffs; the rest home, old

folks rocking on the porch. Attempting to be more precise, however, one finds that there is no simple set of characteristics by which all institutions called nursing homes or rest homes may be distinguished from other institutions, nor is there a set of characteristics to distinguish all institutions called nursing homes from those called rest homes.

It is, of course, possible to devise distinguishing lists of characteristics—that is, to employ real rather than nominal definitions. In practice, researchers and government data collectors rely on state license categories to distinguish OAIs from chronic disease hospitals, boarding houses, and the like. The validity of this technique lies in the fact that a state license is itself an important linking characteristic of all institutions similarly licensed.

A greater problem arises, however, when we attempt to compare types of OAIs using data from various sources. Each relevant federal department and each state has developed its own distinguishing criteria and nomenclature for types of OAIs. Medicare and Medicaid legislation, by encouraging the concept of levels of care and introducing new terms, has had the most important recent influence on the lexicon of OAIs. Specifically, three new types of facilities have been defined in the Medicare and Medicaid legislation: extended care facilities (ECFs), skilled care facilities (SCFs), and intermediate care facilities (ICFs). Still, as we have pointed out elsewhere (Manard et al., 1975, especially Table 2.3), euphemism also plays a part in the official naming of institutions, with some states rising to heights of verbal delicacy. Just as mental hospital has replaced insane asylum, rest home is giving way to personal care home and retirement facility. What is classified as an extended care facility in Massachusetts may be classified as a skilled care facility in Virginia and a comprehensive care nursing home in Utah. A Massachusetts rest home may be equated with a home for adults in Virginia or a personal care home in Utah.

The fact that there is no universal schema for categorizing OAIs must be a serious consideration for researchers comparing their own work with that of others. Special attention must be paid when the respective works involve different levels of care and different types of facilities. This posed a problem as we reviewed a large number of relevant gerontological studies. Our ability to specify an institutional characteristic which related to quality of care and to summarize the literature surrounding it was limited by the original works themselves. Thus, a study, using nursing homes as the units of analysis, which purports to be investigating the relationship between size of facility and quality of care may be reporting spurious findings if there are no controls for level of care offered at the facilities under study. In such a study the investigator may find himself comparing large ECFs with small ICFs and drawing conclusions about the extent to which size of a facility contributes to quality of care when, in fact, it may be level of care which is the key contributor. Where possible in our discussion we indicated the types of facilities employed in particular studies. Unfortunately, as readers have discovered, only a few researchers offered more specific information than the general nomenclature of nursing homes, rest homes, and homes for the aged. As a result, at this time we are unable to offer any conclusions about the relationship between level of care and quality of care.

The scarcity of institutions that are nonproprietary, relatively small in size, wealthy in resources, sociable, and with a staff that has positive attitudes toward the residents raises another problem with the research literature: its inability to direct us toward answers to the question, "how do we improve the quality of care in the remaining facilities?" As many are aware, sufficient licensing procedures and operating regulations already exist, though cynics (and others) suggest that even the inspectors and regulators themselves admit regulation is a poor tool for assuring quality institutional care (Barney, 1974).

A recent report by Senator Moss's Subcommittee on Long-Term Care (Special Committee on Aging, 1974), in a chapter entitled, Nursing Home Inspections: A National Farce, points out that

there are few weapons other than the threat of license revocation to bring a facility into compliance with operating regulations,

because of legal and administrative procedures required, license revocation is itself ineffective,

in many instances where revocation is implemented, judges are reluctant to close a facility when an operator claims deficiencies are being corrected,

inspections are geared to surveying the physical plant rather than evaluating the quality of care.

What is the answer then? A principle that one hears discussed is accountability—but to whom and for what? Barney (1974) proposes that facilities be accountable to the community for the care they provide, with this accountability ensured by direct community involvement. Gaynes (1973) and Tobin (1974) also suggest "community-based-sponsored institutional facilities" as substitutes for the "worst" homes which do not now provide needed services for the chronically ill elderly. Gottesman (1974) advises administrative changes to make all homes accountable for providing the kind of responsible high quality care we observe in many nonprofit facilities.

The past record on administrative and regulatory changes, however, is not good. As Mendelson and Hapgood (1974) point out, personal connections between the industry and its regulators, occasional instances of blatant corruption and downright bureaucratic weariness have deterred attempts in this sphere before, and new approaches may be necessary (see Anderson, 1974, for a discussion of some possible strategies being attempted in selected areas and facilities). These same authors argue, though, that lack of continued effective public pressure is the most basic reason for the failure of nursing home regulation. It is just this lack of sustained public pressure which may prove problematic for proposals related to community involvement. Still, lack of public pressure itself may be symptomatic rather than causal in nature. On the one hand, while the population of old persons continues to grow faster than any other age group, and the population of OAI is increasing as well, only a small proportion of the general population is believed to have any experience with aged institutionalized individuals. Thus, relatively few of the noninstitutionalized have personal experience with OAIs. On the other hand, lack of public pressure may be symptomatic of an old bugaboo with which gerontologists are quite familiar: deep-rooted fears and attitudes toward aging and death.

In summary, it is fair to say that researchers have been successful in identifying that which constitutes a good OAI but researchers, practitioners, and regulators are operating in an unfocused vacuum when it comes to making an OAI good.

REFERENCES

ANDERSON, N. N. "Approaches to Improving the Quality of Long-Term Care for Older Persons." *Gerontologist*, 14 (1974): 519–524.

ANDERSON, N., HOLMBERG, R. H., SCHNEIDER, R. E., and STONE, L. B. *Policy Issues Regarding Nursing Homes, Findings From a Minnesota Study.* Minneapolis: Institute for Interdisciplinary Studies, American Rehabilitation Foundation, 1969.

BARNEY, J. "Community Pressure as a Key to Quality of Life in Nursing Homes." *American Journal of Public Health*, 64 (1974): 265–268.

BEATTIE, W. M., and BULLOCK, J. "Evaluating Services and Personnel in Facilities for the Aged." In *Geriatric Institutional Management*, edited by, M. Leeds and H. Shore. New York: Putnam, 1964.

BENNETT, R. "The Meaning of Institutional Life." *Gerontologist*, 3 (1963): 117–125.

CURRY, T., and RATLIFF, B. W. "The Effects of Nursing Home Size on Resident Isolation and Life Satisfaction." *Gerontologist*, 13 (1973): 296–298.

DICK, H. R., and FRIEDSAM, H. "Adjustment of Residents of Two Homes for the Aged." *Social Problems*, 27 (1964): 282–290.

GAYNES, N. L. "A Logic to Long-Term Care." *Gerontologist*, 13 (1973): 277–281.

GELFAND, D. E. "Visiting Patterns and Social Adjustment in an Old Age Home." *Gerontologist*, 8 (1968): 272–275.

GOTTESMAN, L. "Nursing Home Performance as Related to Resident Traits, Ownership, Size, and Source of Payment." *American Journal of Public Health*, 64 (1974): 269–276.

GOTTESMAN, L., and BOURESTOM, N. "Why Nursing Homes Do What They Do." *Gerontologist*, 14 (1974): 501–506.

GRANT, D. P. "Architect Discovers the Aged." *Gerontologist*, 10 (1970): 275–281.

GREENWALD, S. R., and LINN, M. W. "Intercorrelations of Data on Nursing Homes." *Gerontologist*, 11 (1971): 337–340.

HOLMBERG, R. H., and ANDERSON, N. N. "Implications of Ownership for Nursing Home Care." *Medical Care*, 7 (1968): 300–307.

JACOBS, R. "One Way Street: An Intimate View of Adjustment." *Gerontologist*, 9 (1969): 268–275.

KAHANA, E., and KAHANA, B. "The Effects of Age Segregation on Interaction Patterns of Elderly Psychiatric Patients." Paper presented at annual meeting of American Psychological Association, Washington, 1967.

KASARDA, J. "The Structural Implications of Social System Size: A Three Level Analysis." *American Sociological Review*, 39 (1974): 19–28.

KOSBERG, J. "The Relationship Between Organizational Characteristics and Treatment Resources in Nursing Homes." PhD dissertation, University of Chicago, 1971.

KOSBERG, J. I. "Differences in Proprietary Institutions Care for Affluent and Nonaffluent Elderly." *Gerontologist*, 13 (1973): 299–304.

LAWTON, M. P. "Social Ecology and Older People" *American Journal of Public Health*, 64, (1974): 257–260.

LEVEY, S., RUCHLIN, H. S., STOTSKY, B. A., KINLOCH, D. R., and OPPENHEIM, W. "An Appraisal of Nursing Home Care." *Journal of Gerontology*, 28 (1973): 222–228.

LIPMAN, A. "A Socio-Architectural View of Life in Three Old Peoples' Homes." *Gerontologia Clinica*, 10 (1968): 88–101.

MANARD, B., KART, C., and VAN GILS, D. *Old age institutions.* Lexington, Mass.: D. C. Heath, 1975.

MENDELSON, M. A., and HAPGOOD, D. "The Political Economy of Nursing Homes." *Annals of the American Academy of Political and Social Science*, 415 (1974): 95–105.

SCHOOLER, K. "The Relationship Between Social Interaction and Morale of the Elderly as a Function of Environmental Characteristics." *Gerontologist*, 9 (1969): 25–29.

Special Committee on Aging, U.S. Senate. *Nursing Home Care in the United States: Failure in Public Policy.* Washington, D.C.: USGPO, 1974.

TAIETZ, P. "Administrative Practices and Personal Adjustment in Homes for the Aged." Cornell Experiment Station Bulletin, Jan., 1953.

TOBIN, S. "How Nursing Homes Vary." *Gerontologist*, 14 (1974): 516–519.

TOWNSEND, P. *The Last Refuge.* London: Routledge & Kegan Paul, 1962.

U. S. Dept. of Health, Education and Welfare. "Nursing and Personal Care Services, U. S., May-June, 1964." Washington, D.C.: USGPO, 1968.

U. S. Dept. of Health, Education and Welfare. "Nursing Homes: Their Admission Policies, Admissions and Discharge, U. S., April-September, 1968." Washington, D.C.: USGPO, 1972.

U. S. Dept. of Health, Education and Welfare. "Characteristics of Residents in Nursing and Personal Care Homes, U. S., June-August, 1969." Washington, D.C.: USGPO, 1973.

Organizational Features of Terminal Status Passage In Residential Facilities for the Aged

Victor W. Marshall

Dying may be viewed sociologically as a career involving a passagee (the dying person) and, in some cases, others who accompany him or who control aspects of his status pas-

"Organizational Features of Terminal Status Passage in Residential Facilities for the Aged" by Victor W. Marshall is reprinted from *Urban Life* Vol. 4, No. 3 (Oct. 1975) pp. 349–368 by permission of the Publisher, Sage Publications, Inc.

sage. In this paper, I focus on a home for the aged (St. Joseph's) and a retirement village (Glen Brae) as representative communities of the aging and dying. The two settings are viewed as sociocultural milieux in which residents live and, potentially, at least, participate in constructing the status passage reality wherein their own dying occurs. This reality includes the organization of their dying careers—involving the development of views of career termination—as well as other aspects of their lives as aging and dying people.

A number of observers have suggested that the extent to which the lives of elderly residents of congregate housing are generally satisfactory is greatly influenced by the degree of independence and resident-initiated organization (Aldridge, 1956; Kalson, 1972; Messer, 1967; Seguin, 1973). My restricted concern here is with the relationship between organizational features and the development among aged individuals of a sense that their dying status passage is appropriate or legitimate. The analysis focuses first on the differing structuring of time and then on the characteristics of the dying career within the two settings. As we shall see, the two communities are widely disparate in terms of their characteristic patternings of living and dying. Comparing them provides an opportunity to theorize about the influence of organizational features of residential settings for the aging on the degree to which and the ways in which passagees construct and legitimize their own dying and deaths.

Data used in this analysis stem from field research supplemented by interviewing in the two settings. Glen Brae is a rambling, modern, 300-apartment structure housing about 400 residents in a campus-like setting in a suburban environment in the eastern United States. Residents purchase their apartments on a "life-care" principle which includes transfer to an attached nursing-care facility should this become necessary. Fully 78 percent of the residents are female, but only 15 percent of females are married. About half the females are widowed, and just under a third have never married. Three-fourths of the males are still living with their spouses, the remainder beiing widowed. These sex and marital-status imbalances are not highly irregular, given the average age of the residents (eighty) and the age range (sixty-four to ninety-six). As in most similar communities, residents are educationally privileged, with less than one-fifth having no more than a high school education. Religious adherence

is mixed, but largely Protestant. The community has been described more extensively elsewhere (Marshall, 1973, 1975).

St. Joseph's, located twenty miles from the retirement village, provides a marked contrast. A decaying red-brick structure in a suburban area, it houses approximately seventy people, plus forty-five on a fully integrated nursing floor. The age range, sixty-four to ninety-eight, is comparable to that at Glen Brae. About 80 percent of the residents are supported through welfare. As at Glen Brae, the residents are primarily female. None, however, live with their spouses. Those able to pay their own way have private rooms; the majority live in dormitories. The infirmary, located on the main floor, houses those in need of more intensive care. A registered nurse is on duty at all times. A minority of residents, because of ethnic background, speak English with difficulty or not at all. All residents are nominally Catholic, and the home is administered by nuns.

TEMPORAL STRUCTURING OF ACTIVITIES

The timing of life in any organized setting depends on the synchronization, sequencing, and frequency of activities as well as on the activities themselves.[1] St. Joseph's Home and Glen Brae present vivid contrasts on the temporal structuring of activities.

At St. Joseph's, as in other relatively "total" institutions (Goffman, 1961: 6), virtually all aspects of life are carried out in the company of others treated in the same way. Activities are, for the most part, regularly sequenced but infrequent. The pace of life is slow. Meals exemplify the important events of the day because, on the typical day, nothing else happens. A bell beckons the residents to preassigned tables of six which are sex-segregated and unchanging. There is little conversation (due perhaps to language differences and to the lack of variety in table mates). Within fifteen minutes, most of the residents have left the dining room. There are no planned daily activity programs.[2] The

Directress is aware of the practice in similar institutions of encouraging residents to participate in planned activities but she thinks it preferable to leave them alone. About mid-morning, three or four residents might be found helping some of the Sisters with sewing and mending. A mid-day walk through the dormitories finds more than half the residents lying on top of their freshly made beds. Other activities are limited to the use of a few television lounges and sunporches and a basement recreation room where the men go for a smoke in the evening, generally sitting in silence. Conversation or any other activity in this room is infrequent—so much so that it took me about three weeks to work up the nerve to venture into it.

There is a monthly party, a birthday celebration for those having a birthday during the period. And the auxiliary does run a monthly bingo game. Yet residents are primarily spectators at these events. During bingo, for example, a volunteer stands over each player and when the number is called, moves the tab on the card.[3] The only event of note which truly breaks routine—a summer bus trip to a beach organized by the administration—does so only because its routine is on a once-yearly basis. In fact, the temporal structuring at St. Joseph's is so routinized and so slow that serious illness and death and its accompanying funeral (see below) become, ironically, the major novelties which interrupt the sameness of daily living. (See Gustafson, 1972, for a similar finding.) My field work at St. Joseph's was intermittent and thus, as a matter of course, I would ask upon my return, "What's new?" Although no one knew that death and dying were of particular interest to me, I was invariably told that what was new was that a death had occurred.

The situation at Glen Brae is a study in contrasts. Meals, for example, are anything but lock-step occasions. Residents may eat in their own kitchen-equipped apartments, in a snack bar, or in the dining room during extensive serving hours (evening meals in the dining room are part of the rental package). Seating arrangements are a matter of choice,

and a hostess will introduce newcomers or isolates to those with whom they may wish to share a table. Table size varies and this, together with the freedom to choose one's partners, leads to broad-ranging and extensive informal interaction. Dining is frequently preceded by small cocktail parties in the apartments, but whether any of these are scheduled or not, the walk to and from meals is customarily made in company.

Like dining arrangements, recreational pursuits are flexible and provide resident-initiated and planned possibilities for interaction with others. Throughout the day, depending on season, one sees the residents busy at lawn-bowls, shuffleboard, swimming, bridge games in the many lounges, or tending small flower gardens outside their apartments. There is a wide variety of scheduled and nonscheduled events, none of which are organized by the administration. A resident-initiated and run house government—the Forum—plans and implements a range of concerts, movies, lectures, religious services, craft and hobby groups, hiking trips, and field trips to neighboring cultural and recreational affairs. The Forum itself, with its many committees, is another source of activity and involvement. Residents produce their own newspaper, run their own library, and field their own choral group. The contrast with St. Joseph's was symbolized for me on the first visit I made to each setting shortly before Christmas: at St. Joseph's, the nuns were putting up Christmas decorations; at Glen Brae, residents were making their own.

In sum, while in neither setting does the administration formally encourage activity, time is structured very differently within each. At St. Joseph's the routine is repetitious, slowpaced, and lacking in novelty. When activities are scheduled, they are rarely done so at the initiative of residents. As one St. Joseph's resident noted, when asked how far ahead he planned, "I really don't, because it's all planned for you here. It's all routine." Asked if he missed that [planning], he said, "I did, but not any more." At Glen Brae, in contrast, the swift pace of activities is initiated by residents who in turn can draw upon them to piece together a day that breaks routine. Even the low activity level of a small minority of Glen Brae residents is higher than that of the most active person at St. Joseph's. I met no resident at St. Joseph's who kept a daily personal calendar, but I seldom met anyone at Glen Brae who did not. I did not have to schedule appointments for interviews at St. Joseph's, but I found it necessary to do so at Glen Brae. The slow pace of St. Joseph's resulted in death being highlighted, whereas the busy round of life at Glen Brae tended to dilute the vivid presence of death. The active involvements of residents in fashioning a way of life at Glen Brae provided, as we shall see, an interactional substratum for dealing with death such as was not developed at St. Joseph's.

THE DYING CAREER

A move to either Glen Brae or St. Joseph's is, virtually for all, the final move. When one of the St. Joseph's residents died unexpectedly, I was told by another, "That's fifteen in five months." Total deaths the year before had been twenty, and just sixteen the year before that, for rates of approximately 17 and 14 percent.[4] All but two had occurred in the home. St. Joseph's is a place where people go to die; and the residents know it. As the resident who kept a tally put it,

> I knew what the home was for. In fact the day I moved in here they had a death. Now for the past three years I write them down. Just for curiosity to keep a law of averages.

Glen Brae is also a place where people go to die and know it. The move to the retirement village heightens awareness of finitude. Considerable financial resources must be expended under the life-care provision, and a commitment is made to pay monthly rental fees until death. Intendedly rational decision making thus involves, for all except the very rich, an estimate of just what the

cost will be over that period before death, and this necessitates some estimate of life expectancy (discussed at length in Marshall, 1973). As one resident described this bargain, "They come here to die, you know, to spend their last days. . . . It's a form of insurance to come here—based on life expectancy."

Both settings, then, are recognized by the residents as places to die. But the impact of this recognition differs because of the differing ways in which dying careers within them are organized.

Dying at St. Joseph's

Dying is a social event; people die in the context of others who define their dying. Glaser and Strauss (1968: 6) use the term "dying trajectory" to refer to an individual's socially defined course of dying. As socially perceived, the dimensions of dying

> depend on when the perceiver initially *defines* someone as dying and on his expectations of how that dying will proceed. Dying trajectories themselves, then, are perceived courses of dying rather than their actual courses.

In this respect, we may note with Sudnow (1967: 62) that

> the characteristics "he is dead" and "he is dying" . . . are the products of assessment procedures, i.e., constitute the outcomes of investigative inquiries of more or less detail, undertaken by persons more or less practically involved in the consequences that discovery of those outcomes foreseeably have.

At St. Joseph's, the term "dying" tends to be reserved for the very last stages. As one aide noted, "When they start dying, they don't last for but a day. Some of them take longer." As such, while the residents may be "socially dead" (Kalish, 1968; Gustafson, 1972) to the outside world, they at least begin their residence in the home defined by staff as alive. The trajectory towards death begins, rather, with a definition of the resident as seriously ill or as needing intensive care. This leads to a move from the dormitory or private room on the second or third floor to the main infirmary floor. Then, if or when the prognosis of "dying" is made, the resident is moved to a special room, called at times the "dying room," but known to both staff and residents as "St. Peter's Room" (not a pseudonym), which, ironically, is room 13. At times there is a waiting list for this room, as my field notes record: "Sally and another aide said there are three people just waiting to die. So one is in St. Peter's Room. The other two are still in their own rooms." The dying trajectory implications of the room are appreciated with great clarity by the residents. One man, for example, who was placed in St. Peter's Room with a "dying" prognosis, got up in the middle of the night and made his way back to his own room.

Through St. Peter's Room, the dying of St. Joseph's residents is symbolically marked off from their living. But ritual, coupled with the fact that death is not disguised, keeps death in a prominent place in the minds of residents. The bodies of the dead were swiftly removed by a mortician, but invariably returned for the public funeral—a ritual which, because of the frequency of its occurrence, must have been important in the lives of the residents. These funerals were the prerogative of a single priest who had very definite ideas as to their ritual value. All dead received the same funeral mass (which, since it replaced the regular daily mass, always received a good turnout). During it, a "respectable" representation of the ambulatory would listen to a lengthy sermon emphasizing the love and mercy of God, the importance of leading a good life, and the privilege of being able to pray for the soul of a community member. When giving his funeral sermon, the priest used a booming voice which could be heard throughout the building, even down on the basement floor, two stories below. This, he indicated, was quite intentional. He wished to be heard both by those residents who were hard of hearing and also by those who had not come to the chapel. At the end of the services, the open coffin would be wheeled to the foot of the chapel, the residents would file past, hesitate briefly and then go out to view the funeral procession leaving the grounds.

This is routine in a setting where fifteen to twenty funerals are held each year. On the day of one funeral, a birthday party was held in the afternoon. No references to the funeral were made as the residents enjoyed the festivities marking off an additional year's passage toward the same fate.

In summary, St. Joseph's Home is a place where people go to die, where an important aspect of daily life centers around the fact that people die there, and where death receives considerable ritual treatment. What is noteworthy about St. Joseph's, as a community where people die, is that dying is organized *for* the residents, not *by* them.

Dying at Glen Brae

As I have discussed the organizational features of dying at Glen Brae at some length elsewhere (Marshall, 1975), I will here only briefly note those features which contrast with the situation at St. Joseph's.

The administration had no formal policy or plans concerning the management of dying and death as a community event, but early on in the history of the village, residents began to organize and to develop informal means of dealing with death. A retired psychologist living in Glen Brae suggested that management avoid euphemisms in referring to the death of a resident, and that simple obituary notices be posted when someone died. By the time the community had been in existence for a little over a year, an editorial written by the head of the Forum appeared in the resident newspaper. It referred to a rising death rate, and urged residents to adopt a determination to "look toward the future and be prepared. . . . It is up to us, not management, to make Glen Brae the haven we desire." Residents were urged not to make vivid displays of grief. Death, then, was to be treated informally and discreetly at Glen Brae; but it was not to be ignored.

As at St. Joseph's, the definition of a resident as dying has interactional consequences. At some point the dying of a resident will lead to his removal to the extended care facility, which is somewhat separated from the residential section, though accessible by an enclosed corridor. This provision serves the function of effectively removing the vivid presence of death from the midst of the community (Friedman, 1966). This is not to say that the residents are unaware that they live in the midst of death. That would simply not be possible, given that so many among them die. But their awareness of the hard, cold fact of death, as opposed to their strong awareness of finitude, is probably somewhat buffered by this geographical segregation of the terminally ill.

Perhaps the most important of the Forum-initiated activities is a "corridor-chairman" system. For each corridor in the village, the Forum appoints one individual to act as "den-mother." This person makes live or telephone contact with each resident on his or her corridor each day, and can mobilize formal and informal community supports when needed. Attempts are made to incorporate isolates, and particular watchfulness is paid to situations of potential crisis, such as bereavement over a spouse or friend. The system serves to define the atmosphere of the community as one of mutual support. As one resident put it, when a spouse dies, "people rally round—make dates for lunch with them."[5]

The majority of residents approve the low-key management of death and grief. In the words of one, "Here we are in the midst of death, so to speak, because you see notices often. I think death is very philosophically treated here." The philosophical treatment of death at Glen Brae rests, however, on a foundation of informal resident interaction.

The administration requires residents to make plans for their own deaths. They must have wills, designated executors, and specific plans for disposition of their bodies. This, however, is the only concrete way in which the administration itself positively intervenes in the ways residents deal with impending death. They have themselves taken other steps—meetings with the medical staff of the infirmary which led to agreements allowing the absence of heroic measures in sustaining life, as an example.

The residents of Glen Brae have developed a system of mutual supports and normative patterns of behavior toward death. Residents see death and, as with residents of most retirement villages, which are initially populated in "batches" when the community begins (Carp, 1972; Rosow, 1966), they are aware of the rising death rate as their overall population ages. Seeing other members of their community die, and thinking about their own impending deaths, they can draw on the informal supports available in their community. Glen Brae is organized to provide such assistance, by encouraging a high level of social interaction and by treating death informally.

Thus, death is neither a taboo topic, nor ritually separated from life. It is planned for, but it is also taken for granted and philosophically accepted. The situation is different from that at St. Joseph's, where individuals do not make specific plans for their dying, other than spiritual plans, and where they do not organize themselves as a community of the dying.

LEGITIMIZING DEATH

Socialization for any aspect of aging is not highly programmed within our society. We have no rites of passage to mark the transition to old age, beyond the perfunctory retirement ritual which, in any case, affects few people making the transition into old age (Crawford, 1973). There are few specialized teachers or programs to prepare people for any aspect of old age (Ross, 1974; Rosow, 1974). Socialization for impending death is no exception to the general inadequacies of aging socialization, yet the anticipation of impending death poses a critical marginal situation for the individual (Berger and Luckmann, 1967: 97). As Hochschild (1973: 85) suggests, "Death is significant to the old in a way it is not to the young, not only because they are nearer to their own death but because they are nearer to other people's." Attaining a view of one's impending death as appropriate, legitimate, and acceptable can be viewed as either a personal or social construction of reality process, in which one's life, as it draws to a close in death, is rendered meaningful.

Impending death was not, on the whole, successfully legitimized by the residents of St. Joseph's, whereas it generally was at Glen Brae. A number of observations and interview responses suggest that, at St. Joseph's, the principal attitude to impending death was one of resignation, usually phrased in terms of relatively nonabstract religious formulae. When it comes to death, in the words of one, "Nobody's the boss but the Lord." Another, asked when she thinks about death, replied "I have nothing to say about that. If I die I'm going to die and there's nothing to it. I know I'm getting older and the day's shorter. But I don't worry about it." Others say, "The time is pre-destined," and, "You are just living until the Good Lord's ready to take you. You're going to die anyway. What's the difference." Impending death had no positive value attributed to it. People were willing either to die or to live longer if it was "God's will;" but death was not actively prepared for: "Don't plan for death because that's a sin. The Lord plans, not me."

One resident told me, "I'd say about 90 percent here are very morbid about death." I think this was an overstatement; rather, they were resigned to death because it would provide a release from present discomforts. As one resident said: "Well, I've seen people here wish they were gone. Your life can get so miserable and helpless they even pray for it." Another resident answered the question, "Would you agree or disagree with the statement, 'Death is sometimes a blessing?' " in general terms, but terms which exactly described his particular situation and that of most of his fellow-residents:

> Sometimes it is. Very much so if the person is poor—no friends or relations, no bankroll. What could you do. If you go into an old folk's home and you take this and take that and can't eat meals to your taste.

And another old man said:

> We old—no good no more . . . when you be old you see you no good no more. Best thing to go away [that is, die] . . . I don't want to live no more I say, I can't eat anything. I can't drink anything. I got to watch myself.

For him, to die was to suffer, but to live was to suffer more.

Both Glen Brae and St. Joseph's are places where people go to die. But at Glen Brae the accent is on living while at St. Joseph's it is on dying. In a sense, indeed, as noted above, the residents of St. Joseph's are already dead—that is, socially dead. As Kalish (1965) notes:

> Social death occurs when an individual is thought of as dead and treated as dead, although he remains medically and legally alive. Any given person may be socially dead to one individual, to many individuals, or to virtually everyone, and perhaps to himself as well.

In short, "The self-perceived socially dead individual has accepted the notion that he is 'as good as dead,' or that he is, for all practical purposes, dead" (Kalish, 1968). And this, as Kalish notes, frequently occurs when a person enters a nursing home or a hospital, knowing he will not leave. Most St. Joseph's residents are largely or completely severed from family contact. They have low levels of contact with each other within the institution, and—while defined as medically alive by staff—they are frequently treated as if socially and psychologically (senile) dead.

One old man provided me with an insightful vignette which seems to capture the attitude of many. It was the day of a funeral, and he said:

> I was talking with a guy this morning and I said when you get to be seventy you should die. He said no he wanted to live. I said, "What for? You produce anything? You bring home bread and butter? Better you die."

I have elsewhere (Marshall, 1975) argued the case that death is relatively successfully legitimated at Glen Brae. There, residents spoke to me as investigator with ease about death and dying generally and about their own. (This was much less the case at St. Joseph's). A number of attitudinal indicators, if viewed in a "language-game"[6] (Simko, 1970; Winch, 1958; Wittgenstein, 1953, 1965) or "vocabulary of motive" (Mills, 1940) framework, provide evidence that the residents of that community have developed and share a number of good reasons why their death is appropriate or legitimate. To summarize briefly some interview data (see Marshall, 1975, for more extensive treatment), 91 percent of a sample of seventy-nine do not feel that death is tragic for the person who dies; 98 percent say that death is sometimes a blessing; and only 12 percent say that death always comes too soon. These responses are much more accepting of death than is the pattern from a representative U.S. opinion survey which raised the same questions (Riley, 1970).[7]

There is additional evidence that a large proportion of the residents of Glen Brae feel that death is likely to come, for them, not too soon but too late. Asked both how long they anticipated living and how long they desired to live, only one-sixth expressed a desire to live longer than they anticipated living. That is, for the majority for whom data are available, death is expected to come either too late or just on time. In additional ways difficult to describe to others, they conveyed to me, during fieldwork and during formal interviewing sessions, a clear impression that they had reached a stage of their lives in which they could feel their impending death was appropriate.

ORGANIZATIONAL FEATURES

Glaser and Strauss (1971: 116) point out that a person can go through a status passage alone, "as a member of a *cohort* that develops a collective or group character, or . . . as a member of an *aggregate* that has minimal collective features." Congregate residential facilities for the aged provide the possibility for either of the last two types of dying status passage. The cases discussed illustrate these alternatives. The issue is one of the extent to which passagees exert some control over their style of life while in passage (Glaser and Strauss, 1971: 64) and the relationship between in-passage control and the anticipations of the end of the passage.

Glen Brae is an organizational milieu where residents develop a shared perspective in dealing with their status passage. Examples of similar development of shared perspective, of course, abound in the literature of sociology (for example, Becker et al., 1961 and 1968; Olesen and Whittaker, 1968; Roth, 1963). St Joseph's Home, on the other hand, provides an instance where passagees exert little collective control over their life style while in passage. Their passages are traversed in aggregate rather than collective fashion. They do not actively contribute to the development of their own subculture or status passage characteristics.

Let me make this distinction clearer by turning to Becker's (1964) analysis of personal change in adult life:

> A group finds itself sharing a common situation and common problems. Various members of the group experiment with possible solutions to those problems and report their experiences to their fellows. In the course of collective discussion, the members of the group

arrive at a definition of the situation, its problems and possibilities, and develop consensus as to the most appropriate and efficient ways of behaving.

This consensus, definition, or subculture can be one in which the inevitable passage toward death is rendered meaningful or legitimate, but it need not develop in that way. A principal vehicle for creating any culture is conversation. As Berger and Kellner (1964) remark:

> The plausibility and stability of the world, as socially defined, is dependent upon the strength and continuity of significant relationships in which conversation about this world can be continually carried on . . . the reality of the world is sustained through conversation with significant others.

At Glen Brae the comparatively well-educated residents utilized high verbal skills in conversation, talking of death as a collective concern. At St. Joseph's, the overall amount of talk, as well as the amount of talk about death, was low. For example, when I asked residents whether people here often talk about losing loved ones through death, the typical reply was a flat, "No," or "I don't bother talking."

Of fundamental importance in the contrast between the two settings is the fact that the overall level of interaction, which is a precondition of conversation, differed so greatly. I have suggested that there is little activity at St. Joseph's[8] and that most of that which does occur is structured by staff. Staff imputations of disability may play a further role in structuring and reducing both staff-resident and resident-resident interaction. Staff sometimes used the phrase, "They're just like children, you know," in discussing residents. More than once I was advised by a staff member "not to bother" to interview a particular resident or patient, because "He's much too senile; you won't be able to talk with him." While true in some cases, I frequently found that I had already spoken with

the resident, carried on a somewhat difficult conversation, and gathered useful data of a verbal nature. This imputation of senility, and its interactional consequence, is not just a staff phenomenon:

> At lunch, Mrs. Brown said, "I see you talked with Miss Harrison. Be careful of what she said. She's senile, you know" [field notes].

On the whole, the attitude of staff toward patients and residents was marked by a benevolent maternalism, as the "just-like-children" remark indicates, or as is evident in a nursing assistant's characterization of her patients: "They're all babies. They all need care. They like to babied." This attitude leads staff to adopt a pattern of high control over the status passagees.[9] As Glaser and Strauss (1971: 120) point out, one tactic of socialization agents who wish to retain control over passagees is to attempt to reduce communication among them. At St. Joseph's the administration seeks to socialize passagees for impending death through the use of formal ritual (funerals), while a high degree of control is manifest over other aspects of their lives.

At Glen Brae, while the administration makes no formal attempts to socialize passagees for impending death, neither does it seek to exert control over other aspects of the residents' lives. This leaves them free to develop their own ways of dealing with death as a community phenomenon.

CONCLUSION

Some tentative conclusions of a more general nature emerge. The vivid presence of death does not in itself lead to acceptance of it. Dying is a status passage, and among the features of any status passage are the extent to which the actions of participants are regulated by others, the amount of control which the participants exercise, and whether the passage is traversed alone or with others (Glaser and Strauss, 1971: 8–9). An administration can allow passagees to exercise a high degree of status passage control, or it can seek to retain control.

At St. Joseph's Home, administrative practices mitigate against interaction so as to create the conditions for death to be faced without community support. Death is both geographically and ritually present at St. Joseph's Home, but positive acceptance of it is minimal. The trajectories of dying, as defined in the Home, serve to deny the reality that all are dying, for the definition is reserved for the very final stages, and leads to increased geographical isolation of the "dying" person on the infirmary floor or in St. Peter's Room. Funeral ritual, as employed in the Home, is formal and fails to involve the other community members in any meaningful way, as is evident from the switch possible from funeral in the morning to birthday party in the afternoon. At St. Joseph's, death has the character of something other than and outside of the individual. Because the organization for death and dying is provided for the residents and not by them, opportunities to construct the meaningfulness of dying are constrained.

At Glen Brae, residents deal with death as a community event. They take the initiative, in the absence of administrative initiatives, in recognizing their mutual terminal status passage, in creating its shape, and in fashioning its character. They make plans for death, and they have developed informal tacit understandings by which to deal with it. As a result, Glen Brae is a community setting where the residents are remarkably successful in legitimating their impending deaths. Highly important in this respect is the interactional and conversational foundation of community life. Low-keyed and resourceful, the residents have developed community control over the dying status passage.

The major organizational factor differentiating the two communities is the degree of resident-initiated social organization for death and dying. Death is frequent, visible, and ritually acknowledged at St. Joseph's Home, but it does not become a matter in which the residents, as members of a community, become involved. Death is frequent,

visible, and informally dealt with by residents themselves at Glen Brae, where it becomes a focus of mutual status passage control and collective community involvement.

NOTES

1. This draws heavily on Wilbert Moore (1963). Lyman and Scott (1970: 195) refer to the pace and sequencing of activities, while Roth (1963: 107–114) emphasizes the negotiated character of timetables in a way complementary to Glaser and Strauss' (1971) emphasis on status passage negotiation, which I discuss later.

2. Interestingly, however, those very few residents who were most active were presented to me and other outsiders as exemplary residents.

3. Observing this phenomenon one evening, I decided to find out what was happening with those residents not at the bingo game. In a darkened, second-floor lounge, I found eight or ten sitting quietly watching a television set. The picture was flipping.

4. Townsend (1962: 95) found an average yearly death rate of 17 percent in his survey of all homes for the aged and nursing homes in England and Wales.

5. St. Joseph's does not present this possibility because there are no married couples living there.

6. Theoretically, I treat certain language occurrences as demonstrating facility with a particular language-game centering on the giving of answers to questions (Wittgenstein, 1965: 67–68), such as interview questions about the appropriateness of each. Methodologically, I participated in such language-games with the subjects in order to make inferences as to their competencies in the language-game of death (see Simko, 1970). Winch (1958: 15) provides a link to the social construction of reality: "Our idea of what belongs to the realm of reality is given for us in the language that we use. The concepts we have settle for us the form of the experience we have of the world."

7. The results are also indicative of higher acceptance of impending death than was found from the small and unrepresentative number of residents of St. Joseph's to whom I put the same questions. Some of the verbatim responses appear earlier in this paper. At St. Joseph's I relied much more exclusively on participant observation, and informal discussion with residents, conducting only nine formal interviews over the five-month period during which I was in the field there.

8. It has been suggested that lower-class people are "reluctant to meet new people . . . to form new social relationships, and above all to initiate interaction with strangers" (Cohen and Hodges, 1963). It has also been argued that members of the lower classes have less facility and fluidity with language (e.g., Bernstein, 1960). While I would not with certainty rule out these possible explanations for the difference between Glen Brae and St. Joseph's, recent studies have demonstrated a high degree of interaction among aged working-class residents of a trailer park (Johnson, 1971), and a high-rise apartment building (Hochschild, 1973). Hochschild notes that the working-class aged she studied taught each other about death (1973:79): "It was a fact of life . . . and there was no taboo against talk about it . . . . Although each individual faced death essentially alone, there was a collective concern with, as they put it, 'being ready' and 'facing up.'"

9. It is beyond the scope of this paper to go into the causes or origins of the organizational patterns in either setting. I suggest, however, that the rigid administrative control of St. Joseph's has a great deal to do with the fact that its clientele has little power. Organizational features in agencies serving powerless clientele tend, I suspect, to evolve in accordance with administrative convenience as a major criterion. For example, as a researcher "guest," I was provided by staff with coffee on demand. No residents had coffee or tea breaks between meals, because staff felt *some* of them could not handle the cups.

REFERENCES

ALDRIDGE, G. "The Role of Older People in a Florida Retirement Community." *Geriatrics* 11 (1956): 223–226.

BECKER, H. "Personal Change in Adult Life." *Sociometry* 27 (March 1964): 40–53.

BECKER, H., GEER, B., and HUGHES E., *Making the Grade*. New York: John Wiley, 1968.

BECKER, H. and STRAUSS, A., *Boys in White*. Chicago: Univ. of Chicago Press, 1961.

BERGER, P. and KELLNER, H., "Marriage and the Construction of Reality." *Diogene* 46 (1964): 3–32.

BERGER, P. and LUCKMANN, T., *The Social Construction of Reality*. Garden City: Doubleday-Anchor, 1967.

BERNSTEIN, B. "Language and Social Class." *British Journal of Sociology* 11 (1960): 271–276.

CARP, F. "Mobility among Members of an Established Retirement Community." *Gerontologist* 12 (Spring 1972): 48–56.

COHEN, A. and HODGES, H., "Lower-Blue-Collar Characteristics." *Social Problems* 10 (Spring 1963): 303–334.

CRAWFORD, M. "Retirement: A Rite de Passage." *Sociology Review* 21, 3 (1973): 447–461.

FRIEDMAN, E. "Friendship Choice and Clique Formation in a Home for the Aged." Ph.D. dissertation, Yale University, 1966.

GLASER, B. Time for Dying. Chicago: Aldine, 1968.

GLASER, B. and STRAUSS, A., *Status Passage*. Chicago: Aldine Atherton, 1971.

GOFFMAN, E. "On the Characteristics of Total Institutions," pp. 1–24 in E. Goffman, *Asylums*. Garden City: Doubleday-Anchor, 1961.

GUSTAFSON, E. "Dying: the Career of the Nursing Home Patient." *Journal of Health & Social Behavior* 13 (September 1972): 226–235.

HOCHSCHILD, A. *The Unexpected Community*. Englewood Cliffs, N.J.: Prentice-Hall, 1973.

JOHNSON, S. *Idle Haven*. Berkeley: Univ. of California Press, 1971.

KALISH, R. "Life and Death: Dividing the Indivisible." *Social Science & Medicine* 2 (1968): 249–259.

KALISH, R. "The Aged and Dying Process: the inevitable decisions." *Journal of Social Issues* 21 (October 1965): 87–96.

KALSON, L. "The Therapy of Independent Living for the Elderly." *Journal of the American Geriatrics Society* 20 (1972): 394–397.

LYMAN, S. and SCOTT, M., "On the Time Track," pp. 189–212 in S. Lyman and M. Scott, *A Sociology of the Absurd.* New York: Appleton-Century-Crofts, 1970.

MARSHALL, V. "Socialization for Impending Death in a Retirement Village." *American Journal of Sociology* 80 (March 1975).

MARSHALL, V. "Game-analyzable Dilemmas in a Retirement Village: A Case Study." *International Journal of Aging & Human Development* 4, 4 (1973): 285–291.

MESSER, M. "Possibility of an Age-Concentrated Environment Becoming a Normative System." *Gerontologist* 17 (Winter 1967): 247–251.

MILLS, C. W. "Situated Actions and Vocabularies of Motive." *American Sociology Review* 5 (1940): 904–913.

MOORE, W. *Man, Time, and Society.* New York: John Wiley, 1963.

OLESEN, V. and WHITTAKER, E., *The Silent Dialogue.* San Francisco: Jossey-Bass, 1968.

RILEY, J. "What People Think About Death," pp. 30–41 in O. Brim, Jr., H. Freeman, S. Levine and N. Scotch (eds.) *The Dying Patient.* New York: Russell Sage, 1970.

ROSOW I. *Socialization to Old Age.* Berkeley: Univ. of California Press, 1974.

ROSOW, I. "Discussion Following Maurice B. Hamovitch's Paper," pp. 127–135 in F. Carp (ed.) *The Retirement Process.* Washington, D.C.: U.S. Public Health Service Pub. No. 1778, 1966.

ROSS, J-K. "Learning to be Retired: Socialization into a French Retirement Residence." *Journal of Gerontology* 29, 2 (1974): 211-223.

ROTH, J. *Timetables.* Indianapolis: Bobbs-Merrill, 1963.

SEGUIN, M. "Opportunity for Peer Socialization in a Retirement Community." *Gerontologist* 13 (Summer 1973): 208–214.

SIMKO, A. "Death and the Hereafter: The Structuring of Immaterial Reality." *Omega* 1 (May 1970): 121–135.

SUDNOW, D. *Passing On: The Social Organization of Dying.* Englewood Cliffs, N.J.: Prentice-Hall, 1967.

TOWNSEND, P. *The Last Refuge.* London: Routledge & Keagan Paul, 1962.

WINCH, P. *The Idea of a Social Science and its Relations to Philosophy.* London: Routledge & Keagan Paul, 1958.

WITTGENSTEIN, L. *The Blue and Brown Books.* New York: Harper & Row (Torchbook ed.), 1965.

WITTGENSTEIN, L. *Philosophical Investigations* (G. Anscombe, trans.). New York: Macmillan, 1953.

Stratum Contrasts and Similarities in Attitudes Toward Death

Vern L. Bengtson
José B. Cuellar
Pauline K. Ragan

Death is a highly personal issue. Its meaning undoubtedly varies from individual to individual, depending on events and situations unique to each person's biography. The loss of a friend or family member, a serious illness, an accident, psychic states such as depression—these are examples of experiences which probably affect orientations toward death in idiosyncratic ways.

But attitudes toward death are also the product of collective experience. On one level are influences of the broader culture, perspectives about death communicated via mass media and through institutions such as the medical care system. On another level are factors related to an individual's location within the broader social structure. Mortality occurs at earlier ages in lower socioeconomic levels and among racial minorities, so it is plausible that death is perceived differently by members of different social strata. Belief systems and value orientations manifest in different subcultures or strata may result in contrasting meanings attributed to death.

To what extent are attitudes toward death predictable from location in the social structure; and to what extent are they individuated, not explainable by such dimensions of collective experience? What patterns

From *Journal of Gerontology* 32, 1 (1977), pp. 76–88. Reprinted by permission.

of death orientation characterize different levels of social strata, in terms of contrasts between races, age groups, occupational status categories, males and females?

Background

Attitudes toward death have recently been explored in a variety of empirical investigations (for example, Feifel and Branscomb, 1973; Glaser and Strauss, 1968; Jeffers, Nichols, and Eisdorfer, 1961; Kalish and Reynolds, 1976; Marshall, 1975a, b; Riley, 1970; Swenson, 1961). Relatively little evidence, however, has been accumulated to answer questions concerning the extent of collective influence, as contrasted with unique or individuated experience, on orientations toward death. Nor is there much basis for making predictions concerning the degree of similarity or contrast among various social categories within the larger population regarding death attitudes.

It is often suggested, for example, that *age* is related to death orientations, in the sense that older people evidence greater preoccupation with death (Jung, 1959; Kalish and Reynolds, 1976; Munnichs, 1968), or fear death more (Cameron, 1972) than do the middle-aged or young. But this view does not appear supported by other analyses (Feifel and Branscomb, 1973; Jeffers et al., 1961).

Similarly it might be expected that race or ethnic differences are predictive of attitudes toward death, because of the marked contrasts in longevity and life quality evident betweeen minorities and the Anglo-white population in the United States. Although too few studies are available to make any very general statement, one survey (Reynolds and Kalish, 1974) reports minimal ethnic differences in fear of death. Socioeconomic status differentials in death orientations have been found in some research (Diggory and Rothman, 1961; Riley, 1970; Swenson, 1961) while in other analyses minimal class differences are noted (Jeffers et al., 1961). In terms of sex there is also conflicting evidence: Christ (1961) reports females have higher fears of death, while no male-female differences are noted by Diggory and Rothman (1961) and Reynolds and Kalish (1974).

Several reasons may be noted for the lack of consistency among research reports concerning orientations toward death among various social categories. First, many of the studies available are based on small samples of respondents or of individuals from selected populations (e.g., medical or psychiatric patients, residents in retirement communities). Second, no study to date has attempted to assess the relative contribution of various social location factors—age, sex, race—in a single large sample using a multivariate and comparative design. Third, attidues toward death are complex and may be difficult to conceptualize and measure adequately. Critics may question the validity of survey responses elicited within the confines of a structured questionnaire instrument; similarly, the case study approach raises questions of generalizability beyond small samples and possible bias introduced by the close relationship with the interviewer.

These issues suggest the desirability of a research strategy which combines both large-scale survey and ethnographic methods. The joint use of these two approaches is, of course, rare (see Cuellar, 1974; Seiber, 1973). The combination of quantitative and qualitative investigative techniques, however, seems particularly appropriate when reaching a relatively unexplored and potentially affect-laden topic such as orientations toward death.

Focus

The purpose of this research is to examine patterns of contrast or similarity in attitudes toward death among various social categories. The specific analytic questions can be stated as follows: 1) to what extent are attitudes toward death predictable from location in the social structure—from strata defined by race, age, occupational status, sex—and to what extent do they appear individuated, not explained by dimensions of collective experience? 2) which of the four stratum variables accounts for greater variation in predicting attitudes toward death? 3) what consistent patterns of variation emerge as one examines specific social categories—for example, trends among age groups and contrasts between racial groups?

To explore these issues two modes of investigation have been employed: a large-scale survey applying quantitative methods and multivariate statistical tests; and an ethnographic analysis of qualitative data gathered by one of the authors in field interviews within one of the ethnic populations included in the survey. Selected data published in records of other ethnographic investigations are also reviewed in order to enhance generalizability beyond the one ethnic group.

THE SURVEY METHODS AND PROCEDURES

Three aspects of orientation to death and dying constituted the focus of both the survey and the ethnographic interviews: 1) expressed fear of death; 2) how often the respondent reports thinking about death; 3) awareness of finitude or proximity of death, indexed by the number of years the respondent feels he has left to live.

The general hypothesis tested is that these orientations vary by location in the social structure, specifically by the stratum characteristics of age (forty-five to seventy-four years); race* (black, Mexican American, and white); social status (measured by the Duncan [1961] Socio-Economic Status index); sex. Differences in attitudes by social location are analyzed in a four-way analysis of variance design ($3 \times 3 \times 3 \times 2$ factorial). Additionally, in order to estimate the relative amount of variance explained by each main effect, and by the interaction of main effects, the data are examined using Multiple Classification Analysis (Morgan and Sonquist, 1963). The $p < .01$ level is used as determining statistical significance.

Sample

Research in social gerontology is particularly vulnerable concerning representativeness of samples in relation to target populations. Samples are often either under- or over-representative of senile or chronically ill older persons, of those confined to their homes, or of single individuals. Research that focuses on ethnic groups faces the additional problem of comparability across populations, where the confounding of race and socioeconomic status makes strict comparability difficult.

The objectives of this study required a probability sample of residents of Los Angeles County with specified race and age characteristics, stratified by socioeconomic status. The population was stratified conceptually into eighteen cells on the basis of three variables: age, race, and socioeconomic status. A specification of the study was the equal allocation of cases within the sample to the nine age by race cells, with at least a minimally equitable distribution on socioeconomic status within each of these cells. This specification made it necessary to sample for rare traits, for example, to obtain approximately equal numbers of: 1) high SES Mexican Americans ages sixty-five to seventy-four; and 2) low SES whites aged forty-five to fifty-four ("high" and "low" SES were defined as below or above thirty-one on the Duncan (1961) scale, a comparatively low cutting point).

In order to obtain a sample representative of the area population, and at the same time have enough "rare" cases to allow comparison across SES groups, a multi-stage sampling frame was employed. Over 15,000 screening interviews were required in order to produce the eventual sample. The screening interview involved an assessment of age, ethnicity, and occupation, among members of households sampled from 184 census tracts in Los Angeles County. The final sample to emerge numbered 1269 individuals (Table 1) and reflects a response rate of over 80 percent.

The sampling procedure allows adjustment to account for bias that occurred in over-sampling for rare cases. In the analysis to follow weighted data will be used: individuals within each age-race-SES cell are weighted according to the probability of their having been sampled from the area population, relative to other individuals in the cell. This procedure affords considerable confidence that individuals in the study are representative of the population within each age-race-SES category.

Instrument and Data Gathering

The interview schedule was designed over a period of eighteen months in consultation with a Community Research Planning Committee, comprised of representatives from the Los Angeles black and Chicano

---

* The term "race" as used throughout this research report reflects socially perceived distinctions between three groups, not genetic differences. Although some might question choice of race as opposed to "ethnicity," the latter term is often used to contrast white immigrant groups in the United States, for example Italians, Poles, and Irish, who are not identified in this study. Moreover Mexican Americans often define themselves of *la raza* (the race), descendents of the indigenous inhabitants of the territory of Aztlan (precolonial Mexico) who share a distinctive historical and cultural tradition (see Rendon, 1971). Also, although the terms "Mexican American" and "Chicano" may perhaps be used interchangeably, the older respondents in our studies appear to prefer the former. "Chicano" was often a pejorative term in the 1930s and 1940s and even today is more often used by younger members of the community.

TABLE 1

Sample distribution by race, age, and socioeconomic status.

SOCIOECONOMIC STATUS	BLACK AGE			MEXICAN AMERICAN AGE			WHITE AGE		
	45–54	55–64	65–74	45–54	55–64	65–74	45–54	55–64	65–74
Low[a] (1–17)	47	65	77	47	62	71	22	21	19
Medium (18–24)	43	44	37	51	61	59	46	43	46
High (43+)	37	32	31	44	26	28	66	69	75
Subsample Totals		413			449				407

[a] SES levels categorized according to the system of Duncan (1961).

communities. This group had initially been opposed to the research program, which they felt to be potentially exploitative and nonrelevant. Following months of negotiation and a series of adjustments in the initial research plan, the Committee has worked with the research staff in an unusual instance of collaboration between academic researchers and minority community representatives spanning over four years (Bengtson, et al., 1977). For example, the Committee has read and given input to the materials and interpretations presented in this paper, in order to minimize possible misrepresentations from the perspective of the groups from whom data were gathered.

Data were gathered by structured interviews administered by the Survey Research Center of UCLA from June 1974 to January 1975. The questionnaire, which contained over one hundred and fifty items and lasted over one hour, was pretested in two stages with ninety respondents similar to the eventual sample. Interviewers were matched to respondents by ethnicity and, as much as possible, by age. About half the Mexican American interviews were conducted in Spanish, using a schedule that had been back-translated twice to insure linguistic equivalence of questions.

The data to be reported here are based on three items. Because attitude toward death may be an emotion-laden topic, we were initially unsure as to how to proceed asking these questions in the context of a survey covering many topics about problems of aging. A "de-briefing" session with interviewers following the completion of the survey proved to be useful in evaluating the validity of the data on death. Most of the interviewers felt that the section of the interview on attitudes toward death was *not* more problematic than other sections. Some respondents, however, did appear to the interviewers to be evasive or to want to hurry through these particular questions. Other respondents, on the other hand, appeared to be glad to have the chance to talk about the subject of death (a similar experience is reported by Kalish and Reynolds, 1976). We prefaced this section of the interview schedule with the statement, "The question of people's attitudes toward death is receiving a lot of attention right now. I'd like to ask you about your own feeling on this subject." (The wording of individual items is given below).

RESULTS OF THE SURVEY

Expressed Fear of Death

To measure the degree of negative affect associated with the topic of death, we asked directly: "How afraid are you of death? Would you say you are: not at all afraid? somewhat afraid? or very afraid?" The overall distribution of responses was skewed, although it indicated somewhat greater variability than we had anticipated. Sixty-three percent responded "not at all afraid." 33 percent "somewhat," and about 4 percent "very afraid" (we had been concerned that the results would be even more highly skewed, with most persons denying any fear of death).

Differences in response by social stratum location were examined in a four way analysis of variance (Table 2). The results indicate *significant contrasts only in terms of age group membership* ($F = 28.82, p = .001$). There were no meaningful differences among the three racial groups nor by socioeconomic status. The main effect by sex approached statistical significance ($F = 4.218, p = .038$) and inspection of means indicated that females expressed greater fear than did males. None of the interaction effects were significant with the exception of occupational status by sex ($F = 6.504, p = .002$).

If there are significant contrasts by age, which age group expresses the greatest fear of death? Figure 1 shows the percentage of the sample in each racial group who responded "very afraid" and "somewhat afraid." The data are presented by six age categories, rather than the three used in ANOVA, to allow more precise assessment of age trends. Across the three groups it can be seen that expressed fear of death tends to *decrease with age* in this sample of middle-aged and elderly individuals. Within each

Figure 1

Percentage responding "very afraid" or "somewhat afraid" of death, by age and ethnicity.

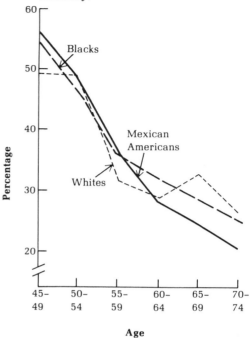

racial group it is respondents aged forty-five to fifty-four years expressing the greatest fear of death, and among the oldest blacks only 26 percent expressed fear.

The pattern of decreased fear by age is pronounced in the two minority racial groups. In Figure 1, of all the subgroups in the sample it is the forty-five to forty-nine-year-old Mexican Americans who expressed the greatest fear of death (57 and 55 percent, respectively). The subgroup indicating the least fear was the oldest (seventy to seventy-four-year-old) Mexican Americans (22 percent); among the oldest blacks only 26 percent expressed fear.

With respect to the general analytic question of this study—how much variation can be attributed to the four stratum location factors taken together, and what is the relative contribution of each—we employed

TABLE 2

Fear of death: analysis of variance summary.

SOURCE	df	SS	F
Race (A)	2	0.20	
Age (B)	2	17.73	28.82***
Social status (C)	2	0.04	
Sex (D)	1	1.30	4.22*
A × B	4	1.32	
A × C	4	3.11	2.53*
A × D	2	0.44	
B × C	4	0.85	
B × D	2	0.33	
C × D	2	4.00	6.50***
A × B × C	8	2.97	
A × C × D	4	1.33	
B × C × D	4	0.29	
A × B × C × D	8	2.45	
Error	1,202	0.31	

*$p < .05$
**$p < .01$
***$p < .001$

Multiple Classification Analysis. This procedure gives what amounts to a standardized partial regression coefficient (beta) for each main effect, allowing comparison of their relative prediction of the dependent variable. It also produces a multiple correlation coefficient between the dependent variable and all factors (as well as factor-by-factor interaction terms) as an estimate of over-all prediction by the independent variables.

The results indicate only a slight level of prediction by stratum variables on this question. The beta for age was .21 and for sex, .06, suggesting that of the four independent variables age is indeed the most effective predictor (race = .02, occupational status = .01). But the multiple R was only .219, indicating that all four independent variables accounted for only about 5 percent of the total variation of this item (MCA summary tables are available for the authors but omitted here to conserve space).

In summary, the results suggest that fear of death is related to age, but in a direction that runs counter to common stereotypes: in this sample *middle-aged* respondents indicated the *greatest* fear of death, while the *oldest* age categories stated the *least*. Furthermore, this trend is accentuated in the two minority racial groups. But all in all, expressions of fear about death do not appear highly predictable from social stratum location, especially in terms of race or socioeconomic status (Table 1).

Frequency of Thinking About Death

Salience of death as a personally relevant issue is difficult to measure. In this survey we simply asked, "How often do you think about your *own* death?" Responses varied among "not at all" (33 percent), "occasionally" (58 percent), and "frequently" (9 percent).

Results of the analysis of variance suggest *little systematic variation predictable by the four stratum indicators*. Only age approaches statistical significance ($F = 3.557$, $p = .028$) with a beta of only .07; the multiple

Figure 2

Percentage who think about death "frequently," by age and ethnicity.

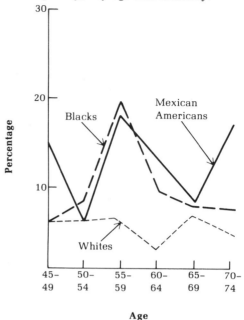

r is .105, yielding a minimal estimate of over-all prediction (1 percent).

Inspection of frequency distributions suggests that the trend by age is curvilinear (Figure 2); moreover, the source of this curve is in the two minority ethnic groups. Among the whites there is no substantial age difference, but for both the black and Mexican American subsamples the middle-aged segments—fifty-five to fifty-nine years—report very high responses of "frequently". In contrast, only 6 to 8 percent of the sixty-five to seventy-year-olds responded "frequently" across the three racial groups (the high percentage of seventy to seventy-four-year-old Mexican Americans answering "frequently" is somewhat anomalous and difficult to interpret, given the upper age range of the sample). Such evidence again runs counter to a popular conception that old age is characterized by a preoccupation with death (see Jung, 1959).

Perceived Proximity of Death

A different method of assessing orientations to the personal meanings of mortality is to ask respondents to estimate the amount of time left to them to live. This has been termed "awareness of finitude" (Marshall, 1974a; Munnichs, 1968); it should be noted that the conceptualization is restricted to the cognitive (how long to live) level, neglecting the affective component (whether living long is worthwhile), a distinction discussed by Marshall (1975b). These estimates may be expected to vary by social location as mortality rates indicate significant contrasts between males and females, between racial groups, and among economic status levels. Or, conversely, expectations of personal longevity may be much more individuated, varying by such factors as the age-at-death of parents, comparison with significant others (siblings or friends), or health status—rather than by the stratum dimensions of race, occupation, and sex examined here.

The results on this variable, however, indicate the four *stratum variables are highly*

predictive, much more so than on the other indicators of death orientations. Race and age differences were highly significant (Table 3), socioeconomic status marginally significant, and sex was not a factor. Significant interaction effects were noted between race and age, and between age, occupation, and sex.

The beta coefficient for race was .26; for age .41; for occupation .07. The multiple r was .485, the four factors thus explaining about 24 percent of the variance. As would be anticipated, the younger age groups expected to live longer (27 years for the forty-five to fifty-four-year-old group compared to twenty and fifteen for the older groups). But unanticipated contrasts are evident between racial groups.

The black subsample as a group expressed the greatest longevity expectancy (mean of twenty-six years) and the Mexican Americans the least (nineteen years). Figure 3 portrays the interaction between ethnicity and age. It can be seen that the Mexican Americans in the middle years (forty-five to fifty-nine) have the most modest expectations of longevity; blacks report the highest expec-

TABLE 3

Estimated years to live: analysis of variance summary.

SOURCE	df	SS	F
Race (A)	2	8,541.28	46.80***
Age (B)	2	22,162.71	121.30***
Social status (C)	2	540.49	2.96*
Sex (D)	1	67.55	
A × B	4	919.95	2.52*
A × C	4	426.15	
A × D	2	345.47	
B × C	4	439.19	
B × D	2	219.85	
C × D	2	278.29	
A × B × C	8	1,070.89	
A × B × D	4	822.07	
A × C × D	4	650.71	
B × C × D	4	1,517.97	4.15**
A × B × C × D	8	565.73	
Error	1,026	93,728.31	

*p < .05
**p < .01
***p < .001

Figure 3

Mean number of years expected to live, by age and ethnicity.

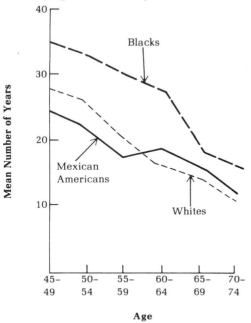

tations at all ages; while the elderly (seventy to seventy-four) whites and Mexican American predict the fewest years to live of all the age-ethnicity groups. The patterns of black responses here are in marked contrast to age-specific mortality data showing differences between minorities and whites. Additional life expectancy at age fifty for whites is 26.4 years, while that for non-whites is 23.8 years. At age seventy it is 12.2 years for whites, 12.0 for non-whites (USDHEW, 1973).

Correlational Analyses

Before concluding the description of survey findings we wish to comment on two additional issues related to the problem of measuring and predicting orientations toward death. First, to what extent are the three attitude items related to each other? Death orientations obviously represent a complex cognitive domain (Kalish, 1976) in which one component may or may not covary with another. For example, thinking about death frequently could reflect high fear of death; it may indicate acceptance with low fear; or the two phenomena may be quite unrelated. In this study expressed fear is moderately associated with frequency of thinking about death (r = .11). There is a slight negative association between proximity of death and frequency of thinking about death (r = −.12). Other inter-item correlations are even lower. One must conclude that the three items do not appear to reflect one single underlying dimension but rather somewhat separate attitudinal components concerning death. These findings—in particular the low degree of covariation between sense of proximity of death and other attitudes toward death—run counter to some current existentialist theory among thanatologists (see the review by Marshall, 1975b).

A second question concerns additional predictors of death attitudes. Given the modest level of variation explained by the four social stratum variables, are there other factors which appear more highly predictive of orientations toward death? We examined four on which data from the survey were available: self-rated health status, happiness, subjective age, and religious affiliation.* With one exception none of the four accounted for substantively significant variation. Health status was moderately related to perceived proximity of death (r = −.36), less so to frequency of thinking about death (r = .14) but not to fear of death (r = .02). Health was inversely related to increased fear of death, but at a low level (r = −.08) (unfortunately measures of religious involvement,

---

* The four factors analyzed were operationalized as follows: Health status was measured by a six-item scale of functioning, from ability to take care of one's self to the ability to hold a regular job. Happiness was tapped by the question, "Taking all things together, how would you say things are these days? Would you say you are very happy, pretty happy, or not too happy these days?" Respondents were asked to characterize the way they thought of themselves as far as age goes (middle aged, young, elderly, or old) for a measure of subjective age. Religious affiliation was indicated simply as religious preference (denomination).

such as church attendance, devoutness, and beliefs were not available; those would afford more adequate test of religious correlates of attitudes toward death than denominational affiliation, which was in this study uncorrelated with the dependent variables). We conclude, therefore, that of these variables only health status appears to be a useful additional predictor of attitudes toward death and that the variation it accounts for is less than that predicted by the variable of age.

Summary of the Survey Data

In terms of the three analytic questions stated at the beginning of this paper, the results of the survey data can be summarized as follows:

1. Orientations to death are, to a limited extent, predictable from location in the social structure as indexed by race, age, occupational status, and sex. But the level of prediction afforded by these four factors taken together is slight (only 5 percent on fear of death, for example), which suggests greater similarity across social categories than had been anticipated. One must look beyond social stratification theory to account for variation in attitudes toward death. Plausible alternative models are idiographic life history analysis (discussed in the next section) and social comparison theory (see Marshall, 1975b) in predicting death orientations.

2. Of the four stratum indicators, age appears to be the most significant factor in predicting attitudes toward death—but not in the direction often supposed. These data suggest that *increasing age is associated with decreased fear of death*, at least in the limited age range of adulthood included in this survey. It is the forty-five to fifty-four-year-old group which expresses the most fear of death; there is no evidence that preoccupation with death increases with age. The eldest respondents may have resolved the crisis

of finitude to a greater extent than the middle-aged, who may be struggling with this issue. Although this is a "maturational" interpretation of data which are cross-sectional in nature, and in the absence of longitudinal data cannot be proved nor disproved, the ethnographic materials to be reviewed in the next section support a developmental explanation. Much less plausible is a "cohort" explanation of these data, which would infer that successive cohorts would have greater fears of death.

3. Contrasts among racial groups can be noted in attitudes toward death, although these are not as strong as contrasts among age groups. Ethnicity does predict some variance in attitudes toward death, but primarily in interaction with age. The eldest Mexican Americans, for example, exhibited the least fear of death in the total sample, while the youngest Mexican Americans (along with the youngest blacks) expressed the greatest. The strongest ethnic differences are evident in awareness of finitude. Blacks expected to live the longest at every age level, and Mexican Americans the least long at the middle-years age level.

4. Neither sex nor socioeconomic status were factors that explained much variance in attitudes toward death. Females tended to express more fear of death but did not think about death more frequently than did males; nor were there sex contrasts in estimation of years left to live, as would be predicted from life expectancy data.

THE ETHNOGRAPHIC FINDINGS

Assessing orientations toward death is obviously a complex and sensitive research task. The findings reported above may be questioned in terms of the adequacy of survey methods and quantitative approaches for exploring attitudes toward death, particularly with single-item indicators. Especially given the modest amount of variance in the survey data that could be explained by the four indicators of social position, it appears valuable to address the issue posed in this research with an ethnographic approach: information collected through repeated observations and in-depth interviews by investigators who have established a close rapport over an extended period of time with informants. Such data are of particular utility in interpreting data on social groups with distinctive historical experiences and cultural traditions.

The ethnographic data presented below were collected as part of a larger study concerning the status of the elderly in an urban Chicano community (Cuellar, 1976). In-depth interviews and life histories were conducted with a total of eighty-seven Mexican Americans during the same time period that the survey was being conducted. Some respondents (n = 34) were members of a senior citizen voluntary organization; others (n = 53) were residents of an age-segregated low cost housing project in East Los Angeles.

Because of the volume and richness of data based on life histories and observations repeated over long periods of time, ethnographic studies commonly accentuate differences between individuals and between groups. Consequently it was of interest to note the high degree of congruence between the qualitative material gathered in the course of the ethnographic analysis and the results of the survey presented above. Juxtaposition of the survey and ethnographic findings suggests four themes. First, the life histories and in-depth interviews reinforce the theme of age contrasts found in the survey data; but second, they provide additional evidence of the importance of biographical and social comparison factors in shaping attitudes toward death. Third, the data highlight some of the indications of cultural heterogeneity, both within and between groups; finally, they reinforce the unanticipated lack of socioeconomic variation found in the sur-

vey, suggesting that age may be a leveler of prior socioeconomic distinctions with regard to death attitudes.*

Crisis and Resolution in Middle and Old Age

Ethnographic evidence supports the proposition of age contrasts in attitudes toward death. Life history materials suggest that the degree to which death is feared, the degree of conscious preoccupation with death, and "awareness of finitude" often can be linked to evidence of "the crisis of middle age" and to the resolution of death fears in old age.

For example, the preoccupation with the issue of death in middle age is evidenced in the remarks of a fifty-five-year-old widow whom we will call Mrs. Martinez, who recently moved into an age-segregated housing project:

> Around here I think about death all the time. Two people have died in this building already. And even though they were much older than I am, I can't help but wonder if I'm going to be next . . . . I want to see my grandchildren somewhat grown! I want to enjoy being a grandmother! But if my husband died when he was fifty-nine, what can I expect? I *have* to live at least ten more years, but I'm afraid I won't make it. I don't want to think about dying but what can I do?

Her response typifies the reaction of many middle-aged respondents who have suddenly been faced with the situation of being alone, who sense their personal finitude more pointedly than ever before in their lives, and

---

* It would be even more valuable to have comparable ethnographic data gathered from the black and white populations represented in the Community Survey. Although such data are not available from this study we have included evidence from other ethnographic investigations dealing with other ethnic groups in an attempt to enhance generalizability.

who express considerable anxiety about death. As Marshall (1975c) has pointed out, with middle-age occurs a convergence of a number of "developmental" tasks in connection with awareness of finitude.

A quite different perspective on mortality is manifested by a sixty-seven-year-old widower whom we will call Mr. Aguilar:

> Although I know I am going to die soon, or rather that I could die at any time, I really try not to think about death . . . . I know I'm going to die, it's something that we all have to go through. When it happens it happens, and there's nothing I can do about it. I'll cross that bridge when I come to it. But for now, I don't think I even want to talk about it.

Similar comments are evident in ethnographic data presented by other investigators. Clark and Anderson (1967) conclude that the typical attitude of mentally healthy older persons in San Francisco, a decade ago, was "I'm not afraid; it happens to everyone at one time or another." or "Let it come when it will, I'm going to live till I die." Marshall (1975a) characterizes such resolution as "the successful legitimation of death" in the retirement community he studied. One woman said, "I feel I've lived my life, and I don't want to be a care to anybody . . . I've had a good life. It's time." While another noted there was "no point" in living to one hundred: "I have no one dependent on me. I've looked after my few descendents I have. And I haven't any great problem to resolve."

Effects of Biographical and Situational Events

Ethnographic data are particularly well-suited to assessing the impact of personally important life events on an individual's orientations toward death. Such events may be historical (participation in warfare, or redefinitions of religious dogma such as the 1965 Ecumenical Council)* or situational (living in an age-segregated environment) or they may relate to the experiencing of different situations in the course of life.

An example of idiographic events influencing death attitudes is reflected in the account of Mr. Cardenas, a seventy-four-year-old security guard who participated in the Mexican Revolution:

> Since I ran away from home to join the *revolución* at the age of thirteen I have always flirted with death. For some reason I have never been afraid to die. If it's my turn, it's my turn. Maybe that is why I've lived so long. I have always liked to play cards and chase women; two very dangerous interests.
>
> I guess I was shot five times before I was twenty years old. Now that I'm old . . . it seems that *la pelona* ("the bald one"—death) is always near. Six years ago . . . teenagers tried to jump me and rob me at the point of a knife. Two years age two *tecatos* (heroin addicts) shot me when they tried to rob the market. One can say that I have been living on borrowed time since I was very young . . .
>
> What I do know is that whenever it comes, in whatever form it comes, I know I am going to die like I have lived, *con huevos* (with balls).

A variation on the theme of life events influencing perspectives on death is suggested by the sixty-four-year-old Mrs. Garcia:

* Vatican II dictated significant changes in the Roman Catholic death ritual. Instead of "dark" vestments, the priests are expected to wear "white" or light vestments. And the rosary to be recited at the death ceremony is supposed to be "the joyous mysteries" rather than "the sorrowful mysteries" as had been the practice prior to the Ecumenical Council. These changes reflect a serious alteration in Roman Catholic philosophy of death: death is joyous, not sorrowful. This conflicts with the lifelong death philosophy of most older Mexican Americans in this study.

It's interesting you should ask me if I fear death. I don't want to die any more than you do, but I'm not afraid of death. Why? Because I'm a woman. I have lived with a man who drank too much and was always running around, and I've sent two sons to war. Every time the phone rang or there was a knock at the door I would die. I've died a thousand times. Why should I be afraid of death? But, I still don't *want* to die.

Although the survey data do not support Mrs. Garcia's contention that women, by virtue of their role socialization, have different attitudes toward death than men, her statement reflects the preparation which certain life circumstances may afford in facing death.

Other historical events alter the meaning and interpretation of death. Manchester (1967) provides insightful evidence that President Kennedy's assassination caused many people to examine their own orientations toward death. A different kind of event, changes produced by the Ecumenical Council (Vatican II) in church dogma regarding death and dying, appears to have caused attitude alterations—and some anxiety—in some of the elderly Mexican Americans as reflected in the ethnographic data. Perhaps the changes—more perceived than real—brought about by Vatican II may explain an anomaly in the survey data: the higher percentage of elderly Mexican Americans (seventy to seventy-four) who reported thinking frequently of death (Figure 2). This evidence of greater concern with death, not found in the other two radical groups, may perhaps be attributed to those religious elderly Chicanos whose religious socialization earlier in life seemed threatened by Church changes, at a time when their non-Catholic cohorts had resolved feelings about death.

Situational factors also define the meaning of death through a process of *social comparison*. One might turn to the experience of parents or siblings in estimating longevity (Marshall, 1975b), and might turn to one's peers in attempting to achieve resolution. In the age-segregated housing project

from which fifty-three ethnographic interviews were collected, many residents made reference to the constant reminders of death in that residential context (see the comments of Mrs. Martinez, above). But rather than being the source of anxiety, the reminders of finitude in an age-segregated setting may lead to acceptance, to legitimation and routinization of the inevitable. Marshall (1975a) describes this process as "socialization for impending death," suggesting that congregate living facilities can provide optimal settings for this kind of socialization. Hochschild (1973) notes that one is better able to face impending death if deaths occur within a taken-for-granted framework where they are considered appropriate. This suggests the importance of role models in the dying process and the rendering of death as appropriate by one's immediate community. Myerhoff (1975) describes the death of an elderly *shtetl* immigrant in the midst of the celebration of his ninety-fifth birthday. She documents the way in which this group of senior citizens drew upon its unique community rituals and symbols to give collective meaning to the event of death.

Cultural Heterogeneity: Within and Between groups

Ethnographic analysis frequently reminds us of differences *within* strata or subcultures, as well as the more often noted contrasts *between* social groups. In a sense the survey data illustrate this point. For one thing, the absence of significant racial contrasts on two of the three dependent variables suggests greater variation within these groups than between them. For another, examination of frequency distributions reveals greater variation within some groups than others. On "fear of death" (Figure 1) for example, Mexican American age categories were both most afraid (the forty-five to forty-nine-year old) and least afraid (the sixty-five to seventy-four-year-old) when comparing groups across the total sample. The white sample evidenced the least heterogeneity by age on this item, the Mexican Americans the greatest.

Two respondents quoted above, Mrs. Martinez and Mr. Cardenas, represent two polar points on the continuum of age-related attitudes toward death. And in a number of other respects, these two individuals reflect the substantial heterogeneity that can be found among Chicanos in general, *viejos* (older persons) in particular. Their life histories are indicative of such within-group contrasts. The fifty-six-year-old Mrs. Martinez was born in Los Angeles, the seventy-four-year-old Mr. Cardenas in rural Mexico. The most significant historical event in her life was World War II; for him it was the Mexican Revolution. She has lived in the Los Angeles area all her life, while he has traversed Mexico and worked throughout the United States. She has a sixth grade education; he never went to school. She is fully bilingual while he has a limited vocabulary in English. Her oldest daughter is married to an Anglo white collar worker; his children have all married Mexican nationals or Chicanos. While she is a non-voting political conservative, he is an apolitical former revolutionary. Thus it can be expected that the variants of these and other individual contrasts, distributed throughout the Los Angeles population of middle-aged Mexican Americans, should result in widely diverse orientations, particularly those regarding death.

Despite such within-group heterogeneity, there are some significant dimensions on which the Chicanos as a group contrast with other segments of the population. For example, the normative boundaries of "middle-age" and "old age" may be defined differently, and perhaps more definitively, in the Chicano subculture. Senior citizen clubs in the predominantly Mexican American Community of East Los Angeles generally defined the lower boundary of old age as fifty (an earlier age than is observed in similar Anglo organizations). The lower boundary of "middle-age" in this community may be somewhere about thirty-five; indeed, the founding in 1974 of a "Young-at-Heart" Club

for individuals between thirty-five and fifty is concrete evidence of this social norm. As such it is not unexpected that Chicanos in their middle years, forty-five to fifty-nine, would have lower expectations of the number of years left to live than other groups (Figure 3).

Another study contrasting the death attitudes of various ethnic or racial groups in Los Angeles supports the conclusion of between-culture variation. Kalish and Reynolds (1972) observed that in comparison with other groups the adult Chicanos were "less capable of dealing with the general notion of the dying process, either their own or others." Their interpretation is that there is generally a higher level of fear of death among Chicanos and that ceremonies and rituals involving death symbols "are attempts at dealing with matters which are highly anxiety provoking and that not even this is sufficient to alleviate their fears and anxieties." Although the survey data of the present study do not support this sweeping conclusion (perhaps in part because the age range of the Kalish and Reynolds study is younger) their comment is a useful reminder of the complex interaction between ethnicity and age. It also is an indication that ritual does not always alleviate anxiety about death, as Marshall (1975c) notes of his observations in a Catholic home for the aged.

Age as a Leveler: Minimizing Socioeconomic Differentials

Perhaps the most unexpected finding from the survey data was the lack of significant socioeconomic status contrasts in fear of death or thinking about death. However, this negative finding may represent support for the the proposition that aging may exert a certain leveling influence on previous socioeconomic distinctions. That is, "the differences that derive from prior social class position, racial grouping, and environmental circumstances may be blurred by decrements of age, the problems incident to the later years, and by social and personal mechanisms developed to cope with them" (Hirsch, Kent, and Silverman, 1968).

While this idea has only recently received some survey research support (Dowd and Bengtson, 1975), enthnographic data reported by Jacobs (1974) illustrate the lack of socioeconomic differences within an age-segregated retirement village. In part these may reflect a sense of common fate, a shared awareness of finitude:

> We don't talk about (death). It will talk for itself. . . . I look at people down here, there have been some really big shots. . . . We have a saying out here: "You may have been bred in Kentucky, but you're nothing but a crumb out here." That's the way I feel about all of us out here. . . . We've got fellas like the Banana King here. He's worth millions. . . . We've got a lot of very well-to-do people in here. But they're not going to live too long. . . . All that you have here is the past. There is no future.

Other data collected in East Los Angeles reinforce the idea that distinctions made between social classes, whether real or artificial, become blurred in later life. This may be even more marked among whites; for among blacks and Mexican Americans occupational status is considerably lower, with less spread among individuals. Given these considerations the failure to account for variance in attitudes toward death according to socioeconomic status is not surprising. Age may indeed be a leveler of prior circumstances which differentiate among individuals, particularly when the issue is orientation to death.

CONCLUSIONS

This study has employed both survey and ethnographic data to explore differences between members of contrasting social categories in orientations toward death. The survey involved 1269 individuals, age forty-five to seventy-four, identified from three racial groups in Los Angeles county: blacks, Mex-

ican Americans, and whites. Ethnographic observation and in-depth interviews about death were undertaken among Mexican Americans in East Los Angeles over a two-year period, involving eighty-seven informants. In both the survey and the ethnographic interviews, respondents were asked about their fear of death, how often they think of death and how many years they anticipate living.

Analysis focused first on the extent to which attitudes toward death are predictable from location in the social structure (defined by race, age, socioeconomic status, and sex) and second, on patterns of death orientation that appear to characterize different levels of social strata. The results suggest that orientations toward death are related to social location, but the level of prediction is much less than would be predicted from the perspective of stratification theory (see the review by Bengtson, Kasschau, and Ragan, 1976). The data indicate greater similarity across social categories than had been anticipated. The hypothesis that common experiences within strata strongly influence death attitudes cannot be supported in light of the high degree of individual variation. A more plausible explanation involves idiographic life events or social comparison processes affecting orientations toward death.

However, of the four stratum indicators, age contrasts were significant in predicting attitudes toward death. The relationship with age in this sample is inverse: it was the middle-aged (forty-five to fifty-four) who expressed the greatest fears of death and the elderly (sixty-five to seventy-four) the least. In a sense these results reinforce the argument by Riley (1971) and Riley, Foner, and Johnson (1972) concerning the utility of age as a stratum-defining characteristic—in this case more so than race or socioeconomic status. Contrasts by race were apparent in the data but evident primarily in differences among age trends in each ethnic group. While the eldest Mexican Americans expressed the least fear of death, the middle-aged Chicanos expressed the greatest fear. Blacks expected to live the longest, Mexican

Americans the least long. There was little evidence of systematic differences between males and females or among socioeconomic status groupings.

The ethnographic analyses offer amplification of these findings, especially in terms of biographical and situational factors influencing attitudes toward death. Four themes appear to summarize the juxtaposition of survey and ethnographic data: 1) the crisis experienced by many middle-aged people in suddenly confronting death and the resolution exhibited by older individuals toward death; 2) the effects of historical and biographical events in shaping orientations toward death; 3) heterogeneity within, as well as between, groups in dealing with death; 4) age as a leveler of prior social distinctions, as aging individuals of various walks of life deal with the common biological imperatives of dying.

REFERENCES

BENGTSON, V. L., CORRY, E. M., GRIGSBY, E. D., and HRUBY, M. "Community Concern and Academic Research: A Case Study." *Journal of Social Issues*, 34 (1977).

BENGTSON, V. L., KASSCHAU, P. L., and RAGAN, P. K. "The Impact of Social Structure on the Aging Individual." In *Handbook of the psychology of aging* edited by J. E. Birren and K. W. Schaie. New York: Van Nostrand Reinhold, 1976.

CAMERON, P. "Generational Differences in Death Attitudes." *Developmental Psychology*, 5 (1972): 31–32.

CHRIST, A. E. "Attitudes toward Death of Acute Geriatric Psychiatric Patients." *Journal of Gerontology*, 16 (1961): 56–59.

CLARK, M. M., and ANDERSON, B. G. *Culture and Aging: An Anthropological Study of Older Americans*. Springfield, Illinois: Charles C Thomas, 1967.

CUELLAR, J. B. "On the Relevance of Ethnographic Methods: Studying Aging in an Urban Mexican American Community." Paper presented at the 27th annual scientific meeting of Gerontological Society, Portland, 1974.

CUELLAR, J. B. "La Ultima Patada: The Impact of Age-Graded Voluntary Association on Older Members of an Urban Chicano Community." In *Life's Career—Aging: Cross-Cultural Studies in Growing Old*, edited by B. G. Myerhoff and A. Simic. (in press, 1976)

DIGGORY, J. C., and ROTHMAN, D. Z. "Values Destroyed by Death." *Journal of Abnormal and Social Psychology*, 53 (1961): 205–210.

DOWD, J. J., and BENGSTON, V. L. "Social Participation, Age, and Ethnicity: An Examination of the "Double Jeopardy" Hypothesis." Paper presented at the 28th annual scientific meeting of Gerontological Society, Louisville, 1975.

DUNCAN, O. D. "A Socio-Economic Index for All Occupations." In *Occupations and Social Status*, edited by A. J. Reiss. New York: Free Press, 1961.

FEIFEL, H., and BRANSCOMB, A. B. "Who's Afraid of Death?" *Journal of Abnormal Psychology*, 81 (1973): 282–288.

GLASER, B., and STRAUSS, A. *Time for Dying*. Chicago: Aldine, 1968.

HIRSCH, C., KENT, D. P., and SILVERMAN, S. L. "Homogeneity and Heterogeneity Among Low-Income Negro and White Aged." Paper presented at the 21st annual scientific Meeting of Gerontological Society, Denver, 1968.

HOCHSCHILD, A. *The Unexpected Community*. Englewood Cliffs, New Jersey: Prentice-Hall, 1973.

JACOBS, J. *Fun City: An Ethnographic Study of a Retirement Community*. New York: Holt, Rinehart, Winston, 1974.

JEFFERS, F., NICHOLS, C. R., and EISDORFER, C. A. "Attitudes of Older Persons Toward Death: A Preliminary Study." *Journal of Gerontology*, 16 (1961): 53–56.

JUNG, C. "The Soul of Death." In *The Meaning of Death*, edited by H. Feifel. New York: McGraw-Hill, 1959.

KALISH, R. "Death and Dying in a Social Context." In *Handbook of Aging and Social Sciences*, edited by R. Binstock and E. Shanas. New York: Van Nostrand Reinhold, 1976.

KALISH, R., and REYNOLDS, D. K. "The Meaning of Death and Dying in the Mexican American Community." In Proceedings of the 6th International Conference for Suicide

Prevention, edited by R. E. Linton. Ann Arbor, Michigan: Edwards Brothers, 1972.

KALISH, R. A., and REYNOLDS, D. K. "Death Attitudes in Three Ethnic Communities: An Empirical Investigation." Los Angeles: Andrus Gerontology Center Press, 1976.

MANCHESTER, W. C. *The Death of a President.* New York: Simon & Schuster, 1967.

MARSHALL, V. W. "Socialization for Impending Death in a Retirement Village." *American Journal of Sociology,* 80 (1975): 1124–1144. (a)

MARSHALL, V. W. "Age and Awareness of Finitude in Developmental Gerontology." *Omega,* 6 (1975), 113–129. (b)

MARSHALL, V. W. "Organizational Features of Terminal Status Passage in Residential Facilities for the Aged." *Urban Life,* 4 (1975): 87–95. (c)

MORGAN, J. N., and SONQUIST, J. A. "Problems in the Analysis of Survey Data: And a Proposal." *Journal of American Statistical Association,* 58 (1963): 415–434.

MUNNICHS, J. M. A. *Old Age and Finitude: A Contribution to Psychogerontology.* Basel and New York: S. Karger, 1968.

MYERHOFF, B. G. "A Death in Due Time: Conviction, Order, and Continuity in Ritual Drama." Paper presented at annual meeting of American Anthropological Association, San Francisco, 1975.

RENDON, A. *Chicano Manifesto.* New York: MacMillan, 1971.

REYNOLDS, D. K., and KALISH, R. A. "Anticipation of Futurity as a Function of Ethnicity and Age." *Journal of Gerontology,* 29 (1974): 224–231.

RILEY, J. A. "What People Think About Death." In *The Dying Patient,* edited by O. Brim, H. Freeman, S. Levine, and N. Scotch. New York: Russell Sage Foundation, 1970.

RILEY, M. W. "Social Gerontology and the Age Stratification of Society." *Gerontologist,* 11 (1971): 79–87.

RILEY, M. W., FONER, A., and JOHNSON, M., *Aging and Society.* Vol. 3. *A Sociology of Age Stratification.* New York: Russell Sage Foundation, 1972.

SEIBER, S. "The Integration of Fieldwork and Survey Methods." American Journal of Sociology, 78 (1973): 1335–1359.

SWENSON, W. M. "Attitudes Toward Death in the Aged Population." *Journal of Gerontology,* 16 (1961): 49–52.

U. S. Dept. of Health, Education and Welfare. "Vital Statistics of the United States: Life Tables." Vol. 2, Sec. 5. Washington: USGPO, 1973.

Black Ageism

Herbert M. Golden

A director of social services in California noted, "When one reviews the research on the black aged, one is depressed to find so many unanswered questions and the lack of definitive data . . . we do not yet know the real conditions of the aging blacks in this country."[1] Her concern and the concern of many dedicated professionals in the field of aging is that in the absence of reliable data on older blacks, there is an increasing tendency on the part of planners to rely on research findings more appropriate to middle-class white elderly for the design of programs intended for blacks. An example of this type of "expedient planning" that can prove dys-

From *Social Policy* 7, 3 (1976), pp. 40–42. Published by Social Policy Corporation, New York, New York 10036. Copyright 1976 by Social Policy Corporation.

functional for black elderly has been offered by Hobart Jackson in testimony before a United States Senate committee. He pointed out that because of the universal focus on providing alternatives to institutionalization for frail or otherwise dependent elderly, the problem among black elderly, which has been overlooked, is actually the reverse: "The problem . . . is not one of how to keep the older black person out of a nursing home or similar institution," he said, "it is rather, how to get him or her in a good one."[2]

Jacquelyne Jackson, a cofounder with Hobart Jackson of the National Caucus on the Black Aged and probably the most prominent black gerontologist in the country, summed it up this way: "If one seeks information on the Negro aged specifically, few data exist. By and large, a trend of systematic exclusion of Negro aged has characterized most sociocultural and psychological studies of the aged."[3]

The concern of professionals has had its impact on governmental agencies; a report of the Senate Special Committee on Aging stated:

> It is becoming increasingly clear that the problem [of elderly blacks in need] is really one of multiple jeopardy, compounded by a shortage of reliable statistical information on key matters. In fact, this information gap has emerged as a vital issue in all Committee on Aging research related to minority groups.[4]

It should be pointed out that by no means is there unanimous agreement regarding the "multiple jeopardy" concept of black elderly. A recent report by the Rand Corporation acknowledges that government data are fairly available to enable researchers "to chronicle the relatively disadvantaged position of black and black elderly populations." But the report then states:

> Although such studies are important, they are potentially misleading if they look only at racial aggregates. All too often socioeconomic controls are not imposed on interracial socioeconomic analyses, so that class or occupational differences are incorrectly attributed to race. Such a failure to differentiate analytically, seriously weakens existing research in terms of its usefulness for improving social services delivery to minority elderly.[5]

In essence, this is the critical conflict for those responsible for planning and implementing programs for the elderly: are the problems faced by elderly Americans essentially the same for most, or do black older persons have special needs warranting differential treatment from white elderly?

To begin, let us consider some of the basic census data that compare black and white elderly.

DEMOGRAPHIC OUTLOOK

In 1974 blacks age 65 and over comprised 7.2 percent of the entire black population in the United States, while whites 65 and over comprised 10.8 percent of the total white population.[6] But blacks over 65 are increasing at a higher rate: over the period 1960 to 1970, blacks over 65 increased by 33.6 percent, whereas whites over 65 increased by only 19.8 percent.

Three-fifths of the black elderly live in the South, and about half live in central cities compared with less than one-third of white elderly. Four out of 10 black elderly living in central cities are below poverty level as defined by the Bureau of Labor Statistics; in nonmetropolitan areas, over two-thirds of black elderly live in poverty, not to mention that needed services are often less available in rural and semirural areas than they are in cities.

In 1970 the percentage of black elderly who had incomes below the poverty level (47.7 percent) was more than twice that of white elderly (22.6 percent). Cost of living increases in Social Security benefits and Supplemental Security Income (SSI) payments introduced in January 1974 have done something to reduce the high levels of poverty among white and black elderly—in 1974, 13.8 percent of white elderly and 36.4 percent of black elderly had incomes below poverty—but the reduction in white elderly below poverty level was 39 percent, while the corresponding decrease for blacks was only 24 percent.

An argument has been made for earlier retirement ages for blacks entitling them to receive Social Security benefits at age 55 or 58, rather than partial benefits at 62 and full benefits at 65, given the documented shorter life expectancy of black men and women in this country. At this time, on the average, blacks do not live long enough to enjoy equal retirement benefits with whites.

With regard to the income gap between older blacks and whites, Jacquelyne Jackson has point out that

> despite the games which people play, for example, of telling us that blacks are making great progress in this country, the absolute gap between old blacks and old whites has not only continued to increase over the past several decades, but is continuing to increase . . . old blacks, in comparison to old whites, have less money now than they did 10 years ago and 20 years ago and 30 years ago.[7]

The 1973 poverty level income for persons age 65 and over as designated by the Bureau of Labor Statistics was $2,360 for an unrelated individual (usually living alone) and $2,980 for a two-person household with the head aged 65 or older. The median income for a 65-year-old black man in 1973 ($2,281) was below poverty level and only 53 percent of his white counterpart ($4,317), while the median income for black women 65 and over was $1,519 (69 percent of her white counterpart). Over 81 percent of black women and 59 percent of white women age 65 and over had incomes under $2,500.

Some insight as to the causes of lower incomes of black elderly compared with whites is provided by employment data that show a greater decrease in elderly blacks still in the labor force. While the number of black males age 65 and older in the labor force decreased by 27 percent from 1964 to 1974, the decrease was only 19 percent for white males in the same age group. Even more significant is the longer term comparison between elderly black and white women. Between 1940 and 1974, among women age 65 and older, the percentage of blacks in the labor force *decreased* 20 *percent* while the percentage of white women working full- or part-time *increased* 43 *percent*. And yet, Jacquelyne Jackson points out that "in 1970, slightly more than one-half of all elderly [black] . . . women living in families . . . were the chief income recipients for their families."[8]

It is common knowledge that black elderly have had less formal schooling than whites, but what is less well known is the extent of illiteracy among blacks 65 and over: in 1969, 31 percent of elderly blacks were illiterate compared to 15 percent of elderly whites. This factor could account at least in part for what is widely recognized to be an under-utilization of services by poor black elderly. Furthermore, the effects of illiteracy tend to be compounded by the fact that black elderly may receive less support from family and live alone more frequently than elderly whites. Kent, for example, found that 11 percent of black elderly were without living relatives compared to 6 percent white elderly.[9] Moreover, in 1974, 70.8 percent of black females and 36.1 percent of black males over age 65 lived alone compared to 29.8 percent white females and 22.9 percent white males.

A "BLACK PROBLEM"?

Barbara Solomon, a black sociologist, points out that "it is not consistent with reality to talk about the black aged as if they were a homogeneous group, all having the same kind of life experience and having had the same kinds of things happen to them."[10] Jacquelyne Jackson, while not denying the heterogeneity among black elderly, forcefully argues that "race is a reality and we should not deny it. . . . Insofar as black old people are concerned, I think that we should not now begin to treat them as if they were the same as white old people. They are not. Racism has adversely affected their preparation for old age."[11]

The Rand authors disagree with Jackson. They assert that the theory of relative deprivation may appropriately be applied to black elderly who have "fewer felt needs for services" because their sense of well-being is relatively high compared to their own earlier lives and the lives of their contemporaries. This could be important in explaining underutilization of social services, they point out. Yet they proceed, where it suits, to deny validity of such resort to cultural homogeneity, declaring it "purely academic for the most part and [serving] little purpose in improving service delivery."[12]

The kind of reasoning Robert Butler advances succinctly in his book *Why Survive?* calls into question the Rand authors' assertion that black elderly's "fewer felt needs for services" may account for their underutilization. Rather, Butler looks to more sensitive treatment of minority aged at the point of service provision as a factor that could be effective in increasing their utilization of social services. Noting that minority groups are extremely poorly represented in the service professions as doctors, nurses, and social workers, Butler suggests that those providing services to minority aged "should have the assistance of interpreters and training with respect to language and culture when this is appropriate. The service provider must understand the differing patterns of behavior that affect the giving and receiving of service."[13]

An important study by Manuel and Bengtson (not listed among the Rand report references) comparing 413 Black, 499 Mexican American and 407 white middle-aged and elderly men and women found that "ethnicity [used interchangeably with "race"] remained a highly important variable in predicting variation in familial network patterns, whether examined alone or in the controlled context of additional, potentially confounding variables." They found further that "relative to age, socioeconomic status and sex . . . ethnicity is a much more consistently important factor in accounting for the variation."[14] Manuel and Bengtson confessed that they began the study with a bias that minimized ethnicity or race *per se* in accounting for variations in family forms, and even after careful re-analysis could not find support for the theory that age is a leveler of prior social distinctions and that racial contrasts would disappear when appropriate controls are introduced for socioeconomic status, sex, or age.

Other scholars have doubts, however; Kent and Hirsch's survey of elderly in Philadelphia[15] and the New York City Department for the Aging's study[16] of the inner-city elderly give persuasive warning against blurring of subgroup distinctions among the black elderly, and even Manuel and Bengtson found "little support for a consistent ethno-minority pattern: blacks and Mexican-Americans did not appear to be more similar to each other than to whites."

But despite the warnings which must be heeded when it comes to making policy for older people, it is important to remember that it is frequently only through identification with a group that may be distinguished from others that programs are effectively executed.

Byron Gold, in an incisive assessment of the present and future roles of the federal government in the provision of social services to older persons, pointed out that prior to the passage of the Older Americans Act in 1965, an argument advanced against separate programs focused on the unmet needs of the elderly was that these unmet needs were not exclusive to older persons with low incomes. The counterargument which won the day and saw the passage of the act was "that the elderly would receive the attention they deserved only if their unmet needs were separated from the problems of other groups and action to deal with them was taken independently."[17] In effect, Gold points out, programs such as the Title VII federal nutrition program (authorized under the Older Americans Act) were designed to assure access to free or low-cost meals on a continuous basis and, therefore, the approach taken was "age-based instead of income-based" (which had been the established welfare policy approach).

With specific reference to elderly blacks, there is little evidence that those responsible for major planning efforts have accepted the concept of differential treatment. Notwithstanding the Department of Health, Education and Welfare's claim that it supports 130 different projects addressed to solving problems of aging in American society, Butler has noted "no evidence . . . that any of these projects dealt specifically with minority elderly. Organized interest in the plight of minority elderly and their lack of service began in the late 1960s and is still in its formation stages."[18] What exists instead is a plethora of generalizations regarding the black elderly, and because empirical evidence is sparse, the operational validity of focusing policy on the heterogeneity of black elderly is largely denied.

What is clear is that attempts to apply research findings based on undifferentiated comparisons between black and white elderly toward the solution of problems faced by black elderly are doomed to ineffectiveness. Social scientists by and large agree that race is an American social reality and as such must be regarded as an independent variable in any study attempting to offer policy and/or planning objectives. It is then only when blacks are studied as a group without necessarily making comparisons to the larger white elderly population that we will have a good base for attacking the unique problems that this minority group membership imposes on people's adaptation to aging.

NOTES

1. Bernice Harper, "Physical and Mental Health Services," in *Community Services and the Black Elderly* (Los Angeles:

Andrus Gerontology Center, University of Southern California, 1972), p. 27.

2. U.S., Congress, Senate, Special Committee on Aging, *Trends in Long Term Care*, 92d Cong., 1st sess., 1972. Testimony by Hobart Jackson at public hearing on August 10, 1971, pp. 2475, 2476.

3. Jacquelyne J. Jackson, "Social Gerontology and the Negro," *The Gerontologist* 7 (Fall 1967), p. 168.

4. U.S., Congress, Senate, Special Committee on Aging, *A Pre-White House Conference on Aging: Summary of Developments and Data*, 92nd Cong., 1st sess., 1971, Rpt. 92-505, p. 4.

5. Duran Bell, Patricia Kasschau, and Gail Zellman, *Delivering Services to Elderly Members of Minority Groups: a Critical Review of the Literature* (Santa Monica, Calif.: Rand Corporation, April 1976), p. 77.

6. The data in this section, unless otherwise noted, are from the U.S. Bureau of the Census, Current Population Reports, Special Studies Series P-23, No. 54, *The Social and Economic Status of the Black Population in the United States, 1974*; Series P-60, No. 102, *Characteristics of the Population Below the Poverty Level: 1974*; *Statistical Abstract of the United States, 1973*; Series P-23, No. 57, *Social and Economic Characteristics of the Older Population: 1974*.

7. Jacquelyne J. Jackson, "Action and Non-Action," in *Action for Aged Blacks: When?* Proceedings of the annual conference of the National Caucus on the Black Aged, Washington, D.C., May 16–17, 1973, p. 13.

8. J. J. Jackson, "The Plight of Older Black Women in the United States," *The Black Scholar* 7, no. 7 (April 1976), p. 49.

9. Donald P. Kent. "Changing Welfare to Serve Minority Aged," in *Minority Aged in America*, proceedings of a symposium, "Triple Jeopardy: the Plight of Aged Minorities" (Detroit: Institute of Gerontology, University of Michigan-Wayne State University, April 17, 1971), pp. 25–26.

10. Barbara Solomon, "Social and Protective Services," in *Community Services*

and the Black Elderly (Los Angeles: Andrus Gerontology Center, University of Southern California, 1972), pp. 1–2.

11. J. J. Jackson, "Black Aged in Quest of the Phoenix," in Triple Jeopardy—Myth or Reality (Washington, D.C.: National Council on the Aged, 1972), p. 32.

12. Bell et al., p. 77.

13. Robert N. Butler, Why Survive? Being Old in America (New York: Harper & Row, 1975), p. 163.

14. Ron C. Manuel and Vern L. Bengtson, "Ethnicity and Family Patterns in Mature Adults: Effects of Race, Age, SES and Sex," paper presented at the annual meeting of the Pacific Sociological Association, San Diego, Calif., March 26, 1976.

15. Donald P. Kent and Carl Hirsch, Needs and Use of Services Among Negro and White Aged (2 vols.) (University Park, Pa.: Pennsylvania State University, 1971). In-depth interviews were held with 762 black and 260 white low income elderly 65 and over.

16. New York City Department for the Aging, The Elderly in the Inner City, forthcoming.

17. Byron D. Gold, "The Role of the Federal Government in the Provision of Social Services to Older Persons," The Annals 415, (September, 1974), pp. 55–69. Gold is former special assistant to the U.S. Commissioner on Aging.

18. Butler, Why Survive?, p. 164.

The World of the Elderly Asian American

Richard A. Kalish
Sharon Moriwaki

When the White House Conference on Aging was originally planned (for November 1971), special concerns sessions were arranged for minority groups. Those selected were blacks, Spanish speaking, and native Americans. "The decision to hold a Special Concerns Session for Asian Americans was made only one month prior to the Conference and only because a special request was made by concerned Asian Americans [The Asian American Elderly, 1972, p. 2]." Why this oversight? "The Asian-American elderly are severely handicapped by the myth that pervades society at large and permeates the policy decisions of agencies and governmental entities . . . that Asian-American aged do not have any problems, that Asian Americans are able to take care of their own, and that Asian-American aged do not need or desire aid in any form [The Asian American Elderly, 1972, p. 2]."

Again the stereotype which is perpetuated is that of the Asian Americans as people without pressing problems, whose needs are basically cared for within the ethnic group, and whose ethnic values have made accommodation to their North American homeland a simple matter (see Kitano, 1969). Against this lovely tableau are the vivid pictures of the conference participants:

From Journal of Social Issues 29, 2 (1973), pp. 187–209. Reprinted by permission.

Cultural barriers that exclude them from receiving their rightful benefits. . . . They do indeed have problems . . . in many respects . . . more intense and complex than the problems of the general senior citizen population . . . suicide rate in certain areas is three times the national average . . . impossible . . . to look only to their families for help. . . . Those who hold the responsibility to assist . . . have turned their backs . . . among the people most neglected by programs presumably serving all elderly.

We will not judge the veracity of the statements in the Asian American White House Conference on Aging document, nor do we wish to produce a polemic attacking some vaguely defined "establishment" for their past neglect. Rather, we will describe the psychosocial aspects of the past and the present living situation for today's elderly Chinese and Japanese Americans. (With apologies to Filipinos, Koreans, Samoans, Hawaiians, and others, who are being ignored not because they are less important, but because the authors understand so much less about them.)

The literature concerning elderly Asian Americans has recently been reviewed by Kalish and Yuen (1971). Needless to say, it is sparse to the point of being virtually nonexistent. However, work is in progress that will provide at least a little data. Ongoing research is being conducted by Kiefer in San Francisco; the Japanese American History Project at UCLA has data on all age groups now waiting analysis; Ohlsen and Leong are just beginning to study the elderly Chinese in San Francisco's Chinatown; Yuen, through Self-Help for the Elderly, is also compiling data on Chinatown; Kalish and Reynolds are completing a study of attitudes toward death among Japanese Americans. Other research projects, given impetus by the White House Conference on Aging, are undoubtedly also in process or getting under way.

Except for earlier work by Caudill (1952) in Chicago, most studies of Asian Americans have been conducted in Hono-

lulu, Los Angeles, San Francisco, and Seattle. Given the geographical distribution of these groups, this is understandable. However, we wish to emphasize the importance of making certain that the excitement of finding "hard data" reported in terms of percentages, means, and correlations not obscure the tremendous diversity of behavior, values, motives, expectations, roles, and so forth found among the elderly Chinese and the elderly Japanese in the United States and Canada.

AN OVERVIEW

Few behavioral scientists ever touch upon *oldness* in their academic training, in their clinical practices, in their community work, or in their research. Hence, in casual discussions or in formal papers, writers who are more familiar with the Issei or first generation Chinese Americans than with the black or white elderly sometimes mistake the qualities and feelings that accompany old age as characteristics associated with ethnicity.

Allowing for the inevitable exceptions—the war brides of the postwar and later years, the students, the recent immigrants from China—first generation East Asian Americans are old. Allowing for inevitable exceptions—the offspring of an early arrival, the descendant of a diplomat—the old East Asian American is first generation.

The age/generation equation is so obvious that its explication seems pontifical, even patronizing. Upon initial glance the exceptions rather than the rule appear to have greater academic implications. Perhaps the relationship between age and generation is so little considered because it is so obvious. We write about elderly Japanese Americans and Chinese Americans as differing from their children and grandchildren because they are not native born, because they often lack fluency in English, because their formal education occurred in their native lands, because they are so often poor. But that they are also old—this is seldom mentioned.

Increasing numbers of persons today are becoming concerned with the elderly

Asian Americans. Whether their intent is to provide adequate services, to improve interpersonal understanding, or to develop social theory, we feel that most of them grasp only the trunk, the tusk, the tail, or the leg of this elephant—they do not know the entire animal. The older Asian Americans cannot effectively be theorized about, understood, or provided for (or, better still, enabled to provide for themselves) without a grasp of four factors: a) their cultural origins and effects of early socialization; b) their life history in the United States and Canada; c) those age-related changes that occur regardless of early learning or ethnicity; and d) their expectations concerning what it means to be old.

These persons share much with their fellow Asian Americans and with their fellow elderly, but the juxtaposition of all elements produces a personal history and a present milieu that is shared neither with younger persons of similar national origins nor with age cohorts of various national origins. The uniqueness of being elderly and Asian American in the first half of the 1970s arises from numerous factors, operating in dynamic interaction. Some of these factors are outgrowths of historical accidents or results of highly situational matters, e.g., the Gold Rush of 1848, the attractiveness of San Francisco's Chinatown as a mecca for older Chinese Americans throughout the United States and Canada, statehood for Hawaii, the changes in relevant immigration acts, the uprooting of families to internment camps during World War II, the counterculture, the system of higher education in California. Other factors depend more upon the results of early socialization in Japan or China, of strongly internalized values regarding proper family roles, of basic goals that were learned early in life and that can never be unlearned with ease.

As these Japanese and Chinese become old, they face the same potential changes that all old people, regardless of geography or ethnicity, face. These include possible reduction of vitality and energy; some decrement in cognitive (e.g., memory, learning new tasks) and sensorimotor (e.g., reaction time,

vision, hearing, movement) capabilities; increased discretionary time (presumably for leisure); the loss of significant others—and the imminence of the loss of self—through death; physical illness, pain, and discomfort; reduced income; reduced futurity; altered and reduced sexuality; and so forth. Similarly, they face the need to cope with changing values, new life styles, and aggressive challenges to established authority.

The authors fully realize that their focus upon the elderly Asian American, while perhaps more cognizant of intragroup differences than presentations totally ignoring age differences, still is too global. Those people we are lumping together include all possible income levels, all possible educational levels, all possible degrees of emotional well-being and emotional disturbance, all possible degrees of loving and being loved; in short, each person is as unique as any individual anywhere. We still believe, however, that these individuals tend to share—relatively—common experiences as a function of the interaction between age and ethnicity, and that certain modal qualities and concerns have thereby emerged. The focus is also on the Pacific Coast situation where conditions were more severe for these Asian immigrants, rather than in Hawaii where there was less prejudice toward these groups.

TRANSPLANTED SOCIAL VALUES

The first generation Asian American, having been socialized in his early years to a Japanese or Chinese value system, is now growing old and facing death in a milieu much at variance with his beginnings. Hsu (1971) states:

> In America the most desired position of the individual is a combination of (a) economic and social independence, (b) successful and rapid achievement of this goal, and (c) the use of creative means in achieving an identity of one's own [p. 86].

Hsu then shows how these values conflict with the values of traditional Chinese society, which discourages financial independence from parents and extended family, while encouraging interdependence, opposes "cutthroat competition for individual ends," [Hsu, p. 87], and rejects "the emphasis upon creativity [which] has given men license for indiscriminate and irresponsible use of any means to pursue an end [Hsu, p. 87]." Hsu subsequently suggests (see his Chapter 10) that the basic root differentiating American and Chinese value systems is the individual-centered orientation and self-reliance of the former vis-à-vis the situation-centered orientation and mutual dependence on the family of the latter.

Financial Independence

For the elderly Chinese American, reared to believe that children should not become financially independent of their parents, contemporary American values must be highly distressing. Except for the handful of very well-to-do, most elderly Chinese have modest or low incomes—some have virtually no income at all. Yet their children, now middle-aged, have undoubtedly received better formal education than their parents, and their present earning power and net worth are probably many times that of their parents. Simmons (1945) has shown that respect for the elderly is highest in societies where the elderly maintain meaningful control of property, income, and jobs. The elderly Chinese Americans have little such control. Their only claim to their children's respect is community pressure (and this can be very powerful), plus the shame, guilt, love, and personal respect that have developed over the years. In a stable society, such as China prior to the postwar period, the wholesale upward mobility of an entire generation would be virtually impossible; in the United States and in Canada, it occurred.

A parallel occurs among the Japanese Americans. Because the first generation could not own real property, real estate was purchased in the name of an American citi-

zen, often the natural child of the alien Japanese, but not infrequently the American born child of a very close friend. Although the right of the American citizen child to receive such a gift from his non-citizen parent (or family friend) was contested, the action was upheld as appropriate.

In effect this meant that the first generation could neither own property nor become citizens until so late in their lives that vocational achievement and financial success were very difficult, although Kitano (1969) can say, "Most of them are in comfortable circumstances [p. 139]." They met many kinds of discrimination in jobs and education and through legal statute that severely limited their progress. The aged Japanese American, with inevitable exceptions, was even less likely to accumulate property because of initial expectations of returning to his homeland. When unable to do so, he was already too late in establishing the game of primogeniture which would assure care in old age by his eldest son. Although even the property owned by the American citizens, i.e., the Nisei children, was often confiscated at the time of the evacuation, various kinds of restitution, including return of property, were required by court order after the war's end—a process which has dragged on even through the summer of 1972, when a bill passed by Congress returned the government-confiscated bank accounts to the original investors (without either interest or allowance for reduction in real value of the amounts).

The relocation camps made matters still worse. The Issei heads of families were unable to forestall the loss of property and were similarly unable to protect their children against incarceration. Not only did their sometimes limited skills in English and their naïveté regarding American laws and bureaucracy impede their receiving a fair response, but no non-citizen was permitted to hold an administrative office in the Evacuation Centers or the War Relocation Camps. Thus the first generation was ignobly stripped of all status and authority and relegated to second-class roles, even within the context of the internment camps. The Nisei, then largely in their teens and twenties, assumed the offices of managers, block captains, council members, and so forth.

Up until the relocation, there was general acceptance of the idea that the parents (primarily Issei) held the reins of the family by tradition, even when they did not have economic power. The camps would appear to have been responsible for forcing the Issei from power and turning it over to the Nisei. The exodus of the Nisei to the armed forces and the opportunity to enter colleges in the Middle West and East both during and after the war were indeed among the more dramatic outcomes of the Evacuation. Opportunities that had been denied the Nisei in a legally and socially racist West Coast society were finally provided as the indirect outcome of the wartime experience. By the middle and late 1940s, the Nisei were, in many instances, well established and scattered all over the United States. Often the Issei found it difficult to get his child back to the West Coast, or to his home community on the West Coast, after the younger generation had savored relative independence, acceptance, and success away from home.

Although the financially and socially successful Issei probably had more to offer to entice his children back, these were relatively few in number. Upon the postwar return to private life, it was the Nisei who was able to take advantage of educational opportunities and to obtain better jobs, while the Issei, the fruits of his most productive years often destroyed by the lengthy incarceration and his dominant role having been effectively undermined, was forced to return to what he had been doing—often required to work with his sons or sons-in-law not as a respected patriarch, but as an equal or even a subordinate.*

Americans, who tend to value financial and social independence, rugged individualism, and freedom from parents, often express deep concern when middle-aged chil-

dren appear to turn from their elderly parents by not showing proper deference and caring. How much more intense this feeling must be in a culture where independence and self-reliance are negatively valued in the first place.

Competition for Individual Ends

Hsu's (1971) second point was opposition among Chinese to "cutthroat competition for individual ends." The important distinction is that aggressive competition between extended family units or between tongs is not deprecated, but the purpose of the competition is to enhance the family or the group rather than the self. Elderly Chinese who are part of an established extended family will probably have some feeling of belonging and of meaning, through group identification and through carrying along a tradition; not infrequently, their effort in working with the family is required. In a distressing number of instances, however, the aged Chinese American is either lacking such close relationships or is unable to capitalize upon them as his tradition has promised him. And some Chinese have never been part of such an association; they were required to enter the general American work arena, where individual competition is socially reinforced.

Creativity

When Hsu speaks of creativity, we surmise his unhappiness is in response to rapid change in social systems. This kind of creativity, which upsets what seems to be the natural order of things, disrupts traditional relationships. Americans at mid-century and thereafter seem to reward innovation for the sake of innovation, changing styles, changing houses, changing spouses, changing jobs, a veritable "future shock" (see Toffler, 1970). The elderly of all cultures are conservative in that they wish to conserve—conserve values, conserve strength, conserve money, conserve energy, conserve relationships. The fast moving world is distressing; new customs

---

* Much of this account is incorporated directly from the notes of Kazue Togasaki, now a San Francisco physician, whose knowledge of the situation was gathered from her own personal experience.

and people and rules are no sooner assimilated than they are passé. As memory and vitality diminish, as time boundaries begin to blur, the aged tend to cling more strongly to the values which are familiar to them.

As with independence and competition, if the elderly in our society which is highly supportive of innovation are disturbed by the rapid change of customs and manners, values, and technology, consider how much more disturbed would be persons reared in societies that looked askance at innovation. For example, East Asian societies were vertical in social structure, with rules and regulations well defined and shared by all members. The individual knew his proper station and could act with confidence in appropriate situations, well aware of the rules of deference and acceptable behaviors.

In discussing the traditional Japanese, Kitano (1969) comments that "Japanese reverence for hard work, achievement, self-control, dependability, manners, thrift, and diligence were entirely congruent with American middleclass perceptions [p. 76]." This is at a different level of abstraction from Hsu's comparison of the Chinese and Americans. Kitano's list of admired qualities points to the norms held by the Japanese immigrants, not their motivations for behavior. These norms derive from values which are similar to those posited by Hsu: the importance of the family and the dependence of the individual on the family group, and obedience and duty to elders.

To an appreciable extent, both Hsu and Kitano have presented values and norms applicable to each other's national group. These cultural maps have been transplanted to a country where the basic axioms of family centered stable life and rules of proper conduct have little relevance, where rules and roles are in constant flux as the individual moves in different circles of others. We are again reminded of how maladaptive even American value systems are to being old in America; the value systems of Japan and China, as transmitted to Japanese and Chinese Americans, are even more maladaptive for these elderly in this country and in Canada.

A LOOK BACKWARDS

In traditional East Asia, the kin group was the functioning unit, and the individual was part of a network of primary relations stemming from the family. Among the Japanese, primogeniture was through the eldest son, and as technology decreased the value of small landholdings, the younger son could do little but go for further schooling or move to the cities. Emigration to America to make their fortunes was an attractive alternative for the ambitious. They form the predominant group of Japanese American aged, the Issei. Although they probably had a moderate education in Japan and were certainly literate in Japanese, they entered the United States as immigrant laborers. For the women, the first sight of California, Washington, or Hawaii was probably as a young wife, an infant, or a picture bride. (Keep in mind that two or even three generations in the same family can all be first generation.)

The Chinese, on the other hand, distributed wealth (land primarily) equally to all sons, and land was felt to belong to the entire family. Thus emigration was due to external causes—the overpopulation problems, political conflicts, and so forth. Both groups of Asians came to the United States and Canada expecting to grow rich in these countries of promise and then to return to leisure and superior status in their own lands. The final result of their migration was to grow old in a foreign land, with a different language, a strange value system, and odd rules of behavior. Changes these immigrants would have encountered in their homeland might have been difficult to accept, but the changes would have occurred in a familiar environment and through a familiar language: they would have been better comprehended, even if not necessarily approved.

If Chinese American, the elderly person is probably a man (the ratio of males to females, all ages combined, in California was 107:100 in 1970; the same ratio among the aged would be higher); although Chinese immigration patterns date back to the middle of the last century, most early arrivals were men and progeny were seldom left to carry on.

If Japanese American, the elderly is more likely a woman (the California ratio of males to females of all ages was 88:100 in the 1970 census, and women tend to live longer than men); the Japanese immigration occurred primarily between the last dozen or fifteen years of the nineteenth century and the first two decades of the twentieth. During 1908, a so-called "gentleman's agreement" between the United States and Japan was implemented, which stipulated that no Japanese laborers were to be admitted into the United States after this time. A modest flow of picture brides, however, continued through the end of 1924; many of these women were the mothers of the Nisei in the relocation camps. They, like their husbands, were often products of the Meiji era of Japan, which, although permitting immense change to occur within Japan, was still restrictive in terms of the values that had to be encountered in the United States.

Almost all of today's elderly Japanese Americans arrived in the United States and Canada during the early part of this century, while a moderate number of elderly Chinese Americans arrived more recently, either coming initially as students or businessmen, perhaps seeking political sanctuary, or as part of the very recent immigrant group following the Immigration Acts of the past two decades. Of 110 Japanese American adults interviewed in a recent study, 31 out of 33 over age sixty were born in Japan and only one was born in the United States (Kalish and Reynolds, 1972). We lack comparable data for elderly Chinese.

GENERATIONAL DIFFERENCES AMONG ASIAN AMERICANS

The elderly Asian American had learned his native language and national customs in his homeland; he was socialized in a milieu where his value system was accepted as a basic "given." Immigration in groups permitted some sense of continuity with the homeland. Organizations and institutions such as the "six companies" in San Francisco and Japanese "ken" were transplanted pos-

sible defenses against the harsh treatment and prejudice of the dominant white society. Further semblance of continuity with the homeland was maintained through living in an ethnic enclave, with close ties to ethnic community and family of procreation, reading ethnic newspapers, and reinforcing an effectively internalized value system through the approval of ethnic age peers.

Since many Chinese and Japanese immigrants in the United States (including Hawaii) and Canada initially anticipated returning to their homeland, we would suppose that they were deeply concerned with providing their children with the kind of early training that would permit them to adjust to subsequent life in East Asia. This would mean that transmitting the values, customs, and languages of their native lands would be vitally important, more important than successful adaptation to the foster homeland.

In contrast, the second generation looked to the country of birth for standards regarding attitudes and behavior. Consciously at least, a member of this group tended to identify more fully with his American age cohorts than with his ethnic elders (Berrien, Arkoff, and Iwahara, 1967). An inevitable set of tensions resulted in many ethnic immigrant communities, although our clinical perceptions suggest that—at least for the Japanese Americans—parental resistance to this change was not intense, especially by those who by this time had accepted the United States, Hawaii, or Canada as their permanent home. Those Issei who had arrived at such an accommodation were probably better able to tolerate the sudden power of their Nisei children and the concomitant Americanization of their behavior.

In the years following the end of World War II, the Nisei GIs began to bring home Japanese war brides. Initially greeted with enthusiasm by their new in-laws, these young women were soon perceived as being part of a modern Japan that the Issei did not effectively understand. While the new wives were drawn from a more emancipated segment of the Japanese population and anticipated new freedom in the United States, their in-laws were seeking traditional relationships. A study conducted in Hawaii found that Nisei men marrying European brides had less stress in their marriages than Nisei men with Japanese brides (Kimura, 1957). Eventually the Issei parents "began to see that a Nisei bride for their son might not be so bad and even preferable to one from Japan who could speak their language but would flaunt New Japan and call them old-fashioned."[1]

The third generation often looks back to cultural roots in their land of origin. With less of their national culture influencing them during their socialization, they have come to grips with their ethnic identity in a totally different fashion than their parents. Rather than accepting the ethnic roles that American society attempted to foist upon them, they made serious efforts to seek the meaning of self and ethnicity through their historical roots in the United States (and Canada) and in their nations of origin.

In seeking their roots, they—as all groups—seek selectively. Most obviously, they do not seek to regain the tradition of filial piety, a sense of obedience to the ruler of the nation in which they live, the encouragement of wars of conquest, nor the adherence to the premise that women are to be subjugated. Rather they look to the arts, the cultural history, some religious involvements, and—to some extent—the martial arts, albeit in the name of peace. In many ways, they are looking to historical values that were of less importance to their parents and grandparents than the historical values the younger Asian Americans are consciously trying to leave behind.

It is ironic, in this regard, that the younger Chinese and Japanese Americans sometimes romanticize the early discrimination that their parents and grandparents faced. In their own attempts to gain a solid feeling of ethnic identity, some third generation Asian Americans have regretted their own relatively easy access to material goods, jobs, and education, and have felt that the suffering of their predecessors offered a significant ethnic experience.

[1] Personal communication, Dr. Kazue Togasaki.

Since most immigrant waves to this country have consisted of the young and the middle-aged, but primarily the young, all have shared one important and often overlooked loss: their ties with kin. They have been unable to relate to their own parents in a fashion that could serve as a model to their own children. They could, of course, preach, admonish, threaten, bribe, cajole, and communicate the folk literature, all in order to socialize their children to the ideal of filial piety, a norm espoused by both Chinese and Japanese (and almost all other American ethnic groups, albeit with more limited recent success).

The ethnic community, through its language schools and other means of social control, may perhaps have been instrumental in teaching some of the later generations the responsibilities of family and community relationships. However, because the second generation of today often did not know their grandparents, they lacked the role model for proper behavior toward the elderly.

Differences and similarities between age groups have been reported in a very small number of studies, Masuda, Matsumoto, and Meredith (1970), studying Japanese Americans in Seattle, found the expected relationship between the individual's generation in the United States and his extent of acculturation. Moreover, among the Issei (but not among the Nisei or Sansei), ethnic identification was related to age. Nonetheless, the authors warn that "considerable residue of ethnic identity [is found in] the third generation Sansei and considerable acculturation [is found in] the Issei [Masuda et al., p. 207]." Two other studies compared university students of different generations but of the same age. Administering the Edwards Personal Preference Schedule to both men and women, Arkoff (1959) found that, compared to Nisei students at the University of Hawaii, the Sansei indicated less need for deference, abasement, nurturance, affiliation, endurance, and intraception, and more need for dominance, achievement, and exhibition. However, the author warns that only two of these differences were statistically significant for women and only one was statistically significant for men!! Considering moderately large Ns (65 male Nisei, 72 female Nisei, 70 male Sansei, and 113 female Sansei), we end up with results that are equivocal. Fong (1965) conducted a similar study of five generations of Chinese Americans, all university students at the time, and also found the expected relationship between generation and assimilation.

A more intriguing study compared males and females both across cultures and across age groups. Berrien et al. (1967) found that Japanese American students resembled non-Japanese American students of their own sex more than they resembled their same-sex parent. The instrument was again the Edwards Personal Preference Schedule. It quickly becomes apparent that none of these studies have included the elderly.

Filial Piety or Egalitarianism

Some traditional East Asian values were related specifically to growing old or being old, and some traditional East Asian customs had special meaning for the elderly. Thus Japanese and Chinese society were both based upon stable family units living in the same locale throughout their lifetimes. The obligation of the family to care for the elderly was beyond questioning. Not only had the parents borne and reared their children, but they had carefully selected their children's mates, based upon a closed system in which marriage was an alliance between families of equal status. The rules were known by all and conformed to with little deviation; the children who did not abide by these rules in caring for their parents were punished by severe social sanctions, but normally the threat of the sanctions was sufficient to control the behavior.

The theme of filial piety is common in Western literature as well as East Asian— "Honor thy father and thy mother." But the themes of independence, self-reliance, and mastery of one's own fate are also dominant in Western thought, while Japan and China honor these values little if at all. Therefore, filial piety in Western cultures tends to be undermined by a vast array of conflicting values, while in Chinese and Japanese cultures, filial piety ranks much higher in the hierarchy of values. The feelings of Western parents regarding the respect of their children would be felt with much greater intensity by Asian-American first generation elderly. (The senior author has often heard elderly white Americans state that they are most anxious to avoid being a burden to their children. His frequent response is, "Why? Weren't they a burden to you for twenty years?")

In addition, today's elderly Asian American recalls his own grandfather controlling the household in which his eldest son lived, along with, perhaps, other adult children. The wives of these sons were extremely attentive to their aging parents-in-law—indeed, this often being their primary charge in the family. The first generation Asian American very likely did not make similar obeisance, since he no longer lived in sufficient proximity to carry out the obligation. Nonetheless, over the decades lingered the notion that his daughters or his daughters-in-law would cater to him in his later years.

Although growing old in all societies implies some losses, it need not imply the loss of status, respect, personal care, health care, or opportunity for activity and involvement. The Asian aged had a position of respect, and to an appreciable extent he perceived growing old as a blessing, as a period in life when he could sit back and enjoy the fruits of his labor while the members of his family sought his advice on important issues and in making decisions. He also had freedom—freedom to express impulses which formerly had been restricted, to tell risqué jokes, to sing off-color songs, to be raucous, to seem foolish. And as long as he was reasonably intact and alert, he retained a status that was raised rather than lowered by his age. He had the self-esteem that comes with being an integral and accepted member of the community.

The Chinese and Japanese immigrants came to a new country, expecting to be rewarded in later years for their labors with a status respected in the community and by their families. However, in a society where the rewards for achievement and productivity accrue to the individual rather than to the family or group, and where future potential is more important than past accomplishments in evaluating the worth of a person, the wisdom and the accomplishments of the elderly were often perceived as irrelevant or were forgotten and ignored.

A View from the Middle Generation

Society needs its villains, and the contemporary folk wisdom—not only of Asian Americans, but of virtually all Americans— is that elderly parents are treated badly by their middle-aged children, probably worse than ever before in history. Like much folk wisdom, this is supported by horror stories, innumerable individual incidents, and reference to the literature of the past in which the aged are extolled. Perhaps the folk wisdom has a basis in truth, perhaps not. More to the point, the knowledge and memories of today often ignore some of the realities of the past, when a mobile society pressed on to new frontiers (for white Americans, the press was westwards—for Asians, the press was to the East), leaving the elderly behind without either social welfare or social security to ameliorate their plight. Moreover, when life expectancy was in the forties, relatively few persons became old, and these were more easily accommodated (not so incidentally, these old also held power over land, goods, and jobs).

The elderly have been caught on the horns of a dilemma. On the one hand, they recognize and at least to some extent accept the values of their adopted homeland that being a burden to children is bad, that having the privacy and independence of one's own home is good, that the education of grandchildren should not be sacrificed for the care of grandparents. On the other hand, they recall their early learning that the old person is entitled not only to financial support, but to personal care, to virtual devotion. Although they themselves had usually escaped the demands of filial piety, they have not escaped the acceptance of its importance.

To claim that the second generation Chinese Americans and Japanese Americans are calloused about their parents or love them less than in earlier centuries is unfair. In the China or Japan of a century ago, the social structure of the community would have made life miserable for an adult child who ignored his parents. Moreover, where could the elderly be sent? And who would pay? Convalescent care facilities, welfare, and social security payments did not exist. We cannot project ourselves back in history to learn what Tanaka-san and Mr. Chen would have done in their homelands in 1830, but we need to take care that we do not make villains of today's middle-aged child because the world for him is different from that of his predecessors and successors.

The shame and guilt identified with what is considered inappropriate care for elderly parents is still much in evidence. It can have amusingly painful ramifications, such as the accidental meeting of two middle-aged Japanese American men while each was visiting his elderly parent in a nursing home, requiring them to consume ten minutes with apologetic explanations as to why it was necessary to have "put mama here." And it can have unpleasant ramifications, such as the elderly Asian-American woman who was placed in a care facility fifty miles from her home community and many miles from any Asian friends so that her children would not have to deal with exactly the experience described previously.

An intriguing question emerges: Will the third-generation Asian American, when he is middle-aged and his parents old, take better care of his elderly, both in terms of money and of personal care, than did his second-generation parent?

THE UNIQUENESS OF ASIAN AMERICANS

The prejudice and discrimination faced by Asian Americans half a century ago was faced, to a greater or lesser extent, by immigrants from Ireland, Poland, Italy, Greece, Armenia, Russia, and Finland, and by Jewish immigrants from everywhere. The Asians were unique, however, in that they were visibly different from the general population and thus regarded as unassimilable. Further, they suffered from discrimination that was codified in law and that explicitly listed them as the victims of the overtly discriminatory laws. The Alien Land Acts, the Alien Exclusion Act, miscegenation laws, the World War II treatment of the Japanese Americans are the most conspicuous of these laws and regulations (although relatively few of Hawaii's Japanese were interned).

Not until 1952 could first-generation Asians become citizens. They were thus unable to vote or exert any but the most marginal political influence. Moreover, they were left in legal jeopardy since they could readily be deported. Even today, first-generation Asian Americans, all but the most recent arrivals having become citizens, are reluctant to become involved with the legal and bureaucratic mechanisms of this nation. Those who have entered in the past few years or those who arrived earlier but who remained illegally in this country (although granted citizen status subsequently) are even less likely to wish to encounter the authorities. Therefore they may refrain from seeking medical care, legal advice, or financial help until their difficulties have reached an extreme stage. If the problems are medical, institutionalization is often required, bringing about an even more stressful situation—alone in an unfamiliar and incomprehensible environment.

The actual validity of their fear of deportation as well as the decades of fear of encountering the legal forces and the courts may well have led to a feeling of helplessness and estrangement in their new homeland, whose rules they did not understand but felt they had to obey. This sense of vulnerability and helplessness has never been effectively studied. It may have been somewhat alleviated by their forming ethnic community groups paralleling the dominant culture in part and their cultures of origin in part. However, their political powerlessness and fear of legal sanctions—seeking to conform and yet mistrusting the government in this new

land—may have further alienated them from the society. These governmental strictures may have been accepted by them as a necessary evil and a duty, as they had been socialized to accept the laws of the land as givens. In China the bureaucratic structure had been perceived as having little influence on the lives of the community; it was salient only when family groups needed immediate aid. For the Japanese family, ties with the emperor were also in evidence and duty to obey was an important value, an obligation to be continually reciprocated.

The difference lies in the treatment of the community members. In China and Japan all people deferred to the government and rewards accrued according to one's family status. Everyone knew the proper rules. In the new land, however, Asians were treated harshly because they were Oriental, regardless of their family status.

Studies of stereotypes during the 1930s and 1940s (e.g., Katz and Braly, 1933; Gilbert, 1951) serve as reminders that the elderly Asian American of today faced a very antagonistic white community during his early adult years. The often patronizing, but still favorable, stereotypes their grandchildren complain so vociferously about today would have been a welcome relief from being viewed as inscrutable, superstitious, sly, shrewd, and imitative. Preferred social distances from Japanese and Chinese placed them with fair consistency very near the bottom of the nationality social distance hierarchy. Although prejudice and discrimination are not lacking today, it is difficult to recall the intensity of feelings directed against today's first generation when they were young and middle-aged parents and the second generation was growing up.

Another element unique to the Asian Americans on the contemporary scene is the attempt, primarily by the young, to establish a Pan-Asian American movement. To our knowledge, no other ethnic activist movement attempts to overcome ancient angers and historical antagonisms in the fashion that this one does. The bitter war between Japan and China occurred when today's elderly were already middle-aged; some of them lost sons in World War II, and many second-generation Asian Americans fought against the Japanese. The conflict of this role for the Nisei has received little attention, but, for the middle-aged and the elderly, Chinese American hatred for the Japanese is often great. Whether the motive is primarily political pragmatism or social idealism—or, probably, a bit of both—the younger Asian Americans have made concerted efforts to work together for the betterment, in their view, of all Asian American communities.

Yet in the minds of the elderly these are the same young who are wearing their hair long, who are responsible for thefts and violence, who have established their own codes for sexual behavior, who have espoused the causes of the black and Mexican Americans, who talk about Yellow Power rather than accommodation, and who accuse the Asian American establishment of being "bananas" (the Asian equivalent of calling a black American an "Oreo"). Differences in values between generations are part of the contemporary status quo, but we wonder whether any other group of elderly is being exhorted to make an ally of its most ancient and reviled enemy. (We recognize the rapid accommodation made by Americans with their World War II enemies, the Germans and the Japanese, but these were not historical conflicts.) We are very much aware of the feelings of the Scots for the British, of the Blackfeet for the Sioux, of the Norwegians for the Swedes, of the Indian Hindu for the Pakistani Moslem. How this dilemma will be solved is an interesting study in personal and group adaptation.

And They Are Now Old

The Chinese Americans often lived in Chinese enclaves to which new immigrants came upon entering the country; San Francisco's Chinatown is now drawing elderly Chinese from the entire West Coast (from Vancouver to San Diego) and east to Chicago, perhaps in lieu of their ability to return to China. Elderly Japanese Americans, although torn out of their own communities during World War II and although less likely to re-

side in sections as ethnically dense as Chinatown, have also tended to live an insular existence.

Increasingly over the years return to the homeland became impossible, but effective dealing with the customs, manners, laws, and regulations (most certainly including the bureaucracy) also loomed as impossible. With age come certain kinds of decrements and losses—not inevitably and not for every elderly person (nor only for the elderly), but the relationship between old age on the one hand and illness, reduction of function, and death on the other hand is obvious. The now elderly Asian Americans must face the varied problems of old age not as they had expected—care and respect in one's family and community—but as strangers in a foreign situation.

SERVICES FOR THE ASIAN AMERICAN ELDERLY

What is being done for this group of elderly? Some preparation for the care of the elderly within their ethnic communities has begun. In Los Angeles, Keiro (nursing home for respected elders), a convalescent care center primarily for Japanese Americans, was established in 1969; an extended care facility to meet the needs of semi-independent or intermediate-care-level persons is now in the planning stages, as is a low cost senior citizens' apartment complex. In San Francisco, Self Help for the Elderly provides an active program in Chinatown, including the provision of hot meals, a recreation center, an outreach program, and so forth; here also federal funds have been made available for health care and for a day care center through On Lok Senior Health Services. In Seattle, programs such as a drop-in center are being planned and effected. Facilities available in Hawaii include Kuakini Home Day Care Center which plans day care programs, social activities, ethnic meals, and family counseling.

But the demand exceeds the supply, and many elderly Asian Americans must leave their communities to receive necessary services. An elderly Japanese or Chinese American, at the time of life that—according to his upbringing—would bring him respect, leisure, and attention, now lives in isolation and fear. If he needs long-term care and does not have ethnic facilities available, he will probably be placed in an institution without personnel who speak his language; he will be treated by a physician who understands neither his culture nor his speech; he will eat unfamiliar food (the lack of rice and tea alone would be bad enough); and he may find no one else with whom he can converse or share his thoughts.

We have accumulated a varity of kinds of evidence that sensory isolation and cognitive restrictions both may lead to further reduction in function, yet we continue to place elderly persons, often already somewhat confused and frequently at the time of recovery from an acute physical illness, in settings where neither sensorimotor nor cognitive stimulation is available. Further, we separate them from the familiar environment that they know and from the people they love.

For the Asian elderly, this separation is especially critical for it removes them from their families and the rules and explicit norms for behaviors which they have come to follow. In the institution, because of language difficulties and the ethnic differences between himself and the staff, the elderly Asian cannot learn the rules and cannot adequately verbalize his needs.

We do not wish to exaggerate the situation. Relatively few elderly of any ethnicity are in institutions; many elderly Asian Americans in areas of high Asian American density can find physicians and other health care professionals who do speak their language and do understand their customs. Most elderly Issei have living children who are concerned about their aged parents and who do have a modest or better income. The situation for first-generation Chinese Americans is less optimistic, many falling into the category of "geriatric orphan." i.e., an elderly person with no responsible next-of-kin available; but the Chinese American communities

are actively moving. While the situation may not be drastic in terms of numbers when compared to other ethnic minorities or to poor whites, it is certainly drastic for those who are affected.

What Is To Become of the Elderly Asian American?

The alert elderly Chinese American, living in San Francisco's Chinatown and having enough money to take care of his more important physical and social needs, probably has access to reasonable services and to companionship. If he is one of the many who does not have an adequate income, he is going to have difficulties. If finally he has to enter a convalescent care facility, he may find himself without even one person to whom he can talk and without the comforts of familiar food, reading materials, movies, and with no access to health and social professionals with whom he can converse.

How can services be provided so that they are more acceptable to these elderly, who are family-oriented and to an extent mistrustful of the dominant society? The Kuakini Home Day Care Center provides care during the day when the second generation is out of the house at work; it also offers family counseling. By engaging the different generations to look at their common problems, family solidarity can be restored and communication and understanding fostered. The rules of the present situation can be explained to the elderly in his own language to help him adjust to the new situation, as well as helping the younger generations to understand their parents and themselves.

One possible solution for the elderly who have families would be to seek out their offspring to determine problem areas and needs, emphasizing the supportive environment for these aged. Services may be more palatable if administered indirectly, through family members who can first explain the services to these elderly.

For single individuals without families, a surrogate family—the ethnic community—can be utilized to simulate the family.

Services are more often used if administered by the ethnic community rather than by the dominant white society. Perhaps their not being able to understand their environment and their negative experiences with the dominant society make them passive, with a "shi-ka-ta-ga-nai" [it can't be helped] attitude, while underneath they are harboring tension and unhappiness.

The task of describing how the elderly Asian American live must await another article. And we must reiterate how remiss we have been in restricting ourselves to the Chinese and Japanese even though a decade from now the elderly Filipino will very likely supplant both these groups in terms of his needs for services and for understanding. We have only touched briefly upon the services available or becoming available for older Asian Americans. We have said almost nothing about the ways some younger Asian American activists have tried to improve conditions for their elderly. We barely touched upon the "Asian concerns" session at the November, 1971, White House Conference on Aging or upon any of the conference follow-ups.

At a very personal level, the authors feel that Asian American communities have the ability to provide necessary services and appropriate kinds of human interactions with their elderly, *given their fair portion of funds and services from federal and other agencies.* We are not as pessimistic about the future as we are distressed about the past. The Asian American has considered himself an invisible minority; the elderly are considered an invisible age group. It is only now that the elderly Asian American is being seen.

REFERENCES

ARKOFF, A. "Need Patterns in Two Generations of Japanese Americans in Hawaii." *Journal of Social Psychology* 50 (1959) 75–79.

Asian American Elderly, The. (White House Conference on Aging, 1971.) Washington, D.C.: USGPO 1972.

BERRIEN, F. K., ARKOFF, A., and IWAHARA, S. "Generation Difference in Values: Americans, Japanese Americans, Japanese." *Journal of Social Psychology* 71 (1967): 169–75.

CAUDILL, W. A. "Japanese-American Personality and Acculturation." *Genetic Psychology Monographs* 45 (1952): 3–102.

FONG, S. L. M. "Assimilation of Chinese in America: Changes in Orientation and Social Perception." *American Journal of Sociology* 71 (1965): 265–73.

GILBERT, G. M. "Stereotype Persistence and Change Among College Students." *Journal of Abnormal and Social Psychology* 46 (1951): 245–54.

HSU, F. L. K. *The Challenge of the American Dream: the Chinese in the United States.* Belmont, California: Wadsworth, 1971.

KALISH, R. A., and REYNOLDS, D. K. Untitled. Unpublished manuscript, Graduate Theological Union, Berkeley, 1972.

KALISH, R. A., and YUEN, S. "Americans of East Asian Ancestry: Aging and the Aged." *The Gerontologist* 11 (1971): (Spring), 36–47.

KATZ, D., and BRALY, K. W. "Racial Stereotypes of 100 College Students." *Journal of Social and Abnormal Psychology* 28 (1933): 280–90.

KIMURA, Y. "War Brides in Hawaii and Their In-Laws. *American Journal of Sociology* 63 (1957): 70–76.

KITANO, H. H. L. *Japanese Americans: the Evolution of a Subculture.* Englewood Cliffs, New Jersey: Prentice-Hall, 1969.

MASUDA, M., MATSUMOTO, G. H., and MEREDITH, G. M. "Ethnic Identity in Three Generations of Japanese Americans." *Journal of Social Psychology* 81 (1970): 199–207.

SIMMONS, L. *The Role of the Aged in Primitive Society.* New Haven: Yale University Press, 1945.

TOFFLER, A. *Future Shock.* New York: Random House, 1970.

Effect of Ethnicity on Life Styles of the Inner-City Elderly

Marjorie H. Cantor

Just as individuals are clearly distinguished from one another by physical, social, and psychological characteristics, so aggregates of people in our society can be differentiated by virtue of their shared culture, ethnicity, and socioeconomic status. As we move toward greater acceptance of the value of a pluralistic society, the importance of understanding differences becomes even more critical for environmental or social planning. Increasingly, decision makers are faced with the need for subgroup analysis as they attempt to fairly balance the competing interests of various ethnic and nationality groups. Nowhere is this need more evident than in large urban areas characterized not only by high density of population but by wide diversity of the backgrounds of its citizens.

Yet in planning services for the elderly there has been a tendency to view older people as a homogeneous group, set off from the rest of society by virtue of a single determinant, age.

But older people on reaching sixty-five (or whatever arbitrary figure a society chooses to signify as old age) do not shed their identity as members of racial, ethnic, or socioeconomic subgroups. Rather, it may well be that this subgroup membership is the crucial factor in conditioning how older peo-

Reprinted, with permission, from *Community Planning for an Aging Society: Designing Services and Facilities.* M. Powell Lawton et al., eds. Dowden, Hutchinson & Ross, Inc., Stroudsburg, Pennsylvania, 1976.

ple grow old and in determining the social, physical, and psychological needs to which the planning process should be addressed.

In all stages of life, morale and well-being are related to an individual's ability to successfully perform the tasks set forth for his age group by society. In childhood, control and mastery of environment is a gradual process, with considerable dependency upon adults as mediating agents. Adulthood presumes the ability, skills, and competence to effectively control environment and determine the course of one's own daily existence. The degree to which this is possible determines to a considerable extent the individual's mental health and integrity of personality. A sense of powerlessness is anathema to successful adulthood in industrialized societies.

Similarly, in old age, although social roles change, the basic drives for independence, competence, and mastery of environment remain. At the same time, with deteriorating health and reduced income, frequent concomitants of old age in our society, a countertrend of gradual diminution of mastery occurs. To the extent that an older person can continue to exercise considerable freedom of choice and control, morale will be high and aging successful.

But the form in which the basic needs of all older people are expressed and the relative role of the family and community in providing the necessary assistance for independent living are heavily conditioned by cultural, economic, and kinship patterns. When family structure continues to be strong and cohesive, more help from that source can be expected. When family is dispersed or nonexistent, the community role is of increasing importance. Meaningful social planning requires precise knowledge of both the extent to which the aging process is similar for all older people and the degree to which racial, ethnic, and socioeconomic differences require varying types of community facilities and services to sustain older people independently in the community for as long as possible.

The Urban Elderly Poor

A review of the gerontological literature confirms the paucity of data about the urban poor and particularly the minority-group elderly. In general, much stress has been placed (not inappropriately) on discovering the broad patterns of the aging process. Where subgroups of elderly have been singled out for study, the sample too often consists of white middle-class respondents in medium-sized or suburban communities. Yet, increasingly, the concentration of elderly, in all industrialized societies is in the largest cities—most frequently in the older central or inner city where poverty and social and environmental blight are common conditions of life.

New York City is the home of three major racial ethnic subgroups—white, black, and Spanish-speaking (mainly Puerto Rican). Although at present the vast majority of older New Yorkers are white, there are growing numbers of black and Puerto Rican elderly; this trend is expected to continue. In an attempt to document the basic similarities, but more importantly the differences, in the life styles and needs of the three major groups of elderly and thereby provide the specificity of data needed for immediate and long-range physical and social planning, the New York City Office for the Aging undertook in 1970 one of the first and most comprehensive cross-cultural studies of the urban elderly poor living in the inner city (Cantor et al.,

1975). Findings in several major areas of particular interest to planners will be discussed and the social policy implications highlighted.

Although New York City is in many ways *sui generis*, particularly with respect to size and complexity, the findings have considerable implications for other major urban areas. Perhaps more important than any specific findings, the New York City study provides a case history in the use of subgroup analysis as a tool for meaningful planning.

Study Goals, Population, and Methodology

The study goals were as follows:

1. To describe the life of urban elderly residing in neighborhoods characterized by poverty, decay, and high risk. Highlighted were problems of income maintenance, social isolation, the unique nature of housing and environmental conditions, and patterns of mobility.

2. To determine the effects of subgroup membership on the aging process among white, Spanish, and black elderly and to document areas of similarity and difference.

   Particular emphasis was placed on identifying the factors that enable the elderly to cope with and effectively control their environment. The relative roles of the individual, family, and community were considered for the population as a whole and for each subgroup.

3. To document the needs of the three major subgroups of elderly for supportive community services with a view toward enhancing mastery over environment. Where possible, differential needs were identified and related to the desirability for new services or the improved delivery of existing services.

4. To explore the degree to which positive feelings of mastery over environment are related to the concepts of high morale and successful aging as presently employed in the gerontological literature.

The focal point of the study was the elderly of the inner city rather than a city-wide sample for three major reasons:

1. First, much is known about middle-class older people but little about the lifestyles and support systems of the urban elderly poor. Yet it is among the urban poor that one would expect to find the greatest need for community assistance.

2. A principal goal of the study was to document the effects of subgroup membership on aging and identify the commonalities and differences among the lifestyles and coping mechanisms of the three major ethnic subgroups found in New York. Most of the black and Spanish elderly reside in the inner city, yet the majority of older people in these core neighborhoods are white, as is the case for the rest of the city.

3. In the belief that environment was a key variable in lifestyles, it was desirable to limit the universe to older people living in similar conditions of neighborhood blight and deterioration.

Defining the inner city in New York was somewhat more difficult than in other urban areas of the country. Typically, a central city is an easily identifiable geographic entity with all the classic attributes of environmental and social decline, surrounded by concentric rings of middle-class communities to which the more affluent have fled. In New York, on the contrary, each borough has its blighted areas interspersed amid middle- or upper-class neighborhoods. Sometimes, even on a single block, tenements stand next to luxury apartments.

The central city of New York was, therefore, defined operationally to be the twenty-six neighborhoods designated as poverty areas by the Human Resources Administration. These areas have the highest incidence of crime, infant mortality, welfare case load, and deteriorated housing, and clearly duplicate the objective conditions found in the inner city of other urban centers in the United States.

The criterion of aging was purposely set at sixty, rather than at the more usual sixty-five years, to enable the gathering of information about the lifestyles and needs of those entering the aged cohort as compared with the "older" elderly. The sample was limited to noninstitutional elderly living in the community.

A replicated probability sample was employed, that embodied five randomly selected, stratified, interpenetrating matched samples. Through a two-step enumeration process, 2,180 households were identified as having one or more older persons. Six call-backs ultimately yielded 1,552 interviews, a completion rate of 71 percent—quite good considering the areas in which the study was conducted and the possible fears of older people about opening doors to strangers.

The final sample of 1,552 respondents proved to be highly representative of the approximately 400,000 older persons living in the twenty-six neighborhoods in 1970 when interviewing took place. The ethnic distribution of the sample is remarkably accurate with, if anything, a slight overrepresentation of black and Spanish elderly—the very groups usually underrepresented in most studies. Where possible, any discrepancies arising from sample selection or interviewing were compensated for through weighting. Interviews were held in the home, ran from one to two hours, and elicited information on virtually all aspects of the lives of older New Yorkers.

FINDINGS

An aging population can be subdivided in many ways: well versus sick, the young elderly versus the older elderly, or institutionalized versus community based. From the beginning the cross-cultural approach was chosen. It was hypothesized that the influence of ethnicity and culture on the lifestyles of older people is crucial, particularly in the areas of greatest interest to us—the support system and the relative roles of family and community in enhancing the lives of older people. Furthermore, little or nothing is known about the similarities and differences in lifestyles of the aged among the major ethnic groups in urban society. Finally, inasmuch as New York City contains the largest number of white, black, and Spanish elderly in the country, it seemed most appropriate to place our initial stress on ethnicity and culture.

However, not unmindful of the importance of socioeconomic class, the final study report will attempt to identify the relative importances of ethnicity, culture, and class. The fact that the study population is limited to poverty-area elderly acts to narrow the range of socioeconomic class. But particularly in the case of the white elderly, social class status prior to old age may be unrelated to current income and may well be a determining factor in attitudes and lifestyle. In addition, the white population is not as homogeneous with respect to culture as the black and Spanish. Finally, ethnicity and culture are used interchangeably in this discussion of the findings.

A Brief Profile of the Inner-City Elderly

Who then are the inner-city elderly, what are their general characteristics, and to what extent does ethnicity affect these characteristics? (see Table 1).

First the inner-city elderly are clearly not a homogeneous middle-class white population. Rather, the study population is a low income, urban elderly sample encompassing three distinct ethnic groups. Although inner-city neighborhoods are increasingly nonwhite, at the present time whites still predominate among both young and old alike. Thus, in the sample, 49 percent of the respondents were white, 37 percent black, and 13 percent Spanish-speaking, principally of Puerto Rican origin.

Ethnicity has a considerable effect on age distribution. If old age is conceptualized as a continuum having a beginning, middle, and ending period, the Spanish elderly are the youngest, tending to cluster in the initial period. Two thirds of the Spanish elderly were under seventy. Black elderly tended to

be more in the middle, older than the Spanish but younger than whites. Nearly 60 percent of the blacks were under seventy; among white respondents, the oldest of the three groups, 40 percent were under 70 and 60 percent were seventy or older. Several cultural factors contribute to these age differences. The most important is differential longevity. Black life expectancy is seven years less than that of whites; although exact data with respect to mainland Puerto Ricans are lacking, it is believed that a similar differential exists. In the past, another factor contributed to ethnic differences in age distribution in the city—the tendency for blacks and Puerto Ricans to return "home" upon reaching old age. This out-migration factor is expected to fade in succeeding generations of black and Spanish elderly.

With respect to the presence of a spouse, more Spanish married originally and as the youngest group more were still married and living with spouse (43 percent). Whites were next most likely to still be married (36 percent). Although blacks had the second highest rate of marriage originally and were younger than the white respondents, at this point in their lives they were least likely of the three subgroups to report still being married and living with spouse. Persons who reported never having been married were most likely to be found among the whites.

The health of the inner-city elderly is poorer than older people generally, as measured both by self-assessed health and the Townsend Index of Functional Ability (Shanas et al., 1968). Although younger, Spanish and black elderly appeared to have significantly more health problems than whites, and a higher proportion was found to be severely impaired or incapacitated (see Table 1). However, although most respondents reported at least one chronic illness, they were not homebound and were able to get around. (Only approximately 7 percent were in wheelchairs or bedridden.)

The inner-city elderly, like all older New Yorkers, had lived in the city and in their immediate neighborhoods for a long time. They had deep roots and considerable

TABLE 1

Major demographic characteristics of inner-city elderly respondents (percentages).

	TOTAL	WHITE	BLACK	SPANISH
Age				
60–64	22.0	15.2	26.2	35.8
65–69	28.2	25.1	31.8	30.0
70–74	22.1	22.3	23.5	17.2
75+	27.2	36.9	17.9	17.0
Sex				
Male	41.0	45.2	35.2	41.9
Female	59.0	54.8	64.8	58.1
Ethnicity				
White	49.4	49.4		
Black	37.4		37.4	
Spanish	13.2			13.2
Religious affiliation				
Protestant	43.5	18.3	86.0	17.4
Catholic	35.3	43.2	9.6	78.7
Jewish	14.9	29.5	0.8	0.4
Socioeconomic status				
Hollingshead's ISP (IV and V: working and lower class)	74.7	63.8	85.3	85.3
Income: under $2,500/yr (est. per capita)	63.8	55.6	71.3	73.6
Occupation: manual	67.6	57.3	79.4	72.4
Education: 8th grade or less	59.9	50.1	65.3	80.4
Marital status				
Married	34.3	35.9	29.3	42.6
Widowed	42.0	39.9	45.2	41.1
Never married	13.4	17.3	10.8	6.1
Separated or divorced	10.3	6.8	14.8	10.3
Living arrangements				
Live alone	39.2	47.4	33.1	26.2
Live with spouse	33.4	34.7	29.0	41.0
Live with others (not spouse)	27.4	17.9	37.9	32.8
Health				
Have health problem(s)	67.3	62.8	72.1	70.6
Self-perceived health as poor	23.8	20.6	25.2	31.4
Incapacity index: severely impaired or incapacitated	15.4	13.6	15.5	22.2
Nativity: born on U.S. mainland	53.3	46.5	80.2	3.4
Total respondents	1.552	766	580	205

Source: Cantor et al., *The Elderly in the Inner City.* New York City Office for the Aging, in press.

feelings of belonging, although they recognized the urban blight around them and were often very fearful of the "strangers in the neighborhood." As expected, whites had the longest tenure in the city (mean residency of fifty-two years), followed by blacks (mean residency of thirty-nine years). Relatively recent arrival was characteristic only of the Spanish elderly, most of whom came to the mainland when they were forty years old or more. But even the Spanish in the sample had lived in New York an average of twenty-five years.

The late arrival of the Spanish has had serious implications affecting their ability to learn English, their employment opportunities, and their Social Security coverage, to say nothing of the psychological problems attendant upon uprooting and moving to an alien culture in the middle and later years of life. It is noteworthy that 86 percent of the Spanish elderly spoke Spanish at home. In the case of most other foreign-born elderly, whether white or black, English was the language in the home.

Although it is common to think of the present generation of white elderly in big cities like New York as largely foreign-born, this was far from the case. Almost half the white respondents were native-born, and of this group 40 percent were at least second-generation Americans. The inner-city is apparently the home of a substantial number of white Americans of old stock, mainly Protestant, who are living in hidden "genteel" poverty.

Because they grew up during the period when higher education, including high school, was mainly for the well-to-do, it is not surprising to find little formal education among the inner-city urban poor. Most of the sample had a grade school education or less, with the least amount of formal education being reported by the Spanish. (This lack of education coupled with minority-group status has severely limited the job opportunities available to most black and Spanish elderly during their adult years.)

Although there is considerable occupational and social-class spread among the inner-city elderly, particularly in the case of the whites, 64 percent of the sample was classified according to the Hollingshead Index of Social Position (Hollingshead and Redlich, 1958) as being in the two lowest categories (i.e., working or lower class), and most respondents were involved in skilled or unskilled occupations during their working years. Spanish and black elderly almost exclusively held unskilled or semi-skilled jobs, with only a handful reporting employment in skilled or clerical/sales occupations. White elderly showed a somewhat greater occupational spread. Although the bulk were skilled workers during their adult years, 15 percent held managerial or professional positions and 20 percent were owners of small businesses or held sales or clerical jobs. As is to be expected, there were relatively few upper-middle- or upper-class elderly living in the inner city, no matter what their ethnic backgrounds.

Retirement and Income

If older people, regardless of their ethnicity, are to live independently in the community, two essential requirements are the ability to buy what they need and the physical strength necessary to permit an adequate level of functioning. Since poverty areas contain more families with lower earnings, lower Social Security coverage, and less savings, one might expect that economic pressures would operate to keep more poverty area elderly at work than is usual among older people in general. This was not so. Inner-city elderly were far less likely to be working after sixty-five than their peers nationally.

Even though all males and 70 percent of the female respondents reported gainful employment sometime during their adult years, 78 percent of the inner-city elderly sample were retired. Ethnicity clearly influences the point at which an older person leaves the labor market. The Spanish were forced out of the labor market earliest. Among Spanish males sixty to sixty-four, 61 percent were no longer working. With respect to black males the picture was slightly better than among the Spanish but still very bad; 50 percent of black male respondents in the sixty to sixty-four age cohort were no longer working.

Among whites in our sample the picture was very different and corresponded to the national labor force participation statistics for the age group. Only a relatively small proportion (25 percent) of those sixty to sixty-four were retired. Whites continued to work much longer. Of those in the sixty-five to sixty-nine age cohort, over 25 percent were still working, as compared with only a very small proportion of black and Spanish males. Even among whites seventy and over, 13 percent of the sample were still working.

These patterns clearly reflect the close link between ethnicity and work status; persons in professional, managerial, and higher-skilled jobs tended to continue working longer than the less skilled. Thus a greater proportion of white male respondents was still working in their late sixties and the early seventies than was true for the other two groups. Sadly enough, the very groups in the elderly population with the lowest incomes during adult working years, and therefore the lowest Social Security benefits in old age, were, because of lack of skill and minority-group status, the first groups forced out of the labor market.

It has been pointed out that poor health may also be a cause of early retirement. In our sample, Spanish reported the greatest health deficiencies, followed by blacks; whites reported the best health. Health of course was related to low income.

It is interesting that among nonworking men in the sixty to sixty-four age group, black and Spanish elderly were two and one-half times more likely to consider themselves retired rather than unemployed as compared with similar-aged white men. This undoubtedly represents a reality orientation. Black and Spanish males are more likely to experience chronic unemployment in their adult working years and, therefore, correctly consider themselves out of the labor market by age sixty.

Whereas black men tended to be out of the labor market earlier, black women continued to work longer, certainly through their sixties. Of the black women sixty to sixty-four, 39 percent were still working; in the sixty-five to sixty-nine age cohort, 20 percent of the black women still worked as compared with only 9 percent of the black men.

From this picture of work status, it is no surprise to learn that the income levels of the inner-city elderly were far below those required for adequate living in a city of high costs. Respondents' incomes were abysmally low, significantly below the citywide levels for older people, and sharp ethnic differences existed. In 1970, the median income for white respondents was $2,746, for blacks, $2,166, and for the Spanish, $1,946. Increases in Social Security since 1970 do not appear to have altered the relative income positions of the inner-city elderly or of the three subgroups.

If these figures do not fully convey how poor the inner-city elderly are, New York City's rent increase exemption program set $5,000 as the upper income eligibility limit for elderly households, and the Bureau of Labor Statistics (U.S. Department of Labor, 1969–1970) considered that a retired couple in 1970 needed $3,080 to maintain a minimum living standard and close to $4,700 for a moderate living standard in New York City.

Although Social Security was the principal source of income for all inner-city elderly (73 percent were receiving Social Security), what was less expected was the extent to which Social Security was the *only* source of income. Relatively few elderly received income from pensions, investments, or savings (30 percent), and fewer still, as we have already mentioned, from employment. Despite the low income levels, only 20 percent received Old Age Assistance and only 11 percent reported financial aid from families.

There were major differences among ethnic groups in regard to income sources, which reflect differential occupational history and minority-group status. White elderly were more likely to receive income from Social Security than either of the other two groups—82 percent as compared with 70 percent of the blacks and 50 percent of the Spanish elderly. And the benefit received by whites was larger in the fall of 1970—$139 monthly for white elderly, $118 for blacks, and $107 for Spanish. Inasmuch as some of the elderly (or their spouses) were still working, the proportion receiving income from Social Security is not necessarily identical with coverage. But similar differentials were found with respect to coverage; 93 percent of the whites reported being covered by Social Security compared to only 87 percent of the blacks and 73 percent of the Spanish. The study data raise the question as to whether Social Security should not begin at age fifty-five for Spanish and black elderly, especially since so many are out of the labor market earlier and their life expectancy is so much shorter than whites.

Far fewer black and Spanish elderly received retirement pensions than did whites. One-third of the whites reported pensions compared to only 25 percent of the blacks and 11 percent of the Spanish elderly. Whites were far more likely to have income-producing savings and investments (43 percent) as compared to black (8 percent) or Spanish elderly (9 percent). However, this income was rarely a large amount or a substantial part of the total income of the poverty-area respondent.

In view of the lower coverage of black and Spanish elderly by Social Security and pensions, the fact that more of these two groups received Old Age Assistance (OAA) than did whites is not surprising. Forty-five percent of the Spanish respondents received OAA as compared with 25 percent among Blacks and only 9 percent among whites. Considering the low level of income, it is indeed surprising that more of the respondents were not recipients of OAA.

The question of Old Age Assistance and by the same token the newer Supplemental Security Income (SSI) program appears fraught with cultural implications.

Spanish elderly, whose incomes were lowest, seemed to have the least hesitation accepting OAA—most of those eligible in our sample were covered. Among the black elderly, although a large proportion (60 percent) of those estimated to be eligible were covered, there was a sizable group of apparent eligibles, 40 percent, still uncovered. Some of these undoubtedly were still working, and in answer to a question on whether or not they would turn to OAA in case of need, most blacks indicated a willingness to use the program.

It is among the white elderly that one finds the greatest resistance to entitlement such as OAA or SSI. Thus only 30 percent of the white respondents estimated to be eligible actually used the OAA program, and almost 25 percent flatly said they would never turn to such a program even if in need. In the case of white respondents, some small few may be precluded from OAA because of unwillingness to surrender meager savings, but far more important seems to be the culturally conditioned feeling of lack of dignity and surrender of independence involved in turning to welfare. Early reports on SSI enrollment indicate that this new program also is having difficulty in attracting many of the white elderly who so desperately need the assistance. As long as such programs are seen as based on means tests and as welfare handouts, the potential for reaching the needy eligible of the inner city appears severely limited.

Living Arrangements

A crucial factor affecting an older person's sense of independence and personal integrity is his or her living arrangements. Does the older person live in his own household or is the older person living in the home of a child or other family member? Certainly, in our culture to give up one's home is viewed as a move away from independence toward dependency. Whether or not one lives alone affects the need for support in time of crisis and the potential for social isolation.

What is the picture in the inner-city today and what trends are discernible?

First, whose household is it? The vast majority of older persons in the poverty areas, as in the rest of the city, live independently in their own homes; 91 percent of the sample reported that they or their spouse were head of household; only 8 percent lived in the household of another, usually a child. However, a higher proportion of the inner-city sample maintained their own homes than is true in the city as a whole, and fewer have moved in with families. Thus, although 84 percent of noninstitutionalized elderly sixty-five and older in the city live in their own homes, 91 percent live independently in our sample. Some part of the differential is due to the presence of 60–64-year-olds in the study sample, but not much. More important is the changing nature of the populations of these areas, with considerable out-migration of younger white families and replacement by blacks and Puerto Ricans. As noted previously, the older population is, however, still predominantly white. This white population appears to consist of fiercely independent elderly who prefer to remain in their own homes rather than move in with their children, as well as older persons who have no choice in the matter, either because they cannot afford homes elsewhere or have no families with whom to live.

The strong desire of older people to maintain their own homes is compatible with the cultural norms of the nuclear family so cherished by the dominant white population. Among ethnic groups more accustomed to extended family patterns, one would expect to find a higher proportion of older people giving up their independent residences and moving in with their families. Such was the case among the respondents of Spanish background and to some, although lesser, extent among blacks; 95 percent of the whites and 89 percent of the blacks continued to maintain their own homes. But the proportion of Spanish living independently dropped significantly to 82 percent, in spite of the fact that the Spanish were the youngest of the three groups and more still had a living spouse.

Although Spanish and blacks were less likely to maintain their own homes than their white peers, the proportion who cling to independence was higher than might be expected, given the extended family tradition and the pressures of poverty. With the continuing acculturation of the younger Spanish population and the difficulties of finding suitable apartments for large families, it is likely that in the future few if any older people will live with children, no matter what their ethnic background. As will be noted later, there is evidence of considerable interaction between older people and children despite the existence of separate households. Perhaps urbanized society is developing a new kind of extended family based on mutual help rather than joint domicile.

But living in one's own household is not the whole question. Whether or not an older person lives entirely alone without anyone else in the household has implications for assistance in time of crisis as well as for morale and degree of social isolation. Although a live-alone is not necessarily an isolate, the likelihood of isolation is greater and the potential need for community intervention is increased.

New York City has more older people living alone than is the case throughout the country (30 percent as compared with 22 percent nationally), and the problems of live-alones are particularly acute in the inner-city neighborhoods.

Among persons sixty-five and over in New York City as a whole, 30 percent live alone; in the inner-city the proportion was 41 percent. The proportion of live-alones in the sample as a whole was 39 percent, but this included younger elderly sixty to sixty-four, who are far more likely to be still married. Thus four out of ten of New York's inner-city elderly sixty-five and over had no one else in the dwelling unit with them. This is a much greater proportion of live-alones than found in two other urban poverty samples; only 26 percent lived alone in the low-income areas of Philadelphia (Kent and Hirsch, 1971), and in the model-city neighborhoods of Los Angeles the proportion was 28 percent (Gelwicks et al., 1971). Although age and sex affected the likelihood of living alone (women were more apt to live alone than men and the oldest elderly were more often found alone), ethnicity was perhaps the most decisive factor. As noted previously, white elderly were far less inclined to move in with their children and, instead, cling to independent living in their own households, even when loss of spouse occurs. Thus many more white than black or Spanish elderly in the inner city were found living alone. Among white respondents, 47 percent lived alone as compared with 37 percent among blacks and 27 percent among Spanish. The highest incidence of single-person households was found among the frailest segment of the white population, older people in their seventies and eighties, particularly among widowed or single women. For such elderly the changing ethnic composition of their neighborhoods only compounds the objective conditions of aloneness and isolation. But even among black and Spanish, where the pattern of living alone was not yet as prevalent, a surprisingly high proportion were alone—27 percent among the Spanish and 34 percent among the blacks. It is, therefore, likely that large numbers of older persons living alone will characterize inner-city neighborhoods, even if there should be a continued decline in white residents. Providing support for these live-alones, many of whom are the oldest, frailest, and most isolated elderly, will continue to be a challenging community responsibility.

Family Relationships in the Inner City: Extent of Contact Between Elderly and Children

In urban industrial society, the support system of the elderly increasingly involves an amalgam of services provided by the family and significant others and services offered by large-scale governmental or voluntary organizations. As kinship structure evolves from the extended family to the modified extended family (i.e., a coalition of separately housed semi-autonomous nuclear families in a state of partial dependency; Litwak, 1965), the importance of the familial versus societal role shifts. Thus today it is government that provides the floor of basic services for older people in such crucial areas as income maintenance, health, and transportation. But the family and significant others still retain considerable importance, particularly in meeting the more idiosyncratic human needs of the individual. An elder person without a circle of significant others can be severely disadvantaged.

In most societies, children and immediate kin are looked to as the first line of support in time of crisis. Particularly as freedom of movement is curtailed owing to increased frailty, poorer health, and the resultant lessened capacity to manage one's own life wholly independently, the circle of significant others—children, siblings, friends, and neighbors—becomes increasingly significant. It is therefore, important to know to what extent older inner-city residents have living children, how close they are to these children, and the degree to which relationships are maintained. And, perhaps most crucial, if there are relationships, what is the quality and form that they take?

Contrary to myths that circulate widely about today's parent-child relationships, most inner-city elderly had children and had not been abandoned by their children. Two out of three had at least one living child. Spanish elderly were significantly more likely than either black or white to have had children in the first place, to still have a child in the household, and to have larger families. (Spanish mean number of children was 4.7 as compared with 3.2 for blacks and 2.7 for whites.)

The majority of the children of all three ethnic subgroups lived relatively near their parents, and the two generations had frequent face-to-face and telephone contact with each other. In view of the frequently described flight of children to suburbia, it is significant that 28 percent of all children were within walking distance, living either in the building or immediate neighborhood, while 26 percent lived elsewhere in the five boroughs of New York. Only 13 percent resided in the suburbs, and 32 percent were beyond the metropolitan area. (It should be noted that the sample was heavily weighted toward the working and lower-middle classes. It is likely that among older people in the city as a whole the proportion of children living in suburbia would be greater. Even in our more limited sample there was a significant difference between the proportion of children in suburbia among the highest-income elderly and the lower-income groups.)

According to the respondents, they see half of their children at least once a week and two thirds at least monthly. Even though more white children live in the suburbs (19 percent white, 11 percent Spanish, and 8 percent black), while the children of Spanish and black elderly tend to reside more frequently in the neighborhood or within city limits (47 percent white, 62 percent black, 55 percent Spanish), there was little difference with respect to the proportions of the three groups of children who saw their parents regularly (50 percent white, 48 percent black, 53 percent Spanish). Apparently, the greater affluence and mobility of white children enabled them to keep in contact with parents even though they lived farther away.

But although children as a group may have lived in relatively close proximity and had a high level of interaction with parents, this does not go to the heart of the question of availability of familial support in time of need. The crucial question is how many older people in the inner city are in contact with at least one or more children on a frequent and regular basis.

The study data indicate that the majority of respondents with children (68 percent) saw at least one child once or more per week. In the case of the Spanish elderly, whose children live the closest, the proportion seeing at least one child weekly was over 80 percent; among blacks the figure was 70 percent, and among whites, 62 percent. At this point we do not know whether the frequent visitor was the same child, perhaps a daughter, or whether the responsibility for the weekly or biweekly visitation was shared among all the children. Whatever the case, the majority of all older persons in the sample had a regular weekly visit from at least one child. In addition, face-to-face contact was supplemented by frequent telephoning, especially between white parents and children, who used telephone contact more frequently than Spanish and black families. The greater frequency of telephoning among white respondents and their children was probably a matter of both greater affluence and greater distance rather than availability of telephones, since 87 percent of the whites and blacks in the sample had a phone in their own household, as did 76 percent of the Spanish.

Although most of the sample had considerable contact with living children, one cannot overlook the fact that there was a sizable minority of older people without living children for whom primary support may have had to be from neighbors or the community. One third of both the white and black poverty-area respondents indicated that they were without children. Among the Spanish elderly, more of whom initially married and had larger families, there was only 18 percent who were childless.

Type of Relationship

An older person can see children frequently and not have close, meaningful relationships. When the respondents were asked to evaluate the closeness of their relationships with their children and to delineate what closeness means behaviorally, a fascinating system of mutual assistance emerged. Although many older people may find it difficult to state to an interviewer that they are not close to a child, and favorable responses may, therefore, be somewhat inflated, white and Spanish respondents felt very close to somewhat more than 75 percent of their children and fairly close to most of the remainder. Black respondents reported somewhat less closeness, indicating that they felt very close to 66 percent of their children, fairly close to 17 percent, and not too close to 16 percent. Here it is likely that the strains of long-term poverty and institutionalized racism have had their effects on the family.

Contact between parents and children is not limited to mere visiting or "checking up," valuable as this type of support may be psychologically. In attitudinal questions the respondents expressed strong feelings about the appropriateness of assistance within the kinship structure and the desirability of mutual interdependency between parents and children. The behavior of the generations appears consonant with these attitudes and involves concrete patterns of mutual help between generations, but clear cultural differences in kinds of assistance emerge.

Respondents were given a series of common types of assistance and asked which they performed for their children, which their children did for them, and the frequency of assistance. Four broad categories of help were involved: 1) ongoing assistance in chores of daily living; 2) advice giving; 3) crisis intervention; and 4) gift giving (see Table 2).

Over 75 percent of the elderly reported helping children in some manner, and this type of involvement of children with parents

TABLE 2

Patterns of mutual assistance between inner-city elderly of New York and their children (percentages).

| | PARENTS TO CHILDREN | | | | CHILDREN TO PARENTS | | | |
	TOTAL	WHITE	BLACK	SPANISH	TOTAL	WHITE	BLACK	SPANISH
Crisis intervention	50.7[a]	50.5	49.2	54.8	67.8	67.4	67.7	69.1
Assistance in chores								
of daily living	38.3	35.2	40.9	41.7	65.1	63.1	66.6	67.7
Baby-sit	22.7	21.0	21.9	29.2	—	—	—	—
Shop, errands	17.6	14.0	21.4	19.4	50.5	42.3	57.9	57.5
Fix things in house	11.3	9.5	10.9	17.5	39.4	38.3	42.1	42.1
Keep house	13.0	8.1	17.8	16.0	21.7	13.9	25.9	34.4
Meal preparation	—	—	—	—	16.1	11.5	21.6	17.1
Take away in summer	—	—	—	—	19.2	23.3	10.2	27.2
Drive to store, doctor	—	—	—	—	28.5	33.3	22.1	29.3
Giving advice	35.5	26.7	36.3	52.8	26.0	24.6	27.0	27.9
On child rearing/home								
management	27.3	20.2	29.2	43.5	—	—	—	—
On major purchases	9.4	9.0	8.5	12.8	12.2	15.1	8.7	11.9
On jobs, business, money								
matters	17.1	13.8	18.2	24.3	21.7	17.5	26.0	23.8
Gift and giving	66.6	72.3	64.0	55.2	81.6	83.7	77.9	82.7
Gifts (nonmonetary)	65.0	70.2	63.1	54.1	79.1	82.2	76.5	76.1
Money	19.9	20.6	21.2	14.9	29.0	20.1	33.4	44.8
No assistance	21.6	19.1	23.2	24.9	13.3	10.5	16.1	15.1
Total respondents	1,020	480	374	166	1,020	480	374	166

[a] Respondents could give more than one response in a category. Totals of subcategories are therefore greater than that for the category itself.

Source: Cantor et al., *The Elderly in the Inner City*, New York City Office for the Aging, in press.

Effect of Ethnicity on Life Styles of the Inner-City Elderly **289** was even greater; eighty-seven percent of the respondents reported that their children helped in some way.

Looking first at the flow of assistance from parents to children, among all three ethnic groups, the giving of gifts, baby-sitting, and helping in times of illness were the most often reported forms of parent-child assistance. Spanish parents less frequently gave gifts involving money that did white and black parents, reflecting unquestionably to some degree their lower income. But, more importantly, the Spanish elderly still appeared to have a more direct role in the family than their black or white peers, and were far more often involved in giving advice with respect to running the home, child rearing, and making major decisions on such things as jobs or substantial purchases. They were also more involved in helping to raise grandchildren than were white or black grandparents. Whites and blacks, on the other hand, although available for help to children in times of illness and for occasional baby-sitting, appeared to play a more passive role with respect to family operations. Their main form of assistance on a regular basis appeared to be gift giving.

A similar pattern with respect to degree of actual involvement in day-to-day chores of life is seen when we look at what children did for parents (as reported by the parents). Help from children was, if anything, even more extensive than parents helping children. Almost nine out of ten older people having children reported such help (see Table 2).

As one might expect, gift giving and crisis assistance were the principal forms of assistance reported by respondents of all three ethnic groups. Among all three ethnic subgroups similarly high proportions of respondents received gifts from children (78 percent black elderly, 84 percent white and Spanish). There were, however, some significant differences in the form of gift. Spanish elderly, with the lowest incomes, more frequently received monetary gifts, followed by blacks. Among the white respondents, gifts were generally in the form of objects (a coat or refrigerator) rather than money.

The difference in type of gift may well reflect the greater need for money on the part of Spanish and black elderly, and a reluctance on the part of white elderly to accept monetary gifts that connote greater dependency.

Children of all three ethnic subgroups assisted equally in time of illness; the proportions of respondents receiving crisis intervention were virtually identical (67 percent white, 68 percent black, 69 percent Spanish) (see Table 2).

Although a similarly high proportion (approximately two thirds) of each subgroup reported receiving some assistance from children in the chores of daily living, there were noticeable differences in the form of the assistance. Spanish and black children appeared to be significantly more involved than white children in such things as shopping and running errands, keeping house, and preparing meals. This greater involvement undoubtedly is partially a reflection of the closer geographic proximity of black and Spanish parents to children, but it is probably also a manifestation of the continuing influence of the extended family structure.

Even more significant with respect to the nuclear family and independence, far fewer white respondents reported that children gave advice in matters of daily living than was the case among the black and Spanish elderly. Among blacks and Spanish, at least one quarter received advice regularly from their children.

Our data clearly indicate that the Spanish elderly, and to some extent the black elderly, are still part of an extended family network encompassing frequent contact and much direct mutual assistance. White elderly, although involved with their children, are less directly involved in day-to-day household activities and have a less time-consuming, a less specified, and a less direct role with respect to the lives of their children. It is, of course, impossible to predict how long this extended protective family system will continue for the Spanish and black elderly. From the attitudinal material in our study, it would appear that the impact of the dominant culture is already having its effect and that the Spanish elderly more than any other group are feeling the strains of attempting to bridge two cultures.

DISCUSSION AND IMPLICATIONS

The foregoing findings point to the important strengths held and difficulties faced by the inner-city elderly of New York.

First, with respect to the newest arrivals, the Spanish elderly as a group are at the younger end of the elderly continuum and have fewer years of residency in the city, although still a substantial amount. Spanish elderly tend to be still married and living with a spouse and may even have a younger child still in the household. Economically, they are the worst off, both with respect to when they leave the labor force and to their level of job skills. Because of relative lack of skill and education they held the lowest paying jobs during their adult years and, if covered by Social Security, receive only minimum benefits. Many, however, are not even covered by Social Security, and they are less likely to be covered by Medicare. However, the Spanish elderly, although suffering from communication difficulties (many still speak only Spanish), have turned to Old Age Assistance and, therefore, Medicaid to a much greater degree than either their black or white peers. The municipal hospitals tend to function as their doctors, and without Medicare coverage they use private physicians to a lesser degree than do the black and white elderly. Low incomes and poor nutrition have undoubtedly contributed to their self-assessed poorer health, but here cultural factors are important, for illness is not considered something to hide but rather to talk about widely (especially among the women). But balanced against severe handicaps of language, economic privation, and lack of Social

Security coverage is the fact that the Spanish elderly, more than their peers, are still functioning within the protective environment of the extended family. Many indicate that they still have rights as elders, and they tend to interact strongly with their children in giving both advice and assistance in a variety of tasks from baby-sitting to shopping to fixing things in their childrens' homes. With less money, they are not as apt to give children material gifts but appear to have outlets for giving of themselves and a role to play within the family circle. However, this picture is being eroded as the younger generation of Spanish-background adults becomes more acculturated. Already 27 percent of the Spanish elderly live alone rather than within the extended family, and Spanish elderly show signs of mental stress and worry to a far greater degree than do black or white elderly. The very thing they worry most about—children and family matters—is indicative of the strains that are evident in the changing family situation among New Yorkers of Spanish background. It would appear that the future holds considerable uncertainty for the Spanish elderly, who in coming generations will probably be caught up in the same dilemma of role crisis presently faced by their peers.

The black elderly are facing many of the same economic and minority-group problems as the Spanish elderly without some of the redeeming features of close-knit, extended family life. Although slightly better off economically than their Spanish peers, they too suffer from extremely low incomes, job discrimination, and forced early retirement for the men. Social Security coverage is far from complete, particularly among women, many of whom continue to work into their late sixties and early seventies. Like the Spanish, black elderly tend to receive minimum or near-minimum Social Security benefits. They are more likely to be covered by Medicare and when ill tend to use private physicians or the clinics of the voluntary hospitals.

Because of poverty and discrimination in childhood and adulthood, blacks have seven years less life expectancy than whites and report poorer health and a greater incidence of chronic illness than white elderly. A somewhat different family pattern is evident among the black elderly. Although most married at one time, fewer blacks in old age are still married and living with a spouse than among the other two subgroups. The incidence of divorce and/or separation is more frequent among blacks, and widowhood is as prevalent as among whites. As a result, there are more female-headed homes with younger family members living in the households of the grandmother. Blacks report slightly less emotional closeness to children, although the majority of their children live within the city limits or in the immediate neighborhoods of the elderly and there is contact between the generations. Black parents help children out somewhat less often than Spanish elderly but seem to play a more direct role in the functioning of their childrens' households than do white elderly. They give gifts as freely as their white peers, although they have less income, and in turn children are available for assistance in time of crisis. However, intervention on the part of children on a day-to-day basis is not as frequent as among Spanish families. Black elderly in need seem more willing than whites to accept Old Age Assistance, but not all black respondents estimated as eligible for income maintenance assistance are getting such help. Among the blacks, increasing numbers appear to be living alone in old age, and it is likely that in the future the problem of live-alones will reach proportions similar to that found among the white population.

Of the three subgroups, black elderly express the greatest satisfaction with their lives in old age and worry the least. It is impossible to determine the exact meaning of this higher level of life satisfaction. Are such attitudes genuinely indicative of present happiness or are they perhaps a reaction formed in response to the discrimination suffered by blacks in this country, a psychologically protective stance adapted early in childhood and carried over into old age? Certainly, black elderly face severe problems of

low income, poor health, inadequate housing, and difficulty in obtaining supportive assistance from both the community and often from their families; their high scores on measures of life satisfaction must be accepted with some hesitation. However, just reaching sixty-five may indeed be a cause for considerable satisfaction.

The white elderly in the poverty areas of the inner-city present a conflicting picture. Most have been lower-middle or middle class during their adult years; old age for them brings not only role loss but severe economic and often social discontinuity. Living longer, many more are found living alone; the incidence of live-alones is particularly high in the case of women, who far outnumber men and are not as likely to remarry upon loss of spouse. Residing in changing neighborhoods, often among hostile neighbors whom they cannot understand, there is considerable fear of crime and of persons different from one's self.

On the other hand, the white elderly have lived in New York a long time; they have strong feelings of belonging and are particularly appreciative of the easily accessible neighborhood facilities and the richness and variety of city life. They are staunch New Yorkers and speak about the city with considerable affection, although recognizing the problems inherent in deteriorating neighborhoods.

The white elderly, although slightly better off than their Spanish and black peers, are truly New York's hidden poor. They have strong feelings of pride and are unwilling to accept easily the help available, such as Old Age Assistance, if it means any loss of independence or dignity. Although most have living children in the area with whom they feel close and are in contact, the separation between the generations is complete in most cases. Children and parents help each other in times of crisis, but involvement in the details of daily living is neither expected nor desired on the part of white elderly nor does it appear to be forthcoming from children, many of whom live outside the immediate neighborhood. Love and affection is shown through gifts, money, visiting, phoning, and emergency help or occasional baby sitting; other types of more direct intervention, including advice giving, are rare. Parents and adult children function as two separate nuclear families, and this separation is both accepted and real.

For the black and Spanish elderly the community must be prepared to accept considerable financial responsibility to compensate for low retirement incomes and poor work histories. The entire cost of adequate housing, health, nutrition, and the variety of services needed by older people certainly cannot be assumed by most black or Spanish elderly, given their low incomes. White elderly, given rising Social Security benefits and pensions, may in the future be better able to assume a greater part of the cost of their needs. But problems of greater isolation from family and higher incidence of living alone will continue to require supportive community services for them as well; particularly in the case of the older and more frail elderly and the unattached women, the two groups of white elderly most often found living alone and with the lowest incomes. In addition, many white elderly need economic assistance, but it must be given in a way that does not strip pride and destroy independence. Hopefully, the assumption of Old Age Assistance by the Social Security system will mean greater economic security for the elderly of all three ethnic groups, coupled with a consideration for personal feelings and for a sense of personal dignity. The elderly of the inner city and their peers throughout the city have contributed long hard years of work and they deserve an old age of respect, dignity, and freedom from want. If today's older New Yorkers fail to realize such a life, so will coming generations.

Acknowledgment

The research reported here was supported by Administration on Aging Grant AA-4-70-089-02.

REFERENCES

BLAU, Z. S. *Old Age in a Changing Society, New Viewpoints.* New York: Franklin Watts Press, 1973.

CANTOR, M. H., and MAYER, M. *Health Crisis of Older New Yorkers.* New York: New York City Office for the Aging, 1972.

———. et al. *The Elderly in the Inner City.* New York: New York City Office for the Aging, 1975 (in press).

CLARK, M., and ANDERSON, B. G. *Culture and Aging.* Springfield, Ill.: Charles C Thomas, 1967.

GELWICKS, L., FELDMAN, A., and NEWCOMER, R. J. *Report on Older Population: Needs, Resources and Services.* Los Angeles: Los Angeles Gerontology Center, University of Southern California, 1971.

HOLLINGSHEAD, A. B., and REDLICH, F. C. *Social Class and Mental Illness.* New York: Wiley, 1958.

KENT, D., and HIRSCH, C. *Needs and Use of Services Among Negro and White Aged,* Vols. I and II. University Park, Pa.: Pennsylvania State University, July 1971 and October 1972.

LITWAK, E. "Extended Kin Relations in an Industrial Democratic Society." In *Social Structure and the Family,* edited by E. Shanas and G. Streib. Englewood Cliffs, N.J.: Prentice-Hall, 1965.

ROSE, A., and PETERSON, W. A., eds. *Older People and Their Social World.* Philadelphia: F. Davis, 1965.

ROSOW, I. *Social Integration of the Aged.* New York: Free Press, 1967.

SHANAS, E., et al. *Old People in Three Industrial Societies.* New York: Atherton, Press, 1968.

TOWNSEND, P. *The Family Life of Old People.* London: Routledge & Kegan Paul, Ltd., 1957.

U.S. Bureau of the Census, 1970 Census of Population. Washington, D.C.: USGPO.

U.S. Department of Labor, Bureau of Labor Statistics. *Three Budgets for a Retired Couple in Urban Areas of the United States, 1969–70.* Washington, D.C.: USGPO.

SECTION 5

Life After Work

Work, of whatever kind, is a central organizing feature in every adult life. The character of work changed in the last century in this country, and the extent of worklife has slowly shifted. The question of mandatory retirement, recently the subject of major federal legislation, has occupied theorists, social planners, and the elderly in industrialized countries over the past several decades. The ramifications of forced retirement vary by social position, employment history, individual expectations, and societal norms. While it is not always the case that people enjoy their work so much that they are dismayed at the thought of relinquishing it, it is certainly true that retirement entails serious life changes. For a great number of elderly, withdrawal from active participation in the labor force necessitates both financial re-evaluation as well as a modification of self-concept. The meaning of work in one's life, and the related importance of retirement, constitute two of the most significant variables influencing morale, adjustment, and life satisfaction among the middle-aged and aged.

As Figure 1 indicates, labor force participation rates have declined considerably for American males since 1940, while life expectancy has increased nearly twenty years for American men during the twentieth century. The latter increase in years has not been absorbed into the lifelong patterns of work, however. Thus, males born today can expect to work less than two-thirds of their lives, spending over twenty-five years of their lives outside of active labor force participation. The figures for women, on the other hand, have shown steady increases in both life expectancy and years of active work life. Since 1900 men have added to their years in the labor force by twenty-five percent; women have added to theirs by almost 400 percent (U.S. Department of Labor, 1976).

Figure 1

Labor Force participation rates in the United States: 1940–1975.

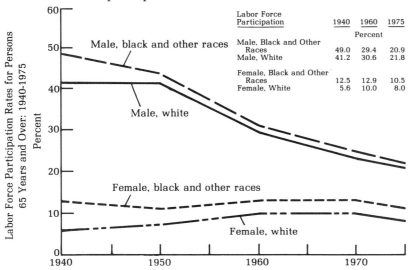

Labor Force Participation	1940	1960	1975
	Percent		
Male, Black and Other Races	49.0	29.4	20.9
Male, White	41.2	30.6	21.8
Female, Black and Other Races	12.5	12.9	10.5
Female, White	5.6	10.0	8.0

Source: *Status: A Monthly Chartbook of Social and Economic Trends,* U.S. Department of Commerce, Bureau of the Census. (Washington, D.C.: Government Printing Office, 1976), p. 30.

The nature of occupational distribution varies by age as well as by gender. In 1975, for example, roughly the same proportion of employed women between the ages of fifty-five and sixty-four, and sixty-five and over, were white collar workers (56 and 54 percent respectively). The distribution differed for the categories of blue-collar and service workers. The proportion of fifty-five to sixty-four year old women employed in blue-collar jobs was twice that for elderly women, 17 to 9 percent. Finally, one-fourth of the middle-aged employed women were service workers, while one-third of the elderly employed women were classified in service jobs. Similar trends are observed among American males, with blue-collar workers predominating among the middle-aged (43 percent, compared to 25 percent of the elderly employed occupying blue collar positions). The disparity is not as great for either white collar or service jobs (U.S. Department of Commerce, 1976).

What has happened since Germany's Chancellor Bismarck established the first integrated pension system in 1884, making benefits payable at age sixty-five? The number of years people can expect to live after retirement has grown from none to five or ten, the numbers of people surviving past retirement have grown dramatically, and the ability of those over sixty-five to continue working has improved. Until the mid-1970s, there was little pressure for the abolition of the mandatory retirement age, established by the Social Security legislation of 1935. In 1978, in response to the influence of heightened public awareness and activity by interest groups representing the elderly, Congress voted to raise the mandatory retirement age to seventy and to abolish forced retirement for federal employees. The changes, which will be phased in over the next two to three years, potentially affect over two-thirds of the labor force. Special exemptions from this extension of retirement age were granted to colleges and universities and businesses with high-level executive positions.

The state of California enacted a law in September 1977 prohibiting forced retirement of private and state employees unless they are proven incapable of performing their jobs. Even critics of mandatory retirement are hesitant to give wholehearted approval to this scheme, maintaining that competency evaluations may prove as traumatic in some instances as an arbitrary retirement age.

The adequacy of pension benefits is a crucial consideration in the timing of retirement. Social security benefits in the United States are modified continuously. A major tax change, approved in December 1977, provides for an increase in the tax base from $16,500 to $17,700 in 1978, with a corresponding increase in the tax rate from 5.85 percent to 6.05 percent; the maximum social security tax to be paid by both employer and employee is $1071 for that year. By 1987 the maximum payment is scheduled to reach $3046, which represents a tax rate of 7.15 percent on the base income of $42,600. These amendments were prompted in part by the declining balance in the social security trust fund. With greater levels of inflation, higher benefit payments, and more retired persons drawing benefits, the drain on the fund has caused considerable consternation. The amendments also offer some incentives for working after retirement. In 1977, people willing to work past age sixty-five received a 1 percent per year increase in benefits; that amount is now raised to 3 percent. In addition, the level at which social security benefits are reduced by one dollar for every two dollars of earnings was increased from $3000 to $4000 for individuals over age sixty-five, with projected increases of $500 each year through 1982.

The amount of benefits received is related to work history. Since women have exhibited entirely different occupational patterns, their treatment under pension programs has varied from that of most male employees. A 1977 task force study of sex discrimination in Social Security regulations by the Department of Health, Education, and Welfare highlighted several major inequities. Because of the types of jobs available to middle-aged and elderly women, a married couple with only one wage earner would qualify for higher social security benefits than a couple with two wage earners who had the same average lifetime earnings. Reflecting our societal norms and values, the Social

Security program gives somewhat better protection to a couple with one spouse who fulfills the role of unpaid homemaker. Previous studies have also urged reform in the social security laws to keep pace with the changing nature of family relationships (United States Senate, 1973), recommending, for example, that homemakers should be given social security coverage in their own right. Recognition that women will continue their active participation in the labor force should be coupled with the fact of limited entry into professional and managerial positions. All these variables must be considered by those attempting to revamp the coverage offered by Social Security. Social insurance programs will continue to be the subject of attention for many years to come.

Retirement brings with it a variety of changes. Not only are financial resources curtailed, but self-concept, health, and family relationships are affected by the passage from the role of worker to retired person. There is no doubt that adequate income is a primary factor in successful adjustment to retirement. Marital and health status are also related to the decision to retire, and will certainly affect satisfaction with retirement. Perhaps of greater interest, from the perspective of intervention, is the finding that planning for retirement enhances one's adjustment to and satisfaction with non-work roles (Barfield and Morgan, 1978).

We often assume that leisure time is automatically pleasurable. It seems a little absurd to say that we must be taught how to play, yet this is more often the case than not. One of the major difficulties confronting those who retire is how to structure their time. Work inscribes a regular pattern on a person's life, and the absence of that pattern may be very disorienting. It would be an impossible task to describe time apart from work, for the variety is infinite. Leisure is not simply free time, or non-work time. Its definition will differ from person to person; for some, leisure means rest or passive relaxation, for others, leisure is one of several work-like activities. Socialization for retirement must include anticipating the significant increase in leisure time, no matter how it is to be spent. Perhaps maximizing the conscious decision-making will further a positive adjustment to retirement. It often requires, after all, as much of a decision to take no action as it does to take some small action (Gordon and Gaitz, 1976).

The readings in this section are concerned with different aspects of work and retirement among the elderly. These concepts can be defined and measured in several ways, though active and continued participation in the labor force is a common measure. The first two selections offer a general overview of work and retirement experiences among the world's aged. The stereotypes that contribute to age discrimination affect the older person's view of himself or herself as much as they influence society's treatment of the elderly. Examination of the notions that older workers are less productive, hinder the advancement of, and are educationally inferior to younger workers reveals the pervasiveness of these ideas within the business sector. In contrast to these not-so-subtle forms of age discrimination, Pendrell details the structural changes that have been made in several European countries to accommodate the large numbers of healthy, active elderly who resist the inflexible retirement mandates common in most industrialized nations. The search for alternatives is being pursued in the United States as well, as our previous discussion of retirement age indicates.

A brief look at the evolution of labor force composition and activity is presented by a Department of Labor report. As we noted earlier, women are increasingly active in the labor force, a trend which is predicted to continue over the next several decades. Jaslow's article on morale among older women lends support to those who advocate the advantages of maintaining a work role if one is able and desires to do so. While he relies on cross-sectional analyses, some of the patterns he describes may well prove valid for studies following women through their work careers.

Just as some are urging total abolition of mandatory retirement, others are espousing the advantages of early retirement. Barfield and Morgan indicate the decision to retire at an age younger than sixty-five may be significantly related to a person's historical experience. Recalling the age-stratification theory described in the first selection of Section 4, the cohort effect has emerged as a possible index to retirement planning and adjustment. Ideally, examination of longitudinal data will validate and expand this finding.

Longitudinal data from the well-known Duke University cooperative research project provides evidence that personal resources are strongly associated with morale and adaptation to retirement. As we would expect, marital and socioeconomic status are correlated with life satisfaction after retirement. Further exploration of the command of personal resources as it relates to aging should prove a fertile ground for gerontological research in areas other than work and retirement.

Finally, John Dyer summarizes public and private pension programs in industrialized countries. He warns that private pensions may not be around forever, though their demise does not appear to be within the foreseeable future.

REFERENCES

1. U.S. DEPARTMENT OF LABOR, Bureau of Labor Statistics, Special Labor Force Report 187, *Length of Working Life for Men and Women, 1970* (Washington, D.C.: USGPO, 1976), p. 32.
2. U.S. DEPARTMENT OF COMMERCE, Bureau of the Census, *Status: a Monthly Chartbook of Social and Economic Trends* (Washington, D.C.: USGPO, 1976), p. 30.

3. U.S. SENATE, Special Committee on Aging, "Future Directions in Social Security," 93rd Cong., 1st Sess., Jan. 1973. (Washington, D.C.: USGPO, 1973).

4. RICHARD E. BARFIELD and JAMES N. MORGAN, "Trends in Satisfaction with Retirement," *The Gerontologist* 18 (1) (1978): pp. 19–23.

5. CHAD GORDON and CHARLES M. GAITZ, "Leisure and Lives: Personal Expressivity Across the Life Span," In *Handbook of Aging and the Social Sciences*, edited by R. H. Binstock and Ethel Shanas (New York: Van Nostrand Reinhold Company, 1976), pp. 310–41.

The Problem of Age Discrimination in Employment

William L. Kendig

It has been said that each day we live we grow wiser. It is certain that each day we live we grow older. In a society that values youth as highly as ours does, after a certain point age is considered a handicap in employment. Not only are older employees usually the most highly paid in the organization, but beliefs persist that older workers are not as productive as younger employees, that they do not keep up with technological changes, and so on and on. These beliefs are generally held toward employees over the age of forty or forty-five, who are frequently among the last hired and the first fired. Day after day each of us relentlessly grows older; day after day each of us not already there moves closer toward the age limits cited previously; each day might be likened to the ticking of a time bomb that could explode our personal lives with the reality of age discrimination. For each of us the time bomb is ticking; for each of us, age discrimination in employment could become a reality.

The president of a consulting firm summed up the corporate environment vis-à-vis age discrimination as follows:

It's amazing to discover the incidence of age discrimination in organizational life. It appears to be the only form of discrimination that has widespread ap-

proval within the structure of corporate life. Racial or religious discrimination has never been touted as a good idea. But how many times have you known of a manager praised and promoted because he headed an organization filled with "young tigers"? "Old lions" just don't seem to boost managers up the corporate ladder.

In the United States we have created and are creating an environment in which "young" is better than "old." Such a philosophy appears to have become an underlying corporate value. . . .

Overt and subtle age discrimination creeps into almost every facet of personnel administration. . . .[1]

Age discrimination is important, because aging is a phenomenon that affects both sexes, all races, creeds, and colors, and members of all religious groups. Like many types of discrimination, age discrimination is often difficult to identify and to prove. Its forms are usually subtle, whether in the workplace or the executive suite. It is often based more upon generally accepted requirements that have never been exposed to the rigors of statistical or scientific testing than on any valid data or studies. While age discrimination exists in all types of jobs, managers and professionals appear to be especially vulnerable to it, since most of them are not organized, and since most of them have no contractual relationship with their employers. Many victims of age discrimination at the professional and managerial levels are hesitant to publicly expose their plight; in most instances they believe they can solve their own problems and that exposure of age discrimination might impede their reemployment elsewhere. However, since passage of the Federal Age Discrimination in Employment Act, many cases have been filed by the Labor Department. These cases provide partial evidence to support the inference of widespread discrimination against older professionals and managers. A summary of a number of these cases will be presented in a later section of this Briefing.

A newspaper article titled "Age Bias Poses A Big Problem" addresses the problem of age discrimination against older employees (executives over forty, in particular) as follows:

> When a business executive over the age of forty is passed for promotion or loses his job, chances are 50-50 he is the victim of age discrimination, although it would be hard to prove.

> "Age discrimination is the most elusive and damaging type of discrimination," says Carin Ann Clauss, associate solicitor of the U.S. Fair Labor Standards Division. "It cuts down workers in their prime."

> Ms. Clauss, a Labor Department expert on age bias, says it is more difficult to prove than race or sex discrimination, because most of its victims are in positions that are difficult to assess for productivity. A short-order cook can be checked to determine whether forty hamburgers still are coming off the grill every hour, but how is the output of a manager measured? If auto sales fall, is it the quality control manager's fault or the energy crisis?

> Since Congress passed the age discrimination law in 1968, nearly 7,000 Labor Department investigations reveal that white collar workers, especially in middle and upper management, are the most common victims. Next are unskilled laborers. Least affected are employees with valuable mechanical skills and union protection. . . .

> An economy move is most effective when you can eliminate executives over the age of forty. These older managers and executives usually are paid more than younger men in similar posts, the opening up of their jobs stimulates younger men with the prospect of promotion and, by turning out a senior executive before retirement age, the company avoids paying full pension benefits.

> With unskilled labor, the financial benefits are not so great on a per capita basis. But releasing scores of older workers whose longevity has brought them higher pay and replacing them with younger people at starting wages is beneficial to the balance sheet.

> Skilled labor is least affected by age discrimination because persons in these jobs usually are in production and companies trying to curb expenses eliminate production workers last. In addition, the shrinking number of skilled workers in many industries enhances their value regardless of age.[2]

Many of the cases that will be cited relate to age discrimination against professionals and managers. In some companies it appears to be accepted that it is cheaper for the company to hire professionals (such as engineers) and retain them for fifteen or twenty years, with little effort to keep them up to date on the latest changes in their fields, and then to let them go, than it is to attempt to update their skills. After all, these professionals can be replaced by beginning-level employees with the latest skills at no training cost to the company.

Not only are the older employees more likely to be eliminated from their positions with a current employer, but if a company goes bankrupt or closes a facility, the older employee has the most difficulty in locating another job. It was reported that when Studebaker Corporation ceased to operate during 1963, more than 8,000 employees lost their jobs; the younger the employee, the easier it was for him or her to find other employment.[3] When the American Viscose Corporation closed its textile plant in Roanoke, Virginia, in 1958, a similar situation occurred. Five years after the plant closed, approximately 60 percent of all prior employees had found other employment, but only 38 percent of those forty-five or older had found employment.[4] When the Packard Motor Company shut its doors, 58 percent of the younger employees obtained positions with the big-three car manufacturers within one year, but only 30 percent of those between forty-five and fifty-four and 15 percent of those between fifty-five and sixty-four were re-employed within the same time period.[5]

What are the possible reasons for age discrimination in employment, and what forms does it take? Most of the reasons usually given are grounded in economics. Some of the more common ones cited are:

1. A belief that older employees are not as efficient as younger employees; hence the retention or hiring of older employees increases the operating costs of the organization. This is based upon the belief that abilities decline with age.
2. Rising costs of such fringe benefits as pensions, health insurance, and life insurance as the average age of employees increases.
3. The belief that employing too many older employees limits the advancement opportunities of more youthful employees, thus encouraging them to seek employment elsewhere.
4. The desire of the organization to present a youthful image; this reason becomes particularly important to some organizations catering to youth.
5. Educational obsolescence in highly technical areas; for instance, in some highly technical areas (such as engineering) it appears to be easier—and cheaper—to hire younger employees with the latest technological training than to attempt to keep the training of those already employed up to date.
6. Employee rigidity; older employees are less likely to accept transfers than are younger employees.
7. Limited number of productive years left after the employee has learned the job. This becomes a critical factor in those positions where it may take a number of years to master a skill.
8. A policy of promotion only from within, with relatively low beginning salaries that would not be attractive to older employees.

Some of the forms taken by age discrimination in employment include:

1. *Dismissal of older employees without cause.* This happens most often in professional, middle management, and white-collar groups and non-union organizations. It seldom happens to employees in strong unions, since labor-management contracts generally contain seniority clauses to protect older members and provide for a grievance procedure whereby the company must prove its reason for dismissal.
2. *Involuntary retirement on an individual basis and not agreed upon as a condition of employment.* Involuntary retirement occurs whenever an individual is required to retire before he chooses to. However, involuntary retirement that is part of an accepted retirement plan is legal. For instance, if a negotiated pension agreement requires everyone to retire at sixty-five, but gives management the option of requesting retirement at sixty-two, it is perfectly legal for it to do so. But, if an employee is not covered by an agreement and is involuntarily retired, age discrimination is usually involved.

3. *Maximum age limitations for initial employment within an organization with little or no supporting justification for such a requirement.* This type of requirement will be commented upon extensively in the review of the case against a transportation firm that has established thirty-five as the maximum entry age for hiring drivers.

4. *Limitations placed upon promotion and/or training based upon age.* This refers to many of the unwritten organizational practices that stop an employee from being considered for training or further promotion if he has not reached a certain level in the hierarchy by a certain age.

5. *Consideration of only younger employees for certain positions without valid occupational reasons for doing so.* This type of discrimination is often identified by the placement of ads that stress "recent college grads," "youthful appearance," "junior executive," etc.

What does the loss of employment mean to the middle-aged or older individual? During 1973 it was reported that more than 867,000 persons over the age of forty-five were out of work.[6] The impact on the individual was described by one author as follows:

> Of the several thousand middle-aged men who will lose their jobs this month, only about 20 percent, one year from now, will have solved their problem to the extent that they are working in jobs as good as the one they lost with salaries as high as before, in a job, in business for themselves or otherwise. Quite a few of these will have lost a substantial part of the savings they had when they lost their job.

> Another 20 percent will still be job hunting and will be quite desperate.

> About an equal number will have gone into business for themselves, and many will have failed or be failing; or will have taken commission selling jobs, with few men succeeding.

> About one-third will either have taken low-paying jobs in which they are unhappy; or will have found, and then lost, one, two, or even three jobs and will be wondering what is wrong.

> Some will have had physical or mental breakdowns, and there will be some suicides. An alarming number of homes and marriages will have been broken up.[7]

It was against this background of human waste and misery brought on by age discrimination in employment that the Federal Age Discrimination in Employment Act was passed.

NOTES

1. Frank P. Doyle, "Age Discrimination and Organizational Life," *Industrial Gerontology* (Summer 1973), pp. 30–31.
2. Leonard Curry, "Age Bias Poses a Big Problem," United Press International: *Washington Evening Star,* June 10, 1974.
3. U.S. Department of Labor, Workplace Standards Administration, Wage and Hour Division, and the Secretary of Labor, "The Law Against Age Discrimination in Employment" (Washington, D.C.: USGPO 1970), p.2.
4. Ibid.
5. Harold L. Sheppard, ed., *Toward an Industrial Gerontology: an Introduction to a New Field of Applied Research and Service* (Cambridge, Mass.: Schenkman Publishing Co., 1970), p. 106.
6. Senator Edward M. Kennedy, "The Age Discrimination in Employment Act: Highlights from a Management Seminar" (keynote address), *Industrial Gerontology* (Summer 1973), p. 3.
7. Louis H. Albee, *Over Forty—Out of Work?* (Englewood Cliffs, N.J.: Prentice-Hall, Inc., 1970), p. 3.

Old Age Around the World

Nan Pendrell

In a little remarked but very important paper, Fred Cottrell made the point, "Business is simply not going to take adequate care of most of the aging."[1] Cottrell is concerned with the convergence of growing populations of the aging and the proliferation of privately owned energy systems. This concern is rooted in his well-known researches into the relationships between energy availability and production, and cultural evolution. Thus a decade ago Cottrell adumbrated Barry Commoner's most recent views: the political and socioeconomic consequences of corporation control of energy production and distribution entail increasing global unemployment along with increasing accumulation and concentration of private profit.[2] In Commoner's view, only socialism can resolve this contradiction.

There is a more or less clear line from Cottrell to Commoner and to other radicals such as Simone de Beauvoir, who holds the view that in a capitalist economy "profit is the only thing that counts" and

> society cares about the individual only so far as he is profitable. . . . The young know this. Their anxiety as they enter in upon social life matches the anguish of the old as they are excluded from it. . . . We cannot satisfy ourselves by calling for a more generous "social pol-

icy". . . it is the whole system which is at issue.[3]

It should be noted that Commoner's *The Poverty of Power* does not isolate the aging as a discrete category; this may be the most significant thing the book teaches us. The contradictions generated by the energy crisis place the aging squarely amidst every group which has been and is being discarded by capitalist technology, regardless of chronological age. The exegesis amounts to marching orders. At the very least we shall have to define precisely what we mean by "retirement," and especially to distinguish between increasing technological umemployment, which decimates the labor force permanently, and other types of unemployment. This would seem to be especially important in the consideration of second careers. Unfortunately, we do not have data from which to determine whether the idea of second careers has any meaning at all for the technologically unemployed or whether it has utility only among restricted categories of professional service workers.

Nor is this merely a national or sectional matter. By the year 2000 the world population aged sixty and over will have reach 585 million—an increase of practically 100 percent in thirty years.[4] Despite the worldwide absolute and relative increase in the size and longevity of the aging population, there is a virtually universal trend toward earlier retirement from industry and even from agriculture. The trend toward increased longevity indicates a general im-

From *Social Policy* 7, 3 (1976), pp. 107–110. Reprinted by permission of *Social Policy* published by Social Policy Corporation, New York, New York 10036. Copyright 1976 by Social Policy Corporation.

provement in health and capability among the aging which is not reflected in retirement policy.[5]

Two sets of data are worth noting. In the more developed countries there is an increase in the number of persons aged seventy-five and eighty-five and over; some estimates suggest that one-third of the sixty-five-plus group is seventy-five and over. "Their proportions among the elderly are increasing more rapidly than those of any other age group sixty years and over."[6] Never before have so many lived so long. Yet persons who are forty-five years and over are "discriminated against in regard to continued employment in the labor force," *particularly in regard to re-entry once the worker has been displaced through technological innovation and change.* Indeed, there is no evidence, at least within highly developed Western technological economies, that throws doubt on the United Nations' conclusion that "employment opportunities are not expanding fast enough to accommodate both the young seeking to enter the labor force and the old seeking to remain in it."[7]

Moreover, despite increasing evidence that the unemployed older worker can compete successfully with younger workers (due to greater experience, more skill, etc.), the "notion of training for 'second careers' has not yet caught on in many developed or developing countries," even though in highly industrialized countries "an individual over the age of forty years begins to consider his age an economic handicap."[8]

The Council of Europe has also exhibited concern about similar socioeconomic implications of aging within its member nations. Longevity in these countries will increase from the present 71.9 years to 74.1 by the turn of the century. "This increase in the dependency ratio—i.e., the number of active versus nonactive members in the labor force—*may even be further aggravated if continuing pressures for earlier retirement succeed*" [emphasis added]. The Council of Europe, in its January 1975 Parliamentary Assembly report, further concluded that "the growing proportion of European elderly will impose a heavier burden on health and social services not necessarily offset by increased productivity or by the diminishing burdens attributable to falling fertility."

The consequences of aging populations were discussed further at a Council of Europe colloquium the following November which was attended by cabinet ministers, parliamentarians, and experts from fifteen European countries and the United States. Some speakers warned of imminent doom; others were more optimistic. None could offer solutions, and there was no consensus. One thought increased social burdens could be assumed provided steps were taken to assure the high productivity of the labor force, such as training and encouraging more women to take jobs. The final speaker's paper advised rethinking the concept of retirement, while, at the same time, he advocated greater humanization of the workplace.

While the problem of retirement is common to most countries, the actual retirement age varies widely (even more widely than the normal retirement age as defined by public policy in various countries—see Table 1. Labor shortage or surplus, type of work, climatic conditions, years of employment, and pension and social security plans are significant variables. In the United States sixty-five is the age at which full Social Security benefits are available, but most workers retire at sixty-two with reduced benefits, and earlier retirement has been noted for fully 50 percent of all male workers. In Canada many men retire as early as fifty-five. For both the United States and Canada, this a reflection of prolonged unemployment among middle-aged workers and of pressures to drop out of the labor force completely. The worker over forty-five years of age faces great difficulty in securing new jobs once be becomes unemployed. (Data from nine countries with mature social security systems and similar economies show increasing rates of unemployment of the aging during 1950 to 1970—see Table 2. In the Netherlands sixty may be the retirement age for those who have been doing heavy work. In France civil servants may retire between fifty-five and sixty.

TABLE 1

Normal retirement age as defined by public policy, selected countries.

COUNTRY	AGE (YEARS) WOMEN	MEN
Norway	70	70
Ireland	70	70
Denmark	67	67
Iceland	67	67
Sweden	67	67
Canada	65	65
Luxembourg	65	65
USA	65	65
Spain	65	65
Portugal	65	65
Netherlands	65	65
Switzerland	63	65
France	65	65
Finland	65	65
Israel	60	65
UK	60	65
East German Democratic Republic	60	65
West German Federal Republic	60	65
Austria	60	65
Poland	60	65
Australia	60	65
Belgium	60	65
Greece	57	62
USSR	55	60
Czechoslovakia	55	60
Japan	55	60
Italy	55	60
Hungary	55	60
Yugoslavia	55	60

Source: U.N., *The Aging*, 1975.

An Australian man who has been unemployed for more than one year may retire at sixty. In the socialist countries of Eastern Europe a number of special situations may reduce the normal retirement age. In the Soviet Union men may retire at sixty, women at age fifty-five; men must have worked a minimum of twenty-five years, females a minimum of twenty. Age requirements are ten years lower for those who work in the far north or in dangerous or hazardous occupations.

In Sweden workers may return from retirement at any time to assume a full-time job; under a flexible new retirement pension system, a Swedish worker may retire at sixty but also choose to work part-time and receive some pension benefits. As long as he or she works at least seventeen hours a week, partial pension and a wide range of fringe benefits are available. Authorities admit the problems or opening up part-time jobs requiring the skill and responsibilities demanded by full-time jobs.[9] The German Democratic Republic, which is experiencing a labor shortage, encourages the aging to remain at work by permitting them to draw a full pension along with salary.

The mounting social costs that inhere in rising longevity rates and in the growth of aging populations are matters of concern among gerontologists as well as among government leaders, economists, and behavioral scientists. At the Kiev International Congress of Gerontology in 1972, B. L. Neugarten called for objectivity in considering the claim of some "enthusiastic" gerontologists that "if life expectancy were increased by only five years, the effects would be so profound as to overturn our present economic and welfare institutions."[10]

A. J. Jaffe also considers that lowering the age of retirement, and thus "undoing the work ethnic," might have a vast effect on our economy. The retirement dilemma (also the title of Jaffe's paper) is the contradiction between a possible leisure-oriented culture and the present work-centered society. Does "training for leisure" place our future economy in jeopardy? On the other hand, he asks whether our society can really provide jobs for all who are able and willing to work.[11] This is a critical question since, as Jaffe reminds us, it is unlikely that our current economy and social norms can afford to maintain people in "idleness" decently and also because older people very often want to continue to work.

Elizabeth L. Meier's comprehensive analysis of the Louis Harris survey for the National Council on the Aging notes substantial differences in reply to the question: "The age at which people are *required* [her

TABLE 2

Rates of unemployment among persons over 65, countries with similar economies and mature social security systems, 1950–1970.

COUNTRY	1950	1960	1970	PERCENTAGE REDUCTION OF THOSE 65+ IN THE LABOR FORCE
USA	23.6	19.0	16.2	31.3
Canada	22.6	17.2	13.0	42.1
Belgium	10.2	6.3	5.6	45.0
France	22.6	17.5	12.5	47.4
West German Federal Republic	19.8	14.2	11.7	40.9
Italy	25.0	12.9	11.1	55.5
Netherlands	17.9	10.7	7.3	59.1
Sweden	21.2	15.1	8.6	59.5
UK	16.4	13.4	13.1	19.5
				Average 39.6

Source: Paul Fisher, "Labor Force Participation of the Aged and the Social Security System in Nine Countries," *Industrial Gerontology*, Winter 1975, pp. 1–14.

emphasis] to retire has gotten younger in recent years. Do you think this is a good thing, or not?" Those under sixty-five said earlier retirement was a good thing by 47 to 39 percent; those over sixty-five disagreed by almost the same proportion: 47 to 33 percent. Younger people felt that earlier retirement "gives people a chance to enjoy life," while those sixty-five and over felt that retirement "ages people."[12]

The Harris report notes that 10 percent of those aged fifty-five to sixty-four considered themselves to be unemployed; that is, in the labor force but currently unable to find a job. The figure of 10 percent is considerably above the official government unemployment figures reported as slightly over 2 percent for males and 3 percent for females in this age category, according to Meier. Marc Rosenblum has noted that because Bureau of Labor Statistics figures categorize "job-discouraged" workers as being totally outside the labor force, true unemployment rates may be skewed and greatly underestimated.[13] Meier adds that such exclusion from the labor force by BLS tabulations may be especially true of older women who have ceased to look for jobs. By statistical evasion and legal disqualification the question of older people's role in society is, without definitive

policy articulation, being resolved through their joining the ranks of the marginal. New public employment jobs fall under the Comprehensive Employment and Training Act (CETA) of 1973 and are determined by BLS unemployment figures. Rosenblum's *discouraged unemployment rate* incorporates the job-discouraged into the labor force and enumerates them as unemployed, instead of expunging them from the labor force tabulations. His figures reveal divergences of as much as over 15 percent from those of the BLS.

Despite the conviction of such organizations as the National Emergency Civil Liberties Committee (NECLC) that the right to a job is a civil liberty, that full employment in meaningful work is required by society to help resolve many social problems, old people remain disproportionately represented among those unemployed in America and they alone among enfranchised American citizens are excluded from all versions of full employment and antidiscrimination protecting legislation successfully established in law.

Indeed, the *New York Times* (June 26, 1976) demonstrated how age discrimination is enshrined in our judicial system of conventional wisdom in their reports on the Supreme Court's upholding a Massachusetts requirement that members of the uniformed branch of the state police retire at age fifty. The court conceded that the "treatment of the aged in this nation has not been wholly free of discrimination" but that the Massachusetts statute "cannot be said to discriminate only against the elderly," hence middle-age and "even old age is not an 'insular group' requiring extraordinary protection. . . ." Thus the states "have the right to set mandatory retirement ages for their employees—so long, that is, as the requirement is relevant to the job being performed." The ordering Court has declared all age-mandatory retirements a matter of states' rights at best; in fact, it may be an invitation to private employers to get the Massachusetts trophy for themselves.

NOTES

1. Fred Cottrell, "Aging and the Political System," in *Aging and Social Policy*, edited by John C. McKinney and Frank T. DeVyver (New York, 1966), pp. 82, 92.

2. Barry Commoner, *The Poverty of Power: Energy and the Economic Crisis* (New York, 1976).

3. Simone de Beauvoir, *The Coming of Age* (New York, 1972), p. 543.

4. United Nations, *The Aging: Trends and Policies*, Department of Economic and Social Affairs, ST/ESA/22 (New York, 1975).

5. See the valuable statement by Juanita M. Kreps, "Sex, Age, and Work," *New York Times*, April 19, 1976. It is a powerful argument for a re-examination of the early-retirement trend, which examination Kreps thinks is "inevitable."

6. U.N., *The Aging*.

7. Ibid., p. 31.

8. Ibid.

9. "Sweden Introduces Flexible Retirement," *Aging International* 3, no. 1 (Spring 1976), p. 11.

10. U.N., *The Aging*.

11. A. J. Jaffe, "The Retirement Dilemma," *Industrial Gerontology*, Summer 1972, pp. 76–77. Professor Jaffe's paper has attained the status of a standard reference in literature dealing with retirement and aging. But rather than endorsing large-scale economic growth to solve the problem of retirement, Jaffe questions how much economic growth is desirable *per se*.

12. Elizabeth L. Meier, "Over 65; Expectations and Realities of Work and Retirement," *Industrial Gerontology*, Spring 1975, pp. 95–109.

13. Marc Rosenblum, "The Last Push; From Discouraged Worker to Involuntary Retirement," *Industrial Gerontology*, Spring 1975, pp. 14–22.

Length of Working Life for Men and Women, 1970

Howard N. Fullerton, Jr.
James J. Byrne

In an industrialized society the average length of working life is an important long-term social and economic indicator. In the United States it has mirrored changes in longevity, labor force participation, and lifestyle. The calculation of working life tables allows estimation of replacement needs in occupations, time lost from work for various reasons, or numbers of separations from and accessions to the labor force. Data from 1970 working life tables indicate that since 1960 worklife expectancy[1] has continued to edge downward for men and to lengthen for women.[2]

CONTINUING TRENDS

The average number of years spent in the labor force by men has been declining since 1950. Largely this has been due to a slow decline in labor force participation among men at the older ages, especially above age fifty-five.

Over this entire century, life expectancy at birth for men has climbed by almost twenty years, while worklife expectancy has increased by less than half of that. Thus, av-

erage time not in the labor force has risen dramatically. (See Table 1). Practically all of the nonwork activity of men at the turn of the century occurred before entrance into the labor force. Now a large proportion of the nonwork years are spent in retirement, though an extended period of education has also delayed labor force entry for many men.

Since 1900 the overall life expectancy of women has increased from 50.7 years to 74.8 years, almost 50 percent. Of the twenty-four additional years, over two-thirds have been added to working life. As Table 1 shows, worklife expectancy of women at birth climbed from 6.3 to 22.9 years, an increase of over 250 percent. Thus, an enormous rise in worklife expectancy has occurred since 1900. After 1950, worklife expectancy among women rose at a faster rate than overall life expectancy, and time spent out of the labor force began to decline.

In 1900 the average man experienced five times as many years of labor force participation as the average woman; by 1970 that ratio had fallen to less than twice as many years. The ratio would be even lower if it were not for the fact that many married women still interrupt their careers to have children, to move to new locations with their husbands, or for other reasons. They also tend to retire somewhat earlier than men, at an average age of about sixty years.

United States Department of Labor, Bureau of Labor Statistics. *Monthly Labor Review* (February 1976): 31–35. (Washington, D.C.: United States Government Printing Office).

TABLE 1

Life and work expectancy at birth, selected years. (In years)

EXPECTANCY	1900[1]	1940[2]	1950[2]	1960[2]	1970
MEN					
Life expectancy	48.2	61.2	65.5	66.8	67.1
Work expectancy	32.1	38.1	41.5	41.1	40.1
Nonwork expectancy	16.1	23.1	24.0	25.7	27.0
WOMEN					
Life expectancy	50.7	65.7	71.0	73.1	74.8
Work expectancy	6.3	12.1	15.1	20.1	22.9
Nonwork expectancy	44.4	53.6	55.9	53.0	51.9
Women's worklife as a percent of men's worklife.	19.6	31.6	36.3	48.6	57.1

[1] Data for 1900 are for white persons in death registration States.
[2] Figures adjusted to remove 14- and 15-year-olds from the labor force to be consistent with 1970 (1900 is not comparable).

WORKLIFE EXPECTANCY OF MEN

As stated earlier, the 1970 data for men indicate a continuation of trends observed between 1950 and 1960; years spent in retirement have increased, because of a drop in labor force participation and a slight rise in longevity.[3] For example, in 1960 a 30-year-old male worker could expect to work for an additional 33.2 years,[4] one-half year less than his counterpart in 1950. By 1970, remaining worklife for the average 30-year-old man had declined to 32.3 years (Table 2), almost a year less than in 1960. Meanwhile, his expected time out of the labor force edged upward from 7.2 to 8.3 years from 1960 to 1970.

The decline in labor force participation among older men, which has led to the recent declines in worklife expectancy, has been a subject of much speculation in recent years. Lower participation has been attributed to numerous factors which have given men the option of earlier withdrawal from the labor force. Prominent among these possible explanations are improved pension plans, higher social security payments, broader government benefits, and greater labor force participation by wives. Thus, older workers who either wanted to retire or found it dif-

ficult to find a new job were better able to leave the labor force.

As shown in Table 3, men in most age groups exhibited similar rates of labor force entry and withdrawal in 1970 and in 1960. The main difference was their higher rate of withdrawal at age sixty and older in 1970, for the reasons discussed above.

WORKLIFE EXPECTANCY OF WOMEN

Marriage, childbearing, divorce, or widowhood affect the probability of women's labor force participation and thus their worklife expectancy. It would be an overwhelming task to calculate an expected worklife for each of the possible combinations of these changes and the ages at which they occur. Short of cataloging all possible variations, one can use either of two techniques for tabulating worklife expectancy: Estimate the experience of a "typical"[5] woman, or assume that women in a given marital or childcare status will remain permanently in that status. Both techniques are employed below.

In the first, the typical experience approach, one derives a worklife expectancy for a woman who marries at a typical age and has an average number of children with normal spacing intervals. Though few persons duplicate the exact experience of this typical woman, many experience patterns which are quite similar; hence, the typical woman's experience can be used as a rough guideline in estimating the length of working life for other women. In this case, we assume that the typical woman joins the labor force at age eighteen, marries at age twenty, and has two children. The first child is born when the mother is age twenty-two and the second when she is age twenty-five. Under 1970 conditions, worklife expectancy for such a woman at age eighteen is 33.9 years.

In the second approach to presenting worklife expectancy, one assumes that a single woman will remain single, a divorced woman will not remarry, and so forth. Using this technique, one obtains the figures presented in Table 2 and discussed below.

Single women. Under the assumption—as in Table 2—of no variation in death rates by marital status, twenty-year-old single women in the labor force in 1970 could expect to live an additional 56.7 years, of which 41.2 years would be spent in the labor force and 15.5 in nonwork activities. This represents an increase from 1960 of more than five years in nonwork expectancy, reflecting a decline of four years in worklife expectancy and an increase of one year in overall life expectancy.

After age thirty-five, worklife expectancy was about three years less than for the comparable age in 1960. For example, at age fifty-five the expected worklife was 10.9 years, down from 13.1. Compared with men in 1970, sixty-five-year-old single women could expect to work about a year less, but have about five more years of retirement due to greater longevity.

Mothers. The different timing of movement in and out of the labor force for childbearing makes it impossible to derive a worklife expectancy applicable to all young mothers.[6] Most childbearing is completed by age thirty-

five, however, and labor force participation becomes relatively continuous. Worklife expectancy of mothers in the labor force after the birth of their last child (Table 2) was somewhat lower at nearly every age than that of single women, though higher at some ages than for ever-married women without children (see Table 2.)

Childless women. Childless married women generally have a worklife expectancy intermediate between that of mothers and single women. At the youngest and oldest ages this pattern held true in 1970; at ages 35—44, their worklife expectancy was even lower than that of mothers in the labor force after the birth of their last child. At age forty-five, for example, childless women had an average of 13.4 years left in the labor force, while mothers in the labor force could expect to work 16.3 more years.

Widowed, Divorced, Separated Women. Women who were widowed, divorced, or separated showed the highest worklife expectancy of any marital status at the younger ages. After age thirty, however, their expectancy fell below that of single women. The long working life of these women was not surprising; many of them head households and have dependents, often experiencing heavy financial pressure. Their worklife expectancy in 1970 was generally about the same as in 1960.

Separations and Accessions among Women. Table 4 presents changes in women's labor force status associated with a number of demographic events in 1970. Rates for separation from the labor force and entry into the labor force (accession) were substantially lower than in 1960[7] for nearly every age, indicating more continuous patterns of labor force participation. Separation rates were much lower in 1970 among women under age thirty, for example, reflecting both low fertility and the tendency for women with young children to continue working.

TABLE 2

Expectancies of life, worklife, and non-labor force activity remaining for men and women in the labor force at selected ages and by marital and child status for women, 1970. (In years)

AGE	MEN	SINGLE WOMEN	EVER-MARRIED WOMEN		
			NO CHILDREN EVER BORN	WOMEN IN LABOR FORCE AFTER BIRTH OF LAST CHILD	DIVORCED, WIDOWED, AND SEPARATED[1]
LIFE EXPECTANCY					
20	49.6	56.7	56.7	56.7	56.7
25	45.2	51.9	51.9	51.9	51.9
30	40.6	47.2	47.2	47.2	47.2
35	36.0	42.4	42.4	42.4	42.4
40	31.6	37.8	37.8	37.8	37.8
45	27.3	33.3	33.3	33.3	33.3
50	23.2	28.9	28.9	28.9	28.9
55	19.5	24.8	24.8	24.8	24.8
60	16.1	20.8	20.8	20.8	20.8
65	13.1	17.0	17.0	17.0	17.0
WORKLIFE EXPECTANCY					
20	41.5	41.2	34.1	([2])	42.3
25	36.9	36.4	29.2	([2])	37.4
30	32.3	32.6	24.3	([2])	32.6
35	27.6	28.5	20.8	26.8	27.8
40	23.2	24.0	17.6	21.2	23.0
45	18.9	19.4	13.4	16.3	18.3
50	14.8	15.0	12.0	11.9	13.6
55	10.9	10.9	10.6	8.2	9.0
60	7.4	7.1	8.9	5.0	6.7
65	5.7	4.4	6.6	4.5	5.3
NONLABOR FORCE ACTIVITY					
20	8.1	15.5	22.6	([2])	14.4
25	8.3	15.5	22.7	([2])	14.5
30	8.3	14.6	22.9	([2])	14.6
35	8.4	13.9	21.6	15.6	14.6
40	8.4	13.8	20.2	16.6	14.8
45	8.4	13.9	19.9	17.0	15.0
50	8.4	13.9	16.9	17.0	15.3
55	8.6	13.9	14.2	16.6	15.8
60	8.7	13.7	11.9	15.8	14.1
65	7.4	12.6	10.4	12.5	11.7

[1] This column includes mothers. Women in these marital statuses were also included in the tabulations for the two previous columns.
[2] Not applicable.

TABLE 3

Estimated rates of men entering and leaving the labor force, 1960 and 1970.[1]

| | | 1960 SEPARATION RATE | | | | 1970 SEPARATION RATE | | |
AGE	ENTRY RATE	TOTAL	DUE TO DEATH	DUE TO WITH-DRAWAL	ENTRY RATE	TOTAL	DUE TO DEATH	DUE TO WITH-DRAWAL
16–19	543.3	1.4	1.4	—	476.0	1.7	1.7	—
20–24	60.0	1.8	1.8	—	84.2	2.3	2.3	—
25–29	14.6	1.7	1.7	—	12.1	2.0	2.0	—
30–34	—	2.1	2.1	0.1	—	2.5	2.3	0.2
35–39	—	3.9	3.9	1.0	—	4.4	3.1	1.3
40–44	—	5.6	4.6	1.0	—	6.7	4.9	1.8
45–49	—	9.7	7.5	2.2	—	11.0	7.6	3.4
50–54	—	19.2	12.3	6.9	—	17.2	11.8	5.4
55–59	—	31.2	18.5	12.7	—	32.9	18.6	14.3
60–64	—	78.2	28.4	49.8	—	103.3	28.4	74.9
65–69	—	162.7	43.4	119.3	—	170.7	43.6	127.1
70–74	—	124.5	59.7	64.8	—	166.4	61.8	104.6
75–79	—	167.5	87.6	79.9	—	169.3	89.6	79.7
80–84	—	249.8	138.3	111.5	—	284.6	130.6	154.0
85+	—	—	—	—	—	—	—	—

[1] Entries per 1,000 persons in the stationary population; separations per 1,000 persons in the stationary labor force.

TABLE 4

Estimated rates of women entering and separating from the labor force, 1970.[1]

| | | ENTRY RATE RELATED TO: | | | | SEPARATION RATE RELATED TO: | | |
AGE GROUP	TOTAL ENTRY RATE	CHILDREN REACHING SCHOOL AGE	LOSS OF HUSBAND	AGING	TOTAL SEPARATION RATE	BIRTH OF CHILDREN	DEATH	AGING
16–19	66.2	0.0	0.0	66.2	24.5	23.8	0.7	0.0
20–24	22.7	1.0	.0	21.7	42.5	41.7	.8	.0
25–29	6.0	5.6	.2	.3	18.4	15.3	.9	2.2
30–34	10.0	8.4	.2	1.4	11.0	7.1	1.2	2.8
35–39	12.2	7.3	.3	4.5	4.8	2.9	1.8	.0
40–44	7.2	3.4	.3	3.5	3.7	.9	2.8	.1
45–49	1.6	.9	.7	.0	15.0	.1	4.2	10.7
50–54	1.8	.0	1.8	.0	33.1	.0	6.2	27.0
55–59	2.3	.0	2.3	.0	61.8	.0	9.0	52.8
60–64	2.4	.0	2.4	.0	165.9	.0	12.8	153.1
65–69	2.3	.0	2.3	.0	193.2	.0	19.8	173.3
70–74	.6	.0	.6	.0	234.8	.0	31.1	203.7
75–79	.6	.0	.0	.0	235.1	.0	51.6	183.4
80–84	.0	.0	.0	.0	244.6	.0	84.0	160.6
85+	.0	.0	.0	.0	1,000.0	.0	354.0	646.0

[1] Entries per 1,000 persons in the stationary population; separations per 1,000 persons in the stationary labor force.

NOTE: Numbers were independently rounded and components do not always add to totals.

CONCLUSIONS

Worklife expectancy in the United States has changed continually, usually growing for both men and women. Between 1960 and 1970 the most pronounced trend was a continued expansion of women's worklife expectancy at birth, which climbed from 20.1 years to 22.9 years during the decade. Combined with a slight decrease in worklife expectancy among men, this means that women are increasing their contribution to wage and salary employment in the United States.

The striking feature about recent growth in women's worklife expectancy is that it has occurred among married women, including those with children. In 1970, one in three women with children under six was in the labor force; this compares with an average of about one in five as late as 1960. Motherhood, traditionally the most important symbol of differentiated sex roles, is less of a barrier to a career than ever before.

NOTES

1. The term "worklife expectancy" is based upon tabulations of the number of persons who are engaged in various types of market employment or who are unemployed. Thus household work and other types of unpaid employment are not counted as part of one's worklife.

2. This is the latest in a series of reports on the length of working life. It will be reprinted with additional tabular data and an explanatory note as a Special Labor Force Report. The most recent report on this subject for men contained data for 1968; it was published in Howard N. Fullerton, "A Table of Expected Working Life for Men, 1968," *Monthly Labor Review*, June 1971, pp. 49–55. The most recent report for women contained data for 1960; it was published as *Work Life Expectancy and Training Needs of Women* (U.S. Department of Labor, Manpower Administration, 1967). Manpower Report No. 12. A table of working life for men in 1960 was published in Stuart Garfinkle, "Table of Working Life for Men, 1960," *Monthly Labor Review*, July 1963, pp. 820–23.

For an extensive description of working life patterns and a detailed exposition of the techniques used in the preparation of tables of working life, see *Tables of Working Life: Length of Working Life for Men*, Bulletin 1001 (Bureau of Labor Statistics, 1950). For a detailed description of the methodology of working life tables for women, see *Tables of Working Life for Women, 1950*, Bulletin 1204 (Bureau of Labor Statistics, 1956).

3. An important problem associated with working life tables is that they are based upon past or current rates of mortality and labor force participation, but are often used to predict the length of future working life. Such predictions are accurate only if these rates remain constant, but in fact the rates are subject to continual change, especially worker rates. If the rate changes are not dramatic, working life tables may provide adequate approximations of future length of working life; otherwise, one must predict future mortality and worker rates in order to calculate worklife expectancy for the future. To illustrate the problem, if the worker rates of women continue to rise sharply during the coming years, then women currently in the labor force will have a longer average worklife than that reflected in the 1970 estimates of worklife expectancy.

4. *The Length of Working Life for Males* (U.S. Department of Labor, Manpower Administration, 1963). Manpower Report No. 8, p. 11.

5. Selection of a "typical woman" was based upon data contained in "Fertility Histories and Birth Expectations of American Women: June 1971," *Current Population Reports*, Series P-20, No. 263 (Bureau of the Census, 1974). This publication gave information on median age at marriage and median intervals in months between successive births, as obtained in a supplement to the Current Population Survey.

6. Comparison of worklife expectancy of mothers for 1970 with 1960 is complicated by several factors: 1) the fact that

the base population used for the 1960 tables was that for married women living with husbands, whereas the 1970 base included all women who had ever been married; 2) compression of the bulk of childbearing into a smaller range of age groups in 1970; 3) the fact that, to in-

crease reliability, the data in 1970 were consolidated into five-year age groups.
7. *Work Life Expectancy and Training Needs of Women*, Manpower Report No. 12, Tables 3 and 4.

Employment, Retirement, and Morale Among Older Women

Philip Jaslow

Substantial increases in both the labor force participation and worklife expectancy of women in America, combined with indications that work (i.e., gainful employment) is increasingly becoming an expressive as well as instrumental role for this group, highlight the growing need for systematic knowledge regarding the non-economic correlates of work and retirement among females in this country. Recent claims by women's rights advocates of extant misconceptions about the meaning and value of work for women notwithstanding, however, the empirically based literature bearing on these issues remains sparse. Except for the work of Streib and Schneider (1971), the plethora of retirement studies over the years has been marked either by the total exclusion of females, small, nonrepresentative samples of women, and/or the omission of analysis by sex (Kutner, et al., 1956; Simpson and McKinney, 1966; Thompson, 1973; Thompson, Streib, and Kosa, 1960). Thus, the extent to which and circumstances under which labor force participation or retirement may be related to

social-psychological well-being among older women has remained largely a matter of conjecture (Maddox, 1968).

The historic exclusion of females from studies in which the adjustment of older workers and retirees has been compared has obviously been a function, to some degree, of aggregate differences between the sexes in the pattern and extent of labor force participation, which have produced much greater variation among women in the timing of occupational retirement regardless of how this concept is operationalized. Defining retirement as the terminal cessation of financially remunerative employment, for example, it is obvious that many women become "retirees" relatively early in life. Doubt may naturally prevail, therefore, not only as to whether occupational retirement is (on the whole) a similar social or psychological experience for women as for men, but also as to whether retirement or continued employment has much non-economic significance at all for most women. Indeed, even where retirement occurs late in life, on the heels of substantial experience in the work force, the tacit assumption seems to have prevailed that it is of little moment in the lives of most women (Donahue, Orbach, and Pollak, 1960).

From *Journal of Gerontology* 31, 2 (1976), pp. 212–218. Reprinted by permission.

Such speculation, of course, rests implicitly on the assumption that the work role itself generally has negligible psychosocial importance among females. If it is essentially an instrumental role, if it contributes little to a woman's psychological identity or self-image, it if is not a point of social integration among females, its loss via retirement should also be incidental to continuing social-psychological adaptation with the exception of indirect effects occurring as a result of income loss.

The traditional approach to the study of retirement among men, in contrast, has been articulated in terms of these very concepts. Hypothesized deleterious social and psychological ramifications of retirement for men have been based essentially on the presumed importance of the work role in integrating a man into the social structure, in conditioning his identity, lifestyle, and participation patterns, and on the assumption that retirement undercuts these patterns by removing him from the world of work in which they are rooted (Havighurst and Friedmann, 1954; Maddox, 1968; Simpson, Back, and McKinney, 1966). The workplace has traditionally been seen for men (but not for women) as a source of many personal satisfactions and affective experiences, providing opportunities for creativity, and giving life enduring significance. The loss of these opportunities and experiences via retirement has therefore been presumed intrinsically demoralizing itself and a precursor of resocialization problems in old age (Donahue et al., 1960; Miller, 1968; Rosow, 1967).

Something certainly must be said for the conventional wisdom which has seen family- and home-oriented roles as the major points around which personal and social identity occur among women. One must be clear, however, that even if this is the case it does not necessarily follow that the work role is or has been of negligible significance for females. In fact, although the empirically based literature in this area is also sparse, several studies have appeared over the years which indicate the importance women have come to attach (or may have always attached)

to work as a personally satisfying and socially meaningful part of their lives (Bower, 1954; Weiss and Samuelson, 1968). More recent study by the Dept. of Labor also strongly indicates that many women enter and remain in the labor force today for reasons unassociated with income (U.S. Dept. of Labor, 1970). While the concept of role change throughout the life cycle is also thoroughly documented in the literature on role theory, little attention has been given to the notion that the work role may be more salient among women at different life stages. Thus, employment may tend to provide the older woman—perhaps more than any other—with a source of dignity, self-esteem, a means for retaining a youthful self-image, opportunities for social participation, or any other integrative or supportive function which has been suggested for older men.

The research reported here represents an effort to explore these notions, or to apply to elderly women hypotheses regarding the theoretical orientation to work and retirement which has evolved for men. More specifically, cross-sectional data are used to test the hypothesis that older working women have better morale than those who do not work. Consistent with the literature on retirement and morale, it is assumed for purposes of this analysis that employment in old age is a cause rather than a consequence of morale.

METHODS

The Sample

This research is based on data originally gathered in 1968 from a multi-stage area probability sample of 3,996 noninstitutionalized persons age 65 and over living in the United States, excluding Alaska and Hawaii. The analysis reported here is restricted to the 2,398 women in the sample. The actual N reported in tables, however, reflects the use of a weighting procedure employed in the parent sample to compensate for the unequal probability of selection of elements and hence to render unbiased estimates of the characteristics of the universe. (This procedure introduced weights proportional to the inverse of the probability of selection, and a constant multiplier designed to render a total weighted frequency as close as possible to the total number of unweighted cases in the sample.)

Of particular relevance to both the substance and methodology of this paper is the recent study by Thompson (1973) reporting on the morale of the *men* from this same parent national sample. Thompson found that variation in morale of the male workers and retirees in the sample could be explained almost entirely by systematic group differences in age, income, and health, thus calling into question some of the long-standing assumptions reviewed above. These same intervening variables are examined here for the women.

The Variables

A large number of items measuring morale and health for the parent sample were submitted by Thompson (1972) to a factor analysis using Hotelling's Principal Components solution, and orthogonally rotated to simple structure by the Varimax method. One of the five morale factors and two of the four health factors extracted by this procedure are employed here.* A brief description of these factors (with rotated loadings for the most influential items), and the other variables, follows.

Morale. The morale factor utilized here reflects essentially the respondents' awareness of and reaction to advancing age. The most heavily loaded items, including some from the Lawton Morale Scale (1972) were:

As you get older, you are less useful (agree or disagree) .668
You have as much pep as you did last year (agree or disagree) .636

---

* Appreciation is acknowledged to Dr. G. B. Thompson for making these analyses available.

Things keep getting worse as you get older (agree or disagree) .563
Age image (positive or negative) .557
As you get older, would you say things are better, worse, or the same as you thought they would be? .398

General Health. This factor correlated most strongly with items representing general health as subjectively assessed by the respondents. Items loading most heavily were:

In general, would you say that your health today is very good, good, fair, or poor? .727
Comparing your health today to how it was when you were sixty, is it better, about the same, or worse? .692
How is your health today compared to how it was last year (better, about the same, or worse)? .654
Would you say that your health is better, about the same, or worse than most people of your age? .643

Physical Incapacity. This factor correlated most strongly with items from the Shanas Index of Incapacity (Shanas et al., 1968). These items, with their rotated loadings, were:

Would you have trouble doing the following without help (never, occasionally, frequently, always):
Getting about the house? .802
Dressing and putting on shoes? .800
Washing and bathing? .784
Going out of doors? .749
Cutting your toenails? .701
Walking up and down stairs? .653

Employment Status. The sample was subdivided into three employment-status categories on the basis of responses to the following questions: "Are you employed now?" and "Since you were twenty-one years old, have you worked a total of at least five years?" Respondents answering "yes" to the first question were classified as employed (whether working full-time or part-time). Respondents answering "no" to the first question but "yes" to the second question were classified as retired. Those answering "no" to both questions were classified as never having worked. By this procedure, 6.3% of the women were found to be employed, 54.1% were designated as retired, and 39.6% were classified as never having worked.

Age. Median age for the sample was 71.7 years; mean age was 72.9 years. Categorically, the women were distributed as follows: 35.5% were age 65-69; 30.1% were age 70-74; 19.1% were age 75-79; 15.3% were age 80 and over.

Income. This variable was measured as the total personal income of the respondent, plus that of her husband (if present), during the twelve months preceding the interview. This included income derived from wages, salaries, and commissions, professional fees, business profits, rent, insurance payments, interest and dividends, Social Security, Veteran's and Old Age Assistance benefits, Unemployment Compensation, and such other sources as sick benefits and alimony. Family gifts and/or allowances were not included. Because of extreme skewness in the income distribution, correlation coefficients involving this variable were based on its logarithm to base 10. Categorically, the sample was distributed as follows: 25.5% under $1,000; 33.7% between $1,000 and $1,999; 16% between $2,000 and $2,999; 15.2% between $3,000 and $4,999; 9.6% with $5,000 and over.

RESULTS

Initial analysis of variance (Table 1) revealed marked differences in morale for the sample by virtue of employment status. The mean morale factor score for the employed women was 0.573, that for the retired group was 0.128, and that for the never-worked group −0.073. Subsequent t-tests also revealed statistically significant differences ($p < .001$) between both the employed and retired groups

TABLE 1

Analysis of variance for morale by employment status.

GROUP		MEAN		N
Employed		.573		150
Retired		.128		1294
Never worked		−.073		948
Source	df	SS	MS	F
Between	2	59.65	29.83	30.59*
Within	2389	2329.28	0.96	
Total	2391	2388.93		

*$p < .001$

as well as between the retired and never-worked groups.

Since it was expected, though, that age, income, and health were each related to employment status (as has been shown for older men), cross-tabulations were also computed for these variables by employment grouping. As Table 2 shows, the employed women were indeed found to be considerably younger as a group than both the retirees and the women who had never worked. The fact that the latter women constituted the oldest group is perhaps an indication of the increased labor force activity of younger cohorts of females in this country.

Table 3 shows that the women still working also tended to express a more positive view of their health than the others, with the never-worked group again scoring somewhat lower than the retirees. In contrast, however, Table 4 indicates a curvilinear re-

TABLE 2

Age by employment status.

	EMPLOYMENT STATUS (%)		
AGE	EMPLOYED	RETIRED	NEVER WORKED
65–69	55.3	35.0	32.8
70–74	27.2	30.2	30.6
75–79	9.3	19.8	19.7
80+	8.2	14.8	16.9
Total	100.0	100.0	100.0
N	150	1287	940

Chi-square = 33.954.
Cramer's V = 0.085.

TABLE 3

General health by employment status.

	EMPLOYMENT STATUS (%)		
HEALTH	EMPLOYED	RETIRED	NEVER WORKED
Good	53.6	38.3	32.8
Average	31.9	33.5	34.6
Poor	14.5	28.2	32.6
Total	100.0	100.0	100.0
N	150	1294	948

Chi-square = 32.014.
Cramer's V = 0.082.

lationship between employment status and degree of physical incapacitation, with the employed group having the lowest percentage of women with both relatively high *and* low degrees of functional disability. While it is certainly no surprise to find the working elderly with the lowest percentage of highly incapacitated women (since this is the youngest group and since many persons with severe functional disabilities are obviously unable to work), it is somewhat puzzling at first blush to find a higher percentage of women with *low* levels of incapacitation among the retired and never-worked groups than among the employed. Perhaps this is a function of the more advantaged life which a larger proportion of the retired and never-worked group may have experienced, and/or of the fact that work itself is a debilitating enterprise for the elderly, the effects of which and are most in evidence among those cur-

rently employed. Whatever the explanation, though, it is noteworthy that so many of the older workers perceived their health so positively (Table 3) despite the fact that many reported at least some degree of functional disability and many were relatively quite incapacitated. While one might conclude from this that older women who work are simply more prone to overestimate the quality of their health, one could also say that they are, rather, more prone to ignore their physical limitations. That is to say, this might be construed in itself as an indication that the experience or state of being gainfully employed does provide psychological benefits to those women who can and do work past age sixty-five.

As expected, Table 5 clearly shows that the employed women were by far the most economically advantaged, with the never-worked group again the most disadvantaged. The poorer circumstances of the retirees in the sample, and particularly of the women who had never worked, provides a striking incidental testimonial to the importance of employment for the financial security of older women in this country (although, as the first column of Table 5 also shows, a paying job alone provides no sure protection from impoverishment). That women in the never-worked group were found to be in the worst economic plight on the whole also points up the importance for females—in the context of existing income maintenance programs for the elderly—of entering old age

TABLE 4

Physical incapacity by employment status.

	EMPLOYMENT STATUS (%)		
DEGREE OF INCAPACITY	EMPLOYED	RETIRED	NEVER WORKED
Low	17.6	27.9	34.5
Average	61.4	45.6	38.5
High	21.0	26.5	27.0
Total	100.0	100.0	100.0
N	150	1294	948

Chi-square = 35.416.
Cramer's V = 0.086.

TABLE 5

Income by employment status.

	EMPLOYMENT STATUS (%)		
INCOME	EMPLOYED	RETIRED	NEVER WORKED
Under $1,000	12.5	23.6	30.1
$1,000–1,999	34.8	35.3	31.5
$2,000–2,999	11.5	15.1	17.9
$3,000–4,999	25.4	14.8	14.0
$5,000+	15.8	11.2	6.5
Total	100.0	100.0	100.0
N	140	1032	767

Chi-square = 49.579.
Cramer's V = 0.113.

with a basis for receipt of work-related retirement benefits, either under Social Security or via private pension.

Since age, income, and health were each found to be related to employment status, then, and since these variables have also been shown repeatedly to be related to measures of life satisfaction and morale (Riley and Foner, 1968), the question arises as to whether their presumed effects as intervening variables can account—either individually or in combination—for the observed relationship between employment status and morale. In other words, do older working women have the best morale *because* they tend to be younger, healthier, and/or wealthier than any others? Similarly, do elderly women with no employment experience have the worst morale because they tend to

be the oldest, poorest, and in the worst health?

In order to answer these questions, cross-tabulations were first computed for employment status and morale between the employed and retired groups, and then between the retirees and women who had never worked, controlling for levels of age, income, and the health factors as a check for interaction effects. One such effect was uncovered, between morale and income, when the employed women were compared with the retirees. As may be seen in Table 6, the relationship between employment status and morale for the workers and retirees remained as initially described but *only* for women with annual incomes below $5,000. For women whose income exceeded this level, however, it was the retired group rather than

TABLE 6

Morale by Employment status controlled for income.

	INCOME LEVEL (%)					
	UNDER $2,999		$3,000–4,999		$5,000 & Over	
MORALE	EMPLOYED	RETIRED	EMPLOYED	RETIRED	EMPLOYED	RETIRED
High	34.7	15.0	54.2	21.9	25.8	51.1
Average	50.1	53.8	40.6	56.0	65.3	33.0
Low	15.2	31.2	5.2	22.1	8.9	15.9
Total	100.0	100.0	100.0	100.0	100.0	100.0
N	82	765	36	153	22	115

Tau C = 0.095	Tau C = 0.235	Tau C = -0.097
Gamma = 0.430	Gamma = 0.597	Gamma = -0.281

the employed which contained a higher percentage of women with high morale and a lower percentage with low morale (although the relationship is not as strong here as indicated by the size of the Gamma coefficients). Thus, for women in the sample with relatively high incomes, retirement rather than employment was associated with better morale. This was the only subgrouping for which this reversal appeared.

As a final step, partial point-biserial correlations between morale and employment status were computed first for the working vs. retired groups, and then for the retired vs. the never-worked groups, controlling for the influence of age, income, and the health factors both individually and in combination. The women with annual incomes of $5,000 or more were excluded from these final analyses since they constituted an exception to the general trend.

A zero-order point-biserial correlation coefficient of .200 was computed for the workers vs. the retirees. As Table 7 shows, age, income, general health, and physical incapacitation, when controlled individually, each reduced the strength of association, with general health constituting the single most important intervening variable. When all four variables were controlled simultaneously, the strength of the relationship between employment status and morale was reduced to its lowest point, producing a partial point-biserial correlation coefficient of

.091. In other words, when the combined effects of age, income, general health, and physical incapacitation are partialled out, the strength of the relationship between employment status and morale is reduced by more than half, with employment status accounting (under these conditions) for slightly less than 1% of the variance in morale. Excluding the high-income group, then, the fact that all other employed women in the sample had better morale than the retirees apparently does stem, in large part, from the joint effects of their being younger, financially better off, less physically incapacitated, and most importantly, more positive about their general health than the retirees. However, these factors do not, in themselves, explain the entire phenomenon, for a small but statistically significant relationship remains.

The comparison of the retirees and women who had never worked produced similar findings, as shown in Table 8. A zero-order correlation coefficient of .098 was reduced slightly when the effects of age, income, and general health were partialled out separately, but with physical incapacitation this time operating as a suppressor variable in the basic relationship. Partialling out age, income, and general health simultaneously reduced the strength of association between employment status and morale to its lowest point, but still left a statistically significant partial correlation coefficient of .077.

While the amount of variance explained by employment status in both cor-

TABLE 7

Partial correlations between morale and employment status for employed vs. retired women.

CONTROL VARIABLES	PARTIAL r	df
Age		
Income	.173*	1029
General health	.176*	1029
Physical incapacity	.131*	1029
Age, income, general health, and physical incapacity	.190*	1029
	.091*	1026

*p < .001.

TABLE 8

Partial correlations between morale and employment status for retired vs. never-worked groups.

CONTROL VARIABLES	PARTIAL r	df
Age	.091*	2224
Income	.095*	2224
General health	.086*	2224
Physical incapacity	.106*	2224
Age, income, & general health	.077*	2222

*p < .001.

relation analyses is under 1%, and while it is certainly possible that other intervening variables could account for these effects, these analyses nevertheless produce some tentative although qualified support for the notion that work itself (or at least some aspect of the experience of being gainfully employed) does tend to be slightly advantageous for the morale of older women *providing* retirement income is not unusually high. Evidentially, it requires an annual income in retirement of approximately $5,000 or more to offset this advantage, underscoring again the importance of adequate financial security for elderly females. That nonworking women with virtually no employment history seem to be the most demoralized in their later years suggests that participation in the labor force may even provide psychosocial benefits which carry over beyond retirement and into old age, thus tending to leave women better off for having had the experience than those whose lives have been entirely leisure-oriented.

SUMMARY

While numerous studies have been reported on the relationship between labor force participation and social-psychological well-being among older men, only speculation has prevailed on this subject regarding elderly women. Such speculation seems to have rested on the assumptions that work provides few psychological benefits or social supports for females, suggesting that occupational retirement is also not psychosocially deleterious in any direct sense. The investigation reported here, in contrast, constituted an effort to test the hypothesis that gainful employment does provide a basis for morale among elderly women, as has been hypothesized for older men.

The analysis revealed that the employed women in a national probability sample of females age sixty-five and over had higher morale than the retirees, with the exception of those women with annual incomes of $5,000 or more among whom the retirees

had better morale than the workers. Women classified as never having worked were found to have the lowest morale as a group. Small but statistically significant differences remained when the intervening effects of age, income, and health were simultaneously isolated, indicating that the group differences in morale stemmed in part—but not entirely—from the fact that the working women tended to be the youngest, the healthiest, and financially better off, while the women who had never worked tended to be the oldest, poorest, and in the worst health. The remaining explained variance, although not large, does lend some tentative support to the hypothesis and would seem to open the door for further speculation regarding the particular kinds of women for whom, and particular circumstances under which, work may have a salutary influence on psychosocial well-being in old age.

It is interesting, finally, to compare these findings with those reported by Thompson (1973) for the men from the same parent sample used here. After controlling for age, income, and health, Thompson could find no employment status effect on morale among the men, concluding that the leisure role for this group may now be an entirely adequate substitute for that of worker. Can it be, then, contrary to the extant literature on adjustment in retirement, that work is actually a more significant factor in the lives of older women than men? Are the non-work roles available to older women actually less fulfilling or rewarding than is leisure for men? At the least, such questions underscore a need for the inclusion of females and analysis by sex in further research in any way concerned with the social or psychological dimensions of work and retirement.

REFERENCES

Bower, J. "The Retail Salespersons: Men and Women." In *The Meaning of Work and Retirement*, edited by R. J. Havighurst and E. A. Friedmann. Chicago: University of Chicago Press, 1954.

DONAHUE, W., ORBACH, H. L., and POL-
LAK, O. "Retirement: The Emerging Social
Pattern." In *Handbook of Social Gerontology*,
edited by C. Tibbitts. Chicago: University of
Chicago Press, 1960.

HAVIGHURST, R. J., and FRIEDMANN, E.
A. *The Meaning of Work and Retirement*.
Chicago: University of Chicago Press, 1954.

KITNER, B., FANSHEL, D., TOTO, A. M.,
and LANGER, T. S. *Five Hundred Over Sixty*.
New York: Russell Sage Foundation, 1956.

LAWTON, M. P. "The Dimensions of
Morale." In *Research, planning, and action
for the elderly*, edited by D. Kent, R. Kastenbaum and S. Sherwood. New York: Behavioral Publications, 1972.

MADDOX, G. L. "Retirement as a social
event in the United States." In *Middle Age
and Aging*, edited by B. L. Neugarten. Chicago: University of Chicago Press, 1968.

MILLER, S. J. "The Social Dilemma of
the Aging Leisure Participant." In *Middle
Age and Aging*, edited by B. L. Neugarten.
Chicago: University of Chicago Press, 1968.

RILEY, M. W., and FONER, A. *Aging and
Society*. Vol. 1. New York: Russell Sage
Foundation, 1968.

ROSOW, I. *Social Integration of the
Aged*. New York: Free Press, 1967.

SHANAS, E., TOWNSEND, P., WEDDER-
BURN, D., FRIIS, H., MILHOJ, P., and STEHOU-
WER, J. *Old People in Three Industrial Soci-
eties*. New York: Atherton Press, 1968.

SIMPSON, I. H., and MCKINNEY, J. D.
(eds.) *Social Aspects of Aging*. Durham: Duke
University Press, 1966.

SIMPSON, I. H., BACK, K. W., and
MCKINNEY, J. C. "Work and Retirement." In
Social Aspects of Aging, edited by I. H. Simpson and J. C. McKinney. Durham: Duke University Press, 1966.

STREIB, G. F., and SCHNEIDER, C. J. *Retirement in American Society*. Ithaca: Cornell
University Press, 1971.

THOMPSON, G. B. "Adjustment in Retirement: A Causal Interpretation of Factors
Influencing the Morale of Retired Men." PhD
dissertation, Brandeis University, 1972.

THOMPSON, G. B. "Work Versus Leisure
Roles: An Investigation of Morale Among
Employed and Retired Men." *Journal of Ger-
ontology*, 28 (1973): 339–344.

THOMPSON, W. E., STREIB, G. F., and
KOSA, J. "The Effect of Retirement on Personal Adjustment: A Panel Analysis." *Journal of Gerontology*, 15 (1960): 165–169.

U.S. Dept. of Labor. "Dual Careers."
Washington, D.C.: USGPO, 1970.

WEISS, R. S., and SAMUELSON, N. M.
"Social Roles of American Women: Their
Contribution to a Sense of Usefulness and
Importance." *Marriage and Family Living*, 20
(1958): 358–366.

Trends in Planned Early Retirement

Richard E. Barfield
James N. Morgan

The size and quality of the labor force depend
heavily on the age at which workers retire.
The liquidity of the Social Security System

From *The Gerontologist* 18, 1 (1976), pp. 13–18.
Reprinted by permission.

is also affected dramatically by early retirement. Some people continue to work, even
after sixty-five and in spite of mandatory retirement, by finding other jobs, while others
retire "early," conventionally defined as before sixty-five. Indeed, the latter behavior has

become the norm: ever since it became possible to retire as early as age sixty-two with actuarially reduced Social Security benefits, a majority of both men and women have been retiring before sixty-five. Various studies, particularly those based on the Social Security Administration's Surveys of Newly Entitled Beneficiaries and its Retirement History Study, have indicated that many of the early retired seemed to have been driven to it by a prior history of unemployment or health difficulties. On the other hand, when a negotiated Supplemental Early Retirement benefit allowed automobile workers to retire still earlier than sixty-two, and even more when a "thirty and out" provision was agreed to, a startlingly large proportion of those who found they could afford it retired early. The growth of private pensions supplementing Social Security is thus likely to have raised the possibility of more voluntary early retirements.

two main findings were that economic and financial factors dominated the retirement decision and that the younger a person was, the more likely to report plans to retire early. The second finding raised the question whether as we get older we all get used to working, less sanguine about the adequacy of our savings program, and less willing to think about retiring; or whether the young in 1966 represented a new and different generation, less imbued with the work ethic, so that over time there would be a trend with each succeeding generation more likely to retire early. The latter is an example of a cohort effect, or generation effect, or (to use more recent terminology) a vintage effect. Of course, it is always possible that a third effect is present, an effect of the current year of history; and it is impossible without special assumptions to sort out the three effects, since the year of history is identical with one's year of birth plus one's age.[1]

PREVIOUS SRC RESEARCH

A decade ago, the Survey Research Center (SRC) of the University of Michigan, with support from the U.S. Department of Health, Education, and Welfare, conducted a survey of a national cross-section asking about retirement plans of working respondents and experiences and satisfaction with retirement of the retired. A parallel survey of auto workers fifty-eight to sixty-one years old, most of them eligible for supplemental early retirement benefits, was conducted and followed up with a re-survey later to assess the progress of the early retirement program (Barfield and Morgan, 1974).

The auto worker surveys showed general satisfaction with the negotiated early retirement program and a high correlation between the amount of benefits a worker could qualify for and whether he or she retired early. The union (UAW) and the auto companies had informed the workers well, and few of them regretted their decisions.

More important in the present context was the cross-section part of the study. Its

NEEDS FOR CURRENT RESEARCH

At any rate, other SRC surveys asking retirement plans seemed to indicate an upward trend within each group in the intention to retire early (see Table 1), but the period was brief and it seemed important to reassess the situation ten years later. The environment has changed dramatically during that dec-

TABLE 1

Plans to retire early, by age.[a]

| | PROPORTION WHO PLAN TO RETIRE BEFORE THEY ARE AGE 65 | | |
AGE	1963 SURVEYS	1966 SURVEYS	1968 SURVEY
35–44	25%	43%	34%
45–54	23	33	35
55–64	21	22	26
Number of Observations	1,853	1,463	852

[a] For family heads in the labor force, age 35 to 64 and with family income $3,000 or more; nationwide samples.[2]

ade. For one thing, there have been gyrating asset values and inflation, with generally dismal impact on the value of most people's savings (it does not necessarily improve retirement prospects, after all, to have a house that has doubled in value if one does not intend to sell it). And for some people at least, there has also been a substantial threat if not experience of unemployment, which should reduce confidence in one's capacity to save enough for an early retirement. Further, there have been scandals about the solvency and equity of private pension plans, but a great increase in their numbers.

Given these historical events, the other main finding of the earlier studies, that financial factors dominated the retirement decision, increased the possibility that people's retirement plans had changed, and thus suggested the need for a reassessment of the situation. Financial factors include not only pension benefits, but such indicators of expected future needs as the duration of mortgage payments and the age at which there would be no more financial obligation to children.

It proved impossible to secure financing for a full-scale study of people's retirement provisions and plans, but we were nonetheless grateful to the Ford Foundation for funding a small reassessment of the current state of people's plans and expectations, with remeasurement only of the previously most crucial explanatory variables. We hoped to be able to see whether plans of various groups had changed, and in particular whether the previous decline in planned early retirement with age reflected a trend, a persistent age effect, or something else.

PROCEDURES OF THE 1976 STUDY

With minor changes to improve clarity, the same question about retirement plans asked in earlier surveys was repeated:

> At what age do you think you will retire from the main work you are now doing?

Of course, some people plan to "retire" only then to find some other, usually part-time work. But that is always true, and we focus here on early retirement from the main job. More important was the impact of societal changes on the possibility of securing precise trend data. Two main problems arose. First, we could no longer interview only the husband in a married couple, the person designated in previous surveys as "head of the family." Instead, we used a random selection within the family, and then asked the respondent about her or his retirement plans *and* those of the spouse. This required a complex questionnaire design, some computer work to reassemble expected retirement plans for "husband or single head" to compare with previous data, and some attention to differences between reports by an individual versus those of a proxy respondent (spouse).[3]

Second, a combination of factors led to substantially increased reported uncertainty about retirement plans and (even more so) about expected retirement benefits. This resulted partly from the brief time and attention given to the subject in an interview devoted to several other topics. But it probably resulted more from inflation, unemployment, fluctuating asset values, and popular articles about the worthlessness of many private pensions. The Pension Reform Act was in place, but the expected increase in the clarity and safety of individuals' rights may well not yet have penetrated to potential beneficiaries. Partially to compensate for the greater expressed uncertainty about age of retirement, we added a follow-up question asking whether or not respondents thought they would retire before sixty-five. The present analysis counts as early retirement plans either an expected age under sixty-five or a positive answer to the second question asked of the uncertain ones. All analysis treats the residual noncommitted as *not* planning early retirement.

The number professing ignorance about the *amount* of retirement pension they could expect was so great that we have not attempted to use it in the analysis, but instead have simply looked at the number of different pension plans from which people expect to get benefits. The main difference, after all, is between those who do and those who do not expect to have a private pension to supplement their Social Security or U.S. Government pension.

Of all the attitudinal and situation factors tried in the previous study, only one appeared to have much effect on early retirement plans—a combination of reported lack of control over work pace and reported difficulty keeping up with the pace. Those two questions were repeated.

In the case of retirement plans for wives, it seemed appropriate to focus on plans to retire before sixty-two, since on the average wives are about three years younger than their husbands, though we shall occasionally comment on differences which appear if one looks at their plans to retire before sixty-five.

We shall look first at trends in planned early retirement by age, but once we get beyond that the usual problems of correlated explanatory factors arise, requiring some kind of multivariate analysis. Our dependent "variable" is really the probability of reporting early retirement plans, a dichotomy for each individual, and we use a form of least squares multiple regression as the analysis technique.[4]

AGE AND OTHER EFFECTS

The top of Table 2 gives the age patterns, unadjusted and adjusted for different compositions of the age groups on the other factors used. Subtracting the overall mean proportion converts the adjusted proportions to dummy variable regression coefficients—adjustments to the mean proportion. Considering the sampling errors associated with these data, it seems clear that if one expected a linear decline with age in plans to retire early, the two groups aged 50-54 and 55-59 are significantly above expectations, whether one looks at the adjusted or the unadjusted proportions. Figure 1 dramatizes the departure from the hypothesis of a trend for each succeeding generation to plan earlier retire-

ment—the hypothesis is pictured by shifting the 1966 data forward ten years, since the 35-39 year old group in 1966 was ten years older in 1976, etc.

Given the small sample, the inevitable changes in procedure, and the limited amount of information collected in this study, we can only speculate as to the reasons for the present state of retirement expectations. It seems clear that different age groups (generations, cohorts) have had different historical experiences. In particular, the two age groups whose retirement plans diverge most dramatically from expectations entered the labor force in the good times just after World War II and thus have had most of their earning lives in prosperity, became well established before the recent unemployment and inflation really hit, probably owned a home before the recent explosion of house prices, and came along late enough to accumulate private pension benefits in many cases.

On the other hand, the age differences are not simply accounted for, and eliminated, by taking account of differences in the number of pensions expected or in the ages when the family will be free of its mortgage and obligations to children, since the adjusted coefficients show much the same pattern. And the wives' plans for retirement before age sixty-two do not form the same pattern (though they do when one focuses on retirement before sixty-five, perhaps because the supplementary question handles the uncertain respondents better).

If, as these data seem to show, particular historical experiences can lead to dramatic differences in planned early retirement, and if the result is a fluctuating proportion retiring early, then the need for regular monitoring of people's retirement provisions and plans would seem important for long-range planning and policy making for both aggregate employment and Social Security funding.

The duration of mortgage payments does seem to affect retirement plans, particularly if they will continue after the person is sixty-two. And responsibilities to children, in these data impressively frequent at advanced ages, affect retirement plans, partic-

TABLE 2

Associations with early retirement planning (gross and adjusted by multiple regression).

| | HUSBANDS AND SINGLE RESPONDENTS | | | HUSBANDS | | | WIVES | | |
| | NO. OF CASES | % PLANNING TO RETIRE BEFORE 65 | | NO. OF CASES | % PLANNING TO RETIRE BEFORE 65 | | NO. OF CASES | % PLANNING TO RETIRE BEFORE 65 | |
		UNADJUSTED	ADJUSTED		UNADJUSTED	ADJUSTED		UNADJUSTED	ADJUSTED
AGE									
35–39	75	60	55	54	54	52	47	40	37
40–44	94	51	50	80	48	45	39	36	38
45–49	84	47	45	70	40	39	29	40	38
50–54	93	52	54	78	53	55	34	40	33
55–59	79	45	45	59	46	47	24	28	32
60–64	61	23	28	53	21	25	*	*	*
AGE FREE OF MORTGAGE PAYMENTS									
Before Age 55; When interviewed; NA, DK	299	46	48	259	46	47	113	34	34
55–62	82	52	45	67	46	41	32	48	48
63 or older	105	47	46	68	39	39	28	33	32
AGE FREE OF RESPONSIBILITY FOR CHILDREN									
Before age 55; When interviewed; No children; NA, DK	279	51	49	216	48	47	103	41	42
55–62	142	47	48	123	43	44	46	38	36
63 or Older	65	34	37	55	35	36	24	17	14
NUMBER OF PRIVATE PENSIONS EXPECTED									
None	165	32	32	117	28	29	50	34	37
One	229	55	55	191	51	52	77	40	40
Two or more	62	60	61	60	58	56	35	35	32
NA, DK	30	50	48	26	41	38	11	24	22
1975 FAMILY INCOME									
Less than $6,000	36	55	55	15	45	59	5	20	21
$6,000–9,999; NA, DK	120	35	38	84	33	40	38	22	23
$10,000–14,999	83	48	46	63	40	38	31	32	32
$15,000–19,999	97	55	52	90	53	49	32	43	43
$20,000 or More	150	51	50	142	48	46	67	45	45
SEX AND MARITAL STATUS									
Single man	32	68	69	*	*		*	*	*
Single woman	60	52	60	*	*	*	*	*	*
Married man; wife working	184	45	43	184	45	* / 44	*	*	*
Married man; wife not working	210	44	43	210	44	45	*	*	*
ABILITY TO KEEP UP WITH PACE OF WORK									
No difficulty	446	47	47	384	44	44	169	36	36
Some Difficulty	10	54	60	10	54	59	4	30	36

* Variable category irrelevant in indicated regression.

Figure 1

Age and plans for early retirement in 1976.

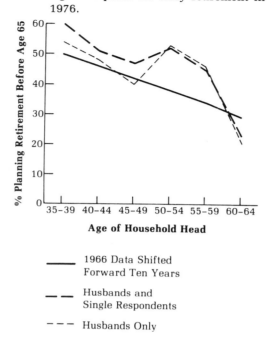

Age of Household Head

———— 1966 Data Shifted
Forward Ten Years

— — Husbands and
Single Respondents

– – – Husbands Only

ularly of mothers. Extra pensions seem to encourage husbands to retire early, but not wives, while higher current family income seems to encourage wives to plan early retirement, but not husbands. Current income supposedly reflects potential capacity to accumulate savings for retirement though it also affects income needs in retirement. Very low income may reflect employment difficulties and plans to escape into an uncomfortable early retirement.

For those interested in a summary of what accounts for differences in early retirement plans, and some sense of statistical significance, Table 3 gives the importance levels of the explanatory characteristics, singly and in multivariate context, using *eta*-squared (the correlation squared) for the former, and an analogue called *beta*-squared for the latter.[5]

There is, of course, a great deal of unexplained variance reflecting both unmeasured

explanatory variables and sheer random variance in people's plans, accentuated by added noise in converting those plans into answers to questions. The differences between husbands and single heads account for the higher correlation in the first regression, since single people, particularly men, are much more likely to plan early retirement. For husbands, it is the young and those expecting extra pensions who are more likely to report planning early retirement. But wives plan to retire early when there is a high family income and no mortgage payments or commitments to children that will continue late in life.

The evidence from our earlier study is that we could have explained more of the plans on the basis of economic factors if we had had better measurement of them. Actually, the ranking of predictors is very much the same for husbands and wives if we deal with wives' plans to retire before sixty-five, perhaps because the added probe question improved the responses; and the age pattern also has an upward bulge for those fifty to fifty-nine. Conversely, if we look at husbands' plans to retire before sixty-two, we find little of the age pattern, though most of the economic factors are still important.

One should not expect, particularly in such a truncated study, to account for much of the interpersonal difference in retirement plans. Our purpose has been to see, generally, whether findings of ten years ago still hold, and, specifically, what the age pattern observed at that time meant. We can conclude that economic factors still matter in retirement decisions, both as measured and as probably represented by the differences between age cohorts. And the economic history of each generation can influence its capacity to retire early.

SUMMARY

A comparison of the age patterns of plans for early retirement with those of a decade earlier was expected to show whether they reflected an age effect or a cohort effect. How-

TABLE 3

Importance of predictors in accounting for plans to retire early (husbands and single respondents aged 35–64; wives aged 35–59).

VARIABLE	NO. OF CLASSES	PLANS TO RETIRE BEFORE 65 HUSBANDS AND SINGLE RESPONDENTS		HUSBANDS		NO. OF CLASSES	PLANS TO RETIRE BEFORE 62 WIVES	
		η^2	β^2	η^2	β^2		η^2	β^2
Age	6	.040	.025	.040	.034	5	.007	.002
Age free of mortgage payments	3	.002	.001	.003	.005	3	.013	.013
Age free of responsibility for children	3	.012	.007	.009	.006	3	.029	.042
Number of pensions expected	4	.051	.052	.052	.049	4	.008	.009
Family income	5	.024	.014	.021	.009	5	.043	.039
Sex/marital status/ working wife	4/2	.015	.028	.000	.000	*	*	*
Ability to keep up with pace of work	2	.000	.002	.001	.002	2	.000	.000
R^2 (adjusted)		.092		.065			.008	
Number of cases		486		394			173	

* Irrelevant in indicated regression.

ever, the data seem to show that recent historic events have been altering the relative position of different cohorts in a nonlinear fashion. It would appear that different age groups are having very different lifetime experiences which are in turn differentially affecting their retirement plans. Further studies getting at financial provision for retirement are required to identify the mechanism at work.

The same studies reported here also asked the already-retired about their satisfaction with retirement, and trends in that satisfaction are reported in a subsequent article.

NOTES

1. There are ways of dealing with the age-period-cohort paradox, mostly by allowing nonlinearity of effects, but they place burdens on the data that this pilot study hardly justifies (Fienberg and Mason, 1977; Glenn, 1976; Mason, Mason and Winsborough, 1976).

2. In surveys conducted in 1963, in connection with a study of individual saving and participation in private pension plans, the following question was asked: "Now I have a few questions about retirement. When do you think you will retire from the work you do; I mean at what age?" In surveys conducted in 1966, in connection with the study of early retirement, the question asked was: "When do you think you will retire from the main work you are now doing—I mean at what age?" The 1966 question followed other questions about retirement and about what things would be like later on. In the 1968 survey, the question was: "At what age do you think you will retire from the main work you are doing now?" The 1968 question was contained in the retirement section of a larger survey.

3. The use of a proxy respondent (the

spouse) in half the cases for married couples produces two independent probability samples, one where retirement plans of husband (or wife) are stated by the spouse and the other where they are given by the person involved. Hence, even without interviewing both spouses, we can assess potential bias by seeing whether the overall proportions are different when there is a proxy respondent. They are not; 48 percent of husbands speaking for themselves said they planned to retire before age sixty-five, while 46 percent of wives reported that their husbands planned to retire early. For retiring before 62 the proportions were 29 and 26 percent, a small bias in the "expected" direction if one thinks wives are more realistic. Since the reduction in sample sizes are more damaging than any potential bias from a proxy respondent, we have not presented the results separately according to who the respondent was.

4.   The overall proportion planning to retire early was close enough to 50 percent (47 percent for heads, 45 percent for husbands only, and 36 percent for wives) and the number of cases sufficiently large, so that the main reasons for complex analysis procedures (logit, probit) do not apply. Ordinary regression with a 1-0 dependent variable and categorical predictors is quite adequate. The use of categorical predictors, indeed, reduces the chances of producing expected proportions greater than 100 percent or less than 0 percent. We use a version called multiple classification analysis, which does not omit one category of each explanatory characteristic but constrains the coefficients so that the weighted mean of each set is zero. Thus, the predicting equation starts with the overall proportion planning to retire early and adjusts that up or down for the effects of membership in one subclass of each explanatory characteristic (Andrews, Morgan, Sonquist, & Klem, 1973). A set of

such coefficients can reveal nonlinear patterns and often is more powerful than a continuous numerical predictor where the characteristic forms a numerical scale (the power loss from grouping is small: $(1-1/k^2)$ where k is the number of classes). With a dichotomous dependent variable, the coefficients can be expressed as subgroup proportions planning to retire early, adjusted for the composition of that subgroup on the other factors used in the regression. The sampling variance of such proportions, like that of any proportion, is largely dependent on the number of cases on which it is based (given in Table 2.) There are sample design effects (more loss from clustering than gain from stratification) which make the sampling error of a percentage larger than pq/n, but the adjusted precentages have smaller sampling errors by a factor of $1-R^2$, so that for percentages around 50 percent and 100 cases, the sampling error is around 5 percent.

5.   Actually, the ratio of the true squared partial correlation to beta-squared is $(1-R^2_A)/(1-R^2_B)$, where R_A is the multiple correlation between the predictor in question and the other predictors, and R_B is the multiple correlation between the dependent variable and the other predictors, excluding the one in question. Thus, if the predictor in question has some explanatory power and is not too highly correlated with the other predictors, beta-squared is a good indicator of its partial correlation squared, its explanatory power, and its significance (Lansing and Morgan, 1971).

REFERENCES

ANDREWS, F., MORGAN, J., SONQUIST, J., and KLEM, L. *Multiple Classification Analysis* (2nd ed.). Ann Arbor, Mich.: Institute for Social Research, 1973.

BARFIELD, R. E., and MORGAN, J. N. *Early Retirement: The Decision and the Ex-*

perience and a Second Look. Ann Arbor, Mich.: Institute for Social Research, 1974.

FINEBERG, S. E., and MASON, W. M. *Identification and Estimation of Age-Period Cohort Models in the Analysis of Discrete Archival Data* (Technical Report #286). Minneapolis: University of Minnesota School of Statistics, 1977.

GLENN, N. D. "Cohort Analysts' Futile Quest: Statistical Attempts to Separate Age,

Period, and Cohort Effects." *American Sociological Review*, 41 (1976): 900–904.

LANSING, J., and MORGAN, J. *Economic Survey Methods.* Ann Arbor, Mich.: Institute for Social Research, 1971.

MASON, W. M., MASON, K.O., and WINSBOROUGH, H. H. "Reply to Glenn." *American Sociological Review*, 41 (1976): 904–905.

Subjective Adaptation to Loss of the Work Role: A Longitudinal Study

Linda K. George

George L. Maddox

Adaptation to changes in or losses of major life roles has received considerable attention from social scientists. The interest of social psychologists has focused particularly on the relationship between the presumed stress of life events and outcomes such as illness or a decreased sense of psychological well-being (see Holmes and Rahe, 1967). Social gerontologists have focused their attention on the correlates of the role losses which commonly accompany the aging process.

Studies of the relationship between retirement and satisfaction or morale, where these indicators of perceived well-being are viewed as valid indicators of subjective aspects of adaptation, illustrate the type of research which predicts that role loss, particularly the loss of central social roles, has a negative effect on an individual's reported

From *Journal of Gerontology* 32, 4 (1977), pp. 456–462. Reprinted by permission.

adaptation. Sociological perspectives generally stress the centrality of the work role and suggest that, in our society at any rate, occupation is a primary claim to social status; that work has a moral as well as a purely utilitarian meaning; and that occupation, along with familial involvement, is a major source of adult identity.

In this paper we address two primary sociological questions about adaptation to the loss of this central life role. The first concerns the amount and direction of change in an individual's reported sense of well-being that occurs after retirement. The second question considers the variables that mediate and condition this outcome. Much recent work (see Streib and Schneider, 1971) has suggested that a multivariate framework is a necessary as well as useful approach to the analysis of adaptation to retirement, a conclusion our analysis supports.

Our choice of analytic techniques was

quided by increasing consensus among social scientists concerning two basic methodological issues involved in assessing the impact of a life event upon some criterion variable. First, methodologically adequate research on social processes requires longitudinal data. In order that amount and direction of change in a particular variable can be determined, the research investigator must have a baseline measure of that outcome variable prior to the occurrence of the event. It is only in this manner that the impact of the event can be distinguished from the effect of the prior level of the outcome variable of interest. Second, multivariate analysis techniques within the general linear model seem best suited to problems of change analysis and are preferable to the use of change scores which have been appropriately criticized by several authors (see Bohrnstedt, 1969; Cronbach and Furby, 1970). The research reported here reinforces these conclusions.

The measurement and analysis of social processes have historically been hindered by a variety of methodological problems. Recently some of these issues have begun to be at least partially resolved, as we will illustrate below. Thus the major purpose of this paper is to illustrate the use of appropriate methodological strategies in a substantive area of interest to social gerontologists. The study sample available to us, while small, is sufficient for illustrating the key methodological points under discussion.

THEORETICAL CONSIDERATIONS

The large and growing literature on life events, stress, and their correlates provides a useful point of departure for the study of role change or loss (e.g., Holmes and Rahe, 1967; House, 1974; Rabkin and Struening, 1976). This perspective emphasizes both the coping behavior occasioned by life events rather than events per se and the multivariate factors which mediate the adaptive or maladaptive outcomes which follow life events. These emphases on process and multiple mediating variables make methodological

demands, the most obvious of which are longitudinal observation and multivariate data analysis techniques. A less obvious demand is that attention must be given to the time of measurement following an event of interest. If a life event activates coping behavior in the interest of adaptation, descriptions of adaptation to the event would necessarily take into account *time since the event*. In the retirement literature, this point has been made by Stokes and Maddox (1967).

The importance of mediating or conditioning variables in understanding coping and adaptive behavior in response to life events is now well established. Life events do not occur in a vacuum. The impact of such events as the change or loss of central social roles is conditioned by a number of factors, including the salience of an event for an individual, the coping skills and resources which can be mobilized, and the social support system which can be activated (Rabkin and Struening, 1976). The literature on retirement has implicitly, sometimes explicitly, stressed the inclusion of mediating variables in the analysis of retirement as a process and adaptation in retirement. Perceived deprivation associated with work loss has been shown to be associated with decreased life satisfaction generally and satisfaction with retirement specifically (Simpson, Back, and McKinney, 1966b). The self-rated importance of work appears to be a measure of the salience of work and personal satisfaction associated with work (Atchley, 1971); hence, differences in the salience of work can be expected to affect the meaning of, and responses to, the loss of work. Health, a basic resource for social role enactment, is a particularly important variable in coping with the role change or loss implied by retirement, since poor health is one of the most commonly stated reasons for retiring from work (Barfield and Morgan, 1969). Indications of maladaptation and dissatisfaction among retired persons might be better explained by poor health than by the event of retirement. The presence of social supports in the form of friends and kin is known to be related to adaptation in retirement (Streib and Schneider, 1971).

In sum, longitudinal observation, control for mediating variables, and multivariate analytic techniques are essential ingredients in studies of adaptation in retirement. A critical illustration of this point is the principal objective of this paper.

METHOD

Subjects

In 1960 Simpson, Back, and McKinney (1966) interviewed in depth a number of retired and pre-retired workers (N = 467) in the Central Piedmont area of North Carolina. In this study purposive sampling was used to insure a variety of occupational types (college faculty, business executives, blue collar skilled workers, and operatives) and work experiences within a relatively small sample. The resulting pool of subjects permitted an assessment of the effect which different orientations to work have on expectations about and adaptation to retirement. Specifically, these investigators explored the impact of such factors as commitment to work, variations in occupational subcultures, and orderliness of work histories on what pre-retired workers expected retirement to be like and what retired workers experienced in retirement. The research design was cross-sectional and inevitably the investigators found themselves speculating about the predictive power of experience and expectations among workers and the accuracy of recall and reporting among retirees. Simpson et al. understood and in their interpretations took into account the importance of mediating variables in the retirement process. They could deal only by inference, however, with the processual aspects of adaptation to retirement.

Six years after the initial study Stokes and Maddox (1967) re-interviewed 130 of the original study population who at the time of the first interview were either pre-retired or within one year of retirement. The re-study was designed to test with longitudinal data some hypotheses derived from cross-sectional data as well as to explore additional hypotheses with detailed data on various subgroups within the longitudinal panel. This paper reports findings from a subgroup of fifty-eight individuals in the re-study. This special study focuses attention on a wide range of mediating variables whose reliability can be stated with some confidence. The subgroup, whose characteristics are summarized in Table 1, are not significantly different from the original sample of 467 studied by Simpson et al. We report this primarily to indicate continuities among the original study, the re-study, and the special study reported here. In this paper we wish to illustrate some basic methodological points about the study of retirement process and adaptation in retirement. We specifically discourage epidemiological generalizations from our data about the distribution of adaptation in retirement among retired persons generally.

TABLE 1

Range, means, and standard deviations of subjects on variables used in analysis.

	(n = 58)		
VARIABLE	RANGE	MEAN	STANDARD DEVIATIONS
Time 1 subjective adaptation (morale)	0–20	17.29	2.41
Time 2 subjective adaptation (morale)	0–20	15.10	1.18
Job deprivation (Time 2)	0–16	12.70	5.28
Occupational prestige	1–3	2.29	.84
Education	1–19	9.09	2.81
Marital status (Time 2)	0–1	.60	.49
Length of time retired (in months)	0–58	25.59	8.05
Self-perceived health (Time 2)	1–4	2.54	.71

We are consciously focusing intensively upon a small group of subjects for whom we have a considerable amount of pertinent longitudinal data primarily in order to argue some methodological issues.

Measures

The morale measure used in this analysis was considered a measure of subjective adaptation and consisted of a modification of the seven-item Kutner Morale Scale (Kutner, Fanshel, Togo, & Langner, 1956). This is one of several widely used instruments in the late 1950s and early 1960s from which Simpson et al. made a reasonable selection. Our five-item modified form was constructed in order to maximize the reliability of the Kutner measure and included the following Likert items:

> As I get older, things seem to get better than I thought would be the case.
> On the whole, I am very well satisfied with my way of life today.
> I deeply regret the chances I have missed during my life to do a better job of living.
> All in all, I find a great deal of unhappiness in life today.
> Things just keep getting worse and worse for me as I get older.

The resulting reliabilities were acceptably high—.89 at Time 1 and .95 at Time 2.

Table 1 displays the range, mean, and standard deviation for the Kutner Scale and other variables used in our analysis. The other variables were used as independent potentially mediating variables which theory suggested were likely to condition the impact of retirement upon subjective adaptation (satisfaction). Job deprivation or missing the intrinsic satisfactions of the job was viewed as a measure of salience of the work role and measured via the Simpson-McKinney Job Deprivation Scale (Simpson et al., 1966) and consisted of four Likert items:

> I often miss being with other people at work.
> I often miss the feeling of doing a good job.

> I often wish I could go back to work.
> I often worry about not having a job.

The reliability of this scale was also acceptable (.86).

Two dimensions of socioeconomic status were included as indications of resources that might be useful in the retirement process. Education was directly coded as years of formal schooling. The Duncan Index of Occupational Prestige (IOP) was used to measure occupational status. The original nine IOP categories were collapsed into three levels of occupational prestige. Although a wide variety of occupational categories were included in the sample, lower levels of occupational prestige were somewhat underrepresented in both the initial study and the special study reported here.

Marital status was used as a dichotomous, "dummy" variable, where 1 represented being currently married and living with spouse and 0 indicated that the subject was not currently married. The presence of a spouse was considered a better measure of potential social support than the comparison of *ever* versus *never* married.

Length of time retired was included in the analysis in order to observe possible differences due to the relative proximity or distance of the retirement event. This variable was coded directly as number of months since retirement.

Subjects' perceptions of their own physical well-being were tapped by a self-health rating, with four alternatives ranging from *good* to *bad*. Health was viewed as a resource which might affect adaptation.

Thus the measures used were relatively standard ways of assessing the information of interest and the derived scales appear to be appropriately reliable.

FINDINGS

Our analysis points overwhelmingly toward stability rather than change in subjective adaptation (satisfaction) over a period of five years for this sample. At t-test for the difference between means using dependent samples indicated that the Time 1 and Time 2 satisfaction means, while exhibiting a decline from Time 1 to Time 2, did not significantly differ. Thus for the sample as a whole, general life satisfaction did not significantly change during the five-year interval between tests. In addition, the zero-order correlation between the two measures of subjective adaptation was .79, which indicates that individuals rank-ordered largely the same on the measures each time.

Multiple regression was used to assess the impact of the conditioning variables as a set and to determine their independent effect upon subjective adaptation among subjects. Subjective adaptation at Time 2 was used as the dependent variable. As suggested by Cronbach and Furby (1970), the variable at Time 1 was always entered in the equation as the first independent variable. Other predictors were then entered to examine their effect net of the Time 1 adaptation measure. In this way both subjective adaptation measures were taken into account without the use of a change score.

Table 2 presents the final equation in which Time 2 adaptation is regressed upon Time 1 adaptation and the other independent variables. Adaptation at Time 1 explained 63 percent of the total of 85 percent explained variance in the variable at Time 2. Occupa-

tional prestige, education, Time 2 marital status, Time 2 job deprivation (i.e., missing the intrinsic satisfactions of employment), and an interaction between occupational prestige and length of time retired were all statistically significant predictors of adaptation at Time 2, net of the Time 1 measure. Net of adaptation at Time 1, the other predictors, as a set, explain about 22 percent of the variance in this variable at Time 2. It is this set of predictors which helps to account for the changes in subjective adaptation that have occurred in our study population. The large amount of variance explained by the Time 1 measure is irrelevant to the issue of changes that occurred and instead reflects the overwhelming stability among our subjects generally.

The standardized *beta* weights of the predictors indicate their relative impact upon Time 2 adaptation. Along with the Time 1 adaptation measure, occupational prestige was the best single predictor of Time 2 adaptation. The higher the prestige of the individual's former occupation, the more likely he was to display a high level of adaptation at Time 2. Occupational prestige was also one component of a statistically significant interaction term which further refines this pattern. Decomposition of this interaction term with dummy variables

TABLE 2

Regression of time 2 upon time 1 subjective adaptation and selected independent variables.

INDEPENDENT VARIABLE	DEPENDENT VARIABLE = TIME 2 SUBJECTIVE ADAPTATION (n = 58)			
	b	B	INCREMENT IN R^2	NET R^2
Time 1 subjective adaptation	.413**	.814**	.636	.479
Occupational prestige	1.145**	.819**	.039	.189
Education	−.166*	−.395*	.082	.043
Occupational prestige × length of time retired	−.127**	−.533**	.037	.087
Job deprivation (Time 2)	−.093*	−.416*	.022	.056
Marital status (Time 2)	.828*	.346*	.036	.036
Constant	−4.235			
Total R^2	.852			

*$p \leq .05$
**$p \leq .01$

TABLE 3

Regression of time 2 subjective adaptation upon time 2 independent variables.

INDEPENDENT VARIABLE	DEPENDENT VARIABLE = TIME 2 SUBJECTIVE ADAPTATION (n = 58)			
	b	B	INCREMENT IN R^2	NET R^2
Marital status (Time 2)	1.711*	.716*	.118*	.168*
Occupational prestige	1.127*	.807*	.096*	.183*
Occupational prestige × length of time retired	−.139	−.587*	.097*	.108*
Education	−.124	−.296	.048	.024
Job deprivation (Time 2)	−.047	−.210	.015	.015
Constant	.678			
Total R^2	.373			

*$p \leq .05$

indicated that for middle level and professional strata, the longer the individual was retired, the more likely he was to have adapted. Within lower occupational groups, on the other hand, the longer an individual has been retired, the more likely he was to be maladapted.

Education appears to have a negative impact upon Time 2 adaptation, although this negative coefficient is somewhat misleading. The zero-order correlation between education and Time 2 adaptation was positive (r = .18), though small. With occupational status and initial level of life satisfaction controlled, however, education was negatively related to adaptation. Even this is somewhat surprising if education is hypothesized as a resource which is positively associated with adaptation in retirement. However, a similar negative relationship between education and life satisfaction was recently reported by Campbell, Converse, and Rodgers (1976). As would be expected, high levels of perceived job deprivation were associated with lower levels of adaptation. Finally, being married was associated with higher levels of adaptation at Time 2.

Table 3 provides an interesting comparison with Table 2. Table 3 shows the same regression equation, but without the inclusion of the baseline (Time 1) measure of adaptation. This equation would represent our estimates for the impact of the independent variables if we were restricted to the use of cross-sectional data. In this sense, this equation is comparable to the many cross-sectional studies previously reported concerning correlates of adaptation in older subjects. In this equation the independent variables explained about 37 percent of the variance in Time 2 adaptation. In the longitudinal equation these same variables, as a set, explained about 22 percent of the variance in adaptation at Time 2. The lower amount of explained variance due to this set of predictors in the longitudinal equation reflects, of course, the effects of intercorrelation between Time 1 adaptation and the other predictors. The first equation, which includes the baseline measure of adaptation, is clearly the better equation as it addresses the question of the impact of various independent variables upon changes in adaptation over time, whereas the second equation merely taps cross-sectional correlates of adaptation.

The *beta* weights associated with the independent variables rank-order largely the same across the two regression equations with the notable exception of the marital status variable. Marital status was a much more important predictor of outcome level of subjective adaptation in the cross-sectional regression equation. This is due to the fact that the relatively strong correlation between initial level of adaptation and marital status $(r = .47)$ was not partialled out in the cross-sectional regression equation.

DISCUSSION

At this point we will consider the substantive and theoretical implications of this research. Generalization from our data should be made with appropriate caution in light of the special sample available for this analysis.

The first and most obvious result in this study has been the overwhelming degree of stability in subjective adaptation measures as evidenced in this sample over a five-year interval, during which time all of the subjects retired. Regardless of the theoretical perspective on which it was based, any expectations that loss of the work role would be accompanied by loss of a sense of general well-being with life is simply not evidenced. Longitudinal data are clearly necessary to address the issue of adaptation to retirement. Cross-sectional data could allow the examination of subjective adaptation level in a sample of retired persons; it could not, however, address the question of the impact of retirement as a process upon adaptation.

Second, as suggested by previous authors, the question of the impact of a life event upon a behavioral or attitudinal outcome frequently is asked and answered in naively simplistic terms. Our multiple regression analysis indicates that complex, multivariate relationships are operating upon the phenomenon of interest. Our analysis also suggests that a number of variables which may be considered as social resources, particularly marital status and various indicators of socioeconomic status, are important predictors of subjective adaptation in retirement. Our results thus support recent suggestions (House, 1974) that it is desirable to orient empirical investigation toward the variables and resources which condition and mediate the relationship between life events and outcome measures. In addition, our analysis suggests that many of the variables previously suggested as bivariate correlates of personal adaptation in retirement, remain sa-

tistically significant predictors of adaptation when controlling upon the impact of other variables. This provides significantly stronger evidence that these variables are indeed important factors in the retirement process and are not merely spurious correlates due to the intercorrelation among various measures of resources and social support.

SUMMARY

In summary, our analysis supports current suggestions that retirement would seem to be most usefully viewed as an event which occasions a complex social process of adaptation conditioned by a variety of resource and temporal variables. The implication is that a complex, longitudinal multivariate model is needed. Multivariate analysis techniques are now available to make this task more manageable. It is hoped that this analysis can serve as an illustration for the application of these multivariate techniques.

Both social psychologists and social gerontologists have expressed considerable interest in adaptation to the loss of or change in central life roles. The relationship between retirement and subjective adaptation is an example of research within this general theoretical framework. Concomitants of this substantive issue are the methodological issues involved in the definition, measurement, and analysis of change.

In this study, longitudinal data for a select panel of fifty-eight male subjects were used to examine the nature of the relationship between retirement and adaptation. These subjects were given a series of social and attitudinal measures shortly before their scheduled retirements. The measures were readministered five years later when they had been retired for varying periods of time. The primary variables utilized in the present analysis include a modified version of the Kutner Morale Scale (as a measure of subjective adaptation), education, occupational prestige, marital status, self-perceived health, and perceived job deprivation. Multivariate methods of analysis were used to examine patterns of change and stability in adaptation over time in the sample.

Our strongest finding was the evidence of overwhelming stability in subjective adaptation over time for these subjects. Evidence for this consisted of a t-test for the difference between paired means and a high ($r = .79$) correlation between the two measures of adaptation.

Multiple regression was used to examine the impact of variables which potentially condition the relationship between retirement and adaptation. Net of the Time 1 baseline measure of adaptation, marital status, occupational prestige, education, job deprivation, self-perceived health, and an interaction between length of time retired and occupational prestige were all significant predictors of adaptation at Time 2. Our results thus support previous studies which suggest that these are important factors in the retirement process. Our results strengthen these previous conclusions by demonstrating that these variables remain significant predictors of subjective adaptation when all intercorrelation among them has been controlled.

REFERENCES

ATCHLEY, R. C. "Retirement and Work Orientation." Gerontologist, 11 (1971): 29–32.

BARFIELD, R., and MORGAN, J. Early Retirement: The Decision and the Experience. Ann Arbor, Mich: Institute for Social Research, 1969.

BOHRNSTEDT, G. W. "Observations on the Measurement of Change." In Sociological Methodology, edited by E. Borgatta and G. Bohrnstedt. San Francisco: Jossey Bass, 1969.

CAMPBELL, A., CONVERSE, P. E., and RODGERS, W. L. Quality of American Life. New York: Russell Sage Foundation, 1976.

CAMPBELL, R. T., and EVERS, M. "An Empirical Comparison of Canonical and Log Linear Approaches to the Analysis of Polytomous Dependent Variables." Paper presented at annual meeting of American Sociological Association, Montreal, 1974.

CRONBACH, L. J., and FURBY, L. "Can We Measure Change—Or Should We?" Psychological Bulletin, 69 (1970): 68–80.

GEORGE, L. D. "An Empirical Comparison of Multiple Regression and Canonical Correlation in the Analysis of Change." In Proceedings of the 1975 Annual Meeting of the Joint Statistical Association, Washington, 1975.

HOLMES, T. H., and RAHE, R. H. "The Social Readjustment Rating Scale." Journal of Psychosomatic Research, 11 (1967): 213–218.

HOPE, K. "Quantifying Constraints on Social Mobility: The Latent Hierarchies of a Contingency Table." In The Analysis of Social Mobility, edited by K. Hope. London: Oxford University Press, 1972.

HOUSE, J. "Occupational Stress and Coronary Heart Disease: A Review and Theoretical Integration." Journal of Health and Social Behavior, 15 (1974): 12–27.

KUTNER, B., FRANSHEL, D., TOGO, A. M., and LANGNER, T. S. Five Hundred Over Sixty. New York: Russell Sage Foundation, 1956.

RABKIN, J. G., and STRUENING, E. L. "Life Events, Stress, and Illness." Science, 194 (1976): 1013–1020.

SIMPSON, I. H., BACK, K. W., and MCKINNEY, J. C. "Attributes of Work, Involvement in Society, and Self-Evaluation in Retirement." In Social Aspects of Aging, edited by I. H. Simpson and J. C. McKinney. Durham, N.C.: Duke University Press, 1966a.

SIMPSON, I. H., BACK, K. W., and MCKINNEY, J. C. "Orientations Toward Work and Retirement, and Self-Evaluation in Retirement." In Social Aspects of Aging, edited by I. H. Simpson and J. C. McKinney. Durham, N.C.: Duke University Press, 1966b.

STOKES, R. G., and MADDOX, G. L. "Some Social Factors in Retirement Adaptation." Journal of Gerontology, 22 (1967): 329–333.

STREIB, G. F., and SCHNEIDER, C. J. Retirement in American Society: Impact and Process. Ithaca, New York: Cornell University Press, 1971.

THOMPSON, W. E., STREIB, G. F., and KOSA, J. "The Effects of Retirement on Personal Adjustment: A Panel Analysis." Journal of Gerontology, 15 (1960): 165–169.

Coordination of Private and Public Pension Plans: An International Summary

John K. Dyer, Jr.

In most of the industrial countries of Europe and North America, some development of private, employer-sponsored pension plans preceded, often by many years, the introduction of social security pensions. Indeed, in many cases it was the very existence of such private plans, tending to be quite restrictive in their coverage, which stimulated the development of the government-sponsored, mandatory old age benefits, paid as a matter of right, which we commonly know as Social Security pensions.

Probably the ideal social security pension system is one that provides a uniform basic pension for all employees, whether in the private or public sector, and regardless of industry, occupation, or earnings level. I know of no such ideal system in existence today, although the Canadian basic old age pension is a close approach, and the British system as it has evolved from Lord Beveridge's proposals of over thirty years ago, also comes close to the ideal.

The pension provisions of the United States Social Security system, some distance from the ideal, seem to be headed *toward* rather than *away* from it. Many of the earlier exclusions, made primarily for administra-

From D. M. McGill, ed., *Social Security and Private Pension Plans: Competitive or Complementary?* (Homewood, Illinois: Richard D. Irwin, Inc., 1977). Reprinted by permission.

tive reasons, have been eliminated. Perhaps we shall see in the not too distant future the inclusion of federal government employees, and even state and local government employees on a mandatory basis, once they recognize that Social Security offers at least a partial answer to the financial difficulties many of them are having with their existing plans.

In other countries specific occupational and industrial groups have typically been excluded from the general social security system. In most cases groups so excluded are covered under special government-administered programs, presumed to be designed so as better to meet their special employment conditions. Our Railroad Retirement System was an illustration of this type of situation, but the recent amendments have now brought railroad employees effectively under the general social security system.

In some countries this fragmentation of social security into a main system and a series of satellite systems for particular industrial and professional groups seems to have become a fixed pattern, with little hope of eventual consolidation. The special systems are often the result of collective bargaining on an industry basis, and in any event the possession of a special social security system tends to become a "status symbol" for the groups so singled out. You will recall that it took a close approach to bankruptcy to bring the railroad employees in the United States into the common fold.

I have mentioned these things about the structure of social security systems since they could be viewed as one approach to the problem of coordinating public and private pensions—the satellite systems are in effect the contracting out of certain employee groups from the main system, in the presence of the real or presumed existence of special conditions or needs. Moreover, in approaching the problem of coordinating public and private pensions, the existence of satellite systems adds an extra dimension to the problem.

However, I shall not pursue this aspect further, but turn now to the problem as it confronts most employers in the private sector, especially the multinational employers—how best to provide for the coexistence to a private occupational pension plan with a mandatory social security system that provides the same employees with pensions as a matter of right.

Briefly, there are two basic alternatives that are generally available:

1. To provide under the Social Security law for "contracting out," that is for permitting individual employers to opt for the exclusion or partial exclusion of his employees from the normally mandatory Social Security system, subject of course to his providing appropriate replacement benefits through a private arrangement.

2. To structure the private plan so that its benefits are "integrated" with those of the Social Security system, that is, so that the two sources combined produce benefits that are adequate but not excessive at all earnings levels.

Combinations of the two alternatives are found. In fact where "contracting out" has been permitted it seldom applies to the full Social Security benefit, so there still remains the problem of integrating the private plan benefits with the residual benefits of the Social Security system.

CONTRACTING OUT

First, I should like to review some of the experiences with "contracting out," not because this is the best or the most prevalent approach, but because the experiences with it are not widely known, and do provide an important part of the background against which the "integration" approach has evolved as the most popular.

I start with a few notes on the "nonhistory" of contracting out in the United States. In 1935, when the Social Security system of the United States was in the process of being legislated, there were not many employers who really believed that the adoption of such a system could be avoided. There was, however, an important and vocal group of employers, encouraged and assisted by insurance companies that were just developing the field of insured pensions, who urged that employers with pension plans for their employees should be permitted to continue these plans unimpaired, and have their employees exempted from Social Security. These fought long and hard for a contracting out amendment, but lost. The effort was never revived, although there was an equally unsuccessful attempt to eliminate the Social Security law as unconstitutional.

Turning now to some more positive experiences, so far as I have been able to discover only four countries have made a serious attempt to use contracting out as a method of coordinating private and public pension plans. These countries are Belgium, Japan, New Zealand, and the United Kingdom.

Belgium may have been the first, but there the experiment was so limited in scope as to be of minor significance. For some years up to 1968, employees covered under the staff social security system of Belgium were permitted to opt that a part of their own social security contributions for retirement and widows' pensions be diverted to a private insurance company for the purchase of similar benefits, enhanced by the inclusion of cash options and other special features.

In 1968 the various Belgium Social Security funds were merged, and a new benefit formula, essentially the one in use today, was introduced for all employees. The individual contracting out feature was eliminated, but the insured benefits secured by the previously diverted employee contributions were preserved for the benefit of those who had them, without any corresponding offset in the new social security benefit formula. Thus the employees who had elected the option were granted a "free ride" to the extent that they received double benefits for the contributions they had diverted to insurance, resulting in a significantly higher total pension, especially for those who were nearing retirement age.

In *Japan*, the problem of coordinating private retirement benefits with social security is of fairly recent origin, and even now has not loomed very large. Japanese employers have provided retirement benefits for a long time. However, the traditional and still prevailing form of such benefits is a lump sum based upon the employee's final earnings level and his length of service. The service usually includes the employee's entire working lifetime, due to the Japanese tradition of lifetime employment. These lump sum retirement benefits have always been looked upon as deferred wages, so when social security pensions were first introduced in 1959 the possibility of coordinating them with the lump sum retirement benefits was apparently not even considered.

In 1962 the Japanese tax law was amended, extending to employer-sponsored annuity plans tax exemptions and deductions quite similar to those provided in the United States. The objective was to give employers encouragement to provide retiring employees with pensions, in lieu of or in addition to the traditional lump sum retirement benefits. Many employers did set up annuity plans, but the annuities provided were, and still are to a large extent, term certain rather than life annuities, and usually include a lump sum option which is almost always elected.

The tax incentive having proved less than satisfactorily effective in stimulating the growth of true pension plans in Japan, the next step, in 1966, was to amend the social security law to permit a measure of contracting out. This was limited in a number of ways:

1. It applied to the wage-related part of the two-tier Japanese social security benefit formula.

2. It required that replacement benefits be at least one-third higher in value than the social security benefits they replaced.

3. The option was available only for employers or employer groups with 1,000 or more employees.

4. Employee and union consent were required.

5. The reduction in employee and employer contributions from contracting out was only about one-third.

6. Lump sum commutation of the replacement benefits could not be permitted.

7. In case of termination of the plan providing the replacement benefits, the actuarial value of accrued benefits must be turned over to the social security reserve fund.

Not surprisingly, contracting out has not proved very popular, although it has been reported that as many as 900 qualifying plans, with 5 million covered employees, are in effect.

The viability of the Japanese contracting out procedure has been impaired by the fact that since 1973 social security benefits have been indexed to the Consumer Price Index. Contracting out, however, is limited to the nonindexed part of the benefit replaced, the increases due to indexing remaining with the social security system. Benefits increased over 40 percent from 1973 to 1975 as a result of the indexing. It is not difficult to visualize the contracted out benefits becoming so insignificant in relation to the whole that there remains little justification for continuing the option. In the absence of a complete overhaul of the Japanese social security system, the need for which is widely recognized quite apart from the question of coordination with private benefits, there are indications that contracting out has a very limited future in Japan.

Contracting out in *New Zealand* has had a very brief history—less than a year—and is now in limbo. In August 1974 the Labour Party-dominated New Zealand Parliament enacted the New Zealand Superannuation Scheme, a compulsory contributory national plan of the money purchase type. This plan became partially effective in April 1975, the beginning of what was to have been a five-year phase-in period. Contracting out was permitted, under conditions that never had a chance to become fully clarified.

In the November 1975 national election the Opposition National Party took over the government of New Zealand. They had made a promise, during the election campaign, to liquidate the New Zealand Superannuation Scheme and to replace it with something much better. One of the first acts of the new government was to discontinue the mandatory contributions, which was done in mid-December. They are now in the process of returning the contributions made, both employee and employer contributions being paid over to the employees, without interest but free of income tax.

During the election campaign the National Party released considerable publicity regarding the plan they would, if elected, substitute for the Labor Government scheme. Contracting out was not among the details mentioned, but it was stated that private schemes were to be treated as a "second tier," and were promised "generous tax concessions." There is nothing I can add at this point, but I rather suspect that contracting out is dead in New Zealand.

Coming finally to the *United Kingdom*, we find that one experiment with contracting out has come to an end, and another is in the process of implementation. From 1946, when Lord Beveridge's national pension program was installed, to 1961, the British system strictly followed the Beveridge pattern of uniform weekly benefits supported by uniform employee and employer contributions, each increased from time to time to keep pace with the rising cost of living.

In 1961 the so-called "graduated scheme" was introduced. This called for matching earnings-related contributions from employees and their employers, and provided fully vested pension benefit accruals directly related to the aggregate amount of the contributions. An employer could contract out his employees by establishing equivalent replacement benefits, under specified conditions, through a private scheme. The contracting out privilege applied initially to the full graduated scheme contributions and benefits, but as increases in contribution rates and the level of earnings to which they applied were introduced from time to time, the increases were not subject to contracting out. Contracting out was permitted only with respect to the original level of contributions, so the scheme developed to an increasing degree as a partially contracted out arrangement.

The financial terms for contracting out were fairly attractive to employers, even with the low rates of interest prevailing fifteen years ago. Many employers, including a large proportion of those in the public sector, opted for a private scheme. As interest rates rose, making contracting out even more attractive to employers, additional employers contracted out. By 1975, when the scheme was terminated, perhaps as many as 50 percent of employees under private schemes had been contracted out.

Discontinuance of the graduated scheme in 1975, with accrued benefits "frozen," was a feature of the Conservative Government's new "Strategy for Pensions," which was to create a full partnership between government and employers in providing employee pensions. This program had a form of contracting out under which the emphasis was focused on the provision of private plan benefits, with a government "reserve scheme" available only for those employees whose employers made no pension provision for them. This somewhat idealistic program was supposed to have become effective in April 1975.

The Labor Government which took over after the February 1974 national elections promptly decided to follow the Conservatives' plan to discontinue the graduated scheme, but to throw out all the rest. In due course the new government came up with its program, which has now been enacted and which is scheduled to take effect in April 1978. It also has a "contracting out" feature, with terms considerably less favorable than those of the 1961 scheme.

So at present British employers and their advisors are struggling with the question of whether or not to contract out of the earnings-related second tier of the Labour Party scheme. There are many complicated issues, not the least of which is a requirement that replacement benefits must be fully indexed, as are the social security benefits they replace, except that at retirement age the national plan will take over the guarantee and payment of subsequent cost of living increases.

It may be that the British are almost alone today in their continuing belief that contracting out is a feasible and desirable concept. Whether or not this faith will sustain them through the many difficulties that lie ahead, both before and after 1978, should be one of the more interesting chapters in the history of public and private pensions.

Looking back through this brief history of contracting out as a device for coordinating public and private pensions, one is struck with the omnipresence of politics as a factor at all stages—adoption, development, and ultimate demise.

Integration

Turning now to the other alternative in coordinating public and private pensions, integration, we find that the political factor is far less important. The reason is fairly obvious—provisions for contracting out generally require specific legislation, in the form of amendments to the social security laws,

while integration is inherently the problem of the employer. He must, of course, satisfy the bureaucrats who must approve his program and verify his tax deductions. Thus the choice, from one viewpoint, depends on whether employers get along better with legislators or bureaucrats.

I happen to belong to that generation of actuaries who started practice in the private pension field during the period when the original Social Security legislation in the United States was being developed, revised, and implemented. Once the possibility of contracting out had been eliminated, as I have described before, the constitutionality of the legislation affirmed, and the 1939 amendments which created the present benefit structure enacted, the major problem of the employer with a pre-existing pension plan became the coordination of that plan with a social security system that had become a reality.

United States

The Revenue Act of 1942 was the first national legislation in the United States to impose detailed control over private pension plans. The primary objective of this legislation was to limit the use of such plans as shelters against the high wartime tax rates, both corporate and individual. The principal provision designed to implement this objective was that which prohibited a tax-qualified plan from "discriminating" in favor of highly compensated employees.

Regulations under the new law did not appear until over a year after its enactment. When the regulations did appear it was found, to the shocked surprise of many employers and their advisors, that the Internal Revenue had interpreted the nondiscrimination provision to limit any and all benefits that might be provided with respect to earnings in excess of those covered by Social Security (then $3,000 per year). Efforts to defeat this interpretation were unsuccessful. The formula limitation for integration is still with us, becoming more complicated with each successive change in Social Security, and with each fresh effort on the part of the tax administrators to refine the formula and its application.

Some details of the first twenty-five years of integration regulations in the United States are contained in Appendix A, which is a paper I prepared in 1968 for the American Enterprise Institute. This paper was prepared primarily to present the arguments against a major reduction (from 37.5 percent to 24 percent) in the integration limit, proposed by the Internal Revenue Service in 1966 on the basis of a stricter interpretation of the concept. A secondary objective of the paper was to show how impractical and unrealistic the whole subject had become. Widespread objection to the IRS proposal resulted in a long delay in its adoption, and after substantial increases in Social Security benefits adopted in 1967 made the proposal even more difficult to justify, it was finally dropped. The 37.5 percent limitation was retained, and this still constitutes the basic limitation on the extent to which benefits on earnings above the Social Security limit may exceed those superimposed upon Social Security in the covered earnings zone. However, the technical details surrounding the adjustment of the basic limit for different types of benefit formula, different compensation bases, death benefits, employee contributions, and other variations continue to complicate the picture. The interpretation and application of the integration regulations has assumed the proportions of a special field of expertise within the Internal Revenue Service and the pension consulting profession.

There has always been a tendency for the integration regulations to lag at least one step behind developments that would normally affect them. Thus, the effect of automatic cost of living indexing of Social Security benefits, introduced some four years ago, has yet to be recognized in the integration regulations. Looking ahead, a new formula for the calculation of Social Security pensions is now before Congress, with an excellent chance of passing, and thereby again rendering the regulations obsolete. Dis-counting the unlikely possibility that the Internal Revenue will finally decide upon a simpler and more practical view of integration, it appears that this aspect of pension plan design and administration will continue to be one of the most complicated and frustrating problems faced by those in the pension field in the United States.

Very early in this process it was recognized that there were two major variations of the integration principle. One was to adopt or continue a benefit formula defining the full objective benefit, deducting from it all or a part of the Social Security benefit. This may be called the "subtractive" approach, although those who prepared plan documents went to great lengths in attempting to avoid the impression that something had been taken away. These efforts often failed, with the result that the so-called "Social Security offset" under this type of plan had a tendency to erode, especially under union pressure, and in some cases eventually to disappear. Where this has happened the loss in terms of redundant benefits is generally permanent; there is no turning back and reintegrating the plan on some other basis.

The other variation on the integration theme, and the one that is probably the most widely used, not only in the United States but in other countries, is to design the private plan benefit formula so that it complements the social security formula. An almost universal characteristic of social security benefit formulas is that they relate to earnings up to some specified level (which of course tends to change), with earnings above that level ignored. Thus the integration formula is generally made up of a certain percentage applied to earnings up to the social security "ceiling," and a higher percentage of earnings above the ceiling. This of course is pretty elementary to all pension practitioners. A subvariation of this type of formula, found in some European countries where the social security benefit is a flat amount, unrelated to earnings or service, consists in omitting entirely from the private plan benefit formula, and from the contribution base as well, all earnings up to a specified level.

The level is determined as that point where the flat social security benefit alone produces a satisfactory benefit in relation to earnings. In Holland this is known as the "franchise" method of integration.

Both of the major variations of integration are found in pension plans in the United States. In the late '30s and early '40s, when employers and their advisors were still uncertain as to the future of social security, the subtractive method was adopted for many of the older plans, sometimes as an interim arrangement pending the development of an entirely new and different pension program. Some employers who started with a subtractive integration, then went to a new plan based on career pay with employee contributions, have completed the full circle and are now back to where they started, with a final pay noncontributory plan.

Europe

Most European countries with a significant development of private occupational pensions have met the integration problem in much the same way that it has been met in the United States. Both variations of the integration approach have been used, but in no country has the application of integration principles been surrounded with anything like the volume of technicalities and formulas that employers in the United States have had to cope with over the past thirty years.

In *Belgium, Germany,* the *Netherlands,* and *Switzerland,* where private occupational pensions have developed along lines quite similar to those with which we are familiar in the United States, both the subtractive and the split formula methods of integration are used. There is probably some increase in the popularity of the subtractive method, since in all of these countries social security pensions are indexed to the cost of living, generally by formula, and subtractive integration seems to be simpler and more satisfactory under these conditions.

The *Republic of Ireland* until very recently had a social security system which excluded from compulsory participation all employees earning above a specified level—a feature which was found in Germany and some other countries some years ago. This led to a practice of limiting participation in private occupational plans to those who were not covered by social security, and the practice of so limiting coverage still persists to some extent in Ireland.

In *France* there is a basic social security system, plus a unique series of complementary pension systems superimposed. For the very high paid employees there is often a third layer of pension coverage. This is a most interesting structure, but much too complicated to discuss here. Suffice it to say that the whole complex is integrated on the basis of salary slices (tranches), although some overlapping has recently crept in through collective bargaining.

Sweden has a flat rate basic pension, plus an earnings-related complementary tier of social security, plus a third tier of privately financed pensions created by industrywide collective bargaining. This may be the most perfectly integrated system to be found, but only because the individual employer has no choice but to go along with the standard pattern. Only at the top levels of salary can the employer make his own deal with his executives.

MANDATORY PRIVATE PENSIONS

As mentioned before, the *Netherlands* and *Switzerland* belong to that group of countries where national and private pensions are coordinated by integration, in much the same way as in the United States. However, in both of these countries it has been decided as a matter of national policy—confirmed by referendum in Switzerland more than three years ago—that, rather than continue expanding social security, every employer should be required by law to maintain an occupational pension plan, privately financed and administered but meeting prescribed minimum standards. The development of these "second pillar" programs has been stalled in both countries by immediate and serious economic problems. In Switzerland, enabling legislation has finally reached the Parliament and will probably be enacted in 1976, with the program starting a five-year phasing-in period on January 1, 1978. The timetable in the Netherlands is not yet clear.

The Swiss and Dutch proposals, it should be emphasized, are not to be confused with the "two-tier with contracting-out" programs in effect in Japan and being implemented in the United Kingdom. The Swiss and Dutch plans do not include any government-administered alternative; they simply call for a second tier private plan as a statutory requirement upon every employer. It might be noted that such a program has been in effect in Finland for over ten years, although on a basis which does not provide much guidance for the larger industrialized countries.

CONCLUSION

In considering this collage of public and private pensions, and their diverse efforts to coexist, one is greatly tempted to look for some common denominator—perhaps a direction in which all of the elements are heading toward some ultimate goal. The pursuit of this line of inquiry, however, quickly involves far greater questions of economic and political evolution, areas in which no actuary would venture. Thus any conclusions that might be derived from the picture as I have drawn it must necessarily be narrow and highly equivocal.

If in any country there is a significant movement in the relative positions of public and private pensions, it will inevitably be in the direction of giving public pensions a larger role. If the cold war between public and private pensions is ever to come to an end, public pensions will be the winner; the rules of the game are so written. Thus, in most of South America the public pension movement developed like any other South American revolution—it was over before most people knew it had started. Private pensions never had a chance.

I am not wholly pessimistic, however, as to the future of private pensions in North America, or even in Europe. Perhaps twenty-five years ago an eminent authority on international benefits predicted that private pensions in Europe had no better than a ten- or fifteen-year life expectancy, so far as rank and file employees were concerned. Today we see that they have virtually disappeared in Italy, and probably must be considered a lost cause in Spain, but they still seem to be alive and in reasonably good health in most of Northern Europe. So I am not about to be a prophet of doom for the private pension movement in my generation.

SECTION 6

Aging Tomorrow: Prospects, Policy, Ethics

What is need not necessarily be so, yet the exigencies of daily life often cloud our realization of that fact. Under any circumstances, looking two or three decades into the future is no easy task. Those who are already old often express impatience with long-range projections, and for those who will be old tomorrow or the day after, the vicissitudes of life in the next century appear insurmountable. While futurology has become something of an academic fancy, the basis for gerontology in the first place is intervention. Using history or the contemporary scene as a guide it is possible to anticipate the approximate proportions of what is to come, but with the world changing ever more quickly and in unforeseen directions, the quality of life for those who will be old in the years following 2000 may be markedly different from what has been described so far. There is, nonetheless, reason as well as opportunity to engage in rational advanced planning; to do otherwise would be to shirk our responsibilities, to undermine the justification of gerontology and the potential for a fulfilling life for tomorrow's elderly.

The future status of the aged hinges not only on factors of their health, psychological and economic well-being, living arrangements and support services, but on a range of issues far beyond an individual's or even an entire cohort's control. A combination of international concerns and demands together with an overarching value or ideological orientation will lend structure to the meaning of life across the lifecourse. It seems clear that the lot of the elderly will likely improve relative to younger age categories on a number of dimensions. In terms of income, occupational indicators, health status, education, and related areas of life there is evidence to support assumptions of continued advancements (Palmore, 1976; Hendricks and Hendricks, 1977). Yet the prospect of shortages in natural resources, reallocation of governmental backing, and the changes associated with lifting the mandatory retirement age render the future more difficult to anticipate. Whatever resolutions do emerge cannot rely solely on technological or scientific skills. As rigorous as science is, it does not operate in a vacuum. If all of us, as the elderly of the twenty-first century, are to face our lives with hope, the time to begin is now; yesterday would have been even better.

For the immediate future, that which will become a reality for those already born, a pragmatically circumscribed orientation can limit the range of alternatives which must be considered (Lakoff, 1977). But there is by no means a consensus as to whether or not the needs of future cohorts of older people can best be met by treating them as a subcategory, apart from the rest of society. Ascribing characteristics to a group numbering upwards of thirty million may be an effective way of designing policy, but at what cost to those involved? Even so worthwhile a goal as flexible retirement policies will pose problems for those who might well desire a change in status but who must also contend with economic realities and social pressures prescribing self-worth on the basis of productivity (Etzioni, 1976). In a pluralistic society such as ours the balancing of individuality against policy positions is a never-ending struggle.

As complicated as it may be to engage in social forecasting some tentative predictions can be made. To begin with, we must have an indication of how many people will be included in the target population. Herman Brotman provides just that information in his projections for the year 2000. Unless the natural processes of aging are somehow arrested, or there is a dramatic breakthrough in medical knowledge—both of which are generally considered to be unlikely since normal physiological changes, cancer and similar ailments all have multiple etiologies which make them poor candidates for a quick cure—demographers know approximately how many people there will be over age sixty-five in the year 2000. What is more problematic is their proportion among the total population. Working with projections of zero population growth Brotman predicts that 15.5 percent of all Americans will be sixty-five or older. If growth rates fall below replacement levels, as they have recently, then the percentages would be higher. Should couples in the United States return to a fertility average exceeding a simple replacement rate, then the percentage of people over sixty-five will fall accordingly. It is among the very old, those over age seventy-five that the greatest change will occur. With a jump of 60 percent expected, the need for social services will be far greater than it is today. The most dramatic increases in the overall number and proportion of older people are likely to be observed among blacks, due primarily to declining mortality rates. As Brotman points out, however, the relative deprivation of the black elderly is not going to improve unless existing social policies are renovated.

What kinds of support services should be available for tomorrow's elderly? Ostensibly they will be designed for the specific needs of that group, but what of the political compromises that characterize even the most fundamental program? David Peterson and his colleagues call for further attention to the issues of cohort alienation, formulation of an identifiable aged subculture, development of gerontology as a field of inquiry, and ethical dimensions of physical and sociological survival. No easy questions these. In fact, so controversial are the elements involved that the editor of the journal in which Peterson et al.'s comments first appeared was stimulated enough to offer his own response. In replying, Elias Cohen challenges several of the predictions and conclusons reached. Disagreeing with Peterson et al. on several criteria, Cohen implies that the wish may be progenitor to the thought, and that more sober reflection is mandated. Both article and reply have been included here to provide a brief glimpse of the vitality of the debate being conducted among gerontologists themselves. Directing further attention to social components in the daily life of older people around the turn of the century, Bernice Neugarten and Robert Havighurst examine the role of the family for the very old, those over seventy-five.

The study of aging is not only a scientific enterprise; the humanities also contribute to our understanding of how people become old. In an affluent society such as ours, technology is frequently perceived to be a panacea for all manner of social ills and difficulties. Yet technology creates as many hurdles as it overcomes. Michel Philibert, by training a French philosopher, is a proponent of an integrative approach to aging. Recognizing that we are more than biological organisms growing old according to predetermined timetables, Philibert reminds us that we impute meaning to the events in our lives, they do not just happen. Much of gerontology, he feels, has become entirely too ahistorical and insulated from the values around which we structure our consciousness. Reviewing the recent history of gerontology he asserts that there may have been some misdirection in the field, but that it is not too late to return to a more holistic approach. Contrasting two distinct philosophical approaches, one eastern, the other our more familiar western way, Philibert musters literary and cross-cultural illustrations applicable to improving the lot of tomorrow's elderly, suggesting in the process the need for a new concept of aging.

REFERENCES

1. ETZIONI, A. "Old People and Public Policy," *Social Policy* 7 (3) (1976): 21–29.

2. HENDRICKS, J., and HENDRICKS, C. D. "The Prospects of Aging." In *Aging In Mass Society: Myths and Realities,* pp. 385–414. Cambridge, Mass.: Winthrop Publishers, Inc. (1977).

3. LAKOFF, S. A. "The Future of Social Intervention." In *Handbook of Aging and the Social Sciences,* edited by R. H. Binstock and E. Shanas, pp. 643–63. New York: Van Nostrand Reinhold Company, 1977.

4. PALMORE, E. "The Future Status of the Aged." *The Gerontologist* 16 (4) (1976): 297–302.

Population Projections

Tomorrow's Older Population (to 2000)

Herman B. Brotman

INTRODUCTION

An adequate data base, designed for planning and evaluation, is one of the most important "inputs" for the determination of social policy, the measurement of the kinds and quantities of unmet needs and their relative priorities, and the development of programs to meet the needs based on knowledge both of the need and of the characteristics of the older people who have the need.

However, since most of the available data were collected in, and therefore reflect, the recent or more distant past, we must be sure not to plan future programs for yesterday's older people but for tomorrow's.

Our data base must conform to the recognized concepts that the older population is not a uniform, monolithic mass and that each succeeding cohort of people in the population who attain old age with the passage of time are rather different in number, composition, and proportion of the population than their predecessors.

This aspect, planning for tomorrow's aged, would be much simpler if we were clairvoyant and could see accurately into the future to predict exactly what the situation will be. Unfortunately, this kind of "prediction" is beyond our present skills, so we substitute "projections" based on the application to the present situation of one or more sets

From *The Gerontologist* 17, 3 (1977), pp. 203–209. Reprinted by permission.

of our best or most reasonable assumptions about what future trends will be in order to produce a single best projection or an array of projections resulting from stated, alternative assumptions.

This article will deal with projections covering approximately one generation, 25 years from 1975 to 2000. An article in a future issue will deal with projections beyond the year 2000.

One of the reasons for the choice of this convenient dividing line is that since all of the persons who will be aged 25 and over in 2000 are already born, the consensus on reasonable assumptions as to future trends for them is easily reached and produces a single set of assumptions. The size and composition projections for the total population, however,

TABLE 1

Rate of increase in population.

PERIOD		TOTAL		65 +
1900–1910.		21.0		28.2
1910–1920.		14.9		24.9
1920–1930.		16.1		34.5
1930–1940.		7.2		36.0
1940–1950.		14.5		36.0
1950–1960.		18.5		34.7
1960–1970.		13.3		21.1
Projection	I	II	III	
1970–1980.	11.1	9.7	8.5	22.3
1980–1990.	14.2	10.0	6.9	18.0
1990–2000.	11.4	7.1	4.0	5.8

depend on assumptions as to future birth rates which will determine the size and the composition of the under-25 population in 2000. Future birth rates do not meet the same degree of agreement because they are influenced by individual decisions based on a large variety of factors.

The procedure, then, is to apply to detailed estimates of the age-sex-color composition of the current population a single set of assumptions to project the number and composition in the future for the persons already born. Then, projections based on the number of women of childbearing ages and a small number of assumptions as to future birth rates are prepared to show the population not yet born.

For this article, the base was the 1974 population distribution. The uniform assumptions for future trends for the population already born were: A small decline from current death rates (no medical miracles like a cancer cure); death rates for blacks decreasing faster to approach more closely those for whites; and a constant net inmigration of 400,000 per year.

Three sets of separate assumptions were used in relation to future birth rates. Series I assumes an ultimate fertility rate (children per female) of 2.7, which represents a large increase over the current low rate of approximately 1.8. This assumption produces the largest number of young persons and thus of the total population and reduces the *proportion* of older people.

Series III assumes the opposite end of the birth rate spectrum by using an ultimate fertility rate (children per female) of 1.7, a further decrease from the current low rate of approximately 1.8. This assumption produces the smallest projections and thus shows an increase in the proportion of older people.

Series II assumes a middle position, a fertility rate of 2.1, a middle-range increase over the current 1.8. A continuing 2.1 rate would result in "zero population growth" (a stable population pyramid) just before the middle of the 21st century. This series is generally considered the "conservative" or "most likely" series for future planning when

there are no overriding reasons for using other assumptions concerning future birth rates.

For ease of use, all of the assumptions are included in the footnotes to Parts A, B, and C of Table 2, which presents the projections and the analysis of the projections for every fifth year from 1975 to 2000 for each of the series. Further, it should be noted that the projections do not show a continuous smooth curve because the existing age cohorts vary in size as a result of previous fluctuations in birth rates; the application of uniform assumptions does not wipe out existing differences. For instance, the post World War II baby boom (late 1940s and early 1950s) shows up as a bulge in each succeeding age group with the passage of time.

GENERAL POPULATION TRENDS

Summary

As may be seen from the summary of the rate of increase in the total and the 65+ population between 1900 and 2000, the older population has consistently increased more rapidly than the younger and thus increased in the proportion of the total from 4 percent in 1900 to well over 10 percent in 1975. The projections show a continuation of this differential until just before the turn of the century when the cohort reaching age 65 reflects the low birth rates during the Depression and World War II period (Table 1).

Series I (Table 2A)

These projections, based on an assumed sharp increase over current birth rates, show a slowing down of the increase in the median age of the population (28.8 in 1975, 31.4 in 2000), a small increase in the proportion of the total population in the under-18 category, a similar decrease in the 18–64 group, and a fairly flat figure for the 65+ population at just under 11 percent.

The gross dependency ratios are very rough indications of the burden carried by the middle group, on whom both the young

Analysis of population projections by major age groups, 1975–2000.
Census series I[1]

ITEM AND AGE	1975	1980	1985	1990	1995	2000
Numbers (000)						
All ages	213,641	225,705	241,274	257,663	272,685	287,007
Under 18	66,465	66,194	71,759	80,267	88,368	91,152
18–64	124,846	134,988	142,856	148,463	154,010	165,255
65+	22,330	24,523	26,659	28,933	30,307	30,600
55+	42,099	45,570	48,124	49,412	50,603	53,537
60+	31,568	34,267	37,136	39,127	39,858	40,590
Median age	28.8	29.5	30.1	30.8	31.4	31.4
% distribution						
All ages	100.0	100.0	100.0	100.0	100.0	100.0
Under 18	31.1	29.3	29.7	31.2	32.4	31.8
18–64	58.4	59.8	59.2	57.6	56.5	57.6
65+	10.5	10.9	11.1	11.2	11.1	10.6
55+	19.7	20.2	20.0	19.2	18.6	18.7
60+	14.8	15.2	15.4	15.2	14.6	14.1
Dependency ratios						
Number per 100 aged 18–64:						
Under 18	53.2	49.0	50.2	54.1	57.4	55.2
65+	17.9	18.2	18.7	19.5	19.7	18.5
Under 18 and 65+	71.1	67.2	68.9	73.6	77.1	73.7

[1] Assumptions: Small decline in death rates with black approaching closer to white rates; constant net immigration of 400,000 per year; ultimate fertility rate (children per female) of 2.7, a large increase over the current rate of approximately 1.8.

Source: Bureau of the Census.

and the old are dependent. For this analysis, two ratios are computed, assuming a so-called productive age group of 18–64. One ratio is the number of persons under 18 per 100 aged 18–64; the other is the number of persons aged 65+ per 100 aged 18–64. The total burden is the sum of these two.

In the Series I projections, there are small increases in both dependency ratios over the 25-year period, so that the total burden on the productive age population rises from about 71 to about 74 per 100.

Series II (Table 2B)

These projections, based on a relatively small increase over current birth rates, show a significant increase in the median age of the population (28.8 in 1975, 34.8 in 2000), a decrease in the proportion of the total population in the under-18 age group, a slightly smaller increase in the 18–64 category, and an increase in the proportion aged 65+ from 10.5 to 11.7% in 2000.

The very small increase in the dependency ratio for older persons (from 18 to 19 per 100 aged 18–64) is more than offset by the sharp decline in the under-18 ratio so that the total burden falls from 71 to 63 per 100 aged 18–64.

Series III (Table 2C)

These projections, based on approximately the current low birth rates, show a rapid increase in the median age of the pop-

TABLE 2B

Analysis of population projections by major age groups, 1975–2000. Census series II[1]

ITEM AND AGE	1975	1980	1985	1990	1995	2000
Numbers (000)						
All ages	213,450	222,769	234,068	245,075	254,495	262,494
Under 18	66,274	63,258	64,553	67,679	71,277	71,079
18–64	124,846	134,988	142,856	148,463	152,911	160,815
65+	22,330	24,523	26,659	28,933	30,307	30,600
55+	42,099	45,570	48,124	49,412	50,603	53,537
60+	31,568	34,267	37,136	39,127	39,858	40,590
Median age	28.8	29.9	31.1	32.3	33.6	34.8
% distribution						
All ages	100.0	100.0	100.0	100.0	100.0	100.0
Under 18	31.0	28.4	27.6	27.6	28.0	27.1
18–64	58.5	60.6	61.0	60.6	60.1	61.2
65+	10.5	11.0	11.4	11.8	11.9	11.7
55+	19.7	20.5	20.6	20.2	19.9	20.4
60+	14.8	15.4	15.9	16.0	15.7	15.5
Dependency ratios						
Number per 100 aged 18–64:						
Under 18	53.1	46.9	45.2	45.6	46.6	44.2
65+	17.9	18.2	18.7	19.5	19.8	19.0
Under 18 and 65+	71.0	65.1	63.9	65.1	66.4	63.2

[1] Assumptions: Small decline in death rates with black approaching closer to white rates; constant net immigration of 400,000 per year; ultimate fertility rate (children per female) of 2.1, a middle-range increase over the current rate of approximately 1.8. A continuing 2.1 rate would produce "zero population growth" (a stable population pyramid) just before the middle of the 21st century. Projection Series II is generally considered the "most likely" or "conservative" series for future planning when there are no over-riding reasons for using other assumptions.

Source: Bureau of the Census.

ulation (28.8 in 1975, 37.0 in 2000), a large decrease in the proportion of the population aged under 18, and fairly large increases in the proportion aged 18–64 and 65+. As might be expected, this low birth rate assumption produces the largest proportion of older persons, 12.5%.

Similarly, the dependency ratio for the under-18 age group drops very sharply and far overbalances the small increase in the 65+ ratio so that the total burden drops from about 71 to 56 per 100 aged 18–64.

The Black Population, All Series (Table 3)

This table summarizes the results of the application of all three sets of assumptions but presents only the 1975 and 2000 figures. Also, gross dependency ratios are not computed, since they have meaning for only the total population which carries the burden of support for the younger and older age groups through both public and private mechanisms.

TABLE 2C

Analysis of population projections by major age groups, 1975–2000. Census series III[1]

ITEM AND AGE	1975	1980	1985	1990	1995	2000
Numbers (000)						
All ages	213,323	220,356	228,355	235,581	241,198	245,098
Under 18	66,147	60,845	58,840	58,185	58,919	57,322
18–64	124,846	134,988	142,856	148,463	151,972	157,176
65+	22,330	24,523	26,659	28,933	30,307	30,600
55+	42,099	45,570	48,124	49,412	50,603	53,537
60+	31,568	34,267	37,136	39,127	39,858	40,590
Median age	28.8	30.3	31.8	33.4	35.2	37.0
% distribution						
All ages	100.0	100.0	100.0	100.0	100.0	100.0
Under 18	31.0	27.6	25.8	24.7	24.4	23.4
18–64	58.5	61.3	62.5	63.0	63.0	64.1
65+	10.5	11.1	11.7	12.3	12.6	12.5
55+	19.7	20.7	21.1	21.0	21.0	21.8
60+	14.8	15.6	16.3	16.6	16.5	16.6
Dependency ratios						
Number per 100 aged 18–64:						
Under 18	53.0	45.1	41.2	39.2	38.8	36.5
65+	17.9	18.2	18.7	19.5	19.9	19.5
Under 18 and 65+	70.9	63.3	59.9	58.7	58.7	56.0

[1] Assumptions: Small decline in death rates with black approaching closer to white rates; constant net immigration of 400,000 per year; ultimate fertility rate (children per female) of 1.7, a small decrease from the current low rate of approximately 1.8.

Source: Bureau of the Census.

Depending on the birth rate assumptions, the black population may be expected to grow from 24.5 million in 1975 to between 31.0 and 36.4 million in 2000. The proportion under 18 shows sizable decreases under all of the series due in part to the uniform assumptions that death rates for blacks will decrease faster than for whites. A reflection of this is the considerable increase in the proportions aged 18–64 and 65+ for all assumptions.

Whereas 65+ blacks represented 7.4 percent of all blacks in 1975, the proportion will grow to between 8.1 and 9.5 percent in 2000. While this is a noteworthy achievement, the rapid growth from 1.8 million older blacks in 1975 to almost 3 million by 2000 will merely exacerbate the problems of this minority unless there is considerable improvement in the relatively disadvantaged position of today's black aged.

OLDER POPULATION TRENDS

Since all persons who will be in the older categories by 2000 are already born and their numbers are not affected by future birth rates, the application of the uniform set of assumptions regarding death rates and net immigration produce a single set of projections for all series. The basic assumption of a very small decrease in death rates (with blacks approaching the rates for whites) presumes

TABLE 3

Analysis of black population projections by major age groups, 1975 and 2000.

ITEM AND AGE	1975	2000 FOR SERIES[1]:		
		I	II	III
Numbers (000)				
All ages	24,517	36,379	33,325	30,963
Under 18	9,547	12,522	9,982	8,110
18–64	13,165	20,915	20,401	19,911
65+	1,805	2,942	2,942	2,942
55+	3,254	5,334	5,334	5,334
60+	2,616	4,011	4,011	4,011
Median age	23.5	27.8	30.9	33.3
% distribution				
All ages	100.0	100.0	100.0	100.0
Under 18	38.9	34.4	30.0	26.2
18–64	53.7	57.5	61.2	64.3
65+	7.4	8.1	8.8	9.5
55+	13.3	14.7	16.0	17.2
60+	10.7	11.0	12.0	13.0

[1] See footnotes to Parts A, B, and C of Table 2 for explanation of assumptions for each Series.

Source: Bureau of the Census.

that there will be no medical breakthroughs like a cancer cure in the next 25 years. While such a medical advance would have a large impact on life expectancy in the upper ages, the chances are that the startling claims of added years and added numbers in the popular literature would not be achieved in full, since death is a result of multiple risks; some of the older people who would not die of cancer at some given age might still die from a variety of other causes.

Tables 4 A, B, and C (all older persons, whites, and blacks, respectively) are designed to serve primarily as reference tables presenting 1975 and 2000 data by sex and by 5-year, 10-year, and summary age groupings for the 55+ segment of the population. Analytical measures include percentage distributions based on 55+ and 65+ totals, sex ratios (women per 100 men), and detailed percentage increases from 1975 to 2000.

In quick summary: the most significant conclusions are 1) that not only is the older population growing faster than the younger but the older population itself is aging since the older part is growing faster than the younger part (between 1975 and 2000, the 55–64 age group will increase by 16 percent, the 65–74 by 23 percent, and the most vulnerable, the 75+, by 60 percent); and 2) that the existing disparity between the numbers of older men and women will increase further (in 1975, there were 144 women per 100 men aged 65+, in 2000, there will be 154; the 75+ ratio jumps from 171 to 191).

Growth rates for white and black aged generally follow the pattern for the total of all races, but the rates for whites are somewhat below the total while those for blacks show considerably higher levels.

TABLE 4A

Analysis of older population projections by sex and race, 1975 and 2000. (numbers in thousands). All races.

AGE	TOTAL			MEN			WOMEN			PER 100 MEN
	#	%		#	%		#	%		
1975										
55+	42,099	100.0	—	18,483	100.0	—	23,616	100.0	—	128
65+	22,330	53.0	100.0	9,147	49.5	100.0	13,182	55.8	100.0	144
55–59	10,531	25.0	—	5,020	27.2	—	5,511	23.3	—	110
60–64	9,238	21.9	—	4,316	23.4	—	4,923	20.9	—	114
65–69	8,097	19.2	36.3	3,581	19.4	39.2	4,515	19.1	34.3	126
70–74	5,784	13.7	25.9	2,446	13.2	26.7	3,337	14.1	25.3	136
75–79	3,998	9.5	17.9	1,570	8.5	17.2	2,428	10.3	18.4	155
80–84	2,629	6.2	11.8	953	5.2	10.4	1,675	7.1	12.7	176
85+	1,822	4.3	8.2	596	3.2	6.5	1,226	5.2	9.3	206
55–64	19,769	47.0	—	9,336	50.5	—	10,434	44.2	—	112
65–74	13,881	33.0	62.2	6,027	32.6	65.9	7,852	33.2	59.6	130
75+	8,449	20.0	37.8	3,119	16.9	34.1	5,329	22.6	40.4	171
2000										
55+	53,537	100.0	—	22,953	100.0	—	30,583	100.0	—	133
65+	30,600	57.2	100.0	12,041	52.5	100.0	18,558	60.7	100.0	154
55–59	12,947	24.2	—	6,224	27.1	—	6,723	22.0	—	108
60–64	9,990	18.7	—	4,688	20.4	—	5,302	17.3	—	113
65–69	9,023	16.9	29.5	4,021	17.5	33.4	5,002	16.4	27.0	124
70–74	8,056	15.1	26.3	3,368	14.7	28.0	4,688	15.3	25.3	139
75–79	6,224	11.6	20.3	2,375	10.4	19.7	3,849	12.6	20.7	162
80–84	4,080	7.6	13.3	1,383	6.0	11.5	2,697	8.8	14.5	195
85+	3,217	6.0	10.5	894	3.9	7.4	2,323	7.6	12.5	260
55–64	22,937	42.8	—	10,912	47.5	—	12,025	39.3	—	110
65–74	17,079	31.9	55.8	7,389	32.2	61.4	9,690	31.7	52.2	131
75+	13,521	25.3	44.2	4,652	20.3	38.6	8,868	29.0	47.8	191
% increases										
55+	27.2			24.2			29.5			
65+	37.0			31.6			40.8			
55–59	22.9			24.0			22.0			
60–64	8.1			8.6			7.7			
65–69	11.4			12.3			10.8			
70–74	39.3			37.7			40.5			
75–79	55.7			51.3			58.5			
80–84	55.2			45.1			61.0			
85+	76.6			50.0			89.5			
55–64	16.0			16.9			15.2			
65–74	23.0			22.6			23.4			
75+	60.0			49.2			66.4			

Source: Bureau of the Census.

TABLE 4B

Analysis of older population projections by sex and race, 1975 and 2000. (numbers in thousands) White

AGE	TOTAL #	TOTAL %		MEN #	MEN %		WOMEN #	WOMEN %		PER 100 MEN
1975										
55+	38,185	100.0	—	16,735	100.0	—	21,450	100.0	—	128
65+	20,317	53.2	100.0	8,278	49.5	100.0	12,039	56.1	100.0	145
55–59	9,521	24.9	—	4,551	27.2	—	4,970	23.2	—	109
60–64	8,347	21.9	—	3,906	23.3	—	4,441	20.7	—	114
65–69	7,267	19.0	35.8	3,217	19.2	38.9	4,050	18.9	33.6	126
70–74	5,298	13.9	26.1	2,225	13.3	26.9	3,073	14.3	25.5	138
75–79	3,678	9.6	18.1	1,431	8.6	17.3	2,246	10.5	18.7	157
80–84	2,418	6.3	11.9	870	5.2	10.5	1,548	7.2	12.9	178
85+	1,657	4.3	8.2	535	3.2	6.5	1,122	5.2	9.3	210
55–64	17,868	46.8	—	8,457	50.5	—	9,411	43.9	—	111
65–74	12,565	32.9	61.8	5,442	32.5	65.7	7,123	33.2	59.2	131
75+	7,753	20.3	38.2	2,836	17.0	34.3	4,916	22.9	40.8	173
2000										
55+	47,101	100.0	—	20,218	100.0	—	26,883	100.0	—	133
65+	27,113	57.6	100.0	10,638	52.6	100.0	16,475	61.3	100.0	155
55–59	11,294	24.0	—	5,472	27.1	—	5,821	21.7	—	106
60–64	8,694	18.5	—	4,108	20.3	—	4,587	17.1	—	112
65–69	7,777	16.5	28.7	3,489	17.3	32.8	4,287	16.0	26.0	123
70–74	7,144	15.2	26.4	2,985	14.8	28.1	4,159	15.5	25.2	139
75–79	5,611	11.9	20.7	2,132	10.6	20.0	3,479	12.9	21.1	163
80–84	3,687	7.8	13.6	1,240	6.1	11.7	2,447	9.1	14.9	197
85+	2,894	6.1	10.7	791	3.9	7.4	2,103	7.8	12.8	266
55–64	19,988	42.4	—	9,580	47.4	—	10,408	38.7	—	109
65–74	14,921	31.7	55.0	6,474	32.0	60.9	8,446	31.4	51.3	130
75+	12,192	25.9	45.0	4,163	20.6	39.1	8,029	29.9	48.7	193
% increases										
55+	23.3			20.8			25.3			
65+	33.5			28.5			36.9			
55–59	18.6			20.2			17.1			
60–64	4.2			5.2			3.3			
65–69	7.0			8.5			5.9			
70–74	34.8			34.2			35.3			
75–79	52.6			49.0			54.9			
80–84	52.5			42.5			58.1			
85+	74.7			47.9			87.4			
55–64	11.9			13.3			10.6			
65–74	18.8			19.0			18.6			
75+	57.3			46.8			63.3			

Source: Bureau of the Census.

TABLE 4C

Analysis of older population projections by sex and race, 1975 and 2000. (numbers in thousands) Black

AGE	TOTAL #	%		MEN #	%		WOMEN #	%		PER 100 MEN
1975										
55+	3,525	100.0	—	1,547	100.0	—	1,978	100.0	—	128
65+	1,805	51.2	100.0	761	49.2	100.0	1,044	52.8	100.0	137
55–59	908	25.8	—	419	27.1	—	489	24.7	—	117
60–64	812	23.0	—	367	23.7	—	445	22.5	—	121
65–69	768	21.8	42.6	329	21.3	43.2	439	22.2	42.1	133
70–74	428	12.1	23.7	191	12.4	25.1	237	12.0	22.7	124
75–79	276	7.8	15.3	118	7.6	15.5	159	8.0	15.2	135
80–84	188	5.3	10.4	73	4.7	9.6	115	5.8	11.0	158
85+	144	4.1	8.0	50	3.2	6.6	94	4.8	9.0	188
55–65	1,720	48.8	—	786	50.8	—	934	47.2	—	119
65–74	1,196	33.9	66.3	520	33.6	68.3	676	34.2	64.8	130
75+	608	17.3	33.7	241	15.6	31.7	368	18.6	35.2	153
2000										
55+	5,335	100.0	—	2,290	100.0	—	3,046	100.0	—	133
65+	2,942	55.2	100.0	1,188	51.9	100.0	1,753	57.6	100.0	148
55–59	1,323	24.8	—	617	26.9	—	707	23.2	—	115
60–64	1,070	20.1	—	485	21.2	—	586	19.2	—	121
65–69	1,075	20.2	36.5	460	20.1	38.7	615	20.2	35.1	134
70–74	775	14.5	26.3	331	14.5	27.9	445	14.6	25.4	134
75–79	505	9.5	17.2	204	8.9	17.2	301	9.9	17.2	148
80–84	326	6.1	11.1	117	5.1	9.9	209	6.9	11.9	179
85+	260	4.9	8.8	76	3.3	6.4	184	6.0	10.5	242
55–64	2,393	44.8	—	1,102	48.1	—	1,293	42.4	—	117
65–74	1,850	34.7	62.9	791	34.5	66.6	1,060	34.8	60.5	134
75+	1,091	20.5	37.1	397	17.3	33.4	694	22.8	39.6	175
% increases										
55+	51.4			48.0			54.0			
65+	63.0			56.1			67.9			
55–59	45.7			47.3			44.6			
60–64	31.8			32.2			31.7			
65–69	40.0			39.8			40.1			
70–74	81.1			73.3			87.8			
75–79	83.0			72.9			89.3			
80–84	73.4			60.3			81.7			
85+	80.6			52.0			95.7			
55–64	39.1			40.2			38.4			
65–74	54.7			52.1			56.8			
75+	79.4			64.7			88.6			

Source: Bureau of the Census.

Aging in America

Toward the Year 2000

David A. Peterson
Chuck Powell
Lawrie Robertson

Large numbers of retired persons, reasonably healthy, geographically separated from their families, and relying on social insurance programs for a living income are a comparatively new phenomenon in this nation. Likewise, the field of research, education, and service created to understand and aid these individuals has only recently acquired significant social impact. The shortness of time to socialize both individuals and professionals has resulted in divergent opinion on the present condition of the field as well as short- and long-range trends. The purpose of this paper is to identify a number of these trends and to make some projections regarding aging in the year 2000. Before suggesting an outline of the future, however, it will be helpful to sketch the contemporary situation briefly.

Today, as in the past, the field needs a clear, coherent, and generally accepted policy on aging. The 1971 White House Conference on Aging, although having the development of a national policy as its theme, was not successful in creating such a statement. A national policy should be enunciated by a public official at the highest level of government. Such a policy would provide an elastic framework which could be adjusted over time. In addition, this orientation would be-

From *The Gerontologist* 16, 3 (1976), pp. 264-275. Reprinted by permission.

come the foundation upon which the numerous programs designed to improve the quality of life for older persons could be built. A good example of such social planning can be found in the Full Employment Act of 1946 which has served American society for some thirty years (Bailey, 1950).

The development of a clear policy is dependent upon the contemporary social and political conditions of the nation. Current conditions, however, are not sufficiently supportive to allow the promulgation of such a statement. In fact, basic and sweeping changes appear to be occurring which will likely retard, for the interim, any consensus on a national policy for the aging. From all indications, present ambivalence in identifying appropriate clientele (i.e., the vulnerable aged or all older people) and in determining the most appropriate programmatic focus (i.e., income support or community programs) will continue. This ambivalent focus has resulted in misunderstanding, counterproductive activities, and inappropriate utilization of resources.

Although policy, change and client ambivalence have hindered the development of the field, significant progress has occurred during the past decade to provide a foundation for rapid future development. An infrastructure has been built which can deliver mandated services and act upon the political system so that the wishes of the constituency are adequately represented at the highest levels of decision making. The U. S. Senate Special Committee on Aging, and more recently the House of Representatives Select Committee on Aging, the Administration on Aging, state units on aging, and area agencies provide for grassroots input while acting at the very heart of decision making at the national, state, and local levels. These are indicative of marked and significant progress beyond that of other eras; for instance, the Townsend Movement could create excessive noise but was not able to successfully affect legislation (Holtzman, 1963; Pinner, Jacobs, and Selznick, 1959; Putnam, 1970). Organizations of older persons alternately support and attack this infrastructure in hope of securing an increasing proportion of the available resources. Their growing concern is for a life with independence and dignity; one in which their contribution to the prosperity of the nation is recognized and in which their individual constitutional rights to life, liberty, and property are respected.

Finally, aging programs today are moving incrementally to improve service, budget, and community support. Through significant increases in Administration on Aging funding since 1972, the past several years have seen steady growth of resources, a development of community interest, and a broadening of the services provided to older people. a national system is slowly taking form which enables professionals to elicit input from clients, convey needs to policy makers, plan strategies, deliver services, and adequately compete for limited resources. This movement has developed slowly and continues year by year to grow in strength and vitality.

DIFFICULTIES IN PREDICTING THE FUTURE

Prediction of events which will occur in the future is a difficult undertaking since there are an unlimited number of unforeseen variables that may intervene at any time. Some of these events are currently beyond the control of man (e.g., floods, drought, earthquakes, and blizzards) others, though created by man, are of such a magnitude that they take on an inertia of their own and are modified only by horrendous effort and agonizing sacrifice (e.g., inflation, war, conflicting ideology, and resource depletion).

Extrapolating from present trends excludes the likelihood of the intervention of the unforeseen. As Ogburn (1964) has pointed out,

> The logic of prediction is that the universe of the future will be much like the universe of the past. If some greatly upsetting factor occurs, such as a war or a revolutionary invention, the conditions are so changed that extrapolation is hardly worth trying.

A classic set of predictions which typifies the tendency to overlook the unforeseen was made in the 1937 National Resources Committee Report to President Franklin D. Roosevelt. In predicting technological developments in the futre, the authors totally overlooked the discovery of nuclear power, jet propulsion, aviation as a primary transportation system, and the transistor, all of which were in use within fifteen years (National Resources Committee, 1937).

Thus the prognosticator is left in the quandary of being forced to describe the future in terms of the present, ignoring the unforeseen, or embarking on the hazardous undertaking of including within the prediction those future events which may be generally obscured from the present view. Recently, gerontologists at the University of Chicago put forth a series of predictions regarding aging in the year 2000 (Neugarten, 1975). Essentially, their study placed heavy emphasis on the demographic, social, health, and program changes that may occur in the next quarter century. At the University of Nebraska at Omaha, we have been examining a somewhat different area feeling that linear projections may overlook certain contingencies. The questions entertained here generally support the Chicago predictions. On the other hand, the comments to follow focus primarily on the political and social policy areas while giving attention to voting and constitutional issues. The basis for these predictions is found in social history and political philosophy. As a consequence, these projections address a variety of macro-changes that are likely to occur in the future. These suggestions are supported by several indicators which suggest that real and massive changes are imminent in our society and that older people will be significantly affected by such events.

PREDICTIONS FOR THE YEAR 2000

There will be a significant shift in political philosophy in the United States. This change in political philosophy should be as great as was the change from Herbert Hoover to his successor, Franklin D. Roosevelt. The nation has undergone several such shifts in the past 200 years. These changes have, for the most part, been marked by three events: 1) a collapse in the old older; 2) a period of instability; 3) a critical election. The cumulative effect of these events generally signaled that the population was ready to move away from the existing political philosophy and its attendant policies into the next segment of the future. With the passage of time these periods became clearly identifiable. The collapse of the old order and the ensuing periods of instability are relatively well defined in terms of the eras of Jefferson (Ellis, 1971), Lincoln (Foote, 1958; Sandburg, 1939), and Franklin Roosevelt (Burns, 1956). Historians will agree that these three presidential periods signaled the emergence of a changed political philosophy that continued over a significant time span.

The critical election theory seems to support the contention that dominant political philosophy has shifted radically at several points in our history. These shifts were indicated by critical elections which show a collapse in partisan allegiances, erratic behavior, voter turnout deviations, and ticket-splitting (Burnham, 1970; Pomper, 1974; Sundquist, 1973). At these intersections, prior partisan loyalties have been permanently and massively reorganized as the society seeks to determine new directions. The elections of 1800–1804, 1828, 1860–1864, 1896, and 1932–1936 can be defined as critical, with the elections of 1828 and 1896 re-enforcing an ongoing political time period. Some would consider the elections of 1968–1972 in a similar light, however, this is a premature judgment.

The several indicators mentioned above do not occur at regular intervals; therefore, it is difficult to predict the time and direction of the coming change in political philosophy. As to time, interpretation of political and historical events indicates that conditions are favorable for such a change. The past several years have seen a collapse in many areas as the citizenry questions the old order and instability results. In terms of direction, the coming change may be toward a more conservative, laissez-faire form of capitalism. However, a more likely outcome would be a move toward the liberal side or toward the protection of individual rights. A post-industrial society seems to point the way toward an improvement in the quality of life and social justice (Bell, 1973). Consequently, our expectation would be that within the next twenty-five years the nation will redefine its political philosophy in such a manner that aging will be given a parity position in society. Aging and the aged will receive an equitable share of the aggregate resources in the more general move to social equality.

A clear national policy for the field of aging will be developed and enunciated. Such a policy statement will militate against the current disorganization and overlap now found in the programmatic approach to the problems of the aged.

For the most part, public policy is formulated, legitimated, and finally applied after passing many strategic check points in the environment (Dommel, 1974). These time-consuming inputs are necessary, inasmuch as proponents and opponents search and negotiate for the proper approach to real or perceived problems in given areas. The process eventually provides the necessary parameters within which a policy can be stated (Dye, 1972; Easton, 1965a, b; Ripley, 1974). In terms of aging, the bulk of this process has passed many of the strategic check points in the movement toward a public policy. When one considers the White House Conferences on aging, advocacy roles played by the many national organizations representing the interests of the aged, and numerous legislative efforts designed to resolve precisely identified problems, it is reasonable to conclude that the stages of acceptability and awareness have been passed. The time has arrived when all efforts can be considered *in toto* for the purpose of placing existing programs under a national policy statement.

A policy statement is a declaration of intent on the part of government. To be most effective and carry maximum impact, the declaration should be highly visible as in a statement by the President or a promulgation by Congress. Implementation in this case should not be problematic, as there are numerous programs in existence that are capable of fitting within the necessary policy framework. Future programs can be merged into this framework for the purpose of additional strength. Therefore, it is reasonable to forecast a forthcoming policy statement that will address aging in the total environment. This occurrence will permit a comprehensive address to aging by replacing the piecemeal approach of the past.

There will develop a voting bloc of individuals who consider themselves to be old and who will, for a time, successfully support legislation for persons in the later stages of life. This prediction runs somewhat counter to the prevailing opinion that the development of voting bloc of the aged is unlikely in the foreseeable future. Binstock (1974), for example, suggests that there are no sound reasons to expect older people to gain more power through voting than they have today. Other writers have supported this position by showing that older Americans have few

common interests (Carter, 1969), are not a homogeneous group (Schmidhauser, 1968), have little cohesion (Binstock, 1972), and have strong party alliances (Campbell, 1964). While examination of the voting behavior of older people shows their propensity to vote, evidence is generally lacking to support the claim of a voting bloc (U. S. Dept. of Commerce, 1973a, b, 1975). Nevertheless, these data provide an accurate and unchallenged description of how many elderly voters cast ballots. They also supply limited insight into the issues and candidates in a given election. Still, they offer little understanding of the reasons for this voting behavior.

While our prediction includes an awareness of this prevailing opinion, our argument is based on other grounds. First, several writers have noted a propensity on the part of older people to turn toward political activity as a means of personal fulfillment, regardless of whether this activity leads to clearly defined ends (Atchley, 1972; Glenn, 1969; Schmidhauser, 1968). Second, although older people may not have accepted a political position, people often shape their attitudes and opinions in response to perceived pressures from the group, even when these pressures are weak or absent (Ripley, 1974). Various organizations of senior citizens, for instance, are actively engaged in assuring that these pressures are strong and obvious. Third, certain factors can operate on individuals and groups to motivate persons into protective activity. Frustration (Knutson, 1972), loss of gratification (Davies, 1973), and loss of material benefits (Wilson, 1973), are strong motivators which can trigger a defensive response among the elderly. When older persons perceive conditions to exist which threaten their economic, physical, or psychological well-being, it is reasonable to expect a protective reaction—even one so unlikely as the formation of a voting bloc.

Evidence that the older population will respond in such a manner may be gleaned from past elections. When candidates are unable or unwilling to address the perceived threat faced by the elderly, they may be confronted by a united opposition. Examination of the 1936 elections in Florida and Montana provide illustrations of this behavior. In Florida, Governor Carlton ignored the income maintenance demands of the elderly and lost the primary election to a relative unknown (*New York Times*, 1936). In Montana, Senator Borah took a supportive, middle-ground position on the same issue and easily defeated a Townsend supported candidate (Holtzman, 1963). While this evidence is only suggestive, it is such as to illustrate that an issue can unite a group of older people into a political bloc, at least for short periods of time.

It is our expectation that the issue which will unite older Americans in the coming years will be the perceived loss or modification of social security payments and Medicare benefits. These programs are widely based and meet the test of significance as they touch all or most of the elderly. A mere suggestion that these programs be tampered with should trigger a perceived threat of the first magnitude with attendant, vigorous reaction by the elderly. Historically, the political system in the United States has provided many such examples which have led to de-stabilization of existing voting patterns. At these intersections, the potential for change is great (Niemi, 1973). Therefore, we expect a voting bloc to emerge based on perceived loss of benefits.

The Supreme Court will declare compulsory retirement at a fixed age unconstitutional. This development will remove the fixed age or length of service requirement now found in the working environment. This prediction will be realized as legal scholars, medical practitioners, and members of the gerontological community undertake revisions in present statutory and administrative laws which have developed over time in support of mandatory retirement.

In approaching this question, it is imperative to recognize that mandatory retirement is cloaked in the respectability of time, with very shallow underpinning in law. Although important, time alone does not answer the question of legality or constitutionality. In a more important sense, legal rules are never clear; accordingly, if a rule had to be absolutely clear prior to implementation our society would be impossible (Levi, 1948). However, there are times when the individual rights of citizens are restricted by the actions of managers and legislators. When this occurs, the actions must be reconciled against the Constitution.

Generally speaking, legislatures pass statutory laws based on some identifiable need (Ripley, 1974; 1975), while administrative agencies generate procedural rules referred to as administrative law (Lorch, 1969). These two instruments stand in law or lie dormant until tested against the Constitution. Prior to becoming a member of the Supreme Court, Charles Evans Hughes made the observation that we live under a Constitution. The Constitution, however, is generally what judges regard it to be and the task of safeguarding our life, liberty, and property falls to the judiciary (Swindler, 1970). This philosophy seems operative currently as the court continues to remove barriers imposed by historical precedent and strike down repressive social or economic legislation (Corwin, 1974).

The constitutionality of mandatory retirement or refusal to hire due to age is questionable; therefore, we may expect additional court battles in these areas (Kaplan, 1971). These court battles will be supported by two significant constitutional guarantees—due process and equal protection. The Fifth Amendment assures that no person will be deprived of life, liberty, or property without due process, while the Fourteenth Amendment restrains states from depriving any person of life, liberty, or property without due process and equal protection under the law.

Three recent cases set the stage for testing the validity of mandatory retirement and refusal to hire due to age. They are *Weiss v. Walsh* (1973), *Weisbrod v. Lynn* (1974), and *Cleveland Board of Education v. LaFleur* (1974). The first case reached the U. S. District Court in 1972 and was dismissed on the rationale that, "despite advances in our knowledge of aging it is nonetheless clear that abilities diminish with age and that age is not discriminatory because it cuts across all categories of race, religion, and national origin" (Butler, 1975). Such a conclusion can and will be tested frequently in the cauldron of Federal Courts as well as public opinion.

A popular, although somewhat unenlightened, rationale has begun to develop. In *Weisbrod v. Lynn*, Justice Department lawyers argued along similar lines by stating that, "age is a classification which cuts across racial, religious, national origin and economic means—which bears a substantial relationship to mental and physical ability" (Mackenzie, 1975). This case reached the Supreme Court during the 1974–1975 session; however, the court refused to hear the case with Justice Blackmun voting to hear the appeal. These two cases nevertheless demonstrate a willingness of the government and the courts to establish a classification based on chronological age which directly conflicts with due process and equal protection.

In *Cleveland Board of Education* v. *LaFleur,* the school board had required teachers who became pregnant to take maternity leave several months prior to giving birth. This position was established in the absence of medical evidence as to the individual teacher's ability to perform assigned tasks. An arbitrary class based on a time frame had been created. The defendent looked to the due process clause of the Fourteenth Amendment for redress. Justice Potter Stewart writing for the majority upheld the defendent's right to individual treatment.

> The provisions amount to a conclusive presumption that every pregnant teacher who reaches the fifth or sixth month of pregnancy is physically incapable of continuing. There is no individualized determination by the teacher's doctor—or the school board's—as to any particular teacher's ability to continue at her job. The rules contain an irrebuttable presumption of physical incompetency, and that presumption applies even when the medical evidence as to the individual woman's physical status might be wholly to the contrary.

This decision seems to set the stage for the overturning of the rationale established in the two previous cases.

The final decision will rest with the court contingent on the arguments presented. Over the years this body has shown a willingness to address significant issues and provide legal answers to societal problems (Abraham, 1974; Friedman and Israel, 1970). Cumulative evidence, then, strongly suggests that mandatory retirement and refusal to hire because of age will be struck down by the court in the next quarter century.

IMPLICATIONS AND CONCLUSIONS

In developing the preceding positions, we have generally supported the University of Chicago's projections as to the future of aging. Our forecasts, however, have concentrated on the aged and their position in the larger society vis-à-vis the governmental and political decision-making process. In this regard, neither the Chicago predictions nor ours are exhaustive. There are numerous areas that should be examined for the purpose of giving the gerontological community a more realistic view of the future. Areas worthy of further scrutiny, for example, include: 1) *cohort alienation,* i.e., to what extent will there be considerable conflict between older people and youth over the issue of resource allocation? 2) *disciplinary development,* i.e., how and to what extent can the field of aging be significantly broadened in future decades? and 3) *physical and sociological survival,* i.e., to what degree will concern be manifested regarding the right of adults to decide how long and under what conditions they wish to live? In the latter instance, to what extent will subsequent advances in medicine impact the aged population?

The future is of utmost importance and is heavily dependent on the activities of the present. The decisions and behavior of persons working in the field of aging today will determine the events of the next twenty-five years. The planning that is done today should be based on valid assumptions as to the conditions that will exist in the next quarter century. If we assume that the future will be an absolute reflection of the present and that a static period is to be expected, then the field of gerontology will find itself in a position of reacting to contemporary events rather than leading in the areas of planning and implementation.

To some extent we are already living in the future as we continually create a framework contingent upon our response to present events. While some of our predictions are obviously advantageous, others are not. The assumptions we choose and the decisions we make will affect both aged persons and professionals alike. As a consequence, in preparing for the future it is essential to provide inputs from numerous areas of expertise. Such an approach will lay the groundwork for future planning as well as assist in the establishment of a more mature and realistic *Weltanschauung*.

REFERENCES

ABRAHAM, H. J. *Justices and Presidents: A Political History of Appointments to the Supreme Court.* New York: Oxford University Press, 1974.

ATCHLEY, R. C. *The Social Forces in Later Life: An Introduction to Social Gerontology.* Belmont, Calif: Wadsworth, 1972.

BELL, D. *The Coming of Post-Industrial Society.* New York: Basic Books, 1973.

BAILEY, S. K. *Congress Makes a Law: The Story Behind the Employment Act of 1946.* New York: Columbia University Press, 1950.

BINSTOCK, R. H. "Interest-group Liberalism and the Politics of Aging." *Gerontologist,* 12 (1972): 265–280.

BINSTOCK, R. H. "Aging and the future of American Politics." *Annals of American Academy of Political and Social Science,* 415 (1974): 199–212.

BURNHAM, W. D. *Critical Elections and the Mainsprings of American Politics.* New York: W. W. Norton, 1970.

BURNS, J. M. *Roosevelt: The Lion and the Fox.* New York: Harcourt, Brace, & World, 1956.

BUTLER, R. N. *Why Survive? Being Old in America.* New York: Harper & Row, 1975.

CAMPBELL, A. *The American Voter.* New York: John Wiley & Sons, 1964.

CARTER, M. K. "Politics of Age: Interest Group or Social Movement." *Gerontologist,* 9 (1969): 259–263.

Cleveland Board of Education v. *LaFleur,* 94 S. Ct. 791 (1974).

CORWIN, E. S. *The Constitution and What It Means Today.* Revised by H. W. Chase & C. R. Cucat. Princeton, New Jersey: Princeton University Press, 1974.

DAVIES, J. C. "Aggression, Violence, Revolution, and War." In *Handbook of political psychology,* edited by J. Knutson. San Francisco: Jossey-Bass, 1973.

DOMMEL, P. R. *The Politics of Revenue Sharing.* Bloomington, Indiana: Indiana University Press, 1974.

DYE, T. R. *Understanding Public Policy.* Englewood Cliffs, New Jersey: Prentice-Hall, 1972.

EASTON, D. A. *A Systems Analysis of Political Life.* New York: John Wiley & Sons, 1965a.

EASTON, D. *A Framework for Political Analysis.* Englewood Cliffs, New Jersey: Prentice-Hall, 1965b.

ELLIS, R. E. *The Jeffersonial Crisis: Courts and Politics in the Young Republic.* New York: Oxford University Press, 1971.

FOOTE, S. *The Civil War,* Vol. I. New York: Random House, 1958.

FRIEDMAN, L., and ISRAEL, F. L. (eds.) *The Justices of the United States Supreme Court, 1789–1969: Their Lives and Major Opinions.* New York: Chelsea House, 1970.

GLENN, N. "Aging, Disengagement, and Opinionation." *Public Opinion Quarterly,* 33 (1969): 17–33.

HOLTZMAN, A. *The Townsend Movement: A Political Study.* New York: Bookman Associates, 1963.

KAPLAN, S. "Too Old to Work: The Constitutionality of Mandatory Retirement Plans." *Southern California Law Review,* 44 (1971): 150–180.

KNUTSON, J. N. *The Human Basis of the Polity.* New York: Aldine-Atherton, 1972.

LEVI, E. H. *An Introduction to Legal Reasoning.* Chicago: University of Chicago Press, 1948.

LORCH, R. S. *Democratic Process and Administrative Law.* Detroit: Wayne State University Press, 1969.

MACKENZIE, J. P. "High Court Upholds U.S. Retirement Age." *Washington Post,* Feb. 25, 1975.

National Resources Committee. Report of the Subcommittee on Technology. *Technological Trends and National Policy, Including the Social Implications of New Inventions.* Washington, D.C.: USGPO, 1937.

NEUGARTEN, B. L. (ed.) "Aging in the Year 2000: A Look at the Future." *Gerontologist,* 15 (1:2 1975): 1–40.

New York Times. Aug. 13, 16, 1936.

NIEMI, R. G. "Political Socialization." In *Handbook of Political Psychology,* edited by J. Knutson. San Francisco: Jossey-Bass, 1973.

OGBURN, W. F. *On Culture and Social Change.* Selected papers edited by O. Dudley. Chicago: University of Chicago Press, 1964.

PINNER, F. A., JACOBS, P., AND SELZNICK, P. *Old Age and Political Behavior: A Case Study.* Berkeley: University of California Press, 1959.

PUTMAN, J. K. *Old-age Politics in California: From Richardson to Reagan.* Stanford, Calif.: Stanford University Press, 1970.

POMPER, G. M. *Elections in America: Control and Influence in Democratic Politics.* New York: Dodd, Mead, 1974.

RIPLEY, R. B. *American National Government and Public Policy.* New York: Free Press, 1974.

RIPLEY, R. B. *Congress: Process and Policy.* New York: W. W. Norton, 1975.

SANDBURG, C. *Abraham Lincoln: The War Years.* New York: Harcourt, Brace, 1939.

SCHMIDHAUSER, J. "The Political Influence of the Aged." *Gerontologist,* 8 (1968): 44–49.

SUNDQUIST, J. L. *Dynamics of the Party System: Alignment and Realignment of the Political Parties in the United States.* Washington, D.C.: Brookings Institution, 1973.

SWINDLER, W. F. *Court and Constitution in the 20th Century: The New Legality, 1932–1968.* New York: Bobbs-Merrill, 1970.

U.S. Dept. of Commerce, Bureau of the Census. Voting and registration in the election of Nov., 1970, Ser. P-20, No. 228. USGPO, Washington, Oct., 1973a.

U.S. Dept. of Commerce, Bureau of the Census. Voting and registration in the election of Nov., 1972, Ser. P-20, No. 253. USGPO, Washington, Oct., 1973b.

U.S. Dept. of Commerce, Bureau of the Census. Voter participation in Nov., 1974 (advance report), Ser. P-20, No. 275. USGPO, Washington, Jan., 1975.

Weiss v. Walsh, 324 F. Supp 75 S.D.N.Y., (1972), Affirmed without opinion, 461 F. 2d 846 2nd Cir. (1972), certiorari denied 409 U.S. 1129 (1973).

Weisbrod v. Lynn, Fd2d, D. C. Ct. of Appeals (Mar. 11, 1974).

WILSON, J. Q. *Political Organizations.* New York: Basic Books, 1973.

COMMENT

Editor's Note

In the course of exercising customary editorial duties, the Editor was so stimulated by the foregoing article that he undertook to engage the authors in some colloquy regarding their predictions and underlying assumptions. They suggested that the comments offered to them might be of interest to the readership and that they would welcome published commentary on their article in the hopes that it would stimulate further discussion and exchange. As a result of that suggestion, I have departed from the customary policy of restricting the editor's effusions to the editorial page to challenge some assumptions and conclusions that Peterson and his colleagues have suggested.

Retrospective futurology is a chastening exercise. As Peterson et al. point out, the

National Resources Committee Report of 1937 overlooked the discovery of nuclear power, jet propulsion, aviation as a primary transportation system, and the transistor, all of which were in use within fifteen years. If prediction is difficult in technological areas where the state of development is on firmer theoretical bases and research building-block techniques may be better developed, how much more difficult is prediction in the political and social sciences. We have difficulty in predicting birth rates, and from a demography standpoint we made egregious errors by predicting increased birth rates five years after the rates had tapered off, largely because changes in social customs had been ignored, and the view was directed at the long-range curve, which had not changed significantly. Nevertheless, if one is going to engage in predicting the future, the predictions should have a good base in a clear view of the present, a clear view of those factors that one can reasonably believe will exist at the point in the future one is offering predictions about and some supportable assumptions.

One of the underlying assumptions is that "basic and sweeping changes appear to be occurring which will likely retard . . . any consensus on a national policy for the aging." Furthermore, there is some suggestion that there is ambivalence in identifying appropriate clientele. If one looks at resource allocation, the ambivalence may be more in the eyes of advocates for community services than it is in the eyes of researchers. Resource allocation has moved clearly and steadily in the direction of improved income maintenance (including supplemental security income and food stamps) and payments for medical services through Medicaid and Medicare. Both may be viewed in terms of income support programs. Resources allocated for services have been miniscule and continue to be so. Indeed, to the extent that Title XX of the Social Security Act represented at least as substantial a resource for the elderly (potentially) as the Older Americans act, the placing of a ceiling on Title XX represented a step backward. There is no indication of intent by the Congress in the long or short run to remove that ceiling and there is little evidence to suggest that there will be great surges forward in appropriations for Titles III and VII of the Older Americans Act. This seems to comport with general trends evidenced in the fields of mental health and child welfare.

A second assumption is that significant progress has occurred during the past decade to provide a foundation for further development. The Area Agencies on Aging no more represent an infrastructure for delivering mandated services and acting upon the political system, "so that the wishes of the constituency are adequately represented at the highest levels of decision making" than do the community mental health centers (or for that matter other human service delivery mechanisms). The fact that Senate and House Committees on Aging hear witnesses from "the grass roots," and the fact that federal and state agencies are required to publish regulations and receive comment on them in the Federal Register and the state equivalent, or the fact that hearings must be held is not to say that there is bona fide grass roots input, much less control. A realistic view would suggest that aside from the abortive experience of Community Action Program agencies operating under the Office of Economic Opportunity, we have not had very serious attempts at grass roots input in the human service field in the United States. Indeed, it may be impossible. It is one thing to hear from the Grey Panthers or the National Council of Senior Citizens or the American Association of Retired Persons/National Retired Teachers Association, and quite another to hear from the most vulnerable of the elderly who are not members or part of any of those organizations. Indeed, very few of the policy statements of those organizations have effectively dealt with the hard-to-reach, inarticulate, and what one might call the defeated elderly.

Furthermore, not all commentators share the view that the Townsend movement was not able to affect legislation successfully. Indeed, some hold that the impact of Townsend was such as to give great impetus to the

Social Security Act which was offered as an alternative to the Townsend Plan. More to the point, however, might be a look at the McClain movement in California which was successful—so much so that it was able to secure a constitutional amendment which, among other things, wrote the name of the individual to administer the old age pension program in California into the constitution. Ultimately, that amendment was repealed, but the power of McClain relative to the elderly and the blind in California is probably one of the most significant chapters in American history on old age politics. It is almost universally overlooked.

At the risk of engendering howls of outrage, let me suggest that the assertions about the growing concern of elderly people for a life "with independence and dignity . . . in which their contribution to the prosperity of the nation is recognized and in which their individual and constitutional rights to life, liberty and property are respected," may or may not be correct. The late Donald Kent, a former Editor of this journal, in a striking article entitled, "Aging: Fact or Fancy" (USGPO, 1965) raised serious questions about what it was elderly people *do* prefer and whether professionals in geronotology accurately understood what the elderly did or did not prefer or aspire to. While the assertions made by Peterson conform to the general rhetoric, some researchers report findings that may question it.

Finally, there is an assumption that aging programs are moving "incrementally to improve service budget and community support." To suggest that there have been significant increases in Administration on Aging funding since 1972 is to take a narrow view based on a start from near zero. Such an approach permits the conclusion of a many-fold increase. However, when measured against Title I of the Older Americans Act, the increases are not significant. They may be politically appropriate, but they do not begin to make much impact on what need is, and there is nothing to suggest that we can predict a budget for the Administration on Aging of several billion dollars a year

even within the next quarter century. Furthermore, it is difficult to suggest at this point that the Area Agencies on Aging represent anything like a national system. It is probably one of the most fragmented approaches to human services that has yet been designed in the United States. It is almost completely divorced from ordinary political processes and, as such, is well insulated from organized pressures operating through political structures.

The Peterson paper offers four predictions for aging in America:

1. There will be a significant shift in political philosophy in the United States such that aging will be given a parity position in society and, further, that aging and the aged will receive an equitable share of the aggregate resources in the more general move to social equality.

2. A clear, national policy for the field of aging will be developed and enunciated.

3. There will develop a voting bloc of individuals who consider themselves to be old and who will successfully support legislation for persons in the later stages of life.

4. The Supreme Court will declare compulsory retirement at a fixed age unconstitutional.

Peterson and his associates muster very little evidence that suggests support for the prediction of a national redefinition of political philosophy moving toward the liberal side or toward protection of individual rights. If one looks at the selection of presidents (to use one criterion) over the last half century, Franklin D. Roosevelt notwithstanding, one must conclude that America selects its presidents from the center of the spectrum rather than from either extreme. There is nothing in that history to suggest a significant re-definition in political philosophy— that term being used to connote some significant shifts in the allocation of power among social classes, between majority and minority groups, or among the holders and nonholders of economic power. Furthermore, one might argue that the very complexity of our society and the extraordinary interdependence that has evolved in the economy have rendered significant shifts in almost any direction nearly impossible. Our national "style" is one of incrementalism, except during those periods of time when survival of the sovereign seems to be threatened. Even there, because of our extraordinary wealth, we have not chosen or found it necessary to choose radical solutions but have been able to proceed largely incrementally and in classical conservative fashion.

If the incrementalism is indeed the style, it is doubtful that twenty-five years will be sufficient to achieve the parity the authors suggest. While the analog is far from perfect, one might suggest that the black, Indian, and Spanish-American segments of our society have been striving for parity for a considerable time and find the progress minimal. It took a century and a half for women to gain the vote, and it has been another half century of striving to secure other rights, not the least of which is equal pay for equal work. Power relationships are not easily changed in our country, and, while I wish no less fervently for the outcome predicted by Peterson and his colleagues, I am much less sanguine about the prospects.

As for the clear national policy for the field of aging, I would suggest that one *has* been clearly enunciated. However, having said that I hasten to ask, "What difference does it make whether there is one or not?"

A stated national policy on aging is anything but self-executing. To state a national policy is not to have one that is the basis for governmental and nongovernmental activity. Title I of the Older Americans Act has not been changed since the bill was signed into law by the President on July 14, 1965—more than a decade ago. The Act sets forth a ten-point declaration of objectives for older Americans in keeping with the traditional American concept of inherent dignity of the individual in our democratic society.

These objectives are as follows:

1. An adequate income
2. The best possible physical and mental health
3. Suitable housing
4. Full restorative services
5. Opportunity for employment without age discrimination
6. Retirement in health, honor, and dignity
7. Pursuit of meaningful activity
8. Efficient community services when needed
9. Immediate benefit from proven research knowledge
10. Freedom, independence, and the free exercise of individual initiative.

And, as if that were not enough, one might look to the presidential messages on aging by the past three elected presidents, each of whom has undertaken what I am sure he perceived to be a clear, national policy for the field of aging. The fact that Title I of the Older Americans Act is honored in breech simply says that it is an ineffective policy statement.

Policy statements abound in statutes and in presidential pronouncements. The Civil Rights Act of 1964 is a policy statement of great significance, but it does not mean that we have secured equal treatment for minorities in all sectors of societal activity. What is perhaps most astonishing is the authors' reliance on the Full Employment Act of 1946 as an example of a policy statement. The Full Employment Act has not provided full employment in this country except for a few brief periods while we were at war during the Korean conflict or the Vietnamese war. Even then it was not so much the Full Employment Act that gave us the condition it sought, as it was the economic activity generated by wartime needs. Furthermore, the Full Employment Act has been a farce for blacks, undereducated whites, and women.

For the last two years unemployment has been incredibly high in this country and hardly within any acceptable limits. Furthermore, it now appears that we must expect to be content with a level of unemployment hovering in the vicinity of seven or eight percent over-all and probably twice that for minority groups. Thus, I would suggest that there must be a distinction between a policy statement and what the policy actually is as it is carried out. The Constitution is a magnificent policy statement; the Bill of Rights is a magnificent policy statement; however, the degree to which these policy statements are honored, even where they seem to be explicit, is something else again.

I believe that it is insufficient to say that the field "needs a clear, coherent, and generally accepted policy on aging" unless the authors are talking about some social consensus on aging. In that connection, I would submit that there is a social consensus that is reflected in the way in which we currently allocate resources. In the view of some, allocations for Social Security, Supplemental Security Income, Medicare, and Medicaid represent substantial allocations. Whether they are such relative to other allocations may be a question. But that is different from suggesting that a clear national policy has not yet been developed and enunciated.

Furthermore, the suggestion that a forthcoming policy statement will address aging "in the total environment" suggests a holistic, integrated, and coordinated approach to the problems besetting the elderly in the population. There is nothing in the area of gerontology nor in any human service field to suggest that this will indeed be the case. If anything, we have proceeded toward greater and greater fragmentation in the human service field than ever before. Community mental health centers, public welfare agencies administering Title XX funds, Area Agencies on Aging, public housing authorities, "236 housing" and other congregate facilities, not to mention intermediate care facilities and skilled nursing facilities may be providing an array of social services to the elderly in the community one way or another without effective coordination, the Area Agencies on Aging notwithstanding. This is not to suggest that the fragmentation is bad (or for that matter, good). It is merely to point out that it exists and that its presence, institutionalized in law and bureaucratic structures, is a fact of life which will militate against addressing aging "in the total environment." Neither child welfare nor community mental health, both of which have considerably longer histories than the field of aging, have come anywhere close to what the predictions suggest. And there is nothing on the horizon to indicate that they will be forthcoming. Neither penal programs nor vocational rehabilitation have experienced in the past what the authors anticipate for aging in the next twenty-five years. Indeed, one might opine that the establishment of Area Agencies on Aging might be taken to represent increasing fragmentation rather than integration of services. The AAA is isolated from Title XX programs, community mental health programs, SSI and SSA, services for the blind, the Health Systems Agencies, and probably some others that I have not thought of.

Policy and administration are closely intertwined. Effective policy integration is difficult, if not impossible, in the absence of some degree of administrative integration. Successful bureaucrats stake out their domains both programmatically *and* organizationally. The territorial imperative is not one easily overcome.

With reference to the third prediction, which holds that the elderly will coalesce into a voting bloc, I would suggest that the wish is father to the thought. Not only is the evidence of political activity among the elderly slim, but those writers who are cited as potentially supporting the proposition either acknowledge that relatively few elderly have turned toward political activity, or do not mention the elderly at all. While it is true that the elderly may vote as a bloc when they perceive their interests as threatened, it is difficult to understand how and why this bloc will develop on the basis of a perceived threat to Social Security payments and Medicare benefits when there is also the prediction that there will be a significant shift in political philosophy in the United States which will yield a more equitable share of the aggregate resources to the elderly. The escalator clauses in the OASDI program will tend to hold the relationships where they are. There may be incremental additions to Social Security and Medicare programs, but they are likely, as in the past, to be just that and, as such, will not significantly alter the current income relationships between the elderly and the nonelderly. In fact, the most significant alteration in income shifts may derive from what happens in the non-Social Security pension benefit arena.

Furthermore, there is no evidence to refute Binstock and other writers who suggest, as the authors point out, that there are no sound reasons to expect older people to gain more power through voting than they have today. Indeed, a look at national, state, and county political committees will reveal very few special concerns for the elderly and very few attempts to enlist the elderly or even perceive the elderly as a viable political force. For a time, the Republican National Committee had a special committee on the aging. The Democrats never followed suit. State and county committees have not done so either despite some very good reasons which can and should be mustered in behalf of special activity with and in behalf of the elderly. While organizations like the American Association of Retired Persons/National Retired Teachers Association, the National Council of Senior Citizens and the Grey Panthers have lobbied and have been articulate spokesmen on behalf of causes for the elderly, they have not, except where the authors point out there is a perceived serious threat to cherished programs, been able to deliver large blocs of elderly voters to one party or another. To be sure, the elderly have defeated some unwanted school district bond issues, have returned votes against anti-Social Security candidates, or forced city hall to rescind higher tariffs for gas, e.g., Phila-

delphia. However, this is significantly different from what is contemplated in the development of a cohesive voting bloc which might be analogized to the farm bloc, the labor bloc, the businessman's bloc, or any other generally recognized bloc.

Finally, one must wonder about the prediction concerning the holding of the Supreme Court relative to mandatory retirement. While I may personally agree that mandatory retirement provisions are constitutionally offensive, I must confess that I do not see equally clearly the evidence that supports the prediction. Sound constitutional argument, unfortunately, is not sufficient to bring about a change in Supreme Court holdings. *Weiss* and *Weisbrod* are powerful suggestions that the trend is the other way. *LaFleur* dealt with an entirely different issue, Rehnquist's dissent, notwithstanding.

While lawyers love to analogize, the fact of the matter is that the Court seemed to believe that *LaFleur* was inapposite to the mandatory retirement issue. There is currently before the Court the case of *Murgia v. Commonwealth of Massachusetts*, a strong case involving the compulsory retirement of a state police colonel at age fifty-five. My hunch is that if the Court *does* come down against compulsory retirement in this case, it will be on such narrow grounds as to have very little effect on the broad issue. The problem here is that twenty-five years is a relatively short time in which to achieve some overturning of a Supreme Court decision. Not only is the court dominated by Nixonian appointees who are conservative, but two of the pre-Nixon holdovers, White and Stewart, are hardly apt to participate in the overturning of *Weiss* and *Weisbrod*. Marshall and Brennan will soon leave the Court, and the likelihood is that their replacements will be along conservative lines regardless of who is the President. What is more significant, however, than the composition of the Supreme Court is the complexion of district and circuit courts, influenced as they must be by the appointments made by Presidents Nixon and Ford during their respective terms of office. My own opinion is that it might be more reasonable to suggest that mandatory retirement provisions will *not* be overturned in the coming twenty-five years, not only because of the conservative nature of the Supreme Court, but also because of the persistence of an adverse employment picture. Some of the same conditions that led to passage of the Social Security Act may be with us and will persist for a considerable time to come. It *is* accurate to suggest, however, that there may be increasing litigation, but I do not believe that we can anticipate overturning mandatory retirement provisions on constitutional grounds. The Age Discrimination in Employment Act, which clearly provides for compulsory retirement as a legitimate device, provided that compulsory retirement age is sixty-five, further supports the contention which I suggest. Here, Congress has legitimized discrimination on the basis of age after age sixty-five. One might prescribe (rather than predict) some activity by elderly people on the political front to amend the Age Discrimination in Employment Act to eliminate the legitimization of compulsory retirement at age sixty-five. In some ways the political solution through statutory amendment may be more achievable than the judicial constitutional solution.

The business of futurology is both stimulating and baffling. After all, is that not what research and inquiry is all about: to establish a better understanding of the world, all that is in it, what the behaviors are, and what the universal laws of science may disclose so that we can better predict what will happen in both the long and short run? Social scientists have been chary about making predictions because predictions have a way of coming home to roost. Peterson and his colleagues, in the tradition of Neugarten et al. have moved ahead. Hopefully, others will follow with more marshalling of evidence and further predictions.

In gerontology we are perhaps more fortunate than researchers and investigators in other fields. All of those who will be elderly twenty-five years or even fifty years hence have been already born and there are data and information available about them. To be sure, we do not have data available about what the political, social, economic, or for that matter, physical environment will be like twenty-five or fifty years hence, but then if we had all the data prediction would not be that interesting. However, Peterson and his colleagues do give us good suggestions for further scrutiny and they are commended to our readership.

More importantly, however, they have offered an example of stimulating prediction which has prompted this response. It is my hope that our readership will respond to the stimulating articles that *The Gerontologist* has the privilege to offer. If they do so, there will be space on these pages for their opinions.

Elias S. Cohen,
Editor-in-Chief

Aging and the Future

Bernice L. Neugarten
Robert J. Havighurst

A wide range of predictions regarding the future of our society have been put before the American public in the past few years. In the flood of statements now appearing there are—to oversimplify it—perspectives that are grandly optimistic, others that are grossly pessimistic. The economy will continue to expand, and the good life will soon be here for us all, or the economy is on the verge of collapse. With continued growth of science and technology, man will solve the problems of overpopulation, food shortages, energy crises, inflation, environmental pollution, and the threat of nuclear war; or because of the very growth of science and technology, such problems are now so unprecedented in scale that man's efforts are doomed to fail.

From one or the other perspective, the future status of the aged is also differently described. In the optimistic world-view, where at least the developed countries are moving from a production orientation to a quality-of-life orientation, it is said that more equitable social systems are arising. Older perons will get their fair share of the new abundance. In the pessimistic view, where among other things there will be increasing alienation, conflict over employment opportunities and competition between age groups, the old will become newly disadvantaged.

From *Social Policy, Social Ethics, and the Aging Society*, edited by B. L. Neugarten and R. J. Havighurst. (Washington, D.C.: National Science Foundation, 1977): 3–8. Reprinted by permission.

We ourselves have taken a conservatively optimistic position. While, in the sections to follow, we shall focus upon the short-run future to the year 2000, we view that twenty-five-year period within a longer time perspective. In the more distant period between 2000 and 2050 we anticipate that a series of crises will arise in the less developed parts of the world, whose resolutions will involve the United States and other developed countries. The goal will become increasingly clear: to create a world in which each nation will have a fair share of natural resources. An equilibrium world society will gradually appear, with a nearly stationary population, and with the consumption of energy and other resources being controlled in such ways that the use of energy, food, and materials will be approximately equal to the supply of new resources.

We are assuming that sensible and constructive measures will be taken in the United States within the next two decades to prevent us from making the world situation so much worse that by the year 2000 corrective measures will have become impossible. For example, in 1970 the United States, with its 6 percent of the world's population, consumed 33 percent of the world's energy. The United States will either reduce its use of energy in the short-run future or work out new supplies which do not take energy away from the rest of the world.

In very brief terms, we are assuming that over the next twenty-five years there will be slowed economic growth in the American society together with slowed population growth (with Zero Population Growth occurring in about seventy-five years); increasing urbanization and growth of metropolitan agglomerations; and continuing technological advances. Levels of education will continue to rise, although at a less dramatic rate than in the past few decades, producing less difference between age groups.

We are assuming a value orientation which—to borrow a phrase from Denis Johnston and others—is neither the "blue" world of the work ethic nor the "green" world of the leisure ethic, but a "turquoise" world in which new concepts of work and new flexible life styles will appear, so that in both the work setting and the leisure setting there will be greater concern for personal growth and fulfillment (Johnston, 1972). We are presuming also a society in which there will be more, rather than less planning, and in which the role of government in the affairs of everyday life will increase rather than decrease. We are assuming that persons of all ages will expect "more" from life, although "more" may mean a changing value system in which the pursuit of affluence may become less significant than the pursuit of meaningful ways of self-enhancement and community enhancement.

HOW MANY OLDER PERSONS WILL THERE BE?

Whatever the uncertainties in other areas, population projections for the middle-aged and old are relatively safe for the next twenty-five years because they depend on mortality rates, not fertility rates. Everybody who will be old by the year 2000 is already alive. But will he live a great deal longer than his predecessors?

Two general strategies for lengthening life are being pursued by biomedical and biological researchers: the first is the continuing effort to conquer major diseases; the other, to alter the intrinsic biological processes which are presumed to underlie aging and which may proceed independently from disease processes—that is, to discover the genetic and biochemical secrets of aging, then to slow the biological clock that is presumably programmed into the human species. This second approach is directed at rate control, rather than disease control.

Thus far all the increases in life expectancy have been due to increased controls over disease and not, so far as is known, to any decrease in the rate of aging. The question then becomes: Are there likely to be dramatic discoveries with regard to rate control that will lead to a mushrooming in numbers of older persons by the year 2000?

In attempting to answer this question, the present authors have made inquiries of leading biological researchers, asking for their assessments. With the striking exception of a few who are saying that if research efforts were generously enough supported, the lifespan could be extended some twenty to twenty-five years within the next two decades (for example, Comfort, 1959; Strehler, 1970) the responses we have thus far received are consistently negative. The overwhelming majority have responded that they see no such possibility. We have therefore proceeded on the conservative view that there will be no dramatic changes in the length of the human lifespan within the next several decades, but that, instead, there will be relatively regular improvements in medical knowledge and health care that will produce steady but slow reduction in mortality rates and small gains in life expectancy.

The population aged sixty-five and over in 1976 is nearly twenty-two million, and constitutes about 10 percent of the total American population. If fertility and mortality rates continue to the year 2000 the same as they were in 1968, there will be 26.5 million people over sixty-five, or about the same 10 percent of the total. But it is expected that mortality rates will be reduced somewhat, and that fertility rates will also be reduced from the 1968 level. Suppose we assume that fertility rates hover around the level which will eventually produce a stationary population, as is now the case. Suppose we assume also that age-specific mortality rates will decrease by 1 percent per year after age twenty, making a cumulative reduction over the next twenty-five years of about 30 percent. Upon that assumption, there will be about thirty-one million people over sixty-five, or 11.5 percent of the total population. The proportion of people over seventy-five, while it is now about 4 percent, would increase to 5.5 percent in the year 2000.

This 1 percent per year reduction in mortality rates would add about three years to average life expectancy for persons aged sixty-five. Thus men who reach sixty-five in the year 2000 could expect to live, on the average, to age eighty-one, and women, to age eighty-four.

THE HEALTH STATUS OF OLDER PEOPLE

Given our assumptions that average life expectancy will increase over the next twenty-five years, and that this increase will come, not from a slowing of the rate of aging, but from continuingly improved health, it follows, by definition, that we are also assuming improved health status for older persons in the future.

In truth, the realities are more complex. The relations of various forms of morbidity to mortality are not well understood, nor the relations of mortality rates at younger ages to mortality rates at later ages; there are various definitions of "health" or "vigor" and various indices that have been used for measurement; levels of education and socioeconomic status are related both to morbidity and mortality; and so on. Suffice it to say that for the future we are presuming better levels of health for older persons because poverty is diminishing over the life-cycles of successive cohorts of persons, because educatioonal levels are rising, and because we predict more effective forms of public health and improved systems of health care.

All this says little, however, regarding the period of disability that can be expected to occur for many people in the very last phase of life; and for the moment, we have little basis for predicting that this period will become shorter.

THE ROLE OF THE FAMILY

Keeping in mind that "family" is not synonymous with "household," and looking first at family structure, it is clear from census data that there has been a significant shift in marital status of older perons in the past twenty years, with an increase in the proportions of both men and women who are married and living with spouses, and with offsetting decreases in the proportions never married, widowed, or divorced. Whether these trends will continue for the next twenty-five years will depend upon a whole host of factors, social as well as economic, not least upon changing attitudes toward marriage, divorce, and remarriage.

With regard to intergenerational family structure, we can be fairly sure that the four- and five-generation family will be the norm because of increasing longevity and because the length of generations has been shortening.

It is often overlooked that for persons who will be old in 2000, there will be more rather than fewer children and other relatives. For example, the average woman of seventy-five now has 2.0 surviving children, but the woman who reaches seventy-five in the year 2010 will have 2.85 surviving children. This is due to the "baby boom" of the 1950–60 period, when the birth rate reached high levels. Because the birth rate then dropped precipitously during the 1960s and 1970s, again there will again be smaller numbers of living children per older woman in the decade 2010.

Numbers of surviving children do not, of course, tell us about interactions or patterns of assistance between parent and child. Projections of the latter type are difficult. We do not, for example, have national data for the 1970s by which to assess present patterns of family interaction, to say nothing of future patterns. Yet a whole range of smaller studies leads to the conclusion that the family has thus far remained a strong and supportive institution for older people. Most old people want to be independent of their families as much as possible, but when they can no longer manage for themselves, they expect their children to come to their aid. Not only do such expectations exist, but they are usually met. A complex pattern of exchange of services exists across generations, and both ties of affection and ties of obligation remain strong. Perhaps expectations will change in these regards by the year 2000, but if so, the changes are likely to be slow.

When it comes to living in the same household, there has been a dramatic trend toward separate households for older persons. While there are more families who have older relatives, fewer are living with them. Yet in 1970, the latest year for which national data are available it was clear that the older the individual, and the sicker, the more likely he would be found living with a child. For persons aged 75+, one of five women and one of ten men were living with a child (a few percent were living with another relative). It is a neglected fact that, in 1970, a total of 2¼ million persons aged 65+ were living in the same household with a child or other relative.

Here again it is not easily predicted whether or not the trend toward separate households will continue. The trends will be affected by economic factors and by housing policies. One significant factor is the increasing number of families in which persons of advanced old age have children who are themselves old, a trend that will become even more marked in the next few decades. What its effects will be is difficult to foresee. If a more effective network of supportive social and home health services arises, more intergenerational households may appear in which both generations are old.

One thing is likely: that families will want more options in the settings and types of care available for an aged family member whose health is failing. Such institutions as

nursing homes may be necessary for a part of the population, but many families may seek ways of maintaining an older person at home, either in his own household or in the child's household.

THE YOUNG-OLD AND THE OLD-OLD

For a number of reasons it is useful to view older persons as consisting of two groups— the young-old who are fifty-five to seventy-five, and the old-old who are seventy-five and above. The young-old begin about age fifty-five because in recent years more and more men and women are choosing to retire at age fifty-five to sixty, rather than after age sixty-five. We anticipate that in the year 2000 people will be in relatively good health up to age seventy-five or thereabouts, and they will participate in civic and social and political activities, especially if they drop out of the labor market.

Whether the recent trend toward earlier retirement persists will depend on economic as well as manpower factors. If monetary inflation continues to increase the cost of living (and to decrease the purchasing power of the dollar) people may not opt for early retirement because their pensions and social security benefits will not be likely to support them adequately. Also, the increasing cost of energy and of food and other necessities may force the whole society to reverse the trends of the 1950–75 period, when the age of retirement was being lowered and the length of the working life was being shortened. Heilbronner's *Human Prospect* (1974) shows this to be a real possibility.

Whichever way the pendulum swings —toward greater leisure and affluence or toward a more Spartan kind of existence, the young-old will become more distinguishable, not only from the middle-aged group below age fifty-five, but also from the old-old who are over seventy-five.

As suggested by our earlier comments on health status, the young-old are already a relatively healthy group. The data have not been aggregated in age categories most appropriate to our purposes, but at present, about 15 percent of the group aged forty-five to sixty-four need to limit their major activities because of health, while for all those sixty-five+, it is about 40 percent. We estimate that, if our young-old group were differentiated in these data, the proportion with health limitations would probably be between 20 and 25 percent.

In distinguishing further between the young-old and the old-old, we should look again at population data and family data. Women do not outnumber men in the 55–75 age group as much as they do in the 75+ group. Furthermore, because most men marry women somewhat younger than themselves, the young-old are more like the middle-aged than like the old-old. About 80 percent of the young-old men, and well over half the women were married in 1970 and living with their spouses. By far the common pattern is a husband and wife living in their own household (some 80 percent own their own homes).

The young-old are already much better educated than the old-old and in the near future they will be in a less disadvantaged educational position in comparison to the young. The gains in educational level in successive cohorts of the population have been so substantial that by 1990 the young-old group will be, on the average, high school graduates. Furthermore, with the anticipated growth in higher education for adults, and the even greater growth in what the Carnegie Commission (1973) calls "further education" (that education, both part-time and full-time, which occurs in settings other than college campuses and which is not aimed at academic degrees) it can be anticipated that the educational differences that presently exist between young, middle-aged, and young-old will be further reduced.

With regard to political participation, the young-old group is a highly active group compared to other age groups. When national data are corrected for income and education, over-all political participation is highest for the age group 51-65 (i.e., voting, persuading others how to vote, actively working for party or candidate, working with others on local problems); and it falls off only a little for persons over sixty-five (Verba and Nie, 1972). Thus, in the electorate as a whole the young-old are disproportionately influential.

These, then, are some of the characteristics of that fifteen percent of the total population who are the young-old. As a group, they are already markedly different from the outmoded stereotypes of old age, and by the year 2000 they will be increasingly so. A vigorous and educated young-old group can be expected to develop new needs with regard to the meaningful use of time and to want a wide range of opportunities both for self-enhancement and for community participation.

THE OLD-OLD

An increasing minority of the old-old will remain active and productive and, because this is true, will want increased options in all areas of life. The majority will probably live independently, but many will need supportive social services, or home health services, or special features in the physical environment to enable them to function as fully as possible. Without taking an overly optimistic view, it is likely that such services will grow, and that they will become more effective not only in slowing physical and mental deterioration, but in preventing unnecessary decline in feelings of self-worth and dignity.

There is no denying the fact that at the end of life there will be a shorter or longer period of dependency. There will be increased numbers of old people who will need economic support, and increased numbers of the old-old who will require special care, either in their own homes or in institutional settings. For persons who are terminally ill or incapacitated, the problems for the society will continue to be how to provide maximum care and comfort and the assurance of dignified death, and also how to provide a greater element of choice for the individual himself or for members of his family regarding how and when his life shall end. The future will probably see the spread of educational programs aimed at the public at large as well as at various professional groups for achieving a "best" death rather than the latest-possible death for each individual.

New and difficult questions will arise regarding what share of the national budget should go to meeting the economic needs of the old, and what share of health and social services should go to the old-old. These are questions which will gain increasing public attention. In the discussion and resolution of these issues, the policy-makers of the society will need the assistance, not only of the biomedical scientist and the economist, but also of the legal scholar, the humanist, and the ethicist.

REFERENCES

CARNEGIE COMMISSION ON HIGHER EDUCATION, *Toward a Learning Society*. New York: McGraw-Hill, 1973.

COMFORT, A. "Longer Life by 1990?" *New Scientist* (Dec., 1959): 549–51.

HEILBRONNER, ROBERT I., *An Inquiry into the Human Prospect*. New York: Norton, 1974.

JOHNSTON, D. F. "The Future of Work: Three Possible Alternatives." *Monthly Labor Review*, U.S. Department of Labor, Washington (May, 1972).

STREHLER, B. "Ten Myths About Aging." *Center Magazine* (July, 1970); 41–48.

VERBA, S. AND NIE, N. H. *Participation in America*. New York: Harper and Row, 1972.

Philosophical Approach to Gerontology

Michel Philibert

From conception to death, the human experience of aging is all at once given to us, and interpreted and managed by us through words and deeds. Humans age; they know they age, anticipate, discuss, and review their aging. Facts, interpretation and management continually interact with one another. Human aging is not factual or biological only, it is also symbolic, social, and cultural.

Human aging is versatile and differential. Though universal insofar as all humans age, human aging exhibits great variations in

Original paper prepared by the author for this volume.

direction, pace, effects, patterns, styles, interpretation, evaluation, and management. Variations do not appear only between functions, or between individuals in the same population but also between populations located in different geographic or cultural areas or different periods. Not only are the variations in interpretation and management of the human lifecourse usually greater than those biologically grounded; social patterns and cultural rules, whether educational, political, medical, or economic, contribute with other ecological factors to variously influence biologic processes of aging.

THE STUDY OF HUMAN AGING: WHAT IT MUST BE

The study of human aging (now currently called gerontology) aims at a better understanding of its variations and ambiguities, through a better knowledge of its conditions, so as to provide us with a better use and control of its course. It derives its theoretical characters and status from the traits of the aging experience described above; namely, it must be comparative, dialectical, hermeneutical, and interventive.

The study of aging must be *comparative*, because only by comparing its variations to one another and to their respective conditions shall we assess what in aging is universal and constant, what is particular and changing, what comes from nature and what from nurture, what is manageable and what is not.

If the study of aging must take into account the full range of its given variations in style and pattern, it must use cross-cultural and historical comparisons, namely, anthropological and historical materials and methods. This necessity provides the first reason why the study of aging must be *hermeneutical*.[1] Human concern for aging has been productive throughout centuries, in all places, of feelings, of fantasies, of observations, of interpretations, and reactions. These have been expressed and embodied in social institutions, in oral tradition, in symbolic forms, and in written texts. They are available in folklore, myths, rituals, tales, religion, drama, art, poetry, songs, proverbs, precepts, recipes, customs, law, in magics and medicine, in essays and novels, in paintings, and in movies.

Such expressions of human thinking about aging, such documents of the human experience in aging are not usually formulated as scientific statements. But in them lies all the available information on the way former generations have, in different historic and social settings, experienced, interpreted, and managed their life cycle. In order to extract from these various documents and sources the latent information they harbour,

to assess their accuracy and probability, to make them comparable to one another and to the results of current scientific investigations, a vast effort in detection, identification, selection, classification, and interpretation lies ahead. All skills and tools recently refined by historians, anthropologists, cultural geographers, linguists, exegetes, semioticians, literary and art critics, who have been in the past decades the most inventive in human sciences, must be tentatively borrowed and adapted to study aging. Because the main bulk of available material on the variations in human aging consists of texts, because these texts call for interpretation, the comparative study of aging must and will be hermeneutical.[2]

The study of aging will be hermeneutical for another reason, the same that makes it also *dialectical*. The reactions of individuals and communities to the processes through which we grow up and older, our attitudes towards and between juniors and elders, our various patterns in organizing our life cycle, are neither mere effects, nor irrelevant and inefficient misconstructions, of some basic natural, biologic mechanisms that experimental scientists could sort out from their social consequences or from fanciful, unsupported speculation. They are constituents of the very experience the students of aging try to ascertain. The continuous, circular interaction between facts and values, nature and culture, between what is inflicted upon us, or granted to us, and what is made by our own reactions to, and management of, our lifecourse, compels the study of aging to use a dialectical approach, and to interpret it as we interpret texts and symbols, hermeneutically.[3]

As in experimental sciences, part of the variations to be investigated in aging must be designed and produced on purpose so as to test hypotheses: this implies that the study of aging has to be *interventive*. But such provoked variations cannot provide us sufficient information. Because of the length of aging in the human individual, many facts defeat the investigator's patience and availability. Because of interaction between biological, social, and cultural conditions, many variables escape control. Ethical, social, and political norms also limit the liberty of investigators in designing experiments—these being inevitably social as well as scientific. Finally, any experimental design and any direct observation of aging people will be limited to the contemporary living and available population, that is, frequently to the same cultural area and necessarily to one and the same generation.

The study of aging must be, or rather, must not deny being interventive. The strongest motivation for studying aging has been throughout history the will to make the best out of it. Intervention has been and still is, the ultimate goal of research in aging.[4] It is also, in experimental science, a specific phase, the deliberate production of variations, so as to test hypotheses. It is currently and erroneously considered as a by-product of science, and called "applied gerontology." Intervention must be understood as pervading the study of aging. While we study aging, we do not stop from experiencing, interpreting and managing our own and others' aging, neither do our social and intellectual strategies in studying aging cease to be influential on, and influenced by, our social and personal policies in aging. the very study of aging contributes to shape the aging process, both by its planned, and by its unpremeditated, effects. It would behoove us to take cognizance of this fact, following Margaret and Paul Baltes' lead when they state: "Behavior in the aged is modifiable, and operant research can likely identify the type of environmental conditions which are appropriate for the control of aging behavior."[5]

GERONTOLOGY: A FALSE START

Concern for aging, speculation and investigation on aging, are as old in mankind as history can trace, yet it is only in the early twentieth century that the words geriatrics and gerontology were coined, and only in the forties that they have been used to label new

social institutions specially set up to provide the care of aged patients and scientific research on aging. The first international congress was held, and the International Gerontological Association established, in Liege in 1950.

The selection of a new label, and the launching of new, specific institutions, such as centers, institutes, societies, journals, committees, conventions, grants, awards, research, teaching and training programs and facilities, handbooks, textbooks, subsidies, and so on, must, I submit, be interpreted as expressing dissatisfaction of the founding fathers of gerontology with former results and methods in the study of aging. Most pioneers who promoted the label "gerontology" considered all previous literature on aging as pre-scientific, as scientifically useless or misleading. They saw it as a confused mixture of common sense observations, unsupported speculation, and erroneous stereotypes. They dropped the habit, observed through centuries in hundreds of books on aging and old age, of reviewing and reinterpreting previous literature and contemporary lay opinions on the subject.[6] A new usage was adopted, to refer only to supposedly scientific gerontological endeavors.

I consider this deliberate rejection and ignorance of pre-scientific and extrascientific literature on aging as ruinous to the study of aging. As I have attempted to suggest, such literature provides us with materials which, adequately treated, can disclose the full range of variations in human aging. To ignore it is not only to deprive oneself of an indispensable source of knowledge; it is also to deprive oneself of the best available detector of our own ethnocentric biases and modernist delusions. But we cannot condemn only, we must understand why gerontology made this false start.

I submit that the Clubs for research on aging, which appeared in the thirties and gave birth to geriatric and gerontological institutions, resulted from the junction of a need and a tool, of a call and an answer. The need or call for (more) research on aging expressed a growing awareness of historic changes having recently affected, in industrialized countries, both the number and the position of the aged in society, and more generally, the whole life cycle and the experience of aging. To face an increasing quantity, and an unprecedented pattern, of difficulties resulting from these historic changes, it was felt that unprecedented and increased efforts had to be made in the study of aging and in the care of the aged. So far, so good.

In order to face the need, to answer the call, attention should have focused on the historic changes, which multiplied the proportion of the aged and modified, perhaps deteriorated, the experience of aging. Recent methods should have been borrowed, new methods designed, to approach a new and unprecedented situation. Unfortunately, the main four scientific tribes who answered the call and devoted themselves to build, as a brand new discipline, the required scientific study of aging—namely, physicians, biologists, pyschologists, and sociologists—themselves victims to then current misconceptions of aging, of science, and of history, misread the situation and took a false start.

Conscious and proud of recent developments in their respective disciplines, they thought that either biology, or medicine, or psychology, or sociology, had achieved a scientific status and was equipped with recently established but sound and standard methods of investigation that would prove adequate and productive in investigating aging. They tended to consider the four disciplines as specific branches of one homogeneous, experimental science of nature, proceeding from observation of facts and hypotheses-testing experiments to laws and theory.[7] They thought that previous and contemporary knowledge of aging was inadequate to explain and control the new situation developing in aging, not so much because that situation had been and was changing—but mostly because previous generations, lacking the scientific tools and approaches, could not apply, in their observation and interpretation of aging, the scientific skills available today. They took into account one important his-

toric change; the rapid increase, in numbers and percentage, of the old in our population, providing more difficulties to cope with (as an incentive to research), and more subjects to observe (as a material for research). But they underestimated or practically ignored the importance of qualitative changes which were affecting the experience of aging, its conditions, and its meaning for the society and for the individual.

Aging was viewed primarily in the first generation of gerontologists, as a natural, universal, mostly biologic, process of decline and deterioration developing in the later part of life.[8] Therefore, direct observation of well selected samples of available older subjects, measurement and analysis of their functions and behavior, of their cells and fluids and organs and metabolism and crystallized intelligence and morale, for the first time scientifically undertaken by biologists, physicians, psychologists, sociologists, using standard concepts and methods of their respective disciplines, would in a few years produce a mass of solid facts. The supposed unity of the aging process[9] and the supposed unity of science, would allow scientists to reveal, through these facts, with adequate use of statistics and computers, the constant links, the underlying mechanisms, the laws of the aging process.

The Development of Gerontology

Such a perspective has witnessed the main efforts made, and the bigger successes obtained, in the quantitative development of gerontology. More research has been done in the past four decades than in the previous four centuries; gerontology has grown and flourished as a social institution. Very few significant or successful efforts have been made in the same time to amend the quality of research on aging, to devise new approaches, to call new disciplines to the field. Riegel recently wrote: "In view of the enormous amount of wasted research efforts, and the concurrent lack of investigation of significant issues, questions need to be raised concerning our concepts of research and theory, communication and education and more generally our concept of man, society and their development."[10]

In fact, aging as deterioration, aging as disengagement were for two or three decades "scientifically" observed as general or average traits in a couple of cohorts of American white middle class, aged citizens born at the end of the nineteenth or at the beginning of the twentieth century. The alleged observation was frequently a naive deduction from age differences measured by transversal studies to supposedly obvious age-changes in the individual life-course; it was also a deduction from a conception of death as universal and total disengagement of the individual from his society (this conception, taken for granted as a scientific one, being a naive and parochial twentieth century misconception) to a conception of aging as an inevitable and gradual preparation for such.[11] The results of such "observations" being considered as exemplifying universal traits of aging, the need for cross-cultural and historic comparisons was either neglected or emphatically denied as useless and irrelevant, as in Cumming and Henry's *Growing Old*.

Thus, devaluation and segregation of the aged, a historic trend and a common stereotype in contemporary western societies, contaminated gerontological thinking; they were considered inherent to the aging process, and their historic, recent, and modifiable character passed undetected. The contempt for pre-scientific and non-scientific literature on aging is largely responsible for this. Their reading would have revealed that alternate conceptions and experiences of aging, linked to different patterns of age grading, exist. In other historic or cultural settings the detection and cultivation of residual or compensatory resources in the aged, or an early and continued cultivation of lifelong skills, fostered in different systems of education and production, are geared to the continued growth and promotion of persons; they influence differently the aging pattern. Premature conclusion from the particular to the universal, naive confusion between the average and the normative, also a frequent disregard for the potential universality latent in accurate analyses or in creative interpretation made by painters or novelists, of individual life course, have severely hampered the early history of gerontology.[12]

Bent by these biases, falling in these traps, gerontology did not harm only itself. Although promising efforts are now being made, although a new gerontology is now emerging, the social development of research, teaching, and training multiplies and reinforces approaches and attitudes which are intellectually outdated and scientifically obsolete, more rapidly than the influence of the few innovators spreads. In the seven published issues of the recent quarterly *Educational Gerontology*, most authors take for granted that the on-going development of training and teaching (both *on* and *to* older subjects) is all for the best; they concern themselves mainly with the "how." I find only David Schonfield and co-author Sally Chatfield soundly remarking that in the task of helping students continue to develop their abilities to think clearly and write concisely, to survey major research findings on age changes in behavior, to develop an appreciation of the problems of the aged, and to understand some of the difficulties in designing and interpreting gerontological investigations, the real difficulty is *the shortage of experienced and knowledgeable instructors.*[13]

More generally a dangerous trend seems to be developing toward what I shall call *gerontologocracy*: a situation in which their alleged knowledge would give power to the gerontologists: a power to teach, to train, to counsel policy makers, social workers, and all kinds of practitioners, by reducing practice to so-called applied gerontology; a power to reduce the aged, once honored and listened to, to material for investigation, or at best to the status of students in need of being told what aging is and means; a power to ignore and to silence the layman, the practitioner, the philosopher, the artist, and the aging; both around them and, more dreadfully, within themselves. This pursuit, or this pretense, of power, might give a scientific caution to, and function as an alibi for those forces in society, whether spontaneous and anonymous, or deliberate and myopic, who conspire through their management of education, production, public health, and power allocation, in making aging, once a meaningful experience to the few, a meaningless experience to the many, and the aged, over researched and under serviced, the shameful image of our alienation.[14]

PHILOSOPHICAL APPROACH TO GERONTOLOGY

A philosophical approach to gerontology is a methodical attempt to critically assess the foundations, the present structure, status and function, the foreseeable and desirable development of gerontology, as the main contemporary accepted form in the study of aging, considered in its two distinct and interrelated aspects of a social institution and an intellectual achievement. A philosophical approach to gerontology must not and could not be reserved to professional philosophers. While not in agreement with J. B. S. Haldane's observation that "the professional philosopher tends to use mental processes of a type which has proved rather a failure in scientific thought," I nevertheless concur with his conclusion: "It is not clear that professionalism is any more desirable in philosophy than in football or religion."[15] A professional philosopher would have to patiently approach gerontology and gerontologists before professing any public statement. However sound the approach to *aging* of Simone de Beauvoir, she did not make a pretense of approaching *gerontology*.

May I suggest the opposite would be equally true, that is, a professional gerontologist, however expert in his field, however suggestive might be his views on his discipline, would be better off not attempting to philosophically approach gerontology without having previously made himself familiar with scholarly methods in history and philosophy.

A philosophical approach to gerontology, as defined above, would, I further suggest, find its best ground and context in a tentative philosophy of aging, while conversely a philosophy of aging makes a critical evaluation of gerontology one of its constituents. Using a Kantian phrase, I define the task of a philosophy of aging as coping with three distinct but interrelated questions: Of aging, what can we know? With aging what must we do? About aging, what may we hope to? What may we expect? Examining the first question implies an evaluation of gerontology as a science, that is, to repeat, as an intellectual undertaking and as a social function. I maintain it cannot be separated from an assessment of the norms governing social activities and institutions that shape the life cycle and influence the experience of aging; such as generalized compulsory retirement schemes for the aged, or compulsory miseducation for the young, or therapeutic revolutions which have created an army of chronically ill aged patients. It cannot be separated, either, from the third question, dealing with the relations of age to life and death, and with those of age to time.

Western Versus Eastern Approaches to Gerontology

Inasmuch as gerontology tends to be a scientific undertaking, and philosophy an exercise in rational thinking, both strive to achieve universality. We should not then, have two different philosophical approaches, one western, one eastern, to *gerontology*. Yet we might, indeed we must, differentiate cultural approaches to *aging*; and considering that philosophical thinking, stirred up by difficulties in living, contradictions in saying, emulation of former philosophers grows roots in different cultural settings in which it finds different incentives and materials, we might after all distinguish between eastern and western philosophical approaches to aging, to its experience and to its study.

In that perspective we might identify as typical of the current western conceptions and attitudes the following: aging as biologically engineered; aging as decline and de-motion; aging as an anticipation of death; aging as the failure or the enemy of growth, life, and happiness; the aged, feared, despised and discriminated against by the many, looked on as a different species, a minority group, a target population, to be cared for, controlled, segregated and investigated. Such western views on aging and the aged might be exemplified in a series of observations. Here are a few illustrations I have selected from both scientific and non-scientific literature.

> These women: he had seen their beauty pass from the smooth bodily complacence of young motherhood to the angular self-possession, slightly gray and wry, of veteran wives. To have witnessed this, to have seen in the side of his vision so many pregnancies and births and quarrels and near-divorces and divorces and affairs and near-affairs and arrivals in vans and departures in vans, loomed, in retrospect, as the one accomplishment of his tenancy here—a heap of organic incident that in a village of old would have mouldered into wisdom. But he was not wise, merely older.[16]

What of this description of the marriage cycle, as supposedly retold by a young Irish peasant girl:

> Sacco began to describe the marriage pattern. He said it was love at first, frequent journeys to the bed, matinee and evening performance, the hay not saved, the calves not fed, then after the first child, a bit of cooling off, the man going out nights and the subsequent children begotten in drink, then squabbles, ructions, first Holy Communions, shoes having to be brought, a lot of troubles and late in life the man back at his own fireplace spitting and banging and grunting inanities to his wife. Your mother was furious.[17]

Dan Greenburg in his humorous *Scoring*,[18] tells of the battle of a young man against the fears and prejudices that would tend to inhibit his readiness to grow up and older:

> I walked through Times Square one day and looked up at the accursed Accutron sign, on which you can watch not only the hours and minutes and seconds but also the tenths of seconds dribble off the end of your life on the huge bulb-studded digital clock, and I figured, All Right. I figured, Why Not. I figured, you've already gotten your first lousy marriage out of the way and possibly even learned a couple of things not to do the next time. I figured, so one of the reaons you're scared of marriage is that it brings you one life process closer to death, so remaining a bachelor isn't going to keep you from aging or from dying either. I figured, so you're scared of the total commitment of marriage, so what, so everybody's scared of that, so big goddam deal. I figured, you're thirty goddam years of age, which is nearly half your life, so what are you waiting for—let's get on with it already. Let's take the next step in life. Let's do it.

Alex Comfort in his earlier writing saw decline as the essence of aging:

> Later we shall undergo a progressive loss of our vigor and resistance which, though imperceptible at first, will finally become so steep that we can live no longer, however well we look after ourselves, and however well society, and our doctor, look after us. This decline in vigor with the passing of time is called aging.[19]

In contrast with this western view on aging, we might be tempted to outline an eastern view, according to which aging would be seen more as a cultural and spiritual process than a biologic one, and as a process of continued opportunity for further growth in knowledge, in experience, in wisdom, that is in understanding the world and in self-mastery; a growth, similarly, in social prestige and authority. The aged consequently would be obeyed, respected, consulted, and envied.

The short autobiography of Confucius, as reported in his conversations with his disciples, might well exemplify this conception of aging as climbing that ladder, each step of which goes higher, higher:

At fifteen, my mind was bent on learning. At thirty, I stood firm, At forty, I was free of delusions. At fifty, I understood the laws of providence. At sixty, there was nothing left in the world that could shock me. At seventy, I could follow the promptings of my heart without trespassing moral law.

From ancient China to modern Japan, we shall compare Hokusai's autobiography, as given in 1835 in his *Preface to a Hundred Drawings of the Fusy-Yama*:

I have been in love with painting ever since I became conscious of it at the age of six. At fifty I had published innumerable drawings, but really nothing I did before the age of seventy was of any value at all. At seventy-three I have at last caught nearly every aspect of nature—birds, fish, animals, insects, trees, grass, all. Thence at eighty I shall have developed still further, and shall at ninety really enter the mystery of reality. When I reach a hundred I shall be truly sublime, and at the age of one hundred and ten, every line and dot I draw will be imbued with life.

This piece was written at age seventy-five, when Hokusai changed his name to that of Gwakio Ropon, "the old man mad with drawing." I suggest its meaning is not much affected by our knowledge that Hokusai died at eighty-nine in 1849, before he could climb up the last steps of its anticipated progression. May I also suggest that the similarities between these two autobiographies strike the western reader more than their differences. Admittedly, Confucius states he has achieved at age seventy a stage of self control, while

at seventy-five Hokusai confesses he is still striving toward a fulfillment yet to come. And whereas Confucius sees aging as a growth in wisdom, Hokusai views it as a growth in art. But both men see life as ascending even through the later years. And Hokusai's anticipated mastery in painting lies more in the eye than in the hand, and even more in the mind than in the eye. His progress as an artist cannot be separated from his progress in understanding, and art to him is rooted in wisdom. Finally, then, the unity of pattern between both texts, and both experiences, outcomes their diversity: *with much dedication, meditation and discipline, human life can be made a way to continued growth in wisdom.*

Two other instances will point out that society and culture can fashion the life cycle according a pattern that Peristiany labelled *age-rank ladder,* so organized as to ascribe the maximum of prestige to old age. Another instance of the eastern conception as we have briefly outlined it is T'ien Ju-K'ang's paper on Pai cults and social age in the Tai Tribes of the Yunnan Burma frontier.[20] According to the author, the Tai life-cycle is organized in four stages, depending much more on social ascription of tasks and cultural rituals than on biology; if all humans, even among those who live a long life, do not enter the fourth stage, through the ritual of the great Pai, those who do so, though economically deprived and politically powerless, enjoy the highest degree of esteem and respect available in their tribes. Finally, according to David Nelson Rowe, a sign of the genuine respect traditionally paid to old age in China may be found in the way Chinese would lie about their age.[21] Whereas in the West people pretend to be, and strive to look or to remain younger than they actually are, in the East one was flattered when said, or treated as, older than one really was.

Despite the instances just reviewed, I would like to hypothesize the two conceptions which we have opposed to one another are less typical of the contrast between East and West than of a contrast between tradition and modernity. Reviewing African, traditional American, or even traditional European literature we might, I think, find a conception of aging as growth in wisdom quite analogous to that we have just assigned to the East. But we shall limit ourselves in the end to show that even in contemporary European literature such a conception, however obfuscated by current prejudices in society and in gerontology, still survives. We shall state that today it is again one of the tasks of philosophy, as it has been in former times, to contribute to restore and rehabilitate, in present science and society, this conception.

I select among many possibilities, two examples of western nineteenth century painters, whose declarations exhibit, on painting and aging, very much the same outlook as their eastern counterpart and contemporary Hokusai. The first is taken from Baudelaire's *Curiosités Esthétiques*:

> At the end of his career, Goya's eyesight had weakened to such an extent that his pencils, so it was said, had to be sharpened for him. Yet even at that time he executed some big and most important lithographs, including a number of bullfights, full of swarming crowds, admirable plates, enormous pictures in miniature—a further proof in support of that strange law governing the destiny of great artists, according to which, since life and intelligence move in opposite directions, they make up on the savings what they loose on the roundabouts, and following a progressive rejuvenation, they grow forever stronger, more jovial, bolder, to the very edge of the grave.[22]

And Paul Valery reports with admiration a saying of Degas, aged seventy, to Ernest Roxart: "One might highly esteem not what one has made but what one will make someday; or else, it's not worth while working."

Would anyone object here that painters do not age as the rest of us, I reply first that even if we have only a few instances of humans maintaining or developing their creativity as they age, that is enough to establish that aging is not universally and totally a

decline. Such instances are worth investigating for how is it that in western, contemporary society, the taste for drawing and painting, so frequent in children, is inhibited for life by the close of adolescence? In any event, we need not enter into a long discussion about painters, because many other witnesses may be called to establish that a positive view of aging survives underground in our western societies.

I have been stricken by the surprise severally and independently expressed by contemporary writers approaching or experiencing old age. They discover with pleasure that aging is much better than they had anticipated. They had been victims of current negative stereotypes, but their knack both in analyzing and expressing their own feelings without falling for the cliches in fashion makes them join in a chorus of denial: no, old age is not what it is currently believed to be. "It is wrong to believe that old age is a slope down," wrote George Sand at age sixty-four in the 1868 volume, *Journal Intime*. "On the contrary: one ascends, and with surprising steps. Intellectual work becomes as fast as in the child. One nevertheless approaches the end of life, but as an aim, not as a reef."

Let me quote a few others who candidly express their surprise:

Paulhan states, "To age is not what one believes. On the whole, you enjoy the same pleasures, only more so. You become freer, think clearer (at least you believe so)."[23]

Or Jouhandeau: "To age is not at all what one believes. It is not at all decline but growth."[24]

St. John Perse in an often quoted verse, cries: "Old age, thou liar! Thou road of glowing embers, not of ash. With face alight and spirit high, to what extreme are we still running? Time measured by the year is no measure of our days. We hold no traffic with the least or with the worst."[25]

Franz Hellens: "For the next guy who figures he's thinking, philosophizing, old age is seen as fate and destruction: or rather, in his perspective, as shrinking, a negative quantity, the very denial of the true meaning of the word: great age is indeed great, the only great. Great age is not what one believes."[26]

Florida Scott Maxwell expresses a like surprise in *The Measure of my Days*: "Age puzzles me. I thought it was a quiet time. My seventies were interesting and fairly serene, but my eighties are passionate. I grow more intense as I age.... To my own surprise, I burst out with hot conviction."[27]

To cut a long list short, I'll end with two quotations that state the possibility of human growth throughout life. Frank Harris writes on Alfred Russell Wallace: "It is by the heart we grow, and Wallace kept himself sincere, so kindly, that he grew in wisdom to the very end of his life, instead of stopping, as most men and women stop growing mentally almost before their bodily growth is completed."[28]

And in the early days of American gerontology, Tibbitts attempted against adverse winds to have old age considered as an opportunity:

> The fact is frequently overlooked that senescence is by no means entirely a period of either relative or absolute decline . . . Welford has shown that one function of maturity is the development of compensations to offset loss of strength and endurance. . . Knowledge and experience are cumulative, thus increasing capacity for making judgments.[29]

Indeed:

> During the last decade or so, there has emerged a new concept of the aging process as it has been developed by medical and social research. Far from being a process of deterioration or regression (the commonly accepted belief), we know now, if proper measures are taken, that the later years can literally be a period of further development.

> An old age environment which encourages activity may convert the later years, despite certain characteristic declines, into an extended period of satisfying growth and development . . . We shall have to recognize maturity as a period of potential growth.[30]

And finally,

> There are positive roles for older people, through which they can make valuable contributions to society. This point of view calls for a new concept of aging—a concept that gives recognition to the positive as well as the negative aspects of maturation.[31]

THE CALL FOR A NEW CONCEPT OF AGING

Tibbitts' call for a new concept of aging is finding more echo, more support, more answer in present day gerontology than it did during the fifties and sixties. What eastern people may perhaps contribute to gerontology, what the historians and philosophers have the duty to contribute, is their awareness that the needed new concept of aging is new only insofar as western twentieth century societies have accentuated as never before, both in thinking and in real life, in interpretation, and in effect, the negative aspects of aging and old age, to the point of oblivion of a traditional, more balanced and more positive view. And the "new" concept, really the rejuvenation of an old one, is needed only insofar as gerontology has willy-nilly conspired, over the past decades, to reinforce, in offering them a pseudo-scientific caution, the biases that in the same process made aging erroneously appear as universal, inevitable decline, and efficiently equated it to real decline for a few cohorts in industrialized countries.

Leo Simmons and many others show that in "primitive" life, in nomadic and illiterate tribes, humans were obliged to exercise, enrich or refine their judgment, memory and skills throughout life. The elders were the more knowledgeable, the more reliable and the more respected. The introduction of writing, the development of larger political entities, the increased division in social work, agriculture, and city life, had among other results the fact that aging ceased to mean necessarily growth and wisdom. People became aware of the ambiguity of aging. Thus Elihu, in the book of Job (32) contests the wisdom of Job's friends:

> Now Elihu had waited till Job had spoken because his three friends were elder than he. When Elihu saw that there was no answer in the mouth of these three men, then his wrath was kindled. And Elihu answered and said, I am young, and you are very old; wherefore I was afraid, and durst now shew you my opinion. I said Days should speak, and multitude of years should teach wisdom. But there is a spirit in man, and the inspiration of the Almighty giveth them understanding. Great men are not always wise, neither do the aged understand judgment.

The dissociation between wisdom and old age was clearly perceived, and therefore the ambiguity of aging. Another trace of such awareness is given by a short reply of Fool to King Lear: "If thou wert my fool, uncle, I'd have thee beaten for being old before thy time." Lear: "How's that?" Fool: "Thou should'st not have been old till thou hadst been wise" (King Lear I. V). You may have perceived an echo of that in what Updike says of his hero: "But he was not wise, merely older." Hence, we may trace the rise of Greek philosophy, developing as a specific kind of discourse and a way of life, to a similar breakdown in the history of Greek society. When aging per se ceased to ensure growth in wisdom, wisdom had to be pursued by deliberate efforts. What way of life must be adopted by everyone and by the community, so as to restore the equation of age to growth, so as to offer to all and each the invigorating prospect of becoming wiser when becoming older?[32] Many traces of that appear in Plato: the Prologue of The Republic is a discussion of old age in which the main points of view that still divide our contemporary gerontologists are clearly stated. I'll restrict myself to a short reply of Socrates, and shall attempt, in a brief commentary, to point out why it opens to us a way to philosophically approach gerontology.

A Socratic Approach

Socrates then, visiting an old friend, replies to his greetings as follows:

> There is nothing which for my part I like better, Cephalus, than conversing with aged men; for I regard them as travellers who have gone a journey which I too may have to go, and from whom I ought to enquire whether the way is smooth and easy or rugged and difficult. And this is a question which I should like to ask of you who have arrived at that time which the poet calls the threshold of old age: is life harder at the end, or what report do you give of it?

The study of aging, which we call gerontology and delegate to specialized scientists, is presented by Socrates as both a personal and a universal concern. We all age, we all know that we age. Inquiring about aging (how is the way), interpreting, evaluating, managing our life course, is our responsibility. Two conclusions must be drawn from that.

First, gerontologists must include in their approach, in gerontology as such, the fact and the responsibility of their own aging, as it has been suggested to them by Kastenbaum:

> We are not completely immune to old age stereotypes prevalent in our culture. Ask gerontologists to examine their own development and aging. It seems to be a soul wrenching experience . . . It is possible that there are some things we really do not want to know about old men and women. Why let ourselves in for vicarious suffering? Why borrow misery from the future? Aversion from intimate contact with the aged is common . . . How many

gerontologic researchers have been encouraged to take a guided tour of their own attitudinal structures? Might a self discovery component add much to the training of psychologists and others preparing for careers with the aged?[33]

Socratic, Kastenbaum is.

Second, gerontology must open itself to the layman: gerontology, just as philosophy, strives for universality. We cannot all make ourselves experts in ice skating, in entomology, in Spanish history. Some of us specialize in these fields. But the very idea that philosophy—how do we live? how must we live—or gerontology—how do we age? how can we make the best out of it?—might be once and for all delegated to specialists is ruinous. Admittedly, these investigations require attention, method, continuity, and we may have learners more advanced than others and some people too busy or too afraid to bother. But gerontology and philosophy are shared undertakings, to which each and all must be welcome.

Professor Junod, recently asked to define geriatrics, answered: "a geriatrician is a physician who strives to make his concern shared by all around him." This seems elusive at first hearing. It says the how, not the what of geriatrics and yet is a most deliberate and deep reply. If all patients and potential patients (all of us), if all the aged and the future aged would share the geriatrician's concern for aging and the aged, the aged would not suffer any more from isolation, rejection, discrimination, despondency, alienation. If one defines health, with Klasi, as "the capacity to stand even illness and invalidity, if not in joy and gratefulness, at least with dignity and profit," they would be healthier; the aim of geriatrics would be, if not achieved, at least approached. A Socratic chap, Junod.

Inquire from the aged whether the way is smooth or rugged, says Socrates. The decision to treat the aged as partners, not as mere objects, in investigations on aging, seems to me of paramount importance. Indeed, it would preserve, as Schonfield and Chatfield observe, the chances of further investigations: "But they (the elderly) are not a captive group, and unlike rats, they are not expendable. If participants reach the conclusion that gerontological studies are pointless, that instructions are un-understandable, that an experimenter knows little about older people, the news spreads quickly, and the volunteer pool may dry up."[34] Beyond this pragmatic perspective, treating aged people as partners helps to restore their feelings of usefulness and their self-esteem. But beyond this ethical perspective, we must point out the junction between the practical and the epistemological perspectives.

To treat the aged as partners, even as teachers, not as pupils or objects, may seem and is indeed a modest attitude, as compared with that of gerontologocrats. It is at the same time, paradoxically, a decisive intervention in our and in their aging. In the *Apology of Socrates*, Plato had Socrates saying that "an unexamined life" is not a life worth living. Similarly, Socrates speaks here on the assumption that "unexamined aging" is meaningless. As younger aging people (we age from birth), we should anticipate the next stages in our life journey, and inquire from our elders. Aging as older people, we should examine, and evaluate our life course, and by comparison with earlier stages, the quality of this our last period; and the specific virtue of being questioned by our juniors, and listened to, is to encourage us in this life-reviewing which happens to be also a life-comforting activity. Sharing our present and our past with our juniors becomes sharing their future and thus nourishes our hopes and expectations.

Thus a mutual discussion between youth and age on the meaning of aging and old age contributes to change the very quality of aging. No study ever is innocent. Always observation troubles the observed phenomenon, and indeed the observer himself. Something that teaches modifies the learner. In assigning to aging, whether in earlier or later phases, the task of investigating and interpreting its own meaning, Socrates makes it exhibit and build up its deepest meaning. In that way stating the problem of aging already facilitates its solution. To look for the meaning of age and life brings it to you; you would not look for it, had you not already found it.

In his book *Senescence*, G. Stanley Hall applied to himself and recommended to others an exercise in life-review:

> As preliminary, it slowly came to me that I must, first of all, take careful stock of myself and now seek to attain more of the self knowledge that Socrates taught the world was the highest, hardest and last of all forms of knowledge. I must know, too, just how I stand in with my present stage of life... This hygienic survey reinforced what I had realized before, namely, that physicians know very little of old age. As a part of the process of reorientation, I felt impelled, as I think natural enough for a psychologist, to write my autobiography and get myself in focus genetically. To this I devoted my first year after retirement.[35]

Further on, devoting his third chapter to literature by and on the aged, Hall comments on an autobiography:

> Perhaps the chief suggestion of this book is that every intelligent man, as he reaches the stage of senescence, should thus pass his life in review and try to draw his lessons, not only for his own greater mental poise and unity but for the benefit of his immediate descendants ... Thus the writing of an autobiography will sometime become a fit hygienic prescription for a rounded-out old age."[36]

A Socratic prescription, to be sure.

I concur with my well-spoken predecessors, and some peers, that the geriatrician should learn not *about* his patient only, but *from* him considering him the geriatrician's teacher. As Richard says, in gerontology and in geriatrics, the progress is not from knowledge to know-how and thence to know-how-to-be, but only the other way round, from a quality of being to intervention and through intervention to knowledge. This philosophical approach at the same time re-enacts the Socratic attitude *and* leads the way to the rejuvenation of our present gerontology.

NOTES

1. Hermeneutics, from the Greek, means the art of interpretation. Exegetes, theologians and philosophers use it mainly to designate problems and procedures in interpreting texts.

2. See, for example, Paul Ricoeur, "The Model of the Text: Meaningful Action Considered as a Text," *Social Research*, 38 (3) (Fall 1971).

3. "In aging, as in other relations considered in science, later events are to be explained by antecedent events"— writes Birren (1959), with a marked preference for closest antecedents versus more remote. A more dialectical view is taken by Jerome Bruner, and should apply to aging: "Sequence is fiction, and in human life what follows may have produced what went before." *On Knowing* (Cambridge, Mass.: Harvard University Press, 1962).

4. Nathan Shock wrote in 1960: "Although advancing age is accompanied by biological impairments that offer fertile ground for the development of disease and pathology, there are compensatory devices which can maintain effective behavior in the human into advanced old age. Investigation of these as yet unmeasured and little understood inner resources over the entire lifespan of the individual is the goal of research in gerontology." "Some of the Facts of Aging," in *Aging, Some Social and Biological Aspects*, edited by N. Shock (Washington, D.C.: American Association, 1960).
Clearly the motivation for investigating those compensatory devices and resources which can maintain effective human behavior into old age is the desire to use and if possible to cultivate them: from knowledge to prevision to action. Shock's perspective is sound, and the more so because he clearly

states that investigation on aging must extend to the entire lifespan; it, however, must be enlarged by stating first that cultivating compensatory resources is alternately (dialectically) end and means to their investigation. Second, that ecological as well as inner resources need investigation. W. Donahue, in "Aging, an Historical Perspective" (Washington, D.C.: Mental Health Study Conference on Research Utilization in Aging, NIMH., (April 30, 1963) made the point very clearly. She wrote: "In its struggle to maintain scientific status and gain acceptance by other disciplines, there is pressure from within to exclude or de-emphasize the more applied aspects of the field and to follow what someone recently characterized as the 'great white knight' of pure research. . . . Yet, I believe, one must agree with the British Scientist, Himsworth, and others that while research is accorded high prestige and is a matter of policy today, its ultimate justification is essentially practical and that its goal is to increase man's power over nature."

5. "The Ecopsychological Relativity and Plasticity of Psychological Aging: Convergent Perspectives of Cohort Effects and Operant Psychology," in *Zeitschrift für experimentelle und angewandt psychologie*, 1977.

6. See also my later discussion of Stanley Hall.

7. Thus Birren stated in 1959: "Broadly speaking the purpose of research on aging is to be able to characterize the nature of the older person and to explain how the organism changes over time, that is, to be able to make succinct statements explaining increasingly large numbers of facts about aging individuals. The role of the scientist studying aging appears to be no different from that in other fields of investigation." "Principles of Research on Aging," in *Handbook of the Individual and Aging* edited by J. Birren (Chicago: University of Chicago, 1969), p. 16.

8. Though Clark Tibbitts was aware of the more ambiguous and ambivalent character of the issue and always insisted on presenting aging in our century as a new opportunity, he somewhat reluctantly had to comply with the then current general agreement of gerontologists to identify aging to decline and to restrict its study to later years: "Aging of the human individual is now regarded as a process or series of changes taking place over a major portion of the lifespan. From one point of view the aging process may be said to cover the entire lifespan. The early years, however, are characterized almost entirely by growth of the organism and by enlargement, differentiation and refinement of capacities. The middle and later years are often characterized by the terms *involution* or *senescence* which imply decline, decrement or loss of function. For the purpose of delineating the field, students are now agreed that gerontology should be concerned with the period which follows the attainment of maximum growth and function. While this is a convenient position to take, aging is a multidimensional process and it is not easy to determine when these changes in direction occur . . . Aging seems to be a developmental process, embodying elements of growth as well as decline throughout most of the lifespan . . . There is a good deal of interrelationship among the several facets of the aging process, and . . . an enormous amount of variation in time of onset of the various changes . . . [Nevertheless], growth may be said to continue as long as gains are exceeding losses; maturity reached and maintained when gains and losses are roughly equal; senescence sets in when losses exceed gains." In Tibbitts, *Handbook of Social Gerontology* (Chicago: University of Chicago Press, 1960), p. 6.

9. A unity which is now strongly questioned, "It is quite unlikely that uniform aging processes can be identified." W. Schaie, see footnote 10.

10. "The history of psychological gerontology," in Carl Eisdorfer, Powell Lawton, *The Psychology of Adult Development and Aging*. (Washington, D.C.: American Psychological Association, 1973). Several authors in the same text reiterate this theme: "What we think we know about the aged and aging is in

need of serious revision, revision of the kind that will invalidate policies based upon some of today's assumed certainties," writes Warner Schaie. "However well justified the initial patterning of research interests may have been, it is unfortunate that the patterns have remained more or less frozen during the last two decades," writes Robert Kastenbaum. And Paul and Margaret Baltes: "Historically, there was a predominant assumption throughout the gerontological literature that aging change was largely one toward deterioration and dysfunctioning and, furthermore, that dysfunctional behavior patterns among the elderly were significantly determined by biological patterns which in themselves showed irreversible decline. Consequently many behavioral researchers shared the belief that any efforts at behavioral intervention or modification were futile ... Thus, during the first decades of behavioral gerontology, there was little or no systematic attempt to delineate environment-behavior interactions in the aged within the framework of ecopsychology."

11. On age changes and age differences and the importance of cohort effects, see the papers by Warner Schaie and by Leonard Cain in *The Gerontologist*, June 1967. On so-called "disengagement theory," see Philibert, "*The Development of Social Gerontology in the U.S.A.*" (unpublished paper, the Division of Gerontology, University of Michigan, September 1964).

12. "It is only out of habit, a habit contracted from the insincere language of prefaces and dedications, that the writer speaks of "my reader." In reality every reader is, while he is reading, the reader of his own self. The writer's work is merely a kind of optical instrument which he offers to the reader to enable him to discern what, without this book, he would perhaps never have perceived in himself." Proust, *Time Regained*, Translated by Andreas Mayor (London: Chatto and Windus, 1972), p. 283.

13. "Goals, Purposes and Future of Undergraduate Education in the Psychology of Aging," *Educational Gerontology* 1 (4) (Oct.–Dec. 1976).

14. I borrow this phrase from Dr. Ian Lawson. See also I. Paull, *Everybody's Studying Us* (San Francisco: New Glide Publications, 1976).

15. "Possible Worlds," in *Possible Worlds and Other Essays*, (London: Chatto and Windus, 1927).

16. John Updike, "I Will not Let Thee Go, Except Thou Bless Me," in *Museums and Women and other Stories* (Greenwich, Conn.: Fawcett, 1960).

17. Edna O'Brien, *A Pagan Place* (Salem, N.H.: Faber & Faber, Inc., 1973) Chapter 1.

18. (New York: Dell, 1972.)

19. *The Process of Aging*, 1961. Comfort grew to give the lie to his juvenile hostility to aging. He now contends that "the things we individually can do to improve our own aging, and that of others, lie overwhelmingly in the sociogenic sector ... By ignoring an oppressed minority which we are inevitably going to join, we do not realize that we are slashing our own tyres. The salient fact is obvious enough. "Old" people are people who have lived a certain number of years, and *that is all*. Unless we are old already, the next "old people" will be us. The real curse of being old is the ejection from a citizenship traditionally based on work. [The answer lies] in life-long education and serial careers ... in recognizing the continued growth and achievement of people. Aging has no effect upon you as a person ... "Oldness" is a political institution and a social convention, based on a system which expels people from useful work after a set number of years. This institution is bolstered by a large body of ignorant folklore (I for one would add: and a large body of "scientific" gerontology), which justifies the expulsion by depicting those expelled as weak-minded, incompetent and increasingly fatuous. None of this folklore is true ... Remember that aging is not a radical change ... But you will have been assiduously trained by past indoctrination to think that aging is a change in yourself ... It isn't. It is much

more like a peculiarly shaped social hat which you are required to put on so that you may become identified as a statutory unperson . . . Getting these attitudes over to people, "old" and not old, is probably the main outstanding task of social gerontology." *A Good Age* (London: Mitchell Beazly, 1977).

20. *American Anthropologist* 51 (1949): 46–51.

21. *China, an Area Manual,* 2 volumes, (Washington, D.C.: Johns Hopkins University Press, 1955).

22. Translated by S. Chauvet. (Baltimore, Md.: Penguin, 1972).

23. Preface a Groethuysen, *Mythes et Portraits,* 1947. I cannot resist adding a second quotation of Paulhan. Grown older, he confirms his surprise and enjoyment: "I am now over eighty—maybe that is more than I deserve. But much to my surprise I realize how delightful is aging; delightful and indeed interesting. You come in the long run to experience so many feelings that you had so far mistaken for sheer writers' inventions and conventions—sheer phoneyness. You understand other feelings that have for so many years remained cloudy. I cannot recommend old age strongly enough to all literary critics to begin with, then to all people whom I enjoy, love and care for, and finally to all and each—except the few bastards I hate who keep my loves genuine." Note,· *Oeuvres Completes,* tome 2 (Paris: Editions du Livre precieux, 1966).

24. "Réflexions sur la Vieillesse," *Nouvelle Revue Française* (July 1951).

25. *Chronique,* translated by R. Fitzgerald (New York: Pantheon, 1961).

26. *Cet Âge Qu'en Dit Grand* (Bruxelles: Jacques Antoine, 1971).

27. (New York: Alfred A. Knopf), p. 13.

28. *My Life and Loves.* 1925, (New York: Grove Press, 1963), p. 968.

29. "A Sociological View of Aging," *Proceedings of the American Philosophical Society* 98 (2) (April 15, 1954).

30. In *Education for Later Maturity: A Handbook,* edited by W. T. Donahue (New York: Whiteside, Inc.; William Morrow & Co., Inc., 1955): 19–35.

31. Tibbitts and Sheldon, "A philosophy of aging," *Social Contribution by the Aging, Annals of the American Academy of Political and Social Sciences* 279 (Jan. 1952): 72–83.

32. May I add that in a positive view of aging, aging is not viewed so much as anticipation of death than as victory over death. Every day the alternative is either to die or to survive, that is, to age. Age, as life itself according to Bichat, expresses the effect of all forces resisting death. At the least, as Montaigne, Maslow and others have said, anticipation of dying may sharpen, instead of ruining life's zest and meaning. Thus Montaigne writes: "Especially at this moment, when I perceive that my life is so brief in time, I try to increase it in weight; I try to arrest the speed of its flight by the speed with which I grasp it, and to compensate for the haste of its ebb by my vigor in using it. The shorter my possession of life, the deeper and fuller I must make it." *Essays,* Ib. III, cap. XIII, translated by Donald Frame (Palo Alto: Stanford University Press, 1958). Another statement, this by Abraham Maslow: "My attitude toward life has changed. The word I use for it now is the post-mortem life. I could just as easily have died so that my living constitutes a kind of an extra, a bonus. It's all gravy. Therefore, I might just as well live as if I had already died. One very important aspect of the post-mortem life is that everything gets doubly precious, gets piercingly important. You get stabbed by things, by flowers, and by babies, and by beautiful things— just the very act of living, of walking and breathing and eating and having friends and chatting. Everything seems to look more beautiful rather than less, and one gets the much-intensified sense of miracles." In Morton Puner, *To the Good Long Life* (New York: Universe Books, 1974), p. 13.

33. "Epilogue," in *The Psychology of Adult Development and Aging,* edited by Eisdorfer and Lawton (Washington, D.C.: A.P.A., 1973).

34. See footnote 13.

35. (New York: Appleton, 1923).

36. Ibid., p. 119.

Index

Blenkner, M., 106
Block, J., 147
Bloom, K. L., 137, 138
Botwinick, J., 134–135
Brim, O., 150
Britton, J. and J., 146
Brotman, Herman, 348–349
Brown-Séquard, Charles E., 24, 75
Bruhn, J. G., 200
Buddhism, 15, 16
Buehler, Charlotte, 121
Buffon, Comte de, 41, 45
Business, attitude toward aging, 21, 27–29
Butler, Robert N., 136, 146, 172, 262, 263

C

Calcium intake, 116
California, 368
Canada, 305
Cancer, 71, 75, 81
Cannon, Walter B., 98–99, 109
Canstatt, 75
Cantor, Marjorie, 189, 278–293
Carrel, Alexis, 76
Caudill, W. A., 265
Cells, 70, 75, 76, 77, 79, 80–81
Cerebral thrombosis, 94–95
Chambers, C. L., 172–173
Charcot, Jean-Martin, 23–24, 25, 75
Chateaubriand, Vicomte, 44–45
Children, 128, 155–156; contact with, 59–60, 115, 287–291; living with, 184–185, 377; and remarriage, 212
China, 10, 13–15, 17–20, 74, 386
Chinese-Americans, 265–277
Chronic illness 91–92, 292
Chu Hsi, 18
Cicero, 40, 42, 43, 45, 49
Circulatory disease, 71, 75
Clark, M. M., 258
Clauss, Carin Ann, 301
Clayton, V., 147
Cleveland Board of Education v. *LaFleur*, 365, 372
Cohort flow, 204
Coles, R., 137
Comfort, Alex 76, 82, 385
Commoner, Barry, 304
Comprehensive Employment and Training Act, 307
Compulsive disorders, 168–169
Confucianism, 13–19, 386
Cottrell, Fred, 304
Council of Europe, 305
Cowgill, Donald, 11–12
Cox, P., and J. Ford, 107
Creativity, 26, 45, 47, 78, 136, 146, 268–269
Cristafalo Index, 76, 77

Cuellar, José B., 188, 244–258
Cult of youth, 30, 62
Cummings, E., 138, 185–186, 193–196, 199
Curry, T., and B. W. Ratliff, 227

D

Daniel, C. W., 79
Darwin, Charles, 21
Darwin, Erasmus, 75
Da Vinci, Leonardo, 74
Day-care centers, 140–141, 275, 276
Death: attitudes toward, 11, 30–31, 32, 78, 129–131, 185–186, 188–189, 244–258; causes of, 232–242; fear of, 247–248; in residential facilities, 232–242
Death rates, 4, 75, 355–356; and public health, 30; and stress, 102–107
Degas, Edgar, 387
Dellas, M., and E. L. Gaier, 136
Denial, 163
Dennis, W., 134
Depression, 126, 128, 164, 167
Despair, 131–132
Diabetes, 79, 80, 91–92
Diet, 43, 57, 72, 113–119
Disabilities, 92, 317
Discrimination, age, 297–298, 300–303, 307–308, 372–373
Diseases of old age, 24, 90–97
Disengagement theory, 138, 185–186, 194–196
Divorce, 158, 210, 292
Dock, William, 94
Dore, R. P., 55
Dorland, W. A. Newman, 26
Drugs, 24, 124–125, 172–181
Druze, 151, 152, 153–154
Duke longitudinal study of aging, 102, 298

E

Education, 44, 60–61, 65, 136, 261, 283, 378
Egyptians, 70, 74
Eifu, Motoda, 19
Eisenstadt, S. N., 55–56, 63
Engel, George, 98, 109
Environment and aging, 100, 187–188, 200–202, 219–221, 227, 279–280
Enzymes, 77
Erikson, Eric, 121, 131, 147, 156–157
Estes, E. Harvey, Jr., 71, 90–97
Evolution, 19–20, 84
Exchange theory, 200–201
Exercise, 43, 81

F

Family, 54, 59–60, 88, 184–185, 187, 220, 287–290, 292; and race, 262, 267–268; in future, 376–377
Fatigue, 167, 168
Farrell, Michael, 150
Federal government, 262–263; and age discrimination, 301; policy on aging, 360–361, 362–363, 368–371; and retirement, 27–28
Filial piety, 14–15, 16–17, 18, 272–273
Filipinos, 277
Finland, 346
Florida, 364
Fong, S. L. M., 272
France, 11, 23, 38–52, 305–306, 345
Free radical theory, 80
Freud, Sigmund, 139
Friedman, M., 158
Full Employment Act, 360, 370–371

G

Galen, 42, 49, 74
Galton, Sir Francis, 26
Gaynes, N. L., 230
Gelfand, D. E., 228
Generational relations, 11, 40–41, 51, 57–58, 61–62, 88; Asian Americans, 270–273; in future, 365
Genetics, 79–80, 85–86
George III, 70
Geriatrics, 70, 75
Germ theory, 11, 57
Germany, 23, 306, 345
Gerontogeny, 71, 85–90
Gerontology, 2, 74–82; history, 2, 8–32, 281–282; philosophy of, 379–391; social, 193–206, 246
Gerovital H3, 81
Glands, 25
Glaser, B., and A. Strauss, 239
Glen Brae retirement village, 232–242
Gold, Byron, 262–263
Golden, Herbert, 189, 259, 263
Gompertz, 75
Gottesman, L., 224–225, 230
Goya, 387
Grandparents, 48, 54, 128, 133
Grant, D. P., 228
Greeks, 11, 74, 389
Grey Panthers, 368, 372
Grief, 107–108, 128, 164, 210, 237
Gutman, David, 123, 124–125, 145–146, 150–159, 172–181

H

Hajime, Nakamura, 13
Haldane, J. B., 384

Hall, G. Stanley, 2, 30
Harman, D., 80
Havighurst, R. J., 138–139
Hayflick, Leonard, 76, 80
Health: and attitude toward death, 251; and elderly, 90–97, 291, 317–318; and life events, 71–72, 98–100; and lifespan, 86–87; and retirement, 284; and status, 198
Hefner, R., 147
Heilbronner, R. I., 377
Hellens, Franz, 387–388
Henry, W. E., 138, 185–186, 193–196, 199
Hindus, 74, 75
Hinton, J., 107, 108
Hippocrates, 42, 74
Hoarding, 165
Hochschild, A., 238
Hokusai, 386
Holmberg, R. H., 226
Holmes, Thomas H., 99, 100, 102, 109
Homes for aged, 104–106, 188, 217, 224–231
Hormones, 49, 80, 99, 108–109
Housing. See Residence
Hsu, F. L. K., 266–267, 268–269
Hsuan-tsung, 16
Hufeland, 75
Hugo, Victor, 40, 42, 45
Hunza, 79
Hursley, Sir Victor, 25
Hutchinson-Gilford disease, 79
Hypertension, 91–92, 116
Hypochondriasis, 167–168
Hysterical neuroses, 169

I

Income, 58, 89, 115, 177; blacks, 260–261, 283–284; and morale, 318, 320–321; and retirement, 283–285, 297
Industrialization, 4, 19, 27–29
Infant mortality, 22, 39, 41
Inner-city elderly, 278–293
Integrity, 131–134
Intellectual faculties, 26, 46, 134–136
Introspection, 132–134, 196
Involutional melancholia, 166–167
Ireland, 345
Iron intake, 116
Issei, 265–277
Italy, 41

J

Jackson, Hobart, 260
Jackson, Jacquelyne, 260, 261–262
Jacobs, R., 227

Socialization, 61, 205, 297
Socioeconomic status, 256–257
Sokichi, Tsuda, 17
Solomon, Barbara, 261
Soviet Union, 41, 63, 79, 306
Stalin, 79
Status of aged, 54, 55, 58, 65, 198
Stearns, Peter, 11
Stenback, A., 109
Stereotypes, 2–3, 9, 274, 297–298
Stokes, R. G., and G. L. Maddox, 333
Strehler, B. L., 71, 80, 82
Stress, 71–72, 80, 81, 98–110, 196, 332
Streib, G., 137, 317
Studebaker Corp., 302
Subculture of aged, 197–198
Suicide, 27
Supplemental Security Income, 260–261, 285, 370
Sweden, 5, 306, 345
Switzerland, 345, 346
Szilard, Leo, 90

T

Tactile relationship, 163
Taiho code, 16
Taoism, 15
Teaff, Joseph, 187–188, 216–223
Tetsujiro, Inoue, 19
Thiamin intake, 116
Thompson, G. B., 317, 322
Todhunter, E. Neige, 72, 113–119
Toju, Nakae, 17
Townsend, P., 226
Townsend movement, 368–369
Travel, effects of, 43
Treas, Judith, 187, 208–212
Tuke, William, 23

U

Undermanning concept, 217, 221
United Kingdom, 343–344, 346
United States: age distribution, 5; attitude toward aging, 10–11, 21–32, 40, 41, 48; education, 61; pensions, 339–340, 343–345; research, 23–25; youth culture, 18
Urbanization, 11, 54, 56, 57, 59–60; and elderly, 278–293

V

Valery, Paul, 387
VanHilst, Anke, 187, 208–212
Veneration, 38–39; see also Filial piety
Virchow, Rudolph, 23
Vitalism, 25
Vitamin A, 116, 117
Vitamin C, 116–117
Voltaire, 45

W

Wallace, Alfred Russell, 388
Wallace, Daniel J., 70–71
Warthin, Aldred, 75
Weber, Max, 63
Weinberg, Jack, 123–124
Weiner, Myron, 56, 64
Weisbrod v. *Lynn*, 365, 372
Weismann, August, 82
Weiss v. *Walsh*, 364–365
Werner's syndrome, 79
White House Conference on Aging, 189, 264, 265, 360, 363
Widowers, 107, 128, 211–212
Widows, 41, 47, 54, 107, 128, 211–212, 215, 311
Williams, R., and C. Wirth, 145
Wilson, R., and G. Maddox, 102–103
Wisdom, 13–14, 35–36, 37, 45, 158
Women, 47–48, 123; death, fear of, 245; death of spouse, 107; drugs, 180, 181; illness, 90; life expectancy, 92, 144; marriage, 210; sex roles, 144–148, 152–157, 194; sexuality, 26, 46–47, 213–216; and stress, 121–122; and work, 204, 311–314, 315–322, 328
Work, 283, 294–295, 305–308; and ethnicity, 283–284; life, 309–314; loss of, 331–338; and morale, 317–322; roles, 11, 58–59; satisfaction, 145, 150, 316; and specialization, 58–59
Work ethic, 63–65

Y

Yatsuka, Hozumi, 19
Youth cultures, 18, 40, 41, 62–63
Yuen, S., 265
Yukichi, Fukuzawa, 19